**lonely planet**

# Java

### Peter Turner

LONELY PLANET PUBLICATIONS
Melbourne • Oakland • London • Paris

# JAVA

**Tanjungpandan**

Pulau
Bangka

Pulau
Belitung

108° E

SUMATRA

4° S

INDONESIA

JAVA SEA

**KRAKATAU**
The legendary volcano
that blew itself apart in 1883

**JAKARTA**
Indonesia's bustling capital,
Java's political and business
epicentre

**CIREBON**
Ancient court city;
succulent seafood

Tanjungkarang
Telukbetung
Panjang

Teluk
Lampung

Bakauheni

6° S

Merak
Krakatau
Islands

Banten
JAKARTA
Tangerang
★ JAKARTA

Selat
Sunda

Serang
Rancam
Danau
Reserve

Bekasi
Karawang

Indramayu

Pulau
Panaitan

Labuan

Rangkasbitung
Cipanas

Cibinong
Bogor
Ciawi

Cikampek
Purwakarta

Subang

Jatiwangi

Cirebon

Tegal
Pekalon

Sumur

Puncak
Pass

Cianjur
**Bandung**
Sumedang

Kuningan
Ciledug

Pemalang

Ujung Kulon
National Park

Tamanjaya

Pelabuhanratu
Cibadak
Sukabumi

Ciwidey

CENTRAL
JAVA

Dien
Plat
Rest
Wonos

Rancabali

Garut

Magenang

Purwokerto

Genteng

Jampangkulon

WEST
JAVA

Ciamis

Kebur

Singdangbarang

Tasikmalaya

Banjar

Pangandaran

Kroya
Cilacap

Pameungpeuk

Cipatujah

Cijulang

Pangandaran
National
Park

**UJUNG KULON NATIONAL PARK**
Superb wildlife, wilderness,
diving and hiking

8° S

INDIAN OCEAN

ELEVATION

2500 m
2000 m
1500 m
1000 m
500 m
0

0    50    100 km

Pangkalanbun

KALIMANTAN

Banjarmasin

Martapura

THAILAND
CAMBODIA VIETNAM
*South China Sea*
PHILIPPINES

BRUNEI

MALAYSIA
PACIFIC OCEAN

SINGAPORE

Sumatra
Kalimantan
Sulawesi
Maluku
Irian Jaya

Jakarta
INDONESIA

Java
*Java Sea*
Nusa Tenggara

Bali
*Timor Sea*

0    500    1000 km

*INDIAN OCEAN*
AUSTRALIA

Karimunjawa Islands

Pulau Bawean

**TROWULAN**
Ancient capital of the Hindu
kingdom of Majapahit

**SEMARANG**
Crumbling but fascinating
old city

**MADURA**
Large, rugged island
famous for its bull races
and strong traditional values

Jepara

Pati

Rembang

Tuban
Paciran

Pulau Madura

Kaliwungu
Demak
Kudus
Blora
Sedayu
Bangkalan
Slopeng
Sumenep
Kalianget

Semarang
Purwodadi
Babat
Lamongan
Camplong
Pamekasan

Ambarawa
Cepu
Bojonegoro
Gresik
Pulau Sapudi

Salatiga
E A S T   J A V A
Surabaya

Temanggung
Ngawi
*Selat Madura*

Magelang
Jombang
Mojokerto
Trowulan

Borobudur
Solo
(Surakarta)
Madiun
Arjuno-
Lalijiwo
Reserve
Pasuruan
Pasir Putih
Situbondo
Baluran National Park

Purworejo
Yogyakarta
Wonogiri
Kediri
Lawang
Probolinggo
Ijen-Merapi-Maelang Reserve

Parangtritis
Ponorogo
Bromo-Tengger-
Semeru
National Park
Bondowoso

Y O G Y A K A R T A
Pacitan
Tulungagung
Malang
Turen
Lumajang
Yang Plateau Reserve
Jember
Banyuwangi
Gilimanuk

Blitar
Tempeh
B A L I

Nusa Barung
Reserve
Watu Ulo
Meru Betiri Reserve
Genteng

Grajagan

Blambangan
Wildlife
Reserve

**BOROBUDUR**
Awe-inspiring Hindu-Buddhist
relics; often described as
Java's most famous attraction

**YOGYAKARTA**
The cultural heart of Java;
traditional arts and crafts

**MERU BETIRI
NATIONAL PARK**
Magnificent coastal rainforest,
exotic wildlife and
egg-laying turtles

# Contents – Maps

# MAP INDEX

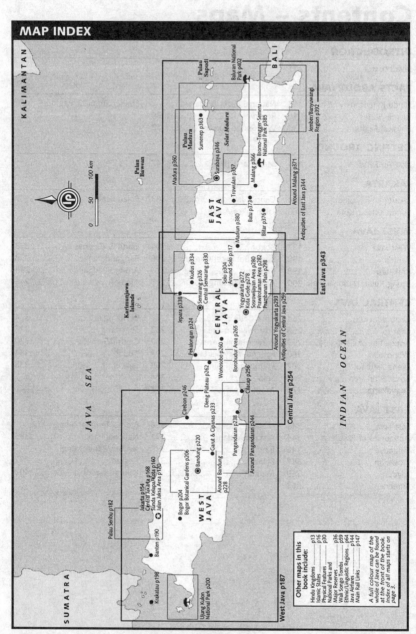

KALIMANTAN

SUMATRA

JAVA SEA

INDIAN OCEAN

BALI

Karimunjawa Islands

Pulau Bawean

Pulau Sapudi

**West Java p187**
- Ujung Kulon National Park p200
- Krakatau p199
- Pulau Seribu p182
- Banten p190
- Jakarta p154
- Central Jakarta p168
- Sunda Kelapa/Kota p160
- Jalan Jaksa Area p170
- Bogor p204
- Bogor Botanical Gardens p206
- Bandung p220
- Around Bandung p228
- Garut & Cipanas p233
- Pangandaran p238
- Around Pangandaran p244
- Cirebon p246
- Dieng Plateau p233

**W E S T   J A V A**

**Central Java p254**
- Cilacap p256
- Borobudur Area p265
- Wonosobo p262
- Pekalongan p324
- Jepara p338
- Kudus p334
- Semarang p326
- Central Semarang p330
- Solo p304
- Around Solo p317
- Yogyakarta p272
- Kota Gede p278
- Sosrowijayan Area p280
- Prawirodirjan Area p282
- Prambanan Plain p298
- Around Yogyakarta p293
- Antiquities of Central Java p259

**C E N T R A L   J A V A**

**East Java p343**
- Madiun p380
- Batu p373
- Blitar p376
- Malang p366
- Around Malang p371
- Trowulan p357
- Surabaya p357
- Madura p360
- Pulau Madura
- Sumenep p363
- Selat Madura
- Bromo-Tengger-Semeru National Park p385
- Baluran National Park p402
- Jember/Banyuwangi Region p392
- Antiquities of East Java p344
- Around East Java p344

**E A S T   J A V A**

0   50   100 km

## Other maps in this book include:
Hindu Kingdoms .......... p13
Islamic States .......... p16
Physical Features .......... p30
National Parks and
Major Reserves .......... p36
Wali Songo Tombs .......... p59
Ethnolinguistic Regions .......... p64
Java Airfares .......... p144
Main Rail Links .......... p147

*A full colour map of the whole of Java can be found at the front of the book. Index of all maps starts on page 3.*

4

# The Author

## Peter Turner

Peter Turner lives in Melbourne, Australia, and has a long held interest in Indonesia and South-East Asia. Since his first extended trip though Indonesia in 1978, he has spent over three years on numerous trips, travelling throughout the archipelago. As well as contributing to *Malaysia, Singapore & Brunei*, *Singapore*, *South-East Asia* and *New Zealand*, he is the author of Lonely Planet's guides to *Jakarta* and *Indonesia's Eastern Islands: From Lombok to Timor*. Peter also coordinates *Indonesia*.

## FROM THE AUTHOR

Of the many people who helped with the preparation of this book, in Jakarta special thanks go to Agus, Ibu Tuti from the Jakarta Tourist Office, and Jeffery Pradjanata. Thanks also to the staff of the West Java Deparpostal, particularly the ever helpful Pak Amir. In Pangandaran, thanks to Kristina and Jajang Nurjaman, and in Mojokerto, cheers to Owen and the Westinghouse gang. In East Java, thanks to the very knowledgable Martin Tyson for help with Baluran and other parks, and to Mark Grantham for all the help in Alas Purwo National Park.

# This Book

The 1st edition of *Java* was researched and written by Peter Turner who returned again to update this 2nd edition.

## From the Publisher

This book was edited by Wendy Owen, assisted by Lara Morcombe, Sally O'Brien, Linda Suttie and Russell Kerr, who stepped into the breach when flu ravaged the Melbourne office. Adrian Persoglia skilfully juggled map drawing, page design and layout to coordinate his first monster manuscript ('it's OK, we've still got another week'). A cast of creative cartographers assisted him, including: Chris Thomas, Leanne Peake, Celia Wood, Chris Love, Lisa Borg, Joelene Kowalski and Mark Griffiths.

New illustrations were drawn by Jenny Bowman. Tim Fitzgerald drew the climate charts and assisted Chris Love with design checks. Marcel Gaston kept a watchful eye on Adrian, Tim (Quark) Uden kept a tracking eye on pages and puns, and Kristin Odijk kept everything together.

Quentin Frayne ensured our Language chapter was linguistically correct and Kusnandar (who, like many Indonesians, really does have only one name – at least he did until he tried to get an Australian driver's licence) cheerfully pointed out our (tiny) mistakes and explained many Javan mysteries. Jamieson Gross came up with some groovy cover ideas and smiled insinuatingly when the gamelan got the gong.

Many thanks again to Barbara Hatley for her contribution to the Arts section, particularly to the Theatre, Folk & Melodrama and Literature sections; to Samantha Slicer for the Religious Architecture of Java section and to Michael Sklovsky for his piece on Furniture in Java.

# Acknowledgments

## THANKS

Many thanks to the travellers who used the last edition and wrote to us with helpful hints, useful advice and interesting anecdotes:

John Ahmad, G Ang, W Ang, Dr B Abtmaier, HJ Cario, Zoe Cameron, Christian Campos, David Coleman, Jeremy Cook, Coco Darmoni, J Dekker, Robyn Dryen, Louisa Ebbeling, Hugh Elsol, Peter Gilet, Natalie Gillespie, Richard & Jenny Hall, Sander Herden, M&J von Hoff, Chris Hogan, Hugo Hopstaken, Paula Hutt, David Kirkby, Jamie Kish, Susie Kong, Georges Krist, Dee Mahan, K Mak, Myumi Matthews, Jon & Phoebe McLeod, Heather Montgomery, Thea Mulder, Kay Munay, Geert Jan van Oldenborgh, Richard Pickvance, Caroline Porcher, Gunter Quaisser, Gerrit Renger, Alex Riley, Peter Roberts, Mikey & Lou Samson, Maria Sarantopoulos, Timothy Shaw, Deanna Sloggett-Behle, Annette Solyst, Cal Spiers, Anika Stokkentre, Geke Stokkink, Christine T Tjandraningsih, L Ta, Shelley Thomas-Benke, David Blair Thomson, Johan Verstraeten, Andrew Wallace, Werner Willemse.

# Foreword

## ABOUT LONELY PLANET GUIDEBOOKS

The story begins with a classic travel adventure: Tony and Maureen Wheeler's 1972 journey across Europe and Asia to Australia. Useful information about the overland trail did not exist at that time, so Tony and Maureen published the first Lonely Planet guidebook to meet a growing need.

From a kitchen table, then from a tiny office in Melbourne (Australia), Lonely Planet has become the largest independent travel publisher in the world, an international company with offices in Melbourne, Oakland (USA), London (UK) and Paris (France).

Today Lonely Planet guidebooks cover the globe. There is an ever-growing list of books and there's information in a variety of forms and media. Some things haven't changed. The main aim is still to help make it possible for adventurous travellers to get out there – to explore and better understand the world.

At Lonely Planet we believe travellers can make a positive contribution to the countries they visit – if they respect their host communities and spend their money wisely. Since 1986 a percentage of the income from each book has been donated to aid projects and human rights campaigns.

**Updates** Lonely Planet thoroughly updates each guidebook as often as possible. This usually means there are around two years between editions, although for more unusual or more stable destinations the gap can be longer. Check the imprint page (following the colour map at the beginning of the book) for publication dates.

Between editions up-to-date information is available in two free newsletters – the paper *Planet Talk* and email *Comet* (to subscribe, contact any Lonely Planet office) – and on our Web site at www.lonelyplanet.com. The *Upgrades* section of the Web site covers a number of important and volatile destinations and is regularly updated by Lonely Planet authors. *Scoop* covers news and current affairs relevant to travellers. And, lastly, the *Thorn Tree* bulletin board and *Postcards* section of the site carry unverified, but fascinating, reports from travellers.

**Correspondence** The process of creating new editions begins with the letters, postcards and emails received from travellers. This correspondence often includes suggestions, criticisms and comments about the current editions. Interesting excerpts are immediately passed on via newsletters and the Web site, and everything goes to our authors to be verified when they're researching on the road. We're keen to get more feedback from organisations or individuals who represent communities visited by travellers.

> Lonely Planet gathers information for everyone who's curious about the planet – and especially for those who explore it first-hand. Through guidebooks, phrasebooks, activity guides, maps, literature, newsletters, image library, TV series and Web site we act as an information exchange for a worldwide community of travellers.

**Research** Authors aim to gather sufficient practical information to enable travellers to make informed choices and to make the mechanics of a journey run smoothly. They also research historical and cultural background to help enrich the travel experience and allow travellers to understand and respond appropriately to cultural and environmental issues.

Authors don't stay in every hotel because that would mean spending a couple of months in each medium-sized city and, no, they don't eat at every restaurant because that would mean stretching belts beyond capacity. They do visit hotels and restaurants to check standards and prices, but feedback based on readers' direct experiences can be very helpful.

Many of our authors work undercover, others aren't so secretive. None of them accept freebies in exchange for positive write-ups. And none of our guidebooks contain any advertising.

**Production** Authors submit their raw manuscripts and maps to offices in Australia, USA, UK or France. Editors and cartographers – all experienced travellers themselves – then begin the process of assembling the pieces. When the book finally hits the shops, some things are already out of date, we start getting feedback from readers and the process begins again ...

---

## WARNING & REQUEST

Things change – prices go up, schedules change, good places go bad and bad places go bankrupt – nothing stays the same. So, if you find things better or worse, recently opened or long since closed, please tell us and help make the next edition even more accurate and useful. We genuinely value all the feedback we receive. Julie Young coordinates a well travelled team that reads and acknowledges every letter, postcard and email and ensures that every morsel of information finds its way to the appropriate authors, editors and cartographers for verification.

Everyone who writes to us will find their name in the next edition of the appropriate guidebook. They will also receive the latest issue of *Planet Talk*, our quarterly printed newsletter, or *Comet*, our monthly email newsletter. Subscriptions to both newsletters are free. The very best contributions will be rewarded with a free guidebook.

Excerpts from your correspondence may appear in new editions of Lonely Planet guidebooks, the Lonely Planet Web site, *Planet Talk* or *Comet*, so please let us know if you *don't* want your letter published or your name acknowledged.

Send all correspondence to the Lonely Planet office closest to you:

**Australia:** PO Box 617, Hawthorn, Victoria 3122
**USA:** 150 Linden St, Oakland, CA 94607
**UK:** 10A Spring Place, London NW5 3BH
**France:** 1 rue du Dahomey, 75011 Paris

Or email us at: talk2us@lonelyplanet.com.au

**For news, views and updates see our Web site: www.lonelyplanet.com**

## HOW TO USE A LONELY PLANET GUIDEBOOK

The best way to use a Lonely Planet guidebook is any way you choose. At Lonely Planet we believe the most memorable travel experiences are often those that are unexpected, and the finest discoveries are those you make yourself. Guidebooks are not intended to be used as if they provide a detailed set of infallible instructions!

**Contents** All Lonely Planet guidebooks follow roughly the same format. The Facts about the Destination chapters or sections give background information ranging from history to weather. Facts for the Visitor gives practical information on issues like visas and health. Getting There & Away gives a brief starting point for researching travel to and from the destination. Getting Around gives an overview of the transport options when you arrive.

The peculiar demands of each destination determine how subsequent chapters are broken up, but some things remain constant. We always start with background, then proceed to sights, places to stay, places to eat, entertainment, getting there and away, and getting around information – in that order.

**Heading Hierarchy** Lonely Planet headings are used in a strict hierarchical structure that can be visualised as a set of Russian dolls. Each heading (and its following text) is encompassed by any preceding heading that is higher on the hierarchical ladder.

**Entry Points** We do not assume guidebooks will be read from beginning to end, but that people will dip into them. The traditional entry points are the list of contents and the index. In addition, however, some books have a complete list of maps and an index map illustrating map coverage.

There may also be a colour map that shows highlights. These highlights are dealt with in greater detail in the Facts for the Visitor chapter, along with planning questions and suggested itineraries. Each chapter covering a geographical region usually begins with a locator map and another list of highlights. Once you find something of interest in a list of highlights, turn to the index.

**Maps** Maps play a crucial role in Lonely Planet guidebooks and include a huge amount of information. A legend is printed on the back page. We seek to have complete consistency between maps and text, and to have every important place in the text captured on a map. Map key numbers usually start in the top left corner.

Although inclusion in a guidebook usually implies a recommendation we cannot list every good place. Exclusion does not necessarily imply criticism. In fact there are a number of reasons why we might exclude a place – sometimes it is simply inappropriate to encourage an influx of travellers.

# Introduction

Java is the political, geographic and economic centre of Indonesia. With an area of 132,000 sq km it is a little over half the size of England, but its population is twice as large at 128 million. With such vast human resources, Java is the powerhouse and dictator of Indonesia.

Java presents vivid contrasts: wealth and squalor, majestic open country and crowded filthy cities, quiet rural scenes and bustling modern traffic. The main cities can be overwhelming, but rural Java is astonishingly beautiful. A string of high volcanic mountains runs through the centre of the island, a smoking backdrop to fertile green fields and terraces. Rich volcanic soils that have long been the secret of Java's richness extend north to the flat coastal plain and the shallow Java Sea, while the south coast fronts the crashing waves of the Indian Ocean.

The Hindu-Buddhist empires reached their zenith in fertile Java and produced the architectural wonders of Borobudur and Prambanan. When Islam came it absorbed rather than banished existing influences and Java is a blend of cultures and religion. The ready Indonesian images of *wayang* shadow puppets, batik and court dances exist alongside the muezzin's call to the mosque.

Java is a long and narrow island, conveniently divided into three provinces: West, Central and East Java. It also includes the special territories of Jakarta – the teeming capital, which is rapidly becoming a megalopolis – and Yogyakarta, a centre for Javanese culture and one of Indonesia's premier tourist destinations.

West Java, home to the Sundanese people, has places of interest like Bandung in the Sundanese heartland, the court city of Cirebon, the beach at Pangandaran, famous Krakatau and the wilds of the Ujung Kulon National Park.

In Central Java, temples and royal cities plot the rise and fall of the Hindu, Buddhist and

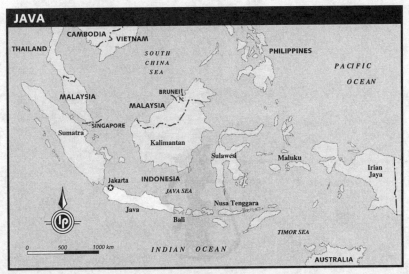

Muslim kingdoms, from which the present-day court cities of Yogyakarta and Solo have evolved. Java is crowded with people, but there are isolated places where you can find yourself out of sight and sound, such as the Dieng Plateau in the beautiful central highlands.

In East Java, spectacular Gunung Bromo volcano is as wild and desolate as you could hope. Off the coast, Madura holds to its independent traditions, and East Java's highlands have some of Java's best hill resorts and hiking opportunities.

# Facts about Java

## HISTORY
### Prehistoric Period
The history of human habitation in Java begins with *Pithecanthropus erectus,* or Java Man, who lived along the banks of the Bengawan Solo River in Central and East Java. During the glacial ages two million years ago, the lowering of sea levels and the existence of land bridges allowed the first humans to migrate down through the Malay Peninsula and Sumatra into Java.

Archaeological sites at Sangiran, Trinil and Ngandong have unearthed Java Man fossils dating to at least one million years ago. Their discovery caused a storm of debate as these oldest humans were held as evidence of the 'missing link', the common ancestor of humans and apes.

*Pithecanthropus erectus* either died out or evolved and intermingled with later migrations. Skulls unearthed at Wajak in East Java give evidence of a later Australoid people, related to Australian aborigines and Melanesians, but the Javanese of today are mostly descended from the Asian migration of Mongoloid people that began around 4000 BC.

Waves of migrants came down through South-East Asia to Java, and the Javanese are an Austronesian people, closely related to the people of Malaysia and the Philippines. The first Austronesians brought their slash-and-burn agriculture and used polished stone axes and adzes, issuing in a new Neolithic era.

By 2000 BC, further migrations showed the influence of the Dongson bronze culture of Vietnam, noted for its bronze drums and ceremonial objects, but in Java iron was also used for tools. Rice was first introduced around this time, and Java's exceptional fertility aided the later development of a sophisticated agricultural system, based on intensive *sawah* (wet rice) agriculture.

The Austronesian people were also experienced seafarers and small river port settlements developed along the coast of Java. As early as the 3rd century AD, merchants from South India traded with Javanese ports, and with them came the influences of Indian civilisation.

### Emergence of Hindu-Buddhism (400-700 AD)
Java's first known Hindu kingdom was that of Tarumanegara, sited just south of Jakarta near Bogor. Near the village of Ciampea, a boulder inscribed with the Palawa script of South India dates from 450 AD and attests to the rule of King Purnawarman. How Hinduism was adopted in Indonesia is still a mystery, but it is likely that the developing Javanese courts invited Brahmin priests

HINDU KINGDOMS

JAVA SEA

Tarumanegara
(5th c)
Pajajaran
(14th c-1580)

WEST JAVA

CENTRAL JAVA

EAST JAVA

Selat Madura

Mataram
(8th-10th c)

Majapahit
(1294-1527)

Kediri
(1045-1222)

Singosari
(1222-92)

YOGYAKARTA

Blambangan
(13th c-1777)

INDIAN OCEAN

0    100    200 km

from India to advise on spirituality and ritual, thereby providing occult powers and a mythological sanction for the new Indonesian rulers.

Other Hindu kingdoms sprang up along the coastal areas of Indonesia, where port towns conducted international trade with China and South-East Asia, where Hindu and Buddhist kingdoms were already flourishing in Cambodia, Burma and Vietnam. The well travelled Chinese Buddhist monk Fa Hsien visited Java in 414 AD and reported the existence of small Hindu trading posts. Other Chinese sources document Hindu courts in Java, some of which sent envoys to China.

The most notable early coastal kingdom was the Sriwijaya Empire, centred in southern Sumatra, which rose to prominence in the 7th century. Sriwijaya controlled the growing trade through the nearby sea lanes and exerted its influence on Java. Though the structure of the kingdom was largely Hindu, it was also a noted Buddhist centre of learning.

Hinduism and Buddhism developed side by side in Indonesia, along with older religious beliefs. The rigid caste system of India was not adopted in Indonesia, and the conflict between Hinduism and Buddhism in India was not played out in Indonesia.

## Mataram & the Golden Age of Central Java (732-900)

In Java, Indian religion reached its zenith with the major civilisations that developed in the fertile valleys and volcanic highlands of Java's interior. The welfare of this primarily agrarian society relied on wet rice, which required an extensive irrigation system, which in turn required close cooperation between villages. From this first need for local government, small kingdoms developed.

Java's village-based social system dependent on mutual cooperation was overlaid with a hierarchical court culture. Clusters of villages gave taxes and labour to a central royal court that adopted Indian religion and was headed by a divine king. The king was

seen as the incarnation of a god, often Shiva or Vishnu, and the court's architecture and organisation symbolised the world of the gods. At the centre, the king was the principal source of spiritual power responsible for leading the necessary rituals and maintaining the harmony of the kingdom.

While Hinduism was eagerly adopted by the courts, the peasantry clung largely to existing animist beliefs. The spirits of nature and the ancestors were still called upon to assist in everything from ensuring an abundant rice crop to healing the sick, and some animist beliefs and rituals were absorbed into court culture and Hindu rites.

The first major principality of interior Java was the kingdom of Sanjaya. The inscriptions of the Canggal Stone, found on Gunung Wakir near Yogyakarta, record the building of a Hindu linga by the new king Sanjaya in 732 AD. He founded the kingdom of Mataram, which controlled much of Central Java. Mataram's religion centred on the Hindu god Shiva, and the kingdom produced some of the earliest of Java's Hindu temples on the Dieng Plateau.

The kingdom of Mataram was to be ruled by competing lines of kings, and Sanjaya's Hindu kingdom was followed by a Buddhist interlude under the Sailendra Dynasty. It was the Mahayana Buddhist Sailendras who began work on Java's most magnificent religious monument, the Borobudur temple complex, around 780 AD.

The Sailendras also exerted some influence over competing Sriwijaya in Sumatra. However, with the marriage of a Sailendra princess to Rakai Pikatan of Hindu Mataram, Hinduism again became dominant. The massive Hindu Prambanan complex was built and consecrated around 856 AD, only 50 years or so after the completion of Borobudur.

## Shift of Power to East Java (900-1016)

By the 10th century, Mataram had declined, leaving only the architectural monoliths of its rule. The construction of these mighty religious monuments must have placed a strain on Mataram's resources and an enormous burden on the peasantry, but whether Mataram's decline can be attributed to internal revolt, invasion from Sriwijaya or volcanic eruptions remains a mystery.

In the early 10th century, King Sendok established his kingdom in the Brantas River Valley in East Java. This major rice-growing area, previously an outpost of the empires of Central Java, became the centre of civilisation on the island. The kingdom flourished, exerting influence on nearby Bali and beyond; but in 1016, under Dharmawangsa, the kingdom was overthrown in a bloody uprising.

## Airlangga & Kediri (1019-1222)

Dharmawangsa's 16-year-old son-in-law, Airlangga, escaped and lived in forest exile where, according to legend, he accumulated wisdom through fasting and meditation. He returned to claim the throne in 1019 AD, and eastern Java's political and cultural ascendancy dates from his reign.

Until his death in 1049, Airlangga set about reclaiming the territory lost since the rule of his predecessor, and Javanese influence grew to its greatest in Bali. Airlangga became one of Java's greatest kings and his court to the north of Kediri adopted a new syncretism of Shivaism and Buddhism, which still has many followers in Java and Bali.

Apart from Airlangga's military conquests, during his reign the arts flourished, particularly literature. The ancient Hindu poem of Arjuna's temptation, the *Arjuna Wiwaha*, was first translated into Old Javanese and it is still one of the most popular *wayang* stories.

Under Airlangga's government, eastern Java became united and powerful but before his death he divided his kingdom between his two sons, creating Janggala, east of the Brantas River, and Kediri to the west. The two rivals struggled for dominance over the next two centuries. The Kediri Dynasty rose to pre-eminence and Chinese reports state that the king of Kediri was second in wealth only to the caliph of Baghdad.

## Singosari (1222-92)

In 1222, in the region of the eastern kingdom of Janggala, a commoner called Ken Angrok usurped power and the Singosari kingdom, based in what is present-day Malang, superseded Kediri. Eastern Java inherited some of its most striking temples from that era, and Singosari pioneered a new sculptural style.

Kertanagara (1262-92) was the last and most important of the Singosari kings. In 1292 the Mongol ruler, Kublai Khan, demanded that homage be paid to China. Kertanagara, however, foolishly humiliated the Great Khan by having the nose and ears of the Mongol envoy cut off and sent back to China.

A Mongol invasion of Java followed, but by this time Kertanagara had already been killed in a civil war. Kertanagara's son-in-law, Wijaya, with Mongol assistance, gained the throne.

## Majapahit Empire (1294-1400)

Wijaya assumed power in 1294 and his new kingdom, Majapahit, was to become the most powerful and famous of all Indonesian kingdoms. Wijaya established his capital at Trowulan, and the kingdom grew in importance under Wijaya's successor, Jayanegara. Trowulan was the largest cultural and administrative city that Indonesia had ever seen.

It was during Jayanegara's reign that Gajah Mada, Majapahit's brilliant military leader, rose to prominence and his power increased after the death of Jayanegara in 1328. The new king, Hayam Wuruk, was too young to rule and Gajah Mada became prime minister and effectively regent of the kingdom from 1336 until his death in 1364. Gajah Mada organised raids into Bali and an expedition against Palembang in Sumatra, and his various military campaigns saw the expansion of Majapahit's suzerainty across much of the Indonesian archipelago and into the South-East Asian mainland. Majapahit also claimed trading relations with Cambodia, Siam, Burma and Vietnam, and sent missions to China.

Under Hayam Wuruk's reign Majapahit reached its golden age, but when he died in 1389, the empire rapidly disintegrated. By the end of the 15th century, Islamic power was growing on the north coast, and less than a century later there were raids into East Java by Muslims carrying both the Koran and the sword.

Many Hindu-Buddhists fled eastwards to Bali. But in the mountain ranges around Gunung Bromo the Tenggerese people trace their history back to Majapahit and they still practise their own religion. This is a variety of Hinduism that includes many proto-Javanese elements.

## Rise of Islam (1300-1550)

Exactly why Islam was adopted in Java remains a debating point for historians, but it was undoubtedly brought by trade. Though initially it was peacefully adopted, even by some of the royalty of the inland kingdoms, once established it was carried further by the sword.

Islam first gained a foothold in Sumatra by the end of the 13th century, and by the early 15th century, Melaka, the region's premier trading port, was Muslim. Melaka's language, Malay, became the lingua franca of trade, and Islam the religion of trade.

The new dynamism of Islam came first to Java's north coast and, in the 15th century, many of the coastal ports came under its sway. Early in the 16th century, Gresik, Tuban, Jepara and Demak were all Muslim,

but it was Demak that rose to become the first great Islamic state in Java as Majapahit, rent by internal conflict, declined.

In 1527 Demak conquered the Hindu-Buddhist kingdom at Kediri, part of Majapahit, and in West Java it took the port of Banten from the Hindu Pajajaran kingdom. Demak went on to control most of East Java, and Banten captured Pajajaran's main port of Sunda Kelapa, renaming it Jayakarta (Jakarta).

The rise of Demak has been attributed to Sunan Gunungjati, one of the *wali songo* (nine saints), who, according to Javanese lore, brought Islam to Java. The stories of the wali are full of tales of mystical powers and occult feats, and today their graves, dotted across the north coast and East Java, attract thousands of pilgrims. Islam in Java absorbed many existing beliefs, and though Islam provided new social and moral codes, Javanese philosophy and traditions continued.

## Arrival of the Europeans (1511-1619)

At the same time as Islam was establishing dominance in Java, the Portuguese and their cannons arrived in South-East Asia to contest the lucrative spice trade controlled by Muslim merchants. Alfonso de Albuquerque conquered Goa in 1510, then Melaka in 1511, before the Portuguese sailed east to find the spice islands of the Moluccas, whose cloves and nutmeg were in great demand in Europe.

**ISLAMIC STATES**

Banten (1527-1682)
JAVA SEA
Cirebon (1552-1705)
Jepara (16th c)
Demak (1505-88)
Giri (16th-17th c)
Selat Madura
Mataram (1575-1755)
Surakarta (1755-1945)
Yogyakarta (1755- )
Pasuruan (16th-17th c)
INDIAN OCEAN
0  100  200 km

In Java, the Portuguese arrived too late. In 1522 they signed a pact with the Hindu Pajajaran kingdom, which sought to stave off the growing power of the Islamic states. By the time the Portuguese returned in 1527 to establish their promised trading post, Sunda Kelapa had already fallen to the Islamic kingdom of Banten. Banten rose to be the most important trading port in the region, attracting Muslim merchants away from Melaka.

The Portuguese were soon followed by other European powers in search of riches. First the Spanish and then various private forays by the British and the Dutch. Cornelius de Houtman lead a disastrous expedition in 1596, losing half his crew, killing a Javanese prince and losing a ship in the process. Nevertheless, he returned to Holland with a boatload of spices that made a profit for the expedition's backers, and soon others followed.

Recognising the potential of the East Indies trade, the Dutch government amalgamated the competing merchant companies into the Vereenigde Oost-Indische Compagnie (VOC), or United East India Company. This government monopoly soon became the main competitor to secure the spice trade.

By 1605 the VOC had defeated the Portuguese and Spanish in the Moluccas, and the Dutch then looked for a base closer to the important shipping lanes of the Melaka and Sunda straits.

The ruler of Jayakarta granted permission for the Dutch to build a warehouse there in 1610. This warehouse soon became a fort, and as relations between the Dutch and the English came to the boil, skirmishes resulted in a siege of the fort by the English and the Jayakartans. The Dutch, under the ruthless empire builder Jan Pieterzoon Coen, razed the town in 1619 and renamed their new headquarters Batavia.

**Rise of Mataram** While the European powers battled for control of the sea lanes, the balance of power shifted in the interior in the second half of the 16th century. Demak was weakened by a protracted, unsuccessful war with the Hindu state of Blambangan and other small Muslim states, such as Jepara and Pasuruan, rose to prominence.

In West Java, around 1580, Banten finally conquered Pajajaran, the last major Hindu kingdom in Java to fall to Islam.

Central Java had languished since the fall of the great Hindu-Buddhist kingdom of Old Mataram that built Borobudur and Prambanan, but around Yogyakarta and Surakarta (now known as Solo), resurgent courts again became the major force in Java.

Central Java had been converted to Islam by Sunan Kudus, one of the wali songo, but while Islam became the state religion, the old court traditions and Javanese philosophy held greater sway away from the north coast. At present-day Solo (Surakarta), the growing kingdom of Pajang was a vassal of Demak, but it was soon overshadowed by the Mataram Empire.

According to legend, the founder of this second Mataram Empire, Senopati, sought the support of Nyai Loro Kidul, the goddess of the South Seas, who was to become the special protector of the House of Mataram. In 1575 Senopati founded his capital at Kota Gede, near Yogyakarta, and went on to conquer Demak in 1588.

Mataram extended its power eastwards, reaching its peak under Sultan Agung (1613-46), one of the classic warrior figures of Java's history. Sultan Agung moved his court to Kerta, south of Kota Gede, and the Mataram Empire eventually dominated Central and East Java and Madura. Agung devastated the north coast and ruled over the greatest empire since Majapahit. The only permanent defeats of his career were his failure to take Dutch Batavia and the sultanate of Banten in the west.

## Foundation of a Dutch Empire (1619-1700)

After the Dutch took Batavia in 1619, the early years were fraught with uncertainty. Governor-General Coen fortified the city, which lived under constant threat of attack from Banten, while the Dutch continued their expansion in the eastern islands.

## Jan Pieterzoon Coen

The far-sighted but ruthless Jan Pieterzoon Coen laid the foundation for a Dutch empire in Indonesia. In 1618, he was appointed governor-general of the small VOC post at Jayakarta and a year later, after skirmishes with the British and Jayakartans, he razed the town and renamed it Batavia. In the Moluccas he destroyed resistance and installed planters to increase spice production with the help of slave labour. Jan Pieterzoon Coen died aged 42, probably of cholera, during the siege of Batavia by Sultan Agung.

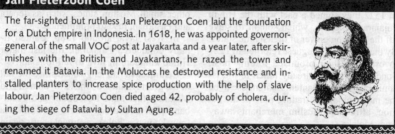

After conquering Central and East Java, Sultan Agung turned his military might westwards. In 1628 Mataram sent a fleet of 60 ships and 10,000 men to attack Batavia. They laid siege to the fort, but the Javanese army was poorly provisioned and had to retreat. An even larger assault the following year also resulted in a humiliating retreat. Batavia was spared further attacks as Sultan Agung had to deploy his armies to crush rebellions in the north coast principalities and wage war with Hindu Blambangan.

When Sultan Agung died in 1646, Mataram rapidly began to disintegrate. Amangkurat I assumed the throne and devoted his reign to destroying all those he suspected of opposing him. His tyrannical policies alienated his subjects and led to revolts on all sides. Recognising the wisdom of an alliance with Dutch military might, Amangkurat I signed a treaty of friendship.

The primary concern of the VOC was to control trade in the archipelago. Initially it shied away from expensive military incursions in Java, but soon became adept at playing off rival Javanese forces.

When a rebellion led by Prince Trunojoyo of Madura broke out in 1675, Amangkurat I called upon the Dutch, who intervened in 1677 but not before Trunojoyo sacked the court of Mataram and retreated to Kediri. In 1678 Dutch and Javanese troops destroyed Trunojoyo's stronghold at Kediri, and in return the Dutch gained concessions on trade and territorial influence.

In the west, Banten continued to flourish as a major trading port, despite unsuccessful attacks from Mataram in 1650 and 1657. Banten reached its peak under Sultan Ageng (1651-83), a firm enemy of the Dutch. A short war broke out in 1656, and the two remained enemies throughout Ageng's rule. In 1680 internal conflict within the royal house led to Dutch intervention on behalf of the ambitious crown prince. In return, the Dutch were granted a garrison in Banten, monopoly of the pepper trade and expulsion of the British and other European traders. It was the beginning of the end for Banten.

With the power of Mataram and Banten in decline, the VOC extended its influence in the interior around Parahyangan (the highlands around Bandung) and Cirebon. It had a garrison stationed at Kartosuro, the new capital of Mataram under Amangkurat II, and a network of trading posts along the north coast, including Semarang and Jepara. Yet while the VOC was a king maker, it never had the military force to control Java. Its military forays were always conducted alongside Javanese armies, and the VOC found itself enmeshed in military campaigns that caused increasing economic problems for the company.

## Javanese Wars of Succession (1704-55)

From the end of the 17th century Java was beset by wars as Mataram fragmented. The VOC, with its allies, the Cakraningrat Dynasty of West Madura, was only too willing to lend military support to contenders to the throne in return for compensation and land concessions.

The First Javanese War of Succession (1704-8) followed Amangkurat II's death. His brother, Pakubuwono I, took the throne with the support of the Dutch, who extracted heavy taxes and gained control of Semarang, East Madura and much of West Java.

The Second Javanese War of Succession (1719-23) followed Pakubuwono's death. Amangkurat IV assumed the throne with Dutch assistance, and was promptly billed by the VOC. The burdens and resentment of the Dutch payments brought further rebellion, which came to a head in 1740 following the Chinese massacre in Batavia.

In Batavia, the large Chinese population had continued to grow, causing suspicion and hostility among the Indonesian and Dutch inhabitants. The government began to deport Chinese labourers to Ceylon, and in 1740 the increasingly desperate Chinese rebelled by attacking outposts and marching on the city. Though the rebels were crudely armed, the good citizens of Batavia panicked and slaughtered 5000 Chinese.

The repercussions spilled into Central Java, and Dutch posts along the north coast were attacked by Chinese from Batavia. Pakubuwono II unwisely joined the fray and Madurese troops marched on the court of Mataram, conquering it in 1742. Pakubuwono was restored to his battered court but more concessions were made to the Dutch.

In 1745 Pakubuwono II established a new court at Surakarta, but it was no more stable than the old. The Third Javanese War of Succession (1746-57) ensued, with Prince Mangkubumi and Mas Said contesting the throne. The Dutch, keen to end its expensive military involvement, forced a solution.

## Mataram Divided; Foundation of Yogyakarta (1755-1800)

In 1755 the former Mataram Empire was split into two rival, self-governing principalities. The Sultanate of Yogyakarta, headed by Prince Mangkubumi, was split off from Surakarta. Mas Said continued to wage war but finally surrendered in 1757 and was granted a smaller domain within Surakarta called Mangkunegaran.

Mangkubumi took the title of Sultan Hamengkubuwono I and was the most able Mataram ruler since Sultan Agung. During his reign the Sultanate of Yogyakarta grew to be the most powerful kingdom in Central Java. Court intrigues continued as Yogyakarta and Surakarta struggled to dominate and reunite Central Java, but the Dutch successfully played the game of divide and rule. Despite a few minor uprisings, Central Java was free of destructive war for the next 70 years, and artistic traditions flowered in the courts.

## A New Colonial Era (1800-11)

Towards the end of the 17th century, the spice trade had declined and the VOC relied increasingly on plantations to prop up falling profits. The Dutch trading monopoly declined, while inefficiency, corruption and expensive military campaigns all helped to bankrupt the company. The Dutch government stepped in and the VOC was finally dissolved in 1799, issuing in a new era of direct colonial government.

Napoleon had conquered Holland in 1795 and installed his brother on the Dutch throne in 1806. In 1808 the government sent pro-revolutionary Governor-General Daendels with the task of reorganising the colony and defending it against the British, who were effectively blockading Batavia's harbour.

Daendels reshaped Batavia, demolishing the old city and developing a new administrative district at Weltevreden to the southeast. Buitenzorg (present-day Bogor) became the official seat of the governor-general. Daendels set about reforming the civil service and attacked corruption, but his reforms had the greatest effect on interior Java, where he sought to establish direct colonial authority over the sultanates. Whereas the Dutch had previously preferred to be the behind-the-scenes power broker, Daendels installed ministers at the courts with the same powers as Javanese rulers. He also claimed Java as Dutch territory and refused to continue to pay rent for Dutch possessions on the coast.

Hamengkubuwono II openly rebelled and Daendels attacked Yogyakarta in 1810, installing the crown prince as Sultan Hamengkubuwono III.

## English Rule (1811-16)

In 1811, after Napoleon's official annexation of Holland, the British, at war with the French, invaded Batavia.

The English ruled the Dutch East Indies for the next five years and Sir Stamford Raffles was appointed lieutenant-governor of Java. Raffles was a reformist in the same mould as Daendels, and was also keen to directly rule Java's principalities. The sultanate of Banten was annexed and the rulers of Cirebon brought to heel. In 1812 the British sent troops to plunder the court of Yogya, supported by the sultan's ambitious brother, who was given the principality of Pakualaman, a small enclave within the sultanate, as reward.

At the end of the Napoleonic wars in 1816, Britain returned the Dutch colonies. Though ambitious and well intentioned, Raffles was not always an efficient administrator. His impact on the colony was minimal, though many ancient sites in Java were catalogued due to his interest in the culture.

## Diponegoro's Java War (1825-30)

Java was in a state of flux due to corruption at court, continual European interference and increased hardship among the Javanese villagers. Into this turbulent picture stepped one of the most famous figures of Indonesian history, Prince Diponegoro.

Diponegoro, the eldest son of Hamengkubuwono III, was brought up in the countryside and became critical of the court culture into which he was born and of the growing European power and influence on Java. In true Javanese mystic tradition, the charismatic prince was a devout Muslim, but also well versed in Javanese philosophy. A visitation from the queen of the South Seas foretold his rise to greatness.

In 1823 the colonial government abolished leases on plantation land owned by aristocrats, thereby depriving them of a large source of revenue. The last straw for Diponegoro came when a road was to be built across his land in 1825. The resultant skirmish launched a bloody five-year war against the Dutch.

Joined by many of his peers at court, and with overwhelming support from the peasantry, Diponegoro soon controlled much of Central Java. The Dutch held the cities but were at sea against Diponegoro's guerrilla tactics in the countryside.

As the war wore on, the Dutch came to terms with the rebel armies. By 1830 the resistance was weak and Diponegoro was treacherously lured into negotiations with the Dutch at Magelang, where he was arrested and exiled to Sulawesi. Over 15,000 government troops had been killed, and 200,000 Javanese lost their lives.

## Culture System (1830-70)

At the end of the Java War, Dutch military and political control of Java was almost complete. However, the war had been fought at enormous financial cost, and the expanded administration needed to control Java was also costly. Plantation crops – primarily sugar along the north coast and coffee in the Parahyangan highlands – had long been the mainstay of the colonial economy. With a deteriorating economy at home, the Dutch wanted Java, the jewel of its colony, to increase profits.

In 1830 Governor-General van den Bosch introduced the infamous Cultuurstelsel (Culture System) in a determined effort to make the colony pay for itself through export crops. Instead of land taxes, peasants had to either cultivate government-owned crops on 20% of their land or work in the government plantations for nearly 60 days of the year. Much of Java became a Dutch plantation, generating great wealth in the Netherlands.

As colonial settlement in the interior spread rapidly, the Javanese aristocracy became effete figureheads. Freed from the responsibilities of rule, they turned their attentions to literature and the arts. For the

Javanese peasantry, this forced-labour system brought hardship and resentment. Forced to grow crops such as sugar instead of rice, the Javanese were subject to famine and epidemics that swept Java in the 1840s, first at Cirebon in 1843 and then Central Java.

## Liberal Policy (1870-1900)

Public opinion in Holland began to decry the treatment and suffering of Indonesians under the colonial government. The so-called Liberal Policy was introduced by liberals in the Dutch parliament who were trying to reform and eliminate the excesses of the Culture System.

Agrarian reform in 1870 freed producers from the compulsion to provide export crops but opened Java to private enterprise, which developed large plantations. Java's population was increasing dramatically, but less land was available for rice production, bringing further hardship to the Javanese. Dutch profits grew dramatically in the latter part of the 19th century.

Java was in transition. The expansion of Dutch rule brought significant changes to Javanese society. To provide labour for the growing bureaucracy, western education became available to the aristocracy, not only for the children of traditional rulers but also for the children from wealthy families who showed talent. At the same time, direct Dutch rule meant the decline of the *bupatis*, or traditional rulers, whom the Dutch had previously supported as their agents. The nature of the elite changed and broadened.

The peasantry, on the other hand, was left stranded without leadership. Islam increasingly became the focus for opposition to exploitation by the colonial administration, local rulers and capitalists.

## 20th Century Colonial Rule (1900-42)

The 20th century heralded a new approach to colonial government as the Ethical Policy was introduced in 1901. Under this policy it became the Dutch government's duty to further the welfare of the Indonesian people in health, education and other social programs.

At the same time, greater development and exploitation of resources in the outer islands saw the bulk of economic activity shift from Java. While Java declined in economic importance, its needs increased, fuelled by its ever growing population. Large increases in public health expenditure were laudable, but ultimately inadequate.

The Ethical Policy gave greater education possibilities for Indonesians, but the vast majority of Indonesians were illiterate. Though primary schools were established and education was now open to all, by 1930 only 8% of school age children received an education.

Much of the increase in education was due to Javanese efforts. The noted author Kartini, through her impassioned writing, inspired education for women and Kartini schools were established in Java. *Pesantren* (religious schools) had always provided religious instruction, but the Modernist Islamic movement gave a new direction. Muhammadiyah, formed in 1912 in Yogyakarta, established schools across Java, teaching fundamental Islamic tenets (sometimes in opposition to Javanese Islamic philosophy) with modern education.

**Nationalism** Western education brought with it western political ideas of freedom and democracy, but the first seeds of Indonesian nationalism were sown by the Islamic movements.

Sarekat Islam was an early, pre-modern nationalist movement, inspired more by Islamic and Javanese mysticism than by notions of independent self rule. It rallied Indonesians under the traditional banner of Islam, in opposition to Dutch influence, but had no national agenda and was often more anti-Chinese than anti-colonial.

The Indonesian Communist Party (PKI), on the other hand, was a fully fledged, pro-independence party inspired by European politics. It was formed in 1920 and found support among workers in the industrial cities. The PKI presumptuously decided to start the revolution in Indonesia in 1926 with isolated insurrections across Java. The panicked and outraged Dutch government arrested and exiled thousands of communists, effectively putting them out of action for the rest of the Dutch occupation.

Despite Dutch repression of nationalist organisations and the arrest of its leaders, the nationalist movement was finding a unified voice. In an historic announcement, the All Indonesia Youth Congress proclaimed its Youth Pledge in 1928, adopting the notions of the one fatherland (Indonesia), one united country and one language (Bahasa Indonesia). In Bandung in 1929, Soekarno founded the Partai Nasional Indonesia (PNI), the most significant nationalist organisation. It was the first, all-Indonesia secular party devoted primarily to independence and not ideology.

Soekarno was educated in East Java and went on to receive a European education before studying at the Bandung Institute of Technology, where he was active in the Bandung Study Club. Bandung was a hotbed of political intellectualism, where the PKI and radical Muslim thought flowered. Soekarno was widely influenced by Javanese, western, Muslim and socialist ideals, and blended these various influences towards a national ideology.

Soekarno was soon arrested and a virtual ban placed on the PNI. Nationalist sentiment remained high in the 1930s, but with many nationalist leaders in jail or exiled, the hope of independence seemed a long way off. Even when Germany invaded the Netherlands in May 1940, the colonial government in exile was determined to continue its rule in the East Indies.

All was to change when the Japanese attacked Pearl Harbor and then stormed down through South-East Asia. After the fall of Singapore, many Europeans fled to Australia, and the colonial government abandoned Batavia, surrendering to the Japanese on 8 March 1942.

## Japanese Rule (1942-45)

The Japanese imperial army marched into Batavia on 5 March 1942, carrying the red-and-white Indonesian flag alongside that of the rising sun. The city's name was changed to Jakarta, Europeans were arrested and all signs of the former Dutch masters eliminated.

Though the Japanese were greeted initially as liberators, public opinion turned against them as the war wore on and Indonesians were expected to endure more hardship for the war effort. The Japanese were keen to impress their superiority on the Indonesian population and soon developed a reputation as cruel masters.

However, the Japanese gave Indonesians more responsibility and participation in government. The very top administrative positions were held by Japanese, but Indonesians from the top down ruled themselves for the first time. The Japanese also gave prominence to nationalist leaders, such as Soekarno and Mohammed Hatta, and trained youth militia to defend the country. Apart from giving Indonesia a military psyche that endured in Indonesian politics, this youthful militia gave rise to the *pemuda* (youth) of the independence movement who would later form the independence army.

## Battle for Independence (1945-49)

As the war ended, the nationalist leadership of Soekarno and Hatta was pressured by radical youth groups to immediately declare Indonesia's independence before the Dutch could return. On 17 August 1945, with tacit Japanese backing, Soekarno proclaimed the independence of the Republic of Indonesia from his Jakarta home.

Indonesians throughout the archipelago rejoiced, but the Netherlands refused to accept the proclamation and still claimed sovereignty over Indonesia. British troops entered Java in October 1945 to accept the surrender of the Japanese. Under British auspices, Dutch troops gradually returned to Indonesia and it became obvious that independence would have to be fought for.

Skirmishes broke out with the new Republican army and things came to a head in the bloody battle for Surabaya as Europeans and Dutch internees returned to the city. Leaders such as Bung Tomo fired the people with their revolutionary rhetoric and the situation deteriorated when British Indian troops landed in the city. Soekarno and Hatta flew to Surabaya to negotiate a ceasefire between the Republicans and General Mallaby, leader of the British forces. Fighting continued, however, and when Mallaby was killed in a bomb blast, the British moved in more troops to prepare for retaliatory action. On 10 November (now celebrated as Heroes Day) the Battle of Surabaya began in earnest, and the British began to take the city under cover of air attacks. It was a bloody retribution and thousands of Indonesians died as the population fled to the countryside. The poorly armed but numerous Republican forces fought a pitched battle for three weeks. The brutal retaliation of the British and the spirited defence of Surabaya by the Republicans galvanised Indonesian support and helped turn world opinion.

The Dutch dream of easy reoccupation was shattered, while the British were keen to extricate themselves from military action and broker a peace agreement.

In Jakarta, the republican government, with Soekarno as president and Hatta as vice-president, tried to maintain calm. On the other hand, youth groups advocating armed struggle saw the old leadership as prevaricating and betraying the revolution.

Outbreaks occurred across the country and Soekarno and Hatta were outmanoeuvred in the Republican government. Sutan Sjahrir became prime minister and, as the Dutch assumed control in Jakarta, the Republicans moved their capital to Yogyakarta. Sultan Hamengkubuwono IX, who was to become Yogya's most revered and able sultan, played a leading role in the revolution. In Surakarta, on the other hand, Pakubuwono XII was ineffectual, to the detriment of Surakarta, when independence arrived.

The battle for independence wavered between warfare and diplomacy. Under the Linggarjati agreement of November 1946, the Dutch recognised the Republican government and both sides agreed to work towards an Indonesian federation under a Dutch commonwealth. The agreement was soon swept aside as the war escalated. The Dutch mounted a large offensive in July 1947 to control much of the north coast, causing the United Nations to step in.

During these uncertain times, the main forces in Indonesian politics regrouped. The communist PKI and Soekarno's old party, the PNI, reformed, while the main Islamic parties were Masyumi and Nahdatul Ulama (NU).

The army also emerged as a political force, though it was split by many factions. The Republicans were far from united and in Java, civil war threatened to erupt when the PKI staged a rebellion in Solo (Surakarta) and then Madiun. In a tense threat to the revolution, Soekarno galvanised opposition to the communists, who were defeated by army forces.

In February 1948, the Dutch launched another full-scale attack on the Republicans, breaking the UN agreement and bringing international condemnation. Under pressure from the USA, which threatened to withdraw its postwar aid to the Netherlands, and a growing realisation at home that this was

Soekarno – first president of Indonesia

an unwinnable war, the Dutch negotiated for independence. On 27 December 1949 the Indonesian flag was raised at Jakarta's Istana Merdeka (Freedom Palace) as power was officially handed over.

## Independence (1949-57)

Across the nation, political and economic uncertainty accompanied the early independence years. The fledgling nation had to contend with secessionist movements in the outer islands, powerful Muslim opposition to the secular state, and unstable government as seven cabinets came and went up to 1955. The economy stagnated and foreign investment went elsewhere, while inflation and corruption increased dramatically.

It was not all bad news for Indonesia though, as the government pressed ahead with social programs providing greater access to education and health services for the majority of Indonesians.

In 1955 Indonesia held its first elections, with the PNI becoming the largest party in a split parliament. The communist PKI had come back from the dead and claimed large support among the peasantry in Java, while the devoutly Muslim population supported the Islamic Masyumi and NU parties. The army was also a key player, but despite attempted coups could not gain power.

All the while, Soekarno was more than a figurehead president answerable to parliament, and held sway by the force of his rhetoric and mass appeal. By 1957 the country was still in turmoil and without clear government. Soekarno, with army support, declared martial law and instigated his era of 'guided democracy'.

## Guided Democracy (1957-65)

Soekarno's 'guided democracy' government was meant to represent all groups in society, working together with mutual cooperation (gotong royong), rather than the competition of parliamentary democracy. The PNI and NU dominated the government, while the major backstage players were the army and the PKI, whose popular support grew dramatically.

Under martial law, the army consolidated its power. Nationalist fervour, inspired by Soekarno's railings against the Dutch refusal to turn over Irian Jaya, resulted in the Indonesian seizure of Dutch properties. Many of these enterprises were administered by the army, which helped to increase its involvement in the economy and also in corruption in general.

Java had always been the focus for politics in Indonesia, but power became increasingly Java-centric. A rebellion in Sumatra only increased the concentration of Javanese in top positions in the government and in the army.

As army interference and power in Indonesia grew, and the PKI, the army's mortal enemy, grew to be the largest communist party outside Russia and China, Soekarno held power in a deft balancing act. All the while, Indonesia's economy languished and inflation spiralled.

In Java, the PKI pushed for land reform through its grass-roots organisation, and sporadic conflicts with Muslim supporters broke out. In the army, Soekarno had managed to manoeuvre the powerful General Nasution away from the top job, but the army expanded with Russian funding.

By 1965 inflation had reached 500%. Soekarno, now convinced that the PKI could not be ignored, gave greater prominence to the communists in Jakarta and courted Beijing. The army grew increasingly uneasy at this new shift in influence. The conflicts came to a head in October 1965.

## New Order (1965-98)

On the night of 30 September 1965, six of Indonesia's top generals were taken from their Jakarta homes and executed in an attempted coup. Led by Colonel Untung and backed by elements of the armed forces, the insurgents surrounded the presidential palace and seized the national radio station. They claimed that they had acted against a plot organised by the generals to overthrow the president.

The army, headed by General Soeharto, quickly crushed the rebellion and Soeharto orchestrated a counter coup. It maintained

## Pancasila

First expounded by Soekarno in 1945 the Pancasila (Five Principles) have remained the philosophical backbone of the Indonesian state. Soekarno meant them to provide a broad base on which a united Indonesian state could be formed. All over Indonesia you'll see the Indonesian coat of arms with its symbolic incorporation of the Pancasila, hung on the walls of government offices and the homes of village heads, on the covers of student textbooks or immortalised on great stone tablets.

In the post-Soeharto era everything is up for re-evaluation and some have suggested that Pancasila should be scrapped. But the idea is likely to continue, with a new reinterpretation, for the principles are sufficiently vague to support both democracy or autocracy. The main message of Pancasila is that religious and ethnic divisions must always take second place to the interests of the state. The principles of Pancasila are:

**1. Faith in God** – symbolised by the star. This is perhaps the most important and contentious principle. As interpreted by Soekarno and the Javanese syncretists who have ruled Indonesia since independence, this can mean any god – Allah, Vishnu, Buddha, Christ etc. For many Muslims, it means belief in the only true God, Allah, but the government goes to great lengths to suppress both Islamic extremism and calls for an Islamic state in multi-ethnic and multi-religious Indonesia.

**2. Humanity** – symbolised by the chain. This represents the unbroken unity of humankind, and Indonesia takes its place among this family of nations.

**3. Nationalism** – symbolised by the banyan tree. All ethnic groups in Indonesia must unite.

**4. Representative government** – symbolised by the head of the buffalo. As distinct from the western brand of parliamentary democracy, Soekarno envisaged a form of Indonesian democracy based on the village system of deliberation *(permusyawaratan)* among representatives to achieve consensus *(mufakat)*. The western system of 'majority rules' is considered to be a means by which 51% oppress the other 49%.

**5. Social justice** – symbolised by sprays of rice and cotton. A just and prosperous society gives adequate supplies of food and clothing for all – these are the basic requirements of social justice.

---

that the Untung coup was organised by the PKI, and an anticommunist pogrom was unleashed. Across the country, but particularly in Java, hundreds of thousands of communists, suspected communists and Chinese were slaughtered. Government arrests and tortures were accompanied by an uncontrolled bloodbath in Java.

**A New Order began with President Soeharto, but 30 years on his regime was in disorder.**

Though Soekarno remained president for two more years, Soeharto and the armed forces called the shots. After suppressing opposition and consolidating power, Soeharto was officially appointed president in 1967 and instigated his era of New Order. Indonesia looked to the west in foreign policy, and western-educated economists set about balancing budgets, controlling inflation and attracting foreign investment.

In 1971 general elections were held to give a veneer of democracy to the new regime. Soeharto used the almost defunct Golkar Party as the spearhead of the army's election campaign. Having appointed his election squad, the old parties were then crippled. Some parties were banned, others had their candidates disqualified and voters were also disenfranchised. Predictably, Golkar swept to power and the PNI was shattered. The new People's Consultative Congress also included 207 Soeharto appointments and 276 armed forces officers.

Soeharto then enforced the merger of other political parties. The four Muslim parties were merged into the Partai Persatuan Pembangunan (PPP; Development Union Party), and the other parties into the Partai Demokrasi Indonesia (PDI).

With the elimination of the communists and the introduction of a more repressive government, political stability returned to Indonesia and the divisions in society were less prominent. A determined effort to promote national, rather than regional, identity was largely successful, but the army's brutal reaction to dissent tarnished Indonesia's international image. Indonesia's invasion of East Timor in 1975 and its subsequent repression of the native people there, and the continuing struggle with Irian Jaya's separatist guerrillas, still hang over the government.

Ever the quiet, smiling general turned president, behind the scenes Soeharto was a consummate power broker, jailing critics and playing off factions to maintain his power base. At the same time, Indonesia prospered and economic progress followed political stability. Soeharto became the 'father of development' and many of his economic achievements were impressive. Burgeoning manufacturing industries, fuelled by massive foreign investment, saw high growth rates and large infrastructure projects, mostly in Java, but the government also spent money improving roads and communications in the more remote areas of Indonesia.

The lot of most Indonesians improved considerably during the 30 years of Soeharto's New Order government. But while life became more tolerable for the poor, the rich became a lot richer. Corruption, an ever-present problem in the country, extended from the lowest paid government official right to the top. The most obvious recipients of the new wealth were the business associates of Soeharto, many of them Chinese Indonesians, and Soeharto's children. The president's family acquired huge business empires, along with prime government contracts, and Indonesian business culture revolved around kickbacks, bribes and official patronage.

Grass-root grumblings increased along with disparity of wealth, but they were ignored by a government entrenched in power and presiding over an economic boom. Greater education also resulted in calls for greater freedom. The political opposition, particularly the PDI, grew in stature and popularity. So much so that in 1996 the government helped engineer a split in the PDI, resulting in its popular leader Megawati Soekarnoputri, Soekarno's daughter, being dumped. PDI supporters rioted in Jakarta, but it was only a foretaste of things to come.

Ageing Soeharto, now well into his 70s, made noises about retirement, but there was no obvious successor and, fearing factional in-fighting, the government reaffirmed his leadership. The business community, both international and domestic, had also become comfortable with Indonesia's brand of crony capitalism and preferred the status quo to the uncertainty of a post-Soeharto Indonesia. Soeharto continued in power, for too long.

## The Fall of Soeharto

All was to change when the Asian currency crisis spilled over into Indonesia. In July 1997 financial markets savaged the rupiah and the Indonesian economy was left teetering on the edge of bankruptcy.

The International Monetary Fund (IMF) pledged financial backing in return for economic reform, abolition of government subsidies on food and fuel, deregulation of monopolies such as the clove monopoly controlled by the president's son, Tommy, and the abandonment of grandiose high-tech, government-sponsored industries, many of which also fell under the huge umbrella of Soeharto Family Inc.

Rising prices resulted in sporadic riots, mostly in Java and southern Sulawesi, as the people, already hard hit by the *krisis moneter* (monetary crisis), looted shops owned by the minority ethnic Chinese, which was a significant business class. The economic miracle of high growth powered by massive foreign investment was over, and the Chinese became the scapegoats for

this sudden, inexplicable loss of faith in the Indonesian economy.

The markets saw chaos and savaged the rupiah. The rupiah bottomed at nearly 17,000Rp to the US dollar in January 1998, down from 2500Rp six months earlier. Foreign debt and inflation skyrocketed, a number of banks collapsed and many companies with foreign loans faced bankruptcy. Millions lost their jobs and Indonesia's impressive gains in eliminating poverty over 30 years were wiped out overnight.

At the same time, President Soeharto was up for re-election. This was a foregone conclusion but, as never before, critics from the Muslim parties, opposition groups and especially student demonstrators demanded that he step down and Indonesia move towards a more open political system.

Soeharto's re-election in February 1998 seemed to at least promise political certainty, and the government moved towards fulfilling IMF demands. The rupiah stabilised but demands for political reform continued as students demonstrated across the country. The demonstrators held banners saying such things as 'Turunkan Soeharto' (Bring Down Soeharto). Once this would have been punishable as treason in Indonesia. The demonstrations were largely peaceful and confined to the campuses, but in late April, violent rioting erupted in the streets of Medan in Sumatra, then in other cities in Indonesia. Adding to the hardship and furthering unrest, the government announced fuel and electricity rises on 4 May 1998, as demanded by the IMF.

Throughout the turmoil the army repeated its support for the government. Tanks and army trucks appeared on the streets of Jakarta to confirm the army's intentions but demands for Soeharto's resignation increased. Student demonstrations would not go away and then, on 12 May, with Soeharto away on a visit to Cairo, soldiers swapped live ammunition for rubber bullets and shot dead four students at Trisakti University in Jakarta.

Jakarta erupted as rioters from outside the campuses went on the rampage. Anarchy ruled in Indonesia's worst civil disturbance since the slaughter of 1965-66. In three days of rioting and looting, over 6000 buildings in Jakarta were damaged or destroyed, and an estimated 1200 people died, mostly those trapped in burning shopping centres. Ordinary people, the urban poor, joined in the looting as law and order collapsed. The army's role was often ineffectual as soldiers looked on, trying to portray the army as the people's ally. Hardest hit were the Chinese, whose businesses were looted and destroyed, and shocking tales of rape and murder emerged after the riots.

The riots finally subsided. But anti-Soeharto demonstrations increased, while the army threatened to shoot rioters on sight. The country feared massive bloodshed and a repetition of history. Still Soeharto clung to the presidency, but with the writing on the wall, some of his own ministers called for his resignation. Soeharto finally stepped down as president on 21 May 1998, ending 32 years of rule.

## The Road to Democracy

Vice-president BJ Habibie was sworn in and quickly set about making the right noises on reform by releasing political prisoners and promising elections. Compared with the reserved Soeharto, who ruled like a Javanese king, civilian Habibie tried hard to cultivate an image as a man of the people. However, as a long-standing minister and close friend of Soeharto, his credentials as a reformer were always going to be questioned.

After the euphoria of Soeharto's demise, the economy was still in tatters and the rupiah plumbed new lows, but Indonesia enthusiastically embraced a new era of political openness. The government talked about political reform, democracy and eliminating corruption but at the same time tried to ban demonstrations and reaffirmed the role of the army in Indonesian politics.

The army's reputation was severely tarnished. Not only had it started the riots by shooting students, then failed to contain the rioting, evidence emerged that military factions used *agents provocateurs* to incite rioting. The newly vocal press also exposed army killings in Aceh and the abduction and murder of opposition activists.

As the government stalled on announcing an election date, it became obvious that it was also stalling on full political reform, preferring to keep democracy within the framework of the old system. The students returned to the streets, demanding elections and Habibie's resignation.

As IMF money flowed into Indonesia, the currency strengthened, but widespread poverty resulted in continuing food riots. People sold their meagre possessions to buy food, while others simply took it, and in uncertain times, old grudges resurfaced. The Chinese continued to be the main scapegoats, while in East Java, bizarre serial killings of black magicians and Muslim clerics claimed the lives of over 200 people.

Student protests came to a head again in November 1998, when thousands rallied as the Indonesian parliament met to discuss terms for the new election. Student demands for immediate elections and the abolition of military appointees to parliament were ignored.

Tension on the streets of Jakarta was fuelled by thousands of pro-government youth militia employed by the authorities. The military, with presidential orders to crack down on dissent, did just that. Three days of skirmishes peaked on 13 November when a student march on parliament was met by military force and gunfire. Clashes left 12 dead and hundreds injured. Jakarta again was in flames, as shopping centres and Chinese businesses were looted and burnt by Jakarta *preman* (thugs) and other opportunists.

Before the smoke had settled, new disturbances in Jakarta took on an even more worrying trend. A local dispute involving Christians from Maluku resulted in rampaging Muslims burning churches throughout the Ketapang district of Jakarta. Christians throughout Indonesia were outraged, and in eastern Indonesia, Christians attacked mosques and the minority Muslim community.

**Megawati Soekarnoputri was the people's choice for president; but can she govern?**

were experienced. In the first free election in over 40 years, thousands took to the streets in support of the new political parties, participating in what was largely a joyous celebration of democracy.

The elections, however, were only the first step to real democratic change. Megawati Soekarnoputri emerged as the most popular choice for president, but her PDIP (Indonesian Democracy Party of Struggle) could muster only around a third of the vote. The government Golkar party, without the benefit of a rigged electoral system, had its vote slashed from over 70% to around 20%. But with strong support from outside Java and Bali, Golkar remains a political force with a number of seats in the DPR lower house.

At the time when this book was being written, the lobbying continued and political deals were still being made. The real struggle has been to try to form a coalition that will satisfy the Indonesian electors. Despite mutterings from Megawati's erstwhile opposition partners that she may not have what it takes to be president, if the opposition parties do not form a united coalition, Golkar may yet be returned to government. Such an event could anger students and the general populace, which is eager for change.

Without a majority government, Indonesia's political scene may remain unstable, but there is a resurgent optimism in the country after the cataclysmic events of 1998/9. Democracy promises hope for a better future, and the economy – while still a long way from recovery – has stabilised and negative growth has been reversed.

The old elite was slow to instigate change and failed to recognise widespread support for the students' demands, but it was acutely aware that political freedom could well mean the reopening of the old divisions in Indonesian society. Communism was no longer a threat, but communal violence was an ever-present danger.

Riots in Kupang, West Timor, were followed by prolonged Muslim/Christian violence in Maluku province and then in Kalimantan in early 1999.

Java, which had seen most of the violence at the onset of the economic crisis, returned to relative order while the outlying areas of Indonesia erupted. There was renewed trouble in the separatist-minded districts of Aceh and East Timor as they saw a real possibility of independence from a weakened Jakarta.

Violence is historically the hand-maiden of political change in Indonesia and democracy will be a rocky road. But despite widespread predictions of violence in the lead up to the June 1999 elections, few problems

## GEOGRAPHY & GEOLOGY

With an area of 132,000 sq km, Java is just a speck on the map of Asia, but with its huge population and economic importance it is a continent in itself.

Colonial travelogues spoke of the emerald isle, a fertile, tropical paradise that was the jewel of the Dutch East Indies. Though most of the primal forest has now gone, and the overcrowded plains appear as a never-ending sea of cities and villages, Java is still an island of astonishing beauty.

Java is dominated by a string of volcanoes running the length of the island, interspersed with brilliant green rice paddies, coconut palms and plantations of sugar cane, rubber and cassava. Its high rainfall is directed into extensive irrigation works, which are the mainstay of sawah, or wet-rice cultivation, the super productive agricultural marvel of flooded rice fields.

The fertile valleys between the volcanoes and along the north coast are the main agricultural regions of Java, and the main population centres.

The south coast also has low limestone hills in the Gunung Kidul region south of Yogya and Solo. The infertile soils and low rainfall make this the poorest region in Java. The south coast, pounded by the Indian Ocean, faces the deep Java Trench.

This trench is the meeting point of the Sunda plate, on which Java lies, and the Australian plate. The collision of these two tectonic plates has produced the volcanic activity and unstable movement that threatens Java with earthquakes and eruptions.

## Volcanoes

Java has over 30 volcanoes, most of which are still active. They stretch from the Ijen Plateau overlooking the straits of Bali to Krakatau, Indonesia's most famous and destructive volcano, which is located in the Sunda Strait between Java and Sumatra.

The spectacular volcanic landscapes of Gunung Bromo in East Java are well known, while nearby Gunung Semeru is Java's highest volcanic peak at 3676m. Semeru is revered as the home of the gods, for the mountains are also centres of spiritual power. In Hindu-Buddhist times, temples

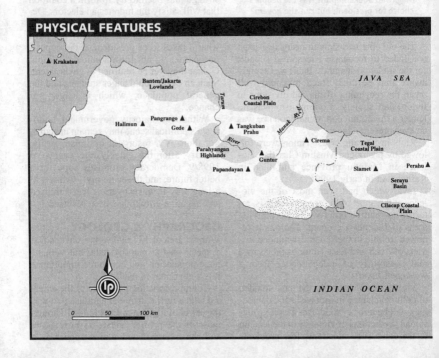

PHYSICAL FEATURES

dotted many of the hillsides and attracted pilgrims offering prayers and appeasement. The mountains still house isolated outposts of the old religion where Hinduism survives.

Most of the volcanoes sit smoking and quiet, with occasional rumblings. Major eruptions in recent time include: Bromo 1972; Raung 1978; Semeru 1978 and 1979; Galunggung 1982; Slamet 1988; Kelud 1990; and Merapi 1972, 1976, 1994 and 1998. Gunung Merapi, overlooking Yogyakarta, features prominently in Javanese folklore and is one of Java's most dangerous volcanoes. Semeru is also very active, but not as close to major population centres.

The rich volcanic soils are the secret to Java's fertility and its ability to support its population. Historically, the volcanoes have also been a barrier between the different regions and cultures, and Java's ethnic diversity is reflected in its geography.

## Coastal Plains & Basins

The major population and agricultural areas are the coastal plains and the basins between the mountains. The Yogya and Solo basins in Central Java, and the Madiun, Kediri and Malang basins in East Java, have long been populated and have given rise to major civilisations. These fertile regions, based around rivers such as the Bengawan Solo and Brantas are extensive rice growing districts. In West Java, the basins in the Parahyangan Highlands also have rich volcanic soils and high rainfall supporting rice and plantation crops. Many parts of West Java, with extensive irrigation and verdant rice paddies, resemble Bali.

The flat coastal plains to the north, lying between the shallow Java Sea and the mountains, are alluvial regions. Rice is grown extensively, as are plantation crops such as sugar cane. Farther east are the

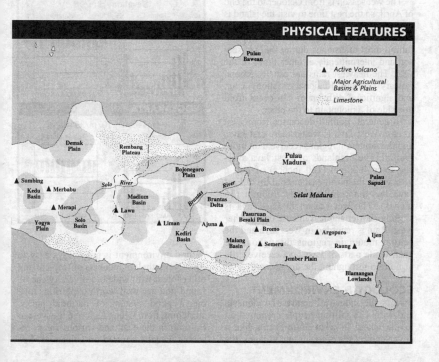

PHYSICAL FEATURES

▲ Active Volcano
Major Agricultural Basins & Plains
Limestone

Pulau Bawean
Demak Plain
Rembang Plateau
Pulau Madura
Pulau Sapudi
Bojonegoro Plain
▲ Sumbing
Solo River
Brantas River
Selat Madura
Kedu Basin ▲ Merbabu
Madium Basin
Brantas Delta
▲ Merapi
▲ Lawu
Pasuruan Besuki Plain
Yogya Plain
Solo Basin
▲ Liman  Ajuna ▲
▲ Bromo
▲ Argopuro  Ijen ▲
Kediri Basin
Malang Basin
▲ Semeru
Raung ▲
Jember Plain
Blamangan Lowlands

limestone hills of the Rembang Plateau that extend into Madura. Here the soils are less fertile, rainfall is lower and it is generally not possible to grow rice. Pockets of the eastern tip of Java are arid and more reminiscent of Australia.

## CLIMATE

Across the island the temperature throughout the year averages 22 to 29°C (78 to 85°F) and humidity averages a high 75%, but the northern coastal plains are usually hotter – up to 34°C (94°F) during the day in the dry season – and more oppressively humid than anywhere else. Generally the south coast is cooler than the north coast, especially in the dry season when it receives the south-east breezes. The mountainous regions inland are much cooler, with temperatures dropping to freezing at night on the mountain peaks.

The wet season is from October to the end of April, so the best time to visit the island is during the dry season from May to September. The rain comes as a tropical downpour, falling most afternoons during the wet season and intermittently at other times of the year. The heaviest rains are usually around January-February. Regional variations occur, and significant differences can occur from one side of a mountain to the other.

In general, rainfall decreases from west to east. West Java is wetter than East Java, and the mountain regions receive a lot more rainfall. The highlands of West Java average over 4000mm (160 inches) of rain a year while the north-east coastal tip of East Java has a rainfall of only 900mm (35 inches). The wet season in East Java is slightly shorter and less intense than farther west. Rain is recorded in West Java and the central mountain regions throughout the year, while parts of East Java receive little or no rain throughout the dry season.

## ECOLOGY & ENVIRONMENT

Java is the industrial centre of Indonesia and with 128 million people crammed on to the island in what often seems like a never-ending sea of towns and villages, the

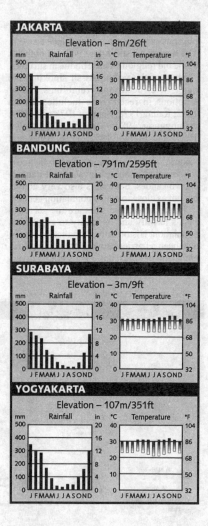

natural environment is not always easy to find. Nevertheless, pockets of tropical and other forest with wide bio-diversity can be found and are well worth exploring. Java has a good system of national parks, stretching from Ujung Kulon in the west to Baluran in the east, and various forest reserves, usually centred on volcanoes. See the following Flora & Fauna section for more information.

Growing industrialisation and population pressures point to ecological degradation in a country that does not have the resources to give environmental issues high priority. In Java's cities, industrial pollution is multiplying and over 30% of Indonesians now live in cities, compared with 15% in 1970. Waste removal services have difficulty coping with the garbage, household and industrial, but the worst threat to living standards is the lack of decent sewerage. Very few cities have a sewerage system and rely on septic tanks or disposal of effluent through the canals and river systems. This in turn is a major source of pollution to water resources. Most Indonesians are simply not supplied with safe drinking water and water has to be boiled. With the increasing wealth of the middle classes, the number of new motor vehicles has increased dramatically, and so too have vehicle emissions.

Despite the problems facing Indonesia, there are environmental protection programs in place but, typically, they are poorly funded and enforcement is difficult or ignored. Indonesia is increasingly looking for help from foreign environmental groups that are involved in a number of research and environmental protection programs right across the country.

· WWF Indonesia (☎ 021-720 3095, fax 739 5907), Jl Kramat Pela 3, Gandaria Utara, Jakarta, has a strong presence in Indonesia and it is a good contact point. LATIN (☎ 0251-379143, 379825), Jl Citarum B/XI No12, Bogor Baru, Bogor, is an Indonesian organisation involved in a variety of projects including rhino research in Ujung Kulon and rainforest medicine at Meru Betiri National Park. Visit their Web site at www.latin.or.id. Yayasan Pembangunan Berkelanjutan (Foundation for Sustainable Development; ☎ 021-8314750, fax 831 4751, email mailadm@ypb.or.id), Jl Tebet Raya 88, Jakarta, conducts environmental training and education programs. The Environmental Impact Management Agency (BAPEDAL), 12th floor, Arthaloka Bdg,

Jl Jend Sudirman Kav 1, Jakarta, is a government agency with wide responsibilities for environmental issues.

Ecotourism has not taken off in a big way in Java but the PPLH Environmental Education Centre near Trawas in East Java runs a variety of environmental programs from paper recycling to water treatment. It has accommodation for visitors and a variety of courses and guided walks. Contact the PPLH Seloliman (☎/fax 0343-880884), email pplh@sby.centrin.net.id), PO Box 03, Trawas 61375 Mojokerto, East Java. It also has an office in Surabaya (☎ 031-5614493) and, if you are coming through from Bali, its Environmental Information Center at the Hotel Santai (☎/fax 0361-287314), Jl Danau Tamblingan 148, Sanur, is a good resource centre. The organisation also runs the hotel.

## FLORA & FAUNA

The western part of Indonesia, comprising Sumatra, Java, Kalimantan and Bali, lies on the Sunda shelf. Known as the Greater Sunda Islands, this part was once linked to the Asian mainland and harboured large Asian land animals, including elephants, tigers, rhinoceroses and leopards, and the dense rainforests and abundant flora of Asia. Overpopulation in Java has seen the forests shrink to isolated pockets and most of the large mammals are now extinct. Many other species have disappeared or are rare. To see what is left, venture to the national parks.

### Mammals

The magnificent tiger once roamed freely throughout Asia and existed in large numbers in Java. A few places in Java claim to be the last refuge of the tiger, notably Meru Betiri National Park in East Java, but tigers in Indonesia are now known only to exist in Sumatra. Leopards (the black leopard or panther is more common in South-East Asia) survive and their small numbers are increasing in protected areas, perhaps because of the extinction of the predatory tiger.

Ujung Kulon National Park is home to panthers and is the last refuge of the almost

## Javan One-Horned Rhino

Standing 1.5m tall and weighing over 1500kg, the Javan one-horned rhino once roamed from India through to Java, but now exists only at Ujung Kulon National Park. Sightings are very rare but numbers of this endangered species have increased to around 60.

extinct one-horned Javan rhinoceros, the largest wild mammal in Java.

Banteng (wild oxen) are large beasts with a slight hump and curving horns. They can be seen at Pangandaran, Ujung Kulon and Baluran national parks. These parks also have populations of the large rusa deer. Muncak (barking deer) and the mouse deer, standing less than half a metre high, are also found in Java.

Java has a number of species of monkey, divided into two groups – the mostly tree-dwelling leaf monkeys and the partly terrestrial macaques. Of the leaf monkeys, the Javan leaf monkey *(Presbytis aygula)* and silvered leaf monkey are important, rare species. The macaques, which are brown coloured with naked pinkish faces, are more common. Java also has an endemic species of the graceful gibbon, the rare Javan gibbon *(Hylobates moloch)*, which still exists at Gede Pangrango National Park.

Musang (civet cats) are common. They look like a cross between a cat and a possum or badger and are found in the wild and also near inhabited areas, where they are often considered to be pests. Java also has

various species of squirrel and the flying lemur *(Cynocephalos variegatus)*.

The fast disappearing ajag (wild dog) is found in Baluran and Alas Purwo national parks and is related to various species of wild dog that are found across Asia. Wild pigs are quite common in forested areas. The work horse of rural life, the kerbau (water buffalo), is wild in some lowland swamp areas.

### Reptiles

Right along the south coast from Ujung Kulon to Alas Purwo National Park, green turtles come ashore to lay their eggs. The giant leatherback turtles are also seen but only in small numbers. Sukamade in Meru Betiri National Park is the best places to see the turtles lay their eggs.

Ujung Kulon is home to the freshwater crocodile, which has all but disappeared elsewhere in Java. Monitor lizards of up to 2m in length are found in the wild and Java has dozens of species of snakes, including the python.

### Birds

Java has around 350 species of birds, which, like their four-legged counterparts, are threatened by the encroachment of human settlement on their habitats. Major areas for birdwatching are in national parks. In West Java, 220 species of bird have been recorded at the Ujung Kulon National Park. These include storks, barbets, bulbuls and hornbills. The hornbills are not common but there are three species to be found in Java.

Pulau Dua and Pulau Rambut reserves, near Banten in West Java, are protected nurseries for many species of coastal bird. They include black-headed ibises, glossy ibises, egrets, herons, darters, mynas, starlings, kingfishers, sandpipers, sea eagles and herons.

The grasslands and mangrove swamps of Baluran National Park are also good for birdwatching and birds seen here include green peafowls, bee-eaters, kingfishers and owls. Also in East Java, more remote

Meru Betiri and Alas Purwo national parks have prolific birdlife.

Undoubtedly, the bird you'll most commonly see in Java is the chicken, scurrying around every kampung. The long-legged Javanese variety makes good eating, but there is one variety bred as a song bird, particularly in Madura and East Java. These prized birds are housed in beautifully carved cages or hoisted on poles to greet the dawn with their 'song'.

## Flora

The landscapes of crowded and heavily cultivated Java are dominated by wet-rice cultivation, but natural forest remains in national parks and in some remote mountain regions. Dense jungle is found along parts of the coasts and contains numerous species of palm and bamboo. Most of Java's volcanoes have forested slopes, and at higher altitudes there are alpine meadows.

Apart from rice and small farm holdings, large tracts of Java are devoted to plantations. In the Parahyangan mountain region of West Java, tea is a major plantation crop and small groves of cloves are found in many mountain areas. The Jember/Banyuwangi area of East Java is a huge plantation region, producing cacao, rubber, cotton, coconuts, tobacco and the famous Java coffee. The north coast, particularly around Cirebon, has large sugar cane plantations.

Less than 10% of Java's once abundant forests remain. Cemara (mountain casuarina) can be found on many of the lower mountain slopes, especially in East Java. Pines, oaks, chestnuts and laurels are also found at higher altitudes. Favourite plantation trees are jati (teak) and mahoni (mahogany). The dewadaru tree is common and is credited with possessing magical powers. It often grows around holy sites, and it is said that good fortune will come to anyone who can catch a falling leaf from the dewadaru tree.

Of all Indonesia's flora, the most spectacular is the rafflesia, the world's largest flower, which grows up to 1m in diameter.

This parasitic plant is found primarily in Sumatra, but a smaller version, *Rafflesia zollingeriana*, is found at Meru Betiri and Gede Pangrango national parks.

Javan edelweiss *(Anaphalis javanica)* grows in alpine meadows. Gede Pangrango National Park is noted for its edelweiss, and the flower can also be seen at Gunung Papandayan. Puspa *(Scima wallichi)* is a hardy bush or small tree, with small wide flowers, found in mountain regions. Pitcher plants, begonias, impatiens and epiphytes are also found in wetter mountain areas. Java also has a species of rhododendron, the orange-flowered *Rhododendron javancum*, and wild orchids.

## National Parks

Indonesian national parks *(taman nasional)* are managed by the Directorate General of Forest Protection and Nature Conservation (Perlindungan Hutan dan Pelestarian Alam), more commonly known as the PHPA. The PHPA offices that manage the parks, usually located in the towns, go under the title of KSDA (Konservasi dan Sumber Daya Alam). Many new national parks have been proclaimed in recent years, mostly because national parks receive greater international recognition and funding than nature, wildlife and marine reserves, of which there are also many in Indonesia.

Java has a number of national parks and reserves that are Java's best kept secret. Some are coastal wilderness regions, but most are mountainous forest areas centred on volcanoes. Almost every volcanic region is a forest reserve and many are in the process of being upgraded to national parks. It is well worth trying to make it to one of the national parks, as a break from the cities and to see the real beauty of Java. Climbing a volcano is the highlight of a trip to Java for many people.

Most of the parks are isolated and have minimal facilities. The park at Ujung Kulon has good but very expensive accommodation on the islands but most parks have only basic huts or accommodation in the nearest town. If the wilderness is your main reason

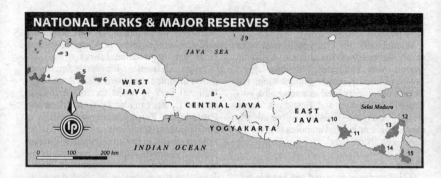

## NATIONAL PARKS & MAJOR RESERVES

1  Pulau Seribu National Park
2  Pulau Dua Reserve
3  Rawa Danau Reserve
4  Ujung Kulon National Park
5  Gunung Halimun National Park
6  Gede Pangrango National Park
7  Pangandaran National Park
8  Dieng Plateau Reserve
9  Karimunjawa National Park
10  Arjuno Lalijiwo Reserve
11  Bromo-Tengger-Semeru National Park
12  Baluran National Park
13  Ijen-Merapi-Maelang Reserve
14  Meru Betiri National Park
15  Alas Purwo National Park

to visit Indonesia, bring a good tent, sleeping bag and kerosene stove. As a general rule, park staff spend little time in the parks and more time in the office, which will be located in the nearest town or city. Call into these offices before heading to the park to check the latest conditions.

The pick of Java's national parks is the one at Ujung Kulon on the south-west tip of the island. Though not easy to reach, it has superb coastal scenery, lush rainforest and coral reefs and is home to the almost extinct Javan rhinoceros and leopards.

In complete contrast, Baluran National Park, on the dry north-eastern tip of Java, one of the most easily visited parks in Indonesia, has grasslands reminiscent of

Africa or Australia. This drive-in park is noted for it buffalos, benteng, deer and birdlife.

Bromo-Tengger-Semeru National Park is justly famous for its spectacular volcanic craters and Gunung Bromo is one of Java's main attractions. The park also contains Java's highest peak, Gunung Semeru, for mountain climbing.

The small Pangandaran National Park is right on the doorstep of a popular beach resort but the trails have been closed for conservation reasons. In the mountains south of Jakarta, Gede Pangrango National Park is good for volcano climbing through submontane forest. Gunung Halimun National Park is nearby but is undeveloped and access is difficult.

One of Java's most spectacular walks is to the active crater lake of Kawah Ijen in the plateau reserve near Banyuwangi in East Java. East Java also has some fine coastal parks, Alas Purwo and Meru Betiri, but access is difficult. Pulau Dua, off the north coast near Banten, is a major sanctuary for coastal sea birds. Pulau Seribu, consisting mostly of resorts, fishing villages and private islands, has rather strangely been made a marine national park.

## GOVERNMENT & POLITICS

*Reformasi* (reform) is the new buzz word in Indonesia. After the repression of the Soeharto years, people now openly talk about what they want and what they don't want.

Demonstrations are a constant in political life, the press enjoys unprecedented freedom and though the road to democracy is a tumultuous one it would be very difficult to turn back. Reform still has a long way to go, especially while members of the old administration remain in government with the army by their side. The process will only be complete after the dust settles following the June 1999 elections and the new political parties set about deciding Indonesia's future.

Though the two houses of parliament have been rejigged, the new system still allows for non-elected appointees, including 38 seats set aside for the military in the 500 seat lower house (DPR). Whatever happens, the DPR looks set to become a real forum for debate, whereas previously it had little say and power resided firmly with the autocratic president and his inner cabinet.

## Political Parties

With the promise of the first open elections in more than 40 years, over 100 new political parties have been formed. Mindful of regional divisions, the government has attempted to restrict parties to those that can claim national representation in at least 14 of the 27 provinces.

Under the old system, the government only allowed three parties: the ruling Golkar party, which controlled the elections, and an emasculated opposition: the Partai Persatuan Pembangunan (PPP), which represented Islamic groups, and Partai Demokrasi Indonesia (PDI), Soekarno's old party, which became an amalgam of nationalists, Christians and 'the rest'.

Golkar, the artificial, all-encompassing, government party of the Soeharto era, used to be the only party of power and influence. Civil servants automatically became members and everyone from village heads to army generals wore the yellow shirts of the party. Now Golkar is desperately trying to throw off its tarnished image as Soeharto's party of corruption and repression.

The PPP now has to compete with other Muslim parties and, if anything, it has become more Islamic.

The PDI is split into two parties. After a government-backed leadership challenge removed popular opposition leader, Megawati Soekarnoputri, in 1996, Megawati has gone on to form her own splinter party of the PDI. Of all the opposition leaders, she has probably the widest popular support. Certainly her enthusiastic supporters, often sporting red bandannas and waving red flags, are the most noticeable. She appeals to Muslims and non-Muslims alike and her party is very much secular. Her lack of support among the army and the old elite is both pro and con.

The other main forces are the Muslim-oriented parties. Amien Rais, the most prominent and effective opposition leader in the months leading up to Soeharto's demise, is a Muslim intellectual whose moderate, modernist line has wide appeal. He now heads the National Mandate Party (PAN). Nahdatul Ulama, the country's largest Muslim organisation, is now again a political force appealing mostly to older, syncretic Muslims. Its ageing and ailing leader, Abdurrahman Wahid, more fondly known as Gus Dur, is more conservative but also commands widespread support.

Amien Rais and Gus Dur are moderates and very keen to keep a lid on communal divisions in multi-religious, multi-ethnic Indonesia. The emergence of fundamentalist Islamic groups would pose the greatest threat to national unity. Though everything is now up for review and there has been talk of scrapping the national ideology of Pancasila (see the 'Pancasila' boxed text in this chapter), the principles for secular government remain strong.

As well as the three main opposition figures, a fourth must be added, Sri Sultan Hamengkubuwono X. Like his father, who was prominent in the independence movement, the present sultan of Yogyakarta came out strongly behind the students and the reform movement in the lead-up to Soeharto's demise. Though without a real power base, the traditional respect the sultan commands as both a traditional and modern leader makes him a highly respected figure.

## Armed Forces

'What are you going to do with your life?' an Indonesian father asks his son.

'I'm not sure', replies the boy. 'I'd like to go into government and maybe become governor or even president, but I'd also like to go into business and become rich. Or perhaps I could go into law and become a judge.'

'In that case', says the father, 'join the army and you can do it all.'

The Indonesian military (ABRI), of which the army is the dominant wing, has always played a prominent role in Indonesian politics and society. Indonesia's military psyche developed during WWII when the Japanese organised village militia to defend Indonesia in the event of reoccupation. When the Dutch returned, independence was gained only after a bloody battle of village armies united under the banner of the new republic.

The Indonesian independence revolution was led by the *pemuda* (youth), and Indonesian freedom fighters became heroes. Their leaders' names adorn Indonesian streets, their exploits are endlessly retold in schools and their homes have become museums. Indonesia's history has become a military one, and even the most obscure leaders of ancient, easily crushed peasant rebellions have become national heroes. The military has been a part of the political process since independence and it hardly regards itself as having usurped power that somehow 'rightfully' belongs to civilians.

Under Soekarno's guided democracy the military's powers and aspirations intensified. In 1958 General Nasution, chief of staff of the army, expounded the doctrine of *dwifungsi* (dual function) to justify the army's expanded role in Soekarno's government after the establishment of martial law. This stated that the army not only played a security role and was responsible to the government, but it also had to play an independent social and political role as 'one of the many forces in society'.

After the 1965 coup the army became not just one of many, but a dominant force in society. The military dwifungsi role strengthened, and military support was necessary for power. As well as automatic military representation in parliament, it was involved in local government right down to the village level. In later years, Soeharto increasingly preferred a civilian image, and his cabinet contained few military men, but military personnel, both former and present, are still widely represented in government and in business.

The military remains a major behind-the-scenes player, and in the turmoil leading up to Soeharto's resignation, all eyes were on ABRI. The top brass came out firmly behind Soeharto, while it was rumoured that the younger level of officers below were pro-reform. A coup looked possible but did not eventuate and in the aftermath, Prabowo Subianto, commander of Indonesia's special forces and son-in-law of Soeharto, was held accountable for the Jakarta riots.

Prabowo was sacked and his main rival, General Wiranto, chief of the armed forces, became top dog. Wiranto assumed a prominent role as a leader of strength and calm throughout the turmoil but, while he remains a leader to defer to, the military's stocks are in decline. The newly free press soon reported atrocities committed by the army over many years.

Political leaders continue to show deference to the armed forces, but more radical reform groups are demanding that the military get out of politics. The students, Indonesia's new revolutionary *pemuda*, are particularly vocal, having borne the brunt of the military's law and order campaigns, which have seen students killed by soldiers.

The military, historically the liberator of Indonesia and the keepers of peace, no longer commands widespread public support. At best it is tolerated as a necessary evil, the only force that can keep Indonesia together in the face of disintegration, but its dwifungsi role is under review and the police have already been separated from ABRI.

A coup is never totally out of the question, especially if a new government should try to forcibly remove ABRI from politics, but without popular support ABRI could only hold power through brutal repression. ABRI has spent decades promoting its role and propagandising itself as the supporter and protector of the people. If that were undone, there might well be some splits in the ranks and the emergence of a new leadership.

## Regional Government

Though national policy, international wranglings and multi-million-dollar deals are the preserve of the central government, for most Indonesians Jakarta is far removed and real government is at the district or village level.

Politically, Indonesia is divided into 27 provinces, including the three special territories of Aceh, Jakarta and Yogyakarta. Java has five provinces: Jakarta, West Java, Central Java, Yogyakarta and East Java.

Each province has its own political legislature, headed by a governor, with extensive administrative powers. The provinces are further broken down into *kabupaten* (districts) headed by a *bupati* (district leader) and *kotamadya* (municipalities) headed by a *walikota* (mayor). The districts are divided into *kecamatan* (subdistricts), each headed by a *camat*. Within the kecamatan, are *kelurahan*, or village groupings.

Each level of government has its own bureaucracy, often with overlapping functions. For example, in one city you may find three or more separate tourist offices – a provincial government tourist office, a district tourist office, a city tourist office and regional representatives of the central government. Between them they may employ dozens, if not hundreds, of people and still not be able to produce a decent map or intelligible brochure. Government is Java's major employer, and its major frustration if you have to deal with it.

But despite this extended hierarchy, often the most relevant level of government is at village level. In the *desa* or *kampung*, the day-to-day running of the village, neighbourhood disputes and local affairs are handled as they always have been. The village elects a *lurah* or *kepala desa*, though often the position of kepala desa is virtually

hereditary, passed within the one family from father to son, even extending back to some long-since-defunct Hindu principality when the kepala desa was *raja* (king). The kepala desa is the government representative at the most basic level, and the person to see if you wander into a village and need to spend the night or resolve a problem.

The village is the main social unit, providing welfare, support and guidance. If a fire destroys a house or a village needs a new well, then everyone pitches in. This grass-roots system of mutual help and discussion is usually presided over by a traditional council of elders, but there are also village organisations or government representatives to carry out government policies and campaigns on economic development, population control, health etc. One of the main community organisations is the *rukun tetangga*, which organises the registration of families and new arrivals as well as neighbourhood security – every village and kampung has a *pos kamling* (security post).

## ECONOMY

Until 1997 all was rosy as the Indonesian economy bounded along like most of Asia with an average annual growth rate of over 6% for 20 years. Only weeks before the monetary crisis swept through Asia, the World Bank declared that Indonesia was performing well and could look forward to more years of high growth. A few months later, Indonesia was bankrupt.

Asia as a whole suffered, but Indonesia, because of the accompanying political strife, was hit the hardest. When the run started on the rupiah in July 1997, 2500 rp would buy US$1. The Indonesian central bank was unable to defend the currency from overseas selling and the rupiah plummeted. Many large corporations had taken out US dollar loans and suddenly, with the fall in the rupiah, these loans trebled, then quadrupled and kept going. Companies went bankrupt overnight and laid off their workers. At the same time prices skyrocketed, mostly for imported items but also for essentials such as rice.

The International Monetary Fund stepped in and promised a US$40 billion bail-out package of grants and soft loans to help Indonesia service its foreign debt and keep the economy afloat. In return, it demanded changes in basic economic fundamentals. Those changes included the lifting of subsidies on fuel and rice, which were destined to hit the poor hardest. When the price of kerosene rose, sporadic rioting broke out in towns across Indonesia, with Chinese shops often being the prime target.

The rupiah fell to almost 17,000 rp to the US dollar in January 1998, recovered substantially after Soeharto's re-election, then plunged again after the Jakarta riots in May 1998. With the disbursement of IMF funds, some stability has returned to the currency but cannot be guaranteed.

Indonesia's economic hole is so deep that recovery seems years away. The swiftness and scope of the human tragedy is difficult to comprehend. Millions lost their jobs overnight, the economy plunged to negative growth of 20% and inflation hit 80%, resulting in starvation as a real possibility for many. Most of the IMF funds had gone into propping up the banking system, and while the government is forecasting inflation to settle in at 20%, economic recovery still has a long way to go.

The gains in the fight against poverty, which for so long were the pride and also the excuse of authoritarian government, have been rapidly reversed. Under the development programs of Soeharto, poverty steadily dropped until, before the crisis, it was estimated that 20 million Indonesians lived below the poverty line, 11% compared with 40% of the population in 1976. In just one year, the figure jumped to 100 million, nearly 50% of the populace, wiping out the gains of a generation. Poverty, unlike in western countries, is defined in Indonesia as earning enough money to buy enough food to avoid starvation.

All is not lost, however. The country has advanced enormously in the last 30 years and has a vastly improved infrastructure of roads, energy and telecommunications. From an economy dependent on oil and gas

for export income, Indonesia started to develop a substantial light industrial base in the mid-1980s. Helped by huge foreign investment in the 1990s, Indonesia is now a major producer of textiles and clothing and is an exporter of footwear, chemicals, fertilisers, cement and glassware.

The manufacturing base remains largely intact, as does oil production, the old mainstay of Indonesia's exports. Indonesia also exports timber and wood products, tin, coal, copper and bauxite, and substantial cash crops like rubber, coffee, copra and fishing. The tourist dollar is also a major industry, but continuing strife has seen a big downturn in visitor arrivals.

Indonesia's main stumbling block is foreign debt. Companies that borrowed overseas but receive much of their income in rupiah are in a hopeless situation. It is also estimated that US$100 billion left the country after the economic crises began. This is not just because many Indonesian Chinese left and took their money with them, as some Indonesian politicians portray it, but because almost anyone with money in Indonesia sold their rupiah in the grab for hard currency.

Hopefully, the only way to go is up for Indonesia's economy. If lasting political stability returns and the rupiah settles in at a realistic exchange rate, the economy can at least begin to arrest negative growth.

Jakarta is the key to Indonesia's economic and political future. The urban poor have been worst hit here, and they have reacted with the most violence. Jakarta, the city of dreams for the rural poor, is now a symbol of dashed hopes. Its ever-present slums are growing and more of its citizens have been forced onto the streets to eke out a living hawking or simply begging. Of those that still have a job, many are forced to survive on the minimum wage of 172,000 rp per month, less than US$25.

Most of Indonesia's industry is based in urban Java: the greater Jakarta area, Bandung, Surabaya and Semarang. While oil, generated in the outer islands, still accounts for around 30% of exports, Indonesia's light industrial base is Java-centric.

## POPULATION

Java, with a population of 128 million people, is one of the most populous islands on earth. Its population was estimated as six million in 1825, 9.5 million in 1850, 18 million in 1875, 28 million in 1900, 36 million in 1925, 63 million in 1961 and 108 million in 1990. Overpopulation in Java remains Indonesia's greatest problem.

The total area of Java and the island of Madura off Java's north coast is 132,000 sq km, or just over half the area of the UK, yet Java's population density of nearly 1000 people per sq km is four times that of the UK and double that of The Netherlands (Europe's most densely populated country). Java with only 6.9% of Indonesia's land mass has 60% of the population.

Jakarta's population is 9.3 million, while the population of greater Jakarta, known as Jabotabek, is 17.5 million, making it one of the world's largest cities. The other major cities in Java are Surabaya with a population of 2.4 million, Bandung, with two million and Semarang, with 1.35 million. Yogya and Solo each have around half a million, while more than a dozen other cities have populations over 100,000. Despite the number of major cities, Java is primarily rural, with the majority of the population involved in agriculture.

### Population Control

Three million people are added each year to the Indonesian population and most of them are in Java. Government efforts to control Java's overpopulation consist of a birth control program and *transmigrasi*, the transmigration program designed to move Javanese to less populated areas like Sumatra, Kalimantan, Irian Jaya and Maluku.

The campaign to reduce the birth rate has been most successful in Java, where many families are now firm believers in the slogan *Dua Anak Cukup* (Two Children Is Enough). Coordinators are also appointed at village level to advise on contraception, monitor birth rates and counsel, if not admonish, families that have more than two children.

These programs started in 1905 with the Dutch, who moved some 650,000 people, mostly from Java to Sumatra, to work as plantation labourers. In the first 18 years of independence (1950-68) only about 450,000 people were moved. But the Soeharto government placed much more emphasis on transmigration and from 1968 to 1994, 6.4 million transmigrants were resettled.

Since the peak five-year plan in 1984-89 when 3.2 million were resettled, transmigration has slowed. Birth control programs proved to be much more effective at reducing population growth and transmigrasi causes other problems. The main problem is that insufficient numbers of people can physically be moved to offset the growth in population. Furthermore, transmigration settlements have developed a poor reputation. Attempts at wet-rice cultivation in unsuitable areas have proved disastrous and settlers have frequently ended up as subsistence farmers no better off than they were back in Java. Many transmigrants are not experienced farmers; two-thirds are landless peasants and another 10% are homeless city dwellers.

Transmigration takes its toll on the natural environment through destruction of rainforest, loss of topsoil and degraded water supplies. Tension, even conflict, with the indigenous people in some settled areas is not uncommon.

The emphasis now is on 'spontaneous' transmigrants who emigrate on their own initiative and can choose where to live. Transmigration is a voluntary program, and more support is now given, such as advice on suitable crops to grow. Some transmigrants are settled on plantations, where they receive a house and land. But their land is part of a plantation and they work on the estate for wages.

### PEOPLE

Indonesia has over 300 ethnic groups, while Java, with three main groups, which share many common cultural attributes, is relatively homogenous. Nevertheless, Java has various ethnic subregions with distinct variations in language and culture.

The three main groups, each speaking its own language, are: the Javanese of Central and East Java, the Sundanese of West Java and the Madurese from Madura island off the north-east coast.

The divisions are blurred – the Madurese, for example, have settled in large numbers in East Java and further afield, and Indonesians from all over the archipelago have come to seek work in the cities. Smaller pockets of pre-Islamic peoples also remain, like the Badui in the mountains of West Java and the Hindu Tenggerese centred on Gunung Bromo in East Java. Polyglot Jakarta identifies its own tradition in the Betawi, the name for the original inhabitants of the city.

## Javanese

The Javanese, from Central and East Java, are the single largest ethnic group in Indonesia and the most dominant. Soekarno was from Java and so is Soeharto and many of the top generals and politicians. The Javanese syncretist world view has shaped the country's policies and philosophy, and the Javanese economic and political dominance is a cause for resentment in many other parts of the archipelago.

Today, the Javanese are Muslim. Though many are *santri*, or devout Muslims, and Java is slowly becoming more orthodox, Javanese culture owes much to pre-Islamic animism and Hinduism. The Javanese cosmos is composed of different levels of belief, stemming from older and more accommodating mysticism, the Hindu court culture and a very real belief in ghosts and numerous benevolent and malevolent spirits.

The rich artistic heritage and refinements of the *kratons*, or palaces, of Yogyakarta and Solo (Surakarta) are perceived as being the benchmarks of Javanese culture. This region of Central Java, known as the *kejawen*, has a long history of resistance to Islam in favour of the Hindu court culture. In contrast to Islam, this Hindu court culture has a hierarchical world view, based on privilege and often guided by the gods or the spirits of nature.

The Javanese language, with its intricate levels of deference, is spoken in its most pure form in the kejawen. Refinement and politeness are highly regarded, and loud displays of emotion and flamboyant behaviour are *kasar* (coarse and rough, bad manners). Self-control and social grace are the hallmarks of the *halus* (refined) Javanese and owe much to the mystical practices of self-denial. Indirectness is a Javanese trait, and stems from an unwillingness to make anyone else feel uncomfortable or ashamed. It is impolite to point out mistakes, embarrassments, sensitive or negative areas, or to directly criticise authority.

However, the common perception of the Javanese as reserved, overly refined and bound by ritual and social constraint is not an accurate one. The Javanese, like all Indonesians, are a very social, outgoing people. Social etiquette is sometimes stiff, but this is because the Javanese place a high price on social responsibility and maintaining harmony in personal relationships.

The more formal aspects of Javanese social interaction are the preserve of the nobility. Javanese peasants, though guided by the same principles, are less concerned with the niceties of etiquette. The other regions of Java, away from the kejawen, are similarly less tied to kejawen philosophy.

The major subvariant of Javanese culture is the *pasisir* culture of the north coast. It is more strongly Islamic, trade oriented and long more open to outside influence than the kejawen culture; its court traditions and hierarchies are much less noticeable. Farther to the east, the down-to-earth *arek* Javanese of the Surabaya region are considered kasar, and don't bother with the various levels of the Javanese language. To the west, around Cirebon and other areas bordering Sunda, Javanese culture and language have absorbed Sundanese influences.

The greatest opposition to traditional Javanese culture comes from the devoutly Islamic *santri* population, and the urban, national culture. For santris, many traditional Javanese values and religious practices are feudal, if not pagan, while urban culture, stressing the more egalitarian Bahasa Indonesia and modern values, is likewise less concerned with tradition.

## Sundanese

The Sundanese of West Java form the second largest ethnic group in Java and in Indonesia. They share many cultural similarities with their closely related Javanese cousins. Their gamelan, puppet theatre and dance have the same roots but are presented in different forms by the Sundanese. The language of the Sundanese is a hierarchical one of different levels.

The Sundanese, because of their mountainous isolation, were less influenced by the major civilisations that developed in Central Java. The Sundanese Hindu kingdoms of Tarumanegara and Pajajaran were smaller than those civilisations and did not produce architectural monoliths like Borobudur. The flourishes, hierarchies and mysticism of the Central Javanese courts were also less evident, and the Sundanese today are an earthy, direct people.

Islam has taken strong root in Sunda, though evidence of Hindu and pre-Hindu traditions remain. Every year, following ancient tradition, ceremonial swords are taken from the village of Panjalu and ritually cleansed. The Badui in the western highlands are distinguished by their history of resistance to Islam.

## Madurese

While the southern and central part of East Java shows a greater Hindu influence, the north coast is the stronghold of Islam and much of the population is Madurese. They came originally from the hot dry island of Madura and are a blunt, strong and proud people who migrated to the north-east coast and then further into East Java. Surabaya is the melting pot of all East Java and, as the gateway to Madura, shows strong influence from the more devoutly Islamic Madurese.

Madurese history and culture has always been linked to Java, though the Madurese have more in common with the seafaring people of the other islands and were often enemies of the Javanese courts. Madura also had its own court traditions, centred on the kraton of Sumenep, but without the highly developed cosmology of the Javanese. The culture from the eastern part of the island around Sumenep is considered more halus, while the west is more kasar. Madura remains one of the most traditional parts of Java, and the Madurese have been shaped by the difficulty of survival on their barren island.

## Betawi

The residents of Jakarta are collectively known as the Orang Betawi (Betawi People), the name derived from the Malay word for Batavia. The name originally referred to Indonesians born in the city and the Betawi developed their own customs, culture and language (a dialect of Malay).

Batavia, as a major port, attracted Sundanese, Javanese, Makassarese and Balinese residents, as well as large numbers of Chinese and Dutch. The cultures of these different groups combined to produce distinctly Betawi music, dance, architecture and customs. One of the largest early groups was the Mardijkers, freed slaves from the former Portuguese colonies captured by the Dutch. The Mardijkers gave Betawi culture unique musical forms and many Portuguese words that have survived in Bahasa Indonesia, now the first language in Jakarta.

In the 19th century, when the city grew only marginally and a large percentage of the population was born there, the Betawi identity was at its strongest. Various waves of migrations since, not least the huge growth since independence, have helped to fragment Betawi culture. As Jakarta continues to grow, and Jakartans try to define themselves, the term Betawi is either an historical one or something that is evolving into a new identity.

## Chinese

Of all the ethnic minorities in Indonesia, few have had a larger impact on the country than the Chinese, or 'overseas Chinese' as they are commonly known. Although comprising less than 3% of the population, the Chinese are the major force in the economy, operating everything from small shops, hotels and restaurants to major banks and industries. The Chinese are by far the wealthiest ethnic group, and there is much anti-Chinese resentment in Indonesia.

The Chinese have long suffered repression and even slaughter in Indonesia. The Dutch used the Chinese as an entrepreneurial middle class, but colonial authorities restricted Chinese settlement and ownership of land. As far back as 1740, anti-Chinese feeling erupted in the massacre of Batavia.

When mass Indonesian organisations emerged in the early 20th century, such as the Muslim organisation Sarekat Islam, frustration with colonialism often resulted, not in attacks on the Dutch, but in attacks on the Chinese.

In post-independence Indonesia the Chinese are seen as an overly privileged group, and their culture has been discriminated against by law. Chinese characters were banned and Chinese schooling was forbidden to Indonesian citizens – thus, those Chinese who had chosen citizenship were forced to drop their language. The issue of citizenship is still a contentious one, with the ever-changing government policies making it hard for Chinese to gain Indonesian citizenship.

Many Chinese took the government's integration line and have adopted the Indonesian language and Indonesian names and blended readily into Indonesian society. They have their own traditions and have developed their own patois, a mixture of Indonesian with Chinese dialects such as Hokkien, but most simply speak Bahasa Indonesia.

Discrimination against the Chinese is again at high levels in the wake of Indonesia's economic crisis. The Jakarta riots of 1998 targeted Chinese businesses, though most rioters were simply looters with little political motivation. But whenever there is unrest in Indonesia, for whatever reason, the Chinese are singled out. In 1965 they were killed for being communists, now they are killed for being capitalists.

Certainly the Chinese are an entrenched and privileged business class but the eagerness of even educated Indonesians to blame their woes on the Chinese shows deep-rooted ignorance and resentment. Unless the government can promote ethnic harmony or increase economic opportunities for ethnic Indonesians to diffuse resentment, then Chinese emigration will increase and with it will go much-needed business expertise and capital.

Though many Chinese fled Indonesia, the majority stayed and many returned. Indonesia is home, as it has been for many generations, and even if they wanted to leave, many Indonesian Chinese cannot afford to and have nowhere else to go.

## Other Groups

Right across Java, outposts of the old religion resisted conversion to Islam. In remote mountain areas, the old cultures survived in a virtual vacuum.

When the nobility of the Majapahit kingdom fled from the Muslim armies to Bali, the common people were left behind. In the inaccessible mountains of the Gunung Bromo region, Hinduism continued to flourish, largely untouched by developments elsewhere in Java. The Tenggerese people of the area are closely related to the Javanese but, in addition to being Hindus, they speak their own Tengger language.

The small Hindu kingdom of Blambangan, the region of Java's far south-east tip, resisted waves of attacks from Demak and Mataram, long after the rest of Hindu Java had fallen. It was finally conquered in 1640, but even then resisted conversion to Islam for over a century. The area still has a large Hindu population and, though a part of Javanese culture, Blambangan has long had cultural ties with Bali. The Osing region around Banyuwangi has its own dialect, a mixture of Javanese and Balinese.

The Badui of West Java resisted conversion to Islam through a strict policy of isolation. Their priests, the 'inner' Badui, have always been sheltered from the outside world by the 'outer' Badui villages, which act as intermediaries. In this way, their religion has been preserved, as has their language, a form of old Sundanese.

## EDUCATION

Indonesian education begins with six years of primary school (Sekolah Dasar, or SD), then three years of junior high school (Sekolah Menegah Pertama, or SMP) and three years of senior high school (Sekolah Menengah Atas, or SMA), leading on to university.

According to official figures released before the economic crisis, the government's education programs had led to a rise in school enrolments – 90% for the seven to 12-year-old age group, though less than half that number makes it to secondary school and less than half again will graduate. The real problem now for Indonesia in the current economic climate is the sudden drop in school enrolments. Parents simply cannot afford to send their children to school and school enrolments dropped to an estimated 60% in 1998. The long-term effects on national education could be drastic, and experts predict that many of the drop-outs will never return to school. Indonesia has made great gains in the literacy rate, currently around 77%, but these gains are now in danger of being reversed.

There are plenty of private schools, many operated by mosques and churches. Muslim schools, with their strict dress codes for girls, are very common in Java. Private schools generally have higher standards, and this is where the upper crust educate their children.

Higher education is concentrated in Java. Number one and biggest in Indonesia is Jakarta's Universitas Indonesia (UI), a government-run university. Yogya is Indonesia's main educational centre, famous for its Universitas Gajah Mada. Bandung has the major high-tech school, Institut Teknologi Bandung (ITB).

## ARTS

Java has an immensely rich artistic tradition that varies from region to region, reflecting the island's social and cultural diversity. The musical styles and instruments of gamelan music vary throughout the island, and each region has its own dances and styles of batik. The regional influences are also seen in wayang puppet theatre, the most readily identifiable Javanese art form. The arts in Java include much more than just the wayang puppet theatre, but this art form is a 'core tradition' that has influenced the other performing arts.

## Wayang Puppet Theatre

Javanese *wayang* theatre has been a major means of preserving the Hindu-Buddhist heritage in Java. The most well known form is the *wayang kulit* – the shadow-puppet theatre that uses leather puppets (*kulit* means leather).

Wayang theatre still teaches traditional Javanese values and has an important ritual function, but today it is also performed largely as entertainment. Each Saturday night, for example, and frequently during the week, full eight-hour wayang performances are broadcast over the radio; shorter versions occasionally appear on television. A *dalang* (the puppeteer, or storyteller) traditionally acquired his skills though inheritance, but now state arts academies and special dalang schools also teach the techniques. Some dalang vary the design of their puppets and add new theatrical and musical elements, maintaining the wayang's age-old function of serving patrons and reflecting on contemporary issues: clown figures now sing and joke about such matters as birth control, agricultural development and paying taxes on time.

The stories in wayang kulit performances are usually based on the Hindu epics the *Ramayana* and the *Mahabharata*. Other forms of wayang draw on the epic stories of Panji, a legendary prince of East Java, and other figures from Javanese court history. A traditional performance, playing out a particular plot *(lakon)* via a series of standard scenes – court audiences, battles, comic interludes – lasts the whole night, from around 9 pm to around 5 am.

**Wayang Kulit** In shadow-puppet theatre, perforated leather figures are manipulated behind an illuminated cotton screen. A dalang animates the puppets and narrates

## Mahabharata, Ramayana & Wayang

Ancient India, like ancient Greece, produced two great epics. The *Ramayana* describes the adventures of a prince who is banished from his country and wanders for many years in the wilderness. The *Mahabharata* is based on the legends of a great war. The first story is a little reminiscent of the *Odyssey*, which relates the adventures of Ulysses as he struggles to return home from Troy; the second has much in common with the *Iliad*.

When Hinduism came to Java so did the *Ramayana* and the *Mahabharata*. The Javanese shifted the locale to Java; Javanese children were given the names of the heroes and by tradition the kings of Java were descendants of the epic heroes.

The *Mahabharata* and the *Ramayana* are the basis of the most important wayang stories in Java and Bali. While they often come across like ripping yarns, both are essentially moral tales, which for centuries have played a large part in establishing traditional Javanese values.

They are complex tales, and the division between good and evil is never absolute. The good heroes have bad traits and vice versa. Although the forces of good usually triumph over evil, more often than not the victory is an ambivalent one; both sides suffer grievous loss and though a king may win a righteous war he may lose all his sons in the process. In the *Mahabharata*, when the great battle is over and the Pandavas are victorious, one of their enemies sneaks into the encampment and kills all the Pandava women and children.

### Mahabharata

The great war portrayed in the *Mahabharata* is believed to have been fought in northern India around the 13th or 14th century BC. The war became a centre of legends, songs and poems and at some point the vast mass of stories accumulated over the centuries were gathered together into a narrative called the 'Epic of the Bharata Nation (India)' the *Mahabharata*. Over the following centuries more was added to it until it was seven times the size of the *Iliad* and the *Odyssey* combined!

The central theme of the *Mahabharata* is the power struggle between the Kurava brothers and their cousins the Pandava brothers. Important events along the way include: the appearance of Krishna, an incarnation of Lord Vishnu, who becomes the adviser of the Pandavas; the marriage of Prince Arjuna of the Pandavas to the Princess Drupadi; the Kuravas' attempt to kill the Pandavas; and the division of the kingdom into two in an attempt to end the rivalry between the cousins. Finally, after 13 years in exile and hiding, the Pandavas realise there is no alternative but war, the great war of the *Mahabharata*, which is a series of bloody clashes between the cousins.

It is at this time that the Pandava warrior Arjuna becomes despondent at the thought of fighting his own flesh and blood, so Krishna, his charioteer and adviser, explains to him the duties and obligations of the warrior in a song known as the 'Bhagavad Gita'. Krishna explains that the soul is indestructible and that whoever dies shall be reborn and so there is no cause to be sad; it is the soldier's duty to fight and he will be accused of cowardice if he runs away.

In the course of the battles many of the great heroes from both sides are slain one by one; many others also lose their lives, but in the end the Pandavas are victorious over the Kuravas.

### Ramayana

The *Ramayana*, the story of Prince Rama, is thought to have been written after the *Mahabharata*. Long before Prince Rama was born the gods had determined that his life would be

## Mahabharata, Ramayana & Wayang

that of a hero, but as with all heroic lives it would be full of grave tests. Rama is an incarnation of the god Vishnu, and it will be his destiny to kill the ogre king Rawana (also known as Dasamuka and Dasakhantha).

Due to scheming in the palace, Rama, his wife the beautiful Sita and his brother Laksamana are all exiled to the forest, where Sita is abducted by the ogre king. Rawana takes the form of a golden deer, luring Rama and Laksamana into the forest as they try to hunt the deer. Rawana then carries off Sita to his island kingdom of Lanka.

Rama begins his search for Sita and is joined by the monkey god Hanuman and the monkey king Sugriwa. Eventually a full-scale assault is launched on the evil king and Sita is rescued.

### Wayang Characters

The wayang characters are often based on figures from the *Mahabharata* and the *Ramayana*. In the *Mahabharata*, the Kuravas are essentially the forces of greed, evil and destruction, while the Pandavas represent refinement, enlightenment and civilised behaviour.

At a wayang or dance performance, if you know the plot well it is easy to identify the characters; otherwise shape, colour, deportment and voice will help.

The noble characters tend to be smaller in size and more elegant in proportion; their legs are slender and close together and their heads are tilted downwards, presenting an image of humility and self-effacement. The *kasar* characters are often enormous, muscular and hairy, with their heads upturned.

Eye shape and the colour of the figures, particularly on the faces, are of great importance. Red often indicates aggressiveness, greed, impatience, anger or simply a very forthright per-

sonality. Black, and often blue, indicates calmness, spiritual awareness and maturity. Gold and yellow are reserved for kings and the highest nobles. White can symbolise purity or virtue, high moral purpose etc. Hair styles, ornamentation and clothing are also important in identifying a particular character.

#### Pandavas

**Bima** Bima is the second-eldest of the Pandavas. He is big, burly, aggressive, not afraid to act on what he believes; he can be rough, even using the language of the man of the street to address the gods. He is able to fly and is the most powerful warrior on the battlefield, but he also has infinite kindness and a firm adherence to principle.

**Arjuna** Arjuna is the handsome and refined ladies' man, a representative of the noble class, whose eyes look at the ground because it's *kasar* to stare into people's faces. He can also be fickle and selfish, but despite his failings, he is *halus* refined in manner, never speaking ill to offend others, polite and humble, patient and careful. Arjuna's charioteer is Krishna, the incarnation of the god Vishnu, a spiritual adviser but also a cunning and ruthless politician.

## Mahabharata, Ramayana & Wayang

**Semar** A purely Javanese addition to the story is Arjuna's servant, the dwarf clown Semar. An incarnation of a god, Semar is a great source of wisdom and advice to Arjuna but his body is squat with an enormous posterior, bulging belly, and he sometimes has an uncontrollable disposition for farting.

**Gareng, Petruk & Bagong** Semar has three sons: Gareng, with his misshapen arms, crossed eyes, limp and speech impediment; Petruk, who, with his hilarious long nose and enormous smiling mouth, lacks proportion in physique and thinking; and Bagong, the youngest of the three, who speaks as though he has a mouthful of marbles. Though they are comic figures, they play the important role of interpreting the actions and speech of the heroic figures in the *wayang kulit* plays. Despite their bumbling natures and gross appearance they are the mouthpieces of truth and wisdom.

### Kuravas
On the Kurava side is Duryudana, a handsome and powerful leader, but too easily influenced by the prevailing circumstances around him and thus often prey to the evil designs of his uncle and adviser, Sangkuni. Karna is the good man on the wrong side, whose loyalty is divided between the Kuravas and the Pandavas. He is actually a Pandava but was brought up a Kurava; adhering to the code of the warrior he stands by his king as a good Javanese should and, as a result, he dies at the hands of Arjuna.

### Ramayana Characters
The characters of the *Ramayana* are a little more clear-cut. Like Arjuna, Rama is the epitome of the ideal man – a gentle husband, a noble prince, a kindly king, a brave leader. His wife Sita (or more often Shinta in Java) is the ideal wife who remains totally devoted to her husband. But not all characters are easily defined: Rawana's warrior brother, Kumbakarna, knows that the king is evil but is bound by the ethics of the Ksatria warrior to support his brother to the end, consequently dying a horrible death by dismemberment.

and chants through the entire night to the accompaniment of the gamelan orchestra. The mass of the audience sits in front of the screen to watch the shadow figures, but some people also sit behind the screen with the dalang to watch the expert at work.

Many of the wayang kulit characters and some of the stories have a specific mystical function. Certain stories are performed in order to protect a rice crop (they incorporate the rice goddess Dewi Sri), for the welfare of a village or even for an individual.

Shadow-puppet theatre is not unique to Java; it can also be found in Turkey, India, China and other parts of South-East Asia, and wayang kulit owes much to Indian tradition. Wayang kulit was flourishing by the 11th century in Hindu-Buddhist Java, but the standardisation of puppet designs is often attributed to Muslim saints who supposedly used wayang to spread their message after the coming of Islam to Java in the 16th century.

The puppets are usually made from water buffalo leather and, after the outline is carved, the fine details are added using small chisels and a hammer. Movable arms are attached and the puppet is painted. Made of the same flexible hide as the puppets, the leaf-shaped *kayon* represents the 'tree of life' or the sacred mountain of Hindu mythology, and is used at the end of scenes or to symbolise wind, mountains, obstacles, clouds or the sea.

The characters in wayang are brought to life by the dalang. To call a dalang a puppeteer belittles the extraordinary range of talents a dalang must possess. Sitting crosslegged on a mat before the white screen the dalang might manipulate dozens of figures in the course of a performance.

The dalang recounts events spanning centuries and continents, improvising from the basic plot a complex network of court intrigues, great loves, wars, philosophy, magic, mysticism and comedy. The dalang must be a linguist capable of speaking both the language of the audience and the ancient *kawi* language used in the songs and narrated passages, and interspersed in the dialogue of the aristocratic characters of the play. The dalang is also a mimic, producing a different voice for each of the characters, and must have great stamina to sustain all-night performances. The dalang must be a musician, poet and comedian and have a deep understanding of history, philosophy and religion.

The dalang also directs the gamelan orchestra using a system of cues, through rehearsed breaks in the plot or by tapping with a wooden *cempala* (mallet). The *kendang* (drum) player liaises with the dalang to set the tempo and to signal the end of pieces.

**Wayang Golek** These three-dimensional wooden puppets have movable heads and arms and are manipulated in the same way as shadow puppets – but no shadow screen. Although *wayang golek* is found in Central Java it is most popular among the Sundanese of West Java. Sometimes a wayang golek puppet is used right at the end of a wayang kulit play to symbolise the transition back from the two-dimensional shadow world of mythical ancestors to the three-dimensional reality of the present day.

Wayang golek uses the same stories as the wayang kulit, including the *Mahabharata* and the *Ramayana* or Panji legends (the heroic exploits of a Javanese prince.) The Muslim *Menak* stories from the Middle East are also popular. These include the elaborate romances inspired by legends about the Prophet Mohammed's uncle Amir Hamzah.

**Wayang Klitik** In East Java the wayang kulit is replaced by the *wayang klitik* or *kerucil*, a flat wooden puppet carved in low relief; this type of wayang is performed without a shadow screen. The wayang klitik is associated with the Damar Wulan stories, which are of particular historical relevance to East Java. The stories relate the adventures of a handsome prince and his rise to become ruler of the Majapahit kingdom.

## Music

The haunting sounds of the gamelan can be heard everywhere in Java, at wayang, dance and theatre performances, bull or ram fights or as musak in hotels. Gamelan can be a few instruments or a full orchestra of 60 to 80 instruments, with sets of suspended and horizontal gongs, gong chimes, drums, flutes, bowed and plucked string instruments, metallophones and xylophones.

Many regional variations occur. Sundanese *gamelan degung* is a dynamic gamelan style played by a small ensemble with the addition of the *degung*, suspended gongs, and the *suling*, a bamboo flute. The *kecapi*, a type of lute, is a unique Sundanese instrument, as is the *angklung*, a frame of bamboo pipes that resonate when shaken.

Jakarta also has some unique musical styles. *Keroncong* music is traditionally sung in a mixture of Portuguese, Dutch and Malay, and is accompanied by groups of keroncong, ukulele-type musical instruments. It was introduced by the Mardijkers, or Black Portuguese, who came from the former Portuguese colonies captured by the Dutch. *Gambang kromong* orchestras accompany Betawi theatre and show Javanese and Chinese influences. These orchestras included a *gambang* (wooden xylophone), *kromong* (bronze bowls), Chinese fiddles, gongs, bamboo flutes, drums and rattles. Another interesting musical style is the *tanjidor* bands, which use European brass and wind instruments, such as clarinets, flutes and trombones. Influenced by Dutch military bands, they were popular street performers.

*Dangdut* music is a very popular Indonesian modern music, characterised by wailing vocals and a strong beat. Though often attributed to Islamic Arabic influences, a major source of this style of music is Indian pop music popularised by Hindi films. This is the music of Jakarta's kampungs, sometimes strongly Islamic in content and seen as rather low class. Yet since its promotion by such figures as singer and film star Rhoma Irama in the early 1980s, it has become popular across the nation among diverse social groups and its appeal continues to grow.

Also ubiquitously popular, particularly among young people, is modern, western-style pop music, dominated by romantic love ballads.

**Gamelan** The word 'gamelan' is derived from the Javanese word *gamel*, which means a type of hammer. The orchestra is composed almost entirely of percussion instruments. Javanese tradition credits a god with the invention of the gamelan orchestra, used to summon the other gods to his palace at the summit of Gunung Lawu, between Solo and Madiun.

There are two types of gamelan styles: a soft style for indoor use and a loud style for outdoor functions. The difference lies in the instruments used. Around the 17th century,

the two styles were blended to form the modern gamelan. It was mainly because of the different ways in which the two styles were mixed and balanced that variations between the gamelan music found in Bali, Central Java and West Java were created. The *gong, kempul, kenong, ketuk* and *kempyang* belong to both the loud and soft styles. The *saron, bonang* and *kendang* belong to the loud style. The *slentem, gender, gambang, celempung, sitar, suling* and *rebab* belong to the soft style.

In a piece of gamelan music, the gong ageng marks the end of each of the phrases of the melody, the saron instruments play the main melody at various ranges of pitch and speed and the bonang play their own rippling configurations at a faster speed than the main melody. The gamelan also uses male and female singers – traditionally they make up part of the soft ensemble. The gamelan orchestra does not accompany the singer as western orchestras do; rather, the singer in a gamelan is really just another instrument, no more or less important than any of the instruments.

Traditionally, gamelan players learnt to play by ear, beginning on the simpler instruments and moving forward as their repertoire and technique developed. A musician did not use notation when playing, although there are systems of written notation. The palaces at Solo and Yogyakarta developed their own systems of notation, but in the late 19th century the *kepatihan* system, now used in Java, was developed and numbers were used for the notes (just as western music uses letters).

The saron and the slentem are the only instruments which can play exactly what is written down, the notation being just a skeleton of everything that is going on in a performance. The phrasemaking instruments – the ketuk, kempul, kenong and gong – give some order and form to these notes, the gong marking the end of the longest musical phrase and the other instruments elaborating on the basic skeleton.

In the loud ensemble the drummer is the leader, the conductor of all the instruments, controlling the tempo, speeding up or slowing down the orchestra, signalling the entrance of the elaborating instruments and shifting the emphasis from the loud to the soft ensemble. Apart from signalling changes within one piece of music the drummer also signals a change from one piece of music to another, because usually at least two or three pieces are combined to form a medley. The rebab (used mainly in Sundanese gamelan) ornaments the music and its line is closely related to the singing.

A gamelan orchestra always accompanies a wayang performance, although the *gamelan wayangan* used for a traditional wayang kulit is much smaller than the usual gamelan seen today. A full-sized gamelan orchestra has instruments with two different tunings – the *slendro* and the *pelog*. A gamelan wayangan only uses instruments with the slendro tuning. Although most gamelan players are men, it is not strictly a male occupation.

## Dance & Theatre

Traditional Javanese theatre and dance are intertwined. Both tell a story to the sounds of gamelan. Dance is an important aspect of theatre, and dialogue is found in some dance performances, or dance may be accompanied by a narrator or singer who tells the story. Dance and theatre rely heavily on the same epics as the wayang – the *Ramayana*, *Mahabharata*, Panji stories etc.

**Court Dances** The most refined dances are the kraton dances of Yogyakarta and Solo (Surakarta). Under official patronage, dancers lived and studied within the kraton walls, developing new styles and refining old. Nowadays, much artistic development comes from government-subsidised art academies, but the kratons still maintain their dance schools with great pride.

The rivalry between the two great kratons continues. The dances of the Solo kraton are considered more refined and feminine, and have influenced the dance styles of the smaller Mangkunegaran and Pakualaman kratons. Dance from the Yogyakarta kraton is considered more robust and masculine,

but the dance of both kratons is of the same tradition and very similar.

The main dances performed for ceremonial occasions are the *bedoyo* and *srimpi* dances. The ritualistic bedoyo is performed by seven or nine female dancers and the story is told through symbolic hand, leg and eye movements, and the relative positioning of dancers on stage. Bedoyo dances can be laboriously slow and difficult to fathom for uninitiated westerners (and for many Javanese). The only animated movement may be the flick of a sash or trailing sarong, and great emphasis is placed on restrained grace and the ability to maintain flowing movement. The srimpi, performed by two or four female dancers, is also restrained but more robust. Small fragments of an epic are performed and end with a battle dance. Taking male roles, the dancers weave and parry blows gracefully.

Kraton dancers perform many other styles and each kraton has its own unique dances, such as Yogyakarta's *beksan lawung* (spear dance). Also in the Yogyakarta kraton, *wayang wong*, a dance drama playing out the wayang kulit repertoire of stories, with human actor/dancers taking the parts of puppet characters, was cultivated on a lavish scale. The *topeng* masked dance, originally performed in villages, was adopted and refined by the kratons and has now become part of court dance tradition.

**Folk & Melodrama** Masked dance is one of the oldest and most widespread of the vibrant and varied performance traditions cultivated outside the courts of Java. The stylisation of human features seen in the shadow puppets is also seen in the topeng masks; elongation and refinement are the key notes of the noble characters, while grotesque exaggeration denotes the vulgar characters. Particular styles of such dance, originally used in ancient animistic rites, and now generally drawn from the stories and characters of the Panji epic of tales, are practised in different geographical areas. One of the most famous of these regional traditions derives from Cirebon, on the north coast, on the border of the provinces of West and Central Java, with its vigorous, dramatic dance style and its loud, forceful musical accompaniment.

Another widespread genre of folk performance is the horse dance, taking varying forms and known by different names according to geographical area *(kuda kepang, jaranan, reyog)*, once again thought to have its origins in long-forgotten spirit beliefs and rites. The performance always involves male figures dancing astride plaited rattan horses, accompanied by pulsating, mesmerising music. Sometimes the horse dancers fall into trance, induced by music, incense and the incantations of the troupe master. They imitate the actions of a horse, eating chaff, drinking from a bucket etc and perform extraordinary feats of strength, such as walking on fire and eating glass.

The spectacular variant of this performance – *reyog Ponorogo* – staged in the Ponorogo region of East Java, involves no trance but, instead, consists of battles between the horse dancers and the *singa barong*, lord of the forest. This figure is depicted by a huge, enormously heavy tigerhead mask framed by peacock feathers, held aloft by a dancer who simply grips it between his teeth by a wooden handle.

Also very popular and frequently performed in rural areas is, or was, a dance involving a single female dancer and serial male partners. Likewise characterised by different styles and terms according to geographic area – *ronggeng, ledek, tayuban* – these performances involve erotic elements and sometimes an association with prostitution. Such connection has incurred official disfavour for these performances in recent years, resulting in certain transformations of the dance forms.

In East Java, tayuban dancers have undergone 'upgrading' courses in dress and deportment, and in West Java, *ketuktilu*, traditionally performed by itinerant dancers with much erotic hip-wiggling, has evolved into the popular dance craze, *jaipongan*, which is practised energetically in the nightclubs of Bandung.

Dance in Java is thus constantly evolving, with new styles being developed and modern elements being introduced. For example, the Ramayana Ballet at the Prambanan temple, probably the most famous Javanese dance performance and very popular with tourists, draws on traditional dance styles and the model of *wayang wong*. But the dialogue has been eliminated and the story is conveyed through choreographed dance incorporating much nontraditional movement, as in modern ballet. Performances of this type, referred to as *sendratari* (a combination of the terms for 'drama' and 'dance'), are cultivated in the performing arts academies and private dance schools, and feature at national and institutional celebrations.

Along with the folk dances and pageants discussed above, which are rooted in ancient animist ritual and have long been performed for community celebrations, the 20th century has seen the development of several new genres of performance which might be referred to collectively as 'popular theatre', performed commercially for entertainment.

These forms are influenced by the model of western theatre in their use of the proscenium arch, painted backdrops and a naturalistic mode of presentation highlighting story and dialogue rather than dance. Yet their stories are taken from local history and legend, they draw on long-established theatrical conventions and dialogue is entirely improvised in regional languages. Moreover, the makeshift conditions of performance – temporary theatre buildings with dirt floors erected by itinerant groups who sleep backstage – plus the relaxed, sometimes raucous, atmosphere accords with the reputation of these forms as entertainment of the common people – the masses.

Different regions have their own performance genres with distinctive story repertoires and styles. In Jakarta, for example, performances of *lenong* theatre employ the local Betawi Malay dialect to play out stories of tough-guy heroes of the colonial period, and of contemporary lower-class life. The repertoire of the East Javanese *ludruk* similarly consists of contemporary domestic melodramas, with the distinctive feature that all female parts, including those of the sexy singers who appear between the acts of the play, are performed by men. The Sandiwara of West Java performs legendary or historical tales in Sundanese language; *ketoprak* theatre, practised in Central Java, particularly Yogyakarta, has a core repertoire of stories drawn from the history of the later Mataram kingdom, but can also include performances of *Aladdin's Lamp* or *Romeo and Juliet*. Yogyakarta's twin court city of Solo (Surakarta) is famed, meanwhile, for its cultivation of a popularised, somewhat 'kitsch', variety of the court dance drama wayang wong.

Movies and especially television have certainly taken their toll on these forms. Commercial troupes have greatly decreased in number, unable to survive the competition. Yet television, radio and the audiocassette industry have also provided new opportunities to perform. The style of presentation necessarily changes in these settings – the precise time constraints of television, for example, demand radical condensation of plot and the use of written scripts. But adaptability to changing conditions and audience tastes is, of course, of the essence in popular theatre – the important thing is that the show goes on.

**Modern Indonesian Theatre** The terms 'modern' and 'Indonesian' here refer to theatre in the national language, Indonesian, which has developed since the 1920s as part of the emerging modern culture of the new Indonesian nation. Employing written scripts and following the model of a western-style play, such theatre at first evolved quite separately from the indigenous traditions described earlier. Contact with European drama via the colonial school system first stimulated the development of this modern theatre and it continued after Independence in 1945 to be characterised largely by wordy, serious plays and association with a small elite, which is western-educated.

In the late 1960s, however, a major shift began to take place, involving rapprochement with indigenous performance styles and a broadening of modern theatre's social base. An important factor influencing this shift was the establishment in Jakarta in 1968 of the Taman Ismail Marzuki (TIM), a complex of performance and discussion sites where modern plays were staged alongside richly varied regional genres; creative horizons expanded and contemporary Indonesian theatre is said to have 'exploded with innovation'.

Another crucial factor was the work of playwright and poet Rendra, who, returning in 1967 from study in the USA, staged several movement-based, avant-garde dramas inspired by this US experience. He then began to produce performances, both original plays and adaptations, incorporating elements of indigenous dramatic structure, acting style, music and folk humour. These were performed throughout the 1970s by Rendra's group, Bengkel Theatre, based in the Central Javanese city of Yogyakarta. Both the style of Rendra's performance and the model of a theatre group led by a single playwright-director-actor-guru have been enormously influential on the subsequent development of modern Indonesian theatre, in Central Java and beyond.

An important element of Rendra's work, prominent also in modern Indonesian theatre generally, is social critique, often conveyed through satirical humour. Kingly figures reminiscent of the wayang tradition are rendered as absurdly flawed, in ways often read as a cheeky slur on contemporary power-holders. Modern theatre is indeed seen to allow a freedom of expression, both artistic and ideological, not possible in older, more stylised theatre forms. Its performers and audiences are constituted overwhelmingly of young people, for whom such freedom in an otherwise strictly controlled social environment is a big attraction. Much of the time these features of modern theatre seem to be begrudgingly tolerated by the authorities, but obtaining permission to perform is nevertheless a lengthy process, and numerous bannings have occurred over the years.

Though much has changed since the heady years of the 1970s, the modern theatre scene in different regions of Java continues to be vibrant, dynamic and varied. In Jakarta, big established groups like Rendra's regrouped Bengkel Theatre, now based in a kind of ashram outside the city, and Teater Koma, led by playwright Riantiarno, stage lavish productions over a number of weeks at venues such as the TIM or at the elegant Gedung Kesenian restored colonial theatre building.

Teater Koma's spectacular productions, involving huge casts, elaborate costumes and sets, singing and dance segments and farcical humour, have proved particularly popular, attracting middle-class viewers not normally fans of modern theatre. Teater Koma plays were also renowned for their daring, blatant political satire, but since the 1990 banning of their play *Suksesi* (Succession), about an elderly king contemplating retirement, their social comment has become more subtle.

Other well-known Jakarta groups include Teater Mandiri, headed by Putu Wijaya, a prolific Balinese writer of absurdist drama and fiction, and Teater Sae and Teater Kubur, directed by the younger figures Boedi S Otong and Dindon. These groups perform intense, abstract works symbolising the psychic fragmentation and confusion of powerless individuals in this globalised, homogenised, post-modern age.

Outside Jakarta, modern theatre in the regions varies in accordance with local culture and conditions, but is generally characterised by less abstract, less glamorous, smaller-scale productions, with more community connection. In Central Java, the cities of Yogyakarta and Solo, and also smaller centres such as the north-coast town of Tegal, have been the site of particularly active and socially engaged modern theatre. In Yogya, connection with prominent national cultural figures, first Rendra, and then outspoken Islamic essayist, public speaker, poet and dramatist Emha Ainun Nadjib, has added vibrancy and controversy to the modern theatre scene.

The indigenous theatrical traditions of Central Java – court, folk and popular – have likewise provided modern theatre groups with a rich store of familiar images and styles to appropriate and subvert, attracting the interest of local audiences. The group Gandrik, for example, has become renowned for its compact, humorous performances on stage and television, incorporating many dramatic elements from and recreating the intimate atmosphere of folk theatre, while also conveying some very contemporary social comment.

Another mode of engagement with the culture and experience of ordinary people is that of the group Gapit in the city of Solo. The language of Gapit plays is not Indonesian but Javanese, the crude, direct local expressions actually used in daily life by its subjects, the urban poor, struggling with the changes brought about by processes of 'development'. Gapit's productions all concern the theme of material and cultural dispossession of the have-nots by the very developments which have brought affluence to opportunistic elites.

Besides such well-known troupes there are also many amateur groups, based in urban neighbourhoods, comprising secondary and tertiary students and other young people. They rehearse enthusiastically and perform at occasions such as the community concert held each year for Independence Day. Nongovernment development groups also use theatre as a channel of self-expression and consciousness-raising for local communities.

## Literature

In a similar fashion to modern theatre, western-style written literature developed as an integral part of Indonesian culture. With strong connections to the development of a nationalist consciousness, pre-war poetry gave expression to sentiments of love of native land, while novels focussed on themes of conflict, both within individuals and in the community, between modern aspirations and traditional social bonds. The period of Japanese wartime occupation and the subsequent revolution against the returning Dutch is documented in brutally realistic fiction by such authors as Idrus and Pramudya Ananta Tur. This period also spanned the short working life of Indonesia's most famous poet, Chairil Anwar, who came to Jakarta from his native Sumatra as a teenager in 1940 and died in 1949. His major themes, however, are not those of the social hardship and military struggle of the time. His stance is instead that of the romantic individualist rebel, demanding freedom from social restrictions in his pursuit of personal fulfilment and artistic perfection.

In the highly politicised climate of the 1950s and early 1960s, as political parties jockeyed for power and three dominant forces – the army, the Communist Party and President Soekarno – confronted each other, literature became caught up in these conflicts. Supporters of a liberal standpoint described as 'universal humanism' were opposed by members of Lekra, a cultural organisation with some association with the Communist Party. The novel *Twilight in Jakarta* by the liberal writer Mochtar Lubis was banned in the late 1950s because of its scathing portrayal of corruption and exploitation by the bureaucracy and powerful leftist political parties. Later, a manifesto of the liberal group, asserting the right to free artistic expression, was also banned.

But when political fortunes changed, and the leftist forces were decimated in 1965-66, many writers were among those imprisoned or killed. These included the man often referred to as Indonesia's greatest writer, Pramudya Ananta Tur, who was detained for 14 years in Jakarta jails and on the prison island of Buru.

The following period, the early years of the New Order regime which succeeded that of Soekarno, is remembered, particularly by its participants, as a time of flourishing creativity in literature, theatre and the arts generally. The establishment of the earlier-mentioned TIM as a site of discussions, poetry readings and exhibitions, as well as the founding of a new literary journal *Horison*, were important stimuli. The

predominant literary style was anti-realist absurdist, fantastic (apolitical according to some critics, allegorical in the view of others) exemplified in the fiction of writers such as Danarto, Budi Darma and Putu Wijaya.

Later, through the late 1970s and 80s, a range of styles and themes emerged – focusing on regional cultural traditions and settings. This is evident in the case of Javanese writers such as Umar Kayam and Arswendo Atmowiloto in fiction and Rendra, Soebagio Sastrowardoyo and Linus Suryadi in poetry; the cerebral, highly personal poetry of Jakarta intellectuals such as Sapardi Jaka Damono, Goenawan Mohamad and Toeti Heraty; and realist, historically based novels in recent works by Ajip Rosidi, NH Dini and, most strikingly, Pramudya Ananta Tur.

Immediately after his release in 1979 Pramudya set to work to publish a series of novels written during his prison years, a quartet set at the turn of the century depicting the birth of the Indonesian nationalist movement. Other works followed in an impressive stream, but all were banned by the Indonesian authorities because of Pramudya's tainted political past. Internationally, however, many of Pramudya's writings are available in translation, including the prison quartet *This Earth of Mankind*, *Child of All Nations*, *Footsteps* and *House of Glass*, and a moving story of class and gender oppression, drawing in part on the experiences of Pramudya's grandmother, *Girl from the Coast*.

The predominance of the institutions of TIM and *Horison*, and the siting of influential daily newspapers and book publishers in the capital, have contributed to a picture of Jakarta as the centre of modern Indonesian literary activity. Aspiring writers in regional towns dream of gaining recognition through publication of their work in *Horison*, or of reading their stories or poetry at TIM. In fact, though many of the leading writers reside in the capital, others live elsewhere – Budi Darma has a university position in Surabaya, Umar Kayam heads a cultural institute in Yogyakarta and NH Dini runs a library and holds writing workshops for children in her home in the Central Javanese city of Semarang. Many young people in the regions participate enthusiastically in literary activities, particularly poetry readings.

Such readings, first popularised by major figures such as Rendra, who dramatically performed rather than simply reading out his lengthy, socially engaged works, are frequent and well attended. Their shared, participatory quality accords perhaps with traditional patterns of oral communication and the value placed on community. Another factor is the focus on freedom of expression similar to that mentioned earlier in relation to contemporary theatre.

Attention has focused so far on works recognised as 'serious' literature, *sastra*, as distinguished from other writing, including popular novels, magazine stories etc, classified as mere entertainment. Since the early 1970s there has been a boom in the publishing of such popular fiction, as economic growth has produced an expanding middle class with money to spend and leisure time to fill.

Prominent among producers of such fiction are women authors, who have produced novels and stories with female heroes and domestic settings. Mainstream literary critics tend to dismiss these 'ladies' novels' as lightweight and trivial, and at the same time to lump women authors together as natural participants in this domain. Very few women are recognised as writers of serious literature; the novelist NH Dini, poet Toeti Heraty and short-story writer Leila Chudori are several key exceptions to this rule. Dini's success has been to write of love, marriage, divorce and domestic tension, the core themes of popular fiction, in ways which have nevertheless attracted the attention of 'serious' readers.

Along with women's fiction, stories that have been written specifically for the youth market have an enthusiastic and growing following. Popular literature provides an important window on the changing nature of Indonesian society, regardless of the quality of such writing.

## Batik

Along with wayang and gamelan, batik is one of Java's most easily recognised and highly developed art traditions.

The technique of applying wax or some other type of dye-resistant substance (like rice paste) to cloth to produce a design is found in many parts of the world. The Javanese were making batik cloth at least as early as the 12th century but its origins are hard to trace. Some think the batik skills were brought to Java from India, others that the Javanese developed the technique themselves. The word 'batik' is an old Javanese word meaning 'to dot'.

The development of batik in Java is usually associated with the flowering of the creative arts around the royal courts – it's likely that the use of certain motifs was the preserve of the aristocracy. The rise of Islam in Java contributed to the stylisation of batik patterns and the absence of representations of living things from most designs. More recently, batik has grown from an art mainly associated with the royal courts into an important industry with a number of noted production centres.

Batik is either *tulis* (hand drawn) or *cap* (stamped), though both may be used on the same piece of fabric. In *batik tulis*, hot wax is applied to the smooth cloth with the *canting*, a pen-like instrument with a small reservoir of liquid wax. The design is first traced out onto the prepared cloth and the patterns drawn freehand in wax on the white cloth, or on to a cloth previously dyed to the lightest colour required in the finished product. The wax-covered areas resist colour change when immersed in a dye bath. The waxing and dyeing are continued with increasingly dark shades until the final colours are achieved. Wax is added to protect previously dyed areas or scraped off to expose new areas to the dye. Finally, all the wax is scraped off and the cloth boiled to remove all traces of the wax. Many hours, days or even weeks of work can go into producing a highly prized piece of intricate tulis batik.

From the mid-19th century, production was speeded up by applying the wax with a metal stamp called a *cap*. The cap technique can usually be identified by the repetition of identical patterns, whereas in the freer composition using the canting, even, repeated geometric motifs vary slightly. It's worth noting that batik cap is true batik; don't confuse it with screen-printed cloth which completely bypasses the waxing process and is often passed off as batik.

**Regional Styles** Java is the home of Indonesian batik, and each district produces its own designs. The court cities of Yogyakarta and Solo are major batik centres. Traditional court designs are dominated by brown, yellow and indigo blue. These days both cities produce a wide range of modern as well as traditional batiks. Solo is a major textile centre and many of the large batik houses are based there.

Batiks from the north coast of Java have always been more colourful and innovative in design. As the trading region of Java, the north coast came in contact with many influences and these are reflected in its batik. Pekalongan is the major batik centre on the north coast, and traditional floral designs are brightly coloured and show a Chinese influence. Floral and bird motifs are popular traditional designs. Many modern designs are now employed and some of Indonesia's most interesting batik comes from Pekalongan. Cirebon also produces very fine, colourful tulis work.

## SOCIETY & CONDUCT

The culture of Java is complex. Religion is a mishmash of eastern thought, language is stratified and everything changes subtly from region to region. Java has many opposing forces: Muslim versus non-Muslim, country versus city, modern versus traditional, rich versus poor, coastal versus interior ... somehow they all manage to exist side by side.

They survive by the principle stressed by Soekarno – *gotong royong*, or mutual cooperation. The village principles of helping one's neighbour, avoiding conflict, showing respect and offering hospitality are very important in overcrowded Java. The village structure still exists, even in Jakarta with its kampungs and neighbourhood organisations.

Java is a society in transition. Over the last decade, both western and Islamic influences have become more noticeable. In the cities, shopping malls and supermarkets have proliferated and motorbikes and cars have replaced bicycles. Jeans, rather than the sarong, is now the norm. Satellite TV dishes are everywhere – atop luxury hotels and in small villages. National culture, through use of Bahasa Indonesia, has stressed an Indonesian rather than a Javanese identity. A growth of orthodox Islam has seen a decline in traditional ritual.

But it is wrong to assume that traditional Javanese culture is weak. The Javanese are very proud of their culture and heritage, and while eager to embrace the benefits of modernity, they hold strongly to Javanese values.

Traditional values of the family and religion are maintained. The head of the family is accorded great respect and children acquiesce to their parents and elders. Beyond the extended family, the main social unit is the village. In Javanese society, the concerns of the individual are of less importance than they are in western society, and western notions of individualism are seen as odd or selfish.

The Javanese are generally a very courteous and hospitable people and great importance is placed on making sure that offence is not given and that a mutual feeling of well being is promoted in dealings with others. Interpersonal dealings are generally amiable and unhurried – even a passing meeting with a stranger is carried out with a smile and a chat. 'Keeping face' is extremely important to Indonesians and criticisms are not voiced directly. It is very bad form to shout at, contradict or embarrass someone in public. Refinement and politeness are highly regarded.

### Dos and Don'ts

The Javanese make allowances for western ways but there are a few things to bear in mind when dealing with people in Java.

Never hand over or receive things with the left hand. It will cause offence – the left hand is used to wash after going to the toilet and is considered unclean. To show great respect to a high-ranking or elderly person, hand something to them using both hands.

Talking to someone with your hands on your hips is impolite and is considered a sign of contempt, anger or aggressiveness.

Hand shaking is customary for both men and women on introduction and greeting. It is customary to shake hands with everyone in the room when arriving or leaving.

The correct way to beckon to someone is with the hand extended and a downward waving motion of all the fingers (except the thumb). It looks almost like waving goodbye. The western method of beckoning with the index finger crooked upward won't be understood and is considered rude. It is fine to point at something or to indicate direction, but rude to point at someone – gesture with the whole hand.

When entering someone's house it is polite to remove your shoes, but this is often disregarded.

Hospitality is highly regarded and when food or drink is placed in front of you, you should wait until asked to begin by your host, who will usually say *silahkan,* or 'please'. It is impolite to refuse a drink but not necessary to drink it all. In more refined Central Java it is considered polite to leave a small amount in the bottom of a glass when finished – drink it all and it will be refilled.

While places of worship are open to all, permission to enter should be requested, particularly when ceremonies or prayer are in progress, and you should ensure that you're decently dressed. Always remove footwear before entering a mosque.

Indonesians will accept any lack of clothing on the part of poor people who cannot afford it; but for westerners, thongs (flip-flops), bathing costumes, shorts or strapless tops are considered impolite except, perhaps, around western-style beach resorts. Elsewhere, you should look respectable and revealing dress is not appropriate. Women are better off dressing modestly – revealing tops are just asking for trouble. For men, shorts are considered low class and only worn by boys.

## What's in a Surname?

To show respect to an older person or someone of high status, *Pak* (Mr) or *Ibu* (Mrs) should always be used, eg Pak Amir or Ibu Tuti, unless you know the person very well or are directed to do otherwise.

Indonesians will use Mr or Mrs, usually attached to your Christian name, eg Mr Peter, when they address you. They are not taking the mickey. This odd appellation comes about because many Indonesians do not have surnames in the western sense. Except in Christian areas, Indonesians are generally given their own, unique names and do not take a family name.

However, most people have two names. The first name is the important one, while the second is rarely used. For example, if a business acquaintance has Amir Syafril written on his card, then he is Pak Amir, not Pak Syafril.

It is common for Javanese to have only one name, eg Soeharto or Soekarno. In case you are wondering, Tommy Soeharto is not the real name of the former president's son, but an Anglicised nickname. His real name is Hutomo Mandala Putra.

It feels strange being called Mr Peter, but people often feel very uncomfortable if you ask them to drop the Mr. For them it seems disrespectful. Put up with it, and imagine what Indonesians go through overseas when asked for a surname. Those with only one name often make up a surname rather than try to explain the lack to dumbfounded officials.

## RELIGION

Indonesia is overwhelmingly Muslim, but communities of Christians, Hindus and Buddhists live in Java. While the Muslim lobby is strong, the government protects the right to freedom of religion, which is enshrined in the state philosophy Pancasila.

### Islam

Indonesia first came in contact with Islam through Muslim traders, primarily from India, who introduced a gentler, less orthodox, form of Islam than that of Arabia. Today it is the professed religion of 90% of Javanese and its traditions and rituals affect all aspects of their daily life.

Javanese Muslims firmly believe in Allah, and that Mohammed is his prophet. The fast during Ramadan is widely observed, as are other Islamic rites, such as circumcision. However, many Javanese also hold other religious beliefs and carry out rituals that are unrelated to and even contradictory with Islam. Like Hinduism and Buddhism before it, Islam also has had to come to terms with older existing traditions and customs. Islam in Java is rooted in Hindu-Buddhism, *adat* (traditional law) and animism.

In Java, Islam first came to the north coast, the *pasisir*, and this is still the stronghold of Islam. Madura is strongly Islamic, as is much of East Java where the Madurese have settled. Islam is dominant along most of the north coast, especially in Surabaya, Jepara, Pekalongan and to the west around Jakarta. Sunda has also been influenced by pasisir and is primarily Islamic. Even some parts of the Javanese heartland are devoutly Muslim, such as Magelang, the home of the Buddhist Borobudur, just north of Yogya.

Yet even in these orthodox regions, Islam was not the all-conquering religion but absorbed existing beliefs. According to Javanese lore, Islam was brought by the wali songo (nine saints) whose feats are imbued with Javanese mysticism. Saint worship has no part in orthodox Islam, yet every year the graves of the wali songo along the north coast attract thousands of pilgrims, offering prayers and rose petals as at Hindu shrines.

In the interior, Islam was adopted with considerable resistance. The Hindu kings

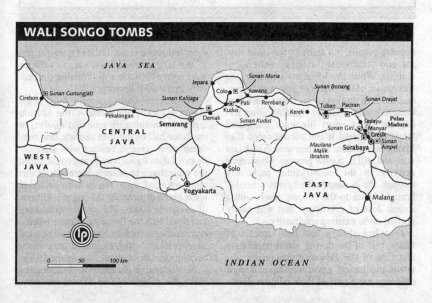

**WALI SONGO TOMBS**

## Wali Songo

According to tradition, Islam was disseminated in Java by the nine guardians of Islam, or *wali songo*. These mystics, warriors, scholars and teachers grafted Islam on to existing Javanese religious thought.

Like all Javanese heroes, their histories are obscured by tales of mystical achievements and legendary deeds. Most are of noble birth, and they are all linked to the great Islamic kingdoms of the north coast, such as Demak, from where Islam was spread across Java.

Today, their tombs are holy pilgrimage sites. Pilgrims chant prayers and scatter rose petal offerings around the graves, even though saint worship is proscribed by orthodox Islam.

**Maulana Malik Ibrahim** The 'father of the wali', his tomb lies in Gresik where he attracted converts until his death in 1404 AD. His origins are unknown, but it is believed he came from either Persia, Turkey or India, and was one of the first teachers to spread Islam.

**Sunan Ampel** One of the most revered of the Wali Songo, Sunan Ampel was the son of a Middle-Eastern Muslim and a prince of the South-East Asian kingdom of Champa (in modern-day Vietnam). He is credited with the conversion of Demak, the first great Islamic kingdom on Java, and was buried in Surabaya in 1479 AD. Two of his sons were also walis.

**Sunan Bonang** The eldest son of Sunan Ampel was instrumental in building Java's holiest mosque at Demak (said to be built by the Wali Songo in a single night) and served as its first imam. He was buried in Tuban in 1525 AD.

**Sunan Drajat** The second son of Sunan Ampel, he settled in the Paciran area and used gamelan music to help in conversion. His tomb lies in Drajat.

became sultans, but many of the court rituals and traditional Javanese beliefs remained. While the Mataram kingdom, the forerunner of the courts of Solo and Yogya, was quick to profess Islam, it was more than keen to preserve Hindu-Buddhist court traditions. Later court literature embraced Islam but related it and subordinated it to Javanese tradition. The conversion to Islam was, and still is, a slow process. Missionary activity in the countryside, especially through the *pesantren* (religious schools), brought Islam to the people, albeit with a strong dose of mysticism that was easily grafted on to existing spirituality.

Java has always had two streams of Islam: that of the devout santri population and that of the Javanese syncretists, for whom meditation, grave worship and spirit offerings are a part of their religion. However, Indonesia is not isolated from the rest of the Islamic world and various reforms have seen a shift towards orthodoxy, especially in the 20th century.

The original santri primarily lived in the towns, typically the *kauman*, the Muslim quarter combining mosque and market. In the latter half of the 19th century, this merchant class came in contact with more orthodox Islam through trade and could afford the pilgrimage to Mecca. Members of this class returned from Mecca with orthodox ideas and a distaste for the pagan traditions of Javanese Islam. The cry for orthodoxy increased with the founding of mass Islamic organisations, such as Muhammadiyah and Sarekat Islam, which claimed a large membership right throughout Java by the 1920s.

Nowadays, eight million Indonesians make the pilgrimage to Mecca annually,

## Wali Songo

**Sunan Giri** Legend has it that Sunan Giri was the son of a Muslim scholar and a prince of the Hindu Blambangan kingdom, who set him adrift on the ocean at birth. He was a student of Sunan Ampel and studied further in Aceh and Gresik before setting up a religious school in Giri. He was the most orthodox of the Wali Songo, and it is said he was elected leader to ensure that orthodoxy would ultimately prevail over the two Wali Songo camps of orthodox and adaptive Islam.

**Sunan Kudus** A great scholar and religious teacher, he also commanded the forces of Demak in battle and went on to found the city of Kudus, where he was buried in 1550 AD. He is credited with bringing Islam to the interior of Java.

**Sunan Kalijaga** The son of the regent of Tuban, he was a great leader and mediator who adapted existing Javanese traditions to Islam. A noted mystic and artist, Sunan Kalijaga developed new forms of wayang and gamelan, and travelled widely through Java and Sumatra as a missionary.

**Sunan Muria** Active around Kudus and Jepara, Sunan Muria was a man of the people, travelling around the countryside and making conversions in the villages. He is one of the most loved of the Wali and is buried on Gunung Muria at Colo.

**Sunan Gunungjati** Sunan Gunungjati was one of the great warriors of Islam and, though his life is shrouded in legend, his deeds are the most historically verifiable. He was born in Sumatra and came to Demak after a pilgrimage to Mecca. He led the Demak forces that attacked Banten, bringing Islam to West Java, and in 1552 moved to Cirebon where he established a new sultanate.

and the trend to Islamic fundamentalism grows. While once it was rare to see women wearing head shawls and covered from head to toe, it is becoming more common in the schools and market places. Yet the government is wary of any Islamic extremism, and the call to introduce Islamic law is likely to land you in jail. Pluralism is enshrined in the constitution and in the Pancasila and is vigorously defended by the government.

**Islamic Customs** Customs in Indonesia often differ from those of other Muslim countries. Muslim women in this country are allowed more freedom and are shown more respect. Indonesia is a traditional society but women do not wear facial veils, nor are they segregated or excluded from the work place.

The laws of Islam require that all boys be circumcised and in Indonesia this is usually done between the ages of six and 11.

One of the most important Islamic festivals is Ramadan, a month of fasting prescribed by Islamic law, which falls in the ninth month of the Muslim calendar. Traditionally, during Ramadan people get up at 4 am to eat and then fast until sunset. Many Muslims visit family graves and royal cemeteries, recite extracts from the Koran, sprinkle the graves with holy water and strew them with flowers. Special prayers are said at mosques and at home. At the end of Ramadan, mass prayers are held in the early morning and these are followed by two days of feasting. Extracts from the Koran are read and religious processions take place; gifts are exchanged and pardon is asked for past wrongdoings in this time of mutual forgiveness.

Friday afternoons are officially decreed as the time for believers to worship and all government offices and many businesses are closed as a result. All over Indonesia you'll hear the call to prayer from the mosques, but the muezzin of Indonesia are now a dying breed – the wailing will usually be performed by a cassette tape.

## Javanese Religion

While the professed religion of the overwhelming majority is Islam, older beliefs also hold great sway. Thus some suggest that Java has two religions – Islam and Agama Jawa (Javanese Religion), which is a mixture of religious beliefs.

Javanese beliefs encompass spirits, deities and magic, and the events of life are accompanied by a wide range of rituals. Orthodox Islam, modernity and urban culture have all helped to undermine Javanese mysticism and magic. Rituals have disappeared or been streamlined and the older beliefs are often ridiculed, but many Javanese still hold strongly to pre-Islamic traditions, particularly in the villages.

Java is primarily an agricultural society and many rituals revolve around the harvest and activities concerning the village.

### Old Javanese Mosques

When Islam came to Java it absorbed existing traditions. Many Javanese mosques even show the same architectural detail found in Hindu temples. The three-tiered *meru* roof, topped by a *mustaka*, found on many Javanese mosques is the same as those on Hindu temples in Bali. In Bali, three tiers represent the Hindu trinity, while 11-roofed temples are devoted to Sanghyang Widi, the supreme Balinese deity. Similarly, some early mosques in Java, such as the Al-Manar Mosque in Kudus, have *candi bentar* (split gateways) found at Hindu temples and designed to keep out evil spirits.

Bersih Dusun, the 'village cleaning' ceremony, is held during the Sela month of the Javanese calendar, when the village is cleansed of bad spirits and misfortune. The village gathers for a ritual feast *(slametan)* and food offerings are made at the grave of the village founder. At other ceremonies the rice goddess, Dewi Sri, may be invoked to ensure a good harvest.

For the royal courts of Central Java, Nyai Loro Kidul (Queen of the South Seas) is an important deity linked to the power and prosperity of the kingdom. The rulers of Yogya and Solo are joined in spiritual marriage to the queen. The current *susuhunan* (sultan) of Solo is a regular visitor to Parangtretes on the south coast, where he communes in meditation with Nyai Loro Kidul. Each year, giant *gunungan* (mountain) rice offerings are taken to the sea from the kratons of Solo and Yogya.

**Slametan** This feast is a central ritual for the Javanese, emphasising the traditional values of community, sharing and mutual cooperation. Though it is social as much as religious, the slametan accompanies all major ceremonies. Slametan can be an expensive affair, involving the whole village, though it is usually held for neighbours and family. At a slametan the food usually consists of cones of rice and a number of side dishes. A religious official reads passages from the Koran or the guests may chant the Muslim profession of faith ('There is no God but Allah') before eating begins.

Both santris and non-santris hold slametans for different events. For non-santris, the slametan not only promotes community spirit but also appeases the spirits. The slametan accompanies the major events of life, when rituals are carried out to ward off evil spirits and to ensure good fortune. Pregnancy, childbirth, circumcision, death etc are accompanied by a slametan.

**Spirit World** Javanese folklore has a plethora of good and evil spirits that for many Javanese are merely superstition but for others have to be appeased or cultivated.

After death, the spirit of the deceased is believed to remain around the house before moving on to the spirit world. Food may be placed under the deceased's bed for 40 days after death and various slametan rites are conducted at intervals up until the 1000th day after death. Ancestral spirits can be called upon by the living for help or guidance and it is important, at least initially, to visit the grave to make offerings and seek blessing. Sacred graves of famous people, such as the wali songo saints, and even that of Soekarno, attract thousands of pilgrims each year. Bad spirits may remain in the village, causing nuisance or even sickness and death.

Besides the spirits of people, various benevolent spirits include the *dayang* (guardians of the village), *widadari* (beautiful fairies) and *ingkang ngemon* (guardian spirits that look after an individual).

The *tuyul* are mischievous and ultimately malevolent spirits that can take the form of children or dwarfs. Through magic or meditation, an individual can gain the help of these spirits to become rich, and theft is often blamed on the tuyul. An alliance with evil spirits can be dangerous and these tuyul require constant appeasement.

Other evil spirits are numerous and usually take ugly or monstrous forms, though some are beautiful sirens, such as the *kuntilanak*, that appear naked and lure men who walk alone on the streets at night.

Ghosts can possess people, causing illness and madness, entering through the soles of the feet or fontanelle (part of the skull). Young children are particularly susceptible to evil spirits and the rites of pregnancy, birth and childhood often involve driving away evil spirits.

**Magic** The mediators with the spirit world are known as *dukun*. For traditional healing, exorcism, numerology or invocation of the spirits at harvest time, the dukun is called upon. Dukuns may be powerful practitioners of magic, sometimes black magic, or meditative mystics, while others are ordinary individuals who are deemed to have a special gift, such as healing. However, dukuns are not necessarily practitioners of magic – midwives and masseurs are also classed as dukun – but they are versed in the rituals required for their special field.

Magic often involves the use of talismans. A practitioner of black magic may use a doll representing a person to inflict harm or cast a love spell. A person's possessions, hair or nail clippings may also be used. Amulets or charms worn around the neck can ward off evil or attract benevolent forces. They may contain parts of the body, such as the stub of a baby's umbilical cord, or inscriptions provided by a dukun or religious teacher. The religious inscriptions, or *mantras,* may be based on Sanskrit religious texts or, more often, they are based on Islamic sources.

Central to the belief in Javanese magic is *kesakten*, the magical energy found in parts of the body, animals, plants and inanimate objects, particularly sacred objects and heirlooms. Sacred heirlooms *(pusaka)*, particularly the kris, gamelan sets, jewellery and precious stones, possess magical power and are used for many ceremonies.

## Kris

Many Javanese families own a *kris*, passed down through generations. The most important part of the kris is the blade, traditionally forged by repeated beating and folding of the metal to form ribbed patterns *(pamor)*. The power of a kris relies on the symbolism of the pamor, and a kris assumes more power through age and the people who have owned it. Like other sacred heirlooms, kris possess *kesakten*, or spiritual energy, which can be harnessed for protection against illness or danger. On a long journey or when undertaking a dangerous task, a Javanese would take a favourite kris for protection, and it is said a kris will rattle in its scabbard at the approach of danger. Many ceremonies involve the ritual cleansing of sacred kris to preserve kesakten.

**Healing** Modern medicine is now the preferred recourse when illness strikes. The pharmacy is often the liveliest place at night in Javanese towns, and the average consumption of pills, along with traditional herbal tonics *(jamu)*, is astonishing. But traditional beliefs persist, such as the idea that too much wind entering the body is the cause for colds and minor aches. No matter how hot it is, Javanese will close bus windows rather than suffer wind.

When all else fails, the dukun is called An expert in traditional herbs and medicines, he also relies on magic. He may use talismans, charms and chants to drive away evil spirits or he may call on the help of benevolent spirits. The dukun as healer is still popular and is often seen at markets. Imitators, travelling charlatans who put on magic shows before selling their cure-all elixirs, provide amusing performances but are now rare in Java.

**Mysticism** The Javanese have a long tradition of mysticism based on asceticism and meditation. Rooted in Hindu-Buddhist spiritualism, Javanese mysticism is also influenced by Islamic mysticism. Orthodox Muslim mystical movements based on Sufism are found in Java, particularly Sunda.

Throughout Javanese literature, revered figures have gained magical powers through self-denial and meditation. The sultans are still expected to fulfil their mystical duties.

Kebatinan is a Javanese religious movement. Some groups are theosophical and preach tolerance and morality, but most concentrate on Javanese mysticism. The court cities of Yogya, and especially Solo, are noted for their Kebatinan societies. Under the guidance of a guru, self-enlightenment is sought through typically *priyayi* pursuits of self-denial, restraint, humility and meditation.

## LANGUAGE

Java's three main languages are Javanese, spoken by nearly 60% of the people in central and eastern Java, Sundanese, spoken in western Java, and Madurese, spoken on the island of Madura and nearby.

Indonesian or Bahasa Indonesia (*bahasa* means language), is the official national language of Indonesia and is spoken as a second language by most Javanese. It is the language of government, commerce and education. In the villages and among older people, it is not always fluently spoken, but all educated people speak it proficiently. English is also widely spoken, particularly in the main tourist areas.

Various dialects are also spoken in Java. Osing, a mixture of Javanese and Balinese, spoken in the very east of Java, around Banyuwangi, is closely related to Tenggerese, the language of the Hindu Tengger people of the Gunung Bromo area. In West Java, the isolated Badui tribe speaks a form of Old Sundanese. In Jakarta, the original inhabitants, the Orang Betawi, used Malay as the common language of communication but developed their own dialect.

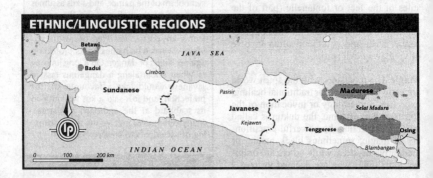

## ETHNIC/LINGUISTIC REGIONS

Betawi

Badui

Cirebon

JAVA SEA

Sundanese

Pasisir

Madurese

Javanese

Selat Madura

Kejawen

Tenggerese

Osing

INDIAN OCEAN

Blambangan

0    100    200 km

# RELIGIOUS
# ARCHITECTURE
# OF JAVA

RELIGIOUS ARCHITECTURE OF JAVA

BERNARD NAPTHINE

The Javanese have a long tradition of mysticism and spiritualism. This tradition of religious syncretism was fertile ground for the spread of Indian religion that was already established in Java by the 5th century AD.

Hinduism, then later Buddhism and finally Islam all flourished on Java, but Java did not simply adopt these religions, it adapted them and allowed the religions to evolve within its society. These religions, their iconography and the ultimate expression of their architecture assumed a quintessential Javanese character.

Hindu kingdoms, though small, first emerged in West Java. The Classical period of Java's great Hindu-Buddhist kingdoms begins in Central Java in the 8th century and extends though to the 14th century. The majority of influences came via the Vajrayana Pala Dynasty in Bengal and the Hindu Chola Dynasty from the region of present-day Madras. The trading ships and Brahman priests that first brought these cultures to the shores of Java also traded with Cambodia, and a comparison may be drawn with temples there, particularly Angkor Wat.

The earliest Hindu temples in Central Java are at the Dieng Plateau, where building began in the late 7th century. From these first small, plain temples, temple architecture blossomed under the great Mataram kingdom, first noted in inscriptions in 732 AD under King Sanjaya. The successors to Sanjaya, the Buddhist Sailendra Dynasty of Mataram, created Borobudur between 750 AD and 850 AD. The second Mataram kingdom constructed the temple complex at Prambanan.

The kingdom of Mataram mysteriously disappeared and the focus for religious architecture shifted to East Java. Under the kingdoms of Airlangga, Kediri, Singosari and finally Majapahit, the East Javanese temple style fused Shivaism, Buddhism and wayang styles to produce a new exuberant architecture.

During the 14th century, Muslims from India, Arabia and Iran arrived in Java seeking new trading opportunities, via the same trading routes used by Hindu and Buddhist traders previously. With the same ease that the people of Java absorbed Hinduism and Buddhism they saw the arrival of Islam, which brought with it new foreign influences. The Indonesian/Javanese interpretation of the mosque was born.

**Title page:** Main temple complex, Prambanan, Central Java (Photo by Glenn Beanland).

**Facing page:** Relief work, Buddhist figure in lotus position, Borobudur, Central Java.

# HINDU ARCHITECTURE

The Hindu temple as a place of worship, no matter how vast in size, was traditionally designed as a sacred monument, not a communal hall of worship. This stems from the central theme in Hinduism that maintains the individual's struggle to escape the eternal cycles of reincarnation and thus achieve spiritual freedom. This idea is reflected in the spaces created for Hindu deity worship (of Shiva, Laksmi etc), where the candle-lit divine image is shrouded by the shadows and darkness of the temple structure, perpetuating the belief of the individual and personal worship (as compared to mass worship) of the appropriate deity. Hindu temples (and, similarly, Buddhist temples) serve as places of contemplation and meditation.

The intense decoration of these monuments existed as an aid to this process, as opposed to being merely idolatry. By depicting various scenes from the epics, the *Ramayana* and, especially, the *Mahabharata*, they resulted in a visual theology lesson. The Hindu ritual of *puja* (worship) also takes place here and is usually performed in front of an image or statue symbolising the deity in question. The architectural components of a Hindu temple comprise:

- the image representing the deity
- a *shikhara* or spire over the sanctuary
- a sanctuary – the Sanskrit word is *garbhagriha* or 'womb-house': the area that houses porch or canopy

PETER TURNER

**Left:** The Gedung Songo (Nine Buildings) temples, scattered across Gunung Ungaran, are some of the oldest in Central Java, built in the 8th and 9th centuries AD. Shown are a Shiva temple and a smaller Vishnu temple.

A Hindu temple operates as a home for the deity and, as a consequence, is comparatively smaller than other places of worship. It also houses the god's consort and other associated deities in different parts of the temple. Other architectural devices employed to elevate the religious experience in Hindu temples, some of which are age-old architectural gestures evident in religious work throughout time, include:

- an enclosure – the pillared gallery of the temple, or the closed passages within that space. The dark enclosed spaces of the temple emphasise the spatial transition of outside to inside (representing the secular to sacred transition) as well as initiating the idea of the worshipper becoming enshrouded by their blessed venerations.
- the use of only one point of entry – this symbolises the Hindu idea of one approach to the divine. Hindu temples, no matter how elaborate the other spatial elements or rituals become, will only have one doorway, often preceded by an entry porch.

**Right:** Shiva Temple at Gedung Songo, featuring Nandiswara and Mahakala statues either side of the doorway.

PETER TURNER

RELIGIOUS ARCHITECTURE OF JAVA

PETER TURNER

PETER TURNER

**Top:** Main temple complex, Prambanan, Central Java.

**Bottom:** Statue detail, Prambanan, Central Java.

GLENN BEANLAND

- an altar – this age-old device for ritual worship is employed by Hindu temples as the base on which to raise the temple
- a pillar or spire – this is used to represent the axis between the earthly worshipper and his deity. The small dome found on the top of Hindu pillars represents the domain of the deity.

# Javanese Interpretation of Hindu Architecture

Candi Bima at the Dieng Plateau temple complex appears to be a typical example of Hindu temple architecture, with its single enclosed shrine with an entrance porch under a multi-tiered tower. The Hindu iconography and narrative is revealed in the sculptural reliefs, as is expected in Hindu temples but, despite the obvious connection to the Hindu epics, the reliefs don't appear to be of Indian origin. Instead, the deities' heads, carved into the niches, appear more like theatre masks, while at the same time suggesting a contemplative calmness which doesn't connect with either the drama of the Hindu epics or the theatre. Similarly, traditional Indian sculptural relief conventions, such as down-turned eyes, eyes with deep-set ridges around them, or lack of expression, are not utilised here. In fact, the sculptural reliefs, despite their content, speak more of a Buddhist tradition than Hindu, communicating the ideas of the eternal, the contemplative etc. This indicates the absorption and interpretation and subsequent expression of new religious ideas.

The temple complex at Prambanan shows a remarkable improvement in building techniques compared with those at Dieng Plateau. Of particular interest is the rebuilt temple dedicated to Shiva, one of the three temples dedicated to the holy trinity of Brahma, Shiva and Vishnu. This temple stands at approximately 47m high and is orientated around the cardinal points. Its spatial arrangement typifies Hindu

**Top:** Main temple complex, Prambanan, Central Java.

architecture, but of note is the composition – the four towers situated around the central tower, accentuating the idea of ascension and centralised space. Enclosed in the inner sanctum is a full-scale representation of the deity Shiva, but interpreted and presented by the Javanese in the form of Mahadeva, the Supreme Being. The Javanese have also chosen to depict scenes from the Ramayana, which in Indian tradition was usually reserved for Vishnu temples.

PETER TURNER

**Left:** Candi Singosari, near Malang, was built in 1304 in memory of King Kertanegrara but was never finished. *Kala* heads over the doorways ward off evil spirits.

PETER TURNER

PETER TURNER

**Top left:** Candi Jawi, near Tretes in East Java, combines elements of Shiva and Buddha worship, a common fusion in later East Javanese religion. This 14th century temple is principally dedicated to Shiva but also features a small Buddhist *stupa* mounted on top.

**Top right:** *Dwarapala* guardian figures are often found at the entrance to temple complexes and palaces. This one is from Singosari, East Java.

**Bottom:** After the enclosed galleries that guide pilgrims on a 5km walk past the sculptured reliefs of Buddhist teachings, the upper galleries, representing the approach to enlightenment, afford fine views of the surrounding area.

# BUDDHIST ARCHITECTURE

The most characteristic and earliest type of Buddhist building is the *stupa*, a Sanskrit word for relic shrine. It is a place of worship where respect is paid to relics by acts or gestures, such as prostration, offerings or chanting. In earlier times these were the actual relics of the Buddha, then those of his disciples, and eventually stupas were erected simply to commemorate a period in the Buddha's life. The stupa evolved to become the most powerful symbol of the Buddha.

The visual appearance of the stupa is thought to have derived from a combination of two forms from pre-Buddhist times: the hemispherical royal burial mound and the shape of a folded umbrella, which was a symbol of regal authority.

GLENN BEANLAND

Buddhist temples generally consisted of the stupa as a central sacred nucleus, surrounded by a ritual hall and enclosed by a court. As architecture, temples are far more regionally specific than the stupa itself, which has remained an architectural embodiment of the Buddhist philosophy. The components of a stupa traditionally are:

- a *medhi* – a circular base
- a dome – representing the shape of an *anda* or 'cosmic egg' and a *garbha*, or 'womb'
- a *vedika* – a square stone railing which is connected to the *chattra* by a short mast
- the *chattra* – the umbrella-like spires, symbolising Indian regality.

BERNARD NAPTHINE

BERNARD NAPTHINE

ANDREW BROWNBILL

**Top left:** Relief work, female deity, Borobudur.

**Top right:** A Buddha image at Borobudur sits on the upper terraces called the *arupadhatu* (sphere of formlessness) representing enlightenment. The *mudra* or position of the hands is symbolically important and here signifies reasoning.

**Bottom:** One of the many stone wallcarvings at Borobudur.

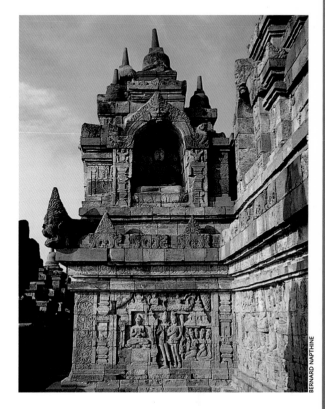

BERNARD NAPTHINE

These components were oriented around the cardinal points, often corresponding with four gateways or four flights of stairs. At Borobudur the four terraces correspond to the cardinal points and contain four Buddha figures respectively.

Javanese Buddhist temples also utilised the *shikhara* (spire) form which later became a Hindu archetype, and more intricately ornamented temples adopted the mandala form.

**Top:** Of the 504 Buddha statues at Borobudur, 432 are contained in open niches on the four galleries leading up to the circular terraces. Water spouting *makara* gargoyles adorn many of the niches.

# Javanese Interpretation of Buddhist Architecture

When examined as a religious monument in a broad architectural context, Borobudur derives its form from an ancient idea of the 'holy mountain'. Religious architecture throughout history has built on (and often included construction of) great mounds to promote the actual, the imagined or hoped for connection between people and their deities.

There is also a more direct connection to Hindu mythology and Meru, the golden mountain, whose foothills were the Himalayas.

The golden mountain was the house of the gods and it extended above and below the earth, symbolising the totality of the universe. This idea directly connects with Javanese mythology, which was inherently aware of the divine powers of mountains due to periodic mass destruction by volcanic eruptions. Ironically, the materials used for Borobudur are sourced from the very volcanoes that were later to bury it in volcanic ash for centuries. Borobudur is not only significant for its beauty and sheer mass (which can be difficult to convey to Westerners as we tend to conceive grand space as something that is contained or enclosed), but also because no other known Hindu or Buddhist architect had ever attempted to combine so many theological concepts in one single built structure. Borobudur has often been described as the most remarkable piece of architecture to emerge from any of the Indian-born religions. Equally remarkable is the complexity of the theological doctrines that it is based on, and it requires more than a broad base of Buddhist understanding to appreciate the intricate details and essences captured in this piece of work.

The three main architectural devices employed at Borobudur are:

- the holy mountain – the ascension of which accentuates the Buddhist idea of rising from the depths of the human condition to ultimate spiritual enlightenment, or nirvana
- the mandala plan pattern – this is used as a circulation device, manipulating the way people move through the spaces. A mandala, meaning circle in Sanskrit, is a pattern of concentric circles, rectangles or interlinked triangles, which visually represent a Buddhist view of the universe as well as being used as a meditation device. Looking at the mandala, the eye follows the pattern to the centre; at Borobudur the entire body and, theoretically, the soul are taken on a 5km-long pilgrimage, representing life's journey, to the centre, which coincides with the summit of the holy mountain – the stupa
- the stupa - this is situated at Borobudur's peak.

Borobudur consists of many stupas leading up to the stupa on its summit, but as an overall object it may also be considered as one stupa (perpetuating a Dutch theory that the monument itself contains relics of the Buddha buried in the hill below). This captures the essence of the inherited Mahayana stream of Buddhism: many Buddhas, yet only One; many universes, yet only One.

The divisions between each of the levels encloses each level without permitting any views to previous or future terraces, serving to represent the different planes of existence which must be experienced individually. The sculptural reliefs of various Buddhist texts and narratives evidenced here, like those in the Hindu tradition, exist as an aid to the pilgrims on their journey. The number and intensity of the scenes shown is concentrated on the lower levels, representing the lower planes of existence and depicting scenes of ceaseless struggle and carnal torment. As one passes through the levels and symbolically rises closer to the planes of spiritual perfection, the relief work appropriately becomes sparser and human images are increasingly replaced by Buddhas. The sculptural works themselves, despite their strong Indian influences, are very Javanese in character, particularly in the non-Indian physical appearance of the figures. These differences can be partially attributed to the volcanic rock material used, not available in India, but also to the Javanese interpretation of Buddhism and its iconography.

# ISLAMIC ARCHITECTURE

The elaborate mosque structures that we recognise today as quintessential Islamic religious architecture originated from humble beginnings in the deserts of Arabia. Simple, unadorned buildings, they contained no sacred relics, images or altars. In fact, the requirements of an Islamic

**Right:** The 18th century Mesjid Jamik in Sumenep, Madura, features Middle-Eastern designs and Chinese porcelain tiles but its gateway and inside tiered roof are Javanese in design.

PETER TURNER

place of worship are very simple, as only an enclosed space to perpetuate the sense of unity and an indication of the direction of Mecca is required to satisfy Islamic law. The prophet Mohammed is believed to have said: 'The most unprofitable thing that eateth up the wealth of a Believer is building'. This was obviously soon forgotten as the Arab Muslims conquered new regions and inherited rich new architectural styles, such as Persian and Syrian. The mosques then saw the development of architectural components that would soon be identified with the Islamic type:

- a dome
- a *mihrab* or niche – showing the direction of prayer – *qiblat*
- the orientation of the mosque towards Mecca
- a *menara*, minaret or tower – this was initially developed by Mohammed as an elevated platform from which the summons to prayer could be issued, in order to produce a different sound from

PETER TURNER

**Left:** The 16th century Mesjid Agung mosque at Banten has a five-tiered *meru* (holy mountain) roof, also found in Hindu temples. The minaret operated as a lookout tower and resembles a lighthouse.

that of the Jews or Christians. Adhan, the formal prayer call, was created and the platform evolved into the minaret form, thus symbolising traditional religious notions of height and, on a practical level, operating as a landmark. In the case of Mesjid Agung (1525) at Banten, the minaret also operated as a beacon or lookout tower and, in fact, closely resembles a lighthouse.

## Javanese Interpretation of Islamic Architecture

The coming of Islam to Java saw the development of the timber mosque as a new type of Islamic place of worship. The new choice of material cannot only be attributed to the availability of materials, but also to the type of skilled labour available; it is suggested that the seafaring traders who brought Islam to Java had considerable timber ship-building skills that were then utilised for mosque building. There are also theories regarding the Chinese influence of these often pagoda-like structures.

The Javanese mosque typically consisted of a tall timber structure, with many roofs, over a centralised timber colonnaded hall. The obvious absence was the dome, which did not appear until around the 19th century. Also absent was the geometric ornamentation that characterised Islamic mosques; Javanese mosques did not become ornamented until the 20th century when government building programmes resulted in a rise of other styles, such as Mughal.

Without the use of a centralised dome, which provides a counterpoint to the direction of entry and prayer, the Javanese used four master columns (though sometimes six or one central column to the

**Left & right:** The dome and minaret of Jakarta's huge Istiqlal Mosque are classically Middle-Eastern in style and typical of modern Indonesian mosques.

GLENN BEANLAND

GLENN BEANLAND

apex of the roof is used), which supported a central higher-hipped roof. This is known as the *saka guru* principle. This tall internal space was further emphasised by other columns, arranged concentrically, which supported the lower tiers of roofs, and by the glimpses of light which filtered through the upper roof layers.

A hierarchy of roof types exists in temple building in Java: the type of roof reflects the type of ritual or activity to be undertaken there. The same principles and the importance of the architectural gesture of 'enclosure' were applied to mosques as they had previously been applied to Hindu temples. For example, an open-ended gable roof would house activities of less importance than a centralised hip roof (ie, folded down at all sides). Similarly, a multiplicity of centralised hipped roofs, in a vertical direction, would again elevate the importance of that ritual or activity; as well, the ascending roof planes symbolised the theological concept of the 'holy mountain'. Mesjid Agung at Banten is particularly notable for its five-tiered roof.

One of the oldest surviving mosques in Java is Mesjid Agung at Demak (1474). Although it has seen a number of renovations, it is believed to be mostly in its original form. The architectural principles of the centralised vertical space supported by the four saka guru columns, enclosed by the multi-tiered hipped roofs, are all adhered to at this mosque. Its orientation towards Mecca, as with other early mosques, is only approximate.

Because of the massive numbers of Muslims in Indonesia and Java, very large mosque complexes, with the ability to accommodate tens of thousands of Islamic worshippers, are now being built. One such mosque can be found in Jakarta: the Istiqlal Mosque. These mosques, as well as other late 20th century mosques, depart from the typical Javanese mosque-building traditions, such as the four-columned central space, and instead respond to global influences and technological advances.

BERNARD NAPTHINE

**Left:** Istiqlal Mosque, Jakarta.

# Facts for the Visitor

## HIGHLIGHTS
### Cultural Centres

Java's number one tourist centre is the cultural city of Yogyakarta, centred around the sultan's palace. Yogya has excellent, cheap facilities and a host of reasonably priced tours to surrounding attractions. It makes an ideal base for trips to awe-inspiring Borobudur, Indonesia's most famous landmark, and the equally impressive temple complex at Prambanan.

Less visited, nearby Solo is another court city and major repository of Javanese culture. It is quieter, without Yogya's range of facilities, but also without Yogya's crowds. Solo can also be used as a base to explore the antiquities of Central Java.

Cirebon, on the north coast, is sleepier than most other Javanese cities, and has its own court culture and palaces. Though not as impressive as Yogya or Solo, it makes a worthwhile stopover.

Well off the beaten tourist track, the north coast of Java is the cradle of Islam and shows another side of Java away from the *kratons*. There are ancient mosques, decaying old trading ports and Muslim pilgrimage sites, which can be interesting diversions for the more adventurous. Madura has an interesting traditional culture, with Sumenep the highlight.

### Antiquities

Magnificent Borobudur and Prambanan are on most itineraries, but dozens of other sites from the Hindu/Buddhist period are scattered across Central and East Java. While most are now restored, few are breathtaking and it usually requires time and effort to reach them. The lesser antiquities are mostly for those with a strong interest in Javanese history, but some are in magnificent natural settings.

In Central Java, the temples of the Dieng Plateau are not stunning, but the surrounding mountains and volcanic sites make up for it. Gedung Songo, between Solo and Semarang, is a small complex with plain temples, but the mountain views looking across the major peaks of Java are magnificent. Candi Sukuh and the more remote Candi Ceto are small, but interesting, temples like no other in Java and make a good day trip from Solo. Imogiri, the burial complex of Mataram kings and the current sultans, is another pleasant day trip into the countryside from Yogya.

In East Java, Trowulan (the ancient city of Majapahit) is the most impressive temple complex. Panataran comes a close second but it requires a detour from most itineraries. There are number of smaller temples scattered around Malang that are easier to reach on a day trip.

### Cities

Java's big cities, such as Jakarta, Surabaya and Bandung, are intense, crowded and disorienting. To appreciate contemporary Indonesia or the Dutch heritage, a visit to Java's cities is essential. For many travellers, however, the cities are mostly transit points with only a few 'must-sees'. For those who thrive on the excitement of big cities and have time, they can be fascinating to explore, but a quick look is usually enough for most visitors.

Smaller cities, like Bogor and Malang, are more manageable and are good stopover points. Neither are packed with attractions but in Bogor you'll find the famous botanical gardens and the cooler elevation and nearby mountains make a welcome break from Jakarta. Malang is a pleasant city and a good base for exploring the surrounding area.

If you only travel the main highway – the great Postweg road laid by the Dutch from Merak to Banyuwangi – Java's procession of cities and towns can blur into greyness after a while. It is important to see some of the countryside.

## Volcanoes & National Parks

Away from the main highway and major cities, Java's vast urban sprawl gives way to some superb natural attractions. A string of volcanoes runs through the island and Gunung Bromo is one of the most spectacular in Indonesia.

Krakatau, Indonesia's most famous volcano, can be visited from the west coast of Java. Other volcanic mountains, such as Ijen, Papandayan, Merapi and Gede, have superb scenery and good trekking, yet see few tourists.

Ujung Kulon National Park has unique wildlife and wilderness in crowded Java. This is Java's premier park, with good hiking and varied coastal and jungle scenery, but access is more difficult. Gede Pangrango National Park is more easily accessible and has thick forest and good walks.

East Java has Java's most impressive natural scenery. As well as the already mentioned Ijen, Meru Betiri is one of Java's most stunning national parks but is undoubtedly the most difficult to reach. Alas Purwo National Park has good beaches and is slightly easier to get to.

See under national parks in the Flora & Fauna section in the Facts about Java chapter for further information.

## Beaches

Java's beaches don't match those of nearby Bali but they can make a pleasant break from the cities and towns. The black sand beach at Pangandaran is no world-beater but it is Java's number one beach resort. The living is cheap and relaxed and a number of interesting side trips can be made.

Java's finest beaches are on the offshore islands of Pulau Seribu, right on Jakarta's doorstep. These beaches have fine white sand, coconut palms and calm waters but the resorts cater to weekend getaways from the capital and are relatively expensive. The west coast of Java, around Carita, also has reasonable beaches. Pelabuharatu is another more upmarket beach resort in West Java and has black sand beaches and some fine coastal scenery.

Java's north coast has calm waters, but the water is murky and the beaches dirty. The south coast has some good coastal scenery, but it is often rocky and pounded by rough surf. There are some beautiful deserted beaches on the south coast and not all are dangerous for swimming, but facilities are lacking and access difficult.

## Hill Resorts

Java's many hill resorts are nothing like the spa resorts of the Swiss Alps, or as interesting as India's hill stations, but they do have good mountain scenery and walks. Some are quite seedy but others can provide the opportunity for a delightfully cool break from the heat of the plains. Hill resorts are overcrowded with daytrippers on weekends but deserted during the week, when accommodation is more reasonably priced. Very few foreign visitors make it to the hill resorts, Java's most underrated attractions. The following are some of the best of the dozens of hill resorts.

In West Java, the Puncak Pass area is a good break from Jakarta but overdeveloped. A very quiet retreat here is Cibodas, with its scenic botanic gardens and walks in the Gede Pangrango National Park. Outside the town of Garut, Cipanas is a pleasant, hot-spring resort with good accommodation and points of interest nearby. Some of the hill resorts around Bandung make pleasant day trips.

In Central Java, Kaliurang is only a short trip from Yogya on the slopes of smoking Gunung Merapi. Dieng is a scruffy village rather than a resort, but it is peaceful, cool and the scenic plateau area can be explored on foot. Baturaden, on the slopes of Gunung Slamet near Purwokerto, is well off the beaten track, but is one of Java's cleanest and prettiest hill resorts. Bandungan, south of Semarang, is another reasonable resort and a good base to visit the Gedung Songo temple complex.

In East Java, Sarangan is one of the highest resorts built around a lake. Batu, close to Malang, has fine mountain scenery and good facilities.

## SUGGESTED ITINERARIES

A personal itinerary depends very much on personal interests, time available, the level of comfort desired and how much money you want to spend. If time is very limited and money no object, you can fly into Yogya and visit Borobudur for a quick snapshot of Javanese culture. Or by hiring a car and driver, you can put together some excellent, flexible itineraries, visiting the main highlights and off-the-beaten-track destinations in comfort. If you have weeks to spend and are prepared to put up with some discomfort, you can wander in gypsy fashion and explore dozens of places of interest very cheaply.

The typical route through Java on to Bali is a variation on: Jakarta-Bogor/Bandung-Pangandaran-Yogya-Solo-Surabaya/Malang-Gunung Bromo-Bali. This route can be done comfortably in about three or four weeks, less if the big cities are bypassed.

Distances are deceptive. Except on the few toll roads, travel by road or rail is slow. The highways are crowded – count on 40 to 50km/hour for journey times.

### One week or less

Yogya is the best place to experience Javanese culture, and the surrounding area has plenty of attractions. In the city, you can visit the kraton and see cultural performances. Numerous cheap tours are available to Borobudur, Prambanan, Dieng etc, and Solo is close by. If you are prepared to rush, in one week you could also take in another place of interest in Java on a through trip – Gunung Bromo in East Java; or, alternatively, a trip to Bandung, Bogor or Cirebon in West Java on the way to Jakarta.

### Two weeks

Two weeks will allow you to add another couple of places of interest to your itinerary. Jakarta-Bandung-Yogya-Gunung Bromo is a possible itinerary, you could spend up to one week in Yogya/Solo and surrounds and a night or two in Bandung to break up the journey from Yogya to Jakarta. It is possible to include extra sidetrips or one other place of interest.

### Three weeks

In three weeks it is possible to explore Java in more depth and get off the well-beaten path. It is a good idea to venture away from the cities and crowds to the mountains or beaches. Many people include Pangandaran on the above two-week itinerary. A good stop between Bandung and Pangandaran is Garut/Cipanas. On the west coast, Krakatau could be visited or Ujung Kulon National Park can be included, but allow at least four days.

In Central Java, more time could be spent in Solo, or up in the mountains at Dieng, Gedung Songo or Kaliuran.

In East Java, Malang can be used as a base for trips to mountains or nearby temples. Or stop in Surabaya and visit the Madura bull races in season. More time can be sent at Bromo for hiking, or walk to Kawah Ijen.

### Four weeks or more

It is impossible to explore every nook and cranny of Java within the 60 day limit of a tourist pass, but with a month you can take in many of the highlights listed above. You can venture farther afield to Madura or the north coast, visit some of the more remote national parks and volcanoes, or even do a batik course in Solo.

## PLANNING
## When To Go

Weather is the main consideration and the dry season from May to October is the best time to visit Java. Rainfall is higher in the mountains, which are usually covered in cloud, and the wet season in the highlands of West Java can put a real dampener on travel plans. Elsewhere, travel in the wet season is not usually a major problem as rain tends to come only in short, early morning or mid-afternoon bursts. East Java is drier and the wet season slightly shorter.

There are also distinct tourist seasons when prices rise, and accommodation and transport bookings can be tight in some places. The main foreign tourist season is during the European summer holidays in July and August. However, even during the peak tourist months you can always find a place away from the crowds.

The main Indonesian holiday periods are the end of Ramadan (when some resorts are packed to overflowing and prices skyrocket), Christmas, and the end of the school year from mid-June to mid-July when graduating high school students take off by the busload to tourist attractions in Java.

The Javanese, all 128 million of them it seems sometimes, love to get away on weekends. If you want peace and quiet, avoid staying in local tourist areas on Saturday nights, and stay in your hotel and write postcards on Sunday. Most of the mountain and beach resorts are deserted during the week, when hotels are cheaper.

## Maps

An essential companion to this book for exploring Java is the Nelles *Java & Bali* map. It is the most accurate and detailed map to all of Java, and is available in Java and overseas.

Periplus also produce good maps to West, Central and East Java, as well as Yogyakarta and Jakarta. The area maps are small, but useful city maps are included. They are available everywhere in Indonesia and overseas.

Maps produced in Indonesia are of variable quality but are much cheaper than the imported maps and some are quite good. PT Karya Pembina Swajaya produce some good travel maps that include city plans to West, Central and East Java, but road priority is sometimes inaccurate. Major bookshop chains in the large cities, such as Gunung Agung and Gramedia, stock a wide range of maps, including city and *kabupaten* (district) maps.

Commercial maps to the main cities are often good, or tourist offices usually have free maps that are quite adequate. The better hotels have photocopied city maps for guests.

## What to Bring

The old rule of travelling light applies, especially if travelling on a budget. In the cities in Java you can buy almost anything you can get at home. Bring as little as possible and try to keep baggage small. Public transport can be packed to the hilt with passengers, with next to no space left over to stow baggage.

Luggage should be lockable. If you have a pack that doesn't lock, sew on a few tabs so you can shut your pack with a padlock. A small daypack or shoulder bag is also very useful.

Temperatures are uniformly tropical year-round in Java, so short-sleeved shirts and T-shirts are the order of the day. Bring at least one long-sleeved shirt for the cool evenings. The mountain areas are cold at night, so long jeans and possibly a jacket are necessary. Clothing is quite cheap in Java and you can always buy more.

Modesty prevails. If you must wear shorts, they should be the loose-fitting type which come down almost to the knees, but shorts are considered very low class in Java and are only for the beach. Higher dress standards apply whenever you're visiting a government office, so have something suitable for more formal occasions.

A hat and sunglasses are essential, and don't forget sunscreen (UV) lotion. A water bottle is a good idea but you can easily buy water in plastic bottles.

A sarong is an all-purpose Indonesian marvel. Besides wearing a sarong you can use it as an impromptu blanket, top sheet, beach mat or even as a towel. A sleeping bag is really only useful if you intend doing a lot of high-altitude camping.

Toiletries and cosmetics are readily available in Java. Dental floss, shaving cream, tampons and disposable nappies are available, but not easy to find, away from the big cities.

The following is a checklist of things you might consider packing, but don't feel obligated to bring everything on this list:

namecards, visa & passport photos, Swiss army knife, electric immersion coil (for making hot water), cup, padlock, camera & accessories, alarm clock, leakproof water bottle, flashlight with batteries, compass, long pants, short pants, long shirt, T-shirt, nylon jacket, sweater, raincover for backpack, rainsuit or poncho, sewing kit, spoon, sunhat, toilet paper, tampons, thongs, nail clipper, tweezers, mosquito repellent and any special medications you use, plus a copy of the prescription.

A final thought: airlines do lose bags from time to time – you've got a much better chance of not losing your bag if it is tagged with your name and address *inside* as well as outside. Other tags can always fall off or be removed.

## RESPONSIBLE TOURISM

Tourism provides much needed foreign income and few places in Indonesia don't want tourism, but it does have negative impacts that you can help to lessen.

Tourism in developing countries attracts much patronising writing but the key word is respect. If you respect culture, customs and the environment and, most importantly, respect and show an interest in the people that you meet, then not only will your own travels be more rewarding, but so will the experiences of your hosts.

**Customs & Culture**  Indonesia is a relatively conservative country where religious, family and social values are still highly respected. Learn something of the customs and culture and avoid behaviour that contradicts those values. Revealing dress, public displays of affection and aggressive behaviour are poor form in Indonesia. They may be tolerated in tourist resorts like Kuta in Bali, but that doesn't mean they are acceptable. Take your cues from Indonesians, not from your fellow travellers. Be aware of religious customs and always ask before entering a mosque, temple, church or sacred site. See Society & Conduct and Religion in Facts about Java for more information on this topic.

**Tourist Economy**  Staying in family-owned budget hotels, eating at *warungs* (food stalls ) and travelling on local transport means your spending money will flow more directly into the local economy. It should also mean that you will meet more Indonesians and gain a wider knowledge of Indonesian society, but how you travel is up to you. Staying in better hotels, travelling first class or taking tours is not a crime, and contributes just as much, if not more, to the economy, which is the main benefit tourism offers to Indonesians. But how you interact with the locals is more important than how much money you spend. For too many budget travellers, 'interaction with locals' boils down to aggressive haggling and not much else.

Bargaining is an essential social skill for Indonesians and you will gain more respect if you know local prices and bargain for goods. At the same time, while overcharging becomes annoying after a while, tourism is a luxury item that attracts a premium, for rich Indonesians as well as for foreign tourists. Increased wealth from tourism and paying a little over the odds may 'distort' local economies, if you think that poverty is a natural order.

**Environmental Concerns**  Environmental issues often seem to be alien to Indonesia, and Indonesians are wont to say to Europeans: 'We are a poor country that needs to exploit our natural resources, and how can you tell us not to cut down our forests when you have already cut down all your own?'. That said, environmental awareness in Indonesia is growing and there are environmental laws, even though they are poorly enforced. Laws are in place to protect endangered species, but you can still see them for sale in local bird markets.

You can lecture all you like, and even report violations to the local authorities, but the best you can hope for is not to add to environmental degradation. Tourist areas are most sensitive to environmental criticism because they may lose their livelihood. Avoid 'eco tours' that trample the flora and harass the fauna.

Snorkellers and divers should never stand on corals and should avoid touching or otherwise disturbing living marine organisms. Hikers should follow the cliché posted in every national park: 'take nothing but photos, leave nothing but footprints'. Minimise disposable waste and take it all out with you, even though the trails may be horrendously littered. Don't depend on open fires for cooking and it is worth bringing a lightweight kerosene stove if you intend to do a lot of camping (other fuels are less readily available in Indonesia).

Many souvenirs are made from threatened species and should be avoided. Turtle shell products, sea shells, snake skin, stuffed birds, butterflies, etc are all too readily available in Indonesia. Not only does buying them encourage ecological damage, their import into most countries is banned and they will be confiscated by customs.

## TOURIST OFFICES
### Local Tourist Offices

Indonesian tourist offices vary enormously in quality but Java has the best overall selection in the country. The main offices have a variety of brochures, often in appalling English with useless information, but some are worth getting, as are the city maps.

The usefulness of tourist offices varies greatly from place to place. The city tourist offices in Jakarta, Yogya, Bandung and Solo attract lots of tourists and provide good maps and information about the city and its immediate vicinity. Offices in the less-visited areas may have nothing at all. They'll always try to help, but it's pretty hopeless if they don't speak English and you don't speak Indonesian.

Indonesia has a large tourism bureaucracy. The Indonesian national tourist organisation, the Directorate General of Tourism (which has its base in Jakarta) maintains tourist offices called Kanwil Pariwisata in each province, but these are not the places to go for information. Each provincial government has a tourist office called DIPARDA, which is usually good. These offices are located in the capital cities of Bandung, Semarang and Surabaya. In addition, many *kabupaten* (regencies) have their own tourist departments and city governments may have their own tourist offices. The sign on the building is usually written only in Indonesian. Look for Dinas Pariwisata (Tourist Office).

For more details of local offices read the information sections listed under the cities.

### Tourist Offices Abroad

Indonesian Tourist Promotion Offices (ITPO) abroad can supply brochures and information about Indonesia. Useful publications are the *Travel Planner*, *Tourist Map of Indonesia* and the *Calendar of Events* for the whole country. ITPO offices are listed below. Garuda Airlines offices overseas are also worth trying for information.

Germany
  (☎ 069-233677) Wiessenhuttenstrasse 17 D.6000, Frankfurt am Main 1
Japan
  (☎ 03-3585 3588) 2nd Floor, Sankaido Building, 1-9-13 Akasaka, Minatoku, Tokyo 107
Singapore
  (☎ 534 2837) 10 Collyer Quay, Ocean Building, Singapore 0104
Taiwan
  (☎ 02-537 7620) 5th Floor, 66 Sung Chiang Rd, Taipei
UK
  (☎ 020-7493 0030) 3-4 Hanover St, London W1R 9HH
USA
  (☎ 213-387 2078) 3457 Wilshire Blvd, Los Angeles, CA 90010

## VISAS & DOCUMENTS
### Passport

Check your passport expiry date. Indonesia requires that your passport have six months of life left in it on the date you arrive there.

### Visas

**Tourist Pass** For citizens of many countries, a visa is not necessary for entry and a stay of up to 60 days. These countries are: Argentina, Australia, Austria, Belgium, Brazil, Brunei Darussalam, Canada, Chile, Denmark, Egypt, Finland, France, Germany, Greece, Hungary, Iceland, Ireland, Italy, Japan, Kuwait, Liechtenstein, Luxembourg, Malaysia, Maldives, Malta, Mexico, Monaco, Morocco, the Netherlands, New Zealand, Norway, the Philippines, Saudi Arabia, Singapore, South Korea, Spain, Sweden, Switzerland, Taiwan, Thailand, Turkey, United Arab Emirates, UK, USA and Venezuela.

For nationals of these countries a 60-day tourist pass (which is a stamp in your passport) is issued on arrival, as long as you enter and exit through recognised entry ports. Officially (but not always in practice), you must have a ticket out of the country when you arrive and you may be asked to show sufficient funds for your stay. Officially (and almost certainly), you cannot extend your visa beyond 60 days.

The best answer to the ticket out requirement is to buy a return ticket to Indonesia, or include Indonesia as a leg on a through ticket. Singapore-Jakarta tickets are a cheap, popular option for satisfying the requirement. Though immigration often won't even ask to see an onward ticket, if you don't have one you may be forced to buy one on the spot. Jakarta has the worst reputation in this regard, while the busy tourist ports of Bali and Batam cater to short-stay package trips so you're unlikely to be troubled.

In addition to (sometimes in lieu of) an onward ticket, you may be asked to show evidence of sufficient funds. US$1000 is the magic number. Travellers cheques are best to flash at immigration officials, credit cards sometimes work but are not guaranteed. Don't show your cash – you may be asked to 'donate' some of it.

**Visitor Visa** For citizens of countries not on the visa free list, a visitor visa must be obtained from any Indonesian embassy or consulate before entering the country. Visitor visas are only valid for one month, not 60 days as for visa-free entry, and are usually only extendable for two weeks.

A visitor visa is also required for entry *or exit* via an obscure port. In general, entry by air on a regular flight or scheduled international ferry does not require a visa. The Indonesian government produces an official list of recognised entry/exit ports, but the list is rarely updated and the carrier will often be better informed than an Indonesian embassy. This 'no visa' list includes all the main airports and regular entry points. For Java this includes Jakarta, Surabaya, Semarang and Solo.

The main crossings that require a visa are between Jayapura (Irian Jaya) and Vanimo (Papua New Guinea), and between Tarakan (Kalimantan) and Tawau (Sabah, Malaysia). Even if you only want to exit through these points, officially, you must enter the country on a visitor visa.

**Study & Work Visas** Visas for overseas students, for short-term research, to visit family etc can be arranged if you have a sponsor, such as an educational institution. These social/cultural *(sosial/budaya)* visas must be applied for at an Indonesian embassy or at a consulate abroad. These are normally valid for three months on arrival, but they can be extended every month after that for up to six months without you having to leave the country.

Limited stay visas (Kartu Izin Tinggal Terbatas or KITAS), valid for one year at a time, are also issued, usually for those given permission to work. Work permits must first be obtained from the Ministry of Manpower and should be arranged by your employer.

Those granted limited stay are issued a KITAS card, still often referred to as the KIMS card.

The 60-day tourist pass supposedly also covers business travel where the holder is not employed in Indonesia. Visits for conventions or exhibitions are not a problem but you may be asked a lot of questions if you put 'business' as a reason for travel on your embarkation card. Enquire at an Indonesian embassy before departure.

**Visa Extensions** Tourist passes are not extendable beyond 60 days. You may get a few extra days in special circumstances, like missed flight connections or illness, on presentation of written evidence, but whatever you do, do not simply show up at the airport with an expired visa or tourist pass and expect to be able to board your flight. You may be sent back to the local immigration office to clear up the matter.

Extensions for visitor, social and work visas have to be applied for at immigration offices in Indonesia.

## Travel Insurance

A travel insurance policy to cover theft, loss and medical problems is a wise idea. There are a wide variety of policies and your travel agent will have recommendations. Some policies offer lower and higher medical expenses options, and a mid-range one is usually recommended for Asia where medical costs are not so high. Check the small print to see if it excludes 'dangerous activities' that you may be contemplating, such as scuba diving, motorcycling or even trekking. Check if the policy covers ambulances or an emergency flight home, which may be useful.

Theft is a potential problem in Indonesia so make sure that your policy covers expensive items adequately. Many policies have restrictions on laptop computers and expensive camera gear, or else refunds may often be made for depreciated value, not for replacement value.

### Driving Licence & Permits

To drive in Indonesia officially you need an International Driving Permit from your local automobile association. In fact, this is often not required but police may ask for it. Take your home driver's licence, which can be useful for identification, even if you won't be driving.

### Hostel Cards

A Hostelling International (HI) card will give you a tiny discount at the few hostels in Indonesia, but it is of very limited use, given the abundance of cheap and often much better alternatives.

### Student & Youth Cards

The International Student Identity Card (ISIC) is useful for discounts on domestic flights, though maximum age limits (usually 26) often apply, and some attractions offer student discounts.

### Photocopies

All important documents (your passport's data page and visa page, your credit cards, travel insurance policy, your air/bus/train tickets, your driver's licence etc) should be photocopied before you leave home. Leave one copy with somebody at home and keep another copy with you (but make sure you keep it separate from the original), with a stash of cash (US$100 or more) for emergency use.

## INDONESIAN EMBASSIES & CONSULATES

Indonesia embassies abroad include:

Australia
  Embassy: (☎ 02-6250 8600) 8 Darwin Ave, Yarralumla, ACT 2600
  Consulates: Adelaide, Darwin, Melbourne, Perth and Sydney
Belgium
  (☎ 02-7711776) Avenue de Turvueren 294, 1150 Brussells, Belgium
Canada
  Embassy: (☎ 613-2310186) 55 Parkdale Ave, Ottawa, Ontario K1Y 1E5
  Consulates: Vancouver and Toronto
Denmark
  (☎ 45-624422) Orehoj Alle 1, 2900 Hellerup, Copenhagen
France
  Embassy: (☎ 01-45 03 07 60)
  47-49 Rue Cortambert 75116, Paris
  Consulate: Marseilles
Germany
  Embassy: (☎ 0228-382990) 2 Bernakasteler Strasse, 53175 Bonn
  Consular offices: Berlin, Bremen, Dusseldorf, Hamburg, Hannover, Kiel, Munich, Stuttgart
India
  (☎ 011-6118642) 50-A Chanakyapuri, New Delhi
Italy
  (☎ 06-4825951) 53 Via Campania, Rome 00187
Japan
  (☎ 03-34414201) 5-9-2 Higashi Gotanda, Shinagawa-ku, Tokyo
Malaysia
  Embassy: (☎ 03-984 2011) 233 Jalan Tun Razak, Kuala Lumpur
  Consulates: Penang, Kuching, Kota Kinabalu and Tawau
Netherlands
  (☎ 070-310 8100) 8 Tobias Asserlaan, 2517 KC Den Haag
New Zealand
  (☎ 04-475 8697) 70 Glen Rd, Kelburn, Wellington
Norway
  (☎ 2244 11 21) Inkonitogata 8, 0258 Oslo 2
Papua New Guinea
  (☎ 3253116) 1+2/410, Kiroki St, Sir John Guise Drive, Waigani, Port Moresby
Philippines
  Embassy: (☎ 02-2855061) 185 Salcedo St, Legaspi Village, Makati, Manila
  Consular office: Davao

Singapore
(☎ 737 7422) 7 Chatsworth Rd
South Africa
(☎ 12-342 3350) 949 Shoeman St, Arcadia, 0083 Pretoria
Spain
(☎ 95-413 0294) 65 Calle de Agastia, Madrid
Sweden
(☎ 08-663 5470) Singelbagken 12, 11521 Stockholm
Switzerland
(☎ 31-3520 9183) 51 Elfenauweg, 3006 Bern
Thailand
(☎ 02-02-252 3135) 600-602 Petchburi Rd, Bangkok
UK
Embassy: (☎ 020-7499 7661) 38 Grosvenor Square, London W1X 9AD
USA
Embassy: (☎ 202-775 5200) 2020 Massachussetts Ave NW, Washington DC 20036
Consulates: Chicago, Honolulu, Houston, Los Angeles, New York and San Francisco

## Foreign Embassies in Java

Countries with diplomatic relations with Indonesia have their embassies in Jakarta. Surabaya also has a few consular representatives of the USA, the Netherlands, France and a few other countries but they handle only limited functions.

Embassies in Jakarta include:

Australia
(☎ 5227111) Jl Rasuna Said, Kav 15-16
Austria
(☎ 3107451) Jl Diponegoro 44
Belgium
(☎ 5710510) Wisma BCA, Jl Jenderal Sudirman, Kav 22-23
Brunei
(☎ 5712180) 8th Floor, Wisma BCA, Jl Jenderal Sudirman Kav 22-23
Canada
(☎ 5250709) 5th Floor, Wisma Metropolitan I, Jl Jenderal Sudirman, Kav 29
Denmark
(☎ 5204350) 4th Floor, Bina Mulia Building, Jl Rasuna Said, Kav 10
Finland
(☎ 5207408) Bina Mulia Building, 10th Floor, Jl Rasuna Said, Kav 10
France
(☎ 3142807) Jl Thamrin 20
Germany
(☎ 3901750) Jl Thamrin 1

India
(☎ 5204150) Jl Rasuna Said S-1, Kuningan
Italy
(☎ 337445) Jl Diponegoro 45
Japan
(☎ 324308) Jl Thamrin 24
Malaysia
(☎ 5224947) Jl Rasuna Said, Kav X/6 No 1
Myanmar
(☎ 3140440) Jl H Augus Salim 109
Netherlands
(☎ 5251515) Jl Rasuna Said, Kav S-3, Kuningan
New Zealand
(☎ 5709460) Jl Diponegoro 41
Norway
(☎ 5251990) 4th Floor, Bina Mulia Building, Jl Rasuna Said, Kav 10
Pakistan
(☎ 3144011) Jl Teuku Umar 50
Papua New Guinea
(☎ 7251218) 6th Floor, Panin Bank Centre, Jl Jenderal Sudirman No 1
Philippines
(☎ 3100334) Jl Imam Bonjol 6-8
Russia
(☎ 522 2913) Jl HR Rasuna Said, Kav X-7
Singapore
(☎ 5201489) Jl Rasuna Said, Block X, Kav 2 No 4
Spain
(☎ 3142355) Jl Agus Salim 61
Sri Lanka
(☎ 3161886) Jl Diponegoro 70
Sweden
(☎ 5201551) Bina Mulia Building, Jl Rasuna Said, Kav 10
Switzerland
(☎ 5526061) Jl Rasuna Said, B-1, Kav X-3
Thailand
(☎ 3904055) Jl Imam Bonjol 74
UK
(☎ 3907484) Jl Thamrin 75
USA
(☎ 3442211) Jl Merdeka Selatan 5
Vietnam
(☎ 3100357) Jl Teuku Umar 25

## CUSTOMS

Customs allow you to bring in a maximum of 1L of alcohol, 200 cigarettes or 50 cigars or 100g of tobacco. Prohibited are: narcotics, ammunition, explosives, arms, laser guns, transceivers, cordless telephones, pornography, printed matter in Chinese characters and Chinese medicines. Film, pre-recorded video tapes, video laser disc or records 'must be declared and censored'.

Duty is payable on goods obtained abroad, which should be declared if they exceed US$250 or US$1000 per family. Personal effects are not a problem. Customs officials rarely worry about how much gear tourists bring into the country – at least if you have a Western face.

There are no restrictions on import or export of foreign currency, but rupiah is limited to five million rp. Between five and 10 million rp must be declared and a form filled out at the airport. Import or export above that amount requires prior written permission from the Bank of Indonesia.

## MONEY
## Currency

The unit of currency in Indonesia is the rupiah (rp). Coins of 25, 50, 100 and 500 rp are in circulation, both the old silver-coloured coins and the newer bronze-coloured coins. A 1000 rp coin is also minted but rarely seen and the 25 rp coin has almost vanished. Notes come in 500, 1000, 5000, 10,000, 20,000 and 50,000 rp denominations.

## Exchange Rates

For many years the Indonesian rupiah was a relatively stable currency based primarily on the US dollar, trading at around 2000 to 2400 rp to the dollar. Since the 1997 Asian monetary crises and the turmoil in Indonesia, the currency has been on a roller coaster ride, trading as low as 17,000 rp to US$1, though it appears to be settling in at around 8000 rp.

| country | unit | | rupiah |
|---|---|---|---|
| Australia | A$1 | = | 4844 rp |
| France | 1FF | = | 1158 rp |
| Germany | DM1 | = | 3883 rp |
| Japan | ¥100 | = | 61 rp |
| Malaysia | RM1 | = | 1934 rp |
| Netherlands | G1 | = | 3446 rp |
| Singapore | S$1 | = | 4317 rp |
| Switzerland | SFr1 | = | 4756 rp |
| UK | UK£1 | = | 11703 rp |
| USA | US$1 | = | 7348 rp |

## Exchanging Money

**Cash & Travellers Cheques** The US dollar is the most widely accepted foreign currency in Indonesia, and it's the best currency to bring. Other major currencies can readily be changed in the main cities in Java, but rates for other currencies are often less favourable than for US dollars.

If you intend changing money in the countryside or farther afield in Indonesia then bring US dollars – either in cash or preferably in safer travellers cheques from a major US company, such as American Express (the most widely accepted), Citicorp or Bank of America. Bring at least some US dollars in cash for emergencies – you can always find someone who will convert them to rupiah.

Rates vary from bank to bank, and from town to town, so it does pay to shop around. Banks in Jakarta offer some of the best exchange rates in Indonesia, and good rates can be found in cities like Surabaya, Bandung and Yogyakarta. Rates are worse in small towns and foreign currency can sometimes be difficult to change in places where there are few tourists. If you are travelling away from the major cities and tourist areas, it pays to change enough money to tide you over until you reach another major centre.

Touristy places, like Yogyakarta, have lots of moneychangers as well as banks, but banks usually have better exchange rates, though moneychangers may offer the best rates for cash. When changing cash, bigger notes are better – a US$100 note will attract a better exchange rate than a US$20 note.

There are other problems to consider: it's often difficult to change big notes – breaking even a 10,000 rp note in a warung (cheap restaurants) can be a major hassle.

**ATMs** Many Indonesian banks have ATMs linked to international banking networks, such as Cirrus and Plus, which allow withdrawals from overseas savings accounts. Cash advances on Visa and MasterCard can also be made via many ATMs that display the relevant symbols (and sometimes those that don't show the symbols). Cards and networks accepted by ATMs among Indonesia's main banks include:

**Bank Bali:** MasterCard, Cirrus, Alto
**Bank Central Asia (BCA):** Visa, Plus
**Bank Duta:** MasterCard, Visa
**Bank Internasional Indonesia (BII):** Master Card, Visa, Cirrus, Plus, Alto
**Bank Negara Indonesia (BNI):** MasterCard, Cirrus
**Lippobank:** MasterCard, Cirrus, Alto

Check with your bank at home to see if you can use ATM facilities in Indonesia, and also check to see what charges apply.

ATMs in Indonesia have a maximum withdrawal limit, sometimes 600,000 or 1,000,000 rp, sometimes as low as 400,000 rp, which is not much in foreign currency terms. Problems can occur if your bank has a minimum withdrawal limit, which may well be higher than the ATM's maximum, and your transaction will be refused.

Indonesian ATMs also experience a lot of downtime. Except in major cities with many ATMs, don't rely on them. Most large towns have banks with ATMs these days, but they can be hard to find and do not always accept foreign cards.

**Credit Cards** If you have a credit card, don't leave home without it. However, if you are travelling on a low budget, credit cards are of limited use for day-to-day travel expenses in Indonesia, as only expensive hotels, restaurants and shops accept them. But they are very useful for major purchases like airline tickets.

Visa and MasterCard (better) are the most widely accepted credit cards. American Express is a long-distant third; cash can be obtained at Amex agents, usually PT Pacto, in the major cities only.

Credit cards can be a convenient way to carry money, especially if your account is always in the black to avoid interest charges. As well as through ATMs, cash advances on Visa and MasterCard can be obtained over the counter at many banks, though some charge transaction fees of around 5000 rp – always ask first.

Cash advances are readily obtainable in the main cities, and most regional towns in Java have banks that accept credit cards, but it is wise to also carry some travellers cheques or cash as a back up. In more remote areas, you're asking for trouble if all you have is a credit card.

Banks are also charging increasing transaction fees for the use of credit cards overseas, often much higher than the 1% commission charged on travellers cheques. Check with your bank. However, credit-card cash advances are the way to go when there are sudden fluctuations in the rupiah. When this happens, Indonesian banks offer conservative rates for cash or travellers cheques and the interbank exchange rates are often better.

**Giro** Dutch travellers with a Dutch post office account can conveniently obtain cash from Indonesian post offices. These *giro-betaalkaarten* are useful in the many Indonesian towns where there is no bank.

## Costs

Costs in Java vary considerably from place to place but, overall, travel is very cheap and the devaluation in the rupiah makes Java one of the cheapest travel destinations in Asia. Even with high inflation, hotels, food and transport are all very cheap in dollar terms.

With continuing inflation, expect costs quoted in this book to rise, but within a week or two of arrival you should get an idea of price rises and be able to estimate current prices. Goods and services with a high import quota, eg air travel, are likely to rise the most, but transport prices have already risen rapidly and these are expected to moderate.

Jakarta is the most expensive city in the country, but empty hotels make for real bargains, while Yogyakarta has some of the best accommodation bargains in Indonesia. How much it will cost to stay in Java largely depends on what degree of comfort you desire, or what degree of discomfort you're prepared to put up with.

The best international-standard hotels start at around US$80 per night, more in big cities like Jakarta and Surabaya, but discounting has seen rates as low as US$30 for a four or five star hotel. Simpler but very comfortable mid-range accommodation with air-con can be had for under US$15. A bare, budget room costs as little as US$1.50, more like US$3 for something clean and reasonably presentable, but the big cities are more expensive.

Food can be very cheap. A good meal in a cheap eating house or at a food stall will cost well under US$1, while at a top restaurant in one of the big hotels a meal can cost over US$30. For around US$2 to US$5, you can find restaurants serving good quality food with high standards of hygiene and service. Indonesian food always tends to be cheaper, while international food is much more expensive.

Transport is very cheap, ranging from crowded intercity public buses that cost next to nothing, to more luxurious buses and trains that are still cheap by most standards, costing under US$1 per 100km. Taxis, *becaks* (bicycle rickshaws) and any of the many other forms of transport are also absurdly cheap. Car hire is more expensive, but very cheap in dollar terms, and a car and driver costs US$15 or less per day if you shop around.

Java has plenty of other items to spend your money on. Clothes and handicrafts are very good value, if you bargain hard.

**Entry Fees & Guides** Almost every *obyek wisata* (tourist attraction) in Java is subject to entry fees. Palaces, sacred graves, volcanoes, caves, waterfalls – just about everything of interest will have an admission fee of 500 rp or more. Prices will be often posted at the entrance gate, but many places are admission by donation, when someone will appear, clutching the ubiquitous visitors' book for you to sign, and you will be expected to dig deep. In these instances,

500 to 1000 rp is customary, 2000 rp or so if it involves a guided tour. Car or motorbike parking is extra and, as everywhere else, a tip of around 300 rp should be given to the attendant.

Guides will often sidle up to you at tourist attractions, follow you around and start explaining points of interest. They may be touts, such as the guides at Yogya's Water Palace, who will steer you in the direction of batik galleries where they get a commission if you buy. Usually they are guides and expect a tip of around 1000 rp. If you don't want a guide, just tell them so and shake them off, but they are usually knowledgeable and their services can be well worthwhile.

## Tipping

Tipping is not a normal practice but is often expected for special service. Jakarta taxi drivers expect (demand?) a tip – the fare is usually rounded up to the next 1000 rp. Hotel porters also expect a few hundred rupiah per bag. Tipping in cheap restaurants is not expected and many of the expensive restaurants add a 10% service charge to the bill. In expensive restaurants where no service charge is added, a small tip is appreciated. Anyone who carries your bags or shopping, parks your car etc will expect a tip of a few hundred rupiah.

Unemployment is very high in Indonesia, and many people have to eke out a bare existence from the service industry. Their methods may be annoying sometimes – at bus or train stations you almost have to fight porters who will whisk your bag away without being asked. But you should bear in mind that most porters, parking attendants, some guides and other people only make their money from tips. Generosity is appreciated, if not expected, from foreigners, who are universally rich when compared with most Indonesians. But it is also important to understand the value of money in Indonesian terms. For instance, it would be inappropriate to tip porters or guides at tourist attractions 5000 rp, which would be over a day's wages for most people.

## Bargaining

Playing 'market' is a favourite children's game in Java, so bargaining skills are honed from an early age. Bargaining is a complex social game that Indonesians love to play well. Given the fact that prices are rarely fixed, it is also a necessary survival skill when even a few rupiah can make a difference for the poor.

Bargaining may be necessary for a wide range of goods. You should always bargain hard for handicrafts and other tourist items, but it may sometimes be necessary to bargain for everyday items such as a bottle of water or even a a bus fare.

Prices are fixed in department stores, supermarkets, book shops and a few of the fancier shops but most other retail outlets (including some 'fixed price' shops) are open to bargaining. Market purchases almost always involve bargaining.

Restaurants usually have fixed prices and bargaining is not necessary, though overcharging can occur at warungs. Many hotels in Java also have fixed prices, but discounts may be available and it pays to ask, especially at luxury hotels. Train and some bus fares are fixed, but unmetered taxis, becaks and most other forms of transport require bargaining. The price should be agreed before the journey begins.

Your first step in bargaining should be to establish a starting price. It's usually easiest to ask for a price rather than to make an initial offer, unless you know very clearly what you're willing to pay. As a rule of thumb your starting price could be anything from a third to two-thirds of the asking price – assuming that the asking price is not completely crazy, which it may be in tourist areas. Then with offer and counter-offer you move closer to an acceptable price. Don't show too much interest when bargaining and if you can't get an acceptable price, walk away. You will often be called back and offered a lower price.

A few rules apply to good bargaining. First, remember it's not a question of life or death, where every rupiah you chisel away makes a difference. Don't pass up something you really want that's expensive or unobtainable at home for the sake of beating the seller down a few hundred rupiah. Secondly, when your offer is accepted you have to buy the article – don't then decide you don't want it after all. Thirdly, while bargaining may have a competitive element in it, it's a mean victory to knock a poor becak driver down from 1000 to 800 rp for a ride.

Bargaining is sometimes fun – and often not. A lot depends on whether you and the vendor are smiling or yelling at each other. Aggression and argument will cause the trader to lose face, and will push the price up. As in all social interaction in Java, it is important to maintain equanimity.

For everyday goods – snacks, drinks, soap, newspapers etc – there is often the normal, local price *(harga biasa)* and another price, depending on how much you are prepared to pay. The local price is only learnt through experience. If you don't know, ask the staff at your hotel or ask Indonesian friends, or observe what other Javanese pay. If you do know what the price should be, such as the correct minibus fare, tender the correct money.

Above all, don't expect to get the local price, often it is simply impossible, and don't go around feeling that you are getting ripped off all the time – too many people do. Just as in most countries the rich pay more tax than the poor, so it is with Indonesian commerce, and this principle is applied to rich Indonesians as well as to foreigners. Expect to pay a little extra.

## POST & COMMUNICATIONS
## Postal Rates

Examples of rates for international airmail *(pos udara)* are:

|  | Australia | Europe | USA |
| --- | --- | --- | --- |
| Postcards | 3400 rp | 6400 rp | 8000 rp |
| Aerograms | 3200 rp | 8500 rp | 10,600 rp |
| Letters (up to 20g) | 6800 rp | 12,800 rp | 15,900 rp |
| Parcels (500g to 1kg) | 162,500 rp | 295,000 rp | 348,000 rp |

## Sending Mail

Post offices (kantor pos) in Java are quite efficient, and sending mail is straightforward once you find the correct window. Outside many post offices, street hawkers sell stationery and envelopes and offer parcel packing services.

Post offices are usually open Monday to Friday from 8 am to 3 pm and on Saturday until around 1 pm. In the larger cities, the main post offices are often open extended hours, until 8 pm or later, including Sunday, for basic postal services. Go during normal hours for poste restante. Warpostels and warparpostels are private post and telephone agencies that are open extended hours and provide an efficient postal service for slightly higher rates.

Though the postal service has improved enormously, international mail is still quite slow. To Australia or the US takes anywhere from one to two weeks, usually around 10 days. To Europe is a little quicker.

Parcels up to a maximum weight of 7kg can be sent by air mail, or up to 10kg by cheaper sea mail.

Letters and small packets bound for overseas or domestic delivery may be registered (terdaftar) for an extra fee at any post office branch.

Mail within Indonesia can take forever and it is better to pay an extra 600 rp for the kilat domestic express service. Kilat khusus provides overnight domestic delivery (a maximum of two days to even the most remote destination) for 1000 rp to 2000 rp. Kilat khusus envelopes, plus aerograms, can be bought at all post offices.

Post offices also offer Express Mail Service to 46 countries with a maximum of three days delivery time. Tariffs are reasonable compared with courier services. Mail is registered and traceable.

## Receiving Mail

Poste restante at Indonesian post offices is reasonably efficient. Expected mail always seems to arrive – eventually. Have your letters addressed to you with your surname in capitals and underlined, the poste restante, Kantor Pos and city in question. 'Lost' letters may have been misfiled under Christian names so always check under both your names.

## Telephone

Telkom, the government-run telecommunications company, has offices (kantor Telkom) in many cities and towns. They are usually open 24 hours, and often offer fax service as well as telephone. These are the cheapest places to make international and long-distance (inter-lokal) phone calls, and they often have Home Country Direct phones or allow collect calls.

Telecommunications agencies, either Telkom or privately run, are called wartel, warpostel or warparpostel and offer the same services. They may be marginally more expensive but are often more convenient. They are usually open from around 7 am until midnight, but sometimes 24 hours. As a rule, wartels don't offer a collect-call service – in the rare cases that they do, a first minute charge may apply.

Domestic calls are charged according to a system of zones – the cost jumps dramatically if you are ringing other provinces.

**Public Phones**   Public phones are either coin phones, card phones (the most common), chip card phones (not numerous but multiplying rapidly) and credit card phones (still rare). Coin and card phones do not support International Direct Dialling, except a few, very rare card phones at big hotels and outside Telkom offices. The new chip card phones do allow international calls.

Most public coin phones are coloured blue and take 50 rp and 100 rp. You can make a local call with a 100 rp coin, but you will have to keep feeding coins in or be cut off. Newer coin phones are grey and take 50, 100 and 500 rp coins.

For the grey card phones (telepon kartu), you can buy Telkom telephone cards (kartu telepon) in a variety of unit denominations – 100, 125, 250, up to 640 units. They currently cost 170 rp per unit, plus 10%, so a 100 unit card is 18,700 rp. They are sold at Telkom offices, wartels, supermarkets and other retail outlets that display the 'Sedia

## Java Telephone Codes

| Area | Code | Area | Code | Area | Code |
|------|------|------|------|------|------|
| Anyer | 0254 | Jakarta | 021 | Pelabuhanratu | 0268 |
| Bandung | 022 | Jajag | 0333 | Probolinggo | 0335 |
| Bandungan | 0298 | Jember | 0331 | Purwokerto | 0281 |
| Banyuwangi | 0333 | Jepara | 0291 | Rangkasbitung | 0252 |
| Blitar | 0342 | Kalibaru | 0333 | Sarangan | 0351 |
| Bogor | 0251 | Kudus | 0291 | Semarang | 024 |
| Borobudur | 0293 | Labuan | 0254 | Solo | 0271 |
| Carita | 0253 | Lembang | 022 | Sukabumi | 0266 |
| Ciater | 0264 | Linggarjati | 0232 | Sumenep | 0328 |
| Cibodas | 0225 | Madiun | 0351 | Surabaya | 031 |
| Cilacap | 0282 | Malang | 0341 | Tasikmalaya | 0265 |
| Cirebon | 0231 | Pacitan | 0357 | Tawangmangu | 0271 |
| Cisarua | 0251 | Pangandaran | 0265 | Wonosobo | 0286 |
| Ciwidey | 022 | Parangtritis | 0274 | Yogyakarta | 0274 |
| Colo | 0291 | Pasir Putih | 0332 | | |
| Garut | 0262 | Pekalongan | 0285 | | |

kartu telepon' sign. Some retailers put a bigger commission on the cards.

The grey chip card *(kartu chip)* phones use a hard plastic card with an embedded electronic chip, unlike the normal card phones that take a flexible card with a magnetic strip. The chip cards can also be bought from wartels and retail outlets for the same price. Chip-card phones are found in the big cities but are not yet common in the countryside.

There are also light-green coloured phones that take both the normal and chip cards.

Home Country Direct phones can also be found at some Telkom offices, airports, luxury hotels etc. Just press the button for your country (Australia, USA etc) and an operator from that country will come on the line for a reverse-charge or international telephone card call.

There's a wide range of local and international phonecards. Lonely Planet's eKno Communication Card (see the insert at the back of this book) is aimed specifically at travellers and provides cheap international calls, a range of messaging services and free email – for local calls, you're usually better off with a local card. You can join online at www.ekno.lonelyplanet.com, or by phone from Indonesia by dialling ☎ 008-800-103-114.

Once you have joined, to use eKno from Indonesia, dial 008-800-103-111.

**International Calls** For international direct dialling (IDD) – dial ☎ 001 or 008, then the country code, area code (minus the initial zero if it has one) and then the number you want to reach. Two companies provide international connections – 001 is for Indosat and 008 is for Satelindo. All top end and many mid-range hotels offer IDD dialling on room phones, but their surcharges can be hefty. Calls from a *wartel* (telephone office) are cheaper.

International calls operate on a zoning system. Zone 1 covers Malaysia and Singapore (3250 rp per minute), Zone II covers most of the rest of South-East Asia (4875 rp), Zone III covers Thailand, Australia and the United States (8750 rp), Zone IV includes Canada and the UK (6875 rp) and Zone V covers most of Europe (7725 rp). You'll pay those rates at a Telkom office, and an extra 10% tax is charged. The rates are subject to change and have been very variable, depending on currency fluctuations. Wartel rates are similar but it pays to check – some charge a big premium.

It is cheaper to ring on weekends and public holidays, when a 25% discount applies, or on weekdays from 9 pm to 6 am for Asia and Oceania, or midnight to 7 am for North America, Europe and Africa.

**Collect Calls** It is not always easy to make reverse-charge calls. Wartels usually don't allow collect calls because they don't make money on them. In the rare cases that they do allow such calls, 5000 rp or so is charged. Many hotels are similarly unhelpful.

The main answer to this problem is to use public phones. You can make a collect call via the Indonesian operator (☎ 101), but make sure it is collect rather than the more expensive person-to-person service. Alternatively, the Home Country Direct service allows you to dial directly to an operator from the country you are calling for a reverse-charge or international telephone card call. This service may be convenient but it is rarely cheaper than phoning from a wartel. Apart from special Home Country Direct phones, the service can also be used from any phone with IDD capability (such as a chip-card public phone). Dial 001 801 and then the country code. Codes for countries with multiple phone companies are listed in Indonesian phone books.

**Cellular Phones** Indonesia has three GSM networks – Telkomsel, Satelindo and Excelcomindo – with wide coverage in Java and Bali and in the main regional centres elsewhere. Telkomsel has the most extensive network.

If your phone company offers international roaming for Indonesia, you can use your handphone (as it is called in Indonesia) and home SIM card in Indonesia. Mobile calls are cheap in Indonesia, but check the roaming rates charged by your company. Some, such as Australia's Telstra, charge many times higher than Indonesian companies.

Indonesian telephone companies sell SIM cards that you can plug into your phone. This

is usually cheaper, especially if you will be making a lot of local calls and the card will give you a local number. Telkomsel's sim-PATI cards are readily available in the big cities (many Fuji photo shops stock them).

**Useful Numbers** Some useful numbers include:

| | |
|---|---|
| Indonesia country code | ☎ 62 |
| Directory assistance, local | ☎ 108 |
| Directory assistance, long-distance | ☎ 106 |
| Directory assistance, international | ☎ 102 |
| Operator assisted domestic calls | ☎ 100 |
| Operator assisted international calls | ☎ 101 |
| International Direct Dial | ☎ 001 or ☎ 008 |
| Police | ☎ 110 |
| Fire Brigade | ☎ 113 |
| Ambulance | ☎ 118 |

### Fax
You can send messages by fax from the government-run telecommunications office in most cities and many mid-sized towns, or from wartels. Many hotels also offer a fax service, even some budget hotels.

### Email & Internet Access
Indonesia has the lowest per capita rate of Internet penetration in Asia at just 1%, but nonetheless, you will find plenty of opportunity to check and send email or surf the web. Post offices in main cities throughout the country have a Warposnet, which is a privately contracted Internet service, usually open until 8 pm. Rates are cheap at around 10,000 rp per hour. In Java, even some surprisingly small cities have a Warposnet, but they may be open office hours only.

Internet cafes are also popular in the main cities and tourist areas. Rates are higher here and cafe service is usually limited to drinks, if anything, but the atmosphere is a bit less business-like than the Warposnet. Almost all luxury hotel business centres offer Internet connection at high rates.

Indonesian servers are very slow, as a rule. It can take forever to log onto popular Web sites and email services such as Hotmail.

## INTERNET RESOURCES

The World Wide Web is a rich resource for travellers. You can research your trip, hunt down bargain air fares, book hotels, check on weather conditions or chat with locals and other travellers about the best places to visit (or avoid!). The Lonely Planet Web site (www.lonelyplanet.com) has succinct summaries of most places on earth, postcards from other travellers, the Thorn Tree bulletin board, travel news and updates, and links to useful travel resources.

Indonesia hasn't exactly jumped on the Web in a big way but a growing number of sites provide sometimes useful information. Web pages on Indonesian ISPs can be very slow and tend to be updated irregularly. Some of the more interesting sites include:

Jakarta City Government Tourist Office
　discover-jakarta.com/
　(the official site of the Jakarta City Government Tourist Office but not regularly updated)
Living in Indonesia
　www.expat.or.id/
　(for anyone planning on living in Indonesia, particularly Jakarta, this essential site has information, advice and links for the expatriate community)
Travel Indonesia
　www.travel-indonesia.com/
　(a commercial travel site with introductions to Jakarta, Yogyakarta and Bali)
Australian National University
　coombs.anu.edu.au/WWWVLPages/
　IndonPages/WWWVL-Indonesia.html
　(the Australian National University's links site is the 'grand daddy' of links site to everything Indonesian)
Auckland University
　www.auckland.ac.nz/asi/indo/links.html
　(another good links page from the University of Auckland)
Batavianet - Indonesian Super Links
　www.batavianet.com/links/
　(a super links site with thousands of Indonesian URLs)
Indonesian Homepage
　indonesia.elga.net.id/
　(a good general introduction to Indonesia with a range of links)
Royal Institute of Linguistics & Anthropology
　oasis.leidenuniv.nl:70/11/kitlv/daily-report
　(a daily news service of the Royal Institute of Linguistics and Anthropology (KITLV) in Leiden, The Netherlands. It has news postings in Indonesian and English with reports that you won't find in the regular press – plenty of East Timor news)
Indonesia Daily News
　www.uni-stuttgart.de/indonesia/news/
　(a similar service from Indonesia Daily News Online)
Tempo magazine
　www.tempo.co.id/
　(Tempo magazine is one of Indonesia's most respected publications and its website offers good daily news articles, in Indonesian and English)
ANTARA, Indonesian news agency
　www.antara.co.id/index-ENG.html
　(news summaries from the official Indonesian news agency, ANTARA, with a searchable database)
Nature Conservation in Indonesia
　www.noord.bart.nl/~edcolijn/general.html
　(an amazing site for information on nature conservation in Indonesia)

## BOOKS

Java is well documented, and hundreds of books have been written that are devoted to Javanese history, society, culture and arts. Dutch scholars have contributed a huge body of literature to the study of the island, but there are also many excellent works available in English. Many general works on Indonesia also devote substantial coverage to Java.

### Lonely Planet

For Jakarta, Lonely Planet's *Jakarta* city guide covers the city in depth, with detailed travel information. Lonely Planet's *Indonesia* covers the whole country for travel farther afield, and *Bali & Lombok* is a good, detailed companion to this guide if you are travelling on to Bali, as is *Indonesia's Eastern Islands*, which covers Lombok to Timor.

A good introductions to Bahasa Indonesia is Lonely Planet's *Indonesia Phrasebook*. This phrasebook is structured to provide travellers with a good working knowledge of basic Indonesian. The book places emphasis on the day-to-day vocabulary that you will most likely need when you travel around the country.

## Travel

A few travel and cultural guides are available for travel in Java, though some are hard to get outside Java.

*Historical Sights of Jakarta* (1982) by Adolf Heuken SJ is mostly a history book but also serves as a good guidebook to Jakarta's colonial past. It gives a wonderful rundown on Dutch architecture around the city, the history of Batavia and the various groups that populated the city.

In the same vein, *The Sultanate of Banten* by Claude Guillot provides a detailed, illustrated history of Banten and catalogues the present ruins. It makes an ideal guide for appreciating Banten.

*All Around Bandung,* written by Gottfried Roelcke & Gary Crabb, is a detailed guide to the city and surrounding districts of West Java. This guide is beautifully photographed and includes shots of dozens of side trips.

Another series guide is the Periplus guide to *Java*, which has some handsome photos and good background articles. In a similar style is the Insight guide to *Java*, and Insight also produces city guides to *Jakarta* and *Yogyakarta*. Times Publishers in Singapore also produce some well-photographed guides to some Indonesian cities, including Jakarta and Cirebon.

Some interesting travelogues dating from colonial times are still in print. *Java Pageant* and *Javanese Panorama* by HW Ponder are affectionate portraits of Java and its people, written by an English woman who lived in Java in the 1920s and 1930s.

## People, Religion & Society

A classic book on Javanese religion, culture and values, which until recently dominated Western scholarship of Java, is *The Religion of Java* (1960) by Clifford Geertz. Geertz divides Javanese society into three streams: the nominal Muslim peasantry *(abangan)*, which is inclined to animism; the more devout urban Muslims *(santri)*; and old aristocracy *(priyayi)*, whose beliefs are rooted in the Hindu court tradition. This book is rather dated and the divisions are more blurred than Geertz's account suggests.

However, it remains a useful model for understanding Javanese religion and society.

*Javanese Culture* (1989) by Koentjaraningrat is one of the most comprehensive studies of Javanese society, history, culture and beliefs. This excellent reference book covers everything from Javanese toilet training to local kinship lines. The studies of Javanese peasant life and Javanese religion are particularly fascinating.

Two book by Neils Mulder that explore Javanese mysticism are *Individual & Society in Java* (1989) and *Mysticism & Everyday Life in Contemporary Java* (1983). Though concerned primarily with the non-mainstream *kebatinan* mystical movements, they are useful elucidations of Javanese mysticism and its world view.

*Indonesia in Focus* (1990), edited by Peter Homan, Reimar Schefol, Vincent Dekker & Nico de Jonge, is an excellent Dutch publication available in English. With numerous glossy photos and well-illustrated articles, it explores all of Indonesia and its rich ethnic diversity. For Java, it has informed articles on the Badui, the courts of Central Java, batik in Tuban and the bull races in Madura.

*Hindu Javanese: Tengger Tradition and Islam* (1985) by Robert Hefner is a detailed study on the Tenggerese people of the Gunung Bromo area in East Java.

The American Women's Association produces *Introducing Indonesia: A Guide to Expatriate Living*, which covers Indonesian society and customs and everyday practicalities for expatriates, with special reference to Jakarta.

## History

An excellent general history is *A History of Modern Indonesia* (1981) by MC Ricklefs. It covers Indonesian history from the rise of Islam, circa 1300, to the present. It mainly covers Java, but ties in what was happening in the outer islands. For an introduction to all the major empires, movements and currents in Javanese history, this book is a must.

Also by Merle Ricklefs, *War, Culture and Economy in Java: 1677-1726* (1993) examines the Dutch incursions and their impact on Java, and *Jogjakarta under Sultan Mangkubumi 1749-1792* (1974) is a fascinating account of the battles for power as the Mataram Empire was split and Yogyakarta was founded.

For the serious student of Javanese history, Thomas Stamford Raffles' *The History of Java*, published in 1817, is a classic work covering all aspects of Javanese history and society. It's available in two hefty and very expensive volumes, with numerous illustrations.

*Jakarta: A History* (1985) by Susan Abeyasekere is the best history of Jakarta and is particularly good for the later colonial period and post-independence Jakarta. Scholarly but very readable, it provides an excellent introduction to the capital.

The period of the cultivation system has inspired a number of books. One of the best scholarly analyses is *Java Under the Cultivation System* (1992) by Robert van Neil.

Of the many general histories on Indonesia, a very readable, popular history is *Indonesia: Land Under the Rainbow* (1990) by the noted Indonesian writer, Mochtar Lubis. This book is interesting for its view of the country through Indonesian eyes.

## Natural History

Books in English on Javanese wildlife don't exist, but two good illustrated books for all-Indonesia are *The Wildlife of Indonesia* by Kathy MacKinnon and *Wild Indonesia* by Tony & Jane Whitten.

*The Birds of Java and Bali* by Derek Holmes & Stephen Nash is a good field guide for birders. Periplus editions produces *The Ecology of Indonesia* series in eight regional volumes, including one volume devoted to Java and Bali. These weighty, scholarly books cover everything from flora and fauna to population distribution.

*The Malay Archipelago* by Alfred Russel Wallace is an 1869 classic of this famous naturalist's wanderings throughout the Indonesian islands. It includes descriptions of Javanese wildlife and the landscape – the way it used to be.

## Arts & Crafts

*Art in Indonesia: Continuities and Change* (1967) by Claire Holt is a good introduction to the arts of Indonesia, with particular relevance to Java. Though its study of modern art is naturally a little dated, the book gives one of the best explanations of Javanese antiquities and traditional performing arts, with useful appendices on Javanese literature and *wayang* stories.

*Culture and Society in New Order Indonesia* (1993), edited by Virginia Matheson Hooker, examines the developments in the arts under the policies of Soeharto's New Order government. It includes some interesting, though sometimes obscure, articles on modern literature, drama, architecture, painting etc, and a particularly interesting piece on the development of Bahasa Indonesia and its relationship to Javanese.

The 'Oxford in Asia' paperback series (Oxford University Press) has a number of excellent books including *Javanese Wayang Kulit – An Introduction* by Edward C van Ness & Shita Prawirohardjo, *Javanese Gamelan* by Jennifer Lindsay and *Borobudur* by Jacques Dumarcay. One of the best guides to the history, archaeology and the symbolism of Borobudur is John Miskic's *Borobudur: Golden Tales of the Buddhas* (1990).

A classic book on Java's wayang traditions is *Javanese Shadow Puppets* by Ward Keeler. *Wayang Golek* (1991) written by Peter Buurman is the best book on West Java's wooden puppets. It is well illustrated, covers different styles and everything from puppet making to an explanation of the different characters.

For an overall guide to Indonesian crafts, *Arts and Crafts of Indonesia* (1990) by Anne Richter is detailed and is beautifully illustrated. *Folk Art of Java* (1994) by Joseph Fischer covers wayang puppets, masks, children's toys, ceramics and woodcarving as they relate to village traditions.

Two excellent books on batik, which contain numerous illustrations and explanations of regional styles are *Batik: Creating an Identity* (1991), written by Lee Chor Lin and *Batik: Fabled Cloth of Java* (1984) written by Inger McCabe Elliot.

There are plenty of glossy coffee table books on Java. One of the more interesting and attractive is *Java Style*, which is a lavishly photographed look at Javanese design, architecture and interior decoration.

## Fiction

Pramoedya Ananta Tur, a Javanese author, is Indonesia's most well-known novelist, and has spent over 14 years in jail under the New Order government because of his political affiliations and criticism of the government. His most famous quartet of historical realist novels, set in the colonial era, includes *This Earth of Mankind*, *Child of All Nations*, *Footsteps* and *House of Glass*. They chart the life of Minke, a Javanese intellectual who has to reconcile his Javanese beliefs with the colonial world around him.

Mochtar Lubis is another well-known Indonesian writer. His most famous novel on Jakarta, *Twilight in Djakarta* is a scathing attack on corruption and the plight of the poor in Jakarta in the 1950s. The book was banned and the author jailed for this book. Much has changed, but the problems still remain.

Christopher Koch's *The Year of Living Dangerously* is an evocative reconstruction of life in Jakarta during the final chaotic months of the Soekarno period and a sympathetic portrayal of the Indonesians and their culture and society. The movie based on the book, made by Australian director Peter Weir, packs a feel for the place that few other movies could ever hope to achieve.

Much of Joseph Conrad's *Victory* is set in Surabaya, in a hotel very reminiscent of the Hotel Majapahit (see the Surabaya section in the East Java chapter). Though not particularly evocative of Indonesia, the novel gives a wonderful account of the sea traders of the time.

*Max Havelaar* by Multatuli (the pseudonym of Douwes Dekker) is a classic Dutch novel, first published in 1860. Written by a Dutch official based in West Java, it highlights the inhumane treatment of the Javanese

under the Dutch Culture System. The public outcry that the book provoked in the Netherlands helped to change government policy.

## Language

Bookshops in Indonesia stock plenty of cheap Bahasa Indonesia/English text books and dictionaries, but most are of poor quality.

For something a little more advanced, *How to Master the Indonesian Language* by AM Almeister will provide a good introduction to the language and its grammar. *Bahasa Indonesia: Langkah Baru – a New Approach*, Book I, by Yohanni Johns is not really designed for self-study, but if you master this one you will have a substantial vocabulary and a solid grounding in Indonesian grammar.

Cheap pocket dictionaries abound in Indonesian bookshops but are riddled with errors and omissions. *Tuttle's Concise Indonesian Dictionary*, widely available in Indonesia, and *MIP Concise Indonesian Dictionary*, on sale overseas, are the best.

*An Indonesian-English Dictionary* and its companion volume *An English-Indonesian Dictionary* by John Echols and Hassan Shadily are by far the best dictionaries, but too weighty to lug around. *Kamus Lengkap* by S Wojowasito & Tito Wasito, despite some odd and inaccurate translations, is about the best comprehensive dictionary in a manageable size for travelling.

Books for learning Javanese and Sundanese are hard to come by, as are dictionaries, but Javanese/Indonesian and Sundanese/Indonesian dictionaries are on sale in bookshops in Java. *Javanese: A Cultural Approach* by Ward Keeler is a standard American text for studying Javanese.

## FILMS

While television production in Indonesia is booming, the movie industry is ailing. Indonesia has produced hundreds of movies since independence but the chances of getting to see them, even in Indonesia, are limited. Hollywood and Hong Kong blockbusters dominate Indonesian cinemas and contemporary Indonesian film makers who explore unacceptable themes, like poverty, have had trouble getting distribution for their films.

Many Indonesian films tend to be low-budget tragic romances, with a bit of titillation thrown in, or glorification of Indonesia's revolutionary spirit. In the latter category is the recent *Fatahillah*, a US$1.24 million blockbuster (that's a big budget in Indonesia) which tells the story of the national hero who defeats Portuguese incursions into present-day Jakarta.

Some good movies exploring contemporary Indonesian society have been produced in recent years. They include *Langitku Rumahku* (My Sky, My Home) a touching 1990 film directed by Siamet Rahardjo, about two boys, one rich and one from the slums of Jakarta, who form a bond and set off on a journey to Yogyakarta. *Istana Kecantikan* (The Beauty Parlour, 1989) by Wahyu Sihombing is about a gay man forced into marriage because of societal pressure.

Indonesia's best-known contemporary director is Garin Nugroho, whose hard-hitting documentaries and feature films have garnered critical acclaim and international awards. His *Bulan Tertusuk Ilalang* (And the Moon Dances, 1995) was voted the best South-East Asian film and grabbed awards at Berlin, Nantes and Japanese film festivals. It is the story of a master of traditional arts and his relationship with two students, who seek to come to grips with Javanese traditions in a modern world. Other feature films by Garin Nugroho are *Cinta Dalam Sepotong Roti* (Love on a Slice of Bread, 1991) and the acclaimed *Surat Untuk Bidadari* (A Letter to an Angel, 1994). *Dongeng Kancil Tentang Kemerdekaan* (Kancil's Tale of Freedom, 1995) is a documentary following the lives of four boys who scratch a living on the streets of Yogyakarta. It drew criticism from within Indonesia for presenting the darker side of Indonesian life to the world.

A few foreign films have been shot in Indonesia and might be available in video stores. *Jakarta* (1988), directed by Charles Kaufman, is a rousing action film starring Christopher North. It provides little insight into Indonesia but was filmed in and around the capital. The best of the foreign movies is *Max Havelaar* (1976), a Dutch/Indonesian co-production that was directed by Fons Rademakers. Based on the classic novel by Multatuli, it is about a Dutch official in 19th century Java who is confronted by the injustices of colonialism.

## NEWSPAPERS & MAGAZINES

The news media now openly publish stories that could only be hinted at during the Soeharto era. Now the media rails against the former president, but other figures are treated with more care, especially the army. The press is now remarkably free but, though the government talks about *transparensi*, it may be some time before repressive press laws are fully repealed and old habits die hard, especially the desire of government to control information.

### Local

The English-language press is limited mostly to the *Jakarta Post*, published daily. In a country where, until very recently, self-censorship applied and stories of corruption and repression never saw the light of day, the *Jakarta Post* was always surprisingly open. As well as forthright reporting, it also gives a useful run down of events in Jakarta and farther afield.

The other main English-language newspaper is the *Indonesian Observer*, but its coverage of local politics is a long way behind that of the *Jakarta Post*.

Two of the leading Indonesian-language newspapers are the Jakarta dailies *Pos Kota* and the respected *Kompas*, each with a circulation of around three million per day. The other main newspapers, in terms of readership, are *Jawa Pos*, *Suara Pembaruan*, *Republika*, *Pikiran Rakyat*, *Harian Terbit* and *Media Indonesia*. Popular tabloids include *Nova*, a women's paper, and *Bola* (as in soccer), while postreform political tabloids such as *Adil* and *Aksi* are also strong performers. *Femina* is a top selling women's magazine, while *Gatra* is a general news and features magazine, as is the once-banned *Tempo*.

## Foreign

The *International Herald-Tribune*, *Asian Wall Street Journal* and major Asian dailies are sold in Indonesia. Western magazines like *Time*, *Newsweek*, *The Economist* and the excellent Hong Kong-published *Far Eastern Economic Review* are available in Indonesia.

For information on what's happening in Indonesia today (including Indonesian politics, history and culture) take out a subscription to *Inside Indonesia*, published in Australia at PO Box 190, Northcote, Victoria 3070, Australia. Excellent articles cover everything from power plays within the army, to the environment. The journal discusses issues not raised in the Indonesian media and rarely covered overseas.

## RADIO & TV

Radio Republik Indonesia (RRI) is the national radio station, which broadcasts 24 hours in Indonesian from every provincial capital. Indonesia also has plenty of privately run stations.

Thanks to satellite broadcasting, TV can be received everywhere in Indonesia. Satellite dish antennas around the country are aimed almost straight up, as broadcast satellites are put in geostationary orbit – the satellites travel around the equator at the same speed as the earth rotates. You'll also see plenty of Indonesians in geostationary orbit around the TV set of any hotel – they are among the world's foremost TV addicts.

Televisi Republik Indonesia (TVRI) is the Indonesian-language TV station, owned by the government, which is broadcast in every province. It broadcasts on two channels, but the second channel is not available in more remote areas.

Private stations are Rajawali Citra Televisi Indonesia (RCTI), Andalas Televisi (AN-TV), Indosair, Surya Citra Televisi (SCTV) and Televisi Pendidikan Indonesia (TPI), originally an educational station but now much the same as the rest.

Most programming revolves around interminable government news broadcasts. Local news is broadcast in English at 6.30 am on TVRI, 7 am on SCTV and 7.30 am on RCTI. Foreign movies, mostly B-grade US adventure flicks, are screened most evenings with Indonesian subtitles (a good way to pick up the language) and an amazing number of advertisements to interrupt the action at the most inappropriate moments.

Satellite dishes also pick up overseas stations transmitting in the region. CNN, BBC, Television Australia, Malaysian and French television can all be received. Some large hotels also have cable television for HBO, Discovery Channel etc.

## VIDEO SYSTEMS

VCR recorders are outdated technology in Indonesia and VCDs (video CDs) are all the rage.

Almost every shopping centre in the big cities of Java has a shop or stalls selling pirate VCDs very cheaply, but the quality is often poor. Some hunting will turn up a good selection of recent release movies, and they are not censored in a country that cuts just about anything more risque than *Bambi*.

Laser discs are also very popular and they can be bought or rented in a number of places. The quality is better than VCDs.

## PHOTOGRAPHY & VIDEO
## Photography

Colour print film is preferred to anything else, so slide film and black & white film are not as readily available. Nevertheless, you can usually find most types of film in the main cities in Java, even Polaroid film, movie film and video tape. Fuji is by far the most widely available brand, for prints and slides, while Kodachrome is rarely seen and has to be sent overseas for developing. Film is cheap.

Developing and printing is quite good and much cheaper than in the West. You can get Ektachrome and Fujichrome slide film developed in two or three days, and colour print film can be done same-day through photographic shops. Many of these have machines which churn out prints in 45 minutes, and the quality is usually good. Camera batteries and other accessories are readily available from photographic shops.

The usual rules for photography in the tropics apply. Shoot early or late – from 10 am to 1 or 2 pm the sun is uncomfortably hot and high overhead, and you're likely to get a washed-out look to your pictures. On sunny days, a polarising filter helps to reduce glare and to darken an otherwise washed-out sunlit sky. A lens hood will reduce your problems with reflections and direct sunlight on the lens. Beware of the sharp differences between sun and shade – if you can't get reasonably balanced overall light you may have to opt for exposing only one area or the other correctly, or use a fill-in flash.

Java is a good place to take people photographs. Most Indonesians are pleased to have their photo taken, but not all are and it pays to ask first with a smile and a gesture of the camera. Similarly, Indonesians on holidays love to have photos of Westerners, and you may find at Borobudur that you are a bigger attraction than the Buddha.

Military buildings and installations are sensitive photographic subjects and may be prohibited. Ask if in doubt.

### Video

Properly used, a video camera can give a fascinating record of your holiday. As well as videoing the obvious things – sunsets, spectacular views – remember to record some of the ordinary everyday details of life in Indonesia.

Video cameras these days have amazingly sensitive microphones, and you might be surprised at how much sound that they will be pick up. This can also be a problem if there is lots of ambient noise – filming by the side of a busy road might seem OK when you are doing it, but when you are viewing it back home you might find there is a deafening cacophony of traffic noise. One good rule for beginners to follow is to try to film in long takes, and not to move the camera around too much. Otherwise, your video could well make your viewers motionsick! If your camera has a stabiliser, you can use it to obtain good footage while travelling on various means of transport, even on bumpy roads.

Make sure you keep the batteries charged, and have the necessary charger, plugs and transformer suitable for Indonesia. It is possible to obtain video cartridges easily in Jakarta and Denpasar and the main tourist areas, but make sure you buy the correct format. It is usually worth buying at least a few cartridges duty free to start off your trip.

Finally, remember to follow the same rules regarding people's sensitivities as for a photograph – having a video camera shoved in their face is probably even more annoying and offensive for locals than being confronted with a still camera. Always ask permission first.

### TIME

All of Java is seven hours ahead of GMT/UTC. Allowing for variations due to daylight saving. When it is noon in Jakarta it is 9 pm the previous day in San Francisco and Los Angeles, midnight in New York, 5 am in London, 1 pm in Singapore and 3 pm in Melbourne and Sydney.

Indonesia has three time zones. Sumatra, Java and West and Central Kalimantan are on Western Indonesian Time. Bali, Nusa Tenggara, South and East Kalimantan and Sulawesi are on Central Indonesian Time, which is eight hours ahead of GMT/UTC. Irian Jaya and Maluku are on East Indonesian Time, which is nine hours ahead of GMT/UTC. When it is noon in Java, it is 1 pm in Bali and 2 pm in Irian Jaya and Maluku.

### ELECTRICITY

Electricity is 220V, 50 cycles AC. Sockets are designed to accommodate two round prongs of the European variety, eg as in France. Recessed sockets are designed to take earth (ground) facilities, but most appliances and the wiring in many cheap hotels aren't earthed, so take care. Adaptors for foreign plugs can be found in supermarkets and department stores but provide a loose connection, so it is better to bring your own.

Electricity is fairly reliable but blackouts occur in Jakarta and some of the smaller towns, usually for only a few minutes. They can last longer. Large hotels have backup generators. Voltage supply is not stable in many parts and a voltage stabiliser/surge guard is recommended for computers.

## LAUNDRY
Virtually every hotel – from the smallest to the largest – has a laundry service, and except for the most expensive hotels, this is usually very cheap. About the only thing you need be concerned about is the weather, as clothes are dried on the line, so a hot, sunny day is essential. Give staff your laundry in the morning – they like to wash clothes before 9 am so it has sufficient time to dry before sunset.

## MANDI
One thing you'll have to learn to deal with is the *mandi*. The word simply means to bathe or to wash. A mandi is a large water tank with a plastic saucepan. The popularity of the mandi is mainly due to a frequent lack of running water in Indonesia – sometimes the tank is refilled by a hose attached to a hand-pump.

Climbing into the mandi is very bad form indeed – it's your water supply and it's also the supply for every other guest that comes after you, so the idea is to keep the water clean. What you're supposed to do is scoop water out of the mandi and pour it over yourself. Most of the tourist hotels have showers, and the more expensive ones have hot water and bathtubs.

## TOILETS
Another thing which you may have to get adjusted to is the Indonesian toilet. It is basically a hole in the ground, footrests on either side, over which you squat and aim. In tourist areas and big cities, Asian toilets are fading away as more places install western-style toilets. The lack of running water makes flushing toilets a problem, so what you do is reach for that plastic saucepan again, scoop water from the mandi and flush it away.

As for toilet paper, it is seldom supplied in public places, though you can easily buy

your own. Indonesians seldom use the stuff and the method is to use the left hand and copious quantities of water – again, keep that saucepan handy. Some westerners easily adapt to this method, but many do not. If you need to use toilet paper, see if there is a wastebasket next to the toilet. If there is, then that's where the paper should go, not down the toilet. If you plug up the hotel's plumbing with toilet paper, the management is going to get really angry.

*Kamar kecil* is Bahasa Indonesia for toilet, but they usually understand 'way-say' (WC). *Wanita* means women and *pria* means men.

## HEALTH
Being a tropical country with a low level of sanitation, Indonesia is a fairly easy place in which to get ill. The climate provides a good breeding ground for malarial mosquitos, but the biggest hazards come from contaminated food and water. You should not worry excessively about all this. By taking some basic precautions and with adequate information few travellers experience more than upset stomachs.

### Predeparture planning
**Immunisations** Plan ahead for getting your vaccinations: some of them require more than one injection, while some vaccinations should not be given together. Note that some vaccinations should not be given during pregnancy or to people with allergies – discuss with your doctor.

It is recommended that you seek medical advice at least six weeks before travel. Be aware that there is often a greater risk of disease with children and during pregnancy.

Record all of your vaccinations on an International Certificate of Vaccination, which is available from your doctor or from a government health department.

Discuss your requirements with your doctor, but vaccinations you should consider for this trip include the following (for more details about the diseases themselves, see the individual disease entries later in this section).

## Medical Kit Check List

Following is a list of items you should consider including in your medical kit – consult your pharmacist for brands available in your country.

- ☐ **Aspirin** or **paracetamol** (acetaminophen in the USA) – for pain or fever
- ☐ **Antihistamine** – for allergies, eg hay fever; to ease the itch from insect bites or stings; and to prevent motion sickness
- ☐ **Antibiotics** – consider including these if you're travelling well off the beaten track; see your doctor, as they must be prescribed, and carry the prescription with you
- ☐ **Loperamide** or **diphenoxylate** – 'blockers' for diarrhoea; **prochlorperazine** or **metaclopramide** for nausea and vomiting
- ☐ **Rehydration mixture** – to prevent dehydration, eg due to severe diarrhoea; particularly important when travelling with children
- ☐ **Insect repellent, sunscreen, lip balm** and **eye drops**
- ☐ **Calamine lotion, sting relief spray** or **aloe vera** – to ease irritation from sunburn and insect bites or stings
- ☐ **Antifungal cream** or **powder** – for fungal skin infections and thrush
- ☐ **Antiseptic** (such as povidone-iodine) – for cuts and grazes
- ☐ **Bandages, Band-Aids (plasters)** and other wound dressings
- ☐ **Water purification tablets** or **iodine**
- ☐ **Scissors, tweezers** and a **thermometer** (note that mercury thermometers are prohibited by airlines)
- ☐ **Syringes** and **needles** – in case you need injections in a country with medical hygiene problems. Ask your doctor for a note explaining why you have them.
- ☐ **Cold** and **flu tablets, throat lozenges** and **nasal decongestant**
- ☐ **Multivitamins** – consider for long trips, when dietary vitamin intake may be inadequate

**Diphtheria & Tetanus** Vaccinations for these two diseases are usually combined and are recommended for everyone. After an initial course of three injections (usually given in childhood), boosters are necessary every 10 years.

**Polio** Everyone should keep up to date with this vaccination, which is normally given in childhood. A booster every 10 years will maintain immunity.

**Hepatitis A** Hepatitis A vaccine (eg Avaxim, Havrix 1440 or VAQTA) provides long-term immunity (possibly more than 10 years) after an initial injection and a booster after six to 12 months. Alternatively, an injection of gamma globulin can provide short-term protection against hepatitis A – two to six months, depending on the dose given. It is not a vaccine but is a ready-made antibody collected from blood donations. It is reasonably effective and, unlike the vaccine, is protective immediately. But because it is a blood product, there are current concerns about its long-term safety. Hepatitis A vaccine is also available in a combined form, Twinrix, with hepatitis B vaccine. Three injections over a six-month period are required, the first two providing substantial protection against hepatitis A.

**Typhoid** Vaccination against typhoid may be required if you are travelling for more than a couple of weeks in most parts of Asia, Africa, Central and South America and Central and Eastern Europe. It is now available either as an injection or as capsules to be taken orally.

**Cholera** The current injectable vaccine against cholera is poorly protective and has many side effects, so it is not generally recommended for travellers.

**Hepatitis B** People who should consider vaccination against hepatitis B include any long-term travellers, as well as those visiting countries where there are high levels of hepatitis B infection, where blood transfusions may not be adequately screened or where sexual contact or needle sharing is a possibility. Vaccination involves three injections, with a booster at 12 months. More rapid courses are available if necessary.

**Rabies** Vaccination should be considered by those who will spend a month or longer in a country where rabies is common, especially if they are cycling, handling animals, caving, or travelling to remote areas, and for children (who may not report a bite). Pretravel rabies vaccination involves having three injections over 21 to 28 days. If someone who has been vaccinated is bitten or scratched by an animal they will require two booster injections of vaccine, those not vaccinated require more.

**Japanese B Encephalitis** Consider vaccination against this disease if spending a month or longer in a high risk area (parts of Asia), making repeated trips to a risk area or visiting during an epidemic. It involves three injections over 30 days.

**Tuberculosis** The risk of TB to travellers is usually very low, unless you will be living with or closely associated with local people in high risk areas such as Asia, Africa and some parts of the Americas and Pacific. Vaccination with the BCG vaccine (against TB) is recommended for children and young adults living in these areas for three months or more.

**Malaria Medication** Antimalarial drugs do not prevent you from being infected but kill the malaria parasites during a stage in their development and significantly reduce the risk of you becoming very ill or dying. Antimalarials are generally recommended for Indonesia. But expert advice on medication should be sought, as there are many factors to consider, including the area you will be visiting, the risk of exposure to malaria-carrying mosquitoes, the side effects of the medication, whether you are a child or an adult or pregnant and your medical history. Travellers to isolated areas in high risk countries may like to carry a treatment dose of medication for use if symptoms occur.

**Health Insurance** Make sure that you have adequate health insurance. See Travel Insurance under Visas & Documents in the Facts for the Visitor chapter for details.

**Travel Health Guides** If you are planning to be away or you will be travelling in remote areas for a long period of time, you may like to consider taking a more detailed health guide.

*CDC's Complete Guide to Healthy Travel*, Open Road Publishing, 1997. The US Centers for Disease Control & Prevention recommendations for international travel.

*Staying Healthy in Asia, Africa & Latin America*, Dirk Schroeder, Moon Publications, 1994. Probably the best all-round guide to carry; it's detailed and well organised.

*Travellers' Health*, Dr Richard Dawood, Oxford University Press, 1995. Comprehensive, easy to read, authoritative and highly recommended, although it's rather large to lug around.

*Where There Is No Doctor*, David Werner, Macmillan, 1994. A very detailed guide intended for someone, such as a Peace Corps worker, going to work in an underdeveloped country.

*Travel with Children*, Maureen Wheeler, Lonely Planet Publications, 1995. Includes advice on travel health for younger children.

## Nutrition

If your diet is poor or limited in variety, if you're travelling hard and fast and therefore missing meals, or if you simply lose your appetite, you can soon start to lose weight and place your health at risk.

Make sure your diet is well balanced. Cooked eggs, tofu, beans, lentils and nuts are all safe ways to get protein. Fruit you can peel (bananas, oranges or mandarins for example) is usually safe (melons can harbour bacteria in their flesh and are best avoided) and a good source of vitamins. Try to eat plenty of grains (including rice) and bread. Remember that, although food is generally safer if it is cooked well, overcooked food loses much of its nutritional value. If your diet isn't well balanced or if your food intake is insufficient, it's a good idea to take vitamin and iron pills.

In hot climates make sure you drink enough – don't rely on feeling thirsty to indicate when you should drink. Not needing to urinate or small amounts of very dark yellow urine are danger signs. Always carry a water bottle with you on long trips. Excessive sweating can lead to loss of salt and therefore muscle cramping. Salt tablets are not a good idea as a preventative, but in places where salt is not used much, adding salt to food can help.

There are also a number of excellent travel health sites posted on the Internet. From the Lonely Planet home page there are links at www.lonelyplanet.com/weblinks/wlprep.htm #heal to the World Health Organisation and the US Centers for Disease Control & Prevention.

**Other Preparations** Make sure you're healthy before you start travelling. If you are going on a long trip make sure your teeth are OK. If you wear glasses take a spare pair and your prescription.

If you require a particular medication take an adequate supply, as it may not be available locally. Take part of the packaging showing the generic name rather than the brand, which will make getting replacements easier. It's a good idea to have a legible prescription or letter from your doctor to show that you legally use the medication, to avoid any problems.

## Basic Rules

**Food** There is an old colonial adage which says: 'If you can cook it, boil it or peel it you can eat it ... otherwise forget it.' Vegetables and fruit should be washed with purified water or peeled where possible. Beware of ice cream which is sold in the street or anywhere it might have been melted and refrozen; if there's any doubt (eg a power cut in the last day or two), steer well clear. Shellfish such as mussels, oysters and clams should be avoided as well as undercooked meat, particularly in the form of mince. Steaming does not make shellfish safe for eating.

If a place looks clean and well run and the vendor also looks clean and healthy, then the food is probably safe. In general, places that are packed with travellers or locals will be fine, while empty restaurants are questionable. The food in busy restaurants is cooked and eaten quite quickly with little standing around and is probably not reheated.

**Water** The number one rule is be careful of the water and especially ice. If you don't know for certain that the water is safe, assume the worst. Reputable brands of bottled water or soft drinks are generally fine. Only use water from containers with a serrated seal – not tops or corks. Take care with fruit juice, particularly if water may have been added. Milk should be treated with suspicion as it is often unpasteurised, though boiled milk is fine if it is kept hygienically. Tea or coffee should also be OK, since the water should have been boiled.

**Water Purification** The simplest way to purify water is to boil it thoroughly. Vigorous boiling should be satisfactory; however, at high altitude water boils at a lower temperature, so germs are less likely to be killed. Boil it for longer in these environments.

Consider purchasing a water filter for a long trip. There are two main kinds of filter. Total filters take out all parasites, bacteria and viruses and make water safe to drink. They are often expensive, but they can be more cost effective than buying bottled water. Simple filters (which can even be a nylon mesh bag) take out dirt and larger foreign bodies from the water so that chemical solutions work much more effectively; if water is dirty, chemical solutions may not work at all. It's very important when buying a filter to read the specifications, so that you know exactly what it removes from the water and what it doesn't. Simple filtering will not remove all dangerous organisms, so if you cannot boil water it should be treated chemically. Chlorine tablets (Puritabs, Steritabs or other brand names) will kill many pathogens, but not some parasites like giardia and amoebic cysts. Iodine is more effective in purifying water and is available in tablet form (such as Potable Aqua). Follow the directions carefully and remember that too much iodine can be harmful.

## Medical Problems & Treatment

Self-diagnosis and treatment can be risky, so you should always seek medical help. Although we do give drug dosages in this section, they are for emergency use only. Correct diagnosis is vital.

In most cases you can buy virtually any medicine across the counter in Indonesia without a prescription. If you need some special medication, take it with you. However, you shouldn't have any trouble finding common western medicines in Indonesia, at least in big cities like Jakarta and Denpasar where there are lots of well-stocked pharmacies *(apotik)*. In rural areas pharmacies are scarce, but grocery shops will gladly sell you all sorts of dangerous drugs, which are often long beyond their expiry dates (check them). Many of the big tourist hotels also have drugstores.

In each apotik there is an English-language copy of the Indonesian Index of Medical Specialities (IIMS), a guide to pharmaceutical preparations available to doctors in Indonesia. It lists drugs by brand name, generic name, manufacturer's name and therapeutic action. Drugs may not be of the same strength as in other countries or may have deteriorated due to age or poor storage conditions.

As for medical treatment, Catholic or missionary hospitals or clinics are often pretty good, and in remote areas may be your only hope other than prayer beads and chanting. Missionary hospitals frequently have English-speaking staff. Back in the developed world, you can often locate a competent doctor *(dokter)*, dentist *(dokter gigi)* and hospital *(rumah sakit)* by asking at hotels, embassies or offices of foreign companies in places where large expatriate communities work. In the towns and cities there seems to be a fair supply of doctors and dentists to choose from. In the outback of places like Irian Jaya there are clinics set up by the missionaries. There are also public hospitals in the cities and towns.

Hospitals are open during the day, but private clinics operate mostly in the evening from 6 pm. It's a first come, first served system, so you should go early and be prepared to wait. Medical costs are generally very cheap, but drugs are expensive.

Jakarta has the best medical facilities in the country (see the Jakarta chapter for details) but a lot of people still prefer to go to Singapore for serious ailments that require hospitalisation.

## Environmental Hazards

**Heat Exhaustion** Dehydration and salt deficiency can cause heat exhaustion. Take time to acclimatise to high temperatures, drink sufficient liquids and do not do anything too physically demanding.

Salt deficiency is characterised by fatigue, lethargy, headaches, giddiness and muscle cramps; salt tablets may help, but adding extra salt to your food is better.

Anhidrotic heat exhaustion is a rare form of heat exhaustion that is caused by an inability to sweat. It tends to affect people who have been in a hot climate for some time, rather than newcomers. It can progress to heatstroke. Treatment involves removal to a cooler climate.

**Heatstroke** This serious, occasionally fatal, condition can occur if the body's heat-regulating mechanism breaks down and the body temperature rises to dangerous levels. Long, continuous periods of exposure to high temperatures and insufficient fluids can leave you vulnerable to heatstroke.

The symptoms are feeling unwell, not sweating very much (or at all) and a high body temperature (39° to 41°C or 102° to 106°F). Where sweating has ceased, the skin becomes flushed and red. Severe, throbbing headaches and lack of coordination will also occur, and the sufferer may be confused or aggressive. Eventually the victim will become delirious or convulse. Hospitalisation is essential, but in the interim get victims out of the sun, remove their clothing, cover them with a wet sheet or towel and then fan continually. Give fluids if they are conscious.

**Jet Lag** Jet lag is experienced when a person travels by air across more than three time zones (each time zone usually represents a one hour time difference). It occurs because many of the functions of the human body (such as temperature, pulse rate and emptying of the bladder and bowels) are regulated by internal 24-hour cycles and when we travel long distances rapidly, our bodies take time to adjust to the 'new time' of our destination. We may experience fatigue, disorientation, insomnia, anxiety, impaired concentration and loss of appetite. These effects will usually be gone within three days of arrival, but to minimise the impact of jet lag:

- Rest for a couple of days prior to departure.
- Try to select flight schedules that minimise sleep deprivation; arriving late in the day means you can go to sleep soon after you arrive. For very long flights, try to organise a stopover.
- Avoid excessive eating (which bloats the stomach) and alcohol (which causes dehydration) during the flight. Instead, drink plenty of noncarbonated, nonalcoholic drinks such as fruit juice or water.
- Avoid smoking.
- Make yourself comfortable by wearing loose-fitting clothes and perhaps bringing an eye mask and ear plugs to help you sleep.
- Try to sleep at the appropriate time for the time zone you are travelling to.

**Motion Sickness** Eating lightly before and during a trip will reduce the chances of motion sickness. If you are prone to motion sickness try to find a place that minimises movement – near the wing on aircraft, close to midships on boats, near the centre on buses. Fresh air usually helps; reading and cigarette smoke don't. Commercial motion-sickness preparations, which can cause drowsiness, have to be taken before the trip commences. Ginger (available in capsule form) and peppermint (including mint-flavoured sweets) are natural preventatives.

**Prickly Heat** Prickly heat is an itchy rash caused by excessive perspiration trapped under the skin. It usually strikes people who have just arrived in a hot climate. Keeping cool, bathing often, drying the skin and using a mild talcum or prickly heat powder or resorting to air-conditioning may help.

**Sunburn** In the tropics you can get sunburnt surprisingly quickly, even through cloud. Use a sunscreen, a hat, and a barrier cream for your nose and lips. Calamine lotion or Stingose are good for mild sunburn. Protect your eyes with good quality sunglasses, particularly if you will be near water, sand or snow.

## Infectious Diseases

**Diarrhoea** Simple things like a change of water, food or climate can all cause a mild bout of diarrhoea, but a few rushed toilet trips with no other symptoms is not indicative of a major problem.

Dehydration is the main danger with any diarrhoea, particularly in children or the elderly as dehydration can occur quite quickly. Under all circumstances *fluid replacement* (at least equal to the volume being lost) is the most important thing to remember. Weak black tea with a little sugar, soda water, or soft drinks allowed to go flat and diluted 50% with clean water are all good. With severe diarrhoea a rehydrating solution is preferable to replace minerals and salts lost. Commercially available oral rehydration salts (ORS) are very useful; add them to boiled or bottled water. In an emergency you can make up a solution of six teaspoons of sugar and a half teaspoon of salt to a litre of boiled or bottled water. You need to drink at least the same volume of fluid that you are losing in bowel movements and vomiting. Urine is the best guide to the adequacy of replacement – if you have small amounts of concentrated urine, you need to drink more. Keep drinking small amounts often. Stick to a bland diet as you recover.

Gut-paralysing drugs such as Lomotil or Imodium can be used to bring relief from the symptoms, although they do not actually cure the problem. Only use these drugs if you do not have access to toilets, eg if you *must* travel. For children under 12 years Lomotil and Imodium are not recommended. Do not use these drugs if the person has a high fever or is severely dehydrated.

In certain situations antibiotics may be required: diarrhoea with blood or mucus (dysentery), any diarrhoea with fever, profuse watery diarrhoea, persistent diarrhoea not improving after 48 hours and severe diarrhoea. These suggest a more serious cause of diarrhoea and in these situations gut-paralysing drugs should be avoided.

In these situations, a stool test may be necessary to diagnose what bug is causing your diarrhoea, so you should seek medical help urgently. Where this is not possible the recommended drugs for bacterial diarrhoea (the most likely cause of severe diarrhoea in travellers) are norfloxacin 400mg twice daily for three days or ciprofloxacin 500mg twice daily for five days. These are not recommended for children or pregnant women. The drug of choice for children would be co-trimoxazole (Bactrim, Septrin or Resprim) with dosage dependent on weight. A five day course is given. Ampicillin or amoxycillin may be given in pregnancy, but medical care is necessary.

Two other causes of persistent diarrhoea in travellers are giardiasis and amoebic dysentery.

**Giardiasis** is caused by a common parasite, *Giardia lamblia*. Symptoms include stomach cramps, nausea, a bloated stomach, watery, foul-smelling diarrhoea and frequent gas. Giardiasis can appear several weeks after you have been exposed to the parasite. The symptoms may disappear for a few days and then return; this can go on for several weeks.

**Amoebic dysentery**, caused by the protozoan *Entamoeba histolytica*, is characterised by a gradual onset of low-grade diarrhoea, often with blood and mucus. Cramping abdominal pain and vomiting are less likely than in other types of diarrhoea, and fever may not be present. It will persist until treated and can recur and cause other health problems.

You should seek medical advice if you think you have giardiasis or amoebic dysentery, but where this is not possible, Tinidazole (Fasigyn) or metronidazole (Flagyl) are the recommended drugs. Treatment is a 2g single dose of Fasigyn or 250mg of Flagyl three times daily for five to 10 days.

**Fungal Infections** Fungal infections occur more commonly in hot weather and are usually found on the scalp, between the toes (athlete's foot) or fingers, in the groin and on the body (ringworm). You get ringworm (which is a fungal infection, not a worm) from infected animals or other people. Moisture encourages these infections.

To prevent fungal infections wear loose, comfortable clothes, avoid artificial fibres, wash frequently and dry yourself carefully. If you do get an infection, wash the infected area at least daily with a disinfectant or medicated soap and water, and rinse and dry well. Apply an antifungal cream or powder like tolnaftate (Tinaderm). Try to expose the infected area to air or sunlight as much as possible and wash all towels and underwear in hot water, change them often and let them dry in the sun.

**Hepatitis** Hepatitis is a general term for inflammation of the liver. It is a common disease worldwide. There are several different viruses that cause hepatitis and they differ in the way that they are transmitted. The symptoms are similar in all forms of the illness and include fever, chills, headache, fatigue, feelings of weakness and aches and pains, followed by loss of appetite, nausea, vomiting, abdominal pain, dark urine, light-coloured faeces, jaundiced (yellow) skin and yellowing of the whites of the eyes. People who have had hepatitis should avoid alcohol for some time after the illness, as the liver needs time to recover.

**Hepatitis A** is transmitted by contaminated food and drinking water. You should seek medical advice, but there is not much you can do apart from resting, drinking lots of fluids, eating lightly and avoiding fatty foods. Hepatitis E is transmitted in the same way as hepatitis A.

There are almost 300 million chronic carriers of **Hepatitis B** in the world and it is estimated that over a third of the Indonesia population are carriers. It is spread through contact with infected blood, blood products or body fluids, for example through sexual contact, unsterilised needles and blood transfusions, or contact with blood via small breaks in the skin. Other risk situations include having a shave, tattoo or body piercing with contaminated equipment. The symptoms of hepatitis B may be more severe than type A and the disease can lead to long term problems such as chronic liver damage, liver cancer or a long term carrier state. Hepatitis C and D are spread in the same way as hepatitis B and can also lead to long-term complications.

There are vaccines against hepatitis A and B, but there are currently no vaccines against the other types of hepatitis. Following the basic rules about food and water (hepatitis A and E) and avoiding risk situations (hepatitis B, C and D) are important preventative measures.

**HIV & AIDS** Infection with the human immunodeficiency virus (HIV) may lead to acquired immune deficiency syndrome (AIDS), which is a fatal disease. Any exposure to blood, blood products or body fluids may put the individual at risk. The disease is often transmitted through sexual contact or by dirty needles – vaccinations, acupuncture, tattooing and body piercing can be potentially as dangerous as intravenous drug use. HIV/AIDS can also be spread through infected blood transfusions. Some developing countries are not able to afford to screen blood used for transfusions and though blood screening occurs in Indonesia, it is not reliable.

If you do need an injection, ask to see the syringe unwrapped in front of you, or take a needle and syringe pack with you.

Fear of HIV infection should never preclude seeking treatment for serious medical conditions.

**Intestinal Worms** These parasites are most common in rural, tropical areas. The different worms have different ways of infecting people. Some may be ingested on food such as undercooked meat (eg tapeworms) and some enter through your skin (eg hookworms). Infestations may not show up for some time, and although they are generally not serious, if left untreated some can cause severe health problems later. Consider having a stool test when you return home to check for these and determine the appropriate treatment.

**Schistosomiasis** This disease, which is also known as bilharzia, is transmitted by minute worms. They infect certain varieties of freshwater snails that are found in rivers, streams, lakes and particularly behind dams. The worms multiply and are eventually discharged into the water. Schistosomiasis mostly occurs in Africa but it is cited as being present in 'central Indonesia', though it is very rare.

**Sexually Transmitted Diseases** Gonorrhoea, herpes and syphilis are among these diseases; sores, blisters or rashes around the genitals and discharges or pain when urinating are common symptoms. In some STDs, such as wart virus or chlamydia, symptoms may be less marked or not observed at all, especially in women. Syphilis symptoms eventually disappear completely but the disease continues and can cause severe problems in later years. While abstinence from sexual contact is the only 100% effective prevention, using condoms is also effective. The treatment of gonorrhoea and syphilis is with antibiotics. The different sexually transmitted diseases each require specific antibiotics. There is no cure for herpes or AIDS.

**Typhoid** Typhoid fever is a dangerous gut infection caused by contaminated water and food. Medical help must be sought.

In the early stages of this illness sufferers may feel they have a bad cold or flu on the way, as early symptoms are a headache, body aches and a fever which rises a little each day until it is around 40°C (104°F) or more. The victim's pulse is often slow relative to the degree of fever present – unlike a normal fever where the pulse increases. There may also be vomiting, abdominal pain, diarrhoea or constipation.

In the second week of typhoid the high fever and slow pulse continue and a few pink spots may appear on the body. Trembling, delirium, weakness, weight loss and dehydration may occur. Further complications such as pneumonia, perforated bowel or meningitis may also occur.

## Insect-Borne Diseases

Filariasis, leishmaniasis, Lyme disease and typhus are all insect-borne diseases, but they do not pose a great risk to travellers. For more information on them see Less Common Diseases later in this section.

**Malaria** This serious and potentially fatal disease is spread by mosquito bites. Java officially falls within the malarial zone but if you are travelling only to the main cities the risk is very minimal. The risk is slightly higher in less populated areas, especially the south coast and the national parks. Jakarta is one of the few places in Indonesia that has been classified as malaria free, but there is nowhere in Indonesia where it can be guaranteed that an outbreak will never occur. The risk is generally higher in the other islands of Indonesia, with the exception of Bali, where malaria is uncommon.

Symptoms range from fever, chills and sweating, headache, diarrhoea and abdominal pains to a vague feeling of ill-health. Seek medical help immediately if malaria is suspected. Without treatment malaria can rapidly become more serious and can be fatal.

If medical care is not available, malaria tablets can be used for treatment. You need to use a malaria tablet that is different from the one you were taking when you contracted malaria. The standard treatment dose of mefloquine is two 250mg tablets and another two six hours later. For Fansidar, it's a single dose of three tablets. If you were previously taking mefloquine and cannot obtain Fansidar, then other alternatives are Malarone (atovaquone-proguanil; four tablets once daily for three days), halofantrine (three doses of two 250mg tablets every six hours) or quinine sulphate (600mg every six hours). There is a greater risk than normal of side effects with these dosages if the drugs are used with mefloquine, so medical advice is preferable. Be aware also that, because of side effects, halofantrine is no longer recommended by the World Health Organisation as emergency standby treatment and it should only be used if no other drugs are available.

Travellers are advised to prevent mosquito bites at all times. The main messages are:

- wear light-coloured clothing
- wear long trousers and long-sleeved shirts
- use mosquito repellents containing the compound DEET on exposed areas (prolonged overuse of DEET may be harmful, especially to children, but its use is considered preferable to being bitten by disease-transmitting mosquitoes)
- avoid perfumes or aftershave
- use a mosquito net impregnated with mosquito repellent (permethrin) – it may be worth taking your own
- clothes impregnated with permethrin effectively deter mosquitoes and other insects

**Dengue Fever** This viral disease is transmitted by mosquitoes and occurs throughout Indonesia. Generally, there is only a small risk to travellers except during epidemics, which are usually seasonal (during and just after the rainy season). Minor outbreaks occur every year in Indonesia but a major outbreak occurred in 1998 and over 500 people died of the more serious dengue haemorrhagic fever.

The *Aedes aegypti* mosquito, which transmits the dengue virus, is most active during the day, unlike the malaria mosquito, and is found mainly in urban areas, in and around human dwellings.

Signs and symptoms of dengue fever include a sudden onset of high fever, headache, joint and muscle pains (hence its old name, 'breakbone fever') and nausea and vomiting. A rash of small red spots appears three to four days after the onset of fever. Dengue is commonly mistaken for other infectious diseases, including influenza.

You should seek medical attention if you think you may be infected. Infection can be diagnosed by a blood test. There is no specific treatment for dengue. Aspirin should be avoided, as it increases the risk of haemorrhaging. Recovery may be prolonged, with tiredness lasting for several weeks. Severe complications are rare in travellers but include dengue haemorrhagic fever (DHF), which can be fatal without prompt medical treatment. DHF is thought to be a result of second infection due to a different strain (there are four major strains) and usually affects residents of the country rather than travellers.

There is no vaccine against dengue fever. The best prevention is to avoid mosquito bites at all times – see the malaria section earlier for more details.

**Japanese B Encephalitis** This viral infection of the brain is transmitted by mosquitoes. Most cases occur in rural areas as the virus exists in pigs and wading birds but it is rare in Indonesia. Symptoms include fever, headache and alteration in consciousness. Hospitalisation is needed for correct diagnosis and treatment. There is a high mortality rate among those who have symptoms; of those who survive, many are intellectually disabled.

## Cuts, Bites & Stings

See Less Common Diseases for details of rabies, which is passed through animal bites.

**Bedbugs & Lice** Bedbugs live in various places, but particularly in dirty mattresses and bedding, evidenced by spots of blood on bedclothes or on the wall. Bedbugs leave itchy bites in neat rows. Calamine lotion or Stingose spray may help.

All lice cause itching and discomfort. They make themselves at home in your hair (head lice), your clothing (body lice) or in your pubic hair (crabs). You catch lice through direct contact with infected people or by sharing combs, clothing and the like. Powder or shampoo treatment will kill the lice and infected clothing should then be washed in very hot, soapy water and left in the sun to dry.

**Bites & Stings** Bee and wasp stings are usually painful rather than dangerous. However, in people who are allergic to them severe breathing difficulties may occur and require urgent medical care. Calamine lotion or Stingose spray will give relief and ice packs will reduce the pain and swelling. There are some spiders with dangerous

bites but antivenenes are usually available. Scorpion stings are notoriously painful and in some parts of Asia, the Middle East and Central America can actually be fatal. Scorpions often shelter in shoes or clothing.

There are various fish and other sea creatures which can sting or bite dangerously or which are dangerous to eat – seek local advice.

**Cuts & Scratches** Wash well and treat any cut with an antiseptic, such as povidone-iodine. Where possible, avoid bandages and Band-Aids, which can keep wounds wet. Coral cuts are notoriously slow to heal and if they are not adequately cleaned, small pieces of coral can become embedded in the wound.

**Jellyfish** Avoid contact with these sea creatures, which have stinging tentacles – seek local advice. Stings from most jellyfish are not fatal but painful. Dousing in vinegar will de-activate any stingers which have not 'fired'. Calamine lotion, antihistamines and analgesics may reduce the reaction and relieve the pain.

**Leeches & Ticks** Leeches may be present in damp rainforest conditions; they attach themselves to your skin to suck your blood. Trekkers often get them on their legs or in their boots. Salt or a lighted cigarette end will make them fall off. Do not pull them off, as the bite is then more likely to become infected. Clean and apply pressure if the point of attachment is bleeding. An insect repellent may keep them away.

You should always check all over your body if you have been walking through a potentially tick-infested area as ticks can cause skin infections and other more serious diseases. If a tick is found attached, press down around the tick's head with tweezers, grab the head and gently pull upwards. Avoid pulling the rear of the body as this may squeeze the tick's gut contents through the attached mouth parts into the skin, increasing the risk of infection and disease. Smearing chemicals on the tick will not make it let go and is not recommended.

**Snakes** To minimise your chances of being bitten, always wear boots, socks and long trousers when walking through undergrowth where snakes may be present. Don't put your hands into holes and crevices, and be careful when collecting firewood.

Snake bites do not cause instantaneous death and antivenenes are usually available. Immediately wrap the bitten limb tightly, as you would for a sprained ankle, and then attach a splint to immobilise it. Keep the victim still and seek medical help, if possible with the dead snake for identification. Don't attempt to catch the snake if there is a possibility of being bitten again. Tourniquets and sucking out the poison are now comprehensively discredited.

## Less Common Diseases
The following diseases pose a small risk to travellers, and so are only mentioned in passing. Seek medical advice if you think you may have any of these diseases.

**Cholera** This is the worst of the watery diarrhoeas and medical help should be sought. Outbreaks of cholera are generally widely reported, so you can avoid such problem areas. Fluid replacement is the most vital treatment – the risk of dehydration is severe as you may lose up to 20L a day. If there is a delay in getting to hospital, then begin taking tetracycline. The adult dose is 250mg four times daily. It is not recommended for children under nine years nor for pregnant women. Tetracycline may help shorten the illness, but adequate fluids are required to save lives.

**Filariasis** This is a mosquito-transmitted parasitic infection found in many parts of Africa, Asia, Central and South America and the Pacific. Possible symptoms include fever, pain and swelling of the lymph glands; inflammation of lymph drainage areas; swelling of a limb or the scrotum; skin rashes; and blindness. Treatment is available to eliminate the parasites from the body, but some of the damage already caused may not be reversible. Medical ad-

vice should be obtained promptly if the infection is suspected.

**Lyme Disease** This is a tick-transmitted infection which may be acquired throughout North America, Europe and Asia. The illness usually begins with a spreading rash at the site of the tick bite and is accompanied by fever, headache, extreme fatigue, aching joints and muscles and mild neck stiffness. If untreated, these symptoms usually resolve over several weeks but over subsequent weeks or months disorders of the nervous system, heart and joints may develop. Treatment works best early in the illness. Medical help should be sought.

**Rabies** This fatal viral infection is found in many countries. Many animals can be infected (such as dogs, cats, bats and monkeys) and it is their saliva which is infectious. Any bite, scratch or even lick from an animal should be cleaned immediately and thoroughly. Scrub with soap and running water, and then apply alcohol or iodine solution. Medical help should be sought promptly to receive a course of injections to prevent the onset of symptoms and death.

**Tetanus** This disease is caused by a germ which lives in soil and in the faeces of horses and other animals. It enters the body via breaks in the skin. The first symptom may be discomfort in swallowing, or stiffening of the jaw and neck; this is followed by painful convulsions of the jaw and whole body. The disease can be fatal. It can be prevented by vaccination.

**Tuberculosis (TB)** TB is a bacterial infection usually transmitted from person to person by coughing but which may be transmitted through consumption of unpasteurised milk. Milk that has been boiled is safe to drink, and the souring of milk to make yoghurt or cheese also kills the bacilli. Travellers are usually not at great risk as close household contact with the infected person is usually required before the disease is passed on. You may need to have a TB test before you travel as this can help diagnose the disease later if you become ill.

**Typhus** This disease is spread by ticks, mites or lice. It begins with fever, chills, headache and muscle pains followed a few days later by a body rash. There is often a large painful sore at the site of the bite and nearby lymph nodes are swollen and painful. Typhus can be treated under medical supervision. Seek local advice on areas where ticks pose a danger and always check your skin carefully for ticks after walking in a danger area such as a tropical forest. An insect repellent can help, and walkers in tick-infested areas should consider having their boots and trousers impregnated with benzyl benzoate and dibutylphthalate.

## Women's Health
**Gynaecological Problems** Antibiotic use, synthetic underwear, sweating and contraceptive pills can lead to fungal vaginal infections, especially when travelling in hot climates. Fungal infections are characterised by a rash, itch and discharge and can be treated with a vinegar or lemon-juice douche, or with yoghurt. Nystatin, miconazole or clotrimazole pessaries or vaginal cream are the usual treatment. Maintaining good personal hygiene and wearing loose-fitting clothes and cotton underwear may help prevent these infections.

Sexually transmitted diseases are a major cause of vaginal problems. Symptoms include a smelly discharge, painful intercourse and sometimes a burning sensation when urinating. Medical attention should be sought and male sexual partners must also be treated. Remember that in addition to these diseases HIV or hepatitis B may also be acquired during exposure. Besides abstinence, the best thing is to practise safe sex using condoms.

**Pregnancy** It is not advisable to travel to some places while pregnant as some vaccinations normally used to prevent serious diseases should be avoided during pregnancy (eg yellow fever). In addition, some diseases are much more serious for the mother (and may increase the risk of a still-born child) in pregnancy (eg malaria).

Most miscarriages occur during the first three months of pregnancy. Miscarriage is not uncommon and can occasionally lead to severe bleeding. The last three months should also be spent within reasonable distance of good medical care. A baby born as early as 24 weeks stands a chance of survival, but only in a good modern hospital. Pregnant women should avoid all unnecessary medication and vaccinations, and malarial prophylactics should still be taken where needed. Additional care should be taken to prevent illness and particular attention should be paid to diet and nutrition. Alcohol and nicotine, for example, should be avoided.

## WOMEN TRAVELLERS
Indonesia is a Muslim society and very much male oriented. However, women are not cloistered or forced to wear purdah and enjoy much more freedom than in many orthodox Middle Eastern societies. Indonesia is a pre-feminist society. Sexual politics are rarely on the agenda and Indonesia has few women's organisations, unlike some Asian countries, but Indonesian women have not been subjected to the extremes of some other parts of Asian. Suttee has never had any place in Indonesian Hindu societies but female circumcision does occur in some Muslim areas. In Java, typically it is done close to birth. A small incision is made, the intention being to draw a few drops of blood, not to remove the clitoris.

Wives are expected to bear children and cater to their husbands, but in the cities, many women are well educated and employed in the workforce. Two-income families are increasingly common and often a necessity. Women are widely represented in the bureaucracy and industry, usually at the lower end, but many hold middle management positions, though executive positions are overwhelmingly held by men. In traditional rural societies, divisions of labour are very well defined and social organisation is male dominated, but women are not excluded and some societies are matriarchal, notably the Minangkabau of Sumatra.

Plenty of western women travel in Indonesia, either alone or in pairs. Most seem to enjoy the country and its people and most seem to get through the place without any problems. But women travelling alone will receive attention and sometimes it is unwanted. Western looks are considered the pinnacle of beauty and desirability in Indonesia (for men as well as women). This, combined with the notion that the west is the home of free sex, and perhaps because of the legendary exploits of the Bali beach boy gigolos, women travelling solo will get plenty of attention from Indonesian men trying their luck.

To avoid unwanted attention, some women invent a boyfriend or husband (better), and it is preferable to be meeting them soon. A wedding ring has limited success. A photo of you and your partner works much better.

While Indonesian men are generally very courteous, there is a macho element that indulges in behaviour typical of a building site circa 1950 – horn honking, lewd comments etc. Ignore these men totally, as do Indonesian women; they are unsavoury but generally harmless troglodytes. Blonde-haired, blue-eyed women seem to have more hassles than dark women. There are some things you can do to avoid being harassed; number one is to dress modestly. You'll see travellers in Bali who dress with complete disregard for local standards of decency, but elsewhere only prostitutes wear revealing shorts and singlets on the street. Take your cue from Indonesian women, not from other travellers.

Indonesians, both men and women, are generally not comfortable being alone – even on a simple errand they are happier having a friend along. Travelling alone is considered an oddity – a woman travelling alone is considered even more of an oddity. Nevertheless, for a woman travelling alone or with a female companion, Indonesia can be easier going than some other Asian countries.

Tampons can be found in supermarkets in the main cities of Java, but only with some difficulty, so bring plenty with you unless you want to use pads, which are widely available.

## GAY & LESBIAN TRAVELLERS

Gay travellers in Indonesia will experience few problems. Physical contact between same-sex couples is quite acceptable, even though a boy and a girl holding hands may be seen as improper. Homosexual behaviour is not illegal, and the age of consent for sexual activity is 16 years. Immigration officials may restrict entry to people who reveal HIV positive status. Gay men in Indonesia are referred to as *homo* or *gay*.

Indonesia's transvestite/transsexual *waria* – from *wanita* (woman) and *pria* (man) – community has always had a very public profile. Also known by the less polite term as *banci*, they are often extrovert performers, as entertainers on stage and as street-walkers. Perhaps because of the high profile of the waria, community attitudes to the wider gay community are surprisingly tolerant in a traditional, conservative family-oriented society. Islamic groups proscribe homosexuality, but such views are not dominant and there is no queer bashing or campaigns against gays. It pays to be less overt in some orthodox areas though, and the rampage against nightclubs in the Mangga Dua/Glodok area of Jakarta is a worrying trend.

Indonesia has a number of gay and lesbian organisations. The coordinating body is GAY a Nusantara (☎ 031-5934924; fax 5939070), Jl Mulyosari Timur 46, Surabaya, which publishes a monthly magazine *GAY a Nusantara*. Good web sites include www.gunung.com/seasiaweb/ and www.utopia-asia.com, which has an extensive list of gay and lesbian venues throughout Indonesia and the rest of Asia.

## DISABLED TRAVELLERS

Laws covering the disabled date back to 1989, but Indonesia has very little supportive legislation or special programs for the disabled. Indonesia is a difficult destination for those with limited mobility.

At Indonesian airports, arriving and departing passengers usually have to walk across the tarmac to their planes, and that includes Ngurah Rai airport in Bali. Check with the airline to see what arrangements can be made and if they can provide skychairs. Jakarta airport has direct access and lifts, but not all flights use these facilities. International airlines are usually helpful, but domestic flights are much more problematic.

No building regulations require disabled access and even international hotels – Sheraton, Hyatt, Hilton, etc – rarely have facilities, but it might be worth contacting these corporations in your home city and asking what facilities their hotels in Indonesia have. Some hotels have easy street access, by accident rather than design, if you can get a ground floor room. Only top end and upper mid-range hotels have lifts.

Footpaths are a minefield of potholes, loose manholes, parked motorcycles and all sorts of street life and are rarely level for long – until the next set of steps. Even the abled walk on the street rather than negotiate the hassle of the pavement.

Public transport is also difficult but cars with driver can be readily hired at cheap rates and are much more common than self-drive. Minibuses are easily hired but none has wheelchair access. Guides are also readily found in the tourist areas and, though this is not usual, they could be hired as helpers if needed.

Java has a developed infrastructure and is easier to get around than many other parts of Indonesia. Indonesia, with its scents, music and people always ready to chat, would be a rewarding destination for the unsighted. With a sighted companion, many places should be reasonably accessible.

## SENIOR TRAVELLERS

Apart from respect, senior travellers don't get a lot in the way of special treatment in Indonesia, except for discounts on domestic air tickets. Garuda, Merpati and Bouraq airlines offer discounts of 35% to passengers who are aged 60 and over. Your passport must be sighted and a photocopy of the front page provided.

## TRAVEL WITH CHILDREN

Travelling anywhere with children requires energy and organisation. The Indonesians are very receptive to children, sometimes too receptive. Most Indonesians adore children, especially cute western kids, and children may find the constant attention overwhelming.

Travelling in some areas of Indonesia is hard going, probably too hard for most people to want to tackle with the additional burden of small children. Bali, with its resorts and facilities, is the best place in Indonesia to take kids, but Java is well developed with a range of amenities, transport, hotel and food options. Indonesians may have to take their toddlers on gruelling eight hour journeys in stuffy sweltering buses, but you'd be well advised to take a luxury train or bus or rent a car, which is easy to arrange in Java. Similarly, many adults can comfortably sample warung food, but parents with kids will want to be more careful.

Many inoculations are contraindicated for young children, as are the effective malarial prophylactics. If you're only travelling to the main cities, the malaria risk is minuscule, but malaria does occur in more rural areas.

Jakarta is hot, crowded and overwhelming for the uninitiated (mostly for parents who have to look after kids as well as battle the city) but it does have a few good family attractions. Kids old and young will love Dunia Fantasi (Fantasy World), the Disney-inspired fun park at Ancol. Ancol also has a swimming pool complex with waterslides, Sea World and other diversions. Ragunan Zoo has plenty of animals from Indonesia and around the world. Taman Mini Indonesia Indah is educational and is good for older children (and adults) who want to gain an understanding of Indonesia.

Other cities in Java are also bustling and disorienting, but Javanese families also like to get out on weekends, and there are a number of family attractions. Beach resorts, like those on the west coast and Pangandaran on the south coast, are relaxing places to take kids.

For more information on travelling with children, with specific examples for Indonesia, Lonely Planet publishes *Travel with Children*.

## DANGERS & ANNOYANCES
### Political Strife

The economic crisis and subsequent political upheaval have produced isolated disturbances across the country. It is unlikely you will come across anything, but it pays to keep abreast of the news if travelling extensively in Java. Most incidents tend to be sudden outbursts or reactions to local grudges and are over in a matter of hours. Foreigners are not targeted and the trouble is invariably away from the tourist centres, but you don't want to get caught up in anything. Hopefully, Indonesia will soon settle and this advice will be redundant.

Java, as the main population centre, has recorded the most incidents, usually attacks and looting of shops and mostly in smaller provincial cities, but there has been no real pattern. Jakarta, as the capital, will always be a centre for political activity and when it blows it really blows, but it is quiet for weeks on end. Demonstrations are overwhelmingly peaceful but it pays to avoid them, and be wary of any large gathering that looks like a potential mob. Violence, when it does occur, is often a result of heavy-handed reactions by the police and army.

The economic crisis means that crime is on the rise. Violent crime, eg muggings, is very rare in Indonesia, but Jakarta is a place to be wary. Follow the usual rules – avoid disreputable areas, don't walk the streets alone at night etc. Jakarta is still safer than many major US cities.

### Theft

While violent crime is very rare in Indonesia, theft can be a problem. If you are mindful of your valuables and take precautions, the chances of being ripped off are small. Most thefts are the result of carelessness or naivety. The chances of theft are highest in crowded places and when travelling on public bemos, buses and trains.

Pickpockets are common and crowded bus and train stations are favourite haunts, as are major tourist areas, such as Yogyakarta. The thieves are very skilful and often work in gangs – if you find yourself being hassled and jostled, check your wallet, watch and bag. The Indonesian word for thief is *pencuri*.

Don't leave valuables unattended, and in crowded places hold your handbag or daypack closely. Don't carry your passport, travellers cheques or wallet in a bag that can be pickpocketed. A money belt worn under your clothes is the safest way to carry your passport, cash and travellers cheques. We get regular letters from travellers whose passport and travellers cheques have been stolen from their bags while they were sitting on a bus. Wear a money belt and make sure you have a separate record of travellers cheques, credit cards, passport etc.

Keep an eye on your luggage if it is put on the roof of a bus, but bag slashing or theft from bags next to you is also a hazard inside the bus. It is good insurance to have luggage that can be locked. It is worth sewing on tabs to hiking packs to make them lockable.

Theft from buses is a problem in Java. Organised gangs board the buses and take the seat behind you. If you fall asleep or put your bag on the floor, they will slash it and be gone with your gear before you know it. Chances of this happening are very slight, but the gangs target tourists. Economy buses are the worst but travelling deluxe is no guarantee against theft.

Always lock your hotel room door and windows at night and whenever you go out, even if momentarily. If you leave small things like sunglasses, sandals and books lying around outside your room, expect them to disappear. Don't leave valuables, cash or travellers cheques lying around in open view inside your room. It is very rare for hotel staff to risk losing their jobs by stealing, but there's no need to tempt them. It is wise to keep valuables hidden and locked inside your luggage, and better hotels have safe storage facilities.

Report any theft to the police but without witnesses don't expect any action. Bus companies and hotels will automatically deny any responsibility. Reported theft is usually termed *kehilangan* or 'loss', ie you lost it and it is your responsibility to prove theft. Police will give you a report though, which is needed to get a replacement passport and travellers cheques, and also for any insurance claims. You do have travel insurance, don't you?

Be wary and know where your valuables are at all times, but at the same time remember that the overwhelming majority of Indonesians are honest and will go out of their way to look after a visitor.

## Scams

As in most poor countries, plenty of people are out to relieve you of your money, in one way or another. It's hard to say when an 'accepted' practice like overcharging becomes an unacceptable rip-off, but plenty of instances of practised deceit occur.

Con artists are always to be found. Usually, those smooth talkers are fairly harmless guides seeking to lead you to a shop where they get commission. Just beware of instant friends and watch out for excessive commissions. Yogyakarta's batik salespeople fall into this category.

Another recent scam involves being invited to someone's house and then being introduced at a card game where you can't lose. Of course you do lose – big time.

There have been reports from Jakarta of police imposters searching foreigners for drugs and trying to extract money. Robberies of foreigners at knife point by Jakarta taxi drivers have also occurred, but these are very rare.

## Drugs

In most of Indonesia, recreational plants and chemicals are utterly unheard of. Being caught with drugs will result in jail or, if you are lucky, a large bribe.

Indonesia has become something of an Asian centre for Ecstasy, which fuels the local rave scenes in Jakarta and other big cities. When the drug first appeared a few years ago there was some confusion as to whether it was actually illegal or not. Make no mistake about it, it is illegal, and possession can land you in jail.

## Noise

If you're deaf, there's no problem. If you're not deaf, you might be after you've spent a few months in Indonesia. The major sources of noise are radios and TVs – Indonesians always set the volume knob up to the maximum. You can easily escape the racket at remote beaches and other rural settings by walking away, but there isn't much you can do if you're on a bus that has a reverberating stereo system. In hotels, the lobby often will contain a booming TV set, but if you choose your room carefully, you might be able to avoid the full impact. If you complain about the noise, it's likely the TV or radio will be turned down but then turned back up again five minutes later.

Another major source of noise is the mosques, which start broadcasting the calls to prayer at 4 am, repeating the procedure four more times during the day. Again, choose your hotel room carefully.

## BUSINESS HOURS

Government office hours are variable (sometimes very variable) but are generally open Monday through Friday from 7 or 8 am to 3 or 4 pm, with a break for Friday prayers from 11.30 am to 1.30 pm, and Saturday until noon. Go in the morning if you want to get anything done.

Private business offices have staggered hours: Monday to Friday from 8 am to 4 pm or 9 am to 5 pm, with a lunch break in the middle of the day. Many offices are also open on Saturday mornings until noon.

Banks are open Monday to Friday, usually from 8 am to 4 pm. In some places banks open Saturday until around 11 am. Foreign exchange hours may be more limited and some banks close their forex counter at 1 pm. Moneychangers are open longer hours.

Shops open around 9 or 10 am and smaller shops may close at 5 pm but in the big cities shopping complexes, supermarkets and department stores stay open until 9 pm. Sunday is a public holiday but some shops and airline offices open for at least part of the day, and the big shopping malls in the cities buzz all day.

## PUBLIC HOLIDAYS & SPECIAL EVENTS

Indonesia has many faiths and many festivals are celebrated on different days throughout the country. Islam, as the major religion, provides many of the holidays. The most important time for Muslims is Ramadan (Bulan Puasa), the traditional Muslim month of daily fasting from sunrise to sunset.

Muslim events are affected by the lunar calendar and dates move back 10 or 11 days each year. Ramadan falls in the ninth month of the Muslim calendar. It's a good time to avoid fervent Muslim areas of Indonesia –

### Ramadan

One of the most important months of the Muslim calendar is the fasting month of Ramadan. As a profession of their faith and spiritual discipline, Muslims abstain from food, drink, cigarettes and other worldly desires (including sex) from sunrise to sunset. Exemptions from fasting are granted to pregnant women, the ill or infirm, young children and those undertaking extreme physical labour.

Ramadan is often preceded by a cleansing ceremony, Padusan, to prepare for the coming fast (puasa). Traditionally, during Ramadan people get up at 3 or 4 am to eat (this meal is called sahur) and then fast until sunset. Many Muslims visit family graves and royal cemeteries, recite extracts from the Koran, sprinkle the graves with holy water and strew them with flowers. Special prayers are said at mosques and at home.

The first day of the 10th month of the Muslim calendar is the end of Ramadan, called Idul Fitri or Lebaran. Mass prayers are held in the early morning, followed by two days of feasting. Extracts from the Koran are read and religious processions take place; gifts are exchanged and pardon is asked for past wrongdoings during this time of mutual forgiveness. This is the big holiday of the year, a time for rejoicing, and the whole country is on the move as everyone goes home to be with their family.

During Ramadan, many restaurants and warungs are closed in Java. Those owned by non-Muslims will be open but in deference to those who are fasting, they may have covered overhangs or will otherwise appear to be shut. Ask around for what is open. In the big cities, many businesses are open and fasting is less strictly observed. For night owls, the cities come alive for the night meal.

Though not all Muslims can keep to the privations of fasting, the overwhelming majority does and you should respect their values. Do not eat, drink or smoke in public and in someone's house. If you must eat, ask and go out the back.

Ramadan is an interesting time to travel but can be difficult. Apart from the fact that you will have to hunt out restaurants and abstain from imbibing in public, you won't find the first few weeks of Ramadan too restrictive. But travel is a real hassle towards the end of Ramadan. Around a week before and a week after Idul Fitri, transport in Muslim Indonesia is chaotic and packed to the gunwales. Don't even consider travelling during this time. You will be better off in the non-Muslim areas of Indonesia – Bali, East Nusa Tenggara, Maluku, Irian Jaya etc – but even these areas have significant Muslim populations and Idul Fitri is a big national holiday of two days duration for everyone. Plan well, find yourself an idyllic spot and stay put.

Ramadan and Idul Fitri move back 12 days or so every year, according to the Muslim calendar. Future dates for Ramadan are:

| | | |
|---|---|---|
| 8 Dec 1999 | to | 8 Jan 2000 |
| 29 Nov 2000 | to | 29 Dec 2000 |

you get woken up in your *losmen* (cheap hotel) at 3 am in the morning to have a meal before the fasting period begins. Many restaurants shut down during the day, leaving you searching the backstreets for a restaurant that's open. Lebaran (Idul Fitri) marks the end of Ramadan and is a noisy two-day public holiday when half the country seems to be on the move and hotels fill up and prices skyrocket.

## Public Holidays

Major public holidays in Indonesia are:

New Year's Day
1 January
Idul Fitri
(8 and 9 January 2000, 29 and 30 December 2001) – also known as Lebaran, this marks the end of Ramadan and is a noisy celebration at the end of a month of gastronomic austerity. It is a two day national public holiday.
Idul Adha
(16 March 2000, 5 March 2001) – this Muslim festival commemorates Abraham's willingness to sacrifice his son, Isaac, and is celebrated with prayers and feasts. Animals (usually goats) are sacrificed at mosques and the meat is distributed to the poor.
Nyepi
Balinese New Year marks the end of the Hindu saka calendar. The day before, evil spirits are chased away with gongs, drums and flaming torches but on Nyepi itself, Balinese stay home and all Balinese businesses close so that bad spirits will see the deserted streets and leave. The date is announced at the start of the year – usually in April, sometimes in March.
Muharram
(6 April 2000, 26 March 2001) – Islamic New Year, the start of the Muslim calendar.
Good Friday
(21 April 2000, 13 April 2001)
Waisak Day
(1 May 1999, 18 June 2000) – marks the Buddha's birth, enlightenment and death.
Ascension of Christ
(1 June 2000, 24 May 2001)
Maulud Nabi Muhammed
(15 June 2000, 4 June 2001) – the birthday of the Prophet Muhammed, also known as Hari Natal.
Independence Day (Hari Proklamasi Kemerdekaan)
On 17 August 1945, Soekarno proclaimed Indonesian independence in Jakarta. It is a national public holiday and the parades and special events are at their grandest in Jakarta.
Isra Miraj Nabi Mohammed
(6 November 1999, 26 October 2000) – celebrates the ascension of the Prophet Muhammed.
Christmas Day
(25 December)

## Special Events

Java has an enormous number of festivals and cultural and religious events. They range from Independence Day on 17 August, which is celebrated with great gusto throughout Indonesia, to numerous local events based on ancient traditions. These latter may be the Madura bull races or a small village ceremony involving the washing of sacred heirlooms.

The national tourism organisation produces an annual *Calendar of Events* for the whole country. The various provincial governments also produce calendars of events. Those for Central Java, East Java and Yogyakarta are informative and worth picking up from the tourist offices.

As well as annual events, there are many dance, theatre and wayang performances, on a regular weekly or monthly basis throughout Java. These are listed under the cities.

Of the many annual events, highlights include:

### May-October
### Ramayana Ballet at Prambanan
Java's most spectacular dance drama, the Ramayana Ballet, is held at the outdoor theatre at the Prambanan temple complex near Yogya. The ballet is performed over four successive nights, twice each month of the dry season.

### June-July
### Jakarta Fair
This one month event is based around 22 June, the founding date of Jakarta, and features a trade exhibit and carnival attractions at the Jakarta Fair Grounds, as well as cultural events staged all around the city.

### 17 August
### Independence Day
Parades are held in every town and village, but the biggest celebrations occur in Jakarta, where carnivals and cultural shows are held all over the city.

## Javanese Calendars

In the modern world, the 365-day Gregorian calendar dominates the life of the Javanese, setting the working week and appointments of business and government. However, as the Indonesian island is largely Muslim, many cultural and religious events are determined by the Javanese Muslim lunar calendar. Java also has various traditional calendars that are used in divination and for setting ritual dates.

### Saka Calendar

Prior to the coming of Islam in Java, the Hindu *saka* calendar was used, as it still is in Bali. This begins in the year 78 AD of the Christian calendar, when legend has it that Hinduism was first brought to Java by Aji Saka from the Champa kingdom in modern-day Vietnam. A few Hindu/Buddhist events are still based on this calendar.

### Javanese Muslim Calendar

With the coming of Islam, the Muslim calendar of 354 days (355 days in a leap year) was introduced. This lunar calendar has 12 months of 30 or 29 days in duration, starting with the month of Sura (the Javanese name; or Muharram is the Arabic name). The other months in order are Sapar, Mulud or Maulud, Bakdamulud, Jumadilawal, Jumadilakir, Rejeb, Ruwah, Pasa (Ramadan in Arabic), Sawal, Sela and Besar. Most cultural and religious events are based on the Javanese Muslim calendar.

Many of the pre-Islamic ceremonies were grafted on to the Muslim calendar, and ancient rituals were moved to coincide with Muslim religious days. The Javanese new year, 1 Sura, is celebrated in a variety of festivals across Java, none of which are Islamic. For example, in Banyuwangi an offering to the sea spirits is made, in Ponorogo a reyog dance is performed, and in Surakarta the palace heirlooms are ritually cleansed during the Kirab Pusaka ceremony. Many non-santri Javanese hold a *slametan* feast on this day.

### Javanese Month (Selapan)

The Javanese calendar originally had weeks of differing numbers of days, but the most important that has survived is the Javanese market week of five days (Legi, Paing, Pon, Wage, Kliwon). Markets were held in five-day cycles (five is an important symbolic number to the Javanese), and some villages still hold markets according to this market week. Calendars in Java often show the market days as well as the normal days.

The five-day market week is combined with the Muslim/western week of seven days (Minggu, Senen, Selasa, Rebo, Kemis, Jumuwat, Sabtu) to form the Javanese *selapan* cycle or 'month'. This consists of 35 days, or seven times five, as the two sets of weeks running parallel to each other produce 35 different combinations eg Minggu-Legi (Legi Sunday), Senen-Paing (Paing Monday) etc and take 35 days to align again.

The Javanese month is still widely used for setting ritual days and in divining auspicious days, such as a wedding. Wayang performances may be held based on this cycle, and a Javanese will always know on which day he/she was born, for this one-month birthday is an auspicious day, if not a cause for celebration. A slametan feast is traditonally held 35 days after the birth of a child, and many other events are based on this cycle. In Cirebon, Sunan Gunungjati's tomb is only opened on Rebo-Kliwon, while in Kudus, the Sukun kretek factory is closed every Kemis-Pon because this is the day the owner died.

**August-September**
**Madura Bull Races**

These famous bull races are held at locations all over Madura, culminating at Pamekasan, usually in September.

**Variable**
**Labuhan Ceremony**

Palace courtiers from the Yogyakarta kraton make offerings to the Queen of the South Seas at Parangkusomo beach near Parangtretes. Similar ceremonies are made at the volcanoes of Merapi and Lawu, in a ceremony to unite the sultan with the spiritual forces of Yogyakarta and ensure the welfare of the state. Various other Labuhan ceremonies to honour the Queen of the South Seas are held in Java, including at Pelabuhanratu in West Java.

**Waisak**

At Borobudur, this Buddhist ceremony celebrates the enlightenment of the Buddha. Thousands of pilgrims gather to offer prayers and join the procession from the Mendut temple to Borobudur. The four day Borobudur Festival is also held at Borobudur at this time, and includes dance and music performances, art and craft exhibits etc.

## ACTIVITIES
### Hiking & Mountain Climbing

Despite being one of the world's most populous islands, Java still has intact forest and rural areas that can be explored on foot. These are primarily in the national parks and on the forested slopes of the volcanoes. Java has plenty of volcanoes for peak bagging, and while Javanese students can be found out hiking on weekends and holidays, very few foreign tourists even know that it is possible to hike in Java.

Walking trails and hiking as a sport are not well developed in Java. Most walks tend to be day hikes or overnight hikes to volcanoes, and guides are usually required. The national parks have the best trails and the PHPA, the national parks body, provides information at the parks. They also provide guides, where necessary.

Most of Java's volcanoes can be climbed, but they should not be underestimated. Apart from the danger of possible volcanic activity, loose scree on the slopes can make climbing difficult. Special climbing equipment is not usually required, but some climbs involve camping overnight on the mountain in near freezing conditions, and climbers must be equipped against the elements.

Following are some of the more rewarding and easily accessible hiking possibilities on Java. See place entries later in the book for more details.

Gunung Bromo is one of the most spectacular volcanoes, but climbing it is really nothing more than a short stroll. In the surrounding Bromo-Tengger-Semeru National Park, the four or five day walk and climb of Gunung Semeru, Java's highest peak, is tough, but one of the most rewarding on Java. A few other walks, mostly along roads, can be done in the area.

The Gede-Pangrango National Park, near Bogor, is well organised, and the volcanoes in the park can be reached on an overnight climb, or a pleasant day walk can be organised short of the summits.

Gunung Merapi, near Yogyakarta, is a tough climb. It starts at night, though it can be done in one day. Climbs are organised from Kaliurang from Selo on the north side of the mountain.

Kawah Ijen, a beautiful crater lake near Banyuwangi in East Java, is a long dayhike from just outside Banyuwangi, but it is relatively easy. If you have your own transport, the walk is an easy one if approached from Bondowoso. Other walking opportunities exist in this plateau area.

Many of the hill resorts are close to forested areas, with short walks and hikes to volcanoes nearby. Around Garut in West Java, day walks or longer include those to Gunung Guntur and Gunung Papandayan. Using Tretes or Batu as a base in East Java, there are also walks in the Arjuna-Lalijiwo National Park.

For jungle trekking and wildlife spotting, the trails in the Ujung Kulon National Park in West Java provide excellent walking with varied scenery. Walks of up to a week can be put together in Java's premier national park.

Hiking is also possible in the other national parks in East Java, but is either uninspiring (Baluran National Park) or access to the parks is very difficult (Alas Purwo and Meru Betiri national parks).

Most of Java's forested areas are reserves managed by the PHPA, and many are being upgraded to national parks. As yet, facilities are limited or nonexistent in most, but Java has plenty of other walking opportunities for the adventurous and well prepared. The Yang Plateau in East Java has good walks and the Leuwang Sancang Reserve near Pameungpeuk in West Java has rugged jungle walks. The trails and walking conditions can be difficult – it is essential to contact the local PHPA post and to rely on local knowledge and guides before you head off into what is largely uncharted territory.

## Surfing

Indonesia has long had a reputation as a surfing Mecca, and intrepid surfers have been roaming the archipelago for decades in their search for the ideal break. Bali is the main destination but Java has some legendary breaks. Java's most famous surfing destination is Grajagan Bay, otherwise known as G-Land, in East Java's Alas Purwo National Park (see under that section in the East Java chapter for details).

The entire south coast of Java is pounded by surf, much of it on shallow reef, but a few less popular surfing destinations can be found right across to Ujung Kulon National Park in the west. Panaitan Island in the park has a well regarded but dangerous left reef break. Both Grajagan and Panaitan are difficult to reach independently and involve expensive boat hire. Surf companies in Bali, with the highest concentration of surf shops and tour operators in Kuta and Legian, run fairly expensive tours to both destinations.

Pelabuhanratu and nearby Cimaja, south of Bogor, have reasonable surf and are easy to reach, while good waves are reported farther to the south near more remote Genteng. OK surf can also be found around Pangandaran, particularly at Batu Karas. Pelabuhanratu and Pangandaran have plenty of accommodation in all price ranges and are well serviced by public transport.

Much of Java's south coast is remote and sparsely populated. Intrepid surfers with their own transport may well discover new surfing destinations. The best conditions occur from June to October.

## Scuba Diving & Other Watersports

With so many islands and so much coral, Indonesia presents all sorts of possibilities for excellent diving. Java, however, is not a prime diving destination in Indonesia, as the waters tend to be less than clear and the island does not possess the well-developed reefs of some of the other islands. Nonetheless, Pulau Seribu, just off the coast north of Jakarta, has reasonable diving opportunities, as do the waters of West Java, around Krakatau and Ujung Kulon National Park. A number of dive operators can be found in Jakarta, which is the best place to arrange diving trips. Most of the Pulau Seribu resorts have dive shops though the crisis closed most of those on the west coat around Carita.

Some reputable dive shops in Jakarta that offer tours and renting equipment are: Aquasport (☎ 7199045, fax 7198974), Jl Bangka Raya 39A, Jakarta Selatan; the related Divemasters International (☎ 570 3600) in the Hilton Hotel; and Spare Air (☎ 7194121) in the Kemang Hotel, Jl Kemang Raya 2H.

For much of Indonesia, diving may not be very good during the wet season, from about October to April, as storms tend to reduce visibility. Bring your scuba certification – most of the main qualifications are recognised, including those of PADI, NAUI, BSAC, FAUI and SSI.

Windsurfing and waterskiing are not well developed on Java and are only found at the expensive resorts at Pulau Seribu and on the west coast around Carita.

For whitewater rafting, the most professional operators are established on the Sungai Citarak, bordering the Gunung Halimun National Park near Bogor. At Borobudur, the Lotus Guest House also offers whitewater rafting on nearby rivers.

## COURSES

Many students come to Java to study Indonesian. Most courses are arranged by universities overseas and are held at Java's more prestigious universities, including the University of Indonesia in Jakarta, Gajah Mada University in Yogya and Salatiga University in Salatiga (Central Java).

The better private courses can charge US$15 or more per hour, though many offer individual tuition. Jakarta and Yogya have schools geared for foreigners wishing to learn Bahasa Indonesia – see the Jakarta chapter and the Yogyakarta section in the Central Java chapter for school listings.

Various other batik, dance and cookery classes are held in other parts of Java, but on an irregular basis, or you sign up for private tuition. In Jakarta, the cultural centres often arrange courses and are good contact points.

Yogyakarta offers a variety of tourist-oriented courses, such as batik courses (see under Yogyakarta). Various introductory cooking, language and culture courses can be arranged through the Via Via Cafe on Jl Prawirotoman. Bagong Kussudiarja has a dance school at Padepokan, 5km south of Yogya, with courses for foreign students.

Many foreign students study Javanese music and dance, usually at the prestigious arts academies, such as the STSI in Solo or Yogya, but these are usually for exchange students and not for casual visitors. Tumpang, in East Java near Malang, is home to the Mangun Dhama Art Centre (☎ 0341-787907), which is well set up for foreigners and offers East Javanese dance classes, gamelan, wayang, batik and wood carving courses.

Those with a spiritual bent can also delve into Javanese mysticism. Solo has a number of meditation centres offering courses. Buddhist meditation courses are sometimes run at the Mendut Buddhist monastery, near Borobudur. See under those sections for more details.

## WORK

It is possible for foreigners to work in Indonesia, provided you are willing to make some long-term commitments. Although Indonesia is still an underdeveloped country, in some situations you can be paid well. Officially, a work permit is required to work in Indonesia (see under Visas earlier in this chapter), and these are very difficult to get and should be arranged by your employer.

The job market was strong before the crash, especially in Jakarta, but it is very difficult now. By far the best way to arrange employment is through a company outside Indonesia.

Work visas are hard to get, as the Indonesian policy is to hire Indonesians wherever possible. In the past, travellers have been able to pick up work as English teachers, for around 50,000 to 60,000 rp per hour, which used to be reasonable money but now hardly seem worth it. Unless you are getting paid in US dollars, forget it.

Apart from expats who are employed by foreign companies, most foreigners working in Indonesia are involved in some sort of business, usually exporting clothing, furniture, crafts and the like.

## ACCOMMODATION
### Hostels

Indonesia doesn't have much in the way of hostels, mainly because there are so many low-cost hotels. One exception is Jakarta, where accommodation is relatively dear, so there are a number of places offering cheap dormitory accommodation. Surabaya also has the famous Bamboe Denn youth hostel.

Be cautious about security in hostels. While it's not a huge problem, it is something to be aware of. Many hostels provide lockers, but bring your own padlock. If no lockers are provided, put all your gear in your pack and keep it locked.

### Hotels

Hotels in Java come in different grades of price and comfort. At the bottom end of the scale is the *penginapan*. A slightly more up-market penginapan is called a *losmen*. *Wisma* and *pondok* are slightly more up-market again, but still cheap.

An official rating system applies: a hotel can be either a flower *(melati* or *yasmin)* hotel, which is relatively low standard, or a star *(bintang)* hotel, which is more luxurious. A hotel at the bottom of the barrel would be one melati whereas a five star hotel *(lima bintang)* occupies the top end. Most star hotels post signs indicating star rating as set by the government. All hotels are required to pay a 10% room tax, and this may be passed on to the customer, but most cheap hotels either avoid the tax or absorb it into their room rates. Upper-crust places charge a whopping 21% tax and service charge.

The real budget hotels are spartan places with shared bath, starting at around 10,000 rp. Mid-range hotel rooms often come with private bath, starting at about 25,000 rp for a double, but more like 35,000 rp for something reasonably comfortable. Most rooms are let on a double basis, and where singles are available, they are usually only slightly cheaper.

The five-star hotels can match the best in the West, with prices piercing the US$100 level, but the drop-off in tourism and business traffic has seen massive discounting. Top-end hotels often quote prices in US dollars, and some mid-range hotels also engage in this dubious practice, though with the fall in the rupiah, US dollar prices are often meaningless and many now quote in rupiah, or convert to rupiah at a rate well below the going exchange rate.

As a general rule, if you are quoted a price in US dollar you are paying too much, and if the US dollar rate is then converted to rupiah at the current exchange rate, you are being ripped off. Most hotels now charge rupiah rates and you can stay at quality hotels for incredibly low prices.

Rates vary throughout Java. Jakarta is the most expensive city, followed by Surabaya and Bandung. Yogya, on the other hand, has some of the best accommodation bargains in Indonesia. Overall, Java is the cheapest place in Indonesia for travel. If you are coming from Bali, where many hotels are still priced at pre-crisis levels, you will find prices in Java absurdly cheap.

You may have to bargain for your room price, just as you do for other purchases.

Rather than argue, the most polite way to do this is to simply ask for a discount. Ask to see the printed price list *(daftar harga)* when you arrive at a hotel. For many cheap and lower mid-range hotels, the price is often fixed to this rate. Seeing the price list will also give you an idea of the range of rooms – many hotels have a huge range of rooms, from cheap to expensive, but you may only be offered the most expensive. If there is no price list, assume you can bargain, but the existence of a price list doesn't necessarily mean you can't bargain. Some hotels, especially in resort areas, have more than one price list, and if a hotel is overpriced or empty they will often give a discount.

The biggest discounts are at the top end. Luxury hotels always have brochures quoting over-the-top published rates, but most of them readily offer discounts from 20% to 50% or even more.

Even the cheapest hotels tend to be reasonably clean, if spartan, though some stand out as long overdue for demolition. Some places can be abominably noisy, with the inevitable television booming in the passageway outside your room or punching up through the floorboards until after midnight. Other hotels are just several layers of hot little sweatboxes and slimy bathrooms. The tendency in the last few years has been to tear down the old firetraps and replace them with more wholesome accommodation. The best way to survive some of the more dismal places is to go to Indonesia with a level of saintly tolerance and a good pair of earplugs, but the devaluation of the rupiah means that better accommodation is now very affordable.

## Staying in Villages

If you are travelling right out in the countryside and get stuck, you'll often be welcome to stay in the villages. Ask for the village head – the *kepala desa*. They're generally very hospitable and friendly people and will offer you not only a bed but also meals. Payment should be offered and is usually expected. Expecting to pay about the same as you would pay in a losmen, more with meals, is a good rule-of-thumb. If you intend to stay with a kepala desa, have one or two gifts to offer – cigarettes, postcards and photographs are popular.

## Rental

Given the wide assortment of cheap hotels, it almost doesn't pay to bother with renting a house or apartment. Trying to find a house for short-term rental, one or two months, is difficult and depends on personal contacts or luck. Real-estate agents are virtually non-existent in Indonesia. Ask your Indonesian friends, at your hotel, restaurants etc. Something may turn up, but it can take time. Negotiating a proper price may also take some time, and it's wise to obtain the help of an Indonesian friend.

However, if you're working in Java for a long time, you will want to get your own place. Rents vary widely, depending on where you want to live. Jakarta's rates are high, and rent is required in advance, even for three-year leases. Prices are much lower elsewhere.

## FOOD

Unlike some parts of Indonesia, Java has a wide range of food options. Dishes from all over the country can be enjoyed, Chinese food is everywhere and the main cities have restaurants serving everything from Mexican to Japanese.

Most of Indonesia's best-known dishes, *sate*, *gado gado* etc, are Javanese in origin, and food carts and restaurants serve a mindboggling array of dishes with regional variations. Almost every city and district will have its own speciality, and some are famed throughout Java. The best *sate* is said to come from Madura, the best *tahu* from Sumedang, the best fried chicken from Yogya, the best *lumpia* from Semarang, the best *soto* from Lumajang etc.

Indonesian food is often very simple and it doesn't take long to get sick of *nasi goreng* or *bakso*. Many restaurants and eating houses are more concerned with churning out cheap, filling meals than with great cuisine. In general, you have to go to the more expensive restaurants to get good Indonesian food but sometimes, excellent dishes and snacks can be found at small warungs. Each city has its well-known little eating houses or food carts, which are packed nightly, turning out specialities that are as good as you'll find anywhere.

Eating street food you run a higher risk of stomach upsets and, as in any restaurant, it pays to check out the standards of hygiene. But if food is cooked fresh before your eyes it may be safer than that served in the restaurants. Be wary of uncooked food, rubbery seafood and drinks made from unboiled water.

## Restaurants

At the bottom of the barrel in terms of price are the *warungs*. These are the poor persons' restaurants, found everywhere. They're usually just a rough table and bench seats, surrounded by sheets or canvas strung up to act as walls. Often the food is as drab as the warung looks, but occasionally you find something outstanding. One thing you can be sure about is that warungs are cheap. A night market *(pasar malam)* is often a congregation point for warungs.

A variation on the more semi-permanent warung is the *kaki lima* food cart. Kaki lima means 'five feet' – the cart has two wheels, a single stand at the other end and, combined with the vendor's two feet, that makes five in all. They usually set up in the evenings and sell food to take away or they may provide a bench or mats spread out on the pavement for diners to sit and eat.

One step up from the warungs, sometimes in name only, is the *rumah makan* – literally the 'house to eat', often only distinguished from the warung by its fixed position and the addition of solid walls – but many such places call themselves warungs, so it's a hazy distinction.

A *restoran* is a restaurant – once again, often nothing more than the name distinguishes it from a rumah makan. But in many cases a restoran will be an upmarket place, often Chinese-run and with a Chinese menu. Chinese food is nearly always more expensive than Indonesian food, but there is usually a more varied menu.

Western fastfood has come to roost in the main cities, complete with air-conditioning, laminex tables as well as a statue of the ever-smiling Colonel or Ronald the clown. Java has a growing contingent of McDonald's, Pizza Hut, Wendy's and other outlets. Every shopping plaza will have fastfood outlets, and usually a Singapore-style hawkers' centre will be found on the top floor where a number of vendors turn out

local dishes. They are clean and efficient, and sometimes the food is very good.

Jakarta has the most cosmopolitan range of culinary delights in Indonesia – European, Mexican, Indian, Chinese, Korean, Thai and Japanese. Surabaya, and to a lesser extent Bandung, also has a wide selection, and the top international hotels throughout Java have varied menus. Foreign cuisine is very expensive by Indonesian standards but if you have dollars you can sample fine dining for a fraction of the price at home.

## Fruit

It's almost worth making a trip to Java just to sample the tropical fruit. Apples and bananas curl and die before the onslaught of nangkas, rambutans, mangosteens, salaks and sirsaks.

In Asia, unripe fruit, such as mango or guava, are also popular sliced and dipped in thick soy sauce with sliced chilli. Here are some of local specialities:

**apel** – apple. Most are imported from Australia, New Zealand and the USA, and are expensive. Local apples are grown in mountain areas, such as Malang in Java, and are much cheaper and fresher.

**apokat** – Avocados are plentiful and cheap. Try an avocado and ice-cream combo.

**belimbing** – The 'starfruit' is a cool, crispy, watery-tasting fruit – if you cut a slice, you'll immediately see where the name comes from.

**durian** – The most infamous tropical fruit, the durian is a large green fruit with a hard, spiky exterior. Inside are pockets of creamy white fruit. The horrific stench that supposedly emanates from them is not so bad, but hotels and airlines often ban them because of their foul odour. The durian season is in the later part of the year.

**jambu air** – water apple or wax jambu. These glossy white or pink bell-shaped fruit are often sold skewered on a sliver of bamboo. The jambu air is crisp and refreshing eaten chilled, but fairly tasteless. The single seed should not be eaten.

**jambu batu** – guava. Also known as jambu klutuk, the guava comes from Central America and was brought to Asia by the Spanish. The fruit comes in many colours, shapes and sizes; the most common are light green and pear-shaped, turning yellow when fully ripe. The pinkish flesh is full of seeds.

**jeruk** – The all-purpose term for citrus fruit. There are several kinds available. The main ones include the huge **jeruk muntis** or **jerunga**, known in the west as the pomelo. It's larger than a grapefruit but has a very thick skin, tastes sweeter, more like an orange, and has segments that break apart very easily. Regular oranges are known as **jeruk manis** – sweet jeruk. The small tangerine-like oranges, which are often quite green, are **jeruk baras**. Lemons are **jeruk nipis**.

**kelapa** – coconut; as plentiful as you would expect! **Kelapa muda** means young coconut and you'll often get them straight from the tree. Drink the milk and then scoop out the flesh.

**mangga** – mango. The best mangos in all of Indonesia are said to come from Java's Probolinggo region. The mango season is the second half of the year.

Dining on straw mats is very popular in Java. Known as *lesahan*, this style of dining may be offered by street vendors who lay straw mats on the pavement on warm evenings, or by restaurants where you dine at low tables. Sundanese restaurants, in particular, offer delightful lesahan dining experiences. A fish pond is *de riguer* in these restaurants, and freshwater fish (usually *gurame* or *ikan mas*) is netted from the pond, freshly cooked and brought to your table with rice and a number of small side dishes. Some of these restaurants have individual pavilions arranged around the fish pond and gardens, where you take off your shoes, dine cross-legged and listen to the sounds of the night.

## Snacks

Indonesians are keen snackers and everywhere you'll find lots of street-stall snacks, such as peanuts in palm sugar, shredded coconut cookies or fried bananas. Potatoes and other starchy roots are eaten as a snack – either steamed, with salt and grated coconut

## Fruit

**manggis** – mangosteen. One of the most famous of tropical fruits, this is a small, purple-brown fruit. The outer covering cracks open to reveal pure-white segments, which have an indescribably fine flavour. Queen Victoria once offered a reward to anyone who might be able to transport a mangosteen back to England while still edible. The mangosteen season is from November to February. Beware of stains from the fruit's casing, which can be permanent.

**nangka** – Also known as jackfruit, this is an enormous yellow-green fruit that can weigh over 20kg. Inside are individual segments of yellow fruit, each containing a roughly egg-shaped seed. The segments are held together by strong white fibres. The fruit is moist and fairly sweet, with a slightly rubbery texture. It is used mostly in cooking. The **cempadak** is a close relative of the nangka, but smaller, sweeter and more strongly flavoured.

**nanas** – pineapple

**papaya** – or paw paw, are not unusual in the west. The fruit is actually a native of South America and was brought to the Philippines by the Spanish, and from there spread to other parts of South-East Asia.

**pisang** – banana. The range in Indonesia is astonishing – from midgets to specimens well over a foot long. A bunch of bananas, by the way, is **satu sisir pisang**.

**rambutan** – A bright red fruit covered in soft, hairy spines; the name means hairy. Break it open to reveal a delicious white fruit closely related to the lychee. From November to February is the rambutan season.

**salak** – Found chiefly in Indonesia, the salak is immediately recognisable by its perfect brown 'snakeskin' covering. Peel it off to reveal segments that, in texture, are like a cross between an apple and a walnut but in taste are quite unique. Each segment contains a large, brown, oval-shaped seed.

**sawo** – Brown-skinned, looks like a potato and has honey-flavoured flesh

**sirsak** – The sirsak is known in the west as soursop or zurzak. The fruit was originally a native of tropical America, and the Indonesian variety is one of the best. The warty green skin covers a thirst-quenching, soft, white, pulpy interior with a slightly lemonish, tart taste. You can peel it off or slice it into segments. Sirsaks are ripe when the skin has begun to lose its fresh green colouring and become darker and spotty. It should then feel slightly squishy rather than firm.

added, or thinly sliced and fried. One of Java's specialities, from Solo, is *srabi*, a small, delicious sweet pancake.

Almost every warung or rumah makan has glass or plastic jars filled with a mind-boggling array of delicious crackers to be eaten with a meal. Just help yourself and pay with the meal. They range from the popular *krupuk* (prawn crackers) and *emping* (crackers made from melinjo nuts), but can be made from rice, beef, cassava and may be studded with peanuts. East Java is the cracker capital of Java, with many regional variations.

## Main Dishes

The food served in Indonesia, particularly meat dishes, is generally Chinese influenced, although there are also a number of purely Indonesian dishes. Pork is not widely used since the meat is regarded by Muslims as unclean, but it does appear in Chinese dishes. Javanese cooking uses fresh spices and a mixture of ingredients; the chilli is mellowed by the use of sugar in many dishes. Sumatran cooking, on the other hand, blends fresh and dry spices to flavour the main ingredient. The types of fresh spices that Indonesians use are usually known to most Westerners only as dried, ground powders. There is also some Dutch influence in some recipes, in the use of vegetables from temperate zones.

Rice is the basis of the meal, with an assortment of side dishes, some hot (with chilli) and spicy, and some just spicy. Many dishes are much like soup, the water being used to moisten the large quantity of rice eaten. Salad is usually served, along with *sambal* (a spicy side dish) and *acar* (pickles). Many dishes are cooked in *santan*, the liquid obtained when grated coconut is squeezed. *Bumbu* is a combination of pounded ingredients used to flavour a dish. Indonesians use every part of a plant, including the leaves of cassavas, papayas, mangoes and beans.

For a few basic words and phrases to help make ordering a meal easier, see the Glossary at the end of this book.

## Self-Catering

In any medium to large-sized city, you'll find supermarkets, well stocked with a wide variety of both local and imported foods. The other alternative is to explore the outdoor markets, where you will find fresh fruits, vegetables, eggs, chickens (both living and having recently passed away), freshly ground coffee and just about anything else. There are no price tags in the market and bargaining is almost always necessary.

An easy guide to the identification of weird-looking food is *A Jakarta Market* by Kaarin Wall, published by the American Women's Association.

## DRINKS

Indonesians have enthusiastically embraced western soft-drink culture. In a country where delicious, fresh fruit juices are sold, you can still rot your teeth on Coca-Cola, 7-Up, Sprite and Fanta.

There is a saying that while the British built roads in their colonies, the Dutch built breweries. Many of these still exist and, while beer is comparatively expensive (normally 3000 rp a large bottle, often more), it's also good. The three most popular brands are Bintang, Anker and Carlsberg. Bintang is the most popular. For other popular Indonesian drinks, both alcoholic and non-alcoholic, see the Glossary at the end of this book.

## ENTERTAINMENT

There is always something to do at night in the cities and towns of Java. The streets have plenty of life, night markets operate, many people go out for a stroll or a meal and want to chat with foreigners. The big night out is Saturday night, the *malam panjang* (long night).

Traditional entertainment is easy to see in Java. Wayang, gamelan, traditional theatre and dance performances are held on a regular basis and for special occasions. Tourist offices can tell you what's on. Yogya is the best place to see traditional Javanese performing arts, almost every night of the week. Solo also has plenty of cultural performances, while Bandung is a good place to see Sundanese performing arts. Jakarta has cultural shows from all over the country, as well as foreign film festivals, modern plays, art exhibitions etc.

Indonesians love music and the cities have discos packed with dancing revellers. Jakarta has the biggest selection with some amazingly sophisticated clubs, though Bandung and Surabaya have their fair share, and smaller cities have a few drinking holes or discos. The cities also have plenty of karaoke bars and lounges, many of them staffed by hostesses. Pretty girls chat to male clients to keep them drinking, or a fee is asked for their time. Their services may be purely social, though extra dalliances are sometimes negotiated. Even the ubiquitous billiard parlours have hostesses, who play a mean game of pool if you need a partner.

Out in the countryside, entertainment revolves around eating, socialising or going to the movies. Apart from in the main cities, the movies are often bad prints of violent, B-grade American adventure films or kung fu extravaganzas.

For specific listings, see under the cities and towns in this book.

## SPECTATOR SPORTS

Many of Indonesia's live spectator sports are male-oriented and associated with illegal gambling. Cockfighting still occurs in parts of Java. Bull racing, horse racing, ram head-butting and other contests are staged all around the country and are usually designed to improve the breed.

Soccer and badminton are the national sporting obsessions, and Indonesians are the world's badminton champions. They fare less well in international soccer competitions, but that certainly doesn't dampen their enthusiasm for *sepak bola*. The average Indonesian male will be able to tell you more about Manchester United than you ever wanted to know, and regional soccer teams in the national league have their own fanatic followers. Surabaya fans are the most fanatic – avoid the same train carriage when Surabaya is playing away.

Volleyball is played in villages everywhere, and you may well get an invite to join in if you show interest. *Sepak takraw*, also known as *sepak raga*, is a unique South-East Asian game and also popular. Played with a rattan ball, it is a cross between volleyball and soccer and, apart from serving, only the feet are used, resulting in amazing acrobatics.

*Pencak silat*, Indonesia's own form of martial arts, is most popular in West Java. This form of fighting uses not only hands and feet, but also some weapons, including sticks and knives.

## SHOPPING
### What to Buy

Java is a great place to buy handicrafts, mostly from Java, but arts and crafts from all over Indonesia are available. The plunge in the rupiah means that almost everything is cheap in Indonesia, especially locally produced clothes and shoes.

Batik is very much a Javanese art form, and each region produces its own styles. Solo is the main centre for batik, but Yogya also has plenty of batik factories and outlets. Pekalongan is another major centre, as is Cirebon. The large factories, such as Batik Semar and Batik Keris, have showrooms and outlets in all the main cities. The cheapest place to shop for batik is in the markets. The quality is not always high, but some good pieces can be found.

Batik paintings are a speciality of Yogya. They are often of unexceptional quality, but some attractive works are on sale.

Wayang puppets – both the leather wayang kulit and the wooden wayang golek – are good buys and typically Javanese, as are wooden topeng masks. Wayang golek puppets usually come from West Java but are available everywhere, while wayang kulit is a speciality of Central Java. You could even buy yourself a gamelan set in Java, or just a single gong.

A kris is another favourite souvenir from Java. Many of these krises are poor quality, with roughly carved handles, and the crudely etched blades are a poor imitation of the real thing. Nevertheless, they are cheap, and some make attractive souvenirs. Quality, antique krises are highly prized family heirlooms, and hard to come by. High-quality pieces bring very high prices.

Java is also a major centre for woodcarving and furniture production. Jepara is the main woodcarving centre and each year mountains of teak furniture are produced. The woodcarvers of Kudus and Madura are also noted for their fine work, but woodcarvers are found throughout Java, producing small figurines, boxes, panels and furniture. Tables, chests of drawers, Madura heirloom boxes, statuettes etc are available, as is heavily carved Chinese furniture, such as beds and altar tables.

Jakarta is the main centre of antiques, and dozens of shops and woodcarving workshops are scattered around the city. Yogya also has plenty of antique shops, and Solo has an interesting antique market. Antique Dutch and Javanese furniture is widely available and shipping can be arranged, though it is too much hassle for the average visitor to bother about. You'll also find a good range of antique ceramics, particularly old Chinese porcelain, antique jewellery, puppets, krises and batik etc. Antiques should be left to collectors who know their stuff as dealers in Indonesia are very good at artificially ageing wood, brass or just about anything. For the uninitiated, it is best to assume that all 'antiques' are new, which in most cases they are.

The main centre for silverware is Kota Gede, a suburb of Yogya. Noted for fine filigree work, the silversmiths here produce a large range of jewellery, cutlery, coffee pots etc.

Gold shops abound in Java and gold jewellery is usually sold by weight, with the design thrown in for free. However, gold jewellery is primarily for investment and the work is not very exciting. Reasonably priced semi-precious stones can be found at jewellers and some craft outlets.

Rattan goods, such as baskets, furniture and bags, are widely available, and Taskimalaya is a major centre. Yogya's leatherware is very good and exceptional value. Pottery ranges from eathernware household items to intricately carved figurines, such as those from Kasongan, near Yogya.

Souvenir and antique shops also stock handicrafts from all over Indonesia, such as ikat weavings from Nusa Tenggara, woodcarvings from Bali, Sumatra, Kalimantan or Irian Jaya, bronze drums from Alor etc. Jakarta is the best place for all-Indonesia crafts. Though the range of non-Javanese crafts is not quite as good as in Bali, prices are often lower. Be wary of that Asmat shield or Kalimantan fertility statue – it may have just been carved out the back of the shop.

Clothes and shoes are cheap and another good buy. The big shopping malls have the best range. For cheaper prices, check out the markets. International brand name goods are much more expensive, even if produced in Indonesia, but often cost much less than in other countries.

Just about everything is cheap in Indonesia. Imported electronics are reasonably priced but not as good as Singapore, but almost everything else, from toothbrushes to guitars, is cheap for anyone with foreign currency.

## Where to Shop

Jakarta and Yogya are the main centres for handicrafts. Jakarta has shops selling a bit of everything scattered all over town. Yogya also has dozens of antique and craft shops, and Jalan Malioboro is one long street-stall of souvenirs. Jakarta's range is better overall, but shopping in Yogya is easier and not so spread out.

Jakarta is a good place to pick up handicrafts from all over the country. Prices are higher than in the region of origin, but you'll find good buys. Sarinah department store is good for reasonably priced souvenirs at fixed prices. Handicrafts can be found in the other cities and tourist centres. Solo has notable antique and batik markets.

Markets are the cheapest places to shop, but the range of handicrafts is often limited. There are no real government craft emporiums, so the trick is to simply do the rounds of the various art and craft shops to see the range and prices. Many of the large hotels and exclusive shopping malls have art shops, where you'll find that prices are often absurd. You can, and should, bargain in these shops.

Java's shopping malls stock just about everything and are great places to browse for quality goods. Prices are higher than at the markets and local shopping areas, but so is the quality. Jakarta has dozens of big western-style malls, and Surabaya is also a great place to shop. Bandung comes in at number three and Yogya has a couple of smaller malls.

Finally, always thoroughly check your purchases for faulty work. Make sure the stitching is good on clothing and leatherwork. Look for cracks or borer in wood.

Cheap timbers, such as jackfruit, often crack or warp in drier climates. Teak is much more stable.

## Bargaining

Bargaining is essential for handicrafts and the first asking price can be outrageously high. This is particularly true for tourist areas, such as the Jalan Surabaya antique market in Jakarta and some handicraft shops in Yogya and Jakarta.

There is no general rule as to what is a good counter offer to the starting price – the asking price may be 50% higher than what the seller is prepared to accept, or 1000% higher. A good price is only learnt through experience. Shop around and look in some of the fixed-priced shops recommended in this book to get an idea of prices.

# Getting There & Away

## AIR

Jakarta is the principal gateway for entry to Java and Indonesia, though because of its tourist trade Bali gets almost as much air traffic. Many visitors to Java fly to Bali first and then travel overland or else they get a connecting internal flight to Java. From Denpasar, you can get connecting flights with Indonesian carriers to Surabaya, Yogyakarta, and Jakarta.

Flights from Singapore to Jakarta are cheap and it may be cheaper to fly to Singapore, from where you can reach Jakarta by air or ship.

## Airports & Airlines

Indonesian airports are dull affairs. Jakarta's Soekarno-Hatta airport is spacious, modern and surprisingly efficient, but only has a few overpriced food and shopping outlets. (See the Jakarta chapter for more information on getting to and from the airport and for a list of domestic airlines operating from Jakarta.)

Air Canada
  (☎ 5738185) Chase Plaza, Jl Jenderal Sudirman, Kav 21
Air France
  (☎ 5202262) 9th floor, Summitmas Tower, Jl Jenderal Sudirman, Kav 61-62
Air India
  (☎ 3858845) Jl Abdul Muis
Air New Zealand
  (☎ 5738195) Chase Plaza, Jl Jenderal Sudirman, Kav 21
British Airways
  (☎ 11500) 10th floor, World Trade Centre, Jl Jenderal Sudirman, Kav 29
Cathay Pacific Airways
  (☎ 3806664) 3rd floor, Hotel Borobudur Inter-Continental, Jl Lapangan Banteng Selatan
China Airlines
  (☎ 10788) Wisma Dharmala Sakti, Jl Jenderal Sudirman
Garuda Indonesia
  (☎ 311801) Garuda Bldg, Jl Merdeka Selatan 13

Japan Airlines
  (☎ 703883) Mid Plaza, Jl Jenderal Sudirman Kav 10-11
KLM-Royal Dutch Airlines
  (☎ 2526730/5) 17th floor, Summitmas Tower II, Jl Jenderal Sudirman, Kav 61-62
Merpati Nusantara Airlines
  (☎ 6544444) Jl Angkasa Blok B/15, Kav 2/3, Kemayoran
  (☎ 3501433) Gambir Train Station, 24 hour ticket office
Lufthansa Airlines
  (☎ 5702005) Panin Centre Bldg, Jl Jenderal Sudirman 1
Malaysia Airlines
  (☎ 229682) World Trade Centre, Jl Jenderal Sudirman, Kav 29-31
Qantas Airways
  (☎ 2300655) 11th floor, BDN Bldg, Jl Kebon Sirih 83
Royal Brunei Airlines
  (☎ 5211842) World Trade Centre, Jl Jenderal Sudirman 29-31
Silk Air
  (☎ 5208023) Chase Plaza, Jl Jenderal Sudirman, Kav 21
Singapore Airlines
  (☎ 5206881) Chase Plaza, Jl Jenderal Sudirman, Kav 21
Thai Airways International
  (☎ 3140607) BDN Bldg, Jl Thamrin 5
United Airlines
  (☎ 5707520) Bank Pacific Bldg, Jl Jenderal Sudirman, Kav 7-8

## Buying Tickets

Your plane ticket will probably be the single most expensive item in your budget, and buying it can be an intimidating business. It is always worth putting aside a few hours to research the current state of the market. Ring a variety of travel agents for the best fare and ticket to suit your needs. The fares vary, depending on the season (high, shoulder or low) and special deals are often available.

Please use the fares quoted in this book as a guide only. They are the official fares provided by the airlines at the time of writing, but you can often find a travel agency that will discount the official fare. Quoted air fares do not necessarily constitute a recommendation for the carrier.

**Shopping Around** Start early as some of the cheapest tickets have to be bought months in advance, and popular flights sell out early. Talk to other recent travellers – they may help you to avoid some of the same old mistakes. Look at the advertisements in newspapers and magazines, consult reference books and watch for special offers.

For bargain fares, it is usually better to go to a travel agent than to the airline, as the latter can only sell fares by the book. (Airlines can supply information on routes and timetables; however, except at times of inter-airline war, they do not normally supply the cheapest tickets.) Budget tickets may come with lots of restrictions. Check for how long the ticket is valid, the minimum period of stay, stopover options, cancellation fees and any amendment fees if you change your date of travel. Plenty of discount tickets are valid for six or 12 months, allowing multiple stopovers with open dates.

An increasingly popular and useful way to get information about current flights and fares, and to even book tickets directly with the airlines or travel agencies, is to surf the Internet. Lonely Planet's Web site (www.lonelyplanet.com) is a good place to look for some useful hints from other travellers, as well as to find links to sites that provide travel details and costs.

You may discover that those impossibly cheap flights are 'fully booked, but we have another one that costs a bit more ...'. Or the flight is on an airline that is notorious for its poor safety standards and leaves you in the world's least favourite airport in the middle of the journey for 14 hours. Or the staff claim to have only two seats left for that country for the whole of July, which 'we will hold for you for a maximum of two hours ...'. Don't panic – look around.

**Precautions** Once you have your ticket, write the ticket number down, together with the flight number and other details, and keep the information somewhere separate. If the ticket is lost or stolen, this will help you to obtain a replacement.

It's sensible to buy travel insurance as early as possible. If you buy it the week before you fly, you may find, for example, that you're not covered for delays to your flight caused by industrial action, or cancellation costs should you unexpectedly become sick.

**Discounts** Some airlines offer discounts of up to 25% to student card holders. Besides having an International Student Identity Card (ISIC), an official-looking letter from your university (college) is also required by some airlines. Many airlines also require you to be aged 26 years or under to qualify for a discount. These discounts are generally only available on ordinary economy-class fares. You wouldn't get one, for instance, on an APEX or an RTW ticket since these are already discounted.

Frequent flyer deals are available on many airlines flying to Java or the general region. If you fly frequently with one airline, eventually you may accumulate enough points to qualify for a free ticket or other goodies. If you fly a lot, contact the airlines for information before buying your ticket.

**Travel with Children** Children under two years old travel for 10% of the standard fare (or free on some airlines), as long as they don't occupy a seat. They don't get a baggage allowance, however. 'Skycots' should be provided by the airline if requested in advance; these will take a child weighing up to about 10kg. Children between two and 12 years can usually occupy a seat for half to two-thirds of the full fare and do get a baggage allowance. Push chairs (prams) can often be taken as hand luggage.

**Travellers with Special Needs**
If you have special needs of any sort – if you have a broken leg, are a vegetarian, are travelling with a baby or are simply terrified of flying – you should let the airline know as soon as possible so the staff can make arrangements accordingly.

## Air Travel Glossary

**Baggage Allowance** This will be written on your ticket and usually includes one 20kg item to go in the hold, plus one item of hand luggage.

**Bucket Shops** These are unbonded travel agencies specialising in discounted airline tickets.

**Bumped** Just because you have a confirmed seat doesn't mean you're going to get on the plane (see Overbooking).

**Cancellation Penalties** If you have to cancel or change a discounted ticket, there are often heavy penalties involved; insurance can sometimes be taken out against these penalties. Some airlines impose penalties on regular tickets as well, particularly against 'no-show' passengers.

**Check-In** Airlines ask you to check in a certain time ahead of the flight departure (usually one to two hours on international flights). If you fail to check in on time and the flight is overbooked, the airline can cancel your booking and give your seat to somebody else.

**Confirmation** Having a ticket written out with the flight and date you want doesn't mean you have a seat until the agent has checked with the airline that your status is 'OK' or confirmed. Meanwhile you could just be 'on request'.

**Courier Fares** Businesses often need to send urgent documents or freight securely and quickly. Courier companies hire people to accompany the package through customs and, in return, offer a discount ticket which is sometimes a phenomenal bargain. In effect, what the companies do is ship their freight as your luggage on regular commercial flights. This is a legitimate operation, but there are two shortcomings – the short turnaround time of the ticket (usually not longer than a month) and the limitation on your luggage allowance. You may have to surrender all your allowance and take only carry-on luggage.

**Full Fares** Airlines traditionally offer 1st class (coded F), business class (coded J) and economy class (coded Y) tickets. These days there are so many promotional and discounted fares available that few passengers pay full economy fare.

**ITX** An ITX, or 'independent inclusive tour excursion', is often available on tickets to popular holiday destinations. Officially it's a package deal combined with hotel accommodation, but many agents will sell you one of these for the flight only and give you phoney hotel vouchers in the unlikely event that you're challenged at the airport.

**Lost Tickets** If you lose your airline ticket an airline will usually treat it like a travellers cheque and, after inquiries, issue you with another one. Legally, however, an airline is entitled to treat it like cash and if you lose it then it's gone forever. Take good care of your tickets.

**MCO** An MCO, or 'miscellaneous charge order', is a voucher that looks like an airline ticket but carries no destination or date. It can be exchanged through any International Association of Travel Agents (IATA) airline for a ticket on a specific flight. It's a useful alternative to an onward ticket in those countries that demand one, and is more flexible than an ordinary ticket if you're unsure of your route.

**No-Shows** No-shows are passengers who fail to show up for their flight. Full-fare passengers who fail to turn up are sometimes entitled to travel on a later flight. The rest are penalised (see Cancellation Penalties).

**On Request** This is an unconfirmed booking for a flight.

## Air Travel Glossary

**Onward Tickets** An entry requirement for many countries is that you have a ticket out of the country. If you're unsure of your next move, the easiest solution is to buy the cheapest onward ticket to a neighbouring country or a ticket from a reliable airline which can later be refunded if you do not use it.

**Open Jaw Tickets** These are return tickets where you fly out to one place but return from another. If available, this can save you backtracking to your arrival point.

**Overbooking** Airlines hate to fly empty seats and since every flight has some passengers who fail to show up, airlines often book more passengers than they have seats. Usually excess passengers make up for the no-shows, but occasionally somebody gets 'bumped' onto the next available flight. Guess who it is most likely to be? The passengers who check in late.

**Point-to-Point Tickets** These are discount tickets that can be bought on some routes in return for passengers waiving their rights to a stopover.

**Promotional Fares** These are officially discounted fares, available from travel agencies or direct from the airline.

**Reconfirmation** If you don't reconfirm your flight at least 72 hours prior to departure, the airline may delete your name from the passenger list. Ring to find out if your airline requires reconfirmation.

**Restrictions** Discounted tickets often have various restrictions on them – such as needing to be paid for in advance and incurring a penalty to be altered. Others are restrictions on the minimum and maximum period you must be away, such as a minimum of 14 days or a maximum of one year.

**Round-the-World Tickets** RTW tickets give you a limited period (usually a year) in which to circumnavigate the globe. You can go anywhere the carrying airlines go, as long as you don't backtrack. The number of stopovers or total number of separate flights is decided before you set off and they usually cost a bit more than a basic return flight.

**Stand-by** This is a discounted ticket where you only fly if there is a seat free at the last moment. Stand-by fares are usually available only on domestic routes.

**Transferred Tickets** Airline tickets cannot be transferred from one person to another. Travellers sometimes try to sell the return half of their ticket, but officials can ask you to prove that you are the person named on the ticket. This is less likely to happen on domestic flights, but on an international flight tickets are compared with passports.

**Travel Agencies** Travel agencies vary widely and you should choose one that suits your needs. Some simply handle tours, while full-service agencies handle everything from tours and tickets to car rental and hotel bookings. If all you want is a ticket at the lowest possible price, then go to an agency specialising in discounted fares.

**Travel Periods** Ticket prices vary with the time of year. There is a low (off-peak) season and a high (peak) season, and often a low-shoulder season and a high-shoulder season as well. Usually the fare depends on your outward flight – if you depart in the high season and return in the low season, you pay the high-season fare.

You should remind the staff when you re-confirm your booking (at least 72 hours before departure) and again when you check in at the airport. It may also be worth ringing round the airlines before you make your booking to find out how they can handle your particular needs.

Airports and airlines can be surprisingly helpful, but they do need advance warning. Most international airports will provide escorts from the check-in desk to the plane where needed, and there should be ramps, lifts, accessible toilets and phones. Aircraft toilets, on the other hand, may present a problem; travellers should discuss this with the airline at an early stage and, if necessary, with their doctor.

## Departure Tax

Airport tax on international flights from Jakarta and Denpasar is 50,000 rp. At other airports the charge on international flights is 25,000 rp. On domestic flights, airport tax is between 5500 and 11,000 rp, depending on the airport, and is not included in the ticket price.

For residents of Indonesia, including foreigners on KITAS (one year temporary stay/work) visas, a *fiskal* tax of 1,000,000 rp is payable when leaving the country.

## Indonesia

Indonesia has an extensive internal air network, and flights operate from Java to all major cities and many minor ones throughout the archipelago. Merpati is the main internal carrier with the most extensive network, Garuda operates jets on all the major runs, and Bouraq and Mandala also have a few flights. See the Getting Around chapter for more information on airlines, ticketing and flights within Java.

Most flights are out of Jakarta, while Surabaya is a secondary hub with some useful routes.

**Air Passes** Garuda issues a Visit Indonesia Decade Pass at US$100 per sector with a minimum of three sectors, ie US$300, plus 10% tax. The pass can be bought overseas or

in Indonesia within one month of arrival. It is only valid for Garuda flights. The pass can be very good value if you are flying half-way across the country, eg Sumatra to Sulawesi or Bali to Irian Jaya, but otherwise savings are minimal. Inquire at Garuda offices.

**Java** Jakarta is no discount centre compared with Singapore or Bangkok, but it is the best place to buy international tickets in Indonesia. Of most interest to travellers are the short-hop tickets, such as the Jakarta-Singapore and Kupang-Dili trips. Small agents specialising in services for travellers may advertise international tickets, but you will usually get much better discounts at one of the bigger flight specialists.

Jakarta's Soekarno-Hatta airport is spacious, modern and efficient but only has a few overpriced food and shopping outlets. Bali's smaller Ngurah Rai international airport is slightly more interesting. Shopping is also overpriced, but more varied and the airport can be exciting if you like crowds. In peak tourist seasons when a few jumbos land, it is standing room only and queues are long. Standard duty-free items are on sale at both airports, but local cigarettes are much cheaper than the duty-free variety and there are no great bargains for alcohol either.

## Asia

Singapore is the cheapest port from which to reach Java by air from overseas, and Jakarta-Singapore flights are very popular. Garuda has the most flights between Singapore and Jakarta, but this route is also serviced by many airlines that offer better discounts. Singapore-Jakarta tickets cost as little as US$65. Gulf Air, Emirates and Air India are regular discounters. Singapore is also a good place to buy a cheap air ticket if you're leaving South-East Asia.

Direct flights connect Jakarta with almost all other Asian capitals, including Kuala Lumpur, Bangkok, Manila, Hong Kong, Taipei, Beijing, Seoul and Tokyo.

Surabaya is also serviced by a few international flights. Singapore Airlines and Garuda fly to Singapore (US$180) and there are also flights from Surabaya to Kuala Lumpur, Bangkok and Hong Kong.

Silk Air also flies direct from Singapore to Solo.

## Australia

The main gateway to Australia is Bali, and almost all flights to and from Java are routed via Denpasar. Qantas and Garuda are the main carriers, and Ansett and Merpati also have a number of useful flights. The only non-stop flights to Java are the following: Perth-Jakarta (Qantas); Melbourne-Jakarta (Merpati); and Sydney-Jakarta (Qantas & Thai).

Fares vary between the low season (from February to December) and the high season (from December and January).

Return tickets are usually limited to 30 or 90-day excursion fares, but six or 12 month return tickets to Jakarta are also available, and you can add on a Bali stopover for around A$100.

One way/return flights from Melbourne, Sydney or Brisbane to Denpasar cost around A$700/900 in the low season, A$900/1200 in the high season. From Darwin or Perth it costs around A$200 less, and Merpati also has a few flights from Darwin and Port Hedland to Denpasar.

From Melbourne or Sydney to Jakarta, a 12 month ticket normally costs around A$900 return in the low season and A$1150 return in the high season, while excursion fares are slightly cheaper. From Perth, fares are about A$200 cheaper. Recent discounts have seen some very cheap flights to Jakarta, which cost considerably less than flights to Bali.

Travel agents are the best place to shop for cheap tickets, but because Bali is such a popular destination flight, discounting on flights to Indonesia is not large. Travel agents to contact include the big networks like STA Travel or Flight Centres International, with offices in the main cities, or check the travel pages of the main newspapers. It may also be worth ringing the airlines direct.

The highest demand for flights is during school holidays and especially the Christmas break, when flights to Java via Denpasar can be full – book well in advance.

## New Zealand

Garuda and Ansett have direct flights between Auckland and Denpasar, with connections to Jakarta. Air New Zealand has suspended its Bali flights. The return economy air fare from Auckland to Denpasar is about NZ$1150 to NZ$1300, depending on the season, and about NZ$100 more to Jakarta with Garuda.

As they are in Australia, STA Travel and Flight Centres International are popular travel agents.

## Europe

**The UK** Ticket discounting is a long-established business in the UK – the various agencies advertise their fares and there's nothing under the counter about it at all. To find out what is available and where to get it, pick up a copy of the giveaway newspaper *TNT* or the weekly 'what's on' guide *Time Out*. Discounted tickets are available all over the UK, they're not just a London exclusive.

A couple of excellent places to look are Trailfinders and STA Travel. Trailfinders is at 194 Kensington High St, London W8 (☎ 020-7938 3939) and at 46 Earls Court Rd (☎ 020-7938 3366). It also has offices in Manchester (☎ 061-839 6969) and Glasgow (☎ 041-353 2224). STA Travel is at 86 Old Brompton Rd, London W7 (☎ 020-7361 6161) and at Clifton House, 117 Euston Rd, NW1 (☎ 020-7361 2163).

Garuda is one of the main discounters to Indonesia and stops over in either Bangkok or Singapore. Many of its Jakarta flights go via Denpasar. Rock-bottom fares (low season) from London to Bali or Jakarta one way/return are around £270/£440. The least loved airlines, like Pakistan Airlines, usually have the cheapest fares to Jakarta. A host of other airlines fly to Indonesia, including Gulf Air to Jakarta and Lauda to Denpasar. These airlines regularly have cheap fares, but plenty of stopovers, while Qantas, Thai and Singapore Airlines are usually more expensive.

**Continental Europe** The Netherlands, Brussels and Antwerp are good places to buy discount air tickets. In Antwerp, WATS has been recommended. In Zurich, try SOF Travel and Sindbad. In Geneva you could try Stohl Travel. In the Netherlands, NBBS is a reputable agency. Many flights go to Denpasar and the cost is around the same to Jakarta. The cheapest flights often go via Bangkok or Singapore, with another stop en route.

From Amsterdam, 60-day return tickets with KLM to Denpasar cost around f1800 in the low season, f2000 in the high season (June to September). Tickets to Jakarta have been much cheaper recently. Garuda flies to Denpasar via Jakarta, and vice versa, for around the same price but recently it has been offering substantial discounts to fill seats. Other airlines, such as Royal Brunei, Kuwait Airlines, Air India and Malaysia Airlines, often have cheaper fares but go via more inconvenient routes or have more stopovers.

From Frankfurt, Garuda flies to Jakarta and Denpasar for around DM1450, but flights with Lauda, Malaysia Airlines and Royal Brunei are often cheaper, while Lufthansa tends to be more expensive.

Garuda has flight connections between Jakarta and several other European cities including Paris, Zurich and Rome. From Paris, Garuda flights to Denpasar cost around 5500 to 6000FF or you can fly with Cathay Pacific via Hong Kong for around the same price. Lauda is also a regular discounter on Paris-Denpasar flights.

## The USA

Some very good open tickets remain valid for six months or one year but don't lock you into any fixed dates of departure. Flights to Indonesia, either Jakarta or Denpasar, go via Taiwan, Hong Kong, Singapore, Malaysia or another Asian destination and will include the country as a stopover (sometimes you have to stop over). Garuda used to have a Los Angeles-Honolulu-Denpasar-Jakarta flight but suspended it in the wake of the currency crisis – it may start up again.

Return fares to Jakarta or Denpasar start at around US$1000 return in the low season (outside summer – June to August – and Christmas) from the west coast, and around US$1200 from New York. Recent discounts have meant some real bargains. China Airlines via Taipei is often one of the cheapest flights, while Singapore Airlines flies one of the most direct routes.

If you are visiting other parts of Asia, some good deals can be put together. For example, there are cheap tickets between the US west coast and Singapore, with stopovers in Bangkok for very little extra money. However, be careful during the high season (summer and Chinese New Year) because seats will be hard to come by unless reserved months in advance.

The *New York Times*, *LA Times*, *Chicago Tribune* and *San Francisco Examiner* all produce weekly travel sections in which you'll find any number of travel agents' ads. Council Travel and STA Travel have offices in major cities nationwide.

## Canada

Getting discount tickets in Canada is much the same process as getting them in the USA. Again, you'll probably have to fly into Hong Kong or Singapore and travel on from there to Indonesia.

CUTS is Canada's national student bureau and has offices in a number of Canadian cities including Vancouver, Edmonton, Toronto and Ottawa – you don't necessarily have to be a student. There are a number of good agents for cheap tickets in Vancouver. The *Toronto Globe & Mail* and the *Vancouver Sun* carry travel agents' ads.

## SEA

Indonesia has one of the most extensive ferry and passenger ship networks in the world, with regular boats running between all the main inhabited islands. Despite this, there are very few international connections. Ferries from Malaysia to Sumatra are numerous, and ferries run from Singapore to the nearby Indonesian islands of Batam and Bintan, from where boats go to Jakarta and Sumatra.

## Singapore

An interesting way to reach Jakarta is from Singapore via the islands of Bintan and Batam in Sumatra's Riau Archipelago. The main stepping stone to Java is the island of Bintan, which is only a short high-speed ferry ride from Tanah Merah in Singapore, costing S$20. Numerous services go throughout the day and Bintan is a visa-free entry point.

From Bintan, two Pelni ships, the *Bukit Siguntang* and *Sirimau,* sail on alternate weeks from the southern port of Kijang to Jakarta. The journey takes 28 hours and costs 107,000 rp in deck class.

Alternatively, the *Samudera Jaya* leaves Tanjung Pinang on Bintan every Thursday and does the trip in 18 hours. It stops en route at Pulau Bangka and Tanjung Pandang on Pulau Belitung. The *Telaga Express* does a similar run to Jakarta, leaving Tanjung Pinang every Monday.

Batam is the bigger travel hub of the two Riau islands, and ferries constantly do the half-hour crossing to Singapore. From Batam numerous speed boats travel to Pekanbaru on the Sumatran mainland in about eight hours. From Pekanbaru, it's a long gruelling bus trip to Jakarta, so this route is really only for those who want to explore some of Sumatra on the way to Java.

## Bali

Ferries run round-the-clock between Banyuwangi/Ketapang harbour on Java and Gilimanuk in Bali. In Bali, buses run to Gilimanuk, from where frequent ferries go to Ketapang, which has numerous buses and trains to the rest of Java.

An easier alternative is to take one of the through buses from Denpasar to any major city in Java. The ferry journey is included in the cost. From Denpasar's Ubung terminal, buses head straight to: Probolinggo (7½ hours) for Gunung Bromo; Surabaya (nine hours); Yogyakarta (16 hours); or even Jakarta. Ticket agents in the resorts of Kuta, Sanur, Ubud etc sell tickets for departures from Ubung for a slight premium – some also arrange transfer to the bus terminal.

Similarly, from Java, buses run from all the main cities right through to Denpasar, and a few go to Lovina, Singaraja and Padangbai.

## Sumatra

Ferries shuttle between Merak in Java and the southern Sumatran port of Bakauheni, 24 hours a day.

Regular buses go to Merak from Jakarta's Kalideres bus terminal. In Bakauheni, buses take you north to Bandarlampung's Rajabasa bus terminal, where other buses can take you all over Sumatra. The easy option is to take the long-distance buses that run from Jakarta (and other cities in Java) straight through to the main Sumatran destinations, such as Padang, Bukittinggi, Sibolga, Prapat, Medan and even Aceh. Most of these leave from Jakarta's Pulo Gadung bus terminal.

The long bus journeys on Sumatra can take their toll and, as most points of interest are in North Sumatra, many travellers prefer to take a Pelni boat or to fly between Jakarta and Padang.

## Other Indonesian Islands

Indonesia has an extensive ferry network shuttling between the islands from Sumatra through Java and Bali to Nusa Tenggara. These ferry services make island hopping all the way east to Timor relatively easy. For the other islands of Kalimantan, Sulawesi, Maluku and Irian Jaya, the alternative to flying is to take one of the many Pelni ships. Java is well connected on Pelni's extensive passenger fleet network.

**Pelni Ships** Pelni is the biggest sea passenger transporter, with services almost everywhere. It has modern, air-con passenger ships that operate on set routes around the islands, either on a two weekly or monthly schedule. The ships usually stop for four hours in each port, so there's time for a quick look around.

The fleet has some 20 ships that cover virtually all of the archipelago. Routes and schedules change every year, sometimes with only minor adjustments, but if new ships are added then major changes may be made. Try to find a copy of the latest schedule from any Pelni office, but the staff may only have schedules for the ships that call at their port.

Because Pelni ships operate only every two or four weeks, regular ferries are much more convenient. You can travel from Sumatra right through to Timor by land/ferry connections, but Pelni ships are often the only alternative to flying for travel to and between Kalimantan, Sulawesi, Maluku and Irian Jaya. Given the current chaos in the aviation industry (see the Getting Around chapter for details), Pelni boats are often more reliable than flights.

Pelni ships have four cabin classes, or you could opt for the Kelas Ekonomi, which is the modern version of the old deck class. There you are packed in a large room with a space to sleep. But even in *ekonomi*, it's air-con and can get pretty cool at night, so bring warm clothes or a sleeping bag. It is possible to book a sleeping place in ekonomi – sometimes – otherwise you have to find your own empty space. Mattresses can be rented and many boats have a 'tourist deck' upstairs. There are no locker facilities in ekonomi, so you have to keep an eye on your gear.

Class I is luxurious with only two beds per cabin. Class II is a notch down in style, with four to a cabin, but still very comfortable. Class III has six beds and Class IV has eight beds to a cabin. Class I, II, III and IV have a restaurant with good food, while in ekonomi you queue up to collect an unappetising meal on a tray and then sit down wherever you can to eat it. It pays to bring some other food with you.

Ekonomi is OK for short trips. Class IV is the best value for longer hauls, but some ships only offer Class I and II or III in addition to ekonomi. With the devaluation of the rupiah, Class I is good value for the comfort on offer. Prices quoted in this book are usually for ekonomi – as a rough approximation Class IV is 50% more than ekonomi, Class III is 100% more, Class II is 200% more and Class I is 400% more.

You can book tickets up to a week ahead; it's best to book at least a few days in advance. Pelni is not a tourist operation, so don't expect any special service, although there is usually somebody hidden away in the ticket office who can help foreigners.

**Pelni Vessels & Routes** Jakarta has the most Pelni connections and the leg from Jakarta to Padang in Sumatra is a popular alternative to long-distance bus travel through southern Sumatra. Jakarta is also good for connections to Kalimantan. Surabaya has extensive connections to Kalimantan, Sulawesi as well as the eastern islands. The Surabaya-Sulawesi route is very popular with travellers. Regular Pelni boats stop at Cirebon and Semarang for connections to Kalimantan. See under those cities for details.

The port for Jakarta is Tanjung Priok, Benoa is the port for Bali and Bitung is the port for Manado. The main Pelni ships, and the routes they ply (all fortnightly for the round trip unless otherwise indicated), are listed using the following abbreviations: Bali (B), Irian Jaya (IJ), Java (J), Kalimantan (K), Maluku (M), Nusa Tenggara (NT), Sulawesi (Sl) and Sumatra (Sm).

*Awu* Benoa (B) – Lembar (NT) – Waingapu (NT) – Ende (NT) – Kalabahi (NT) – Dili (NT) – Maumere (NT) – Ujung Pandang (Sl) – Tarakan (K) – Nunukan (K), and back via the same ports

*Bukit Siguntang* Dumai (Sm) – Kijang (Sm) – Jakarta (J) – Surabaya (J) – Ujung Pandang (Sl) – Bau-Bau (Sl) – Ambon (M) – Banda (M) – Tual (M) – Dobo (IJ) or Kaimana (IJ), and back via the same ports

*Ciremai* Jakarta (J) – Semarang (J) – Ujung Pandang (Sl) – Bau-Bau (Sl) – Banggai (Sl) – Bitung (Sl) – Ternate (M) – Sorong (IJ) – Manokwari (IJ) – Biak (IJ) – Jayapura (IJ), and back via the same ports

*Dobonsolo* Jakarta (J) – Surabaya (J) – Benoa (B) – Kupang (NT) – Dili (NT) – Ambon (M) – Sorong (IJ) – Manokwari (IJ) – Biak (IJ) – Jayapura (IJ), and back via the same ports

*Kambuna* Sibolga (Sm) – Padang (Sm) – Jakarta (J) – Surabaya (J) – Ujung Pandang (Sl) – Balikpapan (K) – Pantoloan (Sl) – Toli-Toli (Sl) – Bitung (Sl), and back via the same ports

*Kelimutu* Shuttles back and forth between Surabaya (J) and Banjarmasin (K) every two days, substituting Semarang for Surabaya twice a fortnight

*Kerinci* Dumai (Sm) – Kijang (Sm) – Jakarta (J) – Surabaya (J) – Ujung Pandang (Sl) – Balikpapan (K) – Pantoloan (Sl) – Toli-Toli (Sl) – Tarakan (K) – Nunukan (K), and back via the same ports

*Lambelu* Sibolga (Sm) – Padang (Sm) – Jakarta (J) – Surabaya (J) – Ujung Pandang (Sl) – Bau-Bau (Sl) – Ambon (M) – Namlea (M) – Bitung (Sl) – Ternate (M), and back via the same ports (except Bitung)

*Lawit* Kumai (K) – Semarang (J) – Pontianak (K) – Tanjung Pandan-Jakarta (J) – Tanjung Pandan-Pontianak (K) – Cirebon (J) – Pontianak (K) – Tanjung Pandan-Jakarta (J) – Tanjung Pandan-Pontianak (K) – Semarang (J) – Kumai (K)

*Leuser* Semarang (J) – Sampit (K) – Surabaya (J) – Batulicin (K) – Pare-Pare (Sl) – Samarinda (K) – Toli-Toli (Sl) – Tarakan (K) – Nunukan (K), and back via the same ports

*Pangrango* Ketapang (J) – Semarang (J) – Sampit (K) – Bawean-Surabaya (J) – Badas (NT) – Labuanbajo (NT) – Waingapu (NT) – Ende (NT) – Sabu (NT) – Roti (NT) – Kupang (NT), and back via the same ports

*Rinjani* Surabaya (J) – Ujung Pandang (Sl) – Bau-Bau (Sl) – Ambon (M) – Banda (M) – Tual (M) – Fak Fak (IJ) – Sorong (IJ) – Manokwari (IJ) – Nabire (IJ) – Serui (IJ) – Jayapura (IJ) and back via the same ports

*Tatamailau* Banyuwangi (NT) – Bima (NT) – Labuanbajo (NT) – Larantuka (NT) – Dili (NT) – Saumlaki (M) – Tual (M) – Dobo (IJ) – Merauke (IJ) – Timika (IJ) – Kaimana (IJ) – Fak Fak (IJ) – Amahai (M) – Ambon (M) – Bau-Bau (Sl) – Ujung Pandang (Sl) – Badas (NT) – Benoa (B) – Banyuwangi (NT); does the trip in the reverse order the next fortnight

*Tidar* Surabaya (J) – Balikpapan (K) – Surabaya (J) – Pare-Pare (Sl) – Pantoloan (Sl) – Nunukan (K) – Tarakan (K) – Balikpapan (K) – Pare-Pare (Sl) – Surabaya (J) – Ujung Pandang (Sl) – Balikpapan (K) – Tarakan (K) – Pantoloan (Sl) – Ujung Pandang (Sl) – Surabaya (J)

*Tilongkabila* Benoa (B) – Surabaya (J) – Kumai (K) – Semarang (J) – Sampit (K) – Surabaya (J) – Semarang (J) – Kumai (K) – Surabaya (J) – Batulicin (K) – Surabaya (J) – Sampit (K) – Surabaya (J) – Benoa (B) – Lembar (NT) – Bima (NT) – Labuanbajo (NT) – Ujung Pandang (Sl) – Bau Bau (Sl) – Raha (Sl) – Kendari (Sl) – Kolonedale (Sl) – Luwuk (Sl) – Gorontalo (Sl) – Bitung (Sl) – Tahuna (Sl) – Lirung (Sl), and back to Benoa via the same ports in Sulawesi, Maluku and Nusa Tenggara; takes four weeks to complete the entire voyage

*Umsini* Dumai (Sm) – Kijang (Sm) – Muntok (Sm) – Jakarta (J) – Surabaya (J) – Ujung Pandang (Sl) – Balikpapan (K) – Pantoloan (Sl) – Kwandang-Bitung (Sl), and back via the same ports

**Other Ships** Getting a boat, unless it's a Pelni one, will generally involve hanging around a port until something comes by. Check with the shipping offices, Pelni and the harbour master's office. Tickets can be purchased at shipping offices, although for some ships and in some ports (big ones like Jakarta and Surabaya aside) it may be possible and cheaper to negotiate your fare on board rather than buying tickets from the office in advance.

Unscheduled cargo and passenger ships are tough going.

## ORGANISED TOURS

Tours to Indonesia tend to be oriented towards Bali, where accommodation and air fare-only packages are very popular. Adventure/trekking tours are offered by various overseas tour operators and may include a stop in Java, but Java-only tours are not as common.

The European market has the biggest selection, especially Dutch tour companies that have very competitively priced tours ranging from big luxury groups to small, interesting off-the-beaten-track tours. Many Dutch tours focus on Java, and often include Bali. Prices range according to the standard of accommodation. Some tours try so hard to maximise luxury and minimise hassles that participants are hermetically isolated from Indonesia and Indonesians. Smaller groups that provide some independence generally provide a more worthwhile experience.

Of course you can make your own way to Java and take day tours to surrounding attractions. Yogyakarta has dozens of small operators offering cheap tours to surrounding attractions and farther afield. Solo, Malang and Bandung are other good places to arrange tours. Jakarta has a host of tour operators, but they tend to be more expensive.

Airlines may also offer tours in combination with air fare sales. Garuda usually has the best deals, which include accommodation, transfers and a day tour.

# Getting Around

## AIR

There's no real need to fly around Java, unless you're in a real hurry or have money to burn, as there's so much transport at ground level. The most useful and popular flights are from Yogyakarta to Jakarta, Surabaya or Bali, but services are limited. If you do take to the air you'll get some spectacular views of Java's many mountains and volcanoes – try to get a window seat.

## Domestic Air Services

The four main airlines operating in Java and farther afield are:

Garuda Indonesia – the national carrier, operates a useful domestic network between the major cities only. It operates most of the flights between the main cities ion Java.

Merpati Nusantara Airlines – the most extensive domestic network with a mind-boggling array of flights throughout the archipelago, but its intra-Java services have been severely cut back.

Bouraq – a smaller airline with some useful flights from Java to the outer islands from Java, but it no longer operates flights within Java.

Mandala – the smallest of the all-Indonesia airlines. It flies main routes connecting Jakarta with the outer islands as well as Yogyakarta-Jakarta.

Domestic air travel in Indonesia is in a real state of flux. In the wake of the economic crisis, one major airline, Sempati, folded and the others are still in financial trouble. Air fares have risen by around 200% since the collapse of the rupiah, making flying many times more expensive than other forms of transport. But air travel for those with hard currency is still very cheap by world standards.

The main problem is that services have also been cut dramatically. Some 54 regional airports throughout Indonesia have closed and the frequency of flights has also been cut, though flights on main routes are

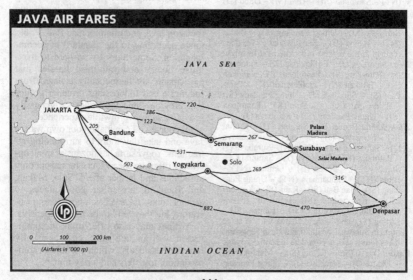

JAVA AIR FARES

still operating. Garuda and Merpati are government-owned and have profitable international flights. Hopefully they will weather the storm and maintain at least the main routes in the national interest. The other thing to be wary of is the fact that flights that have few passengers are often cancelled.

Ticket prices are set by the government and cost the same, regardless of the airline. Discounting is the exception rather than the rule, but a few large travel agents in the main cities sell tickets at a small discount – around 5% on Garuda and Merpati tickets, 10 to 15% on Bouraq and Mandala.

Most airlines offer student discounts of up to 25%. You need a valid International Student Identity Card (ISIC) to take advantage of this. The age limit for claiming the student discount is usually 26. Garuda, Merpati and Bouraq also offer discounts of 35% to passengers aged 60 and over. Your passport must be sighted and a photocopy of the front page provided.

Travel agents overseas can usually include discounted domestic flights with an international ticket, if you enter Indonesia on Garuda. Otherwise domestic tickets bought overseas are quoted in US$ and cost around 50% more than if bought in Indonesia in rupiah.

## Domestic Departure Tax

Domestic departure tax varies from 5500 to 11,000 rp, depending on the airport.

On top of the basic fare quoted by airlines, a 10% tax is charged, and an insurance fee of 2500 rp. Tax and insurance is paid when you buy the ticket, but the departure tax is paid at the airport. Baggage allowance is usually 20 kg, or only 10 kg on the smaller planes, and you may be charged for excess baggage.

## To/From the Airport

Jakarta and Surabaya have official airport buses while in other cities local city buses sometimes pass within easy walking distance of the airport. Taxis operate on the meter, but most airports use a fixed-fare coupon system.

## BUS

Buses are the main form of transport in Java. At any time of the day, thousands of buses in all shapes and sizes are moving thousands of people throughout Java. They are convenient, quick and comfortable if you pay extra. Java has a huge variety of services, from ordinary, public buses that can be very crowded and slow to super luxury coaches that run directly between the main cities.

One drawback to bus travel is that the bus terminal can be a long way from the centre of town, especially in the big cities like Jakarta, Surabaya and Bandung. In these cities the train is often a better alternative because the train stations are more conveniently central.

Small minibuses also cover the shorter routes and back runs. Like the buses, they range from pack-'em-in sweat boxes to a good network of luxury door-to-door minibuses.

Bring as little luggage as possible. Unless you are travelling by luxury bus, there is rarely any room to store anything, so if you can travel with a small bag, do so.

Be careful on the buses. Thievery has always been a problem, but it has increased as the economy has declined. Typically, thieves take the seat behind you and wait for you to fall asleep or put your bag or day pack on the floor. They'll slash your bag, take your belongings and be gone before you know it.

When travelling on the buses, always wear a concealed money belt for your passport, travellers cheques etc. Though the problem is certainly worse on economy buses, travelling deluxe is no guarantee against theft.

## Classes

The bottom line in buses is represented by the ordinary, everyday *ekonomi* buses that run set routes between towns. They stop at bus stations in every town en route, but on the back runs will also stop for anyone, anywhere, in the search for more paying customers – there is no such thing as 'full'. They can be hot, slow and incredibly crowded, but they are also ridiculously cheap and provide a never-ending parade of Javanese life. They are often beatup rattle traps with limited leg room but, if you get a seat and the road is good, they can be quite tolerable for short distances. On the main highways they are faster and stop less. Ekonomi buses are so frequent in Java that you can often just front up to the bus terminal and catch one straight away.

The next class up is the express, or *patas*, bus. They can be much the same as the ekonomi buses but stop only at selected bus stations en route and don't pick up passengers from the side of the road. Air-con patas buses are more luxurious, and seating is often guaranteed. Usually there is no need to book and you can just catch one at bus stations in the big cities.

The luxury air-con buses come in a variety of price categories, depending on whether they have reclining seats, on-board toilets, TV, karaoke, snacks etc. Many of the luxury buses are night buses *(bis malam)*, travelling the highways when the traffic is lighter.

Tickets for express and luxury buses can be bought in advance at bus terminals or, more conveniently, at bus agents in the city centres. Many tourist hotels also arrange tickets. Ticket agents often have pictures of the buses and seating plans, so check to see what you are getting when you buy your ticket.

## Minibuses

Public minibuses are used both as local transport around cities and towns and on short inter-city runs, but their speciality is delivering people out into the hills and villages. They service the farthest reaches of the transport network.

The great minibus ancestor is the *bemo*, a small, three-wheel pickup with a row of seats down each side. These old-style bemos have all but disappeared and are more like regular minibuses these days. The word 'bemo' (a contraction of *becak* and *motor)* is rarely used now but it is still universally understood. Minibuses in Java go by a mind-boggling array of names, with many regional variations, such as *opelet, mikrolet, angkot* or *angkudes*. Just to make things

confusing they are called *taksi* in East Java. Often they will be called simply by their brand name, such as Suzuki, Daihatsu or Toyota, but *colt* (after the ubiquitous Mitsubishi Colt) is the most common term.

Most inter-city minibuses operate a standard route, picking up and dropping off people and goods anywhere along the way. They can be very cramped with even less room for luggage than the buses and, if there is a choice, the buses are usually more comfortable.

Within cities there is often a standard fare, no matter how long or short the distance. On longer routes between cities, you may have to bargain a bit. Minibus drivers often try to overcharge foreigners – more in some places than in others. It's best to ask somebody, such as the staff in your hotel, about the *harga biasa* (normal price) before catching a minibus. Otherwise, see what the other passengers are paying and offer the correct fare.

**Express Minibuses** Java also has an excellent system of door-to-door minibuses (called *travel*), which can pick you up at your hotel (though sometimes you have to go to a depot) and will drop you off wherever you want to go in the destination city. They run all over Java and are usually roomy, deluxe air-con minibuses, though some are getting old, their air-con no longer works and they rattle. Air-con minibuses are almost always newer and more comfortable than the non air-con ones.

## TRAIN

Java has a good rail service running from one end of the island to the other. In the east (at Ketapang/Banyuwangi) it connects with the ferry to Bali, and in the west (at Merak) it connects with the ferry to Sumatra. The two main lines run between Jakarta and Surabaya – the longer central route goes via Yogyakarta and Solo and the shorter northern route goes via Semarang. These main lines are serviced by dozens of trains in all classes – see under the relevant destination for details. A selection of the best services is listed in this book. They are usually those that start in the departure city and travel during the day so that you can see the countryside. Night trains can be very efficient if you are in a hurry, but they may arrive at ungodly hours in the destination city.

A lot of money has been thrown at the rail system in recent years. New signalling systems, luxury trains and a computer booking network have been introduced. Long overruns on scheduled times are now almost a thing of the past. Where you have a choice, trains are usually quicker, more comfortable and more convenient than the buses, especially between main cities.

Choose your trains carefully for comfort and speed. Trains range from very cheap, squalid cattle trains to very comfortable, but expensive, expresses. Fares and journey times for the same journey and in the same class vary from train to train. The schedules change and, although departures may be punctual, arrivals may still be late, particularly on the cheap trains.

When choosing a train, try to get one that begins in the city you are departing from. Seats are more difficult to get on a train coming through from somewhere else and in ekonomi you may be a standing-room-only sardine. Try also to get a train that ends in the city of your destination. Even if you are only going part of the train's journey, the fare is almost the same as you'll pay for the full journey; for example, Jakarta-Yogyakarta on the *Bima* costs the same as Jakarta-Surabaya.

Another factor to bear in mind is that some cities, such as Jakarta and Surabaya, have several stations, and some stations are far more convenient than others. Both these cities have convenient central stations, compared with the bus terminals out in the sticks.

## Classes

*Ekonomi* trains can be no frills, with bare wooden seats, hawkers, beggars and all manner of produce. They can be very crowded and slow, particularly on the back runs. Seats on these trains are hard to get and cannot be booked. However, many ekonomi runs have been upgraded, are limited express and have padded seats that can be booked. The aisles may still fill up but, if you can get a seat, they provide an efficient service. The better trains are usually designated 'ekonomi plus'. In the larger cities, some ekonomi trains may not stop at the main station but at another, less central, station.

Though ekonomi has improved, it is worth shelling out extra for the expresses that offer *bisnis* and *eksekutif* carriages, which are less subject to overruns. In bisnis class you get a guaranteed, comfortable seat with plenty of room and fans (but not air-con). Eksekutif is much more luxurious with air-con, reclining seats, video (maybe) and a snack usually included in the ticket price. Everything else you are offered – from coke to cushions – costs extra.

Top of the range are the fast, new luxury trains that run from Jakarta, such as

MAIN RAIL LINKS

Merak
JAKARTA
Bogor
Bandung
Cirebon
JAVA SEA
Semarang
Pulau Madura
Purwokerto
Solo
Yogyakarta
Kediri
Surabaya
Selat Madura
Problinggo
Jember
Malang
Banyuwangi
Blitar
INDIAN OCEAN
0    100    200 km

the *Argobromo* to Surabaya or the super luxury *Anggrek*, which has fax, telephone and other business services. Other top trains are the *Argo Gede* to Bandung, the *Argo Muria* to Semarang, the *Argo Lawu* and the *Dwipangga* to Solo via Yogyakarta.

## Tickets & Information

Buying tickets is usually straightforward, but ticket windows can be crowded and getting information can be frustrating. Some cities, such as Yogyakarta and Bandung, have helpful tourist information booths at the station, or the station master *(kepala stasiun)* can help. Stations display time-tables, and main stations sometimes provide a printed timetable *(jadwal)*, but an all-Java timetable is impossible to get.

For basic ekonomi trains tickets go on sale an hour before departure – just front up, buy a ticket and hope you can get a seat. The better ekonomi services can be booked up to a week in advance for an extra 1500 rp.

Bisnis and eksekutif trains can be booked weeks in advance at the appropriate ticket windows. The main stations also have a separate, air-conditioned, computerised booking office for eksekutif trains, which are much more civilised, and some English is usually spoken. Or fill in a booking slip if you know what you want. A few travel agents and hotels can buy tickets for you, for a suitable commission, but most do not.

Though it is often possible to get a ticket in any class on the day of departure, you may have to stand in long queues. Seats are hard to get on weekends and impossible in holiday periods. Always try to book at least a day in advance or a few days in advance for travel on public holidays and long weekends.

## CAR & MOTORCYCLE
## Road Rules

There appear to be no road rules in Java, but a logic does exist, based mostly on the rule of 'might is right'. Bicycles give way to motorbikes, motorbikes to cars, cars to trucks and everyone gives way to the buses, which are driven by maniacs. Pedestrians give way to everything.

## Self-Drive

Cars can be hired in Jakarta but the rates are very high. If you use the international companies like Avis and National, typically you'll pay around US$100 per day. Local companies are slightly cheaper. To hire a car you must have a valid local or international driving permit, and the age limit is usually 19, sometimes higher. It is quite easy to rent a car for self-drive in Yogyakarta, but insurance is rarely included.

While it is possible to drive yourself in Java, you need the patience of a saint and the concentration powers of a chess grand master. The main Jakarta-Bandung-Yogyakarta-Solo-Surabaya highway is no fun. Driving along this highway, apart from the odd quiet stretch with stunning scenery, you'll encounter a procession of towns, and villages and constant traffic – buses, trucks, cars, motorbikes, food carts, bicycles, pedestrians and chickens – all competing for the narrow stretch of tarmac. Defensive driving is the name of the game.

Traffic is more manageable away from the main highways, along the south coast, the far west coast and many parts of East Java. Madura has excellent roads and practically no traffic.

## Car Hire With Driver

The most common alternative to self-drive is to rent a car or minibus with driver, which can be a lot cheaper than hiring a self-drive car. The big car rental agencies prefer to rent cars with drivers. Much cheaper are the private operators, which start from as little as 80,000 rp per day with a driver. The *kjang*, an Indonesian built Toyota that is a cross between a family sedan and an off-road vehicle, is a popular model.

Renting a minibus can be a particularly good deal for a group. They are comfortable, sturdy, go-almost-anywhere vehicles and can take up to six people, with luggage, in comfort.

Travel agents in the tourist centres are good places to try for minibus rental. Go to the cheap tour operators – agents in the big hotels will charge big prices. Through the agents you have a better chance of finding a good, experienced driver who speaks some English and knows what tourists want. Failing that, ask at a tourist information centre or your hotel. There is always someone with a vehicle who is looking for work. Good places for hiring cars on this basis are the main cities and tourist destinations, particularly Yogyakarta, but also Bogor, Bandung, Pangandaran, Malang, Jakarta and Surabaya.

Car or minibus rental starts at around 80,000 rp for a day's touring in and around town, including driver but excluding petrol. For longer distances count on at least 100,000 rp. Bargaining is usually required. It is harder, but certainly possible, to find a driver for longer trips lasting a few days or even weeks. Negotiate a deal covering food and accommodation – either you provide a hotel room each night and pay a food allowance, or negotiate an allowance that covers both – figure on about 20,000 to 30,000 rp per day. It pays to see what your driver is like on a day trip before heading off on a lengthy expedition. Check out the driver for experience and language ability, and get licence and identity card details.

For shorter trips around town you can rent taxis or minibuses quite easily through car-rental companies, some travel agents and hotels in main cities. The rates vary but it's likely to be around 10,000 rp an hour for a minimum of two hours, or a flat rate for a set route. It is cheaper through private operators, but heavy bargaining is usually required.

Petrol is reasonably cheap in Indonesia; at the time of writing it was 1000 rp a litre. There are petrol stations around the larger towns, but out in the villages petrol can be hard to find. Small wayside shops sell small amounts of petrol – look for signs that read *press ban*, or crates of bottles with a sign saying *bensin*. Some of the stuff off the roadside stands is said to be of dubious quality, so it's probably best to refill whenever you see a petrol station *(pompa bensin)*.

## Motorcycle

Motorbikes are readily available for hire right across Java. In the tourist centres, agencies will rent motorbikes from around 15,000 rp per day, but just about anywhere else you'll find someone who will rent you their motorbike to make a few extra rupiah. Motorbikes are almost all between 90 and 125 cc, with 100 cc as the usual size. You really don't need anything bigger as the distances are short and the roads are rarely suitable for going very fast. Don't forget to take your motorcycle licence. It is unlikely that you'll be asked to show it in order to hire a bike, but in the rare cases that rental includes insurance, you'll need it to be able make a claim.

Java is not the place to learn how to ride – inexperienced riders would be asking for trouble. The main highways are hectic and the most common form of accident you'll see is a motorcyclist splayed across the road after having been forced off the bitumen by a truck, bus or car.

As well as all the normal hazards of motor bike riding there are narrow roads in Java, unexpected potholes and crazy drivers, buses and trucks which (through size alone) reckon they own the road. Children dart onto the road, bullocks lumber in, dogs and chickens run around in circles and vehicles travel at night without lights. Take it slowly and cautiously around curves so that you avoid hitting oncoming traffic – this includes very large and heavy buses, buffaloes, herds of stray goats and children. Keep to the back roads as much as possible, where riding can be pleasurable.

A motorbike is an ideal vehicle for getting out into the countryside and doing day trips to points of interest. A motorbike gives you enormous flexibility, allowing you to get to places that people without their own transport have to walk to, and it saves having to wait endlessly for transport.

## BICYCLE

Java's crowded highways and traffic-choked cities don't make for ideal bicycle riding, but quiet rural areas do exist. The main highways should be avoided but some of the back roads are suitable for bicycling, particularly along the south coast, Madura and parts of East Java. The large cities are no fun, if not downright dangerous, but a bicycle is an ideal way to get around the towns and villages. In some smaller cities, such as Yogyakarta and particularly Solo, bicycling is still a viable and fun form of transport.

Bicycles can be rented in the tourist centres of Java – Yogyakarta, Solo, Pangandaran – and many backpackers' hotels have bicycles for guests. They are primarily for getting around town, but mountain bikes are readily available for upcountry trips. At markets, post offices and at some tourists sights there are bicycle parking areas (usually 200 rp), where an attendant keeps an eye on your bicycle.

For serious bicycle touring, bring your own. Good quality bicycles and components can be bought in the major cities but are difficult to find elsewhere. Bicycle touring right across Java is not really an option, but it is possible to take bikes on the trains and some buses, thus allowing you to skip the more crowded and dangerous stretches.

## HITCHING

Hitching is not a part of the culture in Indonesia but if you put out your thumb someone may give you a lift. Confusion may arise as to whether payment is required or not. On the back roads where no public transport exists, hitching may be the only alternative to walking, and passing motorists or trucks are often willing to help.

Bear in mind, however, that hitching is never entirely safe in any country in the world, and we do not recommend it. Travellers who decide to hitch should understand that they are taking a small but potentially serious risk. People who do choose to hitch will be safer if they travel in pairs and let someone know where they are planning to go.

## BOAT

There are plenty of ferries and boats from Java to the other islands. Regular daily ferries run between Java and Madura, and between Java, Bali and Sumatra. A couple of Pelni services (see the Getting There & Away chapter) run direct from Jakarta to Semarang and Surabaya, but unless you are desperate to experience boat travel, the train is quicker and more convenient.

The most popular boat journey is the trip across the inland sea between Cilacap and Kalipucang on the south coast, which is really worth doing. If you're travelling between Central Java and Pangandaran in West Java the boat is an excellent alternative to taking the bus and/or train all the way.

There are daily boat services to Pulau Seribu in the Bay of Jakarta, but a trip to the small islands off the coast will usually involve chartering a fishing boat – usually a small motorised boat – and it will be dependent on the weather.

## LOCAL TRANSPORT

Most cities in Java have taxis. Taxis can be found around the big hotels, shopping centres and markets. Most are metered and drivers will use them (Bandung is an exception) – insist if they don't, or catch another taxi. They are available at the airport, train and bus terminals but normally won't use their meters from these destinations (as they may have had to wait for a long time). At most airport terminals and some train stations, taxis operate on a coupon system.

The metered rate is around 1500 to 2000 rp for the first kilometre and 750 to 900 rp for each subsequent kilometre, depending on the city you are in.

Private cars and minivans also operate where taxis don't exist, or sometimes they work in opposition to taxis. Bargaining is definitely the rule with private operators and metered taxis are a better alternative for the uninitiated.

Java has more *becaks* (trishaws) than just about anywhere in the world. They have been removed from Jakarta and are banned from the city centres in some cities, such as Bandung and Surabaya, but are found everywhere else in abundance. Unlike the version found in India, where the driver sits in front of you, or the Filipino version with the driver at the side, in Indonesia the driver sits at the rear, nosing your life ever forwards into the traffic. The becak is a cheap and delightful form of transport and each region in Java

## The Bemo

Of all the weird and wonderful forms of transport that battle for street space in Jakarta, the most revered is the bemo. A bemo is a cute little three-wheeler Daihatsu that looks like a refugee from an early Disney cartoon. It has a rounded front and square and an open back housing two bench rows crammed with passengers. Introduced in 1961 for the ASEAN games, it revolutionised urban transport in Indonesia and spread throughout the archipelago.

Bemo means 'motorised trishaw', a contraction of *becak* (trishaw) and *motor*. Though a whole host of more sophisticated minibus vehicles followed in its wake, the name bemo remains in use in some parts of Indonesia, such as Bali. In Java, though, *mikrolet*, *angkot*, or brand names such as Colt or Daihatsu are often used for minibuses.

Incredibly, the bemo is still used in Jakarta. Though the vehicle belongs in a museum, such as those at Taman Mini's Transport Museum, a few old rattle traps still ply the streets around Glodok and other areas. Though these bemos are rusting and forever breaking down, their owners keep them going with bits of wire and panel bog. Some have lost their panels altogether – spare parts come only from other cannibalised bemos that have finally given up the ghost.

carriage. The fare must be bargained for and fixed before the ride commences.

City minibuses – often called *angkot*, a contraction of *angkutan* (transport) and *kota* (taxi) – ply the cities and towns on fixed routes. Fares may vary with the distance travelled but often a standard fare of around 500 rp applies for any trip within a town, regardless of the length of the journey.

Indonesia has some weird and wonderful means of transport. The *bajaj* (pronounced 'ba-jai') is a farting, noisy three-wheeler, which is a Jakarta speciality that is rapidly disappearing. The horse-drawn *andong* can be found throughout Java. In Jakarta, bicycles with passenger seats on the back can take you around the streets.

### Ojek, Trucks & Pickups

*Ojek* are motorbike riders who take pillion passengers for a bargainable price. They are found at bus terminals and markets, or just hanging around at crossroads. They will take you around town or to villages where no other public transport exists. They can tackle roads impassable to any other vehicle, and are often the only public transport to remote rural destinations. They can also be rented by the hour (starting at around 4000 rp) for sightseeing, though this is unusual.

Where roads are rough and badly potholed, trucks and pickups are used as a form of public transport. One of the great ironies of Indonesia is that farm animals ride in buses and people ride in the backs of farm trucks! In areas where the roads are better, trucks are rare, but they can still be found in the backblocks of East Java. Needless to say, comfort is not one of their virtues.

has its own style. Personal touches include brightly painted pictures, tinkling bells or whirring metal discs strung across the under-

# Jakarta

**• pop 9.3 million**    ☎ 021

Jakarta is all Indonesia rolled into one huge urban sprawl of over nine million people. Indonesians come from all over the archipelago to seek fame and fortune, or just to eke out a living. Bataks and Minangkabau from Sumatra, Ambonese from Maluku, Dani from Irian Jaya, Minahasans from Sulawesi, Balinese, Madurese and Timorese are all united by Bahasa Indonesia and a desire to 'make it' in the capital. For it is in Jakarta that the latest styles and thoughts are formed, and the important political decisions made. Jakarta is the main centre for the economy, the place to do deals and to court government officials.

In the 1980s and 90s, Jakarta underwent a huge transformation. Once, its miserable poverty and crumbling infrastructure made it one of the hell holes of Asian travel. But the city's face was changed forever by skyscrapers, flyovers, luxury hotels and shopping centres.

The showpiece of this new Jakarta is the 'Golden Triangle' central business district bound by Jl Thamrin/Sudirman, Jl Rasuna Said and Jl Gatot Subroto. Viewed from here, Jakarta has all the appearances of a prosperous Asian boom city. Move away from the city centre and it becomes obvious that Jakarta is a big city vortex that sucks in the poor, often providing little more than the hope of hard work at low pay. It was this gulf of opportunity, this huge disparity of wealth that erupted in the Jakarta riots of 1998, an event that finally placed Jakarta on the map, and certainly on the world's television screens.

Jakarta is primarily a city of government and business not a tourist destination, but the old part of the city is not to be missed. Kota is the heart of the 17th century Dutch town of Batavia, centred around the cobbled square of Taman Fatahillah. From the fine old Dutch architecture of Kota you can wander north to the old schooner dock of

- Kota – the heart of the 17th century Dutch city of Batavia, with many examples of Dutch architecture
- Sunda Kelapa – old schooner dock, with an impressive collection of sailing ships, and more Dutch architecture
- National Museum – the finest museum in Indonesia, with an enormous collection of antiquities and exhibits on Indonesia's various ethnic groups
- Taman Mini Indonesia Indah – all-Indonesia theme park
- Dunia Fantasi – Jakarta's answer to Disneyland
- Pulau Seribu (Thousand Islands) – great beaches and resorts right on Jakarta's doorstep

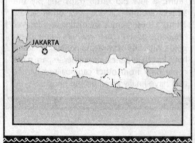

Sunda Kelapa, the most impressive reminder of the age of sailing ships to be found anywhere in the world. Taman Mini Indonesia Indah is one of Jakarta's most popular attractions. The all-Indonesia theme park provides an informative and interesting look at all the regions of Indonesia. Dunia Fantasi (Fantasy World) on the coast at Ancol is Jakarta's answer to Disneyland and a must for the kids. The city also has a few interesting museums, oversized monuments and good shopping possibilities to keep visitors amused.

Jakarta is the most expensive city in Indonesia, the most polluted and the most congested, but if you can withstand its onslaught and afford to indulge in its charms, then it can also be one of Indonesia's most exciting. For this is the 'big durian', the foul-smelling exotic fruit that some can't stomach but others can't resist.

## HISTORY

Jakarta has been the centre of colonial and independent government since the 17th century. There have been at least three towns in the area of Kota or 'Old' Jakarta, all of them centred around the present-day port of Sunda Kelapa, the earliest known settlement, at the mouth of Sungai Ciliwung.

Sunda Kelapa was a port town of the Hindu Pajajaran kingdom, the last Hindu kingdom in West Java. The Portuguese first made contact with Java here in 1522. Pajajaran, keen to stave off the growing power of the Islamic sultanates, signed a treaty with the Portuguese, allowing them to set up a trading post. By the time the Portuguese returned in 1527, Sunda Kelapa had already fallen to the army of the Banten sultanate under the command of Fatahillah.

Renamed as Jayakarta, meaning Victorious City, the town survived unmolested for almost a century as a fief of the Banten sultanate. Today, however, none of the structures of the old town remain.

At the beginning of the 17th century, both Dutch and English merchants had trading posts in Jayakarta. Late in 1618 the British, backed by the Jayakartans, besieged the Dutch United East India Company (Vereenigde Oost-Indische or VOC) fortress. Banten, angered that the vassal Jayakartans had signed a pact with the British, sent its own fleet to oversee the situation and ensure that the British would not dominate. The siege became a standoff and the VOC personnel, holding out in their fortified post, decided to rename the place 'Batavia' after the ancestors of the Dutch.

In May 1619 the Dutch, under General Jan Pieterszoon Coen, stormed the town and reduced it to ashes. A stronger shoreline fortress was built and Batavia eventually became the capital of the Dutch East Indies. Sultan Agung of Mataram twice laid siege to Batavia with massive armies in 1628 and 1629, but his poorly provisioned troops were forced to retreat on both occasions. Banten in the west continued to harry Batavia, but the city was never conquered by an Indonesian power.

Within the walls of Batavia, the prosperous Dutch built tall stuffy houses and pestilential canals on virtual swampland. By the early 18th century Batavia was suffering growing pains as Indonesians and especially Chinese were attracted by its commercial prospects. The growing Chinese population was creating unrest and violence broke out. In October 1740 a general massacre of Chinese took place and a year later Chinese inhabitants were moved to Glodok, outside the city walls.

The city was hit by severe epidemics between 1735 and 1780, and rich Batavians moved away from the port to the south. In 1808, Governor-General Daendels established Weltevreden, situated around the Koningsplein (now Merdeka Square), as the centre of government. Weltervreden became a Dutch showpiece, with grand colonial buildings, leafy residential suburbs, fashionable clubs and shopping precincts. Kebayoran Baru was the last residential area to be laid out by the Dutch after WWII.

Dutch colonial rule ended when the Japanese occupied Java and renamed Batavia 'Jakarta'. At the end of the war, on 17 August 1945, Soekarno declared Indonesia's independence from his Jakarta home, but the Dutch reoccupied the city and the republican government of the revolution retreated to Yogyakarta. When Indonesian independence was finally secured in 1949, Jakarta was made the capital of the new republic.

In 1945 Jakarta had a population of 900,000; since then there has been a continual influx of migrants from depressed

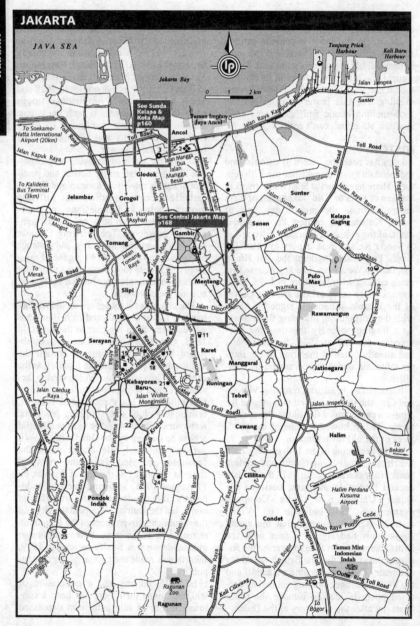

# JAKARTA

JAVA SEA

Jakarta Bay

Tanjung Priok Harbour

Kali Baru Harbour

0    1    2 km

Jalan Jampea

Sunter

See Sunda Kelapa & Kota Map p160

Taman Impian Jaya Ancol

Ancol

Jalan Raya Kampung Bandan

Toll Road

To Soekarno-Hatta International Airport (20km)

Toll Road

Jalan Kapuk Raya

Jalan Mangga Dua

Jalan Mangga Besar

Glodok

Gunung Sahari

Gajah Mada

Jalan Raya Barat Boulevard

Jalan Pegangsaan Dua

To Kalideres Bus Terminal (3km)

Jelambar

Grogol

Jalan Hasyim Asyhari

Jalan Sunter Jaya

Sunter

Kelapa Gading

Jalan Daan Mogot

Banjir Canal

Grogol Canal

Tomang

Jalan Gatah Mada

See Central Jakarta Map p168

Gambir

Jalan Perintis Kemerdekaan

Jalan Perjuangan

To Merak

Toll Road

Jalan Tomang Raya

Jalan Multi

Jalan Husni Thamrin

Menteng

Jalan Kramat Raya

Pulo Mas

Jalan Bekasi Raya

Sekretaris

Slipi

Jalan Diponegoro

Rawamangun

Pesanggrahan

Jalan Perjuangan Panjang

Toll Road

Jalan Sudirman

Karet

Jalan Pramuka

Jalan Matraman Raya

Jatinegara

Serayan

Jalan Asia Afrika

Jalan Jendral

Jalan Rangkay Kusuma Said

Manggaral

Jalan Jendral Gatot Subroto (Toll Road)

Kuningan

Tebet

Jalan Inspeksi Saluran

Kebayoran Baru

Jalan Wolter Monginsidi

Cawang

Halim

To Bekasi

Jalan Panglima Polim

Jalan Ciledug Raya

Jalan Metro Pondok Indah

Jalan Pangeran Antasari

Jalan Kemang

Kali Krukut

Jalan Raya Pasar Minggu

Cililitan

Halim Perdana Kusuma Airport

Outer Ring Toll Road

Jalan Rempoa

Jalan Cipulat Raya

Pondok Indah

Jalan Fatmawati

Cilandak

Jalan Warung Jati Barat

Condet

Jalan Raya Pondok Gede

Jalan Bogor

Taman Mini Indonesian Indah

Jalan Cipulat Raya

Ragunan Zoo

Ragunan

Jalan Bambu Raya

Kali Ciliwung

Jalan Raya Jagorawi (Toll Road)

Outer Ring Toll Road

To Bogor

| PLACES TO STAY | | 4 | Jakarta Fair Grounds | 17 | Jamz |
|---|---|---|---|---|---|
| 12 | Kempinski Hotel Plaza | 5 | Pelni Office | 18 | Sudirman CBD (Industrial Estate); Bengkel |
| 15 | Hotel Mulia Senayan | 6 | Ciputra Mall | | |
| 16 | Hilton Hotel | 7 | Tanah Abang Station | 20 | Plaza Senayan |
| 19 | Hotel Atlet Century Park | 8 | Gambir Station | 21 | Planet Hollywood |
| | | 9 | Senen Station | 22 | Blok M Mall |
| OTHER | | 10 | Pulo Gadung Bus Terminal | 23 | Pondok Indah Mall |
| 1 | Pelni Passenger Terminal | 11 | Jalan Jalan | 24 | Twilite Cafe (TC) |
| 2 | Pasar Pagi Mangga Dua (Shopping Centre) | 13 | PHPA | 25 | Lebak Bulus Bus Terminal |
| | | 14 | Taman Ria Senayan (Fun Park) | 26 | Kampung Rambutan Bus Terminal |
| 3 | Kota Station | | | | |

rural areas and newcomers continue to crowd into the urban slums.

Soekarno's image of Jakarta was of a city of grand structures to glorify the republic and make Jakarta a world centre. The 14 storey Jakarta Hotel broke the skyline, the six lane Jl Thamrin was constructed and a massive sports stadium was erected for the 1962 Asian Games. Work on Jakarta's massive mosque began, and the Merdeka Monument took root.

With Soekarno's architectural ambitions cut short in 1965 (for further information see the Facts about Java chapter), the job of sorting out the city was left to Lieutenant General Ali Sadikin, who held the post of governor of Jakarta from 1966 to 1977. Although he rehabilitated the roads and bridges, encouraged the arts, built several hospitals and a large number of new schools, he also cleared out the slums for new development projects, and tried to eliminate *becaks* and ban street pedlars. To try to stem hopeless overcrowding and poverty he started to control migration to the city.

Jakarta's astonishing growth and prosperity in the 1990s under Soeharto seemed destined to continue forever until the sudden economic collapse of 1997. With the economy in tatters, the capital became a battleground for new political aspirations. Student protests demanding Soeharto's resignation increased in intensity in the early months of 1998, but the army sent tanks onto the streets of Jakarta, determined that the riots and looting that had plagued other parts of Indonesia would not happen in Jakarta.

Then, on 12 May 1998, the army cracked down on students and opened fire with live ammunition, shooting dead four students at Trisakti University in Jakarta. The city erupted in three days of rioting as thousands took to the streets to vent their anger, or simply to loot. Over 6000 buildings were damaged or destroyed and an estimated 1200 people died, mostly those trapped in burning shopping centres. Hardest hit were the Chinese, whose businesses were looted and destroyed, and shocking tales of rape and murder emerged in the aftermath. Jakarta's Chinatown around Glodok was one of the worst hit areas.

The riots lead to the overthrow of Soeharto and the promise of a more democratic Indonesia, but students returned to the streets when the Habibie government stalled on full reform. New riots erupted on 13 November 1998 when, again, student demonstrations were met by military force and gunfire. The clashes left 12 dead, hundreds injured and Jakarta in flames.

Today Jakarta's population is over nine million and, including the adjoining districts in West Java, greater Jakarta, known as JaboJabotabek (a contraction of Jakarta, Bogor, Tangerang and Bekasi), has a population of 17.5 million, making it one of the world's largest cities. While the wealth of the boom times can still be seen, the city is now littered with idle cranes, uncompleted flyovers sprouting grass and deserted building sites awaiting new financing. The downturn in the economy is not likely to slow Jakarta's growth, however. If there is anywhere in Indonesia that money can still be made, it is Jakarta. Despite the high cost of living and widespread poverty, a roadside *parkir* directing traffic and parking cars can earn a fortune compared to a subsistence existence in a village.

## ORIENTATION

Jakarta sprawls over 25km from the docks to the suburbs of South Jakarta, covering 661 sq km in all. The city centre fans out from around Merdeka Square, which contains the central landmark of Soekarno's towering gold-tipped National Monument (MONAS). Merdeka Square itself is just a barren, deserted field, a product of grand urban planning gone wrong. Jakarta's main problem is that it doesn't really have a centre that can be explored on foot, but a number of centres, all separated by vast traffic jams and heat.

For most visitors, Jakarta revolves around the modern part of the city to the south of the monument. Jl Thamrin, running from the south-west corner of Merdeka Square down to the Welcome Monument roundabout, is the main thoroughfare, containing many of the big hotels and a couple of major shopping centres – the Sarinah department store and the Plaza Indonesia.

Just east of Jl Thamrin and south of the National Monument is Jl Jaksa, the main centre for cheap hotels and restaurants.

North of the National Monument, the old city of Jakarta has the city's main tourist attractions. These include the Chinatown area of Glodok, the old Dutch area of Kota and the schooner harbour of Sunda Kelapa. The modern harbour, Tanjung Priok, is several kilometres along the coast to the east past the Taman Impian Jaya Ancol recreation park.

The main train station, Gambir, is just to the east of the National Monument. The intercity bus terminals – Kalideres in the west, Kampung Rambutan in the south and Pulo Gadung in the east – are on the outskirts of Jakarta.

Jl Thamrin, heading south, becomes Jl Jenderal Sudirman, home to more hotels, large banks and office blocks. Farther south are the affluent suburban areas of Kebayoran Baru, Pondok Indah and Kemang, with their own centres and busy shopping districts, such as Blok M in Kebayoran Baru.

## INFORMATION
### Tourist Offices

The Jakarta Tourist Information Office (☎ 3142067) is opposite the Sarinah department store in the Jakarta Theatre building on Jl Thamrin. It can answer most queries and has a good giveaway map of Jakarta and a number of excellent leaflets and publications. It is open Monday to Friday from 9 am to 5 pm, Saturday until noon. It also has a desk at the airport.

The headquarters of the Indonesia Tourist Promotion Organisation is the Directorate-General of Tourism (☎ 3838221) at Jl Merdeka Barat 16-19. This is not the best place to have specific travel queries answered, but it has some useful publications, including the *Calendar of Events* and the *Indonesia Tourist Map*, and you might be able to squeeze a copy of the useful *Indonesia Travel Planner* out of the staff. The office is open government office hours only.

### Money

Jakarta is crawling with banks offering the best exchange rates in Indonesia, though it pays to shop around. The banks offer better rates than moneychangers.

Most banks are open Monday to Friday from 8 am to 4 pm, and Saturday until 11 am. Handy banks to Jl Jaksa are the Lippobank and Bank Duta on Jl Kebon Sirih, both with ATMs for MasterCard withdrawals. Jl Thamrin has plenty of banks, such as the Bank Internasional Indonesia (BII), where rates are usually very good and its ATMs offer cash advances on Visa and MasterCard. The Plaza Indonesia has a selection of banks including the BII bank in the basement level that has an ATM and is open 10 am to 6 pm weekdays and 10 am to 3 pm Saturday and Sunday. The BDNI bank on the 1st level is open from 10 am to 9 pm, but rates are not as good. Many of the big hotels on Jl Thamrin also have bank branches that offer good exchange rates.

Moneychangers, such as the one in Sarinah department store, generally have much poorer rates. One exception is PT Metro Jala Masino in the carpark section of the Jakarta Theatre building, near the Visitor Information Centre.

## Post
The main post office and poste restante is in the octagonal building behind Jl Pos, to the north-east of Monas. It's a good half-hour walk from the city centre, or you can take a No 12 bus from Jl Thamrin. Poste restante at counter 53 is open from 8 am to 6 pm daily and, for basic postal services, a few windows are open until 10 pm daily.

## Telephone
*Wartels* are found all around the city and are usually open from around 7 am until midnight, sometimes 24 hours. As a rule, wartels don't offer a collect-call service. Convenient wartels for those staying around Jl Jaksa are the Duta Perdana Raya Wartel (☎ 3143310, fax 3190460), Jl Jaksa 15a, and the Sapta Persona Wartel, Jl Kebon Sirih Dalam 41, near Borneo Hostel.

## Fax
Faxes can be sent from most wartels and from all major hotels.

## Email & Internet Access
The Warung Pos Internet at the central post office has a bank of terminals at 2000 rp for 15 minutes, 9500 rp per hour. It is open from 8 am to 9 pm weekdays, until 7 pm Saturday and 4 pm Sunday.

The Duta Perana Raya wartel, Jl Jaksa 15a, also has a couple of terminals costing 10,000 rp per hour. Click!, Jl Jaksa 29, is an internet cafe offering access at 8000 rp for 10 minutes, 15,000 rp per half hour and 22,000 rp per hour.

Almost all hotel business centres offer internet connection at high rates.

## Travel Agencies
For international flights the travel agencies on Jl Jaksa are convenient places to start looking: try Robertu Kencana Travel (☎314 2926) at No 20B.

Domestic air tickets usually cost the same at a travel agent as at the airline, but discounts are sometimes available. Raptim Tours & Travel (☎ 335585), Jl Cut Mutiah 8, just to the east of Jl Jaksa, is good for discount ticketing, tours and discounted hotels. Smailing Tour (☎ 3800022), Jl Majapahit 28, past the National Museum on the way to Kota, is one of Jakarta's biggest travel agents, and it has another office in the Skyline Building (☎ 331994), Jl Thamrin 9, just next to the tourist office.

## Bookshops
Times Bookshop in the Plaza Indonesia on Jl Thamrin and also in the Pondok Indah Mall, has one of the best stocks of English-language books and a good range of travel books.

Books Kinokuniya, upstairs at Level 2B of the Sogo department store in the Plaza Indonesia, is slightly better stocked, and also has books in Japanese.

Sarinah department store on Jl Thamrin has a good travel book and map section. Gramedia and Gunung Agung are the two big Indonesian chains with shops all over town.

## Maps
By far the best reference is the *Jakarta Street Atlas* published by Falk but it can be difficult to find. Numerous, detailed single-sheet maps of the city can be found in bookshops. Two of the best produced by international companies are the Periplus map and the Nelles map. They are available overseas but locally produced maps are also quite good and much cheaper: Indo Buwana and Indo Prima Sarana maps are good and have an attached street name index.

Many free maps are available and quite adequate for short-term visitors. Pick up a copy of the *Jakarta City Map* from the Visitor Information Centre or the large hotels.

## Newspapers

The daily English-language *Jakarta Post* (1800 rp from street vendors) gives a useful rundown of what's on, temporary exhibitions and cinema programs. The *Indonesian Observer* has more extensive business coverage and world news but its coverage of local events and politics are a long way behind that of the *Jakarta Post*.

## Film & Photography

Jl Agus Salim, between Jl Jaksa and Jl Thamrin, has photographic shops for film, developing and equipment, but 'tourist prices' may apply and bargaining might be necessary. Otherwise, Jakarta has plenty of places for film developing. Fuji is the most common brand of film and The Plaza Indonesia has a Fuji shop at No 139, which is good for supplies and developing.

## Libraries & Useful Organisations

The various foreign cultural centres have libraries and/or have regular exhibits, films and lectures:

American Cultural Centre
   (☎ 5262834) Wisma Metropolitan II, Jl Jenderal Sudirman
Australian Cultural Centre
   (☎ 5227093) Australian Embassy, Jl Rasuna Said, Kav C15-16
British Council
   (☎ 5206222) Widjoyo Centre, Jl Jenderal Sudirman 71
Centre Culture Français
   (☎ 3908585) Jl Salemba Raya 25
Erasmus Huis
   (☎ 5252321) Jl Rasuna Said, Kav S-3, beside the Dutch Embassy; has a Dutch library and a regular program of cultural events
Goethe Institut
   (☎ 8581139) Jl Mataram Raya 23
The Indonesian/American Cultural Center (Perhimpunan Persahabatan Indonesia Amerika) (☎ 8583241) Jl Pramuka, Kav 30; has exhibits, films and lectures related to Indonesia, and a library

## Language Courses

A few centres offer Bahasa Indonesia courses, but these are mostly long-term courses designed for expatriates. Short intensive courses can be arranged, for a price. Private courses are expensive. Schools with a good reputation are the Indonesian Australia Language Foundation (☎ 521 3350), Jl Rasuna Said Kav C6, and Business Communications Services (☎ 794 1488), Jl Buncit Raya 21B, Mampang. Some embassies arrange courses on a regular basis, or at least have information on teachers and language institutes.

## Medical Services

In South Jakarta, Rumah Sakit Pondok Indah (☎ 7500157), Jl Metro Duta Kav UE, is a perfectly modern hospital that rivals the best hospitals in the west, although it charges modern prices. In central Jakarta (near Jl Jaksa) are the Rumah Sakit Cipto Mangunkusumo (☎ 330808), Jl Diponegoro 71, a government public hospital (reasonably priced with good emergency facilities, but very crowded), and St Carolus Hospital (☎ 3904441), Jl Salemba Raya 41, a private Catholic hospital charging mid-range prices.

Jakarta also has well-equipped, modern medical clinics that provide a full range of services, including specialists, emergency and dental care. AEA International Clinic/SOS Medika (☎ 7505980), Jl Puri Sakti 10, Cipete, is linked to the insurance schemes widely used by expatriates and is in the southern suburbs. Also popular is Medical Scheme (☎ 5201034, 5255367) in the Setiabudi Building 2, Jl Rasuna Said, Kuningan.

## Dangers & Annoyances

For a city with such a huge population and obvious social problems, Jakarta is surprisingly safe. That said, Jakarta is the most crime-prone city in Indonesia and violent crime, almost unheard of in the rest of the country, is reported and on the increase. Take the usual precautions – avoid disreputable areas and don't walk the streets alone at night. Muggings by taxi drivers have been reported; people alone and drunk in the early hours of the morning seem to be most at risk. The overwhelming majority of taxis are safe, however, and you are better off taking a taxi than walking the streets alone at night.

Jakarta's buses and trains tend to be hopelessly crowded, particularly during rush hours. Its pickpockets are notoriously adept and they're great bag slashers too. So take care.

## OLD BATAVIA (KOTA)

The old town of Batavia, known as Kota today, is the oldest and finest reminder of the Dutch presence in Indonesia. At one time it contained Coen's massive shoreline fortress, the Kasteel, and was surrounded by a sturdy defensive wall and a moat. In the early 19th century Governor-General Daendels did a good job of demolishing much of the unhealthy city but there is still a Dutch flavour to this old part of the town. A few of Batavia's old buildings remain in active use, although others were restored during the 1970s and have become museums.

The centre of old Batavia is the cobblestone square known as **Taman Fatahillah**. A block west is the **Kali Besar**, the great canal along Sungai (river) Ciliwung. This was once the high-class residential area of Batavia, and on the west bank overlooking the canal are the last of the big private homes dating from the early 18th century. The **Toko Merah**, or Red Shop, now occupied by the Dharma Niaga company, was formerly the home of Governor-General van Imhoff. At the north end of the Kali Besar is a small 17th century Dutch drawbridge, the last in the city, called **Chicken Market Bridge**.

To reach Taman Fatahillah, from Jl Thamrin take P-01 or P-10 air-con bus or P11 non-air-con bus. Alternatively you can take a city train from Gongandia, near Jl Jaksa, to Kota station and walk. A taxi will cost around 5000 rp from Jl Thamrin.

## Jakarta History Museum

On the south side of Taman Fatahillah, the museum is housed in the old town hall of Batavia, one of the most solid reminders of Dutch rule to be found in Indonesia. This large bell-towered hall, built in 1627 and added to between 1707 and 1710, served the city administration. It was also used by the

city law courts and its dungeons were the main prison compound of Batavia. In 1830 the Javanese hero Prince Diponegoro was imprisoned here for a time on his way into exile in Ujung Pandang (Sulawesi).

Today, the museum contains lots of heavy, carved furniture and other memorabilia from the Dutch period. Among the more interesting exhibits is a series of gloomy portraits of all the Dutch governors-general and early pictures of Batavia.

In the courtyard at the back of the building is a strange memorial stone to one Pieter Erbervelt, who was put to death in 1722 for allegedly conspiring to massacre the Dutch inhabitants of Batavia.

Admission to the museum is 1000 rp. It opens every day, except Monday, from 9 am to 3 pm (on Friday until 2.30 pm and Saturday until 12.30 pm).

## Wayang Museum

Also on Taman Fatahillah, this museum has one of the best collections of wayang puppets in Java and includes puppets not only from Indonesia but also from China, Malaysia, India and Cambodia.

Formerly the Museum of Old Batavia, the building itself was constructed in 1912 on the site of the Dutch Church of Batavia, which was demolished by Daendels in 1808. In the downstairs courtyard there are memorials to the Dutch governor generals once buried here. These include Jan Pieterszoon Coen, founder of Batavia, who died of cholera in 1629 during the siege by Mataram, and Anthony van Diemen, a governor of the VOC.

Admission and opening hours are the same as the Jakarta History Museum.

## Balai Seni Rupa (Fine Arts Museum)

Built between 1866 and 1870, the Palace of Justice building is now a museum housing a collection of contemporary Indonesian paintings, with works by Indonesia's most prominent painters, including Raden Saleh, Affandi and Ida Bagus Made. Part of the building is also a ceramics museum, with Chinese ceramics and Majapahit terracottas.

The museum is closed on Monday and admission and opening hours are as per the Jakarta History Musuem.

## Cannon Si Jagur

This huge bronze cannon on Taman Fatahillah is adorned with a Latin inscription, *'Ex me ipsa renata sum'*, which means 'Out of myself I was reborn'. The cannon tapers at one end into a large clenched fist, with the thumb protruding between the index and middle fingers. This suggestive fist is a sexual symbol in Indonesia and childless women offer flowers and sit astride the cannon in the hope of gaining children. Si Jagur is a Portuguese cannon brought to Batavia as a trophy of war after the fall of Melaka in 1641.

## Gereja Sion

On Jl Pangeran Jayakarta, near Kota train station, this church dates from 1695 and is the oldest remaining church in Jakarta. Also known as Gereja Portugis or Portuguese Church, it was built just outside the old city walls for the so-called 'black Portuguese' – the Eurasians and natives captured from Portuguese trading ports in India and Malaya and brought to Batavia as slaves. Most of these people were Catholics, but they were given their freedom on the condition that they joined the Dutch Reformed Church, and the converts became known as the Mardijkers, or Liberated Ones.

The exterior of the church is very plain, but inside there are copper chandeliers, the original organ and a Baroque pulpit. Although in the year 1790 alone, more than 2000 people were buried in the graveyard here, very few tombs remain. One of the most interesting is the ornate bronze tombstone of Governor-General Zwaardecroon, who died in 1728 and, as was his wish, was buried among the 'ordinary' folk.

## SUNDA KELAPA

Just a 10 minute walk north of Taman Fatahillah, the old port of Sunda Kelapa has more sailing ships, the magnificent Macassar schooners called *pinisi*, than you ever thought existed. This is one of the finest sights in Jakarta. These brightly painted ships are still an important means of transporting goods to and from the outer islands. Most of them come from Kalimantan, spending up to a week in port unloading

### SUNDA KELAPA & KOTA

### SUNDA KELAPA & KOTA

1  Phinisi Cafe
2  Luar Batang Mosque
3  Museum Bahari
4  Watchtower
5  VOC Shipyards
6  Chicken Market Bridge
7  Omni Batavia Hotel
8  Toko Merah
9  Wayang Museum
10  Caf, Batavia
11  Cannon Si Jagur
12  Balai Seni Rupa
13  Jakarta History Museum
14  Gereja Sion

Youthful plea for reform in Indonesia.

ANDREW BROWNBILL

Waiters at Cafe Batavia, Jakarta.

BERNARD NAPFTHINE

Children in a kampung near Jalan Jaksa, Jakarta.

GLENN BEANLAND

Bajaj – motorised three-wheeler taxi, Jakarta.

BERNARD NAPFTHINE

Javanese woman, Mt Bromo, East Java.

ANDREW BROWNBILL

The Bird Market – cheep, eh?

Don't drink the water, but you can have fun at local food stalls.

Shop front, Glodok, Jakarta.

Market produce, Jakarta.

Fruit market, Glodok, Jakarta.

timber and then reloading cement and other supplies for the return journey.

Entry to the dock costs 250 rp. The guides that hang around can provide some interesting insights and spin a few yarns for a bargainable price, and you can also take a row boat around the schooners and across to the Pasar Ikan for around 5000 to 6000 rp.

## Museum Bahari (Maritime Museum)

Near the entrance to Sunda Kelapa, an old VOC warehouse, built in 1645, has been turned into a maritime museum. It exhibits craft from around Indonesia and has an interesting collection of old photographs recreating the voyage to Jakarta from Europe via Aden, Ceylon and Singapore. The building itself is worth a visit and the sentry posts outside are part of the old city wall.

Admission is 1000 rp (children 300 rp), and the Maritime Museum has the same opening hours as the Jakarta History Museum.

Just before the entrance to the museum is the old **watchtower** back near the bridge. It was built in 1839 so traffic could be sighted and directed to the port. There are good views over the harbour but opening hours are haphazard – ask for the caretaker if the watchtower is closed. Admission is 1000 rp.

Farther along the same street from the museum is the early-morning fish market, **Pasar Ikan**. Around dawn, when the day's catch is sold, it is an intense, colourful scene of busy crowds. Later in the day it sells household items and a growing collection of souvenirs.

## GLODOK

After the Chinese massacre of 1740, the Dutch decided there would be no repetition and prohibited all Chinese from residing within the town walls, or even from being there after sundown. In 1741 a tract of land just to the south-west of Batavia was allocated as Chinese quarters. The area became Glodok, Jakarta's Chinatown and the city's flourishing commercial centre.

Some two and half centuries later, in a repetition of history, the Chinese again were subjected to senseless violence. The Jakarta riots of May and November 1998 destroyed much of the area as rioters went on the rampage, pillaging and looting shops, and then burning the buildings. It will be years before those scars are erased and the burnt buildings replaced.

Glodok is bounded to the east by Jl Gajah Mada, a busy commercial thoroughfare, but if you walk in from Jl Pancoran, old Glodok still consists of winding lanes, narrow crooked houses with balconies, slanting red-tiled roofs and tiny obscure shops. Just south of Jl Pancoran, the main focus is the Chinese **Dharma Jaya Temple**, built in 1650.

Businesses carry on as best they can, but many have moved and Glodok's chief interest now lies in a perverse look at the evidence of the Jakarta riots.

## NATIONAL MUSEUM

On the west side of Merdeka Square, the National Museum, built in 1862, is the best museum in Indonesia and one of the best in South-East Asia. Its collection includes a huge ethnic map of Indonesia and an equally big relief map on which you can pick out all those volcanoes you have climbed.

The museum has an enormous collection of cultural objects of the various ethnic groups – costumes, musical instruments, model houses and so on – and numerous fine bronzes from the Hindu-Javanese period, as well as many interesting stone pieces salvaged from Central Javanese and other temples. There's also a superb display of Chinese ceramics dating back to the Han dynasty (300 BC to 220 AD), which was almost entirely amassed in Indonesia.

One of the best places to start a tour of the museum is the Treasure Room, upstairs from the entrance. The gold exhibits are interesting, but if you have walked to the museum the real attraction is the air-con.

Just outside the museum is a bronze elephant which was presented by the King of Thailand in 1871; thus the museum building is popularly known as the Gedung Gajah or Elephant House.

The museum is open daily, except Monday, from 8.30 am to 2.30 pm (on Friday to

## Jakarta Statues

Inspired tastelessness in the Russian 'heroes of socialism' style best describes the plentiful supply of statues that Soekarno left to Jakarta. Many have acquired descriptive nicknames. At the end of Jalan Jenderal Sudirman in Kebayoran Baru, the Semangat Pemuda (Spirit of Youth) statue is a suitably muscular young man holding a flaming dish above his head. He is more commonly known as the 'Pizza Man'.

On Jalan Thamrin, the Welcome Monument 'Hansel and Gretel' was built by Soekarno as a symbol of Indonesian friendliness for the 1962 Asian Games held in Jakarta. Now that the airport has moved, most visitors' first view of the statue is from behind, so it is really the Selamat Jalan (Goodbye), rather than Selamat Datang (Welcome) Monument.

The propaganda element reaches its peak in the Free Irian Monument at Banteng Square near the Borobudur Inter-Continental Hotel. Here, another muscle-bound gent breaks the chains around his wrists. An almost identical statue can be found a few thousand kilometres away in Dili where, surprise, surprise, the statue is the Free East Timor monument.

The 'farmer's monument', just south of Gambir train station on the Jalan Menteng Raya roundabout, is another heart-rending bronze showing a mother offering rice to her returning hero son after the battle for independence. On the southern side of Merdeka Square, not far from MONAS, is a more classical statue of the 19th century freedom fighter, Prince Diponegoro, astride his horse.

Not all of Jakarta's statues are independence inspired. The Arjuna Statue, at the south-western corner of Merdeka Square, is based on the exploits of Arjuna and Krishna from the Hindu epic, the *Mahabharata*. In Pancoran, the Dirgantara statue, though in the 'heroes of socialism' style, is a statue of Hanuman, the monkey god from the *Ramayana* epic. This muscular human figure with the head of a monkey is mounted on a towering pedestal shaped like a seven, hence the '7-Up Man' nickname.

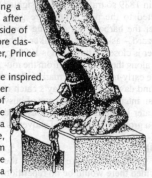
**Chain reaction: Free Irian monument, Lapangan Banteng, Jakarta**

11 am and Saturday to 1.30 pm). Entry costs 750 rp. Conducted tours, in a number of languages, are organised by the Indonesian Heritage Society (☎ 360551 ext 22).

## OTHER MUSEUMS

North-west of the National Museum is the **Taman Prasasti Museum**, or Park of Inscription, on Jl Tanah Abang. This was once the Kebon Jahe Cemetery and some important figures of the colonial era are buried here, including Olivia Raffles (wife of the British Governor-General of Singapore, Sir Stamford Raffles) who died in 1814. The cemetery is open from 9 am to 3 pm Tuesday to Thursday and Sunday, and also until 2.30 pm on Friday and until 12.30 pm on Saturday.

The **Textile Museum** is in a Dutch colonial house on Jl Satsuit Tubun 4, near the Tanah Abang train station. It is open daily (except Monday) from 9 am until 3 pm Tuesday to Thursday and Sunday, until 2.30 pm Friday and 12.30 pm Saturday. Admission is 1000 rp. The building is certainly worth a look, but the Museum Purna Bhakti Pertiwi at Taman Mini has a much better permanent exhibition of Indonesian textiles.

In Menteng, the **Adam Malik Museum**, Jl Diponegoro 29, was the home of the former vice-president and foreign minister. It's now a museum crammed with his private collection of Indonesian wood carvings, sculpture and textiles, a huge display of Chinese ceramics and even Russian icons from when he was ambassador to Moscow. You can wander around the house, a Dutch villa in the old-money suburb of Menteng, not far from Jl Thamrin, and poke into the man's bedroom and even his bathroom, which remain much as he left them in 1984. This excellent museum is open from 9 am to 3 pm every day except Monday.

## NATIONAL MONUMENT (MONAS)

This 132m-high column towering over Merdeka Square is both Jakarta's principal landmark and the most famous architectural extravagance of Soekarno. Commenced in 1961, the monument was not completed until 1975, when it was officially opened by Soeharto. This phallic symbol topped by a glittering flame symbolises the nation's independence and strength (and, some would argue, Soekarno's virility). The National Monument is constructed 'entirely of Italian marbles', according to a tourist brochure, and the flame is gilded with 35kg of gold leaf.

Within the base of the National Monument, the **National History Museum** tells the history of Indonesia's independence struggle in 48 dramatic dioramas. The numerous uprisings against the Dutch are overstated but interesting, Soekarno is barely mentioned and the events surrounding the 1965 coup are a whitewash.

The highlight of a visit is to take the lift to the top, for dramatic, though rarely clear, views of Jakarta. Avoid Sunday and holidays when the queues for the lift are long.

MONAS is open weekdays daily from 9 am to 5 pm. Admission is 600 rp to the museum in the base, or 3100 rp if you wish to include the ride to the top of the monument.

## LAPANGAN BANTENG

Just east of Merdeka Square in front of the Borobudur Inter-Continental Hotel, Lapangan Banteng Square (formerly the Weltevreden) was laid out by the Dutch in the 19th century and the area has some of Jakarta's best colonial architecture.

The **Catholic cathedral**, with its twin spires, was built in 1901 to replace an earlier church. Facing the cathedral is Jakarta's principal place of Muslim worship. The modernistic **Istiqlal mosque**, a Soekarno construction, is reputedly the largest in South-East Asia.

To the east of Lapangan Banteng is the **Mahkamah Agung**, the Supreme Court, built in 1848, and next door is the **Ministry of Finance** building, formerly the Witte Huis (White House). This grand government complex was built by Daendels in 1809 as the administration centre for the Dutch government.

To the south-west, on Jl Pejambon, is the **Gedung Pancasila**, which is an imposing neoclassical building that was built in 1830 as the Dutch army commander's residence. It later became the meeting hall of the Volksraad (People's Council), but is best known as the place where Soekarno made his famous Pancasila speech in 1945, laying the foundation for Indonesia's constitution. Just west along Jl Pejambon from Gedung Pancasila is the **Emanuel Church**, another classic, pillared building dating from 1893.

## TAMAN MINI INDONESIA INDAH

In the south-east of the city, near Kampung Rambutan, Taman Mini is another of those 'whole country in one park' collections, which are popular in Asia. The idea for the park was conceived by Madame Tien Soeharto, and in 1971 the families inhabiting the land were cleared out to make way for the project (then estimated to cost the awesome total of US$26 million) and the park was duly opened in 1975.

This 100 hectare park has 27 full-scale traditional houses from the 27 provinces of Indonesia, with displays of regional handicrafts and clothing and a large 'lagoon' where you can row around the islands of the archipelago or take a cable car across for a bird's eye view. There are also museums, theatres, restaurants, an orchid garden and a bird park with a huge walk-in aviary. There's even a mini Borobudur. The park is quite good value and Indonesians will tell you that if you see this there's no need to go anywhere else in the country!

Other attractions include Keong Mas (Golden Snail) Theatre with its huge Imax screen. Admission is 4000 rp and showings are every couple of hours.

You can walk, or drive your own car, around Taman Mini. Free shuttle buses go regularly, or take the monorail (3000 rp) or cable car (1000 rp) that goes from one end to the other. Bicycles can be hired for 1000 rp per half hour. Free cultural performances are staged in selected regional houses, usually at around 10 am and sometimes in the afternoons. Sunday is the big day for cultural events, but shows are also held during the week. Check the Taman Mini monthly program available from the Visitors Information Centre or call ☎ 840 9237.

Taman Mini is open from 8 am to 5 pm daily, the houses and Museum Indonesia are open from 9 am to 4 pm. Admission is 2500 rp (children 1500 rp).

Taman Mini is about 18km from the city centre; allow about 1½ hours to get out there and at least three hours to look around.

Take any bus to Kampung Rambutan terminal (air-con, patas bus Nos 9, 10 and 11 run from Jl Thamrin) and then a T15 metro-mini to the park entrance. A taxi is much quicker and will cost around 18,000 rp from central Jakarta, plus another 4000 rp for the toll roads.

## TAMAN IMPIAN JAYA ANCOL

Along the bay front between Kota and Tanjung Priok, the people's 'Dreamland,' is built on land reclaimed in 1962. This huge, landscaped recreation park, providing non-stop entertainment, has hotels, nightclubs, theatres and a variety of sporting facilities.

Taman Impian Jaya Ancol's prime attractions include the **Pasar Seni** (Art Market), which has sidewalk cafes, a host of craft shops, art exhibitions and live music on Friday and Saturday nights. The **Seaworld** aquarium, with its walk-through tunnel, a variety of pools and big array of sealife is worth seeing. Ancol also has the **Gelanggang Samudra**, another oceanarium with a boatride and dolphin shows, and the impressive **Gelanggang Renang** swimming pool complex, including a wave pool and slide pool. **Ancol Beach**, so close to the city, is not the greatest place for a swim but you can take a boat from the marina here for day trips to some of Jakarta's Pulau Seribu islands.

The big drawcard at Ancol is **Dunia Fantasi** (Fantasy Land), a fun park that must have raised eyebrows at the Disney legal department. Resemblances to Disneyland start at the 'main street' entrance, and the Puppet Castle is a straight 'it's a small world' replica. Dunia Fantasi is actually very well done and great for kids, with a host of fun rides. It is open from 11 am to 6 pm, Monday to Thursday, 2 to 9 pm Friday and from 10 am to 9 pm on the weekends. Entry costs 21,000 rp on weekdays, 25,000 rp on weekends (not including entry to Ancol).

Basic admission to Ancol is 2500 rp on weekdays and 3000 rp on weekends. The park is open 24 hours but all the attractions have their own opening hours and cost extra, except for the Pasar Seni, which is free. Student discounts are offered. For more information, call ☎ 681511. The park can be very crowded on weekends, but on weekdays it's fairly quiet and a great place to escape from the hassles of the city.

Take a bus or city train to Kota train station, then a No 64 or 65 bus or an M15 mikrolet. A taxi will cost around 10,000 rp from Jl Thamrin.

## TAMAN ISMAIL MARZUKI
On Jl Cikini Raya, not far from Jl Jaksa, the Taman Ismail Marzuki (TIM, ☎ 3154087) is Jakarta's cultural showcase. There is a performance almost every night and here you might see anything from Balinese dancing to poetry readings, gamelan concerts to a New Zealand film festival. The TIM monthly program is available from the tourist office, the TIM office and major hotels, and events are also listed in the *Jakarta Post*.

Jakarta's **planetarium** (☎ 337530) is also here, but shows are generally given in Indonesian. Phone for information about shows in English. The whole complex is open from morning until midnight and there are good outdoor cafes. The No 34 bus from Jl Thamrin stops nearby.

## RAGUNAN ZOO
Jakarta's Ragunan Zoo is about 10km south of the city centre in the Pasar Minggu area. Apart from the usual exotica, this large zoo has a good collection of Indonesian wildlife including komodo dragons and orang-utans. It's not San Diego or even Singapore, but this is by far the best zoo in Indonesia and, though some of the enclosures are depressingly small, for the most part Ragunan is spacious. You can spend a couple of hours wandering around the extensive grounds, which have some remaining stands of bamboo and rainforest flora and a landscaped lake. It's open 7.30 am to 6 pm daily. Admission is 1000 rp, half-price for children. From Jl Thamrin take bus No 19.

## OTHER ATTRACTIONS
Indonesia's independence was proclaimed at **Gedung Perintis Kemerdekaan**, Jl Proklamasi 56 in Menteng, on the site of the former home of Soekarno. A monument to President Soekarno and Vice President Hatta marks the spot.

The **Pasar Burung**, on Jl Pramuka in Jatinegara, is Jakarta's market for captive birds from all over Indonesia.

**Taman Ria Senayan**, near the Olympic Stadium in Senayan, at the corner of Jl Gatot Subroto and Jl Gerbang Pemuda, is a family recreation park with fairground rides. This new complex, built around an attractively landscaped laguna (lagoon), is quite impressive – especially the restaurant complexes, which have an excellent range of dining options and bars (one of the best concentrations of restaurants in Jakarta).

Opening hours are Monday to Friday from 3 to 10 pm, weekends from 10 am to 10 pm, but access to the restaurants is separate and they are open for longer hours. Entry costs 4000 rp (3000 rp for children) or a 15,000 rp ticket includes entry and most of the rides.

## SWIMMING
The swimming pools at Ancol are great, or some hotels let nonguests use the facilities. The Hotel Indonesia has a large pool costing 12,500 rp for nonguests (17,500 rp on weekends).

Orang-utans are found in Rangunan Zoo.

**JAKARTA**

## ORGANISED TOURS

Numerous travel agents offer daily tours of Jakarta, but they tend to be expensive. Bookings can be made through the tourist office and major hotels. Boca Pirento, Panorama and Buana are the main operators. All tour buses pick up from the major hotels, and tour prices and sights are very similar. A four hour morning city tour, for example, costs US$20, and includes the National Museum, National Monument, Sunda Kelapa and Kota.

There are also a variety of tours to nearby towns in West Java, which basically go to Bogor, the Puncak Pass and Tangkuban Prahu volcano near Bandung. An eight hour tour to the Bogor botanic gardens and zoological museum costs US$35; to the Puncak Pass costs US$40.

## SPECIAL EVENTS

The Jakarta Anniversary on 22 June celebrates the establishment of the city by Gunungjati back in 1527 with fireworks and the Jakarta Fair. The latter event is held at the Jakarta Fair Grounds, north-east of the city centre in Kemayoran, from late June until mid-July.

The Jl Jaksa Street Fair features Betawi dance, theatre and music, as well as popular modern performances. Street stalls sell food and souvenirs, and art and photography exhibits are also staged. It is held for one week in August.

Indonesia's independence day is 17 August and the parades in Jakarta are the biggest in the country.

## PLACES TO STAY

Jakarta is the most expensive city in Indonesia for hotels, but in US$ terms, Jakarta has to be one of the world's cheapest cities. The economic meltdown and a drop in tourism has seen big discounts available, especially at mid-range and top-end hotels.

### Places to Stay – Budget

**Jalan Jaksa Area** Jl Jaksa is the main budget accommodation area with a strip of cheap hotels and restaurants, conveniently central near Jakarta's main drag, Jl Thamrin,

and only a 10 to 15 minute walk from Gambir train station.

*Wisma Delima* (☎ 3923850, Jl Jaksa 5) was the original guesthouse and used to be hopelessly crowded and totally chaotic. Now it is quieter but still very hospitable and well run, even though it is now a little down at heel. Dorm beds are 9000 rp (1000 rp less for HI/Hostelling International members and singles/doubles with shared mandi cost 15,000/20,000 rp. Food and cold drinks are available, and the guesthouse has good travel information.

Across the road, the *Norbek Hostel* (☎ 330392, Jl Jaksa 14) is a dark rabbit warren that has a large variety of plywood-walled rooms costing from 15,000 to 40,000 rp with attached bathroom.

Nearby is the *Jusran Hostel* (☎ 3140373, Jl Kebon Sirih Barat VI No 9). Cramped, plywood rooms for 15,000/20,000 rp may be uninspiring, but this is a cosy, quiet, friendly place to stay.

*Nick's Corner Hostel* (☎ 3141988) at No 16 is a more substantial, air-conditioned hostel, but standards have slipped. A bed costs 10,000 rp in cramped dorms or dark, depressing rooms downstairs cost 25,000 to 37,000 rp. Upstairs, air-con rooms with bathroom for 47,000 rp and 65,000 rp are much brighter, but need a good scrub.

*Djody Hotel* (☎ 3151404, Jl Jaksa 35) is another old standby that has lost its shine. It has a pleasant cafe but rooms, while more substantial than the hostels, are dreary and overpriced at 15,500/27,500 rp and up to 55,000 rp with bathroom and air-con. The *Djody Hostel* a few doors up at No 27 is an even drearier offshoot. The rooms are none-too-clean, it's noisy when it fills up and the showers run a murky brown. Singles/doubles/triples with shared bathroom cost 16,000/22,400/35,000 rp.

*Hotel Tator* (☎ 323940, Jl Jaksa 37) is one of the few budget places somewhere between bare basics and mid-range. It has a good little cafe and other touches set it apart, but some rooms are dark and musty, so check a few out. They have showers and

## Jakarta's Kampungs

Jakarta's kampungs, the crowded city 'villages' that are home to millions of Jakarta's residents, have seen major improvements. Over the last 20 years basic amenities have been provided to many of the kampungs, and the appalling conditions that shocked visitors in the '60s and '70s have been greatly alleviated. Though they are poor neighbourhoods, most kampungs are not the shanty-town slums that visitors associate with the term, but are collections of simple dwellings with the amenities of any other village around the country: mosques, shops, schools, community associations etc. The real packing-case slums are now rare and well away from the centre of the city. Even many of the poorer kampungs are now paved.

Kampungs are found all over Jakarta, but right in the city centre you can glimpse one around Jalan Jaksa. Running off the street's strip of backpackers' hostels and eateries, small alleyways lead through the Kebon Sirih kampung crammed with houses, neighbourhood shops and eating houses.

The Kebon Sirih kampung is certainly not rock-bottom poverty, situated as it is on prime real estate. Many of the houses and shanties are being cleared as Jalan Jaksa goes more up-market and becomes the bona fide tourist centre of Jakarta. Other large, central kampungs can be found around Pasar Baru and Tanah Abang.

To visit a kampung it pays to be able to speak some Indonesian. If you don't, ask an Indonesian friend to take you. Kampungs have a definite community feel to them, and, as always in Indonesia, hardship is tolerated with good humour and a remarkable resilience and capacity to survive. Visitors are treated with great hospitality and interest, and to visit a kampung is to experience Jakarta as it is lived in by the majority of its residents.

---

toilets for 30,000/45,000 rp, 55,000 rp with air-con and telephone and 60,000 rp with hot water (if you're lucky).

More places can be found in the small alleys running off Jl Jaksa. Gang 1 is home to two small, quiet places: the *Kresna Homestay* (☎ 325403) at No 175 and the *Bloem Steen Homestay* (☎ 325389), which is next door at No 173. They're a bit cramped, but reasonable value for Jakarta. The Kresna has older rooms for 20,000/25,000 rp without/with mandi; the Bloem Steen is a touch better and has singles/doubles for 20,000/25,000 rp with shared mandi.

Just west off Jl Jaksa, *Borneo Hostel* (☎ 320095, Jl Kebon Sirih Barat 35) is popular and friendly. Rooms cost from 20,000 rp up to 35,000 rp with mandi. The spartan but airy rooms in the same building as the cafe are best. The annexe next door is dank and dungeon-like with dripping plumbing and scurrying cockroaches.

Other places are dotted along this lane, such as *Bintang Kejora* (☎ 323878) at No 52, which has very clean rooms for 15,000/20,000 rp or 35,000 rp with mandi. *Hostel Rita, Pondok Wisata Kebon Sirih* and *Pondok Wisata Jaya Hostel* are all uncomfortably close to the mosque and its early-morning wakeup call.

Just past Hostel Rita, turn left down the alleyway and follow the sign to *Lia's Hostel* (☎ 3162708) in the middle of the kampung at Jl Kebon Sirih Barat 8 No 47. It has a pleasant garden pavilion for sipping coffee and a switched-on manager. This small hostel packs in the rooms, but it is well kept and costs 20,000 rp and 25,000 rp without mandi, or 30,000 rp with mandi.

### Places to Stay – Mid-Range

**Jalan Jaksa Area** *Hotel Le Margot* (☎ 3913830, Jl Jaksa 15) is a relatively new hotel with small, but well-appointed, rooms

JAKARTA

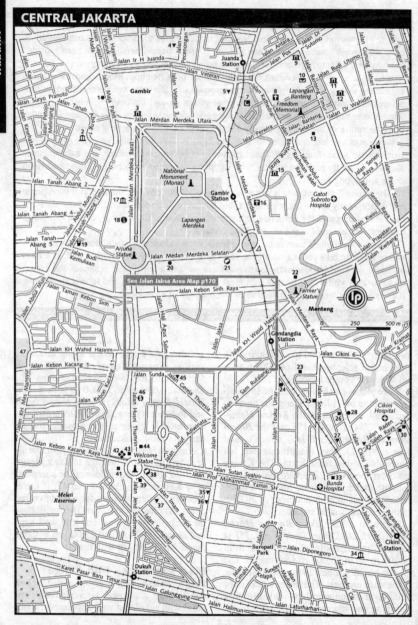

## CENTRAL JAKARTA

Gambir

Jalan Suryo Pranoto
Jalan Kali
Jalan Cideng Timur
Jalan Hayam Wuruk
Jalan Calah Mada
Jalan Ir H Juanda
Jalan Pecenongan

Juanda Station

Jalan Veteran
Jalan Antara
Jalan Dr Sutomo
Jalan Pos
Jalan Budi Utomo
Jalan Gunung Sahari

Jalan Tanah Abang 1
Jalan Petojo
Melintang
Jalan Tanah Abang Timur

Jalan Merdan Merdeka Utara

National Monument (Monas)

Gambir Station

Lapangan Merdeka

Jalan Tanah Abang 2
Jalan Tanah Abang 4
Jalan Abdul Muis
Jalan Tanah Abang 5
Jalan Budi Kemullaan

Arjuna Statue

Jalan Medan Merdeka Barat
Jalan Medan Merdeka Selatan

Lapangan Banteng
Freedom Memorial

Jalan Katbohan
Jalan Perwira
Juang Kuartar
Jalan Abdul Rachman Saleh
Jalan Banteng Selatan

Gatot Subroto Hospital

Jalan Senen Raya 3
Jalan Pasar Senen
Jalan Kwini
Jalan Prapatan
Jalan Kwitang

See Jalan Jaksa Area Map p170

Jalan Kebon Sirih Raya

Farmer's Statue

Menteng

0      250      500 m

Jalan Taman Kebon Sirih 1
Jalan Haji Agus Salim
Jalan Jaksa
Jalan KH Wasid Hasyim

Gondangdia Station

Jalan Cikini 6
Jalan Kramat 4

Jalan Kebon Sirih 1
Jalan KH Wahid Hasyim

Jalan Kebon Kacang 1
Jalan KH Mas Mansyur
Jalan Kebon Kacang 11

Jalan Sunda
Jalan Gereja Theresia
Jalan Husni Thamrin

Jalan Cikini

Cikini Hospital

Jalan Kebon Kacang Raya

Welcome Statue

Jalan Yusuf Adiwinata
Jalan Cokroaminoto
Jalan Dr Sam Ratulangi
Jalan Teuku Umar
Soeroso
Jalan Raden Saleh Raya

Melati Reservoir

Jalan Jend Sudirman
Jalan Imam Bonjol
Jalan Sumenep
Jalan Sutan Syahrir
Jalan Prof Mohammad Yamin SH

Bunda Hospital

Jalan Cikini Raya

Jalan Pegangsaan Timur
Jalan Surabaya

Cikini Station

Suropati Park
Jalan Diponegoro

Jalan Taman Suropati
Jalan Sunda Kelapa
Jalan Cimahi
Jalan Sunder Madiun

Dukuh Station

Jalan Karet Pasar Baru Timur
Jalan Galunggung
Jalan Halimun
Jalan Laturharhari

## CENTRAL JAKARTA

**PLACES TO STAY**
13 Borobudur Inter-Continental Hotel
22 Hotel Aryaduta
23 Gondia International Guesthouse
25 Hotel Menteng I
26 Hotel Alia Cikini
29 Yannie International Guest House
30 Karya II Hotel
33 Hotel Marcopolo
39 Mandarin Oriental Jakarta Hotel
40 Shangri-La Hotel
41 Hotel Indonesia
43 Grand Hyatt Jakarta Hotel
44 President Hotel

**PLACES TO EAT**
4 Jl Pecenongan Night Stalls
5 Queen's Tandoor
6 Sahara Restaurant
27 Art & Curio
31 Oasis Bar & Restaurant
32 Raden Kuring Restaurant
35 Tamnak Thai Restaurant
36 Gandy Steakhouse
37 Lan Na Thai
45 Kafe Pisa

**OTHER**
1 Smailing Tours
2 Taman Prasasti Museum
3 Presidential Palace
7 Istiqlal Mosque
8 Catholic Cathedral
9 Gedung Kesenian

10 Main Post Office
11 Mahkamah Agung
12 Ministry of Finance Building
14 Bharata Theatre
15 Gedung Pancasila
16 Emanuel Church
17 National Museum
18 Directorate-General of Tourism
19 Tanamur Disco
20 Garuda
21 US Embassy
24 Immigration Office
28 Taman Ismail Marzuki (TIM)
34 Adam Malik Museum
38 British Embassy
42 Plaza Indonesia
46 Bank Internasional Indonesia
47 Pasar Tanah Abang

for 115,500 rp (including tax and service). The service is not a strong point but is good value.

*Hotel Karya* (☎ 3140484, Jl Jaksa 32-34) has been recently renovated and is the best in Jl Jaksa. The rooms are well furnished and there is a good restaurant. Posted rates of US$70 are discounted to 125,000 and 150,000 rp, making it a good buy.

Jl Wahid Hasyim has a string of mid-range hotels. *Hotel Indra Internasional* (☎ 3152858) at No 63 is the cheapest, with well appointed but dark rooms for 140,000 rp to 200,000 rp.

The much more impressive *Arcadia Hotel* (☎ 2300050) at No 114 has modern decor and very comfortable rooms for US$90 and US$150, but even with a 50% discount it is still expensive. Its sister hotel, the *Ibis Tamarind* (☎ 3912323), Jl Wahid Hasyim 77, has a pool, fitness centre and a bar. It is edging into the top end but is also overpriced at US$115 and US$160, even with 50% discounts.

The *Cemara Hotel* (☎ 3149985, Jl Cemara 1), on the corner of Jl Wahid Hasyim, has long been a popular hotel in this range and has good rooms and service. Rooms for 250,000 rp and 360,000 rp are competitively priced.

Next door, the *Hotel Bumi Johar* (☎ 3145746, Jl Johar 17-19) is a small, new hotel with a Japanese restaurant. Excellent rooms from 175,000/245,000 rp, even less with discount, make it one of the best buys.

The *Hotel Paragon* (☎ 3917070, Jl Wahid Hasyim 29), is a strangely designed multi-storey hotel with rooms fronting on to open corridors, but the rooms are immaculate and very good value at 165,000 rp after discount.

The *Sabang Metropolitan Hotel* (☎ 3857621, Jl H Agus Salim 11) is an old high-rise with a pool. Despite a recent facelift it is still dog-eared, but the rooms from 140,000 rp are reasonably priced.

**Cikini** The Cikini area, east of Jl Thamrin and close to the TIM cultural centre, has a selection of mid-range hotels and some good guesthouses.

The *Gondia International Guesthouse* (☎ 3909221, Jl Gondia Kecil 22) is in a quiet side street off Jl RP Soeroso. Comfortable air-con rooms around a small garden area cost 140,000 rp, including breakfast. It has a pleasant, homey atmosphere.

A good-value and deservedly popular guesthouse is *Yannie International Guest House* (☎ 3140012, Jl Raden Saleh Raya 35).

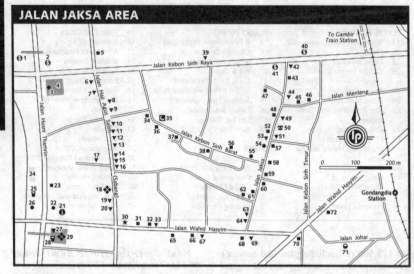

**JALAN JAKSA AREA**

To Gambir
Train Station

There is no sign, just a 'Y' at the front. Very well-kept rooms with air-conditioning and hot water cost 84,000/96,000 rp, including breakfast.

If the Yannie is full, the **Karya II Hotel** (☎ 3101380) next door at No 37 is cheap but drab and has rooms from 66,000 rp to 105,000 rp.

The **Hotel Marcopolo** (☎ 2301777, Jl Teuku Cik Ditiro 19) is a quality, high-rise hotel and always one of Jakarta's best. Though old, the rooms are very well maintained. There is a swimming pool, good service and a restaurant for cheap buffet breakfasts and dinners. Well-appointed rooms with fridge, TV and hot water cost from 149,000 rp, single or double.

**Hotel Alia Cikini** (☎ 3924444, Jl Cikini Raya 32) is right opposite the Taman Ismail Marzuki cultural centre. Though new, it is already starting to fray, but is very good value with rooms for 115,000 rp and 127,000 rp. The rooms have tiled rather than carpeted floors, but are otherwise very well appointed. The hotel also has a small, dirty swimming pool.

**Airport** The cheapest hotel near the airport is the **Hotel Bandara Jakarta** (☎ 6191964, Jl Jurumudi Km 2.5, Cengkareng). There's nothing fancy about it – air-con rooms with bath start at US$35/48.50 and there's a 24-hour coffee shop. It usually has a representative at the airport hotel booth offering free transport and discounts as low as 89,000/99,000 rp.

## Places to Stay – Top End

The **Hotel Indonesia** (☎ 2301008, fax 2301007, Jl Thamrin), built for the Asian Games, which Jakarta hosted in 1962, heralded a new era for hotel development in Indonesia. In 1965 it was the refuge for foreigners surrounded by the turmoil of Soekarno's 'year of living dangerously'. Increasingly shabby rooms start at US$130/140 for singles/doubles but are discounted to as little as 200,000 rp.

Also on the Welcome Statue roundabout, the opulent **Grand Hyatt Jakarta** (☎ 3901234, fax 3906426) is one of the city's best and sits above the Plaza Indonesia shopping centre. Rooms start at US$310.

## JALAN JAKSA AREA

| PLACES TO STAY | PLACES TO EAT | |
|---|---|---|
| 5 Sabang Metropolitan Hotel | 6 Ayam Goreng Jakarta | 64 Mbak Merry |
| 23 Sari Pan Pacific Hotel | 7 HP Gardena | 67 Le Bistro |
| 31 Bali International Hotel | 8 Bakwan Campur | 69 Ayam Goreng Nyonya Suharti |
| 32 Arcadia Hotel | 9 Sakura Anpan Bakery | **OTHER** |
| 34 Pondok Wisata Jaya Hostel | 10 Natrabu Padang Restaurant | 1 Bank Indonesia |
| 36 Pondok Wisata Kebon Sirih | 11 KFC | 2 Bangkok Bank |
| 37 Hostel Rita | 12 Sederhana Padang | 3 Airlines: Garuda, Qantas, |
| 38 Bintang Kejora | Restaraunt | Thai, Ansett & Continental |
| 43 Wisma Delima | 13 Sizzler | 4 BDN Building |
| 45 Bloem Steen Homestay | 14 Kantin 43 | 18 Robinson Department Store |
| 46 Kresna Homestay | 15 Hoka Hoka Bento | 21 Jakarta Theatre & Tourist |
| 47 Jusran Hostel | 16 Kaharu Restaurant | Office |
| 48 Norbek (Noordwijk) Hostel | 17 Paradiso 2001 | 22 Skyline Building |
| 52 Nick's Corner Hostel | 19 Dunkin' Donuts | 24 ATD Plaza |
| 56 Borneo Hostel | 20 Lim Thiam Kie Restaurant | 25 Jaya Pub |
| 57 Hotel Le Margot | 27 McDonald's | 26 Jaya Building |
| 58 Djody Hostel | 33 Hazara Restaurant | 28 Hard Rock Cafe |
| 59 Djody Hotel | 39 Ikan Bakar Kebon Sirih | 29 Sarinah Department Store |
| 60 Hotel Tator | Restaurant | 30 Police Station |
| 61 Hotel Karya | 42 Sate Khas Senayan | 35 Mosque |
| 62 Hostel 36 | 44 Angie's Cafe | 40 Bank Duta |
| 65 Hotel Indra Internasional | 49 Warung Memori | 41 Lippobank |
| 66 Ibis Tamarind | 51 Anedja Cafe | 50 RTQ Warparpostal |
| 68 Cipta Hotel | 53 Rumah Makan Jaksa | 54 Roberto Kencana Travel |
| 70 Cemara Hotel | International | 55 Arfina Margi Wisata Travel |
| 72 Hotel Paragon | 63 Romance Bar & Restaurant | 71 Media Taxis |

Diagonally across from the Hyatt, the *Mandarin Oriental Jakarta* (☎ 3141307, fax 3148680) has rooms from US$180 to US$235. It has no grounds but is an excellent business hotel and the well-furnished rooms have good extras. The nearby *President Hotel* (☎ 2301122, fax 3143631, Jl Thamrin 59) is a smaller, fading luxury hotel with rooms from US$145/155.

The *Sari Pan Pacific Hotel* (☎ 323707, fax 323650), is conveniently located on Jl Thamrin around the corner from the Jakarta Theatre building. The rooms cost US$170/190 and US$200/220.

The opulent *Shangri-La Hotel* (☎ 570 7440, fax 5703531, Jl Jenderal Sudirman Kav 1) has rooms from US$245/275. Farther south, the *Kempinski Hotel Plaza* (☎ 2510888, fax 2511777, Jl Jenderal Sudirman Kav 10-11) is a huge new hotel, just off Jakarta's most prestigious street. The rooms cost US$190 to US$250 but discounts of 50% have been on offer.

Nearby, the *Sahid Jaya Hotel* (☎ 5704444, fax 5733168, Jl Jenderal Sudirman 86) is a rambling hotel with rooms from US$150. Farther south you'll find *Le Meridien Jakarta* (☎ 2513131, fax 5711633, Jl Jenderal Sudirman Kav 18-20). The rooms from US$190 have nice extras.

The *Hilton Hotel* (☎ 5703600, fax 573 3089) on Jl Gatot Subroto is set in large grounds and has good facilities. Rooms cost US$180/195 to US$200/215. Near the Hilton, *Hotel Atlet Century Park* (☎ 571 2041, fax 5712191, Jl Pintu Satu) is a three star hotel, but it has good facilities and well-appointed rooms and is a good alternative to more expensive hotels. Rooms cost from US$95/105. The *Hotel Mulia Senayan* (☎ 5747777, fax 574 7888) in the same area on Jl Asia Afrika, is a new luxury hotel with low opening rates of US$99, while the *Holiday Inn Crowne Plaza* (☎ 5268833, fax 5268832, Jl Gatot Subroto Kav 2-3) has US$210 rooms discounted to same price.

To the north-east of the city centre, not far from the National Monument, the **Borobudur Inter-Continental Jakarta** (☎ 3805555, fax 3809595, Jl Lapangan Banteng Selatan) is one of the older generation of luxury hotels, recently restored and with a large range of sporting facilities. Tastefully furnished rooms start at US$175, or weekend packages are 550,000 rp per night.

Nearby, the **Hotel Aryaduta** (☎ 3861234, fax 380990, Jl Prapatan 44-48) is another of the older breed but still a top business class hotel. Rooms start at US$180.

Other new hotels are springing up everywhere, though these tend to be less central. The **Omni Batavia Hotel** (☎ 6904118, fax 6904092, Jl Kali Besar Barat 44-46) is in the historic Kota district, which is desolate at night. The rooms cost US$120 to US$160 but expect big discounts.

**Airport** For transit visitors, **Quality Hotel Aspac** (☎ 5590008, fax 5590018) is upstairs in departures in the international terminal at the airport. The hotel has a small bar and restaurant, but no other facilities. Rooms for US$100 (US$50 for six hours) are good but very expensive, even with a readily offered discount.

The much more luxurious **Sheraton Bandara** (☎ 5597777, fax 5597700) is 3km from the terminal and the rooms start at US$160 (US$125 on weekends).

## PLACES TO EAT

Jakarta has the best selection of restaurants in Indonesia, everything from street fare to top international restaurants. The restaurants are expensive by Indonesian standards, but the devalued rupiah means you can have fine dining for a fraction of the price it would cost elsewhere in the world.

### Jl Jaksa Area

Jl Jaksa's cafes are convivial meeting places and dish-out the standard travellers' menu. They are certainly cheap and the breakfasts are very good value. The food is either quasi-European or bland Indonesian.

The economic crisis has taken its toll on the number of cafes but one survivor is **Angie's Cafe** (Jl Jaksa 15), with a typical menu. **Mbak Merry** (Jl Jaksa 40) is a very cheap hole-in-the-wall warung with hamburgers and Indonesian dishes. **Pappa Cafe** (Jl Jaksa 41) is the pick of the restaurants, with outside tables and a varied menu that includes Indian food. **Memori** has a remarkably similar menu and screens violent American action videos in the evening. **Margot Cafe** (Jl Jaksa 15C), at the Margot Hotel, is the main backpackers bar and also serves food. At the north end of Jl Jaksa, **Sate Khas Senayan** (Jl Kebon Sirih 31A) is a newly renovated air-con restaurant with a variety of superb sate for 9000 rp to 12,000 rp, gado gado, soto buntut (ox-tail soup) and other classic Indonesian dishes.

The next street west of Jl Jaksa, Jl H Agus Salim, but universally known by its old name of Jl Sabang, has a string of cheap to midrange restaurants. Jl Sabang is famed as the sate capital of Indonesia and dozens of sate hawkers set up on the street in the evening.

Restaurants line both sides of Jl Sabang, and the most famous is **Natrabu** at No 29A, Jakarta's best Padang restaurant. For standard Chinese fare, try the air-con **Lim Thiam Kie** at No 49 or the **Paradiso 2001**, which is a small, basic Chinese vegetarian restaurant. A few modern, spotless restaurants serve cheap noodles, such as the **Bakmi Sabang** at No 43A. The **Pho Hoa**, on the corner with Jl Wahid Hasyim, serves Vietnamese noodles. More expensive restaurants include **Sizzler**, for chain restaurant grills, and **Mel's Drive-In**, an American diner.

At the southern end of Jl Jaksa, Jl Wahid Hasyim has a number of more expensive restaurants. **Ayam Goreng Suharti** at No 51 serves up the famous Yogyakarta-style fried chicken at very reasonable prices. **Tony Roma's** at No 49-51 bills itself as 'a place for ribs' and by god they're right. Bellyextending, melt-in-the-mouth ribs cost around 50,000 rp – there are also half serves available. **Hazara** at No 112 is an expensive Indian restaurant where the food is excellent and the chic decor makes the place special. The long-running *Le Bistro* at No 75 tries but doesn't quite succeed to be French. However the continental food is consistently good and the decor is faded but pleasant. It also has a piano bar.

## Jl Thamrin

The *Sarinah department store* has a very good, if expensive, food-stall area in the basement next to the supermarket. Try the excellent *soto Betawi*. Sarinah is also home to Indonesia's first *McDonald's* and the more expensive *Hard Rock Cafe*. *American Chillis Bar & Grill* on the 2nd Floor has Tex Mex favourites and service by staff who have been over-indoctrinated in American chain restaurant niceties ('Have a nice day!').

The *Green Pub* opposite, in the Jakarta Theatre, has been pumping out Mexican food and grills for years and in the evenings local bands perform in Mexican cowboy garb! *Jaya Pub*, Jl Thamrin 12, at the back of the Jaya building, is another classic music venue that also puts on good grills and pub food.

Farther down Jl Thamrin at the Welcome Statue roundabout, Plaza Indonesia is one of Jakarta's most exclusive shopping centres. The *Cira Food Court* on the 3rd floor is a Singapore-style hawkers' centre with a range of good international food stalls. *Cafe Oh La La*, in the basement, has good pastries and cappuccinos, *Kafe Excelso* has better espresso and light meals. Other fast-food emporia are also in abundance.

*Zigolini*, in the Mandarin Oriental Hotel, is a superb Italian restaurant. Mains such as scaloppine or rack of lamb cost over 100,000 rp, or excellent pizzas and calzones cost around 40,000 rp.

## Other Areas

Menteng, just south of Jl Jaksa, has some good dining options. *Kafe Pisa (Jl Gereja Theresia 1)* has rustic Mediterranean decor, an outside area for al fresco dining and decent pasta, pizza, calamari, scaloppine etc. Housed in a Dutch villa, *Lan Na Thai (Jl Kusuma Atmaja 85)* is one of Jakarta's most stylish restaurants. Rub shoulders with the Indonesian elite and expect to pay at least 100,000 rp per person. The Menteng shopping centre on Jl Cokroaminoto also has a good selection of restaurants. For seafood or steak try the *Gandy Steakhouse* or *Black Angus*. *Tamnak Thai* at No 78 has good, moderately priced Thai food and Chinese seafood.

The Pasar Baru area near the main post office is home to Jakarta's Indian community and some good Indian restaurants are on Jl Veteran 1, opposite the Istiqlal mosque. *Queen's Tandoor (Jl Veteran 1, No 6)* has bright decor, but the good food and reasonable prices make it very popular. *Sahara Restaurant* at No 23 is also good.

One of the best warung areas is on Jl Pecanongan, about a kilometre north of the National Monument. Night warungs start setting up large marquees around 5 pm and serve excellent Chinese seafood and other dishes at cheap prices.

The place to be seen is *Cafe Batavia (Jl Pintu Besar Utara 14)*, which is right in the middle of historic Kota on Taman Fatahillah. Housed in a tastefully renovated Dutch building, the restaurant is not cheap, but the food is excellent.

The historic *Oasis Bar & Restaurant (Jl Raden Saleh 47)* in Cikini, is housed in a large, old Dutch villa and has the feel of an extravagant 1930s Hollywood film set, with prices to match. More than a dozen waitresses serve up a traditional *rijsttafel*, while you are serenaded by a group of Batak singers from Sumatra. Also in Cikini, *Art & Curio (Jl Cikini IV No 8A)* is a delightfully old-fashioned restaurant with dark, bamboo decor and waiters in starched linen jackets. Though not exactly Dutch, it has plenty of colonial ambience. roast beef sandwiches, *bitterballen*, (Dutch-style croquettes) steaks and other grills, all at very reasonable prices.

Jakarta has hundreds of other fine dining establishments scattered around the Golden Triangle (the business district around Jl Jenderal Sudirman and Jl Gatot Subroto) Kebayoran Baru and especially in the wealthy, expat-favoured suburb of Menteng. Closer to the city centre, the Taman Ria Senayan on Jl Gatot Subroto, not far from the Hilton Hotel, has a great selection of stylish restaurants overlooking the lagoon. Wander around to see what takes your fancy – Thai, Balinese, Italian, grills.

## ENTERTAINMENT

Check the entertainment pages of the *Jakarta Post* for films, concerts and special events. Films, lectures and discussions on Indonesian culture are often sponsored by foreign embassies and cultural centres.

### Cultural Performances

The already mentioned *Taman Ismail Mazurki (TIM)* cultural centre in Menteng is one of the best places to see traditional and modern performing arts and cultural events.

The *Gedung Kesenian Jakarta* (☎ 3808283, *Jl Gedung Kesenian 1)* also has a regular program (see the tourist office) of traditional dance and theatre, as well as European classical music and dance.

The *Bharata Theatre* (☎ 4214937, *Jl Kalilio 15)* in Pasar Senen, has *ketoprak* (Javanese folk theatre) performances from 8 pm every Monday and Thursday evening, and *wayang orang* on other nights.

*Wayang kulit* and *golek* puppet shows used to be a regular Sunday event at the *Jakarta History Museum* in Kota but are often cancelled now because of a lack of demand. The various cultural centres, particularly *Erasmus Huis* (see Libraries & Useful Organisations) also have regular cultural events.

### Nightlife

Jakarta is the most sophisticated city in Indonesia, and has nightlife to match. Hundreds of bars, discos, karaoke lounges and nightclubs range from the sleazy to the refined. Jakarta still has plenty of money and people partying until dawn in spite of, or perhaps because of, the crisis. Bands start around 10 or 11 pm and continue until 2 or 3 am, sometimes later on the weekends. During the week, many places close at 1 am.

Some don't have cover charges, though sometimes a first drink cover charge applies in the discos. A beer or a mixed drink costs from 15,000 rp, more in exclusive hotel bars.

**Bars & Live Music** The *Hard Rock Cafe*, on Jl Thamrin, has the usual blend of rock memorabilia, music and food. It is always lively and has decent bands or occasional top-line imports. The music starts around 11 pm, when dinner finishes, and keeps going until 2 or 3 am. The dance floor is dominated by a huge stained-glass portrait of the King, though this Elvis looks vaguely Indonesian. The other chain cafes such as the *Fashion Cafe (Wisma 46, BMI City, Jl Jenderal Sudirman)* and *Planet Hollywood (Jl Gatot Subroto 16)* also have live pub music and are popular on the weekends.

The *Jaya Pub (Jl Thamrin 12)*, next to the carpark behind the Jaya building, is a Jakarta institution that has live pub music most evenings.

A good, smaller pub near the Fashion Cafe is *Elvis Cafe (Jl Sudirman 2)*. While it doesn't exactly rage, it is a friendly place with a mixed crowd and a number of expat regulars and visitors.

The historic, restored *Cafe Batavia* at Taman Fatahillah in Kota is another upmarket venue and a popular spot to be seen. DJs play from 10 am onwards and it is open 24 hours.

Hotel bars can be very lively, depending on the bands. Current favourites include *B.A.T.S* in the Shangri-La Hotel, just off Jl Sudirman; *CJ's Bar*, in the Hotel Mulia Senayan on Jl Asia Afrika; and the nearby *Komodo Airways*, Hotel Century Atlett Park, Jl Pintu Satu Senayan. On Jl Thamrin, *Harry's Bar* in the Mandarin Oriental attracts a business clientele and is one of the best bars in Jakarta for jazz, which plays every night of the week.

The wealthy southern suburb of Kemang also has plenty of bar/restaurants with bands. For something different, *Twilite Cafe (TC, Jl Kemang Raya 24A)* is a fashionable spot for a beer, coffee or light meal and audible conversation. The music is piano, sax, classical or subdued house music. This chic, two-storey complex houses a bar, cafe, Internet cafe, art gallery and bookshop, and is open until 11.30 pm Sunday to Thursday, and until 1.30 pm on Friday and Saturday.

**Discos & Clubs** Jakarta has some sophisticated clubs with high-tech lighting, massive sound systems and pumping dance music. The clubs open around 9 pm, but don't really get going until midnight when the bars close. On weekends they are open to 4 am or later. Cover charges are around 20,000 rp to 25,000 rp.

Jakarta's most infamous disco is long-running *Tanamur (Jl Tanah Abang Timur 14)*. This institution is jammed nightly with gyrating revellers of every race, creed and sexual proclivity, and innumerable ladies of the night. It is unbelievably crowded after midnight on Friday and Saturday nights. Wear what you like here.

Tanamur is the benchmark of Jakarta's nightlife for most visitors, but Jakarta has other amazingly sophisticated clubs. *Bengkel* at Lot No 14 in the backblocks of the sprawling Sudirman Central Business District, off Jl Jenderal Sudirman, is a pyramidal building with a huge dance floor, big screens, dazzling light show, and an eclectic mix of music. The cafe at the front has bands and a billiards area and it goes until 6 am on weekends.

Smaller but also high-tech, *Jalan Jalan*, on the 36th floor of the Menara Imperium on Jl Rasuna Said, is another top spot for house music, with the twinkling lights of Jakarta as a backdrop. It also has a sushi bar, billiard area and bands.

*Jamz*, which is at the front of Lippo Sudirman/Lippo Suites Hotel on Jl Jenderal Sudirman, is the Hard Rock of jazz, with lots of jazz memorabilia. But jazz music is confined to one cramped lounge, while DJs and pop bands ply the other two lounges. It is very popular it and packs in a solidly middle-class crowd every night.

## SHOPPING

Shopping is one Jakarta's biggest attractions. Clothes, shoes and many other goods are very cheap, especially if they are locally made,

while brand name goods are many times more expensive. Jakarta has handicrafts from almost everywhere in Indonesia and, though prices are much higher than in the place of origin, if Jakarta is your first stop, it's a good place to get an overall view of Indonesian crafts. If it's your last stop, then it's always a final chance to find something that you missed elsewhere in the country.

A good place to start is Sarinah on Jl Thamrin. The 3rd floor of this large department store is devoted to batik and handicrafts from all over the country. This floor is divided into different concessions sponsored by the big batik manufacturers like Batik Keris and Batik Danar Hadi. Handicrafts are souvenirs rather than true collectibles, but the quality is high and the prices reasonable.

In the same vein, but even bigger, is the related Pasaraya, Jl Iskandarsyah II/2, in the Blok M shopping centre (see later in this section).

The Pasar Seni, at Ancol recreation park in North Jakarta is a good place to look for regional handicrafts and to see many of them actually being made. Whether it's woodcarvings, paintings, puppets, leather, batik or silver, you'll find it here.

In Menteng, Jl Surabaya is Jakarta's famous fleamarket, with woodcarvings, furniture, brassware, jewellery, batik, oddities like old typewriters and many (often instant) antiques. It is always fun to browse, but bargain like crazy – prices may be up to 10 times the worth of the goods.

Jl Kebon Sirih Timur, the street east of Jl Jaksa, has a number of shops for antiques and curios. The quality is high, but so are the prices.

Jakarta has plenty of shopping centres and markets to explore. Pasar Pagi Mangga Dua, Jl Mangga Besar, is a huge wholesale market with some of the cheapest clothes, accessories and shoes, as well as a host of other goods. Across the road is the Mangga Dua Mall for computers and electronics and the surrounding area has other shopping centres, making it South-East Asia's biggest shopping precinct.

JAKARTA

Pasar Senen, east of Gambir train station, is another lively shopping area with a large, active market.

Jakarta has plenty of big, dazzling malls, such as the exclusive and expensive Plaza Indonesia on Jl Thamrin. It's a great place to browse for designer labels, but the prices are very high. Jakarta has dozens of other shopping centres. Just south of the city centre near the Hilton, Plaza Senayan on Jl Asia Afrika is well stocked, as is the Pondok Indah shopping centre in the southern suburbs.

Blok M is one of the biggest and best shopping areas in Jakarta. Here you'll find the huge Blok M shopping centre above the large bus terminal. This is a more down-to-earth shopping centre, with scores of small, reasonably priced shops offering clothes, shoes, music tapes, household goods etc. More upmarket shopping can be found at the multi-storey Blok M Plaza just across the way. Pasaraya department store is also right next to the shopping centre. Jl Palatehan 1, just to the north of the Blok M bus terminal has some interesting antique and craft shops.

## GETTING THERE & AWAY

Jakarta is the main international gateway to Indonesia; for details on arriving there from overseas see the Getting There & Away chapter. Jakarta is also a major centre for domestic travel, with extensive bus, train, air and sea connections.

## Air

International and domestic flights both operate from the Soekarno-Hatta international airport. Airport tax is 50,000 rp on international departures, 11,000 rp on domestic flights, payable at the airport. From little-used Halim airport, departure tax is 20,000 rp international and 9000 rp domestic. Flights depart from Jakarta to all the main cities across the archipelago. The main domestic airlines have offices open normal business hours, and usually Sunday morning as well. Travel agents also sell domestic tickets.

Following is a list of the main domestic airlines in Jakarta:

Bouraq
   (☎ 6288815) Jl Ankasa 1-3, Kemayoran
Garuda Indonesia
   (☎ 2311801) Garuda Bldg, Jl Merdeka Selatan 13
Mandala
   (☎ 4246100) Jl Garuda 76
Merpati Nusantara Airlines
   (☎ 6544444) Jl Angkasa Blok B/15 Kav 2/3, Kemayoran
   (☎ 3501433) Gambir train station, 24-hour ticket office

For the addresses of some of the international airlines, see the Getting There & Away chapter.

## Bus

Jakarta has four major bus terminals, which are all a long way from the city centre. In some cases the journey to the bus terminal can take longer than the bus journey itself, making the train a better alternative for arriving at or leaving Jakarta. This is especially true for buses to and from Kampung Rambutan bus terminal. When catching buses to Jakarta from West Java note that some 'Jakarta' buses actually go to Bekasi or Tangerang, the districts bordering Jakarta, and are even farther out.

Tickets can be bought from travel agents around town. Jl Jaksa agents not only sell tickets but can include travel to the bus terminals. This will probably cost considerably more, but it can save you a lot of hassle. Advance bookings are a good idea for peak-travel periods, but so many buses operate to the main destinations that if you just front up at the bus terminals you won't have to wait long.

**Kalideres** Buses to the west of Jakarta go from the Kalideres bus terminal, about 15km north-west of Merdeka Square. Frequent buses run to Merak (4000 rp; three hours), Labuan (5000 rp; 3½ hours) and Serang (3000 rp; 1½ hours). A few buses go through to Sumatra from Kalideres, but most Sumatra buses leave from Pulo Gadung bus terminal.

Sunda Kelapa, Kota, Jakarta.

Spires of Jakarta's Catholic Cathedral.

Wayang Museum, Kota, Jakarta.

Free Irian Monument, Lapangan Banteng.

The National Monument (Monas), Jakarta.

Cannon Si Jagur, Taman Fatahillah, Jakarta.

Main altar at Vihara Dharma Bhakti/Temple, Jakarta.

**Kampung Rambutan** The big, new Kampung Rambutan bus terminal handles buses to areas south and south-west of Jakarta. It was designed to carry much of Jakarta's intercity bus traffic, but it mostly handles buses to West Java, including: Bogor (2000/3000 rp normal/air-con; 40 minutes); Bandung (6500 rp to 13,000 rp; 4½ hours); Tasikmalaya (8000 to 15,000 rp; 7½ hours); and Banjar (6500/12,000 to 22,000 rp; nine hours). Buses also go to Merak, Sumatra, Cirebon, Yogyakarta, Surabaya and other long-distance destinations, but Pulo Gadung bus terminal still has most of the long-distance services. Kampung Rambutan is about 18km to the south of the city centre and takes at least an hour by city bus. Take the train for Bogor or Bandung.

**Pulo Gadung** Pulo Gadung is 12km to the east of the city centre, and has buses to Cirebon, Central and East Java, Sumatra and Bali. Many of the air-con, deluxe buses operate from here. This wild bus terminal is the busiest in Indonesia, with buses, crowds, hawkers and beggars everywhere.

The station is divided into two sections: one for buses to Sumatra and the other for all buses to the east.

Most buses to Sumatra leave at between 10 am and 3 pm and you can catch a bus right through to Aceh if you are crazy enough. Destinations and fares include: Palembang (45,000 to 80,000 rp); Bengkulu (60,000 to 90,000 rp); and Padang and Bukittinggi (70,000 to 110,000 rp). Prices are for air-con deluxe buses with reclining seats and toilets – well worth it for those long hauls through Sumatra. Putra Rafflesia has the best bus to Bengkulu at 11 am. For Bukittinggi, two good companies are ALS (☎ 8503446), with buses at 12.30, 2.30 and 4 pm, and ANS (☎ 352411), with buses at 10 am, noon and 2 pm. Both charge 110,000 rp for the 30 hour plus journey.

To the east, frequent buses go to Central and East Java and on to Bali. Destinations include: Cirebon (85000 to 15,000 rp; four hours); Yogyakarta (25,000 to 55,000 rp; 14 hours); Surabaya (30,000 to 68,000 rp; 18 hours); and Denpasar (60,000 to 100,000 rp; 24 hours). Most buses to Yogyakarta leave between 8 am and 6 pm. Some of the better deluxe bus companies are Raya and Muncul.

**Lebak Bulus** This bus terminal, 16km south of the city centre, handles many of the long-distance deluxe buses to Yogyakarta, Surabaya and Bali. Fares are much the same as from Pulo Gadung bus terminal. Most departures are late afternoon or evening.

## Train

Jakarta's four main stations are quite central, making the trains the easiest way out of the city into Java. The most convenient and important is Gambir, on the eastern side of Merdeka Square, a 15 minute walk from Jl Jaksa. Gambir handles mostly express trains to Bogor, Bandung, Yogyakarta, Solo, Semarang and Surabaya. Some Gambir trains also stop at Kota, the train station in the old city area in the north. The Pasar Senen train station, to the east, has mostly economy trains to eastern destinations. Tanah Abang train station, to the west, has economy trains that go to the west.

For longer hauls, the express trains are far preferable to the economy trains, and most have cheaper *bisnis* class in addition to air-con *eksekutif* class. For express trains, tickets can be bought in advance. Gambir station has air-con booking offices at the northern end for advance bookings, while the ticket windows at the southern end are for tickets bought on the day of departure. For schedules and departure times you can ring ☎ 8292151 or ☎ 6927843.

From Gambir train station, taxis cost a minimum of 7000 rp from the taxi booking desk. A cheaper alternative is to go out the front to the main road and hail a bajaj, which will cost at least 2000 rp to Jl Jaksa after bargaining.

**Bogor** Trains to Bogor are either crowded ekonomi trains or the much better Pakuan Express bisnis trains (4000 rp, one hour) leaving Gambir at 7.43, 8.23 (air-con) and 11 am and 2.28, 2.48, 4.23 (air-con), 4.48,

6.38 (air-con) and 7.03 pm. Air-con eksekutif carriages cost 6000 rp. Seats cannot be booked and tickets go on sale one hour before departure. There are also a few ekonomi express trains.

No-frills ekonomi trains are part of the city rail network and can be horribly crowded during rush hour, but at other times they are quite tolerable and provide an efficient service. Their main advantage is that, because they stop at all stations, you can board them at Gondangdia station, only a short stroll from Jl Jaksa. They leave every 20 minutes until around 8 pm and take 1½ hours. The fare is 900 rp from Gondangdia or Gambir, 1000 rp from Kota. Watch your gear on the crowded city trains.

**Bandung** The easiest way to get to Bandung is by train; the journey is very scenic as the train climbs into the hills before Bandung. It is best to book in advance, essential on weekends and public holidays unless you want to stand in a ticket queue for hours.

The efficient and comfortable *Parahyangan* service departs from Gambir station for Bandung (20,000/32,000 rp for bisnis /eksekutif; three hours) roughly every hour between 5 am and 11.30 pm. The more luxurious *Argogede* departs at 10 am and 6 pm, costs 40,000 rp in eksekutif class and takes 2½ hours.

**Cirebon** Most trains that run along the north coast, and those to Yogyakarta, go through Cirebon. One of the best services is the *Cirebon Express* departing from Gambir station at 6.45 and 10.10 am, and 4.55 pm. It costs 18,000/32,000 rp in bisnis/eksekutif and takes 3½ hours.

**Yogyakarta & Solo** The most luxurious trains are the *Argo Lawu* (115,000 rp eksekutif; 7½ hours) departing at 9 pm, and the *Dwipangga* (160,000 rp, eight hours) departing at 8 am. These trains go to Solo and stop at Yogyakarta, 45 minutes before Solo, but cost the same to either destination.

The best-value express services to Yogyakarta are either the *Fajar Utama Yogya*

(36,000/76,000 rp bisnis/eksekutif; eight hours) departing Gambir station at 6.10 and 6.20 am, or the *Senja Utama Yogya* (36,000/72,000 rp) departing at 7.20 and 8.40 pm. The *Senja Utama Solo* goes to Solo (40,000/80,000 rp, 10 hours) at 7.40 pm and also stops in Yogyakarta.

At the other end of the comfort scale are the crowded ekonomi class-only trains departing from Pasar Senen station: the *Gaya Baru Malam Selatan* and *Matamaja*; or the better choice *Empujaya*, leaves Pasar Senen at 9.35 pm and terminates in Yogyakarta. The ekonomi trains cost around 14,000 rp and take 10½ hours to Yogyakarta, but overruns are common.

**Surabaya** Most trains between Jakarta and Surabaya take the shorter northern route via Semarang, though a few take the longer southern route via Yogyakarta. Express trains range from the *Jayabaya Utara* (48,000 rp bisnis; 12 hours) departing Kota at 3 pm, to the luxurious *Argobromo* (140,000 rp eksekutif; nine hours) departing Gambir at 8.05 pm. The *Anggrek* trains (160,000 rp; nine hours), departing Gambir at 9.30 am and 9.30 pm, also have a super eksekutif class (185,000 rp) with computer, telephone and fax services.

The cheapest services taking the north coast route are the ekonomi-class-only *Gaya Baru Malam Utara* (13,500 rp; 13 hours) from Pasar Senen to Surabaya's Pasar Turi train station at 3.40 pm, and the *Parcel* at 8.35 pm. Overruns can turn this into a 20 hour journey on the ekonomi trains.

## Minibus
Door-to-door *travel* minibuses are not such a good option in Jakarta because it can take hours to pick up or drop off passengers in the traffic jams. Some travel agents book them, but you may have to go to a depot on the outskirts. Media Taxis (☎ 323744), Jl Johar 15, near Jl Jaksa, has minibuses to Bandung and beat-up 1970s Australian-made Holdens cars for 25,000 rp.

Mitra Marsada Utama (☎ 3142566), Jl Kebon Sirih Barat Dalam I No 56, just off Jl Jaksa near the Borneo Hostel, was running a tourist bus to Pangandaran (45,000 rp) – check to see if it has started again. Jl Jaksa travel agents also offer direct minibuses to Yogyakarta.

## Boat

See the Getting Around chapter for information on the Pelni shipping services that operate on a regular two week schedule to ports all over the archipelago. The Pelni ticketing office (☎ 4211921) is at Jl Angkasa No 18, north-east of the city centre in Kemayoran. Tickets can also be bought through designated Pelni agents. It costs more to do it this way, but it is more convenient. In central Jakarta, try Menara Buana Surya (☎ 3142464) in the Tedja Buana building, Jl Menteng Raya 29, about half a kilometre east of Jl Jaksa, or Kerta Jaya (☎ 3451518), Jl Veteran I No 27, opposite the Istiqlal Mosque.

Direct Pelni destinations from Jakarta include: Padang, Tanjung Pandan (Pulau Belitung), Surabaya, Semarang, Muntok (Pulau Bangka), Belawan, Kijang (Pulau Bintan) and Batam. Services on the *Lambelu* to Padang (West Sumatra), and the *Sinabong* to Batam (near Singapore) are of most interest to travellers. To Kalimantan, the *Lawit* goes via Tanjung Pandan to Pontianak. A number of Pelni boats go to Ujung Pandang (Sulawesi) via Semarang or Surabaya but there are no direct services.

Pelni ships all arrive at and depart from Pelabuhan Satu (Dock No 1) at Tanjung Priok, 13km north-east of the city centre. Take bus No 81 from Jl Thamrin, opposite Sarinah department store, via Pasar Senen; allow at least an hour. The bus terminal is at the old Tanjung Priok train station from where it is a 600m walk to the dock or 500 rp by ojek (motorcycle or bicycle). From the Tanjung Priok terminal buses run all over Jakarta and to Bogor. A taxi to Jl Jaksa will cost around 15,000 rp (you will have to bargain), a little less on the meter going to the harbour. The information centre (☎ 4301080 ext 2223) at the front of the Dock No 1 arrival hall is helpful.

Other passenger ships also go from Dock No 1 to Bintan and Batam islands, from where it is just a short ferry ride to Singapore. The *Samudera Jaya* is a small but reasonably comfortable air-conditioned hydrofoil, seating up to 300 passengers. It leaves Tanjung Priok on Saturday at 1 pm and sails to Tanjung Pandan (70,000 rp; 12 hours) on Pulau Belitung, before continuing on to Tanjung Pinang (Pulau Bintan; 85,000 rp) and Batam (95,000 rp). Count on a 24 hour trip to Batam. A boat travelling in the reverse direction leaves on Thursday. The *Telaga Express* also leaves Jakarta every Saturday at 6 am to cover the same route (both directions).

To Kalimantan, the *Kapuas Express* departs for Pontianak every Tuesday and Thursday at 10 am, and Saturday at 4 pm.

## GETTING AROUND
### To/From the Airport

Jakarta's Soekarno-Hatta international airport is 35km west of the city centre. A toll road links the airport to the city and a journey between the two takes 45 minutes to an hour, but longer in the rush hour.

Damri airport buses (4000 rp) depart every 30 minutes from around 3 am to 6.30 pm between the airport and Gambir station in central Jakarta. Other airport buses also go to Blok M, Kemayoran, Rawamangun and Bogor. From Gambir to Jl Jaksa take a *bajaj* (3000 rp or less with bargaining), which is a motorised rickshaw taxi, or taxi (7000 rp from the taxi desk), or it is just under a kilometre to walk.

A metered taxi from the airport to Jl Thamrin/Jl Jaksa costs about 35,000 rp, and on top of the metered fare you have to pay around 10,000 rp more, which includes the airport surcharge (2300 rp, payable from, but not to, the airport) and 7500 rp in toll road charges.

### Bus

In Jakarta everything is at a distance. It's hot and humid and hardly anybody walks – you will need to use some form of transport to get from one place to another. Jakarta has probably the most comprehensive city bus network of any major Indonesian city.

Buses cost 400 rp, *patas* (express) buses cost 700 rp and air-con patas buses cost 1800 rp. Jakarta's crowded buses have their fair share of pickpockets and bag slashers. The more expensive buses are generally safer, as well as being more comfortable.

At least a dozen bus companies run a confusion of routes around town. Big regular city buses charge a fixed 400 rp fare. The big express Patas buses charge 800 rp and the air-con Patas buses cost 2000 rp; these are usually less crowded and by far the best option. These services are supplemented by orange toy-sized buses and, in a few areas, by pale blue Mikrolet buses, and other minibus services, which cost between 400 rp and 600 rp. The main terminal for Mikrolet and the numerous red-and-blue Metro Mini buses is at the Pasar Senen market.

The tourist office has information on buses around Jakarta. Some of the useful buses that operate along central Jl Thamrin include:

P1 (ac), P10 (ac) or P11 (non-ac)
    Jl Thamrin to Kota
P11, P10 or 79 (ac)
    Kota to Kampung Rambutan via Jl Thamrin
P15
    Jl Sabang (Jl H Agus Salim) to Jl Ankasa
    (for Pelni, Merpati & Bouraq offices)
P14
    Tanjung Priok to Tanah Abang via
    Jl Kebon Sirih
78 (ac)
    Kota to Kalideres bus terminal

## Taxi

Taxis in Jakarta are metered and cost 2000 rp for the first kilometre and 90 rp for each subsequent 100m. Make sure the meter is used. Many taxi drivers provide a good service, but Jakarta has enough rogues to give its taxis a bad reputation. Tipping is expected, but not obligatory – it is customary to round the fare up to the next 1000 rp. Carry plenty of small notes – Jakarta taxi drivers rarely give change.

Bluebird cabs (pale blue) (☎ 7941234, 7981001) have the best reputation and well-maintained cars.

Typical taxi fares from Jl Thamrin are: to Kota (5000 rp), Sunda Kelapa (6000 rp), Pulo Gadung (8000 rp) and Kampung Rambutan or Taman Mini (18,000 rp). Any toll road charges are extra and paid by the passengers.

## Bajaj & Other Local Transport

Bajaj (pronounced ba-jai) are Indian autorickshaws: orange three wheelers that carry two passengers (three if you're dwarfs) and sputter around powered by noisy two stroke engines. Short trips – Jl Jaksa to the main post office, for example – will cost about 3000 rp. Bajaj are good value, especially during rush hours, but hard bargaining is required. Always agree on the price beforehand. Bajaj are not allowed along main streets such as Jl Thamrin, so make sure they don't simply drop you off at the border.

Jakarta has other weird and wonderful means of getting around. Bemos are the original three wheelers from the 1960s that still operate around Glodok and other parts of Jakarta. In the back streets of Kota, pushbikes with a padded 'kiddy carrier' on the back will take you for a ride! The *helicak*, cousin to the bajaj, is a green motorcycle contraption with a passenger car mounted on the front. Jakarta also has *ojeks* – motorcycles that take pillion passengers – but weaving in and out of Jakarta's traffic on the back of an ojek is decidedly risky. Becaks have been banned from the city and only a few tourist becaks remain at Ancol.

## Car

If you feel up to driving yourself, Jakarta has branches of major rent-a-car firms. Try Avis (☎ 3142900), Jl Diponegoro 25, Bluebird (☎ 7941234), Jl Mampang Prapatan Raya 60, or National Car Rental (☎ 31434-23), Kartika Plaza Hotel, Jl Thamrin 10. But a travel agent may be the cheapest place to hire a car or minibus with driver.

A number of 'transport' guys hang out in Jl Jaksa and they can offer some of the best deals if you negotiate directly with them, avoiding hotel or travel agent commission. Count on paying around 100,000 rp to 150,000 rp for a day tripping around town.

# Around Jakarta

## PULAU SERIBU

• pop 15,000    ☎ 021

Scattered across the Java Sea to the north of Jakarta are the tropical islands of Pulau Seribu, (or Thousand Islands, although there are actually only around 130). The northern half of the area is a marine national park, though 37 of the islands are permitted to be exploited. Apart from a few inhabited islands and a handful of resorts, many islands are the private preserve of the Jakarta rich and famous. Most of the islands have clear waters, coral reefs for diving and beautiful white-sand beaches. Few cities in the world can boast such tropical delights within their municipal boundaries.

Jakarta's offshore islands start only a few kilometres out in the Bay of Jakarta. The most populated island is Pulau Kelapa, while the administrative centre is Pulau Pramuka farther south. Pulau Panjang, which has an airstrip, and Pulau Panggang are other populated islands but most interest focuses on the nine islands that are home to commercial resorts. The waters closest to Jakarta are murky – the better islands are found the farther you go from Jakarta.

All the resorts have individual bungalows with attached bathrooms, and most are air-conditioned. While comfortable, none are international-standard resorts, despite the high prices. Some are quite chic, while others are barely mid-range standard. They have always been expensive, but with the fall in the rupiah they are now much more affordable.

All the resorts have water-sport facilities, with diving and snorkelling equipment, windsurfers, boats for hire etc. Though not one of Indonesia's premier dive destinations, Pulau Seribu is one of the most popular because of its easy access from Jakarta. But pollution is taking its toll on the ever-decreasing live corals.

The resorts have booking offices in Jakarta or at the Ancol Marina. Travel agents at the Ancol Marina also sell packages and are useful for comparing prices. Hikari Multi Sinergi (☎ 6453679), Counter No 6 at the Marina Building, and Mitra Semesta Raya (☎ 6406707), Counter No 9, both book most of the resorts. Resort packages include all buffet meals and transport to the islands, and these work out to be slightly cheaper than taking a room and then paying for meals and transport separately. Prices quoted here are high-season but they are very variable and depend on demand. Prices for children from two to 10 years are usually 50% less than quoted prices. Bring drinks, snacks, cigarettes, your own snorkelling equipment etc – prices are very high at the resort shops. And bring mosquito coils.

### Pulau Bidadari

This is the closest resort island to Jakarta and can be overrun by day trippers. It has a reasonable beach and it can make a good day trip during the week, but the other resorts have more appeal. From Bidadari you can visit other nearby islands like **Pulau Cipir**, **Pulau Kelor** or **Pulau Onrust**, which all have historic interest. Onrust has the remains of an old Dutch VOC shipyard and the island was used by the Dutch from as early as 1615 for ship repairs and then as a base from which to invade Jayakarta. Most of the buildings date from 1786 on, but they were sacked by the British in 1806 and 1810. The other islands, including Pulau Bidadari, have various Dutch ruins, usually controller towers, which were used for defensive purposes and to monitor sea traffic. Kelor has the remains of a 17th century Dutch fort.

*Pulau Bidadari Resort* can be booked at Marina Ancol (☎ 680048), Taman Impian Jaya Ancol. It has a variety of simple cottages accommodating three to eight people costing from 76,000 to 100,000 rp per person during the week, and 91,000 to 122,500 rp on weekends. Boats to Onrust and Kelor can be charted for 180,000 rp for a large passenger boat or around 40,000 rp for a local fishing boat taking five people. At least two boats per day go to and from Bidadari.

JAKARTA

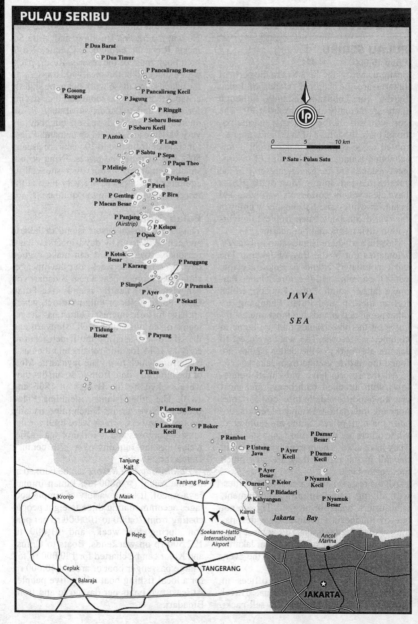

## PULAU SERIBU

P Dua Barat
P Dua Timur
P Pancalirang Besar
P Gosong Rangat
P Pancalirang Kecil
P Jagung
P Ringgit
P Sebaru Besar
P Sebaru Kecil
P Antuk
P Laga
P Sabtu
P Sepa
P Melinjo
P Papa Theo
P Melintang
P Pelangi
P Putri
P Genting
P Bira
P Macan Besar
P Panjang (Airstrip)
P Kelapa
P Opak
P Kotok Besar
P Karang
P Panggang
P Simpit
P Pramuka
P Ayer
P Sekati

P Tidung Besar
P Payung

P Tikus
P Pari

P Lancang Besar
P Laki
P Lancang Kecil
P Bokor
P Rambut
P Damar Besar
P Untung Java
P Ayer Kecil
P Damar Kecil
P Ayer Besar
P Onrust
P Kelor
P Nyamuk Kecil
P Bidadari
P Kahyangan
P Nyamuk Besar

JAVA SEA

0      5      10 km
P Satu - Pulau Satu

Tanjung Kait
Kronjo
Mauk
Tanjung Pasir
Kamal
Jakarta Bay
Ancol Marina
Rejeg
Sepatan
Soekarno-Hatto International Airport
Ceplak
Balaraja
TANGERANG
JAKARTA

## Pulau Ayer Besar

North of Bidadari, Pulau Ayer is another popular day-trip destination. It has a comfortable resort with a swimming pool and a small stretch of good beach, though the waters are still cloudy.

*Pulau Ayer Resort* is booked through PT Sarotama Prima Perkasa (☎ 3842031), Jl Ir H Juanda III/6. Spacious, comfortable cottages range from US$95 to US$200, or US$135 to US$320 on weekends, before discount. The nicest cottages are those built over the water. Discounts have brought prices as low as 262,000 rp (344,000 rp on weekends) for room, breakfast and transport.

## Pulau Kelapa

The entire island group has a population of around 15,000, with the district centre on **Pulau Panggang**, about 15km north of Jakarta, but most people live on just one island, Pulau Kelapa, farther north. Near Kelapa, **Pulau Panjang** has the only airstrip in the islands.

Some 6700 people are crammed onto Kelapa, which is just one big scruffy village that has spread to every corner of the island. This is a poor fishing community and, while some get work on the resorts, very little wealth flows back to the local populace from tourism. Great chunks of coral are used in house construction and you can wander around the narrow alleys between the houses.

The island has a public ferry connection to Ancol. It also has a *penginapan* but there are no good beaches and no reason to stay.

## Pulau Kotok

Kotok has two resorts and a thin but good beach on the north side. The beach is better in front of the Kul Kul resort than it is at the Coconut, which has built an artificial reef along part of it. The island is very popular with divers because of its relatively undamaged reefs. Kotok is also noted for the abundance of *biawak*, giant monitor lizards that grow to 2m, though many other islands are also home to these harmless lizards.

*Coconut Island Resort (☎ 082-8134144)* is on the eastern tip of the island and has an office in Jakarta (☎ 8295074), Jl Tebet Barat Dalam X/3, for bookings. This is a downmarket, tacky looking resort but the bungalows are well-kept, spacious and reasonably priced. Two-bedroom bungalows with sitting room, air-con, fridge and hot water sleep up to six people and cost 250,000 rp (100,000 rp more on weekends). Meals are extra and the boat costs 220,000 rp per person return.

The western two-thirds of the island is home to the *Kul Kul Kotok Island Resort (☎ 082-8121862)*, which can be booked in Jakarta (☎ 6345507), 3rd floor, Duta Merlin Shopping Arcade, Jl Gajah Mada 3-5. This resort is one of the most attractive, with rustic bungalows spaced out in the natural forest, though accommodation is fairly simple. Most bungalows have fan and cold water only, though a few have air-conditioning and hot water. Full-board packages are offered at 500,000 rp per person (10% more on weekends), regardless of the room.

## Pulau Macan Besar (Matahari)

The Matahari Island Resort on Pulau Macan Besar is certainly one of the best equipped resorts. It has very good accommodation and it can provide plenty of activities.It has a disco, its own desalination plant, two helipads and even a handphone transmission tower to ensure the best reception. What more could you want? A beach would be nice. As at a number of other resorts, Matahari has had to build a retaining wall around its investment and there is no beach at all.

*Matahari Island Resort (direct ☎ 641 5332)* can be booked though counter 1&2 (☎ 640338) at the Marina Ancol. The rooms in attractive two-storey bungalows cost from US$50/65 for singles/doubles during the week up to US$60/75 on weekends. However, the resort has been offering some discounted full-board packages from 390,000 rp per person (450,000 rp on weekends).

## Pulau Putri

Pulau Putri has plenty of white sand to lie around on, but the sand is separated from the water by a retaining wall. Accommodation is good and there is a restaurant with a built-in aquarium. In fact, much of the island is an aquarium, with a huge range of tropical fish, sting rays, moray eels and even sharks in the netted baths in front of the resort. An underwater viewing tunnel is moored next to the island's dock.

*Pulau Putri Resort*, PT Buana Bintang Samudra (☎ 8281093), Jl Sultan Agung 21, has a swimming pool and a variety of accommodation, from older but well-appointed cottages with air-con, TV and hot water up to excellent, Balinese-style, thatched-roof cottages. The package rate, including transport and meals, is 460,000 rp per person or 600,000 rp on weekends. Rates for children are around half price.

## Pulau Bira

The newest and one of the best resorts, Bira is one of the largest islands and it has its own nine-hole golf course (a game of golf will set you back around 200,000 rp). It promotes mostly golf packages but even non-golfers will be impressed with the good beach, fine accommodation and facilities that include a large swimming pool.

*Patra Bira Cottages* (☎ 5415103) can be booked though PT Pulau Seribu Paradise (☎ 7975157), Gedung Multika, Mampang Prapatan Raya 71-73, Jakarta. Spacious bungalows have air-con and fridge for 480,000 rp per person, twin share, full board (560,000 rp on weekends) and this is one of the few places to provide mosquito nets. The huge suite bungalows are 800,000 rp per person full board (1,000,000 rp weekends). Return transport is an extra 160,000 rp (200,000 rp on weekends).

## Pulau Pelangi

Pelangi has a retaining wall in parts but in between are some decent stretches of beach and the accommodation is good. It is under the same management as nearby Pulau Bira Besar, so discounts are offered for golfers.

*Pulau Pelangi Resort* can also be booked through PT Pulau Seribu Paradise (☎ 797 5157). Full board packages in older bungalows cost around 500,000 rp (560,000 rp on weekends), including transport.

## Pulau Sepa

This small island is surrounded by wide stretches of pristine sand. Accommodation is simple, the plain food soon palls and mosquitos buzz the rooms at night, but all is forgiven when you step on to the lovely beaches, which are among the best of all the islands. The beaches and the more reasonably priced accommodation means that Sepa is busy when the other islands are empty.

*Pulau Sepa Resort* (☎ 5453375) can be booked through PT Pulau Sepa Permai (☎ 6906968), Jl Kali Besar Barat 29. Rooms have air-con and hot water but are really just a better class of losmen, while bungalows are also simple, but have more character. All-inclusive packages in rooms start at 300,000/465,000 rp for one/two nights, while bungalow packages are 343,000/523,000 rp up to 468,000/773,000 rp.

## Pulau Antuk (Pantara)

Renamed Pulau Pantara from the less-marketable original name of Pulau Antuk (Ghost Island), this resort comprises two islands – Pulau Antuk Timur and Pulau Antuk Barat, separated by a narrow channel. Both house the fanciest resort with the best facilities and being the farthest north of all the resorts, the waters tend to be the clearest.

*Pulau Seribu Marine Resort*, c/- PT Pantara Wisata Jaya (☎ 5723161), Jl Jenderal Sudirman Kav 3-4, is the most up-market of the resorts and is popular with Japanese groups. Antuk Barat has a Japanese restaurant and a swimming pool, while Antuk Timur has the main building, more restaurants, a disco and tennis courts. A regular shuttle connects the two. Bungalows are very comfortable, though not really luxurious. It's the range of other facilities that stand out. Full-board packages cost US$105/165/230 for singles/doubles/triples, slightly more on weekends, and the boat is an extra US$50 return. Even with a favourable conversion rate, this is still the most expensive resort by far.

## Getting There & Away

The resorts have daily boats for guests and day trippers, most leaving at 8 am and returning around 2 pm, which means that an overnight stay is almost two full days at a resort. Jakarta's Ancol Marina is the departure point. Not all resort boats run for just one or two guests, but the Pulau Sepa boats will pick up and drop off at other islands.

Return day-trip rates, including lunch, to the resorts include: Pulau Bidadari (40,000 rp), Pulau Ayer (80,000 rp), Pulau Kotok (250,000 rp), Pulau Putri (240,000 rp), Pulau Sepa (200,000 rp), Pulau Pelangi (300,000 rp) and Pulau Bira Besar (270,000 rp). Transport rates for guests are slightly cheaper but most resorts include transport in their accommodation packages. The resorts provide speed boats and it takes only a little over two hours to get to even the farthest islands.

A local ferry, the *Betok*, operates from Ancol to Pulau Kelapa (8500 rp) on Saturday and Wednesday at 7.30 am, returning Sunday and Thursday, but from Kelapa it is necessary to charter boats to get to other islands. To charter a speed boat from Ancol, prices start at around 1,000,000 rp for a day. No regular flights operate to the airport on Pulau Panjang and planes have to be chartered from Jakarta's Halim airport.

# West Java

The province of West Java, with Bandung as its capital, has a population of 40 million and an area of 46,229 sq km. Historically known as Sunda, it is the home of the Sundanese people and their culture. The name Sunda is of Sanskrit origin and means 'pure' or 'white'.

Away from Jakarta and the flat, hot coastline to the north, West Java is predominantly mountainous and agricultural, with lush green valleys and high volcanic peaks surrounding the capital, Bandung, at the core of the region. West Java is also strongly Islamic, yet in the remote Kendeng mountains there is still a small isolated community known as the Badui, believed to be descendants of the ancient Sundanese who fled from Islam more than 400 years ago.

The Dutch heritage is very noticeable in Bogor and Bandung, and Bandung is also a centre for Sundanese culture. If you want a break from travelling or hiking, the mountains are dotted with resorts, hot springs and volcanoes. West Java has a good beach resort at Pangandaran and a fine backwater trip along the coastal lagoons to Central Java. Other major attractions, though remote and isolated, include the famous Krakatau, off the west coast, and the unique Ujung Kulon National Park in the southwest of the province.

## JAKARTA TO MERAK

Most visitors just head straight through from Jakarta to Merak on their way to (or from) Sumatra, but along this route you can also branch off and head for the west coast. The west coast's greatest attractions are undoubtedly the Krakatau Islands and Ujung Kulon National Park, both of which require some effort to get to, but the beaches are also a welcome break from the noise and hassle of Jakarta. These places can also be reached using Jakarta as a base.

The busy Jakarta to Merak road runs through a flat coastal area that has plenty

## HIGHLIGHTS

- The mighty Krakatau is Indonesia's most famous volcano.
- Bogor's extensive botanical gardens are world class.
- Java's premier national park is Ujung Kulon, with good trekking and varied coastal and jungle scenery.
- Gunung Papandayan is one of the most active and spectacular volcanoes in West Java.
- Gede Pangrango National Park – among Java's more accessible and interesting national parks.
- The volcanically active Gunung Gede is the highlight of Gede Pangrango National Park.
- Puncak Pass is a beautiful 1500m-high pass on a narrow, winding mountain road; it's a popular escape from the heat and crowds of Jakarta.
- Cibodas offers 80 hectares of scenic botanic gardens, over Puncak Pass.
- Cipanas is a resort town with hot springs noted for their curative properties.
- The fishing village of Pangandaran is Java's No 1 beach resort.

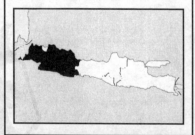

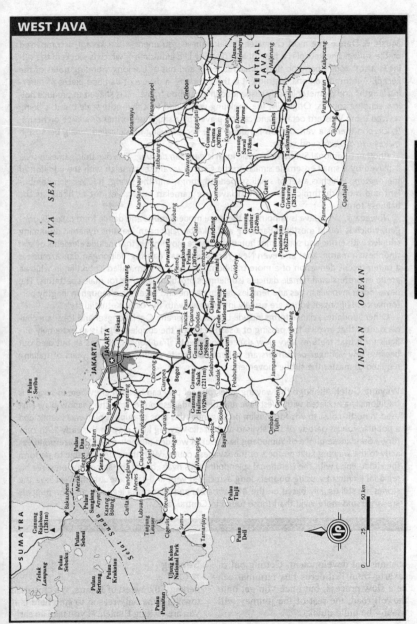

# WEST JAVA

## Sundanese Arts

**Music & Dance** The most characteristic Sundanese instrument is the *kecapi*, accompanied by the *suling*. The kecapi is a type of lute (looking like a dulcimer), which is plucked; the suling is a soft-toned bamboo flute, which fades in and out of the long vibrating notes of the kecapi. Another traditional instrument is the *angklung*, a device of bamboo pieces of differing lengths and diameter loosely suspended in a bamboo frame – it is shaken to produce hollow echoing sounds. Originally, the angklung was tuned to a five-note scale but it is being revived using Western octaves and can be played by a single performer or a large orchestra. In Cirebon there's a variation on Bandung-style kecapi-suling music called *tarling* because it makes use of *guitar* and *suling*.

Another traditional Sundanese music form is *gamelan degung*. This dynamic gamelan style is played by a small ensemble similar to the Central Javanese gamelan with the addition of the *degung*, which is a set of small suspended gongs, and the suling. It is less somnambulant and more rhythmic than Central Javanese gamelan music, yet not as hectic as the Balinese forms.

Nowadays, West Java is famous for the more modern music and dance form called Jaipongan, which is found mostly in Bandung and Jakarta. Jaipongan features dynamic drumming coupled with erotic and sometimes humorous dance movements that include elements of *silat* (Indonesian martial arts) and even New York-style break dancing. Jaipongan dance/music is a rather recent derivation of a more traditional Sundanese form called Ketuktilu, in which a group of professional female dancers (sometimes prostitutes) dance for male spectators. The newer form involves males and females dancing alone and together, although in lengthy performances Jaipongan songs are usually interspersed with the older Ketuktilu style.

Other Sundanese dance forms include Longser, Joker and Ogel. Longser and Joker are couple dances that involve the passing of a sash between the couples. Ogel is an extremely difficult form that features very slow dance movements. Traditional Ogel has all but died out because few younger performers are patient enough to endure the many years of training required to master the subtle movements.

**Wayang Golek** Although the wayang golek puppet play can be seen elsewhere in Java, it is traditionally associated with West Java and the Sundanese prefer it to the shadow play. First used in north-coast towns for Muslim propaganda, this type of puppet play was Islamic and a popular, robust parody of the stylised aristocratic wayang kulit play. In the early 19th century, a Sundanese prince of Sumedang had a set of wooden puppets made to correspond exactly to the wayang kulit puppets of the Javanese courts. With these he was able to perform the Hindu epics with the traditional splendour of his rivals, but at the same time preserve his regional identity by using puppets long associated with anti-Javanese art. In West Java the stories are still usually based on the *Mahabharata* and *Ramayana* legends, and the puppets are larger and more vivid than those found in Central Java.

of industrial development. Getting out of Jakarta from Kalideres bus terminal can be a slow process, but once you get onto the toll road, the rest of the journey will usually be quite quick.

## Serang
☎ 0254

Serang, 90km west of Jakarta, is a crossroad town and the only reason to stop here is if you are visiting Banten. If you take an early morning bus from Jakarta and a late afternoon bus back (or go on to the west coast), you will have plenty of time to explore Banten's ruins.

**Places to Stay** If you get stuck, the *Hotel Abadi (☎ 200641, Jl Jenderal Sudirman 36)*, near the bus station, has a variety of rooms from 15,000 rp with *mandi*, as well as more expensive rooms with air-con.

**Getting There & Away** Buses run to/from Jakarta (Kalideres station, 3000 rp, two hours) and Merak (1000 rp, one hour). Patas buses between Jakarta and Merak bypass Serang, which is south of the highway. From Serang, minibuses run to Banten for 700 rp. Buses also go to Labuan (2500 rp); for Anyer and the coast road, first take a bus to Cilegon.

## Banten

West of Jakarta, on the coast, are the few remaining fragments of the great maritime capital of the Banten sultanate. Banten once thrived on the spice trade of the 16th and 17th centuries, attracting Arab, Indian and Chinese traders as well as the Portuguese, Dutch and English, who established trading posts in what was one of Asia's largest ports.

Today, the historic precinct of Banten Lama (Old Banten) is little more than a dusty fishing village centred on the grand mosque, museum and a gaggle of souvenir stalls. Other tombs, ruined palaces and the remains of a Dutch fort are scattered in the fields over a large area.

Though only a shadow of its former greatness, Banten makes an interesting detour on the way to the west coast and a peaceful break from the busy main highway.

**History** By the time the Portuguese arrived in 1511 after capturing Malacca, Banten was already an established trading centre, noted for pepper. Banten was the coastal port of the Hindu Pajajaran kingdom but Islamic influence, brought by trade, had already penetrated. By 1527, the armies of Demak

under the command of the great Islamic missionary, Sunan Gunungjati, drove out the local ruler and Banten became Muslim.

Conversion helped to increase trade, attracting Muslim traders who preferred to do business in Islamic Banten rather than in Portuguese-controlled Malacca (Melaka).

In 1552 Banten became independent from Demak under Sultan Mauluna Hasanudin and the city grew rapidly with new public works. Around 1580 Banten ventured inland to conquer the last remnants of Pajajaran, effectively ending Hinduism on Java.

The Dutch first arrived in Banten in 1596, initiating a more aggressive era of colonial trade. In 1601 they attacked the Portuguese trading post at Banten and drove the Portuguese out, only to see the English arrive in 1602 to establish their own trading post. Banten became rich as a supplier of pepper direct to European markets but its sovereignty was increasingly undermined.

When Banten attempted to wrest control of trade back from the Europeans and impose taxes, the Dutch and English upped and moved to Jayakarta. After the Dutch took Jayakarta and founded Batavia in 1619, the English moved back to Banten and trade again flourished. Banten became a great city-state, a cosmopolitan melting pot of trade. It was the largest city in Indonesia and one of the largest in Asia with a population of 150,000 in the 1670s.

Banten reached its peak during the reign of Sultan Agung (1651-83), but he unwisely clashed with rising Dutch power in Batavia. In 1680 Agung (not to be confused with the Sultan Agung of Mataram) declared war on Batavia but, before he could make a move, internal conflict within the royal house led to Dutch intervention on behalf of the ambitious crown prince. Agung fled from Banten but finally surrendered in 1683 and his defeat marked the real beginning of Dutch territorial expansion in Java. Not only was Banten's independence at an end but its English East India Company rivals were driven out, effectively destroying British interests in Java.

WEST JAVA

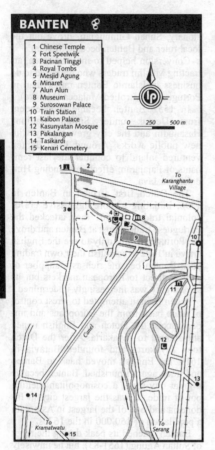

**BANTEN**

1 Chinese Temple
2 Fort Speelwijk
3 Pacinan Tinggi
4 Royal Tombs
5 Mesjid Agung
6 Minaret
7 Alun Alun
8 Museum
9 Surosowan Palace
10 Train Station
11 Kaibon Palace
12 Kasunyatan Mosque
13 Pakalangan
14 Tasikardi
15 Kenari Cemetery

0     250     500 m

To
Karanghantu
Village

To
Kramatwatu

To
Serang

WEST JAVA

The Dutch maintained trading interests in Banten for a time but they did a good job of demolishing the place in the 19th century. At some point too this coastline silted up and Banten became a ghost town, a small dusty fishing village, which is really all that it is today.

**Things to See**  The chief landmark of a prosperous era is the mid-16th century **Mesjid Agung** (Grand Mosque), which dominates the village and is the most impressive sight in Banten. It's a good example of early Javanese Islamic architecture, and it also employed Hindu motifs such as the three tiered *meru* roof of Hindu temples.

Towering above is the mosque's great white lighthouse of a **minaret,** reputedly designed by a Chinese Muslim in 1559. A narrow staircase spirals up through the thick walls of the minaret to two high balconies. From the top are fine views over the coastline, much of which is now fishponds, a sort of local reclamation project made by building retaining walls out into the bay.

Adjoining the mosque are the **royal tombs,** where the leaders of Banten and their families are buried, including Sultan Mauluna Hasanudin, who was the first ruler of an independent Banten from 1552 to 1570. Just to the right inside the door is the small gravestone of a Dutchman, known locally as Hors Kwadil, but historical references suggest his name was Hendrik Cardeel, who converted to Islam and designed the Surosowan Palace. He was accorded the privilege of burial in the royal tombs by the sultan.

The **alun alun**, or main square, was once the centre of Banten. Pride of place here was the Ki Amuk (Raging Fury) cannon, the partner of Si Jagur, which stands in Jakarta's Taman Fatahillah. Legend has it that if the two cannons were to be reunited Banten's power would be restored (though another legend has Si Jagur's partner in Solo). The cannon has now been moved to the front of the museum, partly to stop visitors sitting astride the cannon, which is reputed to have spiritual power and is a symbol of fertility.

Next to the mosque is an **archaeological museum** (open from 9 am to 4 pm, closed Monday) with a modest collection of mostly clay artefacts found in the area, and weapons, including a few of the long, iron, chained spikes which the 'Debus players' are famous for. Banten has long been a centre for practitioners of the Debus tradition, which is supposed to have come from India. These Islamic ascetics engage in masochistic activities such as plunging sharp weapons into their bodies (without drawing blood!), and are able to control pain and fear by the strength of their faith. In Banten this was originally part of the training of the invincible special soldiers attached to the court.

Directly across from the mosque is the large grass-covered site of Hasanudin's fortified palace, the **Surosowan Palace**, which was wrecked in the bloody civil war during the reign of Sultan Agung and rebuilt, only to be razed to the ground by the Dutch in 1832. Excavations have revealed the baths, foundations and walls.

One of the most impressive sights, northwest of the mosque, is the massive ruins of **Fort Speelwijk**, which now overlooks an expanse of sand-silt marsh, although at one time it stood on the sea's edge. The fort was built by the Dutch in 1682, expanded in the 1730s, but finally abandoned by Governor-General Daendels at the beginning of the 19th century. You can wander around inside and up onto the massive ramparts. At the eastern entrance is an old Dutch graveyard with ransacked graves. Opposite the western entrance to the fort is a **Chinese temple**, dating from the 18th century and still in use.

Back along the road to Serang are the huge crumbling walls and archways of the **Kaibon Palace**, which was inhabited by the mother of the last sultan of Banten in the 19th century. Farther south is the **Pakalangan**, tomb of Maulana Yusuf, the second ruler of independent Banten who died in 1580. Nearby, the **Kasunyatan** is a restored mosque dating from the 16th century.

The **Tasikardi** was once a water palace, such as are found in most Javanese royal cities. Here the sultan and his family relaxed, and the artificial lake was once surrounded by royal pavilions. Today, paddle boats, not royal barges, float on the water and this is a popular Sunday picnic spot. Just to the south-east is the **Kenari** royal cemetery. Through the split gateway, a Hindu-influenced architectural detail common in Java and Bali, lie the tombs of Sultan Abulmaali and Sultan Abulmafakhir.

**Getting There & Away** By car, Banten is about a 1½-hour drive from Jakarta, via the western toll road to Merak. Take the Serang turn-off and then the old Cilegon highway to the village of Kramatwatu. The turn-off to Banten is next to the big mosque, through the market.

By public transport, take a bus to Serang, 10km south of Banten, then a minibus (700 rp, half an hour), which will drop you near the Mesjid Agung. A quicker alternative is to take any bus between Jakarta and Cilegon and get off at the mosque in Kramatwatu village, from where *ojeg* motorbike riders can take you the 5km to Banten for around 2000 to 3000 rp.

## Pulau Dua Bird Sanctuary

Off the coast at Banten, Pulau Dua (also known locally as Pulau Burung) is a major bird sanctuary. The island has a large resident population – mainly herons, storks and cormorants – but peak time is between March and July when great numbers of migratory birds (an estimated 50,000) flock here for the breeding season. Pulau Dua is a low swampy island and only hardy, dedicated birders would want to make the trip.

It's a half-hour by chartered boat from the Karanghantu harbour in Banten but you can walk across the fishponds to the island. From Banten, take an *angkot* 5km east to the village of Sawahluhur. Alternatively, from Serang take an angkot to Pasar Rawu (500 rp) and then another to Sawahluhur (700 rp). The village has a mosque and a school and not much else. The trail to the island starts just 100m or so before the village and then it is a hot 1km walk, weaving between the fishponds – just keep heading for the trees on the horizon. There is a PHPA post with a derelict hut that has bare wooden beds and not much else. If you are planning to stay, bring food and water. Very expensive tours are also arranged from Carita.

## Cilegon

Cilegon, 20km north-west of Serang, is a go-ahead town and the centre for one of

Indonesia's most important industrial zones that stretches right through from Jakarta to Merak. On the western outskirts is the vast Krakatau steel plant. This giant enterprise was begun in the early 1960s with Russian aid, partially dismantled when the Russians were expelled after the 1965 coup, but then resurrected with foreign aid and backing from Pertamina.

Cilegon is a modern town with shopping centres and all the amenities you need, including banks – about the only real reason to visit. The Bank BNI is on the main road and Bank Lippo and BII are about half a kilometre off the road in a new middle-class housing estate, one of many around Cilegon. The town even has an international school to cater to expatriate families that are stationed at the large projects in the area. Cilegon's port is a few kilometres north at Bonjonegoro and is being developed to become the biggest container port in Indonesia.

## MERAK
☎ 0254

Right on the north-western tip of Java, 140km from Jakarta, Merak is the terminus for ferries shuttling to and from Bakauheni on the southern end of Sumatra. Merak is just an arrival and departure point and most people pass straight through this noisy, rapidly industrialising town.

**Pantai Florida**, 5km north of Merak, used to be a pleasant beach but the water is dirty and the encroaching industrial development in unsightly. Past Pantai Florida is the huge Suralaya power station, Java's biggest.

## Places to Stay
*Hotel Anda (☎ 71041, Jl Raya Pulorida 5)*, just across the railway line opposite the bus station, has well kept rooms with fan and mandi for 20,000 rp and 23,000 rp, or air-con rooms from 37,500 rp. The *Hotel Robinson (☎ 71960)* next door is similarly priced but not as good.

The new, three-star *Hotel Feri Merak (☎ 572081, Jl Raya Pelabuhan 30)* is 1.5km from the ferry terminal towards Jakarta.

This is far and away the best hotel and has a pool, sauna, fitness centre and Japanese restaurant. Rooms are 140,000 to 160,000 rp, before discount.

*Hotel Pantai Merak (☎ 71015)*, 2km out of town on the road to Jakarta, is sandwiched between the thin strip of beach and the noisy highway. Rooms are comfortable enough and have sea views for 100,000 to 125,000 rp.

## Getting There & Away
The bus and railway stations in Merak are right at the ferry dock.

**Bus** Frequent buses run between Merak and Jakarta (4000 rp, three hours). Most terminate at Jakarta's Kalideres bus station, but buses also run to/from Pulo Gadung and Kampung Rambutan terminals for 6500/10,000 rp ekonomi/air-con. Other buses run all through Java, including Bogor (7000 rp), Bandung (10,000/15,000 to 23,000 rp), Yogya and Solo.

Buses leave from the front of the bus terminal to Serang (1000 rp), Cilegon (700 rp), Labuan (2700 rp) and Rangkasbitung (2200 rp). Buses to Labuan via Anyer and Carita are not frequent so you may have to take one to the Simpang Tiga turn-off on the western outskirts of Cilegon, and then a bus from there.

**Train** An eksekutif train to Jakarta (10,000 rp, three hours) departs at noon and stops at Kota station, otherwise a slower ekonomi train (2500 rp) goes to Tanah Abang station at 1.30 pm.

**Boat** Ferries to Bakauheni in Sumatra depart about every 30 minutes, 24 hours a day. Ferries cost 2900/2300 rp in Ekonomi A/B class and take two hours. Motorbikes cost 5600 rp and cars 96,000 rp. Alternatively, the *Dermaga* is a fast ferry to Bagoni taking 45 minutes and costing 8000/12,000 rp. Through-buses are the easiest option – it takes two hours by bus to Bandarlumpang from Bakauheni – and the cost of the ferry is included in the bus ticket.

# FURNITURE IN JAVA

Interesting furniture can be found in every village in Java. Storage boxes, low stools and work tables are the only 'pure' traditional items, but colonial Indian, Chinese and 20th century influences mean that dressers, chunky rustic tables and unique creations await discovery. Many pieces have a wonderful tropical feel to them.

One noteworthy traditional item is the Jodang. It is a solid rectangular box with high ends that have a central hole. For festivals (eg a marriage) the boxes, laden with treasures, are carried on a bamboo pole. They are often decoratively carved and make interesting chests or low tables. The bigger ones are sometimes modified into seats.

The Dutch introduced teak to Java, and teak is the raw material for much of the finest furniture (split bamboo and other timbers are also common). The main commercial areas of manufacture are close to the ports. There are many workshops along the central north coast, close to the port at Semarang, where much 'antique European'-style furniture is made for export. The level of artisanship varies widely.

You will find the most varied collections of Javanese furniture in the major cities such as Yogyakarta, Solo and Jakarta, although prices are mostly higher than on Bali, even for local pieces. Always remain sceptical about the age of a piece. The word 'antique' is not always used to indicate that a piece is at least 100 years old. Many imitation pieces are to be found, often well made from old timber.

If you are tempted to buy furniture, check that the wood has been properly seasoned, as splitting and contracting in less humid climates is a common problem. You should also realise that the buying price is just one aspect of the deal. To get the item safely home, a good standard of packing is vital. Fumigation of exported woodwork is also required by some countries, so research the total charges before you make decisions. It is not unusual to spend US$600 to get a US$100 item home. The same piece may cost US$60 to send if part of a 20 foot container. There is no shortage of agents with shipping experience.

**Michael Sklovsky**

**Right:** Decorative wood carving, found on much Javanese furniture.

In Jakarta, everything is at a distance. Weaving in and out of the city's traffic is decidedly risky.

Jl Thamrin, the main thoroughfare in modern Jakarta, contains the big hotels and shopping centres.

## WEST-COAST BEACHES

At Cilegon the road branches south to Anyer and runs close to the sea all the way to Labuan. The road passes Cilegon's massive steel works, chemical, cement and other industrial plants until it reaches Anyer market. From here the road runs to Labuan along a flat green coastal strip bordered by a rocky reef-lined coast that is punctuated by stretches of white-sand beach.

This picturesque coast has masses of coconut palms and banana trees and because of its easy access by toll road from Jakarta, it is a popular weekend beach strip. The beaches are good and make a fine escape from Jakarta's heat and crowds. Accommodation is scattered all along the coast from Anyer to Carita.

Anyer tends to be more upmarket, but the whole coast is quite expensive because of its proximity to Jakarta. The only real budget accommodation is in Carita, where tours to Krakatau and Ujung Kulon National Park can also be arranged.

Apart from the multiplying but still spread-out resorts, the area is sparsely populated with small fishing settlements and coconut ports. This is perhaps simply because the land isn't suitable for intensive rice agriculture, but it's also said that survivors of the Krakatau eruption, and succeeding generations, believed it to be a place of ill omen and never returned.

### Anyer
☎ 0254

Anyer, 12km from Cilegon, is an upmarket beach resort popular with Jakarta residents. Anyer was once the biggest Dutch port in Selat Sunda before being totally destroyed by tidal waves generated by Krakatau. The Anyer lighthouse was built after the disaster by the Dutch at the instigation of Queen Wilhelmina in 1885.

Offshore from Anyer is the island of **Sangiang**, which has coral reefs and 7 sq km of jungle, mangrove and monkeys – or at least it used to. A huge resort is now planned for the island but development has stalled with the economic downturn. The resort does have a catamaran, however, which is docked at its own marina just north of the Hotel Mabruk in Anyer and makes trips to the island.

To the south of Anyer, just before Karang Bolong, is the turn-off to **Batu Kuwung**, a hot springs near the town of Padarincang. The springs have a swimming pool and mandi blocks – not exactly a Swiss spa but pleasant enough. No regular public transport runs there from Anyer (it's about half an hour by car or motorbike) but angkot run from Serang on the other side of the mountains.

### Karang Bolong
☎ 0254

There's another good beach here, 11km south of Anyer and 30km north of Labuan, where a huge stand of rock forms a natural archway from the land to the sea. It is a popular local resort – littered and downmarket.

### Carita Beach
☎ 0253

Carita has a wide sandy beach that is good for swimming, and plenty of opportunities to go wandering along the beach or inland. It is the most popular beach for travellers because it has cheap accommodation and is the best place to arrange visits to Krakatau and the Ujung Kulon National Park. That said, Carita is becoming very developed, condominiums now hog the beach and you even get hassling massage ladies, à la Bali. It is still relaxed on weekdays but this is no longer an unspoiled beach village.

About 2km from Carita, across the rice paddies, you'll see the village of **Sindanglaut** (End of the Sea), where the giant tsunami of 1883 ended. The **Hutan Wisata Carita** is a forest reserve with walks through the hills and jungle. The **Curug Gendang** waterfall is a three-hour return hike through the reserve.

Around Carita you'll often see a mass of lights strung out across the sea at night. They're the night fishermen, fishing for shrimp, prawns and lobster from platforms called *bagang* – small bamboo huts on stilts firmly embedded in the sea bottom, way out from the shore.

**Organised Tours** In Carita, a number of small operators offer tours to Krakatau, Ujung Kulon and farther afield. No bargains are on offer but the tours are cheaper than those organised by larger travel agents in the hotels.

The Rakata Tourist Information Service (☎ 81124) at the Rakata Hostel is well run and a good place to start looking. Others offering similar services include the Black Rhino (☎ 81072) and the privately run Tourist Information Service (☎ 81330), opposite the Hotel Desiana.

They all offer almost identical tours to Krakatau, Ujung Kulon (from US$175 per person for four days/three nights) as well as Badui villages (US$150), Pulau Dua (US$150) and even Jakarta (US$100). Expect a very favourable exchange rate for rupiah payment. See under Krakatau for tours to those islands.

The big hotels used to have dive shops but most have closed due to falling demand. Arrange equipment hire and dive trips in Jakarta. Boat hire is easily arranged all along the coast. The best diving is in Ujung Kulon National Park, and Krakatau and Pulau Sanghiang also have diving.

## Places to Stay

Because of the easy access from Jakarta, the resorts along this stretch of coast are expensive, but standards are generally high. Dozens of hotels and villas (many private but some for rent) are spaced out along the 30km stretch from Anyer to Carita, and more are being built. Prices drop the farther south you head from Anyer, and the only cheap accommodation is found in Carita.

On weekends the hotels fill up and prices rise. Prices quoted here are the weekday rates. Weekend rates at the more expensive hotels are usually 20 to 30% more, and 21% tax and service is charged on top of the room rates. However, most hotels are simply overpriced and it pays to inquire about discounts or simply bargain, especially during the week.

**Anyer** Most hotels in Anyer have swimming pools, restaurants and rooms with air-con,

parabola (satellite) TV and hot-water showers. They are spaced out over a 5km stretch and start just south of the Anyer market, but the better places are past the Anyer lighthouse. The first one south of the lighthouse is *Hotel Mambruk Anyer (☎ 601602)*, with large gardens, a swimming pool and tennis courts. It is one of the best in Anyer and discounted rooms with all the trimmings range from 315,000 rp up to the big cottages for 730,000 rp, plus 21%. It has manufactured a small beach, but the coast is still rocky here and unsuitable for swimming.

A little farther south, *Vila Marina (☎ 601288)* has similar facilities, including a boat marina and dive shop, but is not as good. However, weekday rates of 180,000 rp up to 750,000 rp for large, self-contained bungalows are quite reasonable. Speedboats can be hired, starting at 1 million rp per day.

Farther south around the headland is *Ancotte (☎ 601556)*, right on a fine stretch of sandy beach. This hotel is a good mid-range resort and has a pool, restaurant and rooms from 150,000 rp. Old but comfortable bungalows, many with kitchens, cost 275,000 and 325,000 rp. Rates are almost double on weekends.

Past Ancotte is the real centre of the Anyer resort strip. Immediately south of the Patra Jasa hotel is Anyer's most lively stretch with a number of places to stay and a good beach with almost white sand. The beach is dominated by the huge Sol Elite Marbella hotel and condominium complex, which has restaurants, shops and beach stalls to give the scattered developments at Anyer a central focus and a resort feel.

*Patra Jasa Anyer (☎ 602700)* is at the northern end of this good beach but most of the beach in front of the hotel is blighted by a retaining wall. Older motel units are well appointed and start at 350,000 rp. It has an impressive restaurant on a rock outcrop over the sea and the newer section over the road has a swimming pool.

Next along, *Nuansa Bali (☎ 602236)* has a large collection of well appointed but overpriced bungalows starting at 480,000 rp. A little farther south, *Pondok Layung*

(☎ 601870) is a collection of modern three-bedroom bungalows with kitchen for 500,000 rp (10% more on weekends). There is no restaurant or pool but the spacious, well appointed bungalows are good for families and groups. They must be booked in Jakarta (☎ 021-3853520).

In the shadow of the Sol Elite Marbella, the small **Pondok Tubagus Resort** (☎ 601776) is easily overlooked but it is one of the classiest on the coast. Beautifully appointed cottages are furnished in Asian antique style. Rooms cost 500,000 rp and two or three bedroom cottages are 700,000 to one million rp. Most unique are the 'tropical tents' right near the beach, with open living rooms for 300,000 rp.

The biggest place by far is the **Sol Elite Marbella** (☎ 602345) condominium/hotel. It is the best on the coast and this Spanish-owned hotel has real Iberian style. There are swimming pools, shops, restaurants, a host of activities and the good beach is lined with small *warungs* and stalls selling cheap beachwear. Rooms start at 480,000 rp, plus 21%, and even at that price the place can pack them in on weekends.

**Karang Bolong** A few hotels are clustered around the recreational park but there's not a lot of reason to stay. Karang Bolong has a dirty, sprawling warung area around the car park where buses disgorge gawking local tourists. **Lalita Cottages** (☎ 7806514) is on a decent beach and has simple, two-bedroom cottages for a reasonable 150,000 rp. The new **Persona Krakatau** (☎ 650345) is far and away the best place with one, two and three bedroom self-contained cottages from 350,000 to 800,000 rp, 30% less during the week. It has a pool.

Three kilometres farther south, **Puri Retno II** (☎ 201228) has extravagant Balinese-style cottages with extravagant prices – US$125 and US$200 – but no beach. A good beach can be found half a kilometre south and the villas there are worth trying.

Three kilometres south of its sister hotel, the **Puri Retno I** is built in the same style and is even more expensive. At least it has

a thin stretch of beach. Next door, the friendly **Resor Prima Anyer** (☎ 650440) has good mid-range, air-con rooms facing the beach. They cost 170,000 to 423,000 rp but with a big discount they are reasonable value for this part of the world. Other new mid-range hotels can be found in this area, but they are on the other side of the road from the beach.

**Carita** Heading north from Labuan, the usual access point, at the 5 Km marker, is the four star **Pantai Carita Resort** (☎ 81127). It is one of the best on the coast with a swimming pool, tennis courts, diving and windsurfing facilities, restaurants, bars etc. Rooms start at around 500,000 rp and a variety of suites are available. The only drawback is that the beach fronts a rocky reef that is unsuitable for swimming.

Farther north is Carita village and around 1km farther still is the sweeping bay that is the centre for accommodation. The bay has one of the best beaches on the coast and good swimming.

Back in the 1980s, Carita had just one travellers' hotel – the small Carita Krakatau Beach Hotel – started by a German doctor. It was popular for the beach and visits to Krakatau, and other small hotels followed this pioneer. In the 1990s, the big developers moved in, land prices soared and the whole coast became the playground of the Jakarta well-to-do. Even in the current hard times, Carita still pulls big weekend crowds willing to pay high rates. Carita also has some budget and mid-range accommodation, which is hard to find elsewhere on the coast, though prices are still high (bargaining is often possible).

Past the 8 Km mark is the **Resor Lippo Carita/Clarion Suites Hotel** (☎ 81900). This huge condominium/hotel complex hogs the best stretch of beach for almost a kilometre, destroying Carita's character in the process. One/two-bedroom suites are 150,000/225,000 rp on weekdays, and 225,000/375,000 rp on weekends, plus 21%. That is a good rate for the quality on offer, but these are units rather than hotel

**WEST JAVA**

rooms, so there's no pool or restaurant (unless you count the related family fun park across the road).

At the southern end of the Resor Lippo, the new, small **Krakatau Surf Carita** (☎ 83849) is right on the beach and has some of the coast's best accommodation. Very stylish one and two bedroom villas cost US$150 to US$250, plus 21%, but expect big discounts (up to 50%).

Over the road is the popular *Rakata Hostel* (☎ 81171), which has a good restaurant and runs tours to Ujung Kulon and Krakatau. Bright rooms with bathroom for 40,000 and 70,000 rp (50,000 and 90,000 rp on weekends) are a reasonable deal in expensive Carita. More expensive mid-range rooms with air-con and TV cost 100,000 rp (120,000 rp on weekends). All rates are subject to 11% tax.

Farther north is the *Hotel Wira Carita* (☎ 81116), an old-fashioned place with large grounds, a swimming pool and children's playground. It is popular with struggling, middle-class Indonesian families. Simple rooms with mandi cost 50,000 rp or 75,000 rp with air-con, cottages are 200,000 rp, all plus 15.5%. Rates rise on weekends and skyrocket during holiday periods.

Around the 9 Km mark, *Pondok Pandawa* (☎ 82193) is the only cheap place right on the beach but the bungalow rooms with mandi are very basic and overpriced at 40,000 rp (more on weekends).

Next along, the *Carita Baka Baka* (☎ 81126) is also on the beach and has a pleasant restaurant. Expensive rooms with shower and fan are around 60,000 rp or 90,000 rp with air-con, double that on weekends. Try bargaining. Three bedroom bungalows start at 300,000 rp.

Farther north, across the road from the beach, the popular *Sunset View* (☎ 81075) is the best value on the coast for a budget room. Clean rooms with mandi cost only 25,000 rp. Apart from the ping-pong table, there's not a lot else, but the family is friendly. Nearby, the *Badak Hitam* (Black Rhino, ☎ 81072) used to be a budget favourite and may be again if it ever finishes its renovations.

Also in this budget area is the *Ratih Homestay* (☎ 81137), where spartan rooms cost from 30,000 rp. A better option is to keep walking a little farther to the more switched-on **Carita Krakatau Hostel** (☎ 83027). This place caters to travellers, arranges tours and has a good restaurant. The rooms are well back from the road and cost 30,000 rp or 50,000 rp with air-con.

Not far away, around the 10 Km mark, the *Niguadharma Hotel* (☎ 83288) is a new mid-range hotel with a swimming pool and restaurant. It is not right on the beach but it is well appointed and very reasonably priced. Economy rooms with shared bath are 25,000 rp, rooms with bathroom are 50,000 rp or 100,000 rp with air-con, including breakfast.

## Places to Eat

The coast doesn't have a lot of restaurants and dining is usually done at the hotels. It can work out to be quite expensive at the higher priced establishments. Anyer and Karang Bolang have a number of seafood warungs, but unless you have your own transport, you virtually have to eat at your hotel because everything is so spread out.

Good hotel dining options in Anyer include the restaurant at the *Patra Jasa Anyer*, which has fabulous sea views and good Chinese, Indonesian and western food, or the restaurants at the *Sol Elite Marbella*, where you can get a good paella, among other things. Farther south, just before Karang Bolong, *Marina Anyer Kafe* is part of a huge marina/real estate development. The cafe on the waterfront is a very fashionable spot for a drink or light meal and bands play on the weekend.

Carita has plenty of warungs and *rumah makan*. Opposite the Resor Lippo Carita, *Warung Kita* is basic but cheap, or *Rumah Makan Ibu Deni* is also cheap and does a good *ikan bakar* (grilled fish). The beachside restaurant at the *Carita Baka Baka* is very pleasant and reasonably priced and the *Rakata Hostel* has decent food. The *Lesehan Resor Lippo* is a large Indonesian restaurant with dining on mats or at tables.

It is part of the Lippoland development, across the road from the condominiums among the fun rides, mini golf, trail bikes etc.

Farther north on the waterfront, the Lippo Marina is home to the *Kafe Marina*, a more upmarket option for sea breezes and seafood starting at around 20,000 rp. Around the 14 Km mark, the *Cafe de Paris* is an oddity – it has air-con and European food, and it accepts credit cards.

## Getting There & Away
To get to Carita from Jakarta, take a bus to Labuan and then a colt or angkot to Carita (1000 rp). Overcharging is common.

Most visitors to Anyer go by car from Jakarta – 2½ to three hours via the toll road and the turn-off at Cilegon. By bus from Jakarta, take a Merak bus (4000 rp) and get off at Cilegon from where infrequent buses run to Labuan via Anyer and Karang Bolong. Minibuses are much more frequent and run to Anyer market from where you can catch other minibuses farther south. It usually takes three minibuses to get to Carita and Labuan from Cilegon.

## LABUAN
☎ 0252
The dreary little port of Labuan is merely a jumping-off point for Carita or the Ujung Kulon National Park.

### Ujung Kulon Information
Wanawisata Alamhayati (☎ 81217), about 1km from the centre of town on the road to Carita, is the private company that books accommodation on the islands at Ujung Kulon National Park and will also arrange permits. The Labuan PHPA office (☎ 81477), 1km farther along the same road, is also helpful for information, especially if you want to visit Ujung Kulon independently.

### Places to Stay
The *Citra Ayu Hotel* (☎ 81229, Jl Perintis Kemerdekaan 27) is the best in town. Rooms with mandi cost 30,000 rp, or lighter rooms upstairs are 35,000 rp. The *Hotel Caringin* is

much worse but only slighter cheaper at 25,000 rp, or the *Rawa Yana Hotel* is a reasonable option, but Carita is only a few kilometres up the road from Labuan and has much better accommodation.

### Getting There & Away
Frequent buses depart from Kalideres bus terminal in Jakarta for Labuan (5000 rp, 3½ hours) via Serang and Pandeglang. Angkots for Carita (1000 rp, half hour) leave from the market, 100m from the Labuan bus terminal, as do minibuses to Sumur (4000 rp, three hours). Other buses to/from Labuan include: Bogor (5000 rp, four hours); Bandung (9000 rp, seven hours); Rangkasbitung (2500 rp, 1½ hours); Serang (2500 rp, 1½ hours); Merak (3000 rp, two hours); and destinations farther afield such as Garut, Banjar and Kuningan. Frequent buses go from Labuan to Jakarta, Bogor, Rangkasbitung and Serang, but other departures are less frequent and usually leave in the morning only.

## KRAKATAU
The legendary Krakatau lies in the Selat Sunda straits – 50km from the West Java coast and 40km from Sumatra. Today, only a small part of the original volcano remains. But when Krakatau blew itself apart in 1883, in one of the world's greatest and most catastrophic eruptions, the effects were recorded far beyond Selat Sunda.

For centuries Krakatau had been a familiar nautical landmark for much of the world's maritime traffic, which was funnelled through the narrow Selat Sunda straits. The volcano had been dormant since 1680 and was widely regarded as extinct, but from May through to early August in 1883 passing ships reported moderate activity. By 26 August Krakatau was raging and the explosions became more and more violent.

At 10 am on 27 August 1883, Krakatau erupted with the biggest bang ever recorded on earth. On the island of Rodriguez, more than 4600km to the south-west, a police chief reported hearing the booming of 'heavy guns from eastward'. In Alice

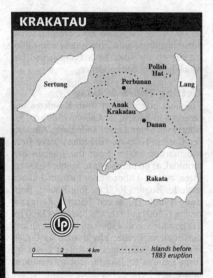

## KRAKATAU

Sertung

Polish Hat

Perbúnan

Lang

Anak Krakatau

Danan

Rakata

0    2    4 km

······· Islands before 1883 eruption

Krakatau) reported odd details such as 'fish dizzy and caught with glee by natives'! Three months later the dust thrown into the atmosphere caused such vivid sunsets in the USA that fire engines were being called out to quench the apparent fires. For three years the dust continued to circle the earth, creating strange and spectacular sunsets.

The astonishing return of life to the devastated islands has been the subject of scientific study ever since. Not a single plant was found on Krakatau a few months after the event; 100 years later – although the only fauna are snakes, insects, rats, bats and birds – it seems almost as though the vegetation was never disturbed.

Krakatau basically blew itself to smithereens but, roughly where the 1883 eruption began, Anak Krakatau (Child of Krakatau) has been vigorously growing ever since its first appearance in 1928. It has a restless and uncertain temperament, sending out showers of glowing rocks and belching smoke and ashes.

Boats can land on the east side, but it is no longer possible to climb right up the cinder cones to the caldera, after Krakatau belched a load of molten rock on one unfortunate tourist who ventured too close. Krakatau is still a menacing volcano, and in its more active phases, intermittent rumblings can be heard on quiet nights from the west coast beaches.

### Getting There & Away

Carita is the usual place to arrange a trip to Krakatau but, more than likely, you will have to charter a boat. The tour operators (see under Carita) will try to arrange a cheap tour by taking down the names of interested travellers wanting to share a boat, but even at peak tourist times this can take two days or more. Usually the numbers just aren't available and you will have to charter.

Prices vary, depending on the quality of the boat, but the cost of chartering is now more affordable, given the rupiah's devaluation. Charter the best boat you can afford.

During the rainy season (November to March) there are strong currents and rough

Springs, Australia, 3500km to the southeast, residents also reported hearing strange explosions from the north-west.

Along with its cataclysmic explosions, Krakatau sent up a record 80km-high column of ash and threw into the air nearly 20 cubic km of rock. Ash fell on Singapore 840km to the north and on ships as far away as 6000km; darkness covered the Selat Sunda straits from 10 am on 27 August until dawn the next day.

Far more destructive were the great ocean waves triggered by the collapse of Krakatau's cones into its empty belly. A giant tsunami more than 40m high swept over the nearby shores of Java and Sumatra and the sea wave's passage was recorded far from Krakatau. It reached Aden in 12 hours over a distance 'travelled by a good steamer in 12 days'. Measurable wave effects were even said to have reached the English Channel. Coastal Java and Sumatra were devastated: 165 villages were destroyed and more than 36,000 people were killed.

The following day, a telegram sent to Singapore from Batavia (160km east of seas, but even during the dry season strong south-east winds can whip up the swells and make a crossing inadvisable. When weather conditions are fine it's a long one day trip, but having visited Krakatau we'd say it's definitely worth the effort – *if* you can hire a safe boat.

Small fishing boats may be cheap, but so are the tales of travellers who spent the night, or longer, adrift in high swells. At the very least, charter one of the large fishing boats, which take up to 10 people. They cost around 800,000 rp per boat if booked through Carita agents, slightly less at Carita village or Labuan.

On the other hand, speed boats from Carita Marina start at around one million rp. They will do the trip in just over an hour instead of three or four hours, life jackets should be provided, and most have radios. The big hotels also arrange speed boats at slightly higher rates.

Most visitors to Krakatau come from Carita or the other beach resorts on the west coast of Java. However, Krakatau officially lies in Sumatra's Lampung Province and it is slightly shorter, and cheaper, to reach Krakatau from the small port of Kalianda.

Green turtles nest in some Ujung Kulon bays.

## UJUNG KULON NATIONAL PARK

Ujung Kulon National Park is on the remote south-western tip of Java, covering about 760 sq km of land area, including the large Panaitan Island. Because of its isolation and difficult access, Ujung Kulon has remained an outpost of primeval forest and untouched wilderness in heavily developed Java. The park was declared a World Heritage Site in 1991. It presents some fine opportunities for hiking and wildlife spotting and has some good beaches with intact coral reefs. Few people visit the park, but despite its remoteness, it is one of the most rewarding national parks in Java.

Ujung Kulon is best known as the last refuge on Java for the once plentiful one-horned rhinoceros, of which there are now only around 60. The shy Javan rhino, however, is an extremely rare sight and you are far more likely to come across less exotic animals, such as banteng (wild cattle), wild pigs, otters, squirrels, leaf monkeys and gibbons. Panthers also live in the forest, and crocodiles in the river estuaries, but these too are a rare sight. Green turtles nest in some of the bays and Ujung Kulon also has a wide variety of birdlife. On Pulau Peucang island, rusa deer, long-tailed macaques and big monitor lizards are common, and there is good snorkelling around coral reefs.

The main park area is on the peninsula but the park also includes the nearby island of Panaitan and the smaller offshore islands of Peucang and Handeuleum. Much of the peninsula is dense lowland rainforest and is a mixture of scrub, grassy plains, swamps, pandanus palms and long stretches of sandy beach on the west and south coasts. Walking trails follow the coast around much of the peninsula and loop round Gunung Payung on the western tip.

### Information

The park office in Labuan is a useful source of information, but pay your entry fee when you enter the park at the PHPA offices in Tamanjaya or on the islands. Pick up a copy of the excellent *Visitor's Guidebook to the Trails of Ujung Kulon National Park*. Entry to the park costs 2500 rp.

WEST JAVA

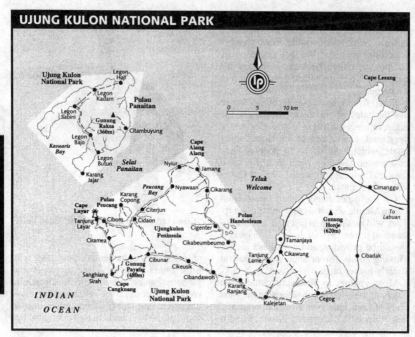

## UJUNG KULON NATIONAL PARK

The best time for visiting Ujung Kulon is the dry season (April to October) when the sea is generally calm and the reserve is not so boggy. Malaria has been reported in Ujung Kulon and, while it is not a high-risk area, anti-malarials are advisable, as are appropriate measures against mosquitos.

Guides must be hired for hiking in the park. The park office in Tamanjaya will arrange this for around 15,000 to 20,000 rp per day, plus food. Bring lightweight food, such as packaged noodles, and drinking water if trekking. Supplies are available in Tamanjaya; Sumur or Labuan have more choice.

### Exploring the Park

The main way to reach the park, and the only cheap option, is by road to Tamanjaya, which has accommodation and a PHPA post where you can arrange guides for the three day hike across to the west coast and on to

Pulan Peucang. This is the most rewarding way to explore the park and its diversity. It can be tackled by anyone of reasonable fitness, but is not an easy walk.

Conditions on the trail are basic – there are rough shelters but some are almost derelict. If you have a tent, bring it. The first part of the trail is a pleasant three hour walk through villages to the south coast at Karang Panjang and then it is another 1½ hours to the hut just back from Cibandawoh beach. The second day is along the beach, five hours to the hut at the Cibunar river. It is tough work in the sand at times and rivers have to be waded, which can be difficult after rain. On the third day, most hikers cross over to the west coast at Cidaon, opposite Peucang. It is a fine, four hour walk up the mountain range and then down through dense forest. This is rhino country – keep your cameras primed, you may be lucky.

An alternative trail with good coastal scenery goes from Cibunar, inland via Gunung Payung to Sanghiang Sirah on the coast. The trail continues along the coast across to the lighthouse at Tanjung Layar, the westernmost tip of mainland Java, before continuing on to Cidaon. The trip can be done as an extension to the main trail or as a two day loop from Peucang.

**Pulau Peucang** is the other main entry into the park but can only be reached by chartered boat from Labuan, Sumur or Tamanjaya. Good but very expensive accommodation and a restaurant are run by a private company, Wanawisata Alamhayati. Peucang also has beautiful white-sand beaches and coral reefs on the sheltered southern coast, making it a resort island for Jakarta residents. Deer are everywhere and a good short walk goes across the island through forest to the surf-pounded north coast. Hikers might be able to hitch a lift on a boat from Peucang, especially on weekends, but don't count on it.

Wanawisata Alamhayati also has comfortable but simple accommodation at **Pulau Handeuleum**, which is ringed by mangroves and doesn't have Peucang's attractions. Boats or canoes can be hired (US$8 including guide) for the short crossing to Cigenter, on the mainland opposite. You can canoe up the Cigenter River and visit a waterfall (US$16), or a hiking trail leads six to eight hours along the coast to the Jamang rangers' hut, where it is possible to overnight. From Jamang the trail continues on past swamp areas rich in birdlife, to Nyawaan beach and through the forest along the coast to Cidaon. Jamang to Cidaon is a full day's hike.

Large Pulau **Panaitan** is more expensive to reach but has some fine beaches and some hiking opportunities. Panaitan is also popular with surfers – tours operate out of Bali – particularly around Legon Bajo where there is a rugged left reef break, and the southern coast also has some good surf. It is a day's walk between the PHPA posts at Legon Butun and Legon Haji, or you can walk to the top of Gunung Raksa, topped by a Hindu statue of Ganesha, from Citambuyung on the east coast.

**Organised Tours**
Wanawisata Alamhayati (☎ 021-641 1124) at the Ancol Marina in Jakarta has two-day/three-night tours to Pulau Peucang from US$256 to US$323 per person, depending on accommodation, for two people. Tours include full board, transfers from Jakarta and a guided walk to Tanjung Layar. Expect discounts of around 40% and prices are more economical for larger groups. Three-day/four-night trips that include Krakatau are also offered.

A typical tour from Carita is four days/three nights with transfer by car to Sumur, then boat to Handeuleum where you camp. Then you trek to Jamang, camp overnight at the rangers' post, explore around Tanjung Alang Alang and the nearby beaches, then return. The all-inclusive tours cost US$175 per person for a minimum of four people, but expect big discounts.

The park office at Tamanjaya can arrange boat hire for 150,000 rp return to Handeuleum, 350,000 to 500,000 rp to Peucang, depending on the boat. Both islands can arrange activities. But they are run by Wanawisata Alamhayati and overpriced. Guides can be hired on the islands or at Tamanjaya for 15,000 to 20,000 rp per day.

**Places to Stay**
The *Wisma Cinta Alam* guesthouse is opposite the national park office at Tamanjaya, in a palm grove near the water. Three-bedroom cottages have a kitchen and sitting area. The cost is 35,000 rp per room or 100,000 rp for a whole cottage. To book, contact the Labuan PHPA office (☎ 81477). The village also has homestays: Pak Kumar's *Sunda Jaya* homestay has rooms for only 10,000 rp per person and meals can be arranged. Tamanjaya is a sleepy, rural village but it does have a few shops and warungs.

The pleasant *guesthouse* at Pulau Handeuleum has doubles/triples for US$15 a double, US$25 a quad, plus 15%. It has a kitchen for guests' use but bring your own food as the island has nothing else.

Pulau Peucang has double rooms in the *old guesthouse* for US$35, which is an outrageous price for losmen-standard accommodation. The much more luxurious *Flora A & B* bungalows have air-con, hot water and refrigerators for US$70 and US$90 a double. Add 15% to all rates, including food in the expensive but very good restaurant. Expect discounts for rupiah payment.

Advance bookings are recommended for both islands, particularly weekends. Contact Wanawisata Alamhayati (☎ 021-6411124 in Jakarta, ☎ 025-1217 in Labuan).

Within the park you can camp or stay at the huts, which are very primitive. The PHPA posts in the park also accommodate hikers for a contribution. Bring food for yourselves and your guide. A tent is handy for the hikes.

It is also possible to stay in Sumur, a large enough fishing village to have warungs, shops and a losmen, the basic *Citra Ayu (☎ 0253-83778)* where the inflated asking rate is 30,000 rp. The *Ciputih Beach (☎ Jakarta 021-8281093)* is a good mid-range resort on the beach 7km south of Sumur towards Tamanjaya, but it is very isolated. Rooms cost US$70, more like 160,000 rp after discount.

### Getting There & Away

The cheapest way to get to the park is by bus to Sumur from Labuan (4000 rp, four hours). A good paved road runs from Labuan to Tanjung Leuser, where there is a big resort complex, about 5km past Citeureup, the turn-off to Sumur. From Sumur to Tamanjaya it is 20km or so along a terrible road and only ojeg (7500 rp) tackle it.

The only other way to reach the park is by boat. You can charter a boat in Labuan or Carita but expect to pay top dollar. Given the long stretch of open sea, which is often subject to large swells, take a good boat, either a large fishing boat or a speed launch, which will cost around 1 million rp. Sumur is the best spot to charter a boat – a good, large fishing boat will cost around 500,000

rp return to Peucang, which can also be reached by charter boat from Tamanjaya.

## BADUI VILLAGES

When Islam swept through Java the temples were sacked and the outward manifestations of Hinduism all but disappeared. Yet throughout the mountains of Java, small isolated pockets of the old religions remain. The Tenggerese in East Java survived the onslaught, but the most mysterious of these groups is the Badui. They have preserved their traditions through a strict policy of isolation, shunning visitors, Indonesian education and attempts by the government to drag them into the modern world. Islam has failed to take root, and reported attempts by a Christian missionary in the 1970s to convert the Badui resulted in him fleeing in fear of his life.

Badui religion is a blend of animism and Hinduism, and the Badui priests are regarded as powerful mystics. This is particularly true of the Badui Dalam (Inner Badui) or 'white Badui' as they are known because of their white dress. The three inner villages of Cibeo, Cikartawana and Cikeusik are off-limits to outsiders and are surrounded by Badui Luar (Outer Badui) villages that have contact with the outside world and act as intermediaries for the Badui Dalam. The Badui live in some 30 villages and number around 5000. The Badui have traditionally spoken a dialect of old Sundanese.

Permits are officially required to visit the Badui villages and access is difficult. Many Badui speak Bahasa Indonesia but English is rarely spoken and a Sundanese-speaking guide is preferable. Though some of the outer villages are used to the steady trickle of visitors who make it to their territory, bear in mind that the Badui are not museum pieces for camera-snapping travellers. You won't be welcome at the inner Badui villages.

The starting point for a trip to Badui territory is Rangkasbitung, 64km east of Labuan and 120km from Jakarta. Obtain permits at the tourist office, (*dinas pariwisata*), Jl Pahlawan 13, before proceeding to Ciboleger, which is the entry point to Badui territory.

Where the buses pull in at the end of the road in Ciboleger, a long flight of steps leads up through the village to the gateway that marks the start of Badui territory. Shops and warungs line the pathway to the top and the Badui come here to trade. You'll probably see the Badui Luar in their distinctive black clothes, and most of the modern clothes sold in the shops are also black. The Badui Dalam sometimes make it to Ciboleger and beyond, but they only travel on foot.

As you pass through the gateway, the change is instantaneous. While litter lines the path to the top, no litter is to be found in Badui territory. From the gateway, walk down the hill and sign in at the house of Pak Usen, the *kepala desa*, and it may be possible to stay there. The village shows a few signs of modernity, such as the incorporation of modern building materials, but there are no television, electricity, roads or schools.

From Ciboleger you can trek to nearby Badui villages. Kaduketug is only a 1km walk to the south, inside Badui territory, and is a very traditional village. Though the Badui wear a mixture of traditional and modern clothing, the houses are all built in traditional style. From Kaduketeg it is an hour or less south-west to Gajeboh, another interesting, more traditional village. You can complete a loop by walking east to Kaduketer and Kadujangkung villages, before returning to Ciboleger via Babakan. This is a long day's hike.

Other Badui villages can be reached from the south and west, but Ciboleger is the only official entry point.

## Places to Stay

Rangkasbitung is a medium-sized, clean, unhurried town. Douwes Dekker, the author of the famous novel *Max Havelaar*, served as a colonial official here. The town has a few cheap hotels, the pick of which is the friendly *Hotel Ksatria (☎ 0252-21208, Jl Ksatria 5)*, about half a kilometre south of the tourist office. Good, clean rooms with

mandi cost 15,000 rp. Cash can be changed at the Bank BNI, Jl Pahlawan 55.

You can stay with the kepala desa in Ciboleger and you may be permitted to stay in other Outer Badui villages. Bring food, gifts, and contribute to your upkeep.

### Getting There & Away

Rangkasbitung is easily reached by bus from Labuan (2500 rp, 1½ hours), Jakarta, Bogor and Serang. The Rangkasbitung bus terminal is 2.5km south of town. Angkot (500 rp) from the bus terminal can drop you near the tourist office and Hotel Ksatria. Rangkasbitung is also serviced by about 10 trains per day from Jakarta's Kota station.

The bus from Rangkasbitung to Ciboleger (4000 rp, 2½ hours) leaves at 6 or 7 am, returning at 11 am. Otherwise, first take a bus to Leuwidamar, where you may be lucky to get a minibus to Ciboleger, but not many go all the way. Most visitors to Ciboleger are small tour groups that make the trip by minibus or car. Tours can be arranged in Carita and Wanawisata Alamhayati (☎ 021-6411124) in Jakarta has expensive tours.

## SOUTH COAST TO PELABUHANRATU

An interesting way to reach Pelabuhanratu from the west coast is along the lightly populated south coast via Malingping. It is time-consuming but possible to go all the way by public transport. From Labuan take any bus to Saketi, 21km east on the main road, and then a 'PS' mikrobus over the hills to Malingping, 68km away. Malingping is a large town and the main bus terminal is 4km south of town.

The main point of interest is the surf-pounded, black-sand beach at Talanca, 2km from the Malingping bus terminal. Here you can stay at *Camp Alpha*, a large, timber lodge just back from the wide beach. Charter an ojeg (1000 rp) or angkot from the Malingping terminal. Simple rooms with mandi cost a hefty 70,000 to 10,000 rp or so extra for meals but it is a beautiful, relaxing spot for walks along the beach and to the nearby lagoon. The educated host speaks English and can fill you in on the area.

From Malingping, angkot take the scenic coast road all the way to Bayah (2500 rp, 35km), the next main town. The lonely *Pondok Arya Perdana (☎ 0252-41013)* is 4km west of town on a rocky but picturesque beach. Rooms and bungalows from 22,000 to 88,000 rp (25% more on weekends and holidays) are good value.

From Bayah, take another angkot to Pelabuhanratu (3500 rp, 63km). The road

travels through the coastal hills with some fine views.

## BOGOR
● pop 712,000    ☎ 0251

In colonial times, Bogor was the most important Dutch hill station, midway between the mountains and the heat-ridden plains of Jakarta, 60km to the south. Governor-General van Imhoff built his large country estate, Buitenzorg (Without a Care), here in 1745 and it became the favoured retreat for

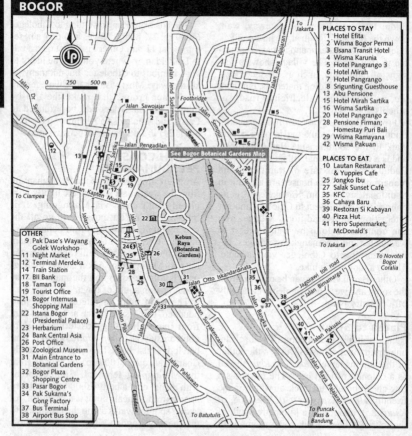

**BOGOR**

**PLACES TO STAY**
1 Hotel Efita
2 Wisma Bogor Permai
3 Elsana Transit Hotel
4 Wisma Karunia
5 Hotel Pangrango 3
6 Hotel Mirah
7 Hotel Pangrango
8 Srigunting Guesthouse
13 Abu Pensione
15 Hotel Mirah Sartika
16 Wisma Sartika
20 Hotel Pangrango 2
28 Pensione Firman;
   Homestay Puri Bali
29 Wisma Ramayana
42 Wisma Pakuan

**PLACES TO EAT**
10 Lautan Restaurant
   & Yuppies Cafe
25 Jongko Ibu
27 Salak Sunset Café
35 KFC
36 Cahaya Baru
39 Restoran Si Kabayan
40 Pizza Hut
41 Hero Supermarket;
   McDonald's

**OTHER**
9 Pak Dase's Wayang
   Golek Workshop
11 Night Market
12 Terminal Merdeka
14 Train Station
17 BII Bank
18 Taman Topi
19 Tourist Office
21 Bogor Internusa
   Shopping Mall
22 Istana Bogor
   (Presidential Palace)
23 Herbarium
24 Bank Central Asia
26 Post Office
30 Zoological Museum
31 Main Entrance to
   Botanical Gardens
32 Bogor Plaza
   Shopping Centre
33 Pasar Bogor
34 Pak Sukarna's
   Gong Factory
37 Bus Terminal
38 Airport Bus Stop

See Bogor Botanical Gardens Map

Kebun Raya (Botanical Gardens)

To Jakarta

To Ciampea

To Jakarta

To Novotel Bogor Coralia

To Puncak Pass & Bandung

To Batutulis

successive governors-general. Daendels made it his semi-official residence in 1808 and during the British interregnum, Sir Stamford Raffles made it his country home. Raffles judged Bogor 'a romantic little village', but Bogor has grown to become almost a suburb of Jakarta and its beauty has faded somewhat.

Bogor's main attraction is its world-class botanical gardens, a vast expanse of luxuriant greenery in the middle of the city. The gardens can be visited as a day trip from Jakarta. Or, since the capital is only one hour away from Bogor, which is cooler and much more relaxed, Bogor can be used as a base to visit Jakarta. From Bogor, you can also venture to the nearby mountains that ring the city, or you can continue to Bandung or Pelabuhanratu.

Though Bogor stands at a height of only 290m, it's appreciably cooler than Jakarta, but visitors in the wet season should bear in mind the town's nickname: the 'City of Rain'. Bogor has probably the highest annual rainfall in Java and is credited with a record 322 thunderstorms a year.

## Information

**Tourist Office** The tourist office (☎ 338 052), on the west side of the gardens at Jl Ir H Juanda 10, has a rough map of the town but not much else. It is open from 7 am to 2 pm Monday to Thursday, until 11 am on Friday and noon on Saturday. It also has a branch at the entrance to the gardens.

At Jl Ir H Juanda 15, next to the main garden gates, is the headquarters of the PHPA – the official body for administration of all of Indonesia's wildlife reserves and national parks.

**Money** Bogor has plenty of banks all over town. The BCA is at Jl Ir H Juanda 28. The BII is near the train station on Jl Dewi Sartika and has an ATM for Visa and Master-Card.

**Post & Communications** The post office is on the west side of the gardens on Jl Ir H Juanda and also has Internet booths open from 8 am to 3 pm Monday to Thursday, to 11 am Friday and to 1 pm Saturday. Wartels can be found next to the post office and at the entrance to the botanical gardens.

## Kebun Raya (Botanical Gardens)

At the heart of Bogor are the huge botanical gardens, known as the Kebun Raya (Great Garden), covering an area of around 80 hectares. They are said to be the inspiration of Governor-General Raffles, but the spacious grounds of the Istana Bogor were converted to botanical gardens by the Dutch botanist Professor Reinwardt, with assistance from Kew Gardens, and officially opened by the Dutch in 1817. It was from these gardens that various colonial cash crops, such as tea, cassava, tobacco and cinchona were developed by early Dutch researchers during the infamous Cultivation Period in the 19th century. The park is still a major centre for botanical research in Indonesia.

The gardens contain streams and lotus ponds and more than 15,000 species of trees and plants, including 400 types of magnificent palms. The garden's orchid houses are reputed to contain more than 3000 orchid varieties but are not open to the general public. Ask when you buy your ticket and you may be granted permission to see them. Close to the main entrance of the gardens is a small monument in memory of Olivia Raffles, wife of the former governor-general, who died in 1814 and was buried in Batavia. Farther behind near the palace is a cemetery with Dutch headstones. The Cafe Botanicus on the eastern side of the gardens has a fine view across the lawns and is a pleasant place for a snack or drink.

The gardens are open from 8 am to 5 pm and although they tend to be very crowded on Sunday, on other days they are very peaceful and a fine place to escape from the hassles and crowds of Jakarta. The entrance fee is 2500 rp during the week and 1500 rp on Sunday and holidays. The southern gate is the main entrance; other gates are only open on Sunday and holidays.

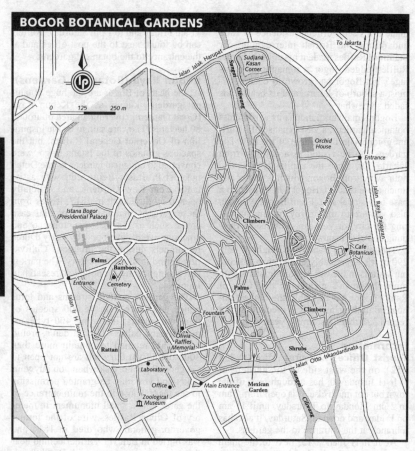

## BOGOR BOTANICAL GARDENS

*To Jakarta*

Jalan Jalak Harupat

Sungai Ciliwang

Sudjana
Kasan
Corner

Orchid
House

*Entrance*

Jalan Raya Pajajaran

Astrid Avenue

Istana Bogor
(Presidential Palace)

Climbers

Cafe
Botanicus

Palms

Bamboos

*Entrance*

Cemetery

Climbers

Fountain

Palms

Rattan

Olivia
Raffles
Memorial

Shrubs

Jalan Otto Iskandardinata

Jalan Ir H Juanda

Laboratory

Office

Sungai Ciliwang

Zoological
Museum

Main Entrance

Mexican
Garden

0      125      250 m

## Zoological Museum

Near the botanical gardens entrance, this museum has a motley but interesting collection of zoological oddities, including the skeleton of a blue whale and a stuffed Javan rhinoceros. If you have ever heard about the island of Flores having a rat problem, one glance at the stuffed Flores version of Indonesian rats in the showcase will explain why. Admission to the museum is 500 rp, and it is open daily from 8 am to 4 pm.

## Istana Bogor (Presidential Palace)

In the north-west corner of the botanical gardens, the summer palace of the president was formerly the official residence of the Dutch governors-general from 1870 to 1942. The present huge mansion is not Buitenzorg though; this was destroyed by an earthquake and a new palace was built on the site a few years later in 1856.

In colonial days, deer were raised in the parklands to provide meat for banquets, and through the gates you can still see herds of white-spotted deer roaming on the immaculate lawns. The Dutch elite would come up from the pesthole of Batavia and many huge, glamorous parties were held there. Following independence, the palace was a much favoured retreat for Soekarno, although Soeharto has ignored it.

Today the building contains Soekarno's huge art collection, much of which lays great emphasis on the female figure, but the palace is only open to groups (minimum 10) by prior arrangement and children are not allowed inside. Contact the tourist office in advance or write directly to the Head of Protocol at the Istana Negara, Jl Veteran, Jakarta. The tourist office may be able to include interested individuals on a tour that is already booked.

## Other Attractions

The **Museum Etnobiologi** at the herbarium on Jl Ir H Juanda was opened in 1982 for research in traditional medicine and medicinal herbs. Many plant species are on display. The museum is open from 7.30 am to 4 pm, Monday to Friday.

The **Batutulis** is an inscribed stone dedicated to Sri Baduga Maharaja by his son King Surawisesa in 1533. Sri Baduga Maharaja (1482-1521) was a Pajajaran king accredited with great mystical power. The stone is housed in a small shrine visited by pilgrims – remove your shoes and pay a small donation before entering. Batutulis is 2.5km south of the gardens, on Jl Batutulis and almost opposite the former home of Soekarno. Soekarno supposedly chose this spot for his home because of the stone's mystical power, but his request to be buried here was ignored by Soeharto who wanted the former president's grave as far away from the capital as possible.

One of the few remaining gongsmiths in West Java is Pak Sukarna, and you can visit his **gong factory** at Jl Pancasan 17. Gongs and other gamelan instruments are smelted over a charcoal fire in the small workshop out the back. A few gongs and *wayang golek* puppets are on sale in the front showroom.

The gong foundry is a short walk south from the garden gates down Jl Empang and west across the river. Look for the 'Pabrik Gong' (Gong Factory) sign.

Pak Dase makes quality wooden puppets at his **wayang golek workshop** in Lebak Kantin RT 02/VI. You can see them being carved and painted and, of course, they are for sale. Lebak Kantin is the *kampung* down by the river, just north of the botanical gardens. Take the footbridge to the Wisma Karunia from Jl Jen Sudirman and ask for Pak Dase in the kampung. Outside the city you can also see wayang golek puppets made at the workshop of Mohammed Ahim, a renowned puppeteer, 15km west of Bogor on the way to Leuwiliang. A little closer to town, near the Cibungbulung turn-off, Mohammad Amsar produces wayang golek and lute-like *rebabs*.

## Places to Stay – Budget

Bogor has a good selection of family-run places which make staying in Bogor a real pleasure. The most popular budget options are close to each other, midway between the railway and bus stations near the botanic gardens.

*Pensione Firman* (☎ 323246, Jl Paledang 48) is friendly, well run and cheap for relatively expensive Bogor. A few basic rooms at the back cost from 17,000 rp and better rooms with mandi are 25,000 and 30,000 rp. The owner speaks excellent English, tours are offered and meals are served.

*Homestay Puri Bali* (☎ 317498), next door at No 50, is more spacious and has large doubles with bathroom for 30,000 and 40,000 rp, including breakfast. One of the best things about this place is the Balinese-style restaurant in a pleasant garden setting.

Around the corner, across from the gardens, the *Wisma Ramayana* (☎ 320364, Jl Ir H Juanda 54) has the most colonial charm. It has a big variety of rooms at the back, with and without bath, from 27,000 to 36,000 rp. The rooms at the front for 37,500 rp have the most style. A couple of huge family rooms are also available for 50,000 and 53,000 rp. Breakfast is included.

The other main hotel geared to the travellers trade is **Abu Pensione** (☎ 322893), near the train station at Jl Mayor Oking 15. This clean, attractive hotel is well set up for information and travel services. It has a few very basic singles for 15,000 rp and more substantial budget doubles for 25,000 rp, but most rooms have attached bath and range from 30,000 up to mid-range quality rooms for 60,000 rp with air-con and hot water. Breakfast is an extra 6000 rp. It also has a good restaurant overlooking the littered river.

Other options include the **Wisma Sartika** (☎ 323747), on the other side of the train station at Jl Dewi Sartika 4D. This family concern is convenient but the simple rooms for 30,000 rp, or 40,000 rp and 50,000 rp with shower, are expensive. North of the botanical gardens, **Wisma Karunia** (☎ 323411, Jl Sempur 33-35) is too far out to be convenient but it is a quiet and very friendly family-run place. It is reasonably priced at 15,000 rp for doubles with shared bath, and from 30,000 to 35,000 rp for rooms with private bath.

## Places to Stay – Mid-Range

**Wisma Pakuan** (☎ 319430, Jl Pakuan 12) is in a large, modern family home southeast of the bus terminal. Well kept rooms with balcony cost 55,000 rp and 66,000 rp with attached bath and hot water, or bigger air-con rooms at the front are 71,500 rp. It is a good buy, breakfast is included, and the family are very helpful.

Bogor has a number of other older guesthouses but most have seen better days and can't keep up with the new hotels. One of the newest and best, halfway between a guesthouse and a hotel, is the smaller **Wisma Bogor Permai** (☎ 381633, Jl Sawojajar 38). Excellently appointed rooms with carpet, TV and minibar cost 100,000 rp for twin rooms or 125,000 rp for doubles. Discounts of 20 to 30% have been on offer, making it exceptional value. Rooms face a courtyard garden and there is a small coffee shop.

Nearby, the **Hotel Efita** (☎ 333400, Jl Sawojajar 5) is bigger and not as cosy but it is also relatively new and has very good rooms with minibar, TV etc for 86,000 rp and 110,000 rp. Large suites for 146,000 rp are also good value. **Hotel Mirah Sartika** (☎ 312343, Jl Dewi Sartika 6A) has older rooms but they are spacious and moderately priced. Rooms, all with hot water and TV, range from 55,000 to 75,000 rp, plus 15%.

Another good hunting ground for mid-range hotels is north-east of the botanical gardens. **Hotel Mirah** (☎ 328044, Jl Pangrango 9A) is a long-running hotel with a small swimming pool. The older rooms for 65,000 to 90,000 rp are very average but rooms in the impressive new wing for 135,000 rp are quite luxurious and among the best in this range. Add 21% tax and service to the rates. Next door, the **Hotel Pangrango** (☎ 328670, Jl Pangrango 23) also has a small pool and a variety of older rooms for 99,000 to 166,000 rp, plus 21%. It's new sister hotel, **Hotel Pangrango 3** (☎ 343433, Jl Raya Pajajaran 1) doesn't have a pool but the rooms are better and good value at 103,000 rp up to 133,100 rp for large suites.

For something smaller, the **Srigunting Guesthouse** (☎ 339661, Jl Pangrango 21) is in a renovated house with a new wing of well appointed rooms but rates of 140,000/158,000 rp for singles/doubles are overpriced. Expect discounts.

## Places to Stay – Top End

The best hotel in the central city is yet another Pangrango, the new **Hotel Pangrango 2** (☎ 321482, Jl Raya Pajajaran 32.) This three-star hotel has a decent-sized pool, restaurant and good rooms for 181,500 and 242,000 rp, as well as suites.

Top of the heap is the **Novotel Bogor Coralia** (☎ 271555), Golf Estat Bogor Raya, but it's a long way from town. From the end of the Jagorawi toll road take the side road for about 5km as it winds its way through a real estate development and then a golf course. This spacious, very tasteful low-rise hotel has a smattering of Indonesian architectural influences and very stylish rooms for US$110 to US$130.

## Places to Eat

Cheap food stalls appear at night along Jl Dewi Sartika, and during the day you'll find plenty of food stalls and good fruit at Pasar Bogor, the market close to the main garden gates. In the late afternoon along Jl Raja Permas next to the train station, street vendors cook up delicious snacks, such as deep-fried *tahu* and *pisang goreng*.

Also near the train station, Taman Topi is a recreational park with fun rides for the kids and a number of good little cafes, such as the *Rumah Makan Wasera*, good for *sate* and *gule kambing* (goat curry).

The *Pujasera* is an air-con hawkers' centre on the top floor of the Bogor Plaza shopping centre opposite the entrance to the botanical gardens. *Es Teler KK* is one of the better stalls for inexpensive lunches and good fruit juices.

The *Salak Sunset Café (Jl Paledang 38)* attached to the Alliance Française, is a chic, cheap little place with river views. Juices, pizzas, spaghetti and Indonesian favourites are featured.

A good restaurant for Sundanese food is the *Jongko Ibu* opposite the post office at Jl Ir H Juanda 36. Prices are moderate and you can dine buffet-style and try a number of dishes. *Restoran Si Kabayan (☎ 311849, Jl Bina Marga I No 2)* is one of Bogor's most pleasant Sundanese restaurants with individual bamboo huts arranged around an attractive garden. You'll need to order a number of dishes to get your fill, but this restaurant is reasonably priced.

Jl Pajajaran, near the end of the Jagorawi toll road, is a good hunting ground for restaurants. The air-con *Cahaya Baru (Jl Pajajaran 7)* is Bogor's best Chinese restaurant, and it is flanked by good Padang restaurants. On the corner of Jl Otto Iskandardinata is *KFC* or farther south is a *Pizza Hut* and *McDonald's* attached to the Hero supermarket.

## Getting There & Away

**Bus** Buses to Bogor from Jakarta (2000/3000 rp, air-con) depart every 10 minutes or so from the Kampung Rambutan bus station and can do the trip in a little over half an hour via the Jagorawi toll road. The only problem is that it takes at least double that time to travel between Kampung Rambutan and central Jakarta.

A Damri bus goes to Jakarta's Soekarno-Hatta airport (7000 rp) every hour from 4 am to 6 pm. It leaves from Jl Bimarmaga I, opposite the Restaurant Yenny, near the end of the Jagorawi toll road.

Buses depart frequently from Bogor for Bandung (4000/7000 rp, three hours). On weekends, buses are not allowed to go via the scenic Puncak Pass (it gets very crowded) and have to travel via Sukabumi (5000/8000 rp, four hours). Other bus destinations from Bogor include Pelabuhanratu (3000 rp), Rangkasbitung (3000 rp), Labuan (5000 rp) and Merak (5000 rp). To Pangandaran (15,000 rp, seven hours), the Sari Bakti Utama bus leaves at 6.30 pm.

Air-conditioned, door-to-door minibuses go to Bandung for 20,000 rp, and there are also connections to destinations farther afield. Travel agents that operate the best buses are Dewa (☎ 653672) and Master (☎ 379184). Ring for pick-up, or the guesthouses can arrange it.

Angkot to villages around Bogor, including Ciampea (No 5), depart from the Terminal Merdeka near the train station.

**Train** The easiest way to reach central Jakarta is to take the trains, which operate every 20 minutes from around 4 am to 8 pm and take 1½ hours. They cost 900 rp to Gambir railway station or 1000 rp to Kota. The ekonomi trains are reasonably efficient but best avoided during peak hours when they can be horribly crowded with commuters. Much more comfortable *Pakuan* express trains leave Bogor at 6.22, 6.45 (air-con) and 9.36 am, and 1.12, 2.48 (air-con), 3.34, 5.24 (air-con) and 5.48 pm. Pakuan trains cost 4000 rp in bisnis, 6000 rp in air-con eksekutif.

Slow ekonomi trains between Bogor and Sukabumi depart at 7.55 am and 1.15 and 5.40 pm, and take about two hours. There is no direct railway service to Bandung.

**Tours & Car Hire** Bogor is a good place to hire a car and driver. Bargaining is essential. Ask at your hotel, or the tourist office may be able to put you in touch with a driver. Drivers also hang out at the front of the botanical gardens but they ask the earth. Bogor has a number of private operators who are used to taking tourists on day trips or extended trips farther afield. Many speak English, some speak Dutch. Prices start at around 100,000 rp per day for a sedan with driver but not including petrol, but the hotels add a large commission.

## Getting Around

Efficient angkot minibuses (300 rp) shuttle around town, particularly between the bus and railway station. Most are green, while the blue angkot run to outlying districts and terminate at Terminal Merdeka. From the bus station, angkot leave from the street behind, Jl Bangka – angkot No 03 does an anticlockwise loop of the botanical gardens on its way to Jl Muslihat, near the train station. To get to the bus station from the tourist office take No 06.

*Becaks* are banned from the main road encircling the gardens. Metered taxis are nonexistent, but you can haggle with the minivan drivers who hang out near the entrance to the botanical gardens.

## AROUND BOGOR
### Purnawarman Stone (Batutulis)

From the village of Ciampea, which is about 12km north-west of Bogor, you can take a colt to the village of Batutulis. There you will find a huge black boulder on which King Purnawarman inscribed his name and made an imprint of his footstep around 450 AD. The inscription on the stone is still remarkably clear after more than 1500 years.

### Gunung Halimun National Park

This new national park is home to some primary rainforest, but the park has mixed usage and also includes plantations such as the Nirmala Tea Estate. The dominant feature of the park is the rich montane forest in the highland regions around Gunung Halimun (1929m), the highest peak.

Visitor facilities at the park are not developed and park administration is handled by the Gede Pangrango National Park at Cibodas. The most visited attractions of Gunung Halimun National Park are the **waterfalls** near Cikidang and those near the Nirmala estate, but the big drawcard is **white-water rafting** which is organised out of the beautiful village of Pajagan on the south-east edge of the park.

Three companies are based in the village and offer a variety of packages, usually including transport from Jakarta. Rafting is on the Sungai Citarak, which comes out at the sea near Pelabuhanratu. Rapids are Class III, suitable for beginners, and most popular is the six hour trip from Pajagan to Pelabuhanratu. It is also possible to start farther upstream at Cialing and do a 2½ trip, or it is five hours to Pajagan.

The three companies, all with depots on the river at Pajagan, are: BJ's Rafting (☎ Jakarta 021-9233312), Jl Duren Tiga Pav 42A, Jakarta; Arus Liar (☎ 081-11103397 or Jakarta 021-8355885, email harsa@rad.net.id) and Citra Jeram (☎ 081-8753614 or Jakarta ☎ 021-7254591). They offer a huge range of options starting at around 125,000 rp per person for Pajagan-Pelabuhanratu, if you make your own way there, up to all-inclusive weekend packages from Jakarta. Trips depend on numbers, so it is essential to book. The companies also have a few huts for campers.

Pajagan can be reached with some difficulty by public transport. Six minibuses per day run from Pelabuhratu along a very scenic but very bad road. Though the trip is only 14km it takes well over an hour. Alternatively, minibuses run from Cibadak, 27km to the east, on the Bogor to Pelabuhanratu road.

From Cibadak, with your own vehicle, you can turn off to Cikadang and then on to Nirmala Tea Estate. Rainfall in the park is around 4000 to 6000mm per year, most of which falls from October to May when a visit is more or less out of the question.

## SUKABUMI & SELABINTANA
☎ 0266

Sukabumi is a thriving commercial town of 120,000 people at the foot of Pangrango and Gede volcanoes. The main reason to visit is for bus connections to Bandung or Pelabuhanratu, or to visit Selabintana, a small hill resort 7km north of town.

Selabintana is much less developed but also much less crowded than the Puncak Pass resort area to the north of Gunung Gede. It is possible to walk up the hillside to **Sawer Waterfall** and on to **Gunung Gede**, but there is no PHPA post in Selabintana. Selabintana has a golf course, swimming pools and a selection of mid-range hotels. Otherwise, Selabintana is simply a quiet place to relax and soak up the mountain air. Selabintana is just 7km north of the city of Sukabumi, which can be reached by bus from Bogor.

### Places to Stay

Minibuses from Sukabumi (take a No 10 from the Yogya department store) to Selabintana run straight up to the foot of Mt Gede and terminate at the old fashioned, slightly faded *Hotel Selabintana (☎ 221 501, Jl Selabintana, 7 Km marker)*. Set on 36-hectare grounds, it has a golf course, tennis and volley ball courts, two swimming pools and a bar/restaurant. Small, dark rooms opposite the golf course cost 40,000 rp, rooms in the hotel section cost 50,000 rp, or huge bungalows with antique furniture are 90,000 rp up to 150,000 rp for those with three bedrooms. Even after you add 20% tax and service to the rates, this hotel is still a bargain.

The Hotel Selabintana is *the* place to stay and there is not a lot to do if you stay elsewhere. Nevertheless, Selabintana has plenty of other hotels. Just below the Hotel Selabintana is the *Pondok Asri Selabintana*, under the same management. Modern, well appointed flatettes cost 75,000 rp, or flatettes with kitchens and two to three bedrooms cost 150,000 rp to 300,000 rp, plus 20%.

Next down the hill is the *Hotel Pangrango (☎ 211532)*, with a huge lobby/convention hall, swimming pool and tennis courts. The older rooms are musty but large and cost 49,000 rp up to 110,000 rp for a two bedroom cottage. Much better are the new, colonial-style chalets. These cute and very well appointed one/two bedroom cottages cost 144,000/192,000 rp. Weekend rates are around 20% higher.

Budget accommodation can be found in the main village, around the 6 Km marker. Best value is the *Hotel Intan (☎ 223031)* at 27,500 rp for good rooms with carpet and attached bathroom. The upstairs rooms are lighter and have views.

## PELABUHANRATU
☎ 0266

Pelabuhanratu, 90km south of Bogor, is a seaside resort popular with Jakarta residents. On a large horseshoe bay, this small fishing town has black-sand beaches and lush scenery, with rice paddies coming almost to the water's edge. Though quiet during the week, it can be crowded at weekends and holidays, and accommodation reflects Jakarta prices, ie expensive.

Swimming is possible when the sea is quiet, but as most of Java's south coast, the crashing surf can be treacherous. Drownings do occur, in spite of the warning signs which went up after the Bulgarian ambassador disappeared here some years ago. If you want to enter the realms of legend, Pelabuhanratu (Harbour of the Queen) is said to have actually witnessed the creation of Nyai Loro Kidul, the malevolent goddess who takes fishermen and swimmers off to her watery kingdom. Don't wear green on the beach or in the water (it's her colour). In the Hotel Indonesia Samudra a room is set aside for offerings to the Queen of the South Seas.

### Orientation & Information

Pelabuhanratu is essentially a two-street town – Jl Siliwangi, which leads into town and to the harbour, and Jl Kidang Kencana, which runs around the harbour and out to the western beaches. The bus station is near the intersection of these two streets. The

## Nyai Loro Kidul

The Queen of the South Seas, Nyai Loro Kidul, is a potent force in Javanese cosmology. Right across the south coast of Java, offerings are made to her to ensure a bountiful fishing catch, but she also plays a special role in the courts of Central Java. As she is a force juxtaposed against the spiritual power of the mountains, the sultans of the kratons of Yogyakarta and Surakarta are required to meditate and seek union with the queen. Senopati, the founder of the Mataram kingdom, learnt of love and war from her and went on to conquer all before him. She also appeared in a vision to Javanese hero Diponegoro, who battled the Dutch.

Perhaps the strangest manifestation of Nyai Loro Kidul is at Room 308 in the Hotel Indonesia Samudra in Pelabuhanratu. The room is decked out in the queen's favourite colour, green, paintings of her adorn the walls and the room is furnished with all the accoutrements a goddess could want when visiting, including hairbrushes and perfume. At least once a week, at 10 pm, interested visitors assemble in the lobby and take the lift to the 3rd floor. It is a parade of the genuinely spiritual, usually elderly Javanese villagers; curious visitors from Jakarta, as well as the half-sceptical who think that they might receive a blessing anyway, and the odd tourist.

After removing shoes in the passageway, everyone files into the room and sits on the floor in a ring, softly chanting and meditating on the queen. A few cameras flash, hoping for a mystic photo, like the one of Nyai Loro Kidul appearing from the waves of the Indian Ocean, supposedly taken by chance, which is often published in Indonesia. After 20 minutes, when the queen may or may not have bestowed her blessing, everyone descends to the lobby for coffee and snacks.

beach road continues on to Cisolok, 15km to the west, and a number of places to stay are scattered along this road.

The tourist office (☎ 433298) is on Jl Kidang Kencana, just west of the fish market, and a *wartel* is next door. A dive shop is also here and, though Pelabuhanratu is not noted for diving, Tinjil and Deli islands, well to the west, have good reefs, clear water and giant clams.

Bank Central Asia on Jl Siliwangi will change US$ cash and travellers cheques – cash only for other currencies and the rates are low. The ATM accepts Visa cards.

### Things to See & Do

Pelabuhanratu town has little of interest, but the harbour is dotted with brightly painted *prahu* and the fish market is lively in the morning. The beaches to the west hold the main interest and some have good surfing. **Cimaja**, 8km west of Pelabuhanratu, has a pebble beach and the best surf when it is working.

Thirteen kilometres west of Pelabuhanratu, at **Pantai Karang Hawu**, is a towering cliff with caves, rocks and pools which were created by a large lava flow that pushed over the beach. According to legend, it was from the rocks of Karang Hawu that Nyai Loro Kidul leapt into the mighty ocean to regain her lost beauty. She never returned. Stairs lead up to a small *kramat* (shrine) at the top.

Farther west, about 2km past Cisolok, are the **Cipanas** hot springs. Boiling water sprays into the river, and you can soak downstream where the hot and cold waters mingle. It is a very scenic area, and you can walk a few kilometres upstream through the lush forest to a waterfall. Cipanas has changing sheds, warungs and crowds on the weekend.

**Goa Lalay** bat cave, about 4km southeast of Pelabuhanratu, is of limited interest, except at sunset when thousands of small bats fly out.

Farther afield, **Cikotok**, about 30km to the north-west, is the site of Java's most important gold mine.

## Places to Stay & Eat

Pelabuhanratu has plenty of mid-range accommodation and a few vaguely cheap options. The beach, and the nicest accommodation, start 1km west from the town.

Cheap options in town are on Jl Siliwangi, a few hundred metres before the harbour. *Penginapan Laut Kidul* at No 148 has simple but clean rooms with bath from 22,500 rp. *Wisma Karang Nara* (☎ 431088) at No 82 is a notch up in quality and priced at 25,000 and 30,000 rp for a room (5000 rp more on weekends). Pick of the town hotels is *Mahkota Pantai* (☎ 432487, Jl Pelita Air Service) overlooking the harbour. Fan rooms are 30,000 rp and air-con rooms, most with good views, are 50,000 to 80,000 rp.

Pelabuhanratu has some excellent Chinese seafood restaurants, the pick of which are the *Restoran Sanggar Sari* (Jl Siliwangi 76) and the *Queen Restaurant* on Jl Kidang Kencana. Lobster will set you back 25,000 rp, and other dishes are moderately priced.

The *Pondok Dewata* (☎ 431022) is the first place in town on the beach. Balinese-style cottages (all air-con) are comfortable but expensive at US$35 to US$60, plus 20% tax and service. Rates are up to 100% more in holiday periods.

Next along on a headland, *Buana Ayu* (☎ 431111) is the best value close to town. Rooms with air-con and bathroom for 75,000 to 85,000 rp are perched above the sea with great views. A few family rooms are also available. The restaurant is the sort of place you could sit all day – good seafood, great views and sea breezes. Farther around the headland is *Bayu Amrta* (☎ 431031), run by the same proprietor and also with great views. The rooms have hot water, air-con, TV etc but are cell-like and expensive at 70,000 to 125,000 rp. Expect discounts.

In Citepus village, 3km from Pelabuhanratu, *Padi Padi* (☎ 42124) has an unprepossessing façade but behind lies the most stylish hotel on the coast. The architecture is Santa Fe, the furnishings are rustic Asian and the rooms all have private porches backing on to a fishpond maze. Superb rooms are US$79, US$89 and US$129, while suites are US$149, converted at a very favourable rupiah rate. The hotel also has a good restaurant.

At the 4 Km marker in Citepus, *Hotel Cleopatra* (☎ 431185) has a pool, restaurant and landscaped gardens. Good-value rooms cost 45,000 to 78,000 rp, while two-bedroom cottages are 150,000 rp and 250,000 rp. Many warung and seafood *rumah makan* are found on the foreshore here. Nearby the *Augusta Hotel* (☎ 42273), a new two star hotel with a swimming pool, is also good value with rooms at 70,000 to 100,000 rp (20,000 rp more on weekends).

About 5km west of town, the *Hotel Indonesia Samudra* (☎ 431200) is one of Soekarno's original luxury hotels built in the 1960s to kick-start tourism in Indonesia. It has a huge pool and some wonderful 1960s touches but this government-run hotel is at least a decade overdue for renovations. Down-at-heel singles/doubles cost US$70/80 but various '*pakets*' are on offer for as little as 150,000/250,000 rp including breakfast and dinner. All rooms have sea views. Regular meditational visits, attended by local mystics and any other interested parties, are held in Room 308, the haunt of the Queen of the South Seas.

Eight kilometres out, Cimaja, the surfing beach, also has a range of accommodation. The *Mustika Rata* (☎ 431233) is a reasonable cheap option with fan rooms from 20,000 to 25,000 rp and air-con rooms from 40,000 to 90,000 rp. The *Hotel Daun Daun* in the village is another budget option with rooms from 25,000 rp. The *Rumah Makan Mirasa* nearby is a favourite with surfers. The best hotel is the *Pondok Kencana* (☎ 431465), up above the main road, which has a small swimming pool and the Ombak 7 pub, with surf flicks and other diversions. Villas with lounge rooms start at 120,000 rp.

A few kilometres farther towards Cisolok is the *Wisma Tenang* (☎ 431365), which has so-so rooms for 40,000 rp and 60,000 rp, but it is right on the beach. On the other side of the road, the *Pantai Mutiara* (☎ 431330) is one of the best places. It has a small swimming pool, fitness centre and restaurant. Standard rooms with bamboo decor cost 35,000 to 59,000 rp, deluxe rooms are 70,000 rp and 105,000 rp, or big family rooms are 140,000 to 170,000 rp. Rates are around 30% more on weekends.

## Getting There & Away

The road from Bogor cuts south over the pass between Gunung Salak and Pangrango through valleys and hillsides of rubber, coconut, cocoa and tea plantations and terraced rice fields. By car, Pelabuhanratu can be reached in four hours from Jakarta. Local buses run throughout the day from Bogor (3000 rp, three hours) and Sukabumi (2500 rp, 2½ hours). Buses from Sukabumi continue on to Cisolok from Pelabuhanratu, and it is possible to continue right along the south coast via Bayah and Malingping. See the South Coast to Pelabuhanratu section earlier in this chapter.

## Getting Around

Angkot run between Pelabuhanratu and Cisolok for 800 rp, less for shorter journeys. They occasionally continue on to Cipanas, otherwise charter them from Cisolok to Cipanas for around 2500 rp. Ojeg at the Pelabuhanratu and Cisolok bus stations can be hired for around 3000 rp per hour for sightseeing. Motorbikes (30,000 rp per day) can be hired at the Hotel Bayu Amrta.

## UJUNG GENTENG

About 80km south-east of Pelabuhanratu, the peninsula of Ujung Genteng is an important turtle-nesting area and a noted surfing destination. To the Sundanese, this area, centred around the town of Jampang, is noted as the home of some of Java's most powerful black magicians.

The small fishing village of Genteng on the east side of the peninsula is the last bus stop, but the main interest lies on the west side at Pantai Ujung Genteng, where *Mama's Losmen* is a well known hangout for surfers in front of a left-hand break. New, much more luxurious accommodation

has also sprung up in the area at *Vila Amanda Ratu* (☎ Jakarta 021-9145688) with rooms and units from 225,000 to 540,000 rp, before discount.

Giant leatherback turtles come ashore in the dry season to lay their eggs at Pantai Pangumbahan, 2km north of Mama's. Ten kilometres farther north is **Ombak Tujuh**, usually reached by chartered boat. It has huge waves and is the most famous surfing destination on the peninsula.

From Pelabuhanratu buses run along the slow, winding road to Ciwaru from where angkot run to Genteng, or buses go from Bogor as far as Surade. From Genteng take an ojeg to the beach.

## BOGOR TO BANDUNG
### Puncak Pass Area

Between Bogor and Bandung you cross over this beautiful 1500m-high pass on a narrow, winding mountain road which passes through small resort towns and tea plantations. At high altitudes it's cool and often misty but in the early mornings the views across the valleys can be superb.

Almost the whole highway is a resort strip crammed with hotels and villas starting about 10km out of Bogor at Ciawi and continuing up through Cibogo, Cipayung and Cisarua to the Puncak Pass and over the other side to Cipanas. The area has fine scenery, a refreshing climate and some good walks, especially from Cibodas, but much of the main highway is an endless, tacky strip of karaoke lounges, rumah makan and overpriced mid-range hotels.

The Puncak area makes a good escape from the city and its attractions can be visited on a day trip. Some lovely quiet spots can be found away from the highway melee for a longer stay. Avoid weekends when the crowds and traffic jams are horrendous.

From Jakarta's Kampung Rambutan station, any Bandung bus can drop you off at any of the resort towns on the highway (but not on Sunday when they aren't allowed to use this highway). From Bogor, frequent buses and Colts (which travel on Sunday) also ply the highway.

If you are wondering why most place names begin with 'Ci', it means water in Sundanese, and the dozens of streams, rivers and waterfalls are a result of the high rainfall that this mountain area receives.

## Cisarua
☎ 0251

Ten kilometres from Bogor on the slopes of the Puncak, there are good walks to picnic spots and waterfalls around Cisarua, which has good budget accommodation. **Curug Cilember** is a waterfall about 30 minutes' walk from Cisarua.

Just east of Cisarua is the turn-off to **Taman Safari Indonesia**, a wildlife park. As well as indigenous and African 'safari' animals in the drive-through game park, there is a bird park, white tiger pavilion, red pandas, children's rides and a program of animal shows. This spacious park with its well tended animals is streets ahead of most of Indonesia's zoos and on Saturday nights it has a night safari (15,000 rp) for viewing nocturnal animals.

Though the park is best explored by car, any Bogor-Bandung bus can drop you at the turn-off, from where minibuses go to the park, 2.5km away. Entry is 12,000 rp for adults, 8000 rp for children under six; cars are 6000 rp or a minibus is 12,000 rp. A park bus does tours of the safari park for those without a car. Park facilities include a swimming pool, restaurants and accommodation.

In the foothills, 7km before the Puncak summit, you finally leave the overdevelopment behind and pass through the tea-carpeted hills of **Gunung Mas Tea Estate**. Stop for a tour of the tea factory, a couple of kilometres from the highway. Tourism is almost as big a business as tea these days, and the estate organises very popular guided tea estate walks, group functions and dinners, and has excellent accommodation. Factory tours cost 1500 rp and guides expect a tip. You can wander at will around the tea estate, which is superb on a sunny day.

Almost at the top of the pass, the **Rindu Alam Restaurant** is a must on every tour itinerary and either has fine views of the surrounding tea estates or is surrounded by ethereal mist. Just below the restaurant you can walk down to **Telaga Warna**, a small 'lake of many colours' – if you're lucky. The colours require sunlight, otherwise the lake is not exciting, but the patch of montane forest around from the lake is an interesting example of the original fauna.

Past the Puncak Pass, at the 86 Km marker, is the turn-off to **Taman Bunga**, large, landscaped private gardens with a few rides and other family attractions. It is 9km from the highway and popular with domestic crowds on weekends.

**Places to Stay** *Kopo Hostel* (☎ 254296, *Jl Raya Puncak 557*) is near the petrol station *(pompa bensin)* in Cisarua. It's excellent value: the four or six bed dorms cost 8000 rp per person or comfortable rooms cost 22,000 to 49,000 rp, including breakfast. HI cardholders can get a small discount. The hostel has a garden, small restaurant, maps of walks and information on places of interest in the area. Good-value walking tours, including transport, are organised to points of interest such as Gunung Gede (25,000 rp per person).

Apart from the Kopo, scores of midrange hotels and villas are spread out along the highway from Ciawi to Cipanas. Some of the villas can be rented.

Typical of the better mid-range hotels is the large *Hotel Safari* (☎ 253000, *Jl Raya Puncak 601*) in the middle of Cisarua, 1km from Kopo Hostel. Owned by the safari park, it has a huge variety of rooms and bungalows in the large grounds from 70,000 rp up to 650,000 rp for a three-bedroom villa. Nearby, the *Hotel Cisarua* is crumbling but cheaper and has plenty of colonial style.

The *Gunung Mas Guesthouse* (☎ 252 501) is a truly tranquil place to stay in the middle of the tea estate. Well-appointed rooms are 160,000 rp or huge VIP rooms with towering ceilings are 200,000 rp. A variety of bungalows sleeping four to 14 people can also be rented from 240,000 to 700,000 rp. Add 50,000 rp to all rates on weekends.

The top hotel, in terms of facilities and elevation, is the *Puncak Pass Hotel* (☎ 263-512503), right near the pass itself. Mostly modern bungalows are scattered over the hillside below the old colonial central building. The views are fantastic and the rates reasonable. Rooms start at 195,000 rp and range up to 600,000 rp for two bedroom bungalows, 20% less during the week.

Not far away, the *Bukit Indah* (☎ 263-512903) is another older hotel with good facilities but slightly cheaper.

**Getting There & Away** From Bogor, take a bus or colt to Cisarua (1000 rp, 45 minutes), or catch a direct bus from Jakarta (1½ hours).

## Cibodas
☎ 0263

At Cibodas, over the Puncak Pass, is a beautiful high-altitude extension of the Bogor botanical gardens, the **Kebun Raya Cibodas**. These are surrounded by thick tropical jungle on the slopes of the twin volcanoes of Gunung Gede and Gunung Pangrango. The 80-hectare gardens were originally planted in 1860. Entry to the gardens is 2200 rp and cars (500 rp) can enter every day except Sunday. Beside the entrance to the gardens is the entrance to the Gede Pangrango National Park.

Cibodas has limited facilities and is more difficult to reach than the resort strip along the Puncak Pass Highway. Consequently, it gets fewer visitors, but it has fine scenery, excellent walks and none of the crowded tat that lines the highway.

**Places to Stay & Eat** In Cibodas village, 500m before the gardens, *Freddy's Homestay* (☎ 515473) is a good option. Bright clean rooms with shared mandi are 20,000 and 25,000 rp upstairs, including breakfast. A bed in a shared dorm room is 15,000 rp. Meals are available and good information is provided.

Located near the PHPA office, the *Pondok Pemuda Cibodas* (☎ 512807) is a HI-affiliated hostel but it caters primarily to school groups. Groups can hire a whole dormitory block for only 80,000 rp, otherwise, a room for up to four people will cost 40,000 rp.

A truly tranquil place to lodge is right within the gardens themselves at the colonial *Wisma Tamu* (☎ 512233). Rooms for 50,000 rp are faded but large and have loads of character. The whole lodge can be hired for 250,000 rp and meals can be ordered. Bookings are essential and you can make reservations at the Bogor Botanical Gardens (☎ 0251-31162) as well as at the Cibodas gardens. It is about a 1km walk uphill from the gate to the guesthouse but cars can enter the gardens every day but Sunday.

There's cheap food at the warungs near the gardens and in the village, 500m down the hill.

**Getting There & Away** The turn-off to Cibodas is on the Bogor-Bandung highway, a few kilometres west of Cipanas. The gardens are then 5km off the main road. Angkot run from Cipanas (800 rp, 30 minutes).

## Gede Pangrango National Park

The Cibodas gardens are also the main entrance to the Gede Pangrango National Park, the highlight of which is the climb to the 2958m peak of volcanically active Gunung Gede. From the top of Gede on a clear day you can see Jakarta, Cirebon and even Pelabuhanratu on the south coast – well, Raffles reported that he could.

Register for the climb and obtain your permit (4000 rp) from the PHPA office just outside the garden entrance. The office has an information centre and pamphlets on the park, which is noted for its montane and alpine forest and birdlife, including the rare Javan eagle.

From Cibodas, the trail passes **Telaga Biru** (15 minutes), a blue/green lake. **Cibeureum Falls** (one hour away) lies just off the main trail. Most picnickers only go this far or some continue on to the **hot springs**, 2½ hours from the gate. The trail continues to climb another 1½ hours to **Kandang Badak**, where a new hut has been built on the saddle between the peaks of Gunung Gede and Gunung Pangrango (3019m). Take the trail to the right for a hard three hour climb to Pangrango. Most hikers turn left for the easier, but still steep, 1½ hour climb to Gede, which has more spectacular views. The **Gede Crater** lies below the summit and you can continue on to the **Suryakencana Meadow**.

The 10km hike right to the top of Gunung Gede takes at least 10 hours there and back, so you should start as early as possible and take warm clothes (night temperatures can drop to 5°C), food, water and a flashlight. Most hikers leave by 2 am to reach the summit in the early morning before the mists roll in. Register at the PHPA the day before. The main trails are well maintained and easy to follow. The hike should only be undertaken in the 'dry' season from May to October.

An alternative approach is to climb Gunung Gede from Selabintana to the south, a steep and slippery 9km path. This path joins the main trail at the Suryakencana Meadow, from where a third trail goes to Gunung Putri, west of Cibodas.

## Cipanas
☎ 0263

Cipanas, 5km beyond the Cibodas turn-off, has hot springs, noted for their curative properties. The **Istana Cipanas** is another seldom-used summer presidential palace favoured by Soekarno. Built in 1750, it is an elegant country house in beautiful gardens but, like the Bogor palace, it is not normally open to the public. Apart from that, Cipanas is another resort town with plenty of hotels and a few restaurants.

The best place to stay is the *Villa Cipanas Indah* (☎ 512513, Jl Tengah 8), a 10 minute walk from the palace. Rooms cost 28,000 rp, and 36,000 rp with hot water. Good information and guides are on offer. The *Hotel Flamboyant* (☎ 512586, Jl Raya Pasekon 69) is another of the cheaper hotels.

## BANDUNG
• **pop 2 million**    ☎ 022

With its population of over two million, Bandung is the capital of West Java and Indonesia's third-largest city. Despite its size, it is a fairly unhurried provincial place and lacks the often suffocating overcrowding of Jakarta and Surabaya. At 750m above sea level, it has a cool and comfortable climate. The majority of the population is native-Sundanese of West Java, who not only have a reputation as extroverted, easy-going people compared with the extremely refined Javanese, but also as zealous guardians of their own ancient culture. In contrast, the city itself is relatively new.

Bandung was originally established in the late 19th century as a Dutch garrison town of some 90,000 Sundanese, Chinese and Europeans. It rapidly acquired importance as a commercial and educational centre, renowned in particular for its Institute of Technology (ITB). Until 1962 there was speculation – and hope – that it was to become the capital of the nation. Bandung's most notable entry in the history books was as host to the Asia-Africa conference in 1955, which placed Bandung in the world spotlight.

On the industrial front, Bandung has maintained some of its European-created production centres and its major concerns include textiles, telecommunications, tea and food processing. It has suffered badly because of the economic crisis, with the collapse of the Timor national car industry and cutbacks to the aerospace industry, but Bandung has been far removed from trouble that has occurred elsewhere in Java.

Although in the past Bandung has been described as the 'Paris of Java', due to its many fine parks and gardens, much of the city's former glamour has faded. As far as its general appearance goes, what exists today is a mish-mash of dilapidated colonial and modern buildings, though the northern suburbs still have graceful residential areas. Art Deco architecture is in abundance, one of the best examples being the Savoy Homann Hotel.

## Colonial Architecture

Of all Java's cities, Bandung has the most noticeable Dutch influence. Jakarta's Dutch heritage is certainly older, and Surabaya and Malang have some fine Dutch buildings, but Bandung's remaining public buildings and leafy colonial suburbs provide Java's greatest concentration of later Dutch architecture.

Dutch interest in Bandung began with the building of the Great Post Road (Groote Postweg now Jalan Asia-Afrika) and in a case of 'if Muhammed won't come to the mountain' Governor General Dandaels ordered the city moved north to meet the road. The local regent, Bupati Wiranatakusumah II, built his residence and **Pendopo** (Meeting Pavilion) just south of the alun alun, in traditional Sundanese style but with obvious Dutch influence.

The city was put on the map with the building of the railway line to Jakarta in the 1880s, and Bandung's cool climate made it something of a resort town. At the turn of the century, with the proclamation of Pax Neerlandica and the formation of a civilian government, decentralisation saw Bandung become an important regional city. Bandung's building boom of the 1920s saw the development of the European district to the north of the centre in the hills, and Bandung acquired its description as the 'Paris of Java'. The period witnessed important architectural developments, particularly the Indo-European style which combined Indonesian architectural motifs with modern architecture, and Bandung's striking Art Deco architecture.

Jalan Braga was a fashionable strip of cafes that appealed to the Dutch elite and visitors escaping to the mountains. On Jalan Asia-Afrika, the **Savoy Homman Hotel** was built in 1880 and became the place to stay. The Savoy Homman was completely refurbished and extended in 1938, and is now best known for its fine Art Deco architecture. The hotel's main competition, then as now, was the **Grand Hotel Preanger**, a mixture of styles with a heavy Art Deco influence. The **Gedung Merdeka** building is another fine Art Deco example along the same stretch. It once housed the Concordia Society, a Dutch social club and centre for Bandung society life.

As you head north along Jalan Braga and then into Jalan Wastukencana, just over the railway line you'll find Merdeka Park and the original **City Hall** built in the 1920s. The park provides a pleasant break from the traffic and all around are fine examples of impressive public architecture. On the park's southern edge, the **Bank Indonesia** building is stoically classical,

Bandung is an excellent place to visit if you are at all interested in Sundanese culture. Otherwise, its main attractions lie in the beautiful countryside that surrounds the city.

To the north and south there is a wild tangle of high volcanic peaks, including the famous Tangkuban Prahu volcano, and several huge tea plantations.

There are also some excellent walks in the area. One of the best walks goes alongside the river, from the village of Maribaya to Dago Hill situated on the outskirts of Bandung.

## Orientation

Bandung sprawls out over the northern foothills of a huge plateau surrounded by high mountain ridges. The main part of the city lies south of the train line and is centred around Jl Asia Afrika and the city square (alun alun). Along Jl Asia Afrika are the tourist office, post office and most of the banks, airline offices, restaurants and top-end hotels. Jl Braga was the ritzy shopping area in Dutch times and has a few useful shops and cafes. The budget hotel area in Bandung is on the south side of the train station.

## Colonial Architecture

while the nearby **Bethel Church** is very Dutch in style. On the Jalan Merdeka side of the park, the **cathedral** with its spires is Bandung's most impressive church while, a little farther north, the **St Angela School** is a fine example of earlier colonial architecture.

The Dutch built a new administrative district to the north-east of the city centre, and in pride of place here is the magnificent **Gedung Sate** building, dating from 1917. The design was strongly influenced by Orientalism fashionable in Europe at the time, though Egyptian and Moorish motifs are more noticeable than Indonesian influences. However, the building is topped by a Javanese-style tiered roof and mounted by a spire that looks like a sate stick, hence the building's name. Farther along Jl Diponegoro, more classically styled Dutch administrative buildings include the **Geological Museum** and the **Gedung Dwi Warna**.

Just to the north of the Gedung Sate building is Bandung's wealthy residential district. This is a wonderfully preserved area of colonial bungalows from the 1920s, with shingled roofs, rounded balconies, bay windows and leadlight. Head over to Jalan Surapati and wander around any of the quiet, leafy back streets just east of Jalan Juanda to savour the life of the Dutch colonial or the present-day Indonesian elite.

One of Bandung's most interesting buildings is found nearby at the Bandung Institute of Technology. The old **ITB building** here was designed by Maclaine Pont and officially opened in 1920. It represents the best example of the Indo-European style, with an expansive shingled roof of Minangkabau design atop a Dutch-style building.

Bandung has plenty of other fine colonial buildings, such as the classical **Governor's Residence** just to the north of the Hotel Guntur, and the **Wisma IKIP** on Jalan Setiabudi to the north of the city. The Wisma IKIP is perhaps Bandung's finest Art Deco building with jutting, rounded curves reminiscent of an ocean liner.

PETER TURNER

**Wisma IKIP building**

---

In colonial times, the railway tracks divided the riff-raff in the south from the people who lived in the Dutch city in the north. During the transitional independence period after the war, the train line was in fact the official partition line between the reoccupied Dutch city in the north and the Republican-controlled Bandung in the south. The railway tracks still represent a social dividing line.

To the north, wealthy residential areas are studded with tree-lined streets and parks bordered on the northernmost edge by the hills of Dago.

## Information

**Tourist Offices** The very helpful Bandung Tourist Information Centre (☎ 4206644) at the alun alun on Jl Asia Afrika is the place to go for detailed information and all the latest on cultural events in and around Bandung. It's open from 9 am to 5 pm daily.

A handy tourist information counter is at the south side of the train station.

**Money** Golden Megah moneychanger, Jl Otista 180 and Jl Lembong 36, usually has the best rates in town and no fees. It is open Monday to Friday from 8.30 am to 4.30 pm,

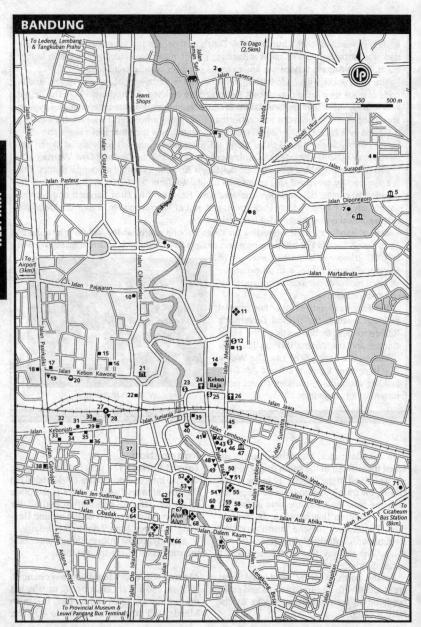

# BANDUNG

To Ledeng, Lembang
& Tangkuban Prahu

To Dago
(2.5km)

Jeans
Shops

Jalan Taman Sari

Jalan Ganeca

Jalan Juanda

Jalan Dipati Ukur

Jalan Surapati

Jalan Diponegoro

Jalan Martadinata

Jalan Pasteur

To
Airport
(3km)

Jalan Cipaganti

Jalan Pajajaran

Jalan Cihampelas

Jalan Pasirkaliki

Jalan Kebon Kawong

Kebun
Raja

Jalan Merdeka

Jalan Jawa

Jalan Suniaraja

Jalan Lembong

Jalan Braga

Jalan Sumatra

Jalan
Kebonjati

Jalan Tamblong

Jalan Veteran

Jalan Naripan

To
Cicaheum
Bus Station
(8km)

Jalan Garduati

Jalan Jen Sudirman

Jalan Asia Afrika

Jalan A Yani

Jalan Cibadak

Jalan Dewi Sartika

Alun
Alun

Jalan Dalem Kaum

Jalan Astana Anyar

Jalan Oto Iskandardinata

Jalan Lengkong Besar

Jalan Karapitan

To Provincial Museum &
Leuwi Pangang Bus Terminal

0   250   500 m

**PLACES TO STAY**
3   Hotel Sawunggaling
4   Wisma Asri
13  Hotel Royal Merdeka
15  Hotel Patradissa
16  Serena Hotel
17  Mutiara Hotel
18  Hotel Cemerlang
22  Hotel Guntur
29  Losmen Sakardana
30  Sakardana Homestay
32  Hotel Patradissa II
33  New Le Yossie
34  Hotel Surabaya
35  Le Yossie Homestay
36  By Moritz
38  Hotel Trio
39  Hotel Kedaton
45  Hotel Panghegar
57  Grand Hotel Preanger
69  Savoy Homann Hotel
70  Hotel Mawar

**PLACES TO EAT**
19  Rumah Makan Mandarin
28  Warungs & Restaurants
44  Braga Permai Cafe
48  London Bakery
49  French Bakery

50  Canary Bakery
51  Sindang Reret Restaurant
53  Night Market Warungs
54  Rumah Makan Tenda Biru
63  Rumah Makan Sari Indah
66  Warung Nasi Mang Udju

**OTHER**
1   Zoo
2   Bandung Institute of
    Technology (ITB)
5   Museum Geologi (Geological
    Museum)
6   Museum Pos dan Giro
    (Post & Giro National Stamp
    Museum)
7   Gedung Sate (Regional
    Government Building)
8   Galael Supermarket
9   Flower Market
10  Bouraq Office
11  Plaza Bandung Indah
    Shopping Mall
12  Bank Duta
14  City Hall (Kantor Walikota)
20  4848 Taxis
21  Governor's Residence
23  Bank BNI
24  Bethel Church

25  Bank Indonesia
26  Catholic Church
27  Train Station
31  Bus Agents
37  Pasar Baru
40  4848 Taxis
41  Braga Disco
42  North Sea Bar
43  Amsterdam Cafe
46  Golden Megah Corp
    Moneychanger
47  Museum Mandala Wangsit
    (Army Museum)
52  Ramayana Department Store
    & Supermarket
55  Sarinah Department Store
56  Wartel
58  Merpati Office
59  Wartel
60  Gedung Merdeka
    (Freedom Building)
61  Bank BRI
62  Main Post Office
64  Golden Megah Corp
    Moneychanger
65  King's Department Store
67  Tourist Information Centre
68  Palaguna Shopping Centre
71  Rumentang Siang

and Saturday until 2 pm. Banks are scattered all around town and have ATMs – try the BNI just west of the Kebun Raja. The biggest selection of banks is on Jl Merdeka, south of the Bandung Indah Plaza.

**Post & Communications** The main post office at the corner of Jl Banceuy and Jl Asia Afrika is open every day from 8 am to 8 pm and has an Internet service. Poste restante is just a tin of jumbled letters out the back. For international telephone calls, a Telkom *wartel* is on the corner of Jl Tamblong and Jl Naripan; there is also a wartel on Jl Asia Afrika, opposite the Savoy Homann Hotel.

**Medical Services** For medical attention, the Adventist Hospital (☎ 234386) at Jl Cihampelas 161 is a missionary hospital with English-speaking staff.

### Gedung Merdeka (Freedom Building)
If you're interested in learning more about the Asia-Africa conference of 1955, visit the Museum Konperensi (Conference Museum) in the Gedung Merdeka on Jl Asia Afrika. There you'll see photographs and exhibits of the meeting between Soekarno, Chou En-Lai, Ho Chi Minh, Nasser and other Third World leaders of the 1950s. The building itself dates from 1879 and was originally the 'Concordia Societet', a meeting hall of Dutch associations and the centre for high society. The museum is open Monday to Friday from 8 am to 6 pm.

### Museum Geologi (Geological Museum)
North across the railway tracks at Jl Diponegoro 57, the museum and the office of the Geological Survey of Indonesia are

housed in the massive old headquarters of the Dutch Geological Service. It has excellent volcano exhibits and an array of fossils, including a model skull of Java Man. It's open from 9 am to 3 pm Monday to Thursday, 9 am to 1 pm Saturday and Sunday. From the train station you can take an angkot bound for 'Sadang Serang' and get off at the Gedung Sate, about 400m from the museum.

## Other Museums

The **Museum Negeri Propinsi Jawa Barat** (West Java Provincial Museum), south-west of the city at Jl Oto Iskandardinata 638, has an interesting display of Sundanese artefacts. It is open every day, except Monday, from 8 am to 2 pm.

The **Museum Prangko** (Stamp Museum) is in the north-east corner of the Gedung Sate (Regional Government) complex on Jl Diponegoro. As well as thousands of stamps from around the world, the museum has everything from post boxes to pushcarts, which have been used since colonial times to ensure that the mail gets through. It is open from 9 am to 3 pm weekdays, 9 am to 1 pm weekends, but closes for lunch, prayer breaks and who knows what else.

The **Museum Mandala Wangsit** (Army Museum), Jl Lembong 38, is devoted to the history and exploits of the West Java Siliwangi division (based in Bandung). The museum is full of grim and explicit photographs of the Darul Islam (Islamic State) rebellion of 1948-62, which was centred largely around Bandung.

## Bandung Institute of Technology (ITB)

North of town on Jl Ganeca is the Bandung Institute of Technology, built at the beginning of the century. The university has large grounds and gardens and the main campus complex is notable for its 'Indo-European' architecture, featuring Minangkabau-style roofs atop colonial-style buildings.

Opened in 1920, the ITB was the first Dutch-founded university open to Indonesians. It was here that Soekarno studied civil engineering (1920-25) and helped to found the Bandung Study Club, members of which formed a political party which grew into the Indonesian Nationalist Party (PNI), with independence as its goal. The institute's students have maintained their reputation for outspokenness and political activism, and in 1978 they published the *White Book of the 1978 Students' Struggle* against alleged corruption in high places. It was banned in Indonesia but later published in the USA. The ITB is the foremost scientific university in the country, but it's also reputed to have one of the best fine arts schools, and its art gallery can be visited. Across from the main gate is a useful canteen in the *asrama mahasiswa* (student dorm complex) where many of the students congregate.

To reach the ITB, take a Lembang or Dago angkot from the train station and then walk down Jl Ganeca.

## Zoo

Bandung zoo's spacious, beautifully landscaped gardens are very attractive, but the animals are few and most are housed in typically cramped conditions. The zoo is a few minutes' walk from the ITB on Jl Taman Sari – the entrance is down the steps past the toy stalls opposite Jl Ganeca. It's open daily from 7 am to 5 pm and admission costs 2000 rp.

## Dago

At the end of Jl Merdeka, Jl Juanda climbs up to Dago Hill to the north, overlooking the city. The famous Dago Thee Huis (Dago Tea House) offers commanding vistas over the bluff and is a fine place to catch the sunset. The complex has an outdoor theatre and an indoor theatre farther down the hill, where cultural events are sometimes held.

On the main road, 100m past the teahouse turn-off, a path leads down to the Curug Dago (Dago Waterfall). From here you can walk along the river to the **Taman Hutan Raya Ir H Juanda** a pleasant forest park with another waterfall, 'caves' and walking paths. By road, the entrance is 2km past the Dago bemo terminal. The Gua Pakar cave is in fact an ammunition store hacked out by the Japanese during the war. Farther north is the Gua Belanda, the same deal, but built by the Dutch. A tunnel leads right though the mountain to the start of the trail that leads all the way to Maribaya along Sungai Cikapundung (see under Maribaya Hot Springs in the North of Bandung section for more information).

## 'Jeans' Street

No discussion of Bandung's sights would be complete without mention of its famous jeans street, Jl Cihampelas, in the more affluent northern side of town. Celebrating the street's standing as a major textile centre, shops with brightly painted humungous plaster statues of King Kong, Rambo and other legendary monsters compete with one another. This kitsch has to be seen to be believed. The jeans are very cheap, though the quality is not fantastic. Denim jackets and T-shirts are a good buy.

## Ram Fights

Noisy, traditional ram-butting fights known as *adu domba* are held in Cilimus, in the northern suburbs of Bandung. They are held most Sunday mornings in the dry season, but not every Sunday.

To the sound of drums, gongs and hand clapping, two rams keep charging at each other. There are about 25 or more clashes of horns with a referee deciding the winner. If a ram gets dizzy they tweak his testicles and send him back into combat until he's had enough! This sport has been popular in West Java for so long that most villages have their own ram-fight societies and there are organised tournaments to encourage farmers to rear a stronger breed of ram. At village level it's just good fun; at district and provincial level there's wild betting.

To reach Cilimus, take an angkot or Lembang minibus (600 rp) to Terminal Ledeng on Jl Setiabudi, the continuation of Jl Sukajadi. Go down Jl Sersan Bajuri directly opposite the terminal, turn left at Jl Cilimus and continue to the bamboo grove.

## Places to Stay – Budget

Bandung's hotels are fairly expensive but Jl Kebonjati, near the train station and the city centre, has some good guesthouses, all providing budget rooms, food and information.

The *By Moritz* (☎ *4205788, Kompleks Luxor Permai 35, Jl Kebonjati*) is a well managed travellers' guesthouse with a good restaurant. Dorm beds cost 10,000 rp and small but spotless singles/doubles/triples with shared bathroom are 15,000/20,000/30,000 rp. Breakfast is included.

*Le Yossie Homestay* (☎ *4205453, 53 Jl Kebonjati*) tends to be overrun with local hangers-on but the rooms are light and there is a downstairs cafe. A dorm bed costs 9000 rp per person; singles/doubles/triples are 12,500/17,500/25,000 rp. An offshoot, the quieter *New Le Yossie* is one street south. Airy rooms around a courtyard garden are a notch above the pack and cost 15,000 rp for singles, 20,000 and 25,000 rp for doubles.

Bandung's original guesthouse, *Losmen Sakardana* (☎ *4209897*) is down a little alley off Jl Kebonjati beside the Hotel Melati I at No 50/7B. Rooms for 12,500/15,000 rp are very basic and past their prime. *Sakardana Homestay* (☎ *4218553, Gang Babakan 55-7/B)* farther along the alley, is better kept but the walls are thin and the alleyway is noisy from nocturnal goings-on. Rooms cost 10,000/15,000 rp.

*Hotel Surabaya* (☎ *436791, Jl Kebonjati 71)* is a rambling old hotel with plenty of colonial ambience (check out the old photographs in the lobby). This would be a superb hotel with renovation but it has been sadly neglected. Spartan rooms range from 13,000/22,500 rp without bath up to 45,000 rp for better rooms with bath and a touch of style.

## Places to Stay – Mid-Range

Bandung has plenty of mid-range hotels, especially north of the train station and along Jl Gardujati, but most are old and faded.

The *Hotel Patradissa* (☎ *4206680, Jl H Moch Iskat 8)* is an older hotel but very well kept and friendly. Rooms, all with bathroom and hot water, cost 25,000/30,000 rp for singles/doubles up to 72,500 rp. Under different owners, **Hotel Patradissa II** (☎ 420 2645, Jl Pasirkaliki 12) is reasonably priced but overdue for a paint job. Spotty rooms with hot water showers cost 35,000 rp.

The best deal at the moment is the new **Serena Hotel** (☎ 4207850, Jl Marjuk 6). Sparkling rooms with hot water, TV and minibar cost 88,000 rp, only 66,000 rp after discount.

**Hotel Guntur** (☎ 4203763, Jl Oto Iskandardinata 20) is a large, older hotel with a manicured garden, and rooms for 60,000 and 80,000 rp. Other central mid-range options include **Mutiara Hotel** (☎ 4200333, Jl Kebon Kawung 60), a motel-style place with a small pool, good cafe and rooms from 89,000 to 138,000 rp. The nearby **Hotel Cermalang** (☎ 671383, Jl Pasirkaliki 45) is newer and better appointed but most rooms, from 129,350 to 186,750 rp, have internal-facing windows.

Just north of the centre near the Plaza Bandung Indah, **Hotel Royal Merdeka** (☎ 4200555, Jl Merdeka 34) is a better class of mid-range hotel with coffee shop, bar, fitness centre and well appointed rooms from 158,400 rp.

**Wisma Asri** (☎ 4521717, Jl Merak 5) is a more homey guesthouse out near the Gedung Sate. Comfortable rooms cost 50,000 to 75,000 rp, plus 20%.

Near the ITB, **Hotel Sawunggaling** (☎ 4218254, Jl Sawunggaling 13) is an attractive hotel with colonial style. Big rooms with minibar and TV cost 110,000 to 155,000 rp.

Spanning the middle and top-end ranges, the **Hotel Panghegar** (☎ 432286, Jl Merdeka 2) is an older business hotel but well positioned and with good rooms from US$100, before massive discount. The new **Hotel Kedaton** (☎ 4219898, Jl Suniaraja 14) is even more central and has a pool and top facilities for the price – rooms cost 150,000/170,000 rp.

## Places to Stay – Top End

Bandung has a glut of luxury hotels, all with swimming pools. Though brochures quote US dollars, they are meaningless and hotels have been offering remarkable discounts to attract weekend visitors from Jakarta – 200,000 rp or less per night. Ring around for the current discount rates.

The very central **Savoy Homann Hotel** (☎ 432244, Jl Asia Afrika 112) is Bandung's most famous hotel, noted for its Art Deco style. Posted rates for singles/doubles start at US$100. The hotel has a garden restaurant and a superb Art Deco dining room facing the street.

Built in 1928, the **Grand Hotel Preanger** (☎ 431631, Jl Asia Afrika 181) competes with the Savoy Homann for colonial style. It doesn't quite match the Savoy Homann on that score but it is one of Bandung's best hotels. Most rooms are in the new tower but the best are the superb rooms in the old wing. Discounting has seen prices drop to 245,000 rp.

Many of Bandung's new hotels are found in the north of the city. On the road to Dago, the smaller **Sheraton** (☎ 2500303, Jl Juanda 390) has rooms from 400,000 rp after discount, and right near the Dago Tea House, **Hotel Jayakarta** (☎ 2505888, Jl Juanda 381) is better value with discounted rooms from 220,000 rp.

North of the zoo on the outskirts of town, **Chedi Hotel** (☎ 230333, Jl Ranca Bentang 56-58) is a small boutique hotel with countryside views, and unique architecture and furnishings. This is one of Java's most stylish hotels and rooms start at US$150.

## Places to Eat

**By Moritz** (See Places to Stay – Budget) is the most popular travellers' bar/cafe. Cheap but fairly grotty warungs and restaurants can be found on the south side of the train station, or Jl Gardujati, opposite the Hotel Trio, has a good selection of night warungs that stay open late.

The best **night warungs** are on Jl Cikapundung Barat, across from the alun alun near the Ramayana department store. Stalls here sell a bit of everything – soto, sate, gado gado, seafood – or try the *soto jeroan*, intestine soup with various medicinal properties,

GLENN BEANLAND

GLENN BEANLAND

Wayang golek puppets: found in West Java ...     ... and in markets throughout Central Java.

SARA-JANE CLELAND

Wayang kulit – shadow puppets – still teach traditional Javanese values and also entertain.

Pulau Antuk Barat, Pulau Seribu, West Java.

Fishing boats at Pangandara, West Java.

mostly designed to stimulate male libido. Nearby on the ground floor of the Ramayana department store is a good, squeaky clean food-stall area.

Bandung also has a number of excellent Chinese restaurants. The *Rumah Makan Mandarin* on Jl Kebon Kawung is a no-frills place with excellent dishes served in steaming cast-iron pans. Seafood is a speciality and the restaurant is popular with Bandung's Chinese community.

Jl Braga is a quasi-European avenue with a string of coffee shops and bakeries. The centrepiece is the *Braga Permai* sidewalk cafe at No 74, a more upmarket restaurant with a mixed menu, a variety of cakes and superb ice cream. On the corner of Jl Braga and Jl ABC/Naripan is the *Canary Bakery*, with hamburgers and western fare; the upstairs balcony is pleasant, if a little noisy. Bakeries include the *Sumber Hidangan Bakery* and the *French Bakery* for a snack or light meal – croissants, Danish pastries or chicken curry puffs. Most popular is the *London Bakery*, which has an espresso machine. The *North Sea Bar* at No 82 and *Amsterdam Cafe* at No 74, specialise in grills, beer and bar girls.

Farther east on Jl Tamblong, the *Rasa Bakery*, housed in a fine colonial building, is a pleasant spot for pastries or a light meal.

All the big hotels have restaurants. For a treat with style try the *rijsttafel* in the *Savoy Homann Hotel* restaurant or the revolving restaurant at the top of the *Hotel Panghegar*.

**Sundanese Restaurants** Bandung is a good place to try traditional Sundanese food. The *Warung Nasi Mang Udju*, on Jl Dewi Sartika just south of the alun alun, is a simple place, but the food is excellent and cheap. *Rumah Makan Tenda Biru* on Jl Braga is a no-frills, cafeteria-style place with good Sundanese food.

*Rumah Makan Sari Indah (Jl Sudirman 103-107)* is much more salubrious, with bamboo decor, an artificial waterfall and huts in the garden at the back for dining on mats. The food is excellent and very moderately priced.

---

## Sundanese Food

Sundanese food is spicy rather than chilli hot. Popular dishes include: *pepes usus*, chicken steamed in bamboo leaf; steamed goldfish; fish flavoured with *laos*, a spice rather like ginger; and spiced buffalo meat, similar to Sumatran rendang. There is often a plate of *petei* (huge broad beans), tempe, salad and sambal. *Soto Bandung*, a soup made from tripe, is another Sundanese speciality of Bandung. In Cirebon, the local speciality is *nasi lengko*, rice with bean sprouts, tahu, tempe, fried onion, cucumber and peanut sauce.

The better Sundanese restaurants are delightful dining experiences, with gardens and a fish pond for netting fresh *garame* and *ikan mas*, popular freshwater fish.

---

The *Sindang Reret Restaurant (Jl Naripan 9)* just around the corner from Jl Braga, is central and has good, if slightly expensive, Sundanese food and Saturday night cultural performances.

For a real treat, take a taxi to the Dago area in the north of the city and the lovely *Penineungan Endah (Jl Tubagus Ismail Raya 60)*. Try Sundanese food in individual tearooms, surrounded by Japanese-style gardens bounded by tranquil brooks. From the waters that surround your teahouse, sizeable goldfish are freshly netted to serve as the Sundanese delicacy, *ikan mas*.

## Entertainment

**Cultural Performances** Bandung is an excellent place to see Sundanese performing arts. Many performances are irregular – the visitor information office can tell you when events are on and can also inform you of special programs.

Bandung's performing arts centre is the *Rumentang Siang* at Jl Baranangsiang 1. Wayang golek puppet performances, *jaipongan*, *pencak silat* (the art of self-defence), *sandiwara* (traditional Javanese theatre), *ketoprak* folk theatre etc are held Saturday nights – check with the tourist office for schedules.

You can catch a scaled-down wayang golek exhibition with a meal every Saturday night from 7 pm at the *Sindang Reret Restaurant*.

*Sanggar Langen Setra (Jl Oto Iskandardinata 541A)* is a Jaipongan dance club that features Ketuktilu and Jaipongan every evening from 8 pm to 1 am. The club is about 2km south of the Jl Jen Sudirman bus terminal. A cover charge applies and you pay extra to join the performers for a dance. While owing much to traditional dance, Jaipongan is a modern social dance and hostesses dance primarily to entertain male clients – something like traditional bar girls.

Every Sunday at the zoo, from 9 am to noon, traditional performances such as pencak silat or wayang golek are held.

*ASTI-Bandung*, in the southern part of the city at Jl Buah Batu 212, is a school for traditional Sundanese arts – music, dancing and pencak silat. Check with the tourist office for events, or it is open to interested visitors every morning, except Sunday.

You can catch angklung performances at Pak Ujo's *Saung Angklung* (Bamboo Workshop), Jl Padasuka 118, east of the city on the way to the Cicaheum bus terminal. You can also see instruments being made. Performances are 12,500 rp and held most afternoons, but they depend on tour group bookings.

**Nightlife** Jl Braga is a good place in the evening for less cultural pursuits. The *North Sea Bar* at No 82 and the similar *Amsterdam Cafe* at No 74 are both popular with expats and visitors. They are crawling with bar girls but get a mixed crowd on weekends and are convivial places. Discos include the *Braga Disco*, just off Jl Braga, and *Polo*, on the 11th floor of the BRI building on Jl Asia Afrika. North-west of the city centre at Jl Dr Junjunan 164, *Laga Pub* is a convivial place that gets some good bands and a fair smattering of expats. *S.O.B Fun Pub (Jl Ir H Juanda 390)* at the Sheraton, has bands and a lively crowd on weekends.

## Shopping

In the city centre, down a small alley behind Jl Pangarang 22, near the Hotel Mawar, Pak Ruhiyat at No 78/17B produces wayang golek puppets and masks, and you can see them being carved.

The Cupu Manik puppet factory is on Jl Haji Akbar, off Jl Kebon Kawung just north of the train station. Traditional Sundanese musical instruments can be bought at Pak Ujo's Saung Angklung (Bamboo Workshop) or the Toko Musik at Gang Suniaraja 3, off Jl ABC.

Jl Cibaduyut, in south-west Bandung, is to shoes as Jl Cihampelas is to jeans, but without the gaudy statues. Leatherwork is a Bandung speciality with dozens of shops selling high-quality shoes and bags at some of the best prices in Java. More central, Jl Jen Sudirman has an excellent selection of shoe shops around the Pasar Kota Kembang, just west of Jl Otto Iskandardinata. For leather jackets, Mirage Leather Wear, shop No 5 on the 2nd floor of Plaza Bandung Indah, has a good range, as does the Leather Palace, Jl Braga No 113, known for its custom-made coats, bags and shoes. The quality of jackets is better but prices are much higher than in Garut, on the way to Pangandaran.

Jl Braga used to be the exclusive shopping street of Bandung, though it is fairly quiet these days. Jakarta's Sarinah department store has a small branch here with a selection of crafts.

These days the shopping malls dominate the town – Plaza Bandung Indah is Bandung's biggest and brightest mall. For everyday goods, the liveliest shopping district is on Jl Dalem Kaum and nearby streets, just west of the alun alun. Supermarkets can be found in the Ramayana department stores on Jl Cikapundung Barat and Jl Dalem Kaum, and in the Plaza Bandung Indah.

Pasar Baru is Bandung's big, somewhat grotty central market, with fruit, vegetables and all manner of goods. Bandung's title of the 'City of Flowers' comes true at the flower market on Jl Wastukencana, on the way to the zoo. Pasar Jatayu, 1km west of the train station on Jl Arjuna, is a flea market where you may be able to find some collectibles if you sift through the junk.

## Getting There & Away
**Air** Merpati Nusantara (☎ 441226), Jl Asia Afrika 73, opposite the Savoy Homann Hotel, has direct flights to Jakarta's Halim airport (205,000 rp) and Surabaya (531,000 rp). Garuda (☎ 4209467) is in the Hotel Preanger on Jl Asia Afrika.

**Bus** The Leuwi Panjang bus terminal, 5km south of the city centre on Jl Soekarno Hatta, has buses west to places like Bogor (4000/7000 rp, three hours), Sukabumi (3500 rp, three hours) and Jakarta's Kampung Rambutan bus terminal (6500 to 15,000 rp, 4½ hours). Buses to Bogor are not allowed to take the scenic Puncak Pass route on weekends. Door-to-door minibuses also go to Bogor (20,000 rp) via Puncak.

Buses to the east leave from the Cicaheum bus terminal on the eastern outskirts of the city. Normal/air-con buses include Cirebon (5000/8000 rp, 3½ hours), Garut (2000 rp, two hours), Pangandaran (10,000 rp, six hours) and Yogya (16,500/25,000 rp, 10 hours).

Sari Harum (☎ 708110) has air-con minibuses to Pangandaran (25,000 rp, five hours). The 4848 company (☎ 4208448), Jl Kebon Kawong 49, has minibuses to Pangandaran, Garut, Cirebon and other destinations but their fleet is decrepit. Their other depot at Jl Suniaraja Timur 39 (☎ 434848) has better minibuses to Jakarta (30,000 rp air-con) or beat-up taxis (25,000 rp).

For luxury buses to long-distance destinations, Kramatdjati (☎ 439860), Jl Kebonjati 96, and Pahala Kencana (☎ 432911), Jl Kebonjati 90, are two convenient agents in the budget accommodation area.

From the Stasiun Hall terminal outside the train station, colts also run to Lembang and Subang (for Tangkuban Prahu and Ciater).

**Train** The Bandung-Jakarta *Parahyangan* (20,000/32,000 rp bisnis/eksekutif; three hours) is the main service with departures to Jakarta's Gambir train station roughly every hour from 4 am to 10.05 pm. The *Argogede* luxury service (40,000 rp, 2½ hours) departs at 6.30 am and 2.30 pm.

Several trains operate on the Bandung-Banjar-Yogya route, most continuing on to Surabaya. Most are night expresses, such as the *Mutiara Selatan* (33,000 rp bisnis) and *Turangga* (45,000/75,000 rp).

## Getting Around
**To/From the Airport** Bandung's Husein Sastranegara airport is 4km north-west of town, 10,000 rp by taxi.

**Bus, Angkot & Taxi** Bandung has a fairly good, if crowded, Damri city bus service which charges a fixed 500 rp. Nos 9 and 11 run from west to east down Jl Asia Afrika to Cicaheum bus terminal.

Angkots run set routes all over town between numerous stations. From Stasiun Hall, on the southern side of the train station, angkots go to Dago, Ledeng and other stations. When returning, catch any angkot showing 'St Hall'. Abdul Muis (Abd Muis), south of the alun alun on Jl Dewi Sartika, and Cicaheum are the other main angkot terminals. Angkots cost 300 to 600 rp (500 rp for most destinations).

Becaks have all but disappeared from central Bandung. Taxis are numerous, both private and metered, but meters are rarely used – they want a minimum of 5000 rp for up to 5km. From the taxi booth at the train station, taxis cost 10,000 rp to any central destination, or fixed charter rates are Maribaya (35,000 rp) and Tangkuban Perahu (60,000 rp).

## AROUND BANDUNG
## Lembang
☎ 022
On the road to Tangkuban Prahu, 16km north of Bandung, Lembang was once a noted hill resort but is now a busy little market town. Most visitors keep heading farther up into the hills, but it is a good place to stop for lunch or a snack. On Jl Raya Lembang, the main Bandung road, excellent fruit and

## AROUND BANDUNG

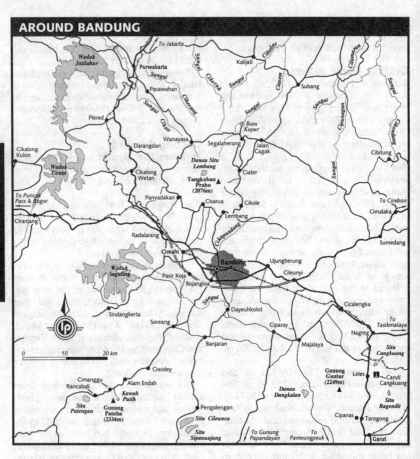

cheap avocados can be found at the Pasar Buah Buahan. Along the same street are a number of good, cheap restaurants. At the market and on the road up to the crater there are stalls selling delicious hot corn on the cob, and *bandrek* (a local ginger drink).

As you enter Lembang, 0.5km before the welcome arch is the turn-off to Lembang's planetarium, the Bosscha Astronomical Observatory. A road winds 2.2km uphill to the telescope set in landscaped gardens with good views across the countryside.

The observatory is run by the ITB (☎ 278 6001), which has a limited program of night viewings.

**Places to Stay & Eat** The *Grand Hotel Lembang* (☎ 2786671, Jl Raya Lembang 272) harks back to the days when Lembang was a fashionable resort for Bandung's Dutch community. It is old-fashioned and comfortable, with beautiful gardens, a swimming pool and tennis courts, as well as a bar and a restaurant. Rooms in the old wing are neglected but have character and attached sitting rooms, and cost 45,000 rp and 60,000 rp. Rooms in the new wing cost from 128,000 rp.

Just past Lembang, the bustle is left behind and the scenery is superb. Here you'll find the very pleasant Sundanese restaurant **Reret II**. A few hotels also have fine aspects. **Puteri Gunung Cottages (☎ 278 6650)** has a pool, tennis court and a commercial flower garden open to the public. Well appointed rooms cost 182,000 to 326,000 rp. The nearby **Panorama Hotel (☎ 2786030)** is also good and aptly named.

### Maribaya Hot Springs

Maribaya, 5km east of Lembang by colt, has a thermal spa, landscaped gardens and a thundering waterfall. It's another tourist spot, crowded on Sunday, but worth visiting. Horses can be hired for around 10,000 rp per hour.

You can extend your Tangkuban Prahu trip by walking from the bottom end of Maribaya's gardens down through a brilliant, deep and wooded river gorge all the way to Dago. There's a good track and if you allow about two to three hours for the walk (6km) you can be at a Dago vantage point for sunset. From there it's only a short trip by colt back into Bandung.

### Tangkuban Prahu

The 'overturned prahu' volcano crater stands 30km north of Bandung. Years ago the centre of Tangkuban Prahu collapsed under the weight of built-up ash and, instead of the usual conical volcano shape, it has a flat elongated summit with a huge caldera more than 7km across.

There is, of course, a legend to explain this phenomenon:

An estranged young prince returned home and unwittingly fell in love with his own mother. When the queen discovered the terrible truth of her lover's identity she challenged him to build a dam and a huge boat during a single night before she would agree to marry him. Seeing that the young man was about to complete this impossible task, she called on the gods to bring the

sun up early and, as the cocks began to crow, the boat builder turned his nearly completed boat over in a fit of anger.

Tangkuban Prahu is easily accessible by car, so it's very much a tourist trap. Up at the crater is an information centre, warungs and a parade of peddlers hustling postcards, souvenirs and other junk. It's a tacky jumble that detracts from the scenery, but you can escape this bedlam of activity and the huge crater is an impressive sight. Tangkuban Prahu still emits sulphur fumes but is not particularly active. Its last serious eruption was in 1969.

Kawah Ratu, the huge 'Queen Crater', is at the top, but you can walk around the rim of the main crater for about 20 minutes for views of the secondary crater, Kawah Upas. The trail leads farther along a ridge between the two craters and returns to the carpark, but it is steep and slippery in parts. Exercise caution. A better walk is to Kawah Domas, a volcanic area of steaming and bubbling geysers that can be reached by a side trail to the top, and few of the busloads make it here. You can also head off across country towards Ciater or Lembang. Guides can be hired for around 10,000 rp.

**Getting There & Away** At 2076m Tangkuban Prahu can be quite cool and around noon the mist starts to roll in through the trees, so try to go early. From Bandung's minibus terminal in front of the train station, take a Subang colt (3000 rp) via Lembang to the park entrance.

Entry is 2550 rp per person. Minibuses to the top officially cost 2500 rp per person but they will probably ask more and if there are not enough people to share you will have to charter anyway. Expect to pay around 15,000 rp with hard bargaining.

Alternatively, you can walk from the gate. It's 4.5km along the road, or take the more interesting side trail via the Kawah Domas crater and its bubbling hot geysers. It is a very steep one hour walk through the jungle – head up the main road and take the trail that branches off at the first small carpark.

WEST JAVA

WEST JAVA

It is much easier to walk this trail from the top down – it starts just behind the information centre and is very easy to follow.

An alternative is to get dropped off at Jayagiri, just outside Lembang, and from there you can walk up through the forest to the crater (about 8km). The trail starts just past the Jayagiri fruit market and comes out near the bus parking area, 1.2km below the main crater. Another less easy-to-follow trail leads off the main crater to Ciater, a two hour walk through forest and tea plantations.

Drivers in Bandung will charge around 60,000 to 70,000 rp for a visit to Tangkuban Prahu, depending on time spent at the crater, including petrol but excluding entry (6000 rp extra for a car). From Lembang count on 35,000 rp return.

## Ciater Hot Springs
☎ 0260

Eight kilometres north-east of Tangkuban Prahu, Ciater is a pretty little place in the middle of huge tea and clove estates. The area has good walks and a tea factory on the south side of Ciater can be visited.

At the end of the road through the village, Ciater's main attraction is the **Sari Ater Hot Spring Resort**. Although quite commercialised, the pools are probably the best of all the hot springs around Bandung, and if you've been climbing around the volcano on a cool, rainy day there's no better way to get warm. There is a 2500 rp admission into the resort area and it costs extra to use the pool. Private baths cost 7500 rp. You can walk to Ciater – about 12km across country – from Tangkuban Prahu, or flag down a colt at the entrance point.

The Ciater Riung Rangga Equestrian Centre (☎ 470969), just north of the turn-off to the hot springs, offers horse riding and professional instruction at reasonable rates. The complex also has tennis courts, a swimming pool, a campground with pre-erected tents and it arranges tea walks.

From Ciater it is possible to visit the less commercialised **Batu Kapur Hot Springs**, 10km from the main road on the way to Subang. From Ciater take a colt to the Jl Cagak junction, then another to Segalaherang, from where ojek will take you to the hot springs.

**Places to Stay** The extensive *Sari Ater Hot Springs Resort* (☎ 460888) has a variety of rustic bungalows spread out in spacious grounds. It has all the facilities of a big hotel but the rooms are crumbling and cost from 154,000 to 533,000 rp for family bungalows, all plus 21%.

Ciater has plenty of small *penginapan* with rooms starting at around 20,000 rp – the ones on the main road are cheaper. *Hotel Permata Sari* (☎ 203891) is close to the hot springs and has good views and rooms from 30,000 rp.

## Waduk Jatiluhur

This artificial lake (*waduk* in Indonesian), 70km north-west of Bandung in the hills near Purwakarta, is a popular resort for swimming, boating and water-skiing. The giant Jatiluhur Dam stretches 1200m across, is 100m high and has created a 80,000-hectare lake surrounded by green hills. It's part of a hydro-electric generating system supplying Jakarta and West Java, and also providing irrigation water for a large area of the province. The dam and hydro-electric station can be inspected with written permission, obtained from the information office at the entrance to the resort village.

The original village was built by the French for their staff when they were building the dam and is now run by a government corporation as tourist accommodation. It's a very peaceful spot during the week, but you really need your own transport to get there and around. Purwakarta is the access point by rail or road either from Jakarta (125km) or from Bandung (65km). From Purwakarta, No 11 angkot run to the resort area and continue a few kilometres farther around the lake to Pelabuhan Biru, the main place to hire boats, canoes, water-skiing gear etc.

About 12km south of Purwakarta, just off the Bandung road, the village of **Plered** produces fine pottery. A number of shops line the road and most have workshops at the back where you can see the pots being made.

## Places to Stay & Eat

Jatiluhur has two hotels and a variety of bungalows that can all be booked through Otorita Jatiluhur (☎ 0264-200525). *Hotel Pesanggrahan* is back from the water but has an elevated position and good views. Well appointed rooms cost 90,000 rp; 20,000 rp more on weekends. *Hotel Istora* has a better position near the lake and a well sited bar/restaurant but is more neglected. Rooms cost 65,000 rp, 10,000 rp more on weekends.

Bungalows are scattered around the streets near the Hotel Pesanggrahan and are good value for groups or families. They range from the small *Puspa*, costing 35,000 rp, up to the much more comfortable, three bedroom *Wisma Jati*, which has a kitchen and some style for 150,000 rp (200,000 rp on weekends).

Apart from the hotel restaurants, eat at the warung area south around the lake from the Hotel Istora. The elevated restaurant at Pelabuhan Biru is a pleasant place to dine overlooking the lake.

## SOUTH OF BANDUNG
☎ 022

The mountains south of Bandung also have popular weekend retreats, though the area is less developed compared with the resorts to the north of the city. The picturesque road south of Bandung through Bojongloa leads to **Ciwidey**, a small town noted for its metalwork, especially knives. For wealthy Bandung residents, Ciwidey is usually just a weekend lunch stop at one of the stylish Sundanese restaurants in and around town. You can stock up on Ciwidey's speciality sweet, *kalua jeruk*, jubes made from citrus rind.

The road winds through the hills to the turn-off to **Kawah Putih**, a volcanic crater with a beautiful turquoise lake. The turn-off is 6km before Rancabali, and then it is 8km to the small crater lake just below **Gunung Patuha** (2334m). Kawah Putih is classed as a 'new' volcano because tourist facilities and the paved road were only built in 1993, but in colonial times the sulphurous water was pumped down the mountain to a chemical plant which extracted the sulphur for use in explosives. A tunnel (Gua Belanda) and the remains of a plant are the only reminders of the Dutch presence. Though only a small crater, Kawah Putih is exceptionally beautiful and eerily quiet when the mists roll in. The surrounding nature reserve has short walks in the dripping, montane forest.

A few kilometres farther south from the turn-off to Kawah Putih is the hot springs at **Cimanggu**, with landscaped gardens and large swimming pools filled by hot water piped from the springs on Gunung Patuha. Nearby is the Ranca Upas deer farm and camp ground. A little farther on is the **Walini Hot Springs**, a newer, more luxurious development, also with a hot water pool.

**Rancabali**, 42km from Bandung, is a tea estate town surrounded by the rolling green hills of the tea plantations. Just 2km south of the town is **Telaga Patenggan**, a pretty lake lined with boats for a leisurely row. You can take a stroll around the lake, and in the nearby forest area; warungs and tea rooms cater to the Sunday crowds.

Also south of Bandung, **Situ Cileunca** is an artificial lake dammed for a hydroelectric scheme. There are bungalows and a campground beside the lake, just outside the hill town of Pengalengan, 36km from Bandung. It is peaceful but of limited interest. The area has a down-at-heel hot spring complex at Cipanas Cibolang, near a thermal energy plant with billowing steam, but the main attraction is the **Malabar Tea Estate**. You can tour the plantations and stay at the wonderful guesthouse, once the home of wealthy plantation owner, Karel Albert Rudolf Bosscha (1865-1925), after whom the observatory at Lembang was named. His grave, a neo-classical pavilion, lies in forest a couple of kilometres from the guesthouse.

## Places to Stay & Eat

Accommodation is limited and empty during the week. In Ciwidey, *Penginapan Sederhana* on the main road opposite the market has dismal rooms for 11,500 rp. The *Sindang Reret Hotel* (☎ 5928205) and *Motel Sukarasa Endah* (☎ 9958311) are both on the highway north of town and have

**WEST JAVA**

large Sundanese restaurants built over fish ponds. The Sindang Reret is slightly better and has comfortable rooms with hot-water showers costing from 72,000 to 151,250 rp during the week, 10% more on weekends.

At Cisondari, just before Ciwidey, take the turn-off to Gambung – 6km along the road is the *Resor Petualangan Alam* (☎ 5928200). This cool, peaceful retreat has great views, a pool, tennis courts and a restaurant. Attractive villas cost 75,000 rp (one room) up to 450,000 rp (six rooms), 25% more on weekends.

At Alam Endah, 5km south of Ciwidey, *Pondok Taman Unyil Lestari* (☎ 5928250), 1km from the main road, has simple cottages with sitting rooms for 66,000 rp, fine views, a nice garden and a good restaurant.

Pengalengan has a number of hotels but the town is of minor interest. Stay at the Malabar Tea Estate, 5km from town. *Malabar Mess* (☎ 5979401) is a delightful colonial guesthouse furnished with Dutch antiques. Rooms cost 75,000 rp in the outside block, but the old rooms in the main house for 120,000 and 150,000 rp are worth the extra. Meals can be arranged.

## Getting There & Away

From Bandung's Leuwi Panjang terminal, frequent buses run to Ciwidey (1200 rp, 1½ hours), as do minibuses (1500 rp). From Ciwidey local angkots run to Situ Patengan (2000 rp). Kawah Putih is not serviced by regular public transport, but you'll find plenty of ojegs in Alam Endah. Buses also run direct to Pengalengan where ojeg hang out at the bus terminal.

## GARUT
☎ 0262

As you travel south-east from Bandung, the road passes through the scenic, fertile hilly countryside and volcanic peaks of the Parahyangan highlands. A southern branch off the main highway leads towards Garut, which is a highland town ringed by impressive volcanic peaks. The fertile valley is a centre for vegetable, orange, tea and tobacco growing.

In Dutch times, Garut was a favourite hill resort. The town itself has lost something of its shine, but the surrounding countryside is very scenic and has a number of attractions. Few tourists visit Garut, but it makes a worthwhile stopover on the way between Bandung and Pangandaran.

On the outskirts of town, 6km to the north-west, are the hot springs at **Cipanas**, an attractive small resort at the foot of Gunung Guntur and an ideal base from which to explore the area. From Cipanas, the **Curug Citiis** waterfall is a one hour walk away up the mountain and it is possible to walk all the way to the peak of Gunung Guntur. The walk to the summit is a hard 10 hour slog there and back. You will be rewarded by fine views but the mountain slopes are not forested.

**Ngamplang**, 5km on the south-eastern outskirts of Garut, has a nine-hole golf course and *adu domba* (ram fights) are held here on the first and third Sunday of the month.

Garut is famed for its *dodol* – confectionery made of coconut milk, palm sugar and sticky rice. At the bus station, hawkers selling tubes of sweet dodol besiege the passing buses and it's sold at many shops around town. The Picnic brand is the best quality and it is possible to visit the Picnic factory on Jl Pasundan.

Garut also has a thriving leatherwork industry, churning out amazingly cheap leather jackets from cow and softer sheep leather. Styles tend to be a bit old-fashioned but there is a big selection – check out the many shops on Jl Sukaregang in the east of town. Also worth a visit is the Sutera Alam silk factory on Jl Otista where you can see cloth woven and the thread being made from cocoons.

## Information

The Garut Tourist Office (Dinas Pariwisata, ☎ 233529), Jl Pamuka 5, has a brochure in Indonesian. The Tirtagangga Hotel in Cipanas has useful maps of Garut and the surrounding area. The best place to change money is the Bank BNI, Jl Ahmad Yani 53.

## Places to Stay & Eat

Garut has plenty of hotels and guesthouses, but Cipanas is the nicest place to stay.

In the centre of Garut, *Wisma PKPN* (☎ *231508, Jl Ciledug 69*) has clean rooms with attached mandi from 16,500 rp. Some good mid-range hotels are on Jl Oto Iskandardinata (Otista) on the outskirts of town in Taragong, such as the *Hotel Sarimbit* (☎ *21033*) at No 236 or the better-value *Hotel Paseban* (☎ *232302*), which has rooms from 25,000 to 50,000 rp.

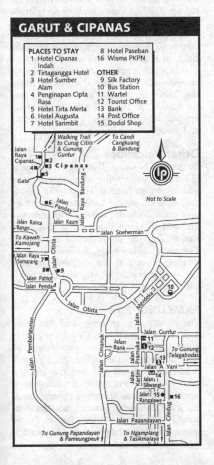

**GARUT & CIPANAS**

PLACES TO STAY
1 Hotel Cipanas Indah
2 Tirtagangga Hotel
3 Hotel Sumber Alam
4 Penginapan Cipta Rasa
5 Hotel Tirta Merta
6 Hotel Augusta
7 Hotel Sarimbit
8 Hotel Paseban
16 Wisma PKPN

OTHER
9 Silk Factory
10 Bus Station
11 Wartel
12 Tourist Office
13 Bank
14 Post Office
15 Dodol Shop

*Hotel Ngamplang* (☎ *21480*) is a big, modern hotel next to the golf course in Ngamplang with good rooms from 90,000 rp.

Cipanas has over a dozen hotels strung along Jl Raya Cipanas, the resort's single road. All have rooms with large baths with water piped in from the hot springs – pamper yourself after a hard day's trekking. Cheap hotels include the basic *Pondok Kurnia Artha* (☎ *232112*), which has dark but OK rooms for 25,000 rp, perhaps less with bargaining. The *Hotel Tirta Merta* (☎ *231422*) is cheerier and has doubles from 25,000 rp. Both hotels charge 10,000 rp or more on weekends. More expensive, but no better, are the *Hotel Banyu Arta* and *Penginapan Cipta Rasa*, both with rooms from 30,000 rp.

As well as hot baths, the following hotels have swimming pools heated by the springs. *Cipanas Indah* (☎ *233736*) is a good mid-range hotel favoured by tour groups. Rooms start at 35,000 rp and good VIP rooms are 50,000 rp (around 10,000 rp more on weekends). The *Sumber Alam* (☎ *231027*) is the most attractive hotel, with rooms built over the water and prices ranging from 60,000 to 245,000 rp (40% more on weekends). The big *Tirtagangga Hotel* (☎ *231811*) is the fanciest hotel, with rooms from 145,000 rp during the week. The new *Hotel Augusta* (☎ *236 801*) is good value, with well appointed rooms from 60,000 to 100,000 rp, but it is more than 1km from the resort area.

Cipanas has a string of warungs serving sate of variable quality at tourist prices. The coffee shop in the *Sumber Alam* is good and moderately priced, as is the *Cipanas Indah* restaurant.

## Getting There & Away

Buses and angkots leave from Garut's Terminal Guntur in the north of town. Garut is easily reached by bus from Bandung (2000 rp, two hours) and Tasikmalaya. For Pangandaran, take another bus from Tasikmalaya. Air-con buses also go to Bogor and Jakarta.

Regular angkots run around town and to Cipanas (angkot No 4, 500 rp), Ngamplang and to the nearby villages. A car or minibus with driver can be rented in Cipanas – ask around the hotels. A trip to Papandayan (see below) will cost around 40,000 rp.

## AROUND GARUT
### Candi Cangkuang

Near Leles, about 10km north of Garut, is Candi Cangkuang, one of the few Hindu temples in West Java. This small temple, renovated in 1976, lies on the edge of Situ Cangkuang, a peaceful small lake. Dating from the 8th century, the temple was in ruins when discovered and logged by the Dutch in 1893. Some of its stones were found to have been carved into tombstones for the nearby Islamic cemetery, which houses the 17th century grave of Arif Muhammad, a Muslim saint. Many pilgrims visit the grave in the Islamic month of Mulud, and the descendants of Arif Muhammad still live next to the temple and have built a new *'rumah adat'* of minor interest. A small museum also lies next to the temple but the main attraction is the trip across the lake and the serene rural surrounds, though tour buses can spoil the peace and quiet.

From Garut, take a No 10 angkot to Leles on the highway, then another angkot or horse-drawn dilman (6000 rp to charter) for the remaining 3km to Candi Cangkuang. Boats across the lake to the temple cost 10,000 rp. A small, basic two bedroom *guesthouse* (☎ *0262-455558)* is just opposite the boat dock and costs 50,000 rp.

### Gunung Papandayan

Twenty-eight kilometres to the south-west of Garut, Gunung Papandayan (2622m) is one of the most active and spectacular volcanoes in West Java. Papandayan has only existed since 1772 when a large piece of the mountain exploded sideways in a catastrophe that killed more than 3000 people. It last erupted in 1925. The large yellow crater (Kawah Papandayan) just below the peak is an impressive sight and clearly visible from Garut valley on fine mornings. The mountain also has good walks.

The bubbling, sulphurous crater is reached by taking an angkot to Bayongbong and then another to Cisurupan, or a Cikajang minibus can drop you at the turn-off on the outskirts of Cisurupan where waiting ojeg cost 3000 rp for the 13km-trip to the crater. It is then an easy half-hour walk to the crater. Guides will offer their services – advisable if you want to explore the bubbling sulphur deposits and their noxious gases at close range – otherwise just keep well to the right inside the crater and continue up to the Pondok Saladah hut at the top lip. For fine views, go very early in the morning before the clouds roll in.

Gunung Papandayan summit is a two-hour walk beyond the crater, and there are fields of Javan edelweiss near the top.

It is possible to camp at Pondok Saladah, an open-sided hut, but the nights are freezing. There are cottages at the warung area for 40,000 rp. The PHPA hut at the parking/warung area arranges camping permits and guides.

### Other Volcanoes

To the east of Garut, **Gunung Telagabodas** (2201m) has a bubbling bright-green crater lake alive with sulphur. To get to Telagabodas, take an angkot to Wanaraja, then an ojeg and walk to the crater. Other craters to the west of Garut that can be visited are **Kawah Darajat**, 26km away, and **Kawah Kamojang**, 23km away, the site of a geothermal plant that has defused the once spectacular geyser activity and replaced it with huge pipes.

## PAMEUNGPEUK

The picturesque, twisting road that leads south from Garut passes through vegetable plots, tea plantations and pine forests to Pameungpeuk, on the south coast. This area is of minor interest and sees few tourists, except for the Garut residents who come on weekends. The coast around Pameungpeuk has some reasonable beaches, though swimming is usually out of the question. Pameungpeuk itself is a large village – big enough to have a small tourist office, PHPA office, and a handful of penginapan.

**Pantai Sayang Heulang** is a small beach-resort 2km west of Pameungpeuk via the main road, then a further 2km down a rough road to the beach. This sleepy village consists of three penginapan and a few warung. The attractive white-coral beach fronts a reef that can be explored on foot at low tide. At high tide, waves break right on the reef – death by coral cuts for swimmers!

Farther west, **Pantai Santolo** has the best beach, which is on a sheltered bay where swimming is usually possible. Fishing boats harbour in the river at the end of the beach and at the mouth of the river is a stone dock built by the Dutch. Prahus can take you across the river, where a walking trail leads through a small forest reserve to the point and to the south beach, with its reef and crashing surf. It is 4km from Pameungpeuk on the main road, and then 2km along a paved road to the beach. Pantai Santolo is also home to an airforce base, which has a good wisma facing the beach. The *Hotel Citra Agung* (☎ 0262-21210) is on the main road directly opposite the turn-off.

Farther west is **Cikelet**, a fishing village, 9km from Pameungpeuk. In the hills outside Cikelet, **Kampung Dukuh** is a traditional Sundanese village that contains many well preserved, thatched *rumah adat*. Beaches farther to the west include **Pantai Cijayana**, which reportedly has good swimming, and **Rancabuaya**. These two beaches are reached via the road through Samudra and Bungbulang, which turns off just before Cikajang.

The main attraction to the east of Pameungpeuk is **Leuweung Sancang**, a nature reserve noted for its bantengs and gibbons. There are trails for jungle trekking in the reserve. Local legend has it that Leuweng Sancang was the centre of an ancient Sundanese kingdom, and the reserve is the site of strong mystical power, but don't bother looking for any lost cities in the forest. For permits and information, check with the PHPA in Pameungpeuk. There is a also PHPA post in Sancang at the entrance to the park. It is quite an expedition to reach Leuweung Sancang, 35km from Pameungpeuk. Buses run to Milamareu, past the turn-off to Sancang. At Milamareu you can try getting an ojeg to the PHPA post, but you might as well get one from Pameungpeuk. Ojeg want 10,000 rp for the trip – the road to the reserve is very bad.

On the way to Leuweng Sancang, 18km from Pameungpeuk, there is another beach at **Cijeruk** that has a government guesthouse where it may be possible to stay.

### Getting There & Away

From Garut, regular minibuses go to Pameungpeuk (1500 rp, three hours) and some continue on to Cikelet. To reach Sayang Heulang or Santolo you either have to walk from the main road or catch an ojeg from Pameungpeuk.

## TASIKMALAYA
☎ 0265

Sixty kilometres east of Garut, this small town is a centre for rattan crafts. Palm leaf and bamboo are used to make floormats, baskets, trays, straw hats and paper umbrellas. For cheaper rattan, visit the village of **Rajapolah**, 12km north of town on the road to Bandung, where many of the weavers work. Tasikmalaya (usually called simply Tasik) also has a small batik industry and is also noted for its *bordel* lacework and *kelom geulis* (wooden sandals).

### Places to Stay

Tasik has plenty of hotels: *Abadi Hotel* (☎ 332789, Jl Empang 58) is a good budget option with rooms from 15,000, while the *Mahkota Graha* (☎ 332282, Jl Martadinata 45) is the best in town and has rooms from 95,000 rp.

### Getting There & Away

From Tasikmalaya buses operate to Bandung (2000/3000 rp, four hours), Garut (1000 rp, 1½ hours), Jakarta (4700/8100 rp, six hours), Banjar, Pangandaran, Cipatujah, Cirebon etc. Tasikmalaya is also on the main railway line.

## AROUND TASIKMALAYA
### Cipanas Galunggung
These hot springs are 20km to the north-west of Tasikmalaya at the foot of Gunung Galunggung, a volcano which exploded in 1982. The hot spring has landscaped gardens and hot water swimming pools, and a walking trail leads to a small waterfall and then on to the Galunggung crater. The crater is 3km and a two-hour walk away. It is a fine walk, through some forest and mountain meadow, but the trail is not always easy to follow. At the gate entrance to Cipanas a road that is suitable only for 4WD vehicles also forks off to the crater and is an easier, if less interesting, walk.

From Tasikmalaya's main bus terminal take an angkot to Bantar on the highway and then an ojeg can take you the 14km along a rough road.

### Situ Lengkong
Situ Lengkong, which is 40km north of Tasikmalaya and half a kilometre from the village of Panjalu, is a serene lake that was formed when the Hindu ruler of Panjalu dammed the valley. A forested island in the middle is home to thousands of flying foxes and contains a *kramat* (shrine) dedicated to the rulers of Panjalu. Boats can be hired to take you around the island, but to visit the kramat involves fetching the key from the village.

The **Bumi Alit**, in Panjalu village, is a small museum containing the heirlooms of the kings of Panjalu and includes a fine collection of *kris*. In the Nyangku ceremony (performed every year in the month of Mulud), ceremonial swords are taken in procession from the Bumi Alit by the ancestors of the Panjalu kings and are washed in the lake. The Bumi Alit is opposite the alun alun and bus station in Panjalu – someone will fetch the key. Entry is by donation.

Ten kilometres from Situ Lengkong is the **Curug Tujuh waterfall**, 200m from the main road to Kawali.

Situ Lengkong can be reached by bus from Tasikmalaya or from Terminal Kawali, where angkots run the 20km to Ciamis.

### Karang Komulyan
On the highway to Banjar and Pangandaran, 16km south-east of Ciamis, Karang Komulyan is the excavated site of the ancient Galuh kingdom. Local guides and tourist literature give a glorified account of the Galuh kingdom as both the first Hindu and the first Muslim kingdom on Java. But this Neolithic settlement dating from around the 5th century points to the pre-Hindu period. Only a few stone walls and foundations remain of the 'palace', store, prayer and bathing areas, but it is a beautiful walk through the jungle and bamboo groves down to the confluence of the swift Ciliwung and Citanduy rivers. A large carpark and government-built cottages next to the park are attempts to make it a major tourist stop.

### Kampung Naga
Halfway between Tasikmalaya and Garut, Kampung Naga is a traditional village and museum piece of Sundanese architecture and village life. The old ways are very much preserved in Kampung Naga – the many tour groups that visit wouldn't come otherwise. Despite the fact that it can be very crowded some mornings when the big busloads arrive, there's no denying the beauty of the place. Kampung Naga, with its thatched roofed houses, is nestled next to a river and surrounded by steep hills terraced with rice paddies – a photographer's dream.

Kampung Naga is 26km from Garut. From Neglasari on the main highway more than 300 steps lead down into the valley.

### BANJAR
Banjar, 42km east of Tasikmalaya, is the junction point where the Pangandaran road branches from the Bandung to Yogya road and rail route. Banjar has some basic hotels if you get stuck en route to Pangandaran – try not to.

### Getting There & Away
The bus terminal is 4km west of town on the highway. Many buses can be caught as they come through the centre of town near the train station. From Banjar, buses go to

Pangandaran (3000 rp, 1½ hours), Bandung, Purwokerto, Jakarta, etc. Buses also go to Jakarta from the Banjarsari bus terminal, half an hour south of Banjar.

Banjar is not a good place to catch trains as most are crowded through-trains. To Yogya, the best options are the *Pajajaran* at 10.50 am or the slower, ekonomi *Cisadane* at 12.50 pm, but they come through from Bandung and it is hard to get a seat. Evening eksekutif trains run right through to Surabaya. Heading to Jakarta via Bandung by train, the *Galuh* originates in Banjar, so seats are easier to get, but it leaves at 6.30 am and takes at least nine hours.

## PANGANDARAN
☎ 0265

The fishing village of Pangandaran is Java's most popular beach resort. It lies on the narrow isthmus of a peninsula with broad sandy beaches that sweep back along the mainland. At the end of the bulbous peninsula is the Pangandaran National Park.

Pangandaran has black sand beaches and dangerous swimming (except for the more sheltered southern end of the west beach), but despite these drawbacks it is an idyllic place to take a break from travelling. The people are exceptionally friendly, accommodation is cheap and the seafood excellent. If lazing around the beaches begins to pall, you can head off east or west to other quieter beaches and attractions nearby.

On weekends Pangandaran is popular with Bandung residents, though the *krismon* (monetary crisis) has slowed things down. During holidays – Christmas and the end of Ramadan in particular – the beaches have a temporary population of thousands. At other times this is just an overgrown fishing village, where brightly painted prahu fish the waters and whole families work together to pull in the nets.

## Orientation & Information

Pangandaran extends for about 3km from the bus terminal and market to the national park boundary in the south. The town is flanked by the west and east beaches and dissected by the main street, Jl Kidang Pananjung. The west beach is a wide sweep of sand and the main resort strip. The east beach is a quieter fishing beach and not much sand remains since a retaining wall was built.

A 2000 rp admission charge is levied at the gates as you enter Pangandaran. It costs another 1250 rp for each visit to the national park.

**Money** The Bank Rakyat Indonesia on Jl Kidang Pananjung changes most currencies and major brands of travellers cheques but rates are poor. It is open from 7.30 am to 4.30 pm Monday to Friday but closed for a 'rest' from noon to 1 am (12.30 to 1.30 pm Fridays). For after-hours transactions, moneychangers have even poorer rates.

**Post & Communications** The post office and Telkom wartel (open 24 hours) are both on Jl Kidang Pananjung. The Telkom wartel has a Home Country Direct phone. For Internet access, head to the Bus-Stop Cafe on Jl Pamugaran.

## Things to See & Do

Cloaked in jungle, **Pangandaran National Park** has banteng, *kijang* (barking deer), hornbill and monkeys, including Javan gibbon, and small bays within the park enclose tree-fringed beaches. The park is divided into two sections – the recreation park and the jungle. Due to environmental degradation, the jungle is now off-limits, but some guides still offer illegal tours and when we visited, a tour group was emerging from the jungle trails. Apart from it being dubious practice to ignore park rules, the trails are very muddy and not easy to follow – don't enter alone.

You can walk the stone paths in the recreation park, which has a few nondescript caves and a couple of nice beaches on the eastern side. The best walk is the Boundary Trail, a natural trail that skirts the jungle. Starting at the east entrance, take the trail along the coast past Wisma Cirengganis. The Boundary Trail starts 150m before Goa

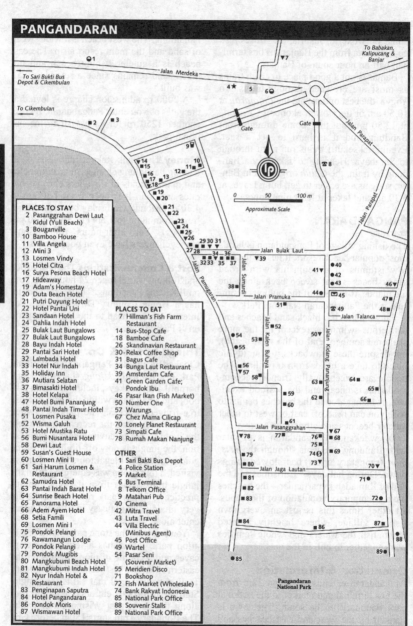

# PANGANDARAN

To Babakan, Kalipucang & Banjar

Jalan Merdeka

To Sari Bukti Bus Depot & Cikembulan

To Cikembulan

Gate

Gate

Jalan Parapat

Jalan Bulak Laut

Jalan Pramuka

Jalan Talanca

Jalan Pasanggrahan

Jalan Jaga Lautan

0        50        100 m

Approximate Scale

Pangandaran National Park

**PLACES TO STAY**
2 Pasanggrahan Dewi Laut Kidul (Yuli Beach)
3 Bouganville
10 Bamboo House
11 Villa Angela
12 Mini 3
13 Losmen Vindy
15 Hotel Citra
16 Surya Pesona Beach Hotel
17 Hideaway
19 Adam's Homestay
20 Duta Beach Hotel
21 Putri Duyung Hotel
22 Hotel Pantai Uni
23 Sandaan Hotel
24 Dahlia Indah Hotel
25 Bulak Laut Bungalows
27 Bulak Laut Bungalows
29 Bayu Indah Hotel
29 Pantai Sari Hotel
32 Lambada Hotel
33 Hotel Nur Indah
36 Holiday Inn
36 Mutiara Selatan
37 Bimasakti Hotel
38 Hotel Kelapa
47 Hotel Bumi Pananjung
48 Pantai Indah Timur Hotel
51 Losmen Pusaka
52 Wisma Galuh
53 Hotel Mustika Ratu
58 Bumi Nusantara Hotel
58 Dewi Laut
59 Susan's Guest House
60 Losmen Mini II
61 Sari Harum Losmen & Restaurant
62 Samudra Hotel
63 Pantai Indah Barat Hotel
64 Sunrise Beach Hotel
65 Panorama Hotel
68 Adem Ayem Hotel
68 Setia Famili
69 Losmen Mini I
75 Pondok Pelangi
76 Rawamangun Lodge
77 Pondok Pelangi
79 Pondok Mugibis
80 Mangkubumi Beach Hotel
81 Mangkubumi Indah Hotel
82 Nyur Indah Hotel & Restaurant
83 Penginapan Saputra
84 Hotel Pangandaran
86 Pondok Moris
87 Wismawan Hotel

**PLACES TO EAT**
7 Hillman's Fish Farm Restaurant
14 Bus-Stop Cafe
18 Bamboe Cafe
26 Skandinavian Restaurant
30 Relax Coffee Shop
31 Bagus Cafe
34 Bunga Laut Restaurant
39 Amsterdam Cafe
41 Green Garden Cafe; Pondok Ibu
46 Pasar Ikan (Fish Market)
50 Number One
57 Warungs
67 Chez Mama Cilicap
70 Lonely Planet Restaurant
73 Simpati Cafe
78 Rumah Makan Nanjung

**OTHER**
1 Sari Bakti Bus Depot
4 Police Station
5 Market
6 Bus Terminal
8 Telkom Office
9 Matahari Pub
40 Cinema
42 Mitra Travel
43 Luta Travel
44 Villa Electric (Minibus Agent)
45 Post Office
49 Wartel
54 Pasar Seni (Souvenir Market)
55 Meridien Disco
71 Bookshop
72 Fish Market (Wholesale)
74 Bank Rakyat Indonesia
85 National Park Office
88 Souvenir Stalls
89 National Park Office

Cirengganis cave. It leads uphill and then down along the river for 30 minutes to the Wisma Cikumal and the western entrance.

Like most south coast **beaches**, Pangandaran has black-sand beaches and the surf can be treacherous. The northern end of the west beach is dangerous and people still drown regularly, including foreigners. South from Bumi Nusantara Hotel, the beach is patrolled (sometimes) and is sheltered by the headland, so swimming is safer. Pangandaran's best beach, Pasir Putih, on the western side of the national park, is now off limits to stop the hordes that have destroyed the reef.

## Organised Tours

Pangandaran has a host of tour operators who are constantly thinking up new tours and hyperbole to describe them. Popular tours are to Green Canyon (30,000 rp per person), and 'countryside' or 'home industry' tours (20,000 to 25,000 rp), which take you to plantations and local industries to see the making of tofu, *krupuk*, sugar etc, as well as a wayang golek maker.

Mitra Marsada Utama (☎ 639733), Jl Kidang Pananjung 163, has tours to the untouched island of Nusa Kambangan. They cost 40,000 rp.

Then there are cycling, boating, walking and snorkelling tours to just about anywhere within a 50km radius of Pangandaran. Tours are usually well run, informative and good value.

## Places to Stay

Pangandaran has over 100 places to stay. At Christmas and Lebaran (the end of Ramadan) holidays, Pangandaran is packed and prices sky rocket. It can also get busy during school holidays and in the peak European holiday season, around August, but for much of the year most hotels are empty and Pangandaran is quiet.

Prices are very seasonal and in busy periods may be higher than quoted here. First night prices are often higher because of the commission system employed by becak drivers and guides. Many hotels, especially the budget places, charge a two night minimum, but like the rates this is often negotiable.

The Bulak Laut area around on the west beach is the best area to stay. Though the swimming is dangerous, the beach is uncluttered and Jl Bulak Laut has good restaurants and plenty of travel services.

## Places to Stay – Budget

**Pangandaran** Most places around Bulak Laut tend to be mid-range, but there are some budget options.

The *Holiday Inn* (☎ 639285, Jl Bulak Laut 50) is the cheapest but it's rough. Singles/doubles cost 7500/10,000 rp with mandi in the rundown wooden rooms or 20,000 rp in the marginally better concrete block rooms. At least that is their posted rates for stays of more than one night, but rates are very variable. Next door, *Mutiara Selatan* (☎ 639416, Jl Bulak Laut 49) is better value. Simple rooms with porch and attached bathroom cost 10,000/15,000 rp. Beds are lumpy but the place is well kept.

Closer to the beach, *Pantai Sari Hotel* (☎ 639175) has a good restaurant and roomy doubles with fan and mandi for 25,000 rp, or brighter air-con rooms upstairs are 35,000 rp. Check a few out as the quality varies, as does the price, depending on the season and length of stay.

Farther north down the alleyway next to the Bamboe Cafe, *Losmen Vindy* (☎ 639 641) is a small new place with neat bamboo rooms for 15,000 rp or 30,000 rp with mandi. Enquire at the cafe if no one is around.

On the same alley, *Mini 3 Homestay* (☎ 639436) is another good option. Slightly dark but comfortable rooms with bathroom cost 20,000/25,000 rp including breakfast or the cute bungalows in the attractive garden cost 30,000 rp. It has a pleasant dining area and good travel services.

*Bamboo House* (☎ 639419) is to the north and away from the beach, but this small, family-run place is well worth considering. Attractive singles/doubles cost 15,000/20,000 rp, or bungalow rooms with mandi costs 30,000 rp.

WEST JAVA

Jl Samudra also has a few options, the pick of which is the *Hotel Kelapa* (☎ *639 329)*. Fairly basic but good-sized rooms with shower cost 20,000 rp. What makes this place special is the wonderful, spacious garden and the attractive cafe.

Farther south, Pangandaran has plenty of other cheap hotels catering mostly to the weekend crowds. The basic *Losmen Mini I* on Jl Kidang Pananjung costs 10,000/15,000 rp for rooms with mandi. Across the road, the rougher but friendly *Rawamangun Lodge* is only 6000/9000 rp. Once popular with travellers, it now attracts only the desperately impecunious.

The small *Pondok Moris* (☎ *639490, Gang Moris 3)* is near the national park. Well kept rooms with porch face an attractive garden and cost 20,000/25,000 rp. Service is very good in this friendly place – if only it wasn't so close to the mosque.

On the eastern beach, the *Panorama Hotel* (☎ *639218)* has pleasant rooms with verandah from where you can watch the fishers haul in the nets. It's a good deal at only 20,000 rp with attached bathroom.

Farther north near the post office, the small *Pondok Ibu* (☎ *639166, Jl Kidang Pananjung 116)* is attached to the tranquil Green Garden Cafe. Three simple but comfortable rooms cost 20,000/25,000 rp each, including breakfast, and come with their own sitting areas.

**Around Pangandaran** The quiet beaches outside Pangandaran are increasingly popular places to hang out and relax, especially when Pangandaran is crowded during the main holiday periods. Most of the following guesthouses are run by westerners who have settled in Pangandaran, and are on the ball with information and services.

Cikembulan, 4km along the beach road to the west, has a small enclave of guesthouses. Electricity is not yet the norm but the room lamps add to the atmosphere. *Delta Gecko* (☎ *630607)* run by the ebullient Kristina is a very popular travellers guesthouse with excellent information, a library and a cultural/BBQ night once a week. Individually

styled bungalows all with bathroom start at 10,000 rp for a bed in a share room, and from 15,000/20,000 rp up to 40,000 rp for the elevated bungalows with seaviews. Full travel services and tours are offered. Its neighbour, the *Losmen Kalapa Nunggal* (☎ *630285)* is another that receives rave reviews for hospitality and home atmosphere. It has just four spotless rooms with bathroom for 20,000 and 25,000 rp and meals are available for guests. Also here is the *Francisco Brillo Losmen & Pizzeria*, currently in limbo with its owner in Italy, but hopefully it will resume operation. About half a kilometre back towards Pangandaran on the beach road, *Tono Homestay* (☎ *630371)* is a friendly, small place with rooms from 35,000 rp.

Four kilometres east of Pangandaran in Babakan, the *Laguna Beach Bungalows* (☎ *639761)* offers stylish mid-range accommodation and has a good restaurant. Delightful bungalows facing the beach cost 50,000 and 57,500 rp, or rooms over the fish pond are 35,000 and 45,000 rp. Ring for pick-up.

## Places to Stay – Mid-Range & Top End

The west beach strip along Jl Pamugaran near Jl Bulak Laut is Pangandaran's Riviera, with a host of good value mid-range hotels popular with Europeans.

*Bulak Laut Bungalows* (☎ *639377)*, opposite the beach on Jl Pamugaran, 100m north of Jl Bulak Laut, is excellent value. Spacious rooms have TV and rock garden bathrooms (cold water) from 20,000/25,000 rp for singles/doubles, or stylish bungalows that have their own sitting rooms are dotted around the lush garden at the back and cost 30,000/35,000 rp. There is one bungalow that has air-con for 50,000 rp. A second *Bulak Laut Bungalows* (☎ *639171)*, which is down the street on the corner of Jl Bulak Laut, is under different management and has just four similarly styled bungalows for 35,000 rp.

*Hotel Nur Indah* (☎ *639349)* on Jl Bulak Laut is a bigger hotel with a pool and restaurant. Comfortable rooms have air-con, hot water and TV for 135,000 rp but they lack character.

Farther back from the beach, the **Bimas-akti Hotel** (☎ 639194, Jl Bulak Laut 12) has a restaurant, small pool and good air-con rooms with hot water and TV for 66,000 and 88,000 rp, more on weekends.

Opposite the beach on Jl Pamugaran, **San-daan Hotel** (☎ 639165) has plain fan rooms with shower costing 40,000 rp and air-con rooms with TV for 75,000 rp; the new rooms with hot water for 100,000 rp are far and away the best. The tariff includes breakfast and dinner. The main attractions are the small swimming pool and the restaurant.

The delightful **Adam's Homestay** (☎ 639164) has eclectic architecture, a book shop, good cappuccinos and a small pool. This excellent establishment has uniquely styled rooms from 54,000/63,000 rp, up to 261,000 rp for a luxury family bungalow with its own pool. Most are in the 90,000 to 126,000 rp range.

Down the alley beside Adam's, the new **Villa Angela** (☎ 628641) has copied the architectural style. Though not in the same league as Adam's, this small place has attractive air-con rooms for 100,000 rp and two fan rooms downstairs for 75,000 rp, before discount. Families can rent a whole floor with sitting room – enquire at the nearby Bamboe Cafe.

One of Pangandaran's bigger resort hotels is **Surya Pesona Beach Hotel** (☎ 639428). It has a swimming pool, expensive restaurant and good rooms with balcony and all the trimmings for 120,000 rp – a good deal.

The **Pasanggrahan Dewi Laut Kidul** (better known as Yuli Beach, ☎ 639375) has delightful boutique bungalows (160,000 rp) with sunken lounge areas in a lush garden with a pool. New rooms for 100,000 and 120,000 rp out the back also have style. All have cold water showers and fan, so expect discounts. Don't expect much in the way of service and the lousy breakfasts are overpriced, but this is one of Pangandaran's most attractive hotels.

More mid-range hotels can be found towards the southern end of the west beach.

**Susan's Guest House** (☎ 639290, Jl Kalen Buhaya 20) is a cheaper option with fan rooms for 30,000 rp or air-con rooms with hot water for 50,000 rp. It is quiet with a garden and rooms are off a central sitting area with kitchen. You can rent a complete four-bedroom unit for 150,000 rp.

**Pondok Pelangi** (☎ 639023, Jl Pasang-grahan 7) is also good for families and has self-contained two/three bedroom bungalows in an attractive garden for 150,000/250,000 rp. The bungalows are old but well kept and come with a fully equipped kitchen.

**Hotel Bumi Nusantara** (☎ 639032) facing the western beach is a big, old hotel with a swimming pool and restaurant. It has a variety of rooms from worn bungalows for 100,000 rp to big family rooms for 300,000 rp. The best mid-range buy would be the stylish rooms in the new block, which have air-con, TV, hot water and minibar for 175,000 rp down to 120,000 rp after discount.

**Sunrise Beach Hotel** (☎ 639220, Jl Ki-dang Pananjung 175) on the east beach, is one of the most pleasant hotels. It has a swimming pool, a good restaurant and attractive rooms but tour groups stay here so rates are over the top at US$50 to US$195. Negotiation will bring the price of a room down to around 260,000 rp, but that is still expensive for Pangandaran.

Across the street from the Sunrise, the **Pantai Indah Barat** (☎ 639006), along with its plush cousin on the east beach **Pantai Indah Timur** (☎ 630714), offer top-of-the-range accommodation, but both are usually empty. The Timur has a huge pool and tennis courts, while the Barat has a more modest pool, tennis courts and a restaurant. They also quote high rates – from 235,000 rp at the Barat and 310,000 rp at the Timur – but discounts of 40% are readily offered.

## Places to Eat

Pangandaran is famous for its excellent seafood (prawns, squid and fish). For cheap Indonesian food, the town has dozens of warungs, especially along the southern end of western beach. The little eateries in front of the Pasar Seni are very cheap and have a good selection.

The Bulak Laut area has travellers' eateries with western-style breakfasts, pancakes and a variety of fruit juices and fruit salads. On Jl Bulak Laut, the pleasant *Pantai Sari Hotel* has a limited menu, but does a good spaghetti and is a top spot for breakfast. The popular *Holiday Inn* has a big menu and passable food at cheap prices though the drinks are more expensive than elsewhere. *Bagus Cafe* across the road is part of the Number One chain and is a pleasant little spot for pizzas and other fare. The Swiss-run *Relax Coffee Shop* is one of Pangandaran's fanciest restaurants and, though expensive, it has delicious, weighty volkenbrot bread and great milkshakes. The dinner menu has superior European dishes and Indonesian selections. For good Sundanese and Javanese food, head to the *Bunga Laut Restaurant*. Food is not blandified for western tastes and it does good soups, chicken and tempe dishes.

Pangandaran's newest travellers' cafe is the *Bus-Stop Cafe* to the north on Jl Pamaguran. Run by Delta Gecko, this switched-on place overlooks the sea and has a wide range of booking services.

The main street, Jl Kidang Pananjung, also has some good restaurants. *Chez Mama Cilacap (Jl Kidang Pananjung 187)* is one of Pangandaran's best restaurants with an extensive menu, moderate prices, fresh fish and icy fruit juices. Farther north, the ever-popular *Number One* has a varied menu and good food. The owner, Dallan, is one of Pangandaran's experienced restaurateurs. The new *Green Garden Cafe* at No 116 has a delightful garden setting and its Indonesian dishes, steak, seafood and salads are served with some style.

For seafood, the most varied selection is found at the excellent *Pasar Ikan* (Fish Market) on the east beach. Pick out what you want from the selection of fresh seafood at the front of the warungs here and pay according to weight. The market is to the north near the post office (not the wholesale fish market to the south). The main market near the bus terminal is the place to stock up on fruit and groceries.

Farther south, overlooking the eastern beach, *Lonely Planet Restaurant (Jl Jaga Lautan 2)* – no relation! – comes with basic warung decor but the seafood is excellent. Choose dishes from the menu or select fish and prawns at the front and pay by weight.

*Inti Laut*, at the front of the Hotel Pantai Uni on Jl Pamaguran, is another excellent spot for fresh seafood with a Chinese bent. Farther south on the west beach, the restaurant at the *Nyur Indah Hotel* is a little expensive but one of Pangandaran's best Chinese seafood restaurants. Nearby, the no-frills *Rumah Makan Nanjung* has sea breezes and does a mean barbecued fish.

Top of the range for seafood is *Hillman's Restaurant*. It's expensive and the service can be slow, but it's worth it for the serene surrounds overlooking the fish ponds (a successful seafood export business operates from here). The food is superb and this is one of the few places you can regularly get lobster.

## Getting There & Away

Pangandaran lies halfway between Bandung and Yogya. Coming from Yogya by bus or rail, Banjar is the transit point, though the most popular way to reach Pangandaran is via the pleasant backwater trip from Cilacap to Kalipucang. From Bandung, plenty of direct buses go to Pangandaran, or it's possible to change for connections in Tasikmalaya.

Pangandaran has a small airport at Nusawiru, 20km to the west, but no scheduled flights.

**Bus** Local buses run from Pangandaran's bus terminal to Tasikmalaya (5000 rp, three hours), Ciamis (4500 rp, 2½ hours), Banjar (3000 rp, 1½ hours), Kalipucang (1000 rp, 40 minutes) and Cilacap (3500 rp, 2½ hours). Buses also run along the west coast as far as Cijulang (1500 rp, 40 minutes).

The large patas (express) buses leave from the Sari Bakti Utama and Budiman bus company depots about 2km west of Pangandaran along Jl Merdeka. Frequent non-air-con buses go to Bandung (10,000 rp, six hours) between 6 am and 9 pm, and Sari Bakti Utama also goes to Bogor (15,000 rp, nine hours) at 7.15 am and 7.30 pm. Buses to Jakarta (16,500/19,500 rp non-air-con/air-con) terminate in Bekasi, 22km east of Jakarta, or Tangerang to the west of Jakarta.

The most comfortable way to Bandung is with the Sari Harum door-to-door minibus for 25,000 rp. The very convenient Mitra (☎ 639180) door-to-door bus to Jl Jaksa in Jakarta is no longer operating but may start up again.

Agents in Pangandaran sell bus tickets for a premium, but they can save you a lot of hassle and their tickets usually include transport to the depots. Commission can be high – it pays to shop around.

The best way to reach Central Java is via the Kalipucang-Cilacap ferry (see Boat later in this section), with bus connections at either end. If the boat doesn't appeal, take a bus to Cilacap from where buses go to Yogya or Wonosobo. You can take the train to Yogya from Banjar, but seats are hard to get.

**Car** Most travel agents rent minibuses with driver for about 150,000 rp per day, including petrol. Put together your own tour and you may be able to negotiate a better rate, especially for an older vehicle. The most popular trip is a three day tour to Yogya. The usual route is via the ferry (the driver drops you in Kalipucang, then picks up in Cilacap) and on to Wonosobo for the first night. The second day goes to Dieng for the sunrise, then on to Borobudur for the night. The final day is to Yogya via Prambanan.

**Boat** One of the highlights of a trip to Pangandaran is the interesting backwater trip between Cilacap and Kalipucang. From Pangandaran it starts with a 17km bus trip to Kalipucang (1000 rp, 40 minutes). From Kalipucang the ferry travels across the wide expanse of Segara Anakan and along the waterway sheltered by the island of Nusa Kambangan. It's a fascinating, peaceful

trip, hopping from village to village in a rickety 25m wooden boat, or a larger boat also operates if the number of passengers warrants. As well as carrying a regular contingent of tourists, it's a very popular local service. Hope for fine weather. In the rain the plastic sheeting comes down to block the views and four hours becomes a long time on a basic boat.

Ferries (3200 rp, four hours) leave from Kalipucang at 8 am, noon and/or 1 pm. A car ferry also operates from the new Majinklang harbour to the south of Kalipucang but this is much less atmospheric.

From the Cilacap harbour it is about 1km to the main road (no more than 1000 rp by becak), from where bemos go to the Cilacap bus terminal (500 rp) or a becak all the way to the terminal costs around 2500 rp. From Cilacap direct buses go to Yogya or Wonosobo for the Dieng Plateau. The last Yogya bus leaves at 9 pm.

The trip is made very easy by the door-to-door services between Pangandaran and Yogya. Bus-ferry-bus services (30,000 rp, 10 hours) are sold all around Pangandaran and will drop you at your hotel in Yogya. Connections to Wonosobo are also advertised, but these are on Yogya buses which will drop you in Kebumen, from where you are put on a public bus to Wonosobo.

### Getting Around
Pangandaran's brightly painted becaks start at around 1000 rp and require heavy negotiation, unless they are taking you to a hotel when the fare will be less than the commission they receive. Bicycles are also an ideal way to get around and can be rented for as little as 5000 rp per day. Motorcycles cost around 20,000 rp per day and are ideal for exploring the area around Pangandaran.

## AROUND PANGANDARAN
The scenic coast road west from Pangandaran to Cipatujah skirts along the surf-pounded beaches and runs through small villages and paddy fields. **Cikembulan**, 4km from Pangandaran, has accommodation (see under Pangandaran) and local industries that

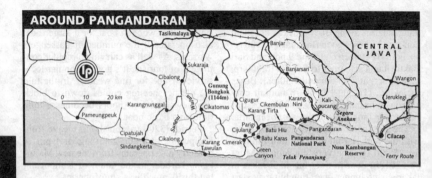

**AROUND PANGANDARAN**

can be visited, including the krupuk factory and a wayang golek workshop.

**Karang Tirta**, 16km from Pangandaran and 2km from the highway, is a lagoon set back from the beach with *bagang* fishing platforms that catch squid, fish and shrimp. The seafood is used especially for making *terasi*, the Indonesian fish paste used widely in cooking and sambals. **Batu Hiu** (Shark Rock), 23km from Pangandaran and 1km from the highway, has a recreational park atop the cliffs with views along the coast. Entry to the cliff park is through a giant concrete shark, and warung along the beach cater to the weekend crowds. Batu Hiu also has basic penginapan, but there is little reason to stay.

Inland from Parigi, near Cigugur, **Gunung Tilu** has fine views and is included in some of the tour itineraries. The **Sungai Citumang**, reached by a rough and hard-to-find inland road from Karang Benda, (watch for a sign and ask for directions) has a small dam from where you can walk upstream to a beautiful gorge – 'Green Canyon II' in Pangandaran tour parlance.

**Batu Karas**, 42km from Pangandaran, is a relaxed fishing village with a surf beach, one of the best on the coast, sheltered by a rocky promontory. Snorkelling is supposedly possible at Genteng Parakan just west of the village. Accommodation, favoured by surfers, can be found 1km beyond the fishing village at the headland beach. *Hotel Melati Indah* is the best value and has well

kept rooms with mandi for 20,000 rp. *Teratai Cottage* has a rundown, empty swimming pool, and rundown rooms for 30,000 and 50,000 rp. Next door, *Alana's Bungalows* has bamboo decor, surf culture and rooms for 20,000 to 35,000 rp with mandi. Good rumah makan include the *Kang Avi* and *Sederhana*. Right in the village, the new *Hotel Pondok Putri* (✆ 6650370) has a pool and very good rooms with hot water for 80,000 rp with fan or 100,000 and 120,000 rp with air-con. On the other side of the village to the east, the *Cijulang Permai* (✆ 0811 854359) has a pool and excellent mid-range rooms for 125,000 rp before discount, but it is a long way from anywhere and the beach is ordinary. Batu Karas can be reached from Pangandaran by taking a bus to Cijulang and then an ojeg for 2500 rp.

Pangandaran's No 1 tour is to **Green Canyon** (Cujang Taneuh is the real name). Many tour operators in Pangandaran run trips here for around 35,000 rp to 40,000 rp and include 'countryside' excursions on the way to make a full-day tour. To get there yourself, hire a boat from the Green Canyon river harbour on the highway, 1km before the turn-off to Batu Karas. Boats cost 23,500 rp for five people and operate from 7.30 am to 4 pm (1.30 to 4 pm Fridays). They travel up the emerald-green river through the forest to a waterfall and a steep rock canyon, and stop for swimming. Count on around 1½ hours for this excellent trip, but it has become so popular that there can be a flotilla of boats on the river and serene nature is giving way to litter and crowds. Go as early as possible at peak times to avoid the crush.

Farther along the coast, about 70km from Pangandaran, is **Karang Tawulan**, another cliff viewing area with rocky outcrops and small rock islands battered by the sea.

The coast road ends at the village of **Cipatujah**, which has a wide but uninspiring beach with dangerous swimming, and a couple of cheap hotels. Five kilometres before Cipatujah is a small PHPA post that monitors the green turtles that lay their eggs at **Sindangkerta** beach. The post welcomes interested visitors.

To the east of Pangandaran, **Karang Nini** is a recreational park perched high on the cliffs with fine views across to the Pangandaran Peninsula. Trails lead down the cliff face to the beach and crashing surf below. Apart from the occasional pair of young lovers, Karang Nini is deserted during the week. The park is run by the PHPA and it is possible to stay in its guesthouse.

### Getting There & Away

Regular buses run between Cijulang and Pangandaran (1500 rp). Buses run from Cijulang west to Cikalong (3000 rp) but buses on to Cipatujah are rare and *ojegojeg* may be the only option. Cipatujah is well serviced by buses from Tasikmalaya and some continue to Ciparanti and even Jakarta. The best way to see this stretch of coast is to hire a motorcycle in Pangandaran.

For Karang Nini, take any Kalipucang-bound bus to the Karang Nini turn-off, 9km east of Pangandaran on the highway. It is then a 3km walk to the park.

## SUMEDANG

The tidy provincial city of Sumedang, 40km from Bandung on the Cirebon road, was once the centre of one of Sunda's most powerful kingdoms. Sumedang rose to prominence under Prabu Geusan Ulun, who broke away from the Hindu Pajajaran kingdom in 1578, but by the 1630s Sumedang was subjugated by Sultan Agung of Central Java's Mataram kingdom.

The **Museum Prabu Geusan Ulun** on the main street, Jl Pangeran Guesan Ulun, is one of West Java's more diverting museums. Once the royal palace, it houses some interesting artefacts, including the royal treasures – crowns and kris inlaid with precious stone. On 12 Mulud of the Islamic calendar, these *pusaka* (treasures) are ritually cleansed and carried in procession around the town. The museum also has furniture, weaponry, ceremonial dresses, royal carriages, gamelan sets and paintings showing earlier greatness. One such painting depicts Pangeran Kornel Kusumadinata IX (1791-1828) shaking hands with Governor-General Daendals in 1818 but using his left hand – a symbol of protest. Many of the prince's subjects were employed in the building of the Great Post Road, Daendals' highway across Java, with great loss of life before the prince withdrew his cooperation. The museum is open daily from 8 am to 12.30 pm. *Srimpi* dance practice is held every Sunday from 8 to 11 am.

Sumedang is also known for its delicious *tahu* (been curd), which is famed throughout Java. Deep fried bean curd is served piping hot with *kecap manis* (sweet soy sauce) and chilli, which you mix together to form a dipping sauce. Try it in one of the many tahu Sumedang restaurants around town.

## CIREBON
☎ 0231

Few people make the trip out to Cirebon but it's an interesting seaport and the seat of an ancient Islamic kingdom with a number of attractions for visitors. Located on the north coast, right on the border with Central Java, the city's history has been influenced by both the Javanese and Sundanese with a bit of Chinese culture thrown in for good measure. Many of the people speak a local dialect blending Sundanese and Javanese, and it has been suggested that the name Cirebon comes from 'Caruban' which is Javanese for 'mixture'. The more direct Sundanese translation is 'prawn waters' from 'ci' (water) and 'rebon' (prawn), and Cirebon is known as Kota Udan, 'Prawn City'.

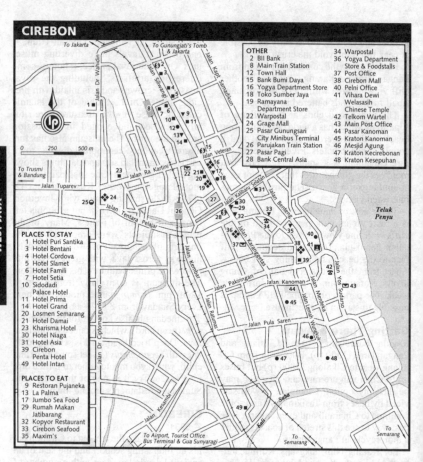

# CIREBON

**OTHER**
2  BII Bank
8  Main Train Station
12  Town Hall
15  Bank Bumi Daya
16  Yogya Department Store
18  Toko Sumber Jaya
19  Ramayana
    Department Store
22  Warpostal
24  Grage Mall
25  Pasar Gunungsari
    City Minibus Terminal
26  Parujakan Train Station
27  Pasar Pagi
28  Bank Central Asia
34  Warpostal
36  Yogya Department
    Store & Foodstalls
37  Post Office
38  Cirebon Mall
40  Pelni Office
41  Vihara Dewi
    Welasasih
    Chinese Temple
42  Telkom Wartel
43  Main Post Office
44  Pasar Kanoman
45  Kraton Kanoman
46  Mesjid Agung
47  Kraton Kecirebonan
48  Kraton Kesepuhan

**PLACES TO STAY**
1  Hotel Puri Santika
3  Hotel Bentani
4  Hotel Cordova
5  Hotel Slamet
6  Hotel Famili
7  Hotel Setia
10  Sidodadi
    Palace Hotel
11  Hotel Prima
14  Hotel Grand
20  Losmen Semarang
21  Hotel Damai
23  Kharisma Hotel
30  Hotel Niaga
31  Hotel Asia
39  Cirebon
    Penta Hotel
49  Hotel Intan

**PLACES TO EAT**
9  Restoran Pujaneka
13  La Palma
17  Jumbo Sea Food
29  Rumah Makan
    Jatibarang
32  Kopyor Restaurant
33  Cirebon Seafood
35  Maxim's

*Teluk Penyu*

To Jakarta
To Gunungjati's Tomb & Jakarta
To Trusmi & Bandung
To Airport, Tourist Office Bus Terminal & Gua Sunyaragi
To Semarang
To Semarang

Cirebon was one of the independent sultanates founded by Sunan Gunungjati of Demak in the early 16th century. Later, the powerful kingdoms of Banten and Mataram fought over Cirebon, which declared allegiance to Sultan Agung of Mataram but was finally ceded to the Dutch in 1677. By a further treaty of 1705 Cirebon became a Dutch protectorate, jointly administered by three sultans whose courts at that time rivalled those of Central Java in opulence and splendour. During the Dutch 'Culture System'

period, a flourishing trade in colonial crops attracted many Chinese entrepreneurs, and the Chinese influence can still be seen in the batik designs for which Cirebon is famous. Two of Cirebon's *kratons* (palaces) are open to visitors and, although a bit run-down compared with the palaces of Yogya and Solo, they still deserve more recognition.

Although Cirebon has long been a major centre for batik, it is also famous for its Tari Topeng Cirebon, a type of masked dance peculiar to the Cirebon area, and tarling, a musical tradition reminiscent of Bandung's *kecapi-suling* music, except that it features guitar, *suling* (bamboo flute) and voice. Cirebon is also important as the major port and fishing harbour between Jakarta and Semarang, with the added bonus that it has excellent seafood.

The north coast, can be a sweltering contrast to the cooler heights inland, particularly in the dry season. Other than that, Cirebon is a well kept city small enough not to be overwhelming, and it makes a worthwhile stopover.

## Orientation

Jl Siliwangi is the main boulevard which runs from the train station to the canal by the Pasar Pagi (Morning Market) and then changes name to Jl Karanggetas. Along this road there are banks, restaurants and the bulk of Cirebon's hotels.

## Information

**Tourist Office** The tourist office (☎ 208 856), Jl Dharsono 5, is 5km out of town on the bypass road, near Gua Sunyaragi. It has a few brochures in Indonesian – not worth the trip.

**Money** Bank Central Asia, Bank Bumi Daya and Bank BII are all on the main street and have ATMs. More banks are on Jl Yos Sudarso near the post office.

**Post & Communications** Cirebon's main post office, with a Warposnet for Internet terminals, is near the harbour on Jl Yos Sudarso. A post office branch is just across the canal on Jl Karanggetas.

For international telephone calls and faxes, the Telkom wartel is on Jl Yos Sudarso and has a Home Country Direct phone. Warpostals at Jl Kartini 7 and Jl Bahagia 40 offer the same services but don't allow collect international calls.

## Kraton Kesepuhan

At the south end of Jl Lemah Wungkuk, the Kraton Kesepuhan is the oldest and best preserved of Cirebon's kratons. It was built in 1527 and its architecture and interior are a curious blend of Sundanese, Javanese, Islamic, Chinese and Dutch styles. Although this is the home of the Sultan of Kesepuhan, part of the building is open to visitors. Inside the palace is a cool pavilion with whitewashed walls dotted with blue-and-white Delft tiles, a marble floor and a ceiling hung with glittering French chandeliers.

The kraton museum has an interesting, if somewhat run-down, collection of wayang puppets, kris, cannon, furniture, Portuguese armour and ancient royal clothes. But the *pièce de résistance* of the sultan's collection is the Kereta Singa Barong, a 17th century gilded coach with the trunk of an elephant (Hindu), the body and head of a dragon (Chinese-Buddhist) and wings (Islamic)! It was traditionally pulled by four white buffalo. It's near the entrance of the Gedong Singa carriage museum.

Entry to the kraton is 1000 rp and includes a guided tour; camera fees are an extra 500 to 2000 rp. The kraton is open from 8 am to 4 pm daily except Friday (7 to 11 am and 2 to 4 pm) and Sunday (8 am to 5 pm).

The guided tour may finish at the Museum Kereta Singa Barong, but behind in the large grounds of the palace is a new dance pavilion, where practice is sometimes held.

## Mesjid Agung

On the west side of the field in front of the Kraton Kesepuhan, the Mesjid Agung, with its tiered roof, is one of the oldest mosques in Java and is similar in style to the Mesjid Agung in Banten.

## Kraton Kanoman

A short walk from Kraton Kesepuhan and approached through Pasar Kanoman, this kraton was constructed in 1588. Kraton Kanoman was founded by Sultan Badaruddin, who broke away from the main sultanate after a lineage dispute with the sixth sultan's heir. Outside the kraton is a redbrick, Balinese-style compound and a massive banyan tree. Farther on past the white, stone lions is the kraton, a smaller, neglected cousin of Kraton Kesepuhan.

Go to the right past the lions, sign the register and a guide will unlock the museum. It's worth it – among the museum's small holdings of mostly carved doors is a stunning sultan's chariot, in the same style as the one in the Kraton Kesepuhan. It is claimed that the one in the Kraton Kesepuhan is a newer copy – the rivalry over the sultanate still exists it seems. You can also visit the *pendopo* (large open-sided pavilion) and its inner altar. Antique European plates, some with Dutch Reformist scenes from the Bible, can be seen before you enter.

Opening hours are haphazard and the guide's fee is by donation – 1000 rp seems appropriate but guides will ask for more.

The colourful **Pasar Kanoman** market, just in front of the kraton, is at its most vibrant in the morning and worth a visit in its own right.

### Kraton Kecirebonan

Although it's classed as a kraton, this is really only a house occupied by members of the current royal family, descendants of Raja Kanomin who broke away from the 10th Kesepuhan sultanate. Wander in and knock on the door and someone will be happy to show you around. A donation is expected. Built in 1839, the house has fine colonial architecture and a small collection of swords, documents and other royal memorabilia.

### Gua Sunyaragi

About 4km south-west of town is this not-to-be-missed attraction – a bizarre ruined 'cave' (*gua*), a grotto of rocks, red brick and plaster, honeycombed with secret chambers, tiny doors and staircases leading nowhere. It was originally a water palace for a sultan of Cirebon in the early 18th century and owes its present strange shape to the efforts of a Chinese architect who had a go at it in 1852.

### Other Attractions

Cirebon's **harbour** is always an interesting place to wander around to see the sailing schooners and freighters unload their wares. Around the port area are several old Dutch

East Indies warehouses – used at a time when opium, tobacco and sugar were shipped out from Cirebon – and other fine examples of Dutch architecture.

The **town hall** (*balai kota*) is a good example of Art Deco architecture, but the crowning glory is the large plaster stucco prawns on the top of the building, attesting to Cirebon's title of 'Prawn City'.

Cirebon has a large Chinese population and a number of interesting Chinese temples.

### Places to Stay – Budget

Inexpensive hotels can be found directly opposite the main train station, but conditions are not good. The *Hotel Setia* (☎ 207 270, Jl Inspeksi PJKA 1222) is the best, but expensive at 30,000 rp a double with mandi.

Jl Siliwangi is the main drag for hotels. On the corner near the main train station, the *Hotel Famili* (☎ 207935, Jl Siliwangi 66) is another basic place, with singles/doubles from 17,500/22,000 rp. Other cheap but uninspiring hotels in the centre of town on Jl Siliwangi are the *Hotel Damai* (☎ 203045), at No 130, where doubles with mandi cost 16,000 to 25,000 rp, or the *Losmen Semarang*, next door at No 132.

The best bet is the *Hotel Asia* (☎ 202183, Jl Kalibaru Selatan 15) alongside the tree-lined canal near the Pasar Pagi. This fine old Dutch-Indonesian inn has a terraced courtyard where you can sit and have breakfast. It's about a 15 minute walk or 1500 rp by becak from the main train station. This very well kept and friendly hotel has a variety of rooms from 17,900 rp without mandi, from 37,800 rp with.

### Places to Stay – Mid-Range

The *Hotel Grand* (☎ 208867, Jl Siliwangi 98) is a pleasantly old-fashioned place with a big front verandah. Worn but large rooms with separate sitting areas have air-con, hot water and TV. They cost 46,000 rp for dark internal rooms, 58,000 rp for those with a view of the alun alun and 70,000 rp for suites with office areas.

The *Hotel Cordova* (☎ 204677, Jl Siliwangi 87) near the main train station, is one of the better buys. Good, renovated rooms with air-con and hot water cost 38,000 to 72,000 rp.

The *Sidodadi Palace Hotel (☎ 202305, Jl Siliwangi 74)* is a pleasant motel-style place built around a quiet courtyard. Comfortable rooms with air-con, hot water and parabola TV range from 76,000 to 96,000 rp. The *Hotel Slamet (☎ 203296)* at No 95 is a cheaper hotel, with reasonable fan rooms with mandi for from 27,000 rp, air-con rooms with hot water from 38,500 rp.

The *Hotel Niaga (☎ 206718, Jl Kalibaru Selatan 47)* is rather dull but has large, clean rooms with air-con, TV, telephone and hot water for 45,000 and 60,000 rp.

*Hotel Intan (☎ 244788, Jl Karan Anyar 36)* is a new hotel with excellent rooms from only 25,000 rp, or 60,000 and 75,000 rp with air-con – one of Cirebon's best buys. The only drawback is that it is well south of the city centre.

Cirebon has a selection of more expensive mid-range hotels. Most are older hotels that have fallen from grace but offer attractive discounts. The large *Kharisma Hotel (☎ 207668, Jl Kartini 60)* is typical, and has old rooms from 169,000 rp or better rooms in the new section from 236,000 rp, and a further discount may be available.

## Places to Stay – Top End

Cirebon's better hotels charge 21% tax and service but include breakfast. Competition is stiff and large discounts (up to 50%) are readily available, making them good value.

The very central *Cirebon Penta Hotel (☎ 203328, Jl Syarif Addurakhman 159)* is small but classy. Excellent rooms cost from US$60, before big discounts. The hotel has a rooftop garden and a health centre. It is above the KFC restaurant, opposite the Cirebon Mall.

Close to the train station, *Hotel Bentani (☎ 203246, Jl Siliwangi 69)* has a variety of rooms from uninspiring mid-range for 190,000 rp to newer luxury for 249,000 rp, and a small pool.

The large *Hotel Prima (☎ 205411, Jl Siliwangi 107)* has a pool, tennis court, health centre, business centre, restaurants and bar. The rooms, from US$50/60, are well appointed but faded.

The *Hotel Puri Santika (☎ 200570, Jl Dr Wahidin 32)* is of a similar standard to the Prima, but newer and the best in town. Rooms start at US$85.

## Places to Eat

Apart from Cirebon's fine seafood, a local speciality to try is *nasi lengko*, a delicious rice dish with bean sprouts, tahu, tempe, fried onion, cucumber and peanut sauce. The *Rumah Makan Jatibarang*, on the corner of Jl Karanggetas and Jl Kalibaru Selatan, has nasi lengko as well as other Indonesian dishes.

The central market, or Pasar Pagi, has a great array of fruits and basic warungs that stay open until evening. Good warungs serving seafood, *ayam goreng* and sate can be found along Jl Kalibaru Selatan between the Asia and Niaga hotels. The *Moel Seafood* warung has delicious, cheap prawns in oyster sauce and *Seafood 31* is also good.

*Yogya department store (Jl Karanggetas 64)* – not the older Yogya store on Jl Siliwangi – has a *food-stall area* on the ground floor. On the 4th floor, *Marina* is a big Cantonese-style banquet hall specialising in seafood. It is one of Cirebon's best restaurants. The *food-stall area* upstairs at the back of *Ramayana Department Store* has authentic dishes and is the pick of Cirebon's food-stall centres.

Jl Bahagia has a number of seafood restaurants, such as *Cirebon Seafood* at No 9. One of Cirebon's best Chinese seafood restaurants is the cavernous *Maxim's* at No 45. Shrimp and crab dishes are a speciality. *Jumbo Sea Food (Jl Siliwangi 191)*, next to Yogya department store, does great seafood grills.

Jl Siliwangi has a few good options. *Restoran Pujaneka* at No 105 is a mid-range, buffet-style eatery, with Sundanese and Cirebon specialities as well as western dishes. *La Palma* at No 86 is a very pleasant bakery in an old Dutch villa with tables where you can sit down and enjoy a snack or a drink.

Cirebon Mall and Grage Mall are the places for western fast food and supermarkets.

## Entertainment

At the Penggung Cerubon, in the grounds at the front of the Hotel Prima on Jl Siliwangi, changing cultural events are held every Saturday night from 8 pm. You might see *topeng* dances, jugglers or just about anything.

## Shopping

Toko Sumber Jaya (Jl Siliwangi 211 & 229), has all sorts of *oleh-oleh* (souvenirs) from Cirebon, mostly of the syrup, dried prawn and krupuk variety; but pottery, bamboo crafts and other interesting knick-knacks are on sale too.

Cirebon is famed for its rattan furniture, made in the surrounding villages. For some superb and very expensive modern rattan furniture, visit the Yama Mutiara studio in the Hotel Bentani. Una Creasi Persada, Jl Rajawali Timur 1 No 88, in a residential suburb, makes an amazing variety of pots, lamps and flowers, all from rattan. The Asia department store, Jl Karanggetas, also has a selection of woven palm and rattan goods from Tasikmalaya.

Though Cirebon is noted for its batik, shops mostly sell batik from other regions. The nearby village of Trusmi is the best place for local batik. Batik Purnama, Jl Karanggetas 16, has a general selection. The biggest concentration of batik shops is on the ground floor under the Matahari department store on Jl Pekiringan.

The Grage Mall is Cirebon's biggest and brightest shopping mall. The Cirebon Mall is also well stocked.

## Getting There & Away

The road and rail route to Cirebon from Jakarta (256km) follows the flat north coast. From Bandung (130km) the road runs through scenic hilly country. Heading east to Pekalongan (137km) and Semarang (245km), the road runs just inland from the coast and is one of the busiest and most traffic-clogged in Java.

**Air** Cirebon has an airport to the south-west past the bus terminal, but there are no flights from here.

**Bus** The Cirebon bus terminal is 4km south-west of the centre of town.

Regular air-con buses run between Cirebon and Jakarta (8000/12,000 rp, five hours), Bandung (5000/8000 rp, 3½ hours), Pekalongan (4000/7000 rp, four hours), Semarang (7500/13,000 rp, seven hours), as well as Yogya, Bogor, Solo, Merak, Surabaya and other destinations. For Pangandaran, first take a bus to Ciamis along a winding but paved, quiet and very scenic road.

For express minibuses from Cirebon, the ACC Kopyor 4848 office (☎ 204343) is conveniently located in town at Jl Karanggetas 7, next door to the Kopyor Restaurant. It has air-con minibuses to Bandung (13,500 rp, 3½ hours), Semarang (20,000 rp, six hours), Yogya (25,000 rp, eight hours) and Cilacap (12,500 rp non-air-con, five hours). Ring to arrange pick-up from your hotel.

**Train** Cirebon is on both the main northern Jakarta-Semarang-Surabaya train line and the southern Jakarta-Yogya-Surabaya line, so there are frequent day and evening trains. The better services leave from Cirebon's main train station just off Jl Siliwangi, where you'll find a computerised booking office. Crowded ekonomi trains leave from the Parujakan train station farther south.

To Jakarta's Gambir train station, the *Cirebon Express* (18,000/32,000 rp bisnis/eksekutif, 3½ hours) departs from Cirebon at 5.50 am, 1 and 3.30 pm. It is much quicker and more convenient than the buses.

To Yogyakarta, the *Fajar Utama Yogya* (36,000/76,000 rp, five hours) departs at 9.20 am. To Semarang, via Tegal and Pekalongan, the *Fajar Utama Semarang* (32,000 rp bisnis, four hours) departs at 10.45 pm.

**Boat** The Pelni office (☎ 204300) is at the harbour past the harbour entrance. The KM *Lawit* stops in Cirebon to and from Pontianak in Kalimantan.

## Getting Around

Cirebon's city minibus *(angkutan kota)* service operates from Pasar Gunungsari, a couple of blocks west of Jl Siliwangi. The minibuses are labelled G7, GG etc, and charge a fixed 400 rp fare around town – some even offer 'full music'!

Cirebon has hordes of becaks ringing through the streets. A becak from the train station to Pasar Pagi costs around 2000 rp. Taxis congregate around the bus and train stations but are unwilling to use their meters from these destinations and are hard to find elsewhere. The going rate from the bus terminal to the train station is 6000 rp.

## AROUND CIREBON
### Sunan Gunungjati Tomb

In the royal cemetery, 5km north of Cirebon, is the tomb of Sunan Gunungjati, who died in 1570. The most revered of Cirebon's kings, Gunungjati was also one of the nine walis who spread Islam throughout Java and his tomb is still one of the holiest places in the country. The inner tombs are only open once a month on Kliwon Thursday of the Javanese calendar, and at Idul Fitri and Maulud Nabi Mohammed. Pilgrims sit in contemplation and pray outside the doors on other days. Along from Sunan Gunungjati's tomb is the tomb of his first (Chinese) wife, and this tomb attracts Chinese worshippers.

The spiritualism of the tombs are spoiled by the crowds of peddlers, beggars and children chanting *kasih uang* (receive money) at the entrance. At the entrance gate, put a small donation in the donation box and shake off the guides who follow you. Inside, ignore other aggressive demands to contribute to various funds. At the top, inside the tombs, tourists are expected to sign the guest book and pay another small donation.

When leaving the tombs, put your shoes on and go to your right (as you face the tombs), through the kampung. The alleyway leads to the main road and over the road is the public cemetery. The revered Datuk Kahfi, an Islamic missionary reputed to have been Sunan Gunungjati's teacher, is buried on top of the hill.

## Trusmi

Some of Cirebon's finest batik is made in the village of Trusmi, 5km west of town. You can get there by taking the G4 or GP angkot from Gunungsari station to Plered, on the Bandung road. Walk past the market from the main road and then down a country lane of whitewashed cottages, or take a becak. At the end of the lane, Ibu Masina's is the best-known studio where you can see batik tulis being made. Her showroom has a wide range of colours and designs and excellent silk batik. Also worth visiting is the workshop of Ibu Ega Sugeng – before you enter the lane to Ibu Masina's, follow Jl Trusmi around to the right and continue 200m to No 218. Collectors will be interested in the intricate, finer pieces, as well as in simple, cheaper pieces such as those showing the range of Cirebon court designs.

It's also worth wandering through the lanes to see the work in progress at the many small home workshops in Trusmi and the adjacent village of Kalitengah. Prices are no lower than those in the shops in Cirebon, but there is a wider selection of batik to choose from.

Surrounding villages, each specialising in their own crafts, include Tegalwangi, where rattan workshops line the Bandung road, 1km on from Plered.

## Plangon

This forest park, 15km from Cirebon on the road to Linggarajati, is a popular picnic spot, crawling with monkeys. At the top of a long flight of stone steps is the grave of a local saint and behind the shrine a trail leads across the ridge for fine views of the countryside. The trail ends at four small headstones, said to be of a Muslim preacher from Persia and another from Brunei, while the other two graves are for their swords.

## Linggarjati & Sangkan Hurip
☎ 0232

In 1946 Linggarjati's place in the history books was assured when representatives of the republican government and the returning Dutch occupying forces met to negotiate a

British-sponsored cooperation agreement. Terms were thrashed out in a colonial hotel at the foot of Gunung Cirema, once a retreat from the heat for Cirebon's Dutch residents. Soekarno briefly attended, but the Linggarjati Agreement was soon swept aside as the war for independence escalated. The hotel is now the **Gedung Naksa**, a museum recreating the events.

Linggarjati is not one of Java's premier hill resorts, but it is peaceful and makes a pleasant sojourn from the heat of the northern plains. It is possible to climb **Gunung Cirema** (3078m), which errupted last century, but a guide is necessary to negotiate the 10 hour walk through the forested slopes to the crater.

**Sangkan Hurip**, 3km downhill, is a hot-springs resort with a large hot-water swimming pool, hot baths and a dozen hotels. It has a good range of accommodation but not Linggarjati's fine aspect.

**Places to Stay** Linggarjati's large resort, *Linggarjati Indah* (☎ 63188), has a camping area, public swimming pool and a host of rooms and bungalows for 55,000 to 195,000 rp. The cheaper *Linggarjati Hotel* (☎ 63185) has simple rooms with bath overlooking the hotel swimming pool for 45,000 rp, more comfortable rooms cost 55,000 and 75,000 rp. The new *Hotel Ayong M* (☎ 63644) has a swimming pool and well appointed rooms for 100,000 rp and suites for 150,000 rp, before discount.

Sangkan Hurip has a bigger range of accommodation: from the very basic *Penginapan Camperik* and *Losmen Witi Sari* to the luxurious *Tirta Sanita Hotel* (☎ 63061), the area's best. Most are mid-range hotels, with swimming pools and hot-water baths.

**Getting There & Away** Linggarjati and Sangkan Hurip are 23km south of Cirebon, lying 2km to the west of the Kuningan road and 1km to the east respectively. From Cirebon, take a Kuningan bus to Cilimus (1000 rp), then an angkot (500 rp) to either resort. Andongs also go to Sangkan Hurip.

## Taman Purkabala Cipari

Just before the town of Kuningan, 35km south of Cirebon, is the turn-off to this museum, built on the site of a Neolithic compound dating back 3000 years. Discovered in 1972, the site is of great archaeological importance as one of the earliest known settlements on Java. Great shards of stone and boxed graves can be seen in the reconstructed compound, and the museum houses pottery and other artefacts found at the site. The Taman Purkabala Cipari is 3.6km west of the highway and then a further 0.7km through the village.

## Pamuan

Some say the 'very best' Cirebon batik comes from the small workshops of Pamuan village near Indramayu, 30km north along the coast. The patterns of the batik are more involved and some of the batik tulis is still coloured with traditional vegetable dyes. You can get there by taking a colt to Indramayu; from the colt station it's about a 1.5km walk or becak ride to the village of Pamuan.

# Central Java

Central Java has a population of 30 million and an area of 34,503 sq km. Semarang is its capital city.

This region is at the heart of Java and is also the heart of Javanese culture. It was the centre of Java's first great Indianised civilisation and much of the island's early culture. Later, the ascendency of Islam in the area created powerful sultanates centred around the *kratons* (walled city palaces) of Yogyakarta and Solo (Surakarta).

Although the north coast was the early Muslims' first foothold on Java, farther inland this new faith was gradually infused with strong Hindu-Buddhist influences and even older indigenous beliefs. The old Javanese traditions and arts, cultivated by the royal courts, are at their most vigorous in Central Java.

As a testament to Java's cultural resilience, it is noteworthy that the long years of Dutch colonial rule made little lasting impact on the island, and even though the Indonesian revolution of the 1940s stripped the sultans of their political powers, the influence of kraton culture still lingers in the minds of many Javanese.

Within the province, the 'special territory' of Yogyakarta ('Yogya') forms an enclave shaped like a triangle with its base on the south coast and its apex at the volcanic Gunung Merapi.

Although the capital of Central Java is formally the north-coast port of Semarang, the cities of Yogya and Solo are the emotional and cultural centres, having both been capitals of old Javanese kingdoms and, frequently, rival cities. Yogyakarta also lives on as the political capital of the Javanese imagination, since it was here that resistance to the colonial regime was the strongest and most effective.

Most of Central Java's main attractions are in, or close to, these two cities, including the magnificent Borobudur and Prambanan temple complexes. There are also

## HIGHLIGHTS

- Yogyakarta is the cultural heart of Java and the island's No 1 tourist centre.
- Borobudur's temples are among the greatest Buddhist relics of South-East Asia and Indonesia's most famous attraction.
- Prambanan Temple Complex is the largest collection of Hindu temples on Java, with a wealth of sculptural detail.
- Dieng Plateau features a collection of the oldest Hindu temples on Java, set in a beautiful landscape.
- Solo (Surakarta) is a major repository of Javanese culture, and the town can be used as a base to explore the antiquities of Central Java.
- Gunung Merapi, the smoking 'Fire Mountain', is one of Java's most active (and destructive) volcanoes.

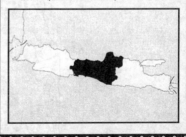

earlier temples in Central Java, most notably the simple, ancient shrines of the beautiful Dieng Plateau. The province also has some fine hill resorts like Kaliurang.

Despite its population pressure, Central Java is a relaxed, easy-going province. The enclave of Yogyakarta in particular remains one of Indonesia's most important tourist destinations.

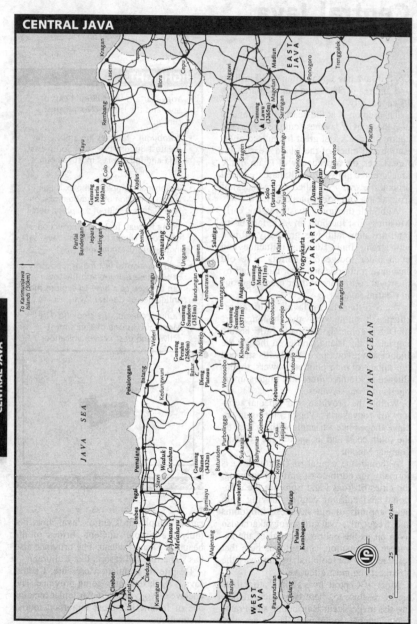

# CILACAP

☎ 0282

Cilacap, just over the border from West Java, is a medium-sized city in a growing industrial area and has the only natural harbour with deep-water berthing facilities on Java's south coast. Cilacap is quite a pleasant town – the river is littered with brightly painted fishing boats and it has an interesting fort to explore, but the main reason to come here is to make the backwater trip to Kalipucang for Pangandaran.

The tourist office (☎ 34481), Jl A Yani 8, is opposite the Hotel Wijayakusuma. It has a few brochures and can arrange a permit to the island of **Nusa Kembangan**, site of one of Java's most infamous prisons, but the island has good beaches and caves to explore. A car ferry runs there on weekends.

Cilacap is famous for **Sidikah Laut**, the sea festival held on 1 Suro in the Javanese calendar (around May), when offerings are made to the sea.

## Things to See

**Benteng Pendem** This is an impressive fort complex at the entrance to the old harbour. Though sometimes erroneously referred to as the 'Portuguese fort', it is in fact a Dutch fort built between 1861 and 1879. With intact barracks, gun rooms and massive ramparts, it is one of the best preserved forts on Java, and relatively little stone has been carted off for use in local construction. Bring a flashlight to explore some of the tunnels and rooms, and wear sandals – one tunnel leads to the sea and lies in shallow water. It is open from 7 am to 5 pm, and entry is 600 rp.

The fort overlooks a long stretch of dirty sand, **Pantai Teluk Penyu**, which (rather sadly) is a very popular local beach where souvenir stalls sell an array of shells and other ecologically fragile items.

All over crowded Java, young lovers seek out solitude in parks. This is the case at **Hutan Payau**, a few kilometres north of town on the road to the airport, but the difference is that this is a mangrove swamp. Wooden walkways have been built through the mangroves, and here and there secluded sitting areas house canoodling couples. It is also possible to rent canoes to take you through the park.

## Places to Stay & Eat

The friendly *Losmen Tiga* (☎ 33415, Jl Mayor Sutoyo 61) is in the centre of town and gets a steady trickle of travellers. The rooms don't come much rougher, but you won't find anything cheaper at 5500/7700/11,000 rp for singles/doubles/triples with shared *mandi* (Indonesian-style bath).

Around the corner, the well kept *Hotel Anggrek* (☎ 33835, Jl Anggrek 16) is a better bet for a decent room, starting at 12,000 rp. Larger rooms with shower are 24,000 rp, and air-con rooms with bath are 40,800 rp.

The *Hotel Teluk Penyu* (☎ 53212, Jl Dr Wahidin 57) is slightly characterless, but rooms are good value: from 20,000 rp with fan and TV, or 50,000 rp to 60,000 rp with air-con.

The *Cilacap Indah* (☎ 33543, Jl Sudirman 1) is a well kept mid-range hotel. Air-con rooms with hot water, TV and minibar cost from 51,000 rp to 90,000 rp, including breakfast.

*Hotel Graha Indah Cilacap* (☎ 33706, Jl Dr Wahidin 5) was formerly the Grand Hotel, but has lost its shine since those days. Nevertheless, it has a pool, restaurant, disco, and rooms with air-con, hot water and TV from 60,000 rp to 110,000 rp.

At the top end is the *Hotel Wijaya-kusuma* (☎ 34871, Jl A Yani 12A) on Cilacap's main central street. It has a pool, restaurant, pub, and excellent new rooms for 292,000 rp and 337,000 rp; but they have been offering specials for as low as 149,000 rp, including breakfast.

The other top-end hotel is the large *Hotel Mutiara* (☎ 31545, Jl Gatot Subroto 136), about half a kilometre to the north of Cilacap, south of the bus terminal. It also has a large pool, and good rooms from 296,000 rp, before discounts of up to 40%.

*Restaurant Perapatan/Sien Hieng (Jl A Yani 62)*, in the very centre of town, is a Cilacap institution and the town's best restaurant, with a large Chinese menu.

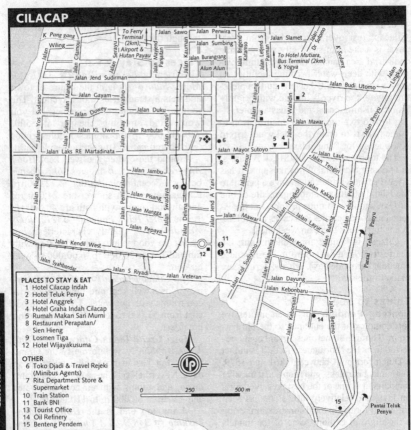

**CILACAP**

PLACES TO STAY & EAT
1  Hotel Cilacap Indah
2  Hotel Teluk Penyu
3  Hotel Anggrek
4  Hotel Graha Indah Cilacap
5  Rumah Makan Sari Murni
8  Restaurant Perapatan/
   Sien Hieng
9  Losmen Tiga
12 Hotel Wijayakusuma

OTHER
6  Toko Djadi & Travel Rejeki
   (Minibus Agents)
7  Rita Department Store &
   Supermarket
10 Train Station
11 Bank BNI
13 Tourist Office
14 Oil Refinery
15 Benteng Pendem

More eateries can be found along Jl Mayor Sutoyo, east of Losmen Tiga, including the good *Rumah Makan Sari Murni*.

## Getting There & Away

**Air** Cilacap has an airport 14km north of the city next to the golf course, but at the time of writing, scheduled flights were suspended.

**Bus** The bus terminal is 3km north of the city centre on Jl Gatot Subroto. Buses travelling to/from Cilacap include Pangandaran (4500 rp, 2½ hours), Yogya (6000 rp, five hours, 232km), Purwokerto (2000 rp, 1½ hours) and Wonosobo (4500 rp, four hours).

For door-to-door minibuses, check the Jl A Yani agents: Toko Djadi (☎ 33490) at No 72 and Travel Rejeki (☎ 33371) at No 68. Destinations include Yogya (15,000 rp), Semarang (17,500 rp) Jakarta (40,000 rp).

**Train** Cilacap's neglected train station (☎ 33842) is very central, just off Jl A Yani, and not far from the Hotel Wijayakusuma.

# GAMELAN INSTRUMENTS

**Bonang** The bonang consists of a double row of bronze kettles (like small kenongs) resting on a horizontal frame. There are three kinds, although the lowest in pitch is no longer used in gamelan orchestras. The bonang is played with two long sticks bound with red cord at the striking end. Although in modern Javanese gamelan, the bonang has two rows of bronze kettles, originally it had only one row, as it still has in Bali.

**Celempung** This is a plucked, stringed instrument, a bit like a zither. It has 26 strings arranged in 13 pairs, stretched over a coffin-shaped resonator. It is plucked with the thumb nails. The sitar is a smaller version of the celempung, with fewer strings and a higher pitch.

**Gambang** The gambang is the only gamelan instrument with bars made not of bronze but of hardwood, laid over a wooden frame. It is struck with two sticks made of supple buffalo horn, each ending with a small, round, padded disc.

**Gender** This is similar to a *slentem* in structure but there are more bronze keys, and the keys and bamboo chambers are smaller. The gender is played with two disc-shaped hammers. Each hand must simultaneously hit a note and damp the preceding one.

**Gong Ageng** The gong ageng or *gong gede* is suspended on a wooden frame. There is at least one such gong, sometimes more, in a gamelan orchestra. Made of bronze and about 90cm in diameter, it is used to mark the end of the largest phrase of a melody.

**Kempul** A small hanging gong that marks a smaller musical phrase.

**Left:** The saron is played with a mallet and the other hand is used as a dampener.

**Right:** The basis for the Gamelan and its unique sounds are the gongs, such as the gong ageng and the bonang shown here.

RICHARD I'ANSON

RICHARD I'ANSON

**Kendang** These drums are all double-ended and beaten by hand (with the exception of the giant drum, the *bedug*, which is beaten with a stick). The drum is an important leading instrument; it is made from hollowed sections of the jackfruit *(nangka)* tree with cow or goat skin stretched across the ends. The middle-sized *kendang batangan* or *kendang ciblon* is chiefly used to accompany dance and wayang performances; the drum patterns indicate specific dance or wayang puppet movements.

**Kenong** The kenong is a small gong laid horizontally on crossed cord and sits inside a wooden frame.

**Ketuk** The ketuk is a small kenong, tuned to a certain pitch, which marks subdivisions of phrases. The sound of the ketuk is short and dead compared with the clearer, resonant tone of the kenong.

**Rebab** The rebab is a two stringed, bowed instrument of Arabic origin. It has a wooden body covered with fine, stretched skin. The bow is made of wood and coarse horsehair tied loosely. The rebab player sits cross-legged on the floor behind the instrument.

**Saron** This is the basic instrument-type of the gamelan, a xylophone with bronze bars that are struck with a wooden mallet. There are three types of saron: high, medium and low pitched. The high one, called *saron panerus* or *saron peking,* is played with a mallet of buffalo horn.

**Slentem** The slentem carries the basic melody in the soft ensemble, as the saron does in the loud ensemble. It consists of thin bronze bars suspended over bamboo resonating chambers; it is struck with a padded disc on the end of a stick.

**Suling** This flute is the only wind instrument in the gamelan orchestra. It is made of bamboo and played vertically.

RICHARD I'ANSON

**Left:** The kratons of Central Java have their own gamelan orchestras and the gamelan sets are sacred heirlooms credited with mystic power.

Just three trains operate: the *Purwojaya* to Jakarta (28,000/48,000 rp in bisnis/eksekutif) at 6 pm; and the ekonomi *Capbaya* to Yogya (4500 rp) and *Seraya* to Bandung (7000 rp), both departing at 5.45 am.

**Boat** Boats to Kalipucang (3200 rp, four hours) leave from the jetty a few kilometres north-west of town, inland on the river estuary, at 8 am and noon and/or 1 pm. Take a bemo (500 rp) to the jetty turn-off, then a becak for the 1km or so to the jetty (1000 rp). A becak from the bus terminal all the way to the jetty should cost about 2500 rp. The jetty is near the big Pertamina installations – no photography! The last ferry leaves at 1 pm, so start early if you are coming from Yogya or Dieng, unless you want to spend the night in Cilacap. See under Pangandaran later in this chapter for full details of this interesting trip.

## PURWOKERTO
☎ 0281

This medium-sized city is primarily a transport hub, and you may find yourself here en route between Wonosobo or Cilacap, or on the way to Baturaden. Purwokerto is an unhurried, remarkably clean city with some architectural reminders of Dutch colonialism.

### Places to Stay & Eat

For a cheap hotel, the *Hotel Sampurna* (☎ 37394, Jl Gerilya 47) is near the bus terminal and has rooms to suit most budgets. The basic *Hotel Baru* (☎ 34085, Jl Pasarwage 27) is in the centre of town near the market. Near the train station, the *Hotel Budi* has rooms for 15,000 rp and 20,000 rp.

*Hotel Borobudur* (☎ 37747, Jl Yosodarmo 32) is a reasonable mid-range option just off the main street, Jl Jenderal Sudirman. Rooms cost 65,000 rp with fan and bath, or 85,000 rp with air-con, hot water and minibar. Ask for a discount.

The big *Dynasty Hotel* (☎ 34321, Jl Dr Angka 71) is by far the best, with a huge pool, bar and restaurant. Rooms start at 137,500 rp; up to 295,000 rp for suites.

Jl Jenderal Sudirman has plenty of restaurants, including the *Ikan Bakar*

*Pringsewa* for grilled fish and the *Holan Bakery*. Farther north on Jl Overste Isdiman, the road to Baturaden, the *Rumah Makan Indonesia* has a varied menu and an Internet cafe. On the same street, *Rumah Makan Selera Remaja* is a bright, modern restaurant with good Indonesian food.

For superb fried chicken, the *Rumah Makan Kalibogor (Jl Yos Sudarso 34)* is about 2km west of town on the main road. The bar/restaurant at the *Hotel Borobudur* overlooks the pool, and has superior Indonesian and Western dishes. For packaged food, check out the huge *Moro Supermarket* on Jl Perintis Kemerdekaan.

### Getting There & Away

Purwokerto's bus terminal is about 2km south of town. Buses run to all major centres, including Cilacap, Wonosobo, Banjar and Yogya. Infrequent direct buses go to Baturaden (1500 rp), or catch an *angkot* (small minibus) from the Pasar Wage (1000 rp) in town. Purwokerto is also a major rail hub, and the train station is close to the centre of town. Numerous trains run to Jakarta, but most are night trains. To Yogya and Solo, the luxury *Dwipangga* departs at 12.58 pm and costs 160,000 rp, or the ekonomi *Tirtonadi* (9000 rp) leaves at 3.26 pm; other trains run at night. The *Purwojaya* goes to Cilacap (1½ hours) at 12.12 pm.

### BATURADEN
☎ 0281

Baturaden, 14km north of Purwokerto, is one of Java's most attractive mountain resorts, on the slopes of Gunung Slamet. Savour the mountain air on quiet weekdays and go for walks through forested slopes to waterfalls and hot springs. The recreation park also has a swimming pool, boat rides and zoo (a tiger, bear and kangaroos etc in depressingly small cages).

From the main entrance, it is about a 2km walk to **Pancoran Tujuh** waterfall through beautiful forest. Before the trail begins to climb steeply, you reach the small **Pancoran Tiga** waterfall and hot springs, where the cold water mixes with the hot and there are bathing facilities. It is then a hard grunt up to the road (cars can drive to Pancoran Tujuh via a long back-road), then another half kilometre to the main waterfall and **Goa Sara Badak**, where hot water gushes through a canyon.

**Gunung Slamet**, the second-highest peak on Java at 3432m, is a Fujiesque volcanic cone that dominates the landscape of western Central Java. Trails lead from Baturaden to the peak, but this is a very tough route. The usual ascent is from Bambangan village to the east or Serang from the north side, and you have to overnight on the mountain.

### Places to Stay

Baturaden has dozens of hotels. *Wisma Kartika Asri* is in a good position opposite the gates to the recreation park. Basic but clean rooms with mandi cost 20,000 rp. Nearer the bus terminal, the *Hotel Sari* is a little better, and costs 30,000 rp. The rock-bottom *Hotel Teluk Penyu* costs just 12,500 rp.

Top of the range is the big *Hotel Rosenda* (☎ 32570), with a pool and rooms from 175,000 rp, before discount; the older *Rosenda Cottages* is simpler and costs 125,000 rp. The other big resort hotel is the *Queen Garden* (☎ 38388), 2km east. It also has a pool and good rooms from 190,000 rp.

### KELAMPOK

Forty kilometres west of Purwokerto on the road to Wonosobo, Kelampok is one of Java's main pottery centres. A string of shops line the road just outside town and a large ceramic factory can be visited. Pots, figurines and even pottery tables and stools are produced, and Kelampok pottery employs interesting latticework, bright colours and innovative designs. Much of the pottery you see for sale on Bali comes from here.

### GUA JATIJAJAR

This huge limestone cave, which is about 130km west of Yogya and 21km south-west of Gombong, is a popular local

## Antiquities of Central Java

The Canggal stone on Gunung Wakir, dated 732 AD, is the oldest antiquity and the first sign of a major Hindu civilisation in Central Java. It attests to the rule of Sanjaya, who founded the Mataram kingdom, which produced some of the most magnificent temples in South-East Asia.

Within 100 years of Sanjaya, temple complexes dotted Central Java. The early temples were principally Shivaite, but Vishnu, Brahma and Buddha were also represented in temple sculpture. The Dieng Plateau was a major temple city with over 400 temples. The earliest temples were squat and boxlike with relatively little sculpture, but around 800, temple art changed and reached its peak on Java.

Under the Buddhist Sailendra dynasty, Borobudur was begun in the late 8th century and completed after nearly 70 years. This monumental work was followed by Prambanan, another enormous Hindu complex completed in 856. Not long after it was built, the Mataram kingdom mysteriously declined and Central Java languished.

Power shifted to East Java and no significant new temples were built in Central Java until the 15th century, when Candi Sukuh and Candi Ceto were erected. These Hindu temples, showing strong fertility and cult worship, were built when Islam was already conquering Java.

tourist attraction. From the parking area, make your way through the group of souvenir sellers to the recreation park and up to the cave, which is spattered with graffiti. A concrete path wends its way over natural springs and through the halls of the cave, which are decorated with life-sized statues that relate the story of legendary lovers Raden Kamandaka and Dewi Ratna Ciptarasa. It is all very tacky, which is unfortunate, because this is an otherwise impressive natural cave.

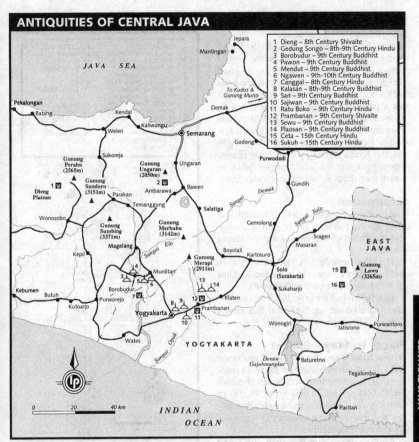

ANTIQUITIES OF CENTRAL JAVA

1 Dieng – 8th Century Shivaite
2 Gedung Songo – 8th-9th Century Hindu
3 Borobudur – 9th Century Buddhist
4 Pawon – 9th Century Buddhist
5 Mendut – 9th Century Buddhist
6 Ngawen – 9th-10th Century Buddhist
7 Canggal – 8th Century Hindu
8 Kalasan – 8th-9th Century Buddhist
9 Sari – 9th Century Buddhist
10 Sajiwan – 9th Century Buddhist
11 Ratu Boko – 9th Century Hindu
12 Prambanan – 9th Century Shivaite
13 Sewu – 9th Century Buddhist
14 Plaosan – 9th Century Buddhist
15 Ceta – 15th Century Hindu
16 Sukuh – 15th Century Hindu

CENTRAL JAVA

More difficult to explore, but larger and unspoilt, **Gua Petruk** is 7km south of Gua Jatijajar. It has impressive stalactite and stalagmite formations – a guide has to be hired from the PHPA (Indonesia's national parks service) post at the caves.

Other attractions in the area are the black-sand beaches to the south. **Pantai Indah Ayah** (also called Pantai Logending), 5km beyond Gua Petruk, is a sheltered bay with a reasonable beach. It has a camping ground and a lake area for boating. Farther

east along the coast is **Pantai Karang Bolong**, where many of the local people make a living collecting the nests of sea swallows from the steep cliff faces above the surf. The nests are collected every three months and sold to Chinese restaurants at home and abroad.

The nearest accommodation is in Gombong, 21km north of Gua Jatijajar on the main road and rail line between Yogya and Bandung. Regular microbuses run from Gombong to Gua Jatijajar.

## WONOSOBO

● **pop 25,000**        ☏ **0286**

Wonosobo is the main gateway to the Dieng Plateau. At 900m, in the hills of the central mountain range, Wonosobo has a good climate and is a fairly typical country town with a busy market. For most of the year it's not a particularly interesting place, but on national holidays it comes alive as people from the surrounding villages gather for festivities held in the main square. You might see the Kuda Kepang dance from nearby Temanggung, or the local Lengger dance, in which men dress as women and wear masks.

### Information

The tourist office (☏ 21194), Jl Kartini 3, is open during business hours, and has maps and brochures of Wonosobo and the Dieng Plateau.

The BNI bank on Jl A Yani changes cash and travellers cheques at low rates, and has an ATM for credit card withdrawals.

The Telkom office is on Jl A Yani near the *alun alun* (main square), and has Home Country Direct phones.

### Places to Stay – Budget

*Wisma Duta Homestay* (☏ *21674, Jl Rumah Sakit 3*) is the best budget option, with comfortable, bright rooms with attached mandi for 15,000 rp and 20,000 rp, or 40,000 rp with shower. Breakfast and free tea and coffee are included. The homestay provides good travel information.

Another good guesthouse is the small *Citra Homestay* (☏ *21880, Jl Angkatan 45*). Large rooms with shared bathroom cost 20,000 rp, and it has a pleasant sitting area. The price includes breakfast.

Wonosobo also has plenty of cheap, uninspiring *losmen* (basic accommodation, often family-run), such as those on Jl Resimen 18 just south of the Hotel Nirwana. The poorly run, crumbling *Hotel Jawa Tengah*. *Hotel Petra* (☏ *27152, Jl A Yani 97*) is more welcoming. Singles are 7000 rp and 11,000 rp, doubles 20,000 rp and 25,000 rp, and a few expensive rooms at back with TV and hot water cost 55,000 rp.

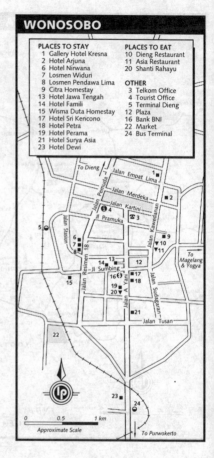

**WONOSOBO**

**PLACES TO STAY**
1  Gallery Hotel Kresna
2  Hotel Arjuna
6  Hotel Nirwana
7  Losmen Widuri
8  Losmen Pendawa Lima
9  Citra Homestay
13  Hotel Jawa Tengah
14  Hotel Famili
15  Wisma Duta Homestay
17  Hotel Sri Kencono
18  Hotel Petra
19  Hotel Perama
21  Hotel Surya Asia
23  Hotel Dewi

**PLACES TO EAT**
10  Dieng Restaurant
11  Asia Restaurant
20  Shanti Rahayu

**OTHER**
3  Telkom Office
4  Tourist Office
5  Terminal Dieng
12  Plaza
16  Bank BNI
22  Market
24  Bus Terminal

If you can't be bothered heading into town, you could do a lot worse than the well run *Hotel Dewi* (☏ *21813, Jl A Yani 90A*), right opposite the bus terminal. It has economy rooms for 15,000 rp, mid-range rooms with mandi are 30,000 rp, or from 40,000 rp with hot water.

### Places to Stay – Mid-Range

Mid-range pickings are lean. *Hotel Nirwana* (☏ *21066, Jl Resimen 18 No 34*) is secure, quiet and the most popular. Rooms with hot shower are immaculate but over-priced at 50,000 rp, or 100,000 rp for large family rooms, and the staff are surly.

The quiet *Hotel Arjuna* (☎ 21389, *Jl Sindoro 7A*) is farther out, and has rooms around courtyard areas from 30,000 rp to 70,000 rp with sitting room.

The *Hotel Sri Kencono* (☎ 21522, *Jl A Yani 81*) is the best of the older hotels. The tiled rooms are well kept, and have hot water showers and TV for 44,000 rp. Breakfast is included.

## Places to Stay – Top End

*Hotel Surya Asia* (☎ 22992, *Jl A Yani 137*) is an excellent three star hotel with a good restaurant and well appointed rooms from 136,000 rp, including tax, service and breakfast.

Top of the range is the new *Gallery Hotel Kresna* (☎ 24111, *Jl Pasukan Ronggolawe 30*), which has a pool, restaurant and bar. This stylish boutique hotel was originally built in 1921 as a retreat for Dutch planters. The old dining room remains, but the rest of the hotel is new. Rooms start at US$80, discounted to as low as 180,000 rp.

## Places to Eat

The popular *Dieng Restaurant* (*Jl Kawedanan 29*) has good Indonesian, Chinese and European food, served buffet-style. The owner, Mr Agus Tjugianto, is an inspirational source of information on Dieng and sometimes arranges Dieng tours. The photograph albums are worth a look. This long-running institution may move out near the new bus terminal.

The *Asia*, two doors down, is one of Wonosobo's best restaurants, and serves Chinese food. The *Shanti Rahayu* (*Jl A Yani 106*) is a spick-and-span place specialising in excellent fried chicken.

## Getting There & Away

Wonosobo's bus terminal is 2km south of the town centre, but plans are afoot to move it 3km out of town on the road to Magelang.

From Yogya, take a bus to Magelang (2000 rp, one hour), then another bus to Wonosobo (2200 rp, two hours). Rahayu Travel (☎ 21217), Jl A Yani 111, and Rama Sakti Travel (☎ 21236) have door-to-door minibuses to Yogya (8000 rp, three hours). Hotels can arrange pick-up.

Hourly buses go to Semarang (4000 rp, four hours) via Secang and Ambarawa (3000 rp).

Direct buses run to Cilacap (4500 rp, four hours), but are not frequent. Otherwise, take a bus to Purwokerto (3000 rp, three hours) and change there. Leave early in the morning to catch the ferry to Kalipucang and on to Pangandaran.

Frequent buses to Dieng (1500 rp, one hour) leave from Terminal Dieng throughout the day and continue to Batur.

## Getting Around

Yellow angkots run around town and to nearby villages, and cost 400 rp for most journeys. *Andongs* (horse-drawn carts) from the bus terminal to the town centre cost 500 rp per person.

## AROUND WONOSOBO

The Dieng Plateau is the major attraction of the area, but there are other attractions on the way to Dieng and farther east. About 3km from Wonosobo on the Dieng road, **Kalianget** is a hot springs complex with a swimming pool.

Some 15km towards Dieng, the western slopes of **Gunung Sundoro** (3136m) are carpeted with tea estates which can be toured. A rough road to Ngadirejo branches off to the east and provides access to the village of Sigedang at 1800m, which is the starting point to climb Sundoro. It is a five to six hour climb to the top of this holy mountain, which attracts hundreds of pilgrims on 1 Suro, the start of the Javanese new year. After taking in the fabulous views from the top, you can backtrack or else you can descend to Kledung Pass on the Wonosobo-Magelang road, where there is a good restaurant and hotel.

From the road to Ngadirejo you can also reach **Jumprit** at the source of the holy Sungai Progo. During the Buddhist celebration of Waisak at Borobudur, monks make the pilgrimage to Jumprit to collect water from the river. **Pring Abus Temple**, 5km from Jumprit, is a small Hindu temple dedicated to Nandi.

**Gunung Sumbing** (3371m) can also be climbed using Kledung as a base. The trail starts from Garungrejo village, but this is a steeper and harder climb, and involves crossing deep valleys.

## DIENG PLATEAU
☎ 0268

The oldest Hindu temples on Java are found on this lofty plateau, 2000m above sea level. The name 'Dieng' comes from 'Di-Hyang', meaning 'abode of the gods', and it is thought that this was once the site of a flourishing temple-city of priests.

The temples, mostly built between the 8th and 9th centuries, covered the highland plain, but with the mysterious depopulation of Central Java this site, like Borobudur, was abandoned and forgotten. The holy city reputedly had over 400 temples, but it was buried and overgrown, then plundered for building material. It was not until 1856 that the archaeologist Van Kinsbergen drained the flooded valley around the temples and catalogued the ruins. The eight remaining temples are characteristic of early Central Javanese architecture – stark, squat and box-like.

These simple temples, while of great archaeological importance, are not stunning. Rather, Dieng's beautiful landscape is the main reason to make the long journey to this isolated region. Steep mountainsides terraced with vegetable plots enclose the huge volcanically active plateau, the marshy caldera of a collapsed volcano. Any number of walks to cool mineral lakes,

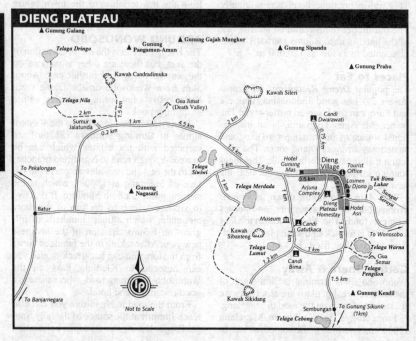

**DIENG PLATEAU**

- ▲ Gunung Galang
- *Telaga Dringo*
- ▲ Gunung Pangamun-Amun
- ▲ Gunung Gajah Mungkur
- ▲ Gunung Sipandu
- ▲ Gunung Prahu
- Kawah Candradimuka
- *Telaga Nila*
- Kawah Sileri
- Gua Jimat (Death Valley)
- 2 km
- 1.5 km
- Sumur Jalatunda
- 1 km
- 0.2 km
- 4.5 km
- 2 km
- Candi Dwarawati
- 0.75 km
- 1.5 km
- To Pekalongan
- *Telaga Siwiwi*
- 1 km
- 1.5 km
- Hotel Gunung Mas
- Dieng Village
- Tourist Office
- Tuk Bima Lukar
- ▲ Gunung Nagasari
- *Telaga Merdada*
- 1 km
- 0.5 km
- Losmen Bu Djono
- Arjuna Complex
- Sungai Serayu
- Batur
- Museum
- Dieng Plateau Homestay
- Hotel Asri
- Candi Gatutkaca
- 1.5 km
- To Wonosobo
- Kawah Sibanteng
- *Telaga Lumut*
- 1.2 km
- Candi Bima
- 1 km
- *Telaga Warna*
- Gua Semar
- *Telaga Pengilon*
- 1.5 km
- To Banjarnegara
- Kawah Sikidang
- Not to Scale
- Sembungan
- To Gunung Sikunir (1km)
- ▲ Gunung Kendil
- *Telaga Cebong*

steaming craters or other quiet, lonely places can be made around Dieng – including to the highest village on Java if you're feeling energetic.

To really appreciate Dieng, it is best to stay in Dieng village. Alternatively, Wonosobo has better facilities and can be used as a base. Yogya companies also run tours to Dieng. The temples and the main natural sights can be seen in one day on foot – be in Dieng in the morning before the afternoon mists roll in. It is a pleasant three or four hour loop south from Dieng village to Telaga Warna, Candi Bima, Kawah Sikidang, then back to Candi Gatutkaca, the Arjuna Complex and the village. Many other lakes and craters around Dieng are scattered over a large area, but they are difficult to reach.

### Information

In Dieng village, a kiosk sells tickets to Dieng for 3000 rp. The Bank Rakyat Indonesia near the Hotel Gunung Mas changes US dollars cash at poor rates.

### Temples

The five main temples that form the **Arjuna Complex** are clustered together on the central plain. They are all Shiva temples, but (like the other Dieng temples) they have been named after the heroes of the *wayang* stories of the *Mahabharata* epic – Arjuna, Puntadewa, Srikandi, Sembadra and Semar. Raised walkways link the temples (as most of the land on which they stand is waterlogged), but you can see the remains of ancient underground tunnels that once drained the marshy flatlands.

Just to the south of the Arjuna Complex is **Candi Gatutkaca** and a small site **museum** containing statues and sculpture from the temples. The museum is open weekends – ask around for the caretaker at other times. The statuary inside reveals interesting carvings, including an unusual representation of Nandi the bull, Shiva's carrier. Nandi has the body of a man and the head of a bull, a unique representation in Hindu iconography found nowhere else. Another gargoyle-like figure sporting an erection is distinctly animist.

Farther south, **Candi Bima** is unique on Java, with its *kudu*, strange sculpted heads like so many spectators looking out of windows.

The restored **Candi Dwarawati** is on the northern outskirts of the village. Near the entrance to Dieng at the river, **Tuk Bima Lukar** is an ancient bathing spring where water spouts from the stone wall. It was once holy and is the setting for a 'fountain of youth' legend.

### Other Attractions

The road that runs south from the Dieng Plateau Homestay passes a mushroom factory and a flower garden before the turn-off to beautiful **Telaga Warna** (Coloured Lake). This lake is coloured with turquoise hues from bubbling sulphur deposits around its shores. A trail leads anticlockwise around the lake to the adjoining lake, **Telaga Pengilon**, and the holy cave of **Gua Semar**, a renowned meditational cave. Return to the main road via the indistinct trail that leads around Telaga Pengilon and up the terraced hillside before eventually returning to the road. The colours of the lakes are better from up high.

A turn-off just south of here leads to a large geothermal station, which has expanded with deeper drilling to become a major electricity supplier. Its pipes run all over the valley.

From Telaga Warna, it is 1km along the main road to Candi Bima, then another 1.2km to **Kawah Sikidang**, a volcanic crater with steaming vents and frantically bubbling mud ponds. Exercise extreme caution when you are here – there are no guard rails to keep you from slipping off the sometimes muddy trails into the scalding hot waters, as one tourist discovered recently. **Kawah Sibentang** is another less spectacular crater nearby, and you can also visit **Telaga Lumut,** another small lake.

South of the geothermal station, the paved road leads to **Sembungan**, reputed to be the highest village on Java at 2300m.

Potato farming has made this large village relatively wealthy, especially since the sharp rise in the price of potatoes. Dieng has a reputation for producing the best potatoes in Indonesia, and demand for this produce has meant that Sembungan has been able to afford to send an inordinately large number of pilgrims on the hajj. The large new mosque is a testament to their faith.

The main attraction is **Gunung Sikunir**, 1km past Sembungan and the shallow Telaga Cebong lake. Views from Sikunir are spectacular. On a clear day.you can see across Dieng and east as far as the Merapi and Merbabu volcanoes. The favourite viewing time is at sunrise. Start at 4 am from Dieng village – it is one hour to Sembungan and about 30 minutes more to the top of the mountain (more a hill). The Dieng Plateau Homestay and Losmen Bu Djono both offer guides for 10,000 rp per person (perhaps less with bargaining).

Other attractions to the west are more difficult to reach. **Telaga Merdada** is a large lake which has a large mushroom factory alongside. **Kawah Sileri**, 2km off the main road and 6km from Dieng, is a smoking crater area with a hot lake. **Gua Jimat** is a 1km walk through the fields from the main road.

Nine kilometres from Dieng village is the trail to **Kawah Candradimuka**, and it's a pleasant 1.5km walk to this crater through the fields. Another trail branches off to two lakes: **Telaga Nila** and a longer two hour walk to the further **Telaga Dringo**.

Just a few hundred metres past the turnoff to Kawah Candradimuka is **Sumur Jalatunda**. This 'well' (as 'sumur' translates) is in fact a deep hole, some 100m across, whose vertical walls plunge down to bright green waters.

Another popular spot for watching the sunrise and for great views of the valley is from **Gardu Pemandangan** lookout point on the Wonosobo road, 5km before Dieng. This is the 'golden sunrise' of the tourist literature. The 'silver sunrise' comes a little later to Dieng itself.

## Places to Stay & Eat

Dieng has a handful of spartan hotels.

The *Dieng Plateau Homestay* (☎ 92823) and the *Losmen Bu Djono* next door are perennial competitors, and both have cafes and information on Dieng. The Dieng Plateau is better maintained and has singles/doubles for 10,000/15,000 rp. A couple of rooms have mandi (but no water as yet). The Bu Djono is friendly, but asks 15,000 rp for a decrepit room. It also has a 'VIP' room with sitting room and hot water for an overpriced 50,000 rp. The *Hotel Asri* has passable rooms for 20,000/25,000 rp. *Hotel Gunung Mas* (☎ 92417) is the best in town, just, but the mosque is right behind and rooms cost a ridiculous 50,000 rp and 70,000 rp. Though it is undergoing renovation it is unlikely the rooms will be worth that price.

Don't expect much in the way of culinary delights. The food at *Losmen Bu Djono* wins back a few points from the *Dieng Plateau Homestay*, and has cold beer. There are some *warungs* (food stalls) opposite the Hotel Gunung Mas, including a good Madurese *sate* place.

## Getting There & Away

Dieng is 26km from Wonosobo, which is the usual access point. Buses from Wonosobo to Dieng village take an hour and continue to Batur. They cost 1500 rp for lowlanders, only 1200 rp for Plateauns, and maybe 2000 rp for tourists. From Batur, 750 rp by bus from Dieng, pick-ups with two rows of seats in the back may not be comfortable, but they'll take you to Pekalongan (1500 rp, three hours, 90km). The road is steep but paved. The usual way to reach the north coast is to head down to Wonosobo and then take a bus to Semarang.

You can reach Dieng from Yogya in a day, including a stop at Borobudur, provided you leave early enough to make the connections: Yogya-Borobudur-Magelang-Wonosobo-Dieng. Yogya travel agents have day tours that include Borobudur, but you'll spend most of your time on a bus.

*continued on page 271*

# BOROBUDUR

From the plain of Kedu, 42km north-west of Yogya, a small hill rises up out of a pattern of palm trees and fields of rice and sugar cane. It's topped by one of the greatest Buddhist relics of South-East Asia – up there with Cambodia's Angkor Wat and Myanmar's Bagan.

Rulers of the Sailendra dynasty built the colossal pyramid of Borobudur some time between 750 and 850 AD. Little else is known about Borobudur's early history, but the Sailendras must have recruited a huge workforce, for some 60,000 cubic metres of stone had to be hewn, transported and carved during its construction. According to tradition, the main architect was Gunadharma. The name Borobudur is possibly derived from the Sanskrit words *Vihara Buddha Uhr*, which mean 'the Buddhist monastery on the hill'.

With the decline of Buddhism and the shift of power to East Java, Borobudur was abandoned soon after completion and for centuries it lay forgotten, buried under layers of volcanic ash. It was only in 1815, when Raffles governed Java, that the site was cleared and the sheer magnitude of the builders' imagination and technical skill was revealed. Early in the 20th century the Dutch began to tackle the restoration of Borobudur, but over the years the supporting hill had become waterlogged and the whole immense stone mass started to subside. A mammoth US$25 million restoration project was undertaken between 1973 and 1983.

Although easily forgotten, standing as they do in the shadow of the great Borobudur, two smaller structures – the Mendut and Pawon temples – form a significant part of the complex.

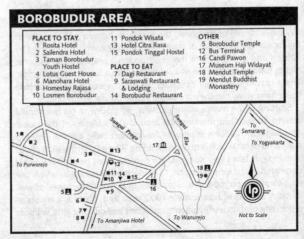

## BOROBUDUR AREA

**PLACE TO STAY**
1 Rosita Hotel
2 Sailendra Hotel
3 Taman Borobudur
 Youth Hostel
4 Lotus Guest House
6 Manohara Hotel
8 Homestay Rajasa
10 Losmen Borobudur

11 Pondok Wisata
13 Hotel Citra Rasa
15 Pondok Tinggal Hostel

**PLACE TO EAT**
7 Dagi Restaurant
9 Saraswati Restaurant
 & Lodging
14 Borobudur Restaurant

**OTHER**
5 Borobudur Temple
12 Bus Terminal
16 Candi Pawon
17 Museum Haji Widayat
18 Mendut Temple
19 Mendut Buddhist
 Monastery

To Semarang
To Yogyakarta
To Purworejo
To Amanjiwo Hotel
To Wanurejo

Sungai Progo
Sungai Elo

Not to Scale

**Top:** Photo by Bernard Napthine.

# Orientation & Information

The small village of Borobudur consists of warungs, souvenir stalls and a few hotels that face the monument. The bus terminal is less than 10 minutes' walk from the monument.

The temple site is open from 6 am to 5.15 pm daily. Admission is 10,000 rp, which includes entrance to the archaeological museum just north of the monument. To hire a guide costs 15,000 rp for one to 20 people. These guides are usually very knowledgable. An audio-visual show at the Manohara Hotel costs 4000 rp, and Borobudur has a few other attractions, including a children's playground and elephant rides.

Borobudur is Indonesia's single most popular tourist attraction and it can be crowded and noisy, especially on weekends. Hawkers outside and inside the archaeological park are becoming increasingly aggressive. The finest time to see Borobudur and capture something of the spirit of the place is at dawn or sunset, but you won't have the place to yourself. These are also popular times for the bus-loads of package tourists.

# Borobudur Temple

Borobudur is a broad, impassive monument, built in the form of a massive symmetrical stupa, literally wrapped around the hill. It stands solidly on its base of 118m x 118m. Six square terraces are topped by three circular ones, with four stairways leading up through finely carved gateways to the top. The paintwork is long gone, but it's thought that the grey stone of Borobudur was at one time washed with white or golden yellow to catch the sun. Viewed from the air, the whole thing looks like a giant three dimensional tantric mandala. In fact, it has been suggested that the Buddhist community that once supported Borobudur consisted of early Vajrayana or Tantric Buddhists who used it as a walk-through mandala.

The entire monument was conceived as a Buddhist vision of the cosmos in stone, starting in the everyday world and spiralling up to nirvana – eternal nothingness, the Buddhist 'heaven'. At the base of the monument is a series of reliefs representing a world dominated by passion and desire, where the good undergo reincarnation as some higher form of life and the evil are destined to a lowlier reincarnation. These carvings and their carnal scenes are covered by stone to hide them from view, but they are partly visible on the south side.

Starting at the main eastern gateway, go clockwise (as one should around all Buddhist monuments) around the galleries of the stupa. Although Borobudur is impressive for its sheer bulk, it is the close-up sculptural detail which is quite astounding. The pilgrim's walk is about 5km long. It takes you along narrow corridors past nearly 1460 richly decorated narrative panels and 1212 decorative panels in which the sculptors have carved a virtual textbook of Buddhist doctrines, as well as many aspects of Javanese life 1000 years ago. There is a continual procession of ships and elephants, musicians and dancing girls, warriors

# BOROBUDUR

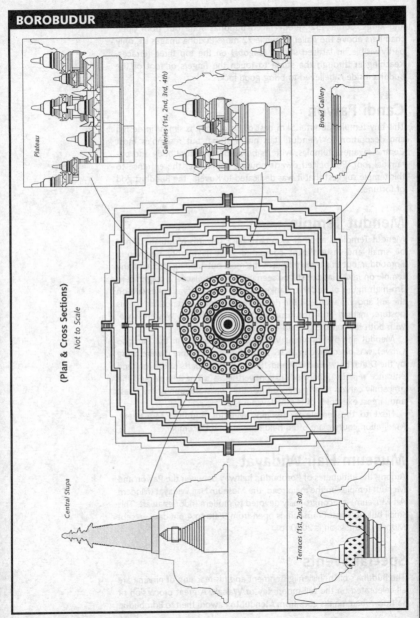

Plateau

Galleries (1st, 2nd, 3rd, 4th)

Broad Gallery

(Plan & Cross Sections)
Not to Scale

Central Stupa

Terraces (1st, 2nd, 3rd)

and kings. Some 432 serene-faced Buddhas stare out from open chambers above the galleries, while 72 more Buddha images sit, only partly visible, in latticed stupas *(dagobs)* on the top three terraces. Reaching in through the stupa to touch the fingers or foot of the Buddha inside is believed to bring good luck.

## Candi Pawon

This tiny temple, about 1.5km east of Borobudur, is similar in design and decoration to Mendut. It is not a stupa, but resembles most Central Javanese temples, with its broad base, central body and pyramidal roof. Pot-bellied dwarfs pouring riches over the entrance to this temple suggest that it was dedicated to Kuvera, the Buddhist god of fortune.

## Mendut Temple

Mendut Temple is another 2km east, back towards Muntilan. It may be small and insignificant compared with its mighty neighbour, Borobudur, but this temple houses the most outstanding statue of any temple on Java that can still be seen in its proper place – a magnificent 3m-high figure of Buddha, flanked by the Bodhisattvas Lokesvara on the left and Vairapana on the right. The Buddha is also notable for his posture: instead of in the usual lotus position, he sits western-style, with both feet on the ground.

Mendut Temple, or Venu Vana Mandira (Temple in the Bamboo Grove), was discovered in 1836, and attempts to restore it were made by the Dutch between 1897 and 1904. Although parts of the roof and entrance remain unfinished, it is nevertheless a fine temple and the gracefully carved relief panels on its outer walls are among the finest and largest examples of Hindu-Javanese art.

Next to the temple is the new Mendut Buddhist Monastery. Meditation courses are often held here around December.

## Museum Haji Widayat

Among the antiquities of Borobudur, halfway between the Pawon and Mendut temples on the main road, the Museum Haji Widayat (Modern Art Museum) is incongruously devoted to modern Indonesian art. This small but significant museum is open from 9 am to 4 pm daily, except Monday. Admission is 2000 rp.

## Special Events

The Buddha's birth, his enlightenment and his reaching of nirvana are all celebrated on the full-moon day of Waisak. A great procession of saffron-robed monks goes from Mendut to Pawon, then to Borobudur,

**DUR**

where candles are lit and flowers strewn about, followed by praying and chanting. This holiest of Buddhist events attracts thousands of pilgrims. Waisak usually falls in May.

Around June, the Festival of Borobudur kicks off with a *Ramayana*-style dance, with a cast of over 300, but based on an episode of the Buddhist Manohara. Folk-dancing competitions, handcrafts, white-water rafting and other activities add to the carnival atmosphere.

## Places to Stay & Eat

The area code for Borobudur is ☎ 0293.

The popular **Lotus Guest House** (☎ *88281, Jl Medang Kamulan 2)*, on the east side of the temple near the main parking area, is the place to head for. Rooms with mandi cost 20,000 to 35,000 rp, including breakfast and free tea and coffee throughout the day. This welcoming, well run losmen has a good cafe, and information on things to do in

**Right:** View from atop the Temples of Borobudur.

BERNARD NAPTHINE

the area. It rents bicycles for countryside touring and organises white-water rafting trips.

Other cheap options on the south side directly opposite the temple are the basic *Losmen Borobudur*, with rooms for 15,000 to 20,000 rp, and the equally simple *Pondok Wisata* (☎ 88362), with rooms from 10,000 to 15,000 rp.

One kilometre from Borobudur, the flash *Pondok Tinggal Hostel* (☎ 88245) has bamboo-style rooms around an attractive garden. A bed in the spotless, often empty, dorms costs 7500 rp. Comfortable, well appointed rooms with attached bathroom cost 33,000 rp, or larger rooms with sitting rooms cost from 44,000 to 125,000 rp. Add 15% to all rates. The hostel also has a good restaurant.

The *Manohara Hotel* (☎ 88131) has an unbeatable position within the monument grounds. Pleasant air-con rooms, most with porches facing the monument, have private bath, hot water and TV for US$47 and US$50, but expect large discounts. Breakfast and unlimited entry to Borobudur are included. It also runs the *Taman Borobudur Youth Hostel*, which is primarily for groups.

A number of other hotels are scattered around the village. The most pleasant is the new *Homestay Rajasa* (☎ 88276, Jl Badrawati 2), which has a small restaurant. Attractive, if slightly expensive, rooms overlook the rice paddies and cost 60,000 rp with fan, or 100,000 rp with air-con.

Last but by no means least, the *Amanjiwa* (☎ 88333) rivals Borobudur in architectural extravagance. Lying at the foothills of the Menoreh Hills, 3km south of Borobudur, it overlooks the monument and mimics its style with extensive use of stone. Exclusive suites, many with their own pool, cost US$665 to US$2260, making it Java's most expensive hotel.

In addition to the hotel restaurants, dining options include the pleasant *Borobudur Restaurant* and the more expensive *Dagi Restaurant* near the Manohara Hotel. The *Saraswati Restaurant* has good food, reasonable prices and the elderly woman who runs it is a gracious and educated host. New hotel rooms are also being built here.

# Getting There & Away

From Yogya's Umbulharjo bus terminal, direct buses go to Borobudur (2000 rp; 1½ hours) via Muntilan. These buses skirt the central city but can also be caught at Jombor, about 4km north of Yogya on Jl Magelang, near the northern ring road. Bus No 5 runs from Jombor to the city centre.

From Borobudur terminal, buses also go to Muntilan (500 rp), Magelang (1000 rp) and Purworejo.

In Borobudur, the hotels are within walking distance of the bus terminal, or a becak will cost no more than 1000 rp anywhere in the village. It's a fine walk to Mendut and Pawon; otherwise, a bus or bemo is 300 rp to hop from one temple to the next, or hire a becak.

Tours of Borobudur are easily arranged in Yogya, at the Prawirotaman or Sosrowijayan area agents, for as little as 25,000 rp per person.

*continued from page 264*

## MAGELANG
- **pop 122,000**

Magelang was once a Dutch military garrison, and it was here that the Javanese hero, Prince Diponegoro, was tricked into captivity in 1829. In the house where he was captured is a **museum** of Diponegoro memorabilia.

Magelang is 42km north of Yogya, on the main road to Semarang. Shortly before the town is **Gunung Tidar**, which legend credits as the 'nail of Java', a mountain planted there by the gods to stop Java from shaking.

## YOGYAKARTA
- **pop 425,000**     ☎ **0274**

Daerah Istimewa (Special District) Yogyakarta is the cultural heart of Java, lying between two of Java's most potent mystical symbols – explosive Gunung Merapi in the north and the Indonesian Ocean, home of the Queen of the South Seas, in the south. Yogyakarta, or Yogya (pronounced 'Jogja') for short, is the most active centre for Javanese arts, and spoken Javanese is at its most *halus* (refined) here. It is also an intellectual centre, crammed with prestigious universities and academies, and Yogya's influence and importance far outweigh its size.

Yogya has always strived to maintain its independence, clinging proudly to its traditions, and it is still headed by its sultan. The sultan's kraton remains the hub of traditional life. The district of Yogyakarta has a population of 3.2 million and an area of 3186 sq km, while the population of the city itself is under 500,000. No longer the city of bicycles, Yogya has noisy and chaotic traffic like any modern Javanese city, but just a short stroll behind the main streets are *kampungs* (neighbourhoods) where life is still unhurried. Despite its veneer of modernity and westernisation, Yogya clings strongly to its traditional values and maintains its traditional philosophies.

The city provides easy access for an insight into Javanese culture. Batik, silver, pottery, *wayang kulit* (shadow-puppetry) and other craft industries are easy to visit, traditional

### Prince Diponegoro

Prince Diponegoro of the Yogyakarta royal house was the charismatic leader of a bloody guerrilla war against the Dutch from 1825 to 1830. Diponegoro was treacherously lured to discuss peace terms with the Dutch at Magellan, then arrested. He was exiled to Sulawesi, where he died in 1856.

performing arts can readily be seen and the contemporary arts are also flourishing. Yogya is also a good base to explore numerous nearby attractions, including Indonesia's most important and awe-inspiring archaeological sites, Borobudur and Prambanan.

Yogya is Java's No 1 tourist centre and Indonesia's most popular city for visitors. It's easy to see why. Apart from its many attractions, Yogya is friendly and easy-going, with an excellent range of economical hotels and restaurants.

### History

Yogyakarta owes its foundation to Prince Mangkubumi who, in 1755, after a land dispute with his brother, the *susuhunan*

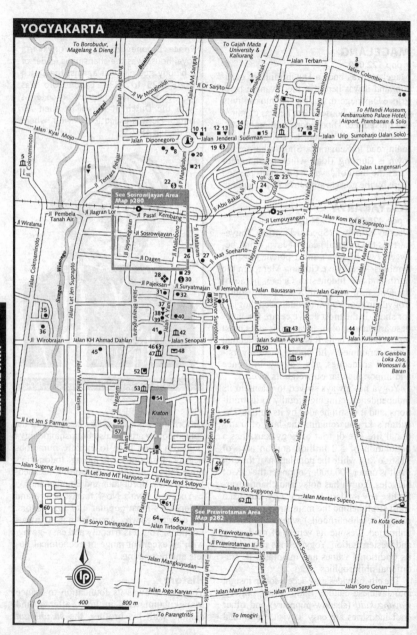

YOGYAKARTA

## YOGYAKARTA

**PLACES TO STAY**
2  Indraloka Home Stay
11  Phoenix Heritage Hotel
12  Hotel Santika
15  Java Palace Hotel
17  Novotel Hotel
21  New Batik Palace Hotel
26  Hotel Ibis
29  Mutiara Hotel
33  Melia Purosani Hotel

**PLACES TO EAT**
1  Pujayo
6  Pesta Perak
10  Pizza Hut
13  Rumah Makan Tio Ciu
37  Cherry Cafe
38  Griya Dahar Timur;
    Cirebon Restaurant
64  Kedai Kebun
65  Dutch Cafe

**OTHER**
3  ISI Dance Faculty
4  RRI Auditorium

5  Museum Sasana Wiratama
   (Monumen Diponegoro)
7  Merpati
8  Minibus Agents
9  Tugu Monument
14  Colt/Bus Terminal to
    Kaliurang & Prambanan
16  Army Museum
18  Galeria Shopping Mall
19  Bank Exim
20  Garuda Office
22  BCA Bank
23  Telkom Office
24  Public Swimming Pool
25  Lempuyangan Train Station
27  Bouraq
28  Matahari Department Store
30  Tourist Information Office
31  Toko Ramai Department Store
32  Terang Bulan Batik Shop
34  Mandala
35  Amri Yahya's Gallery
36  ISI (Fine Arts Faculty)
39  Mirota Batik
40  Pasar Beringharjo Market

41  Gedung Negara
    (Governor's Building)
42  Benteng Vredeburg
43  Pakualaman Kraton
44  Batik Research Centre
45  Nitour
46  BNI Bank
47  Sono-Budoyo Museum
48  Main Post Office
49  Vihara Buddha Prabha
50  Museum Biologi
51  Sasmitaluka Jenderal Sudirman
52  Mesjid Besar
53  Museum Kareta Kraton
54  Kraton Entrance
55  Pasar Ngasem (Bird Market)
56  Purawisata Theatre
57  Taman Sari (Water Palace)
58  Sasono Hinggil
59  Dalem Pujokusuman Theatre
60  Agastya Art Institute
61  Swasthigita Wayang Kulit
    Workshop
62  Museum Perjuangan
63  Umbulharjo Bus Terminal

(king) of Surakarta, returned to the former seat of Mataram and built the kraton of Yogyakarta. He took the title of sultan and adopted the name of Hamengkubuwono, literally 'the universe on the lap of the king', which all his successors have used. He created the most powerful Javanese state since the 17th century. His son was less competent, however, and during the period of British rule the Yogya kraton was sacked, Hamengkubuwono II exiled and the smaller Paku Alam principality created within the sultanate.

For the Javanese, Yogya has always been a symbol of resistance to colonial rule. The heart of Prince Diponegoro's Java War (1825-30) was in the Yogya area. More recently, Yogya was again the centre of revolutionary forces and became the capital of the Republic from 1946 until independence was achieved in 1949. As the Dutch took control of other Javanese cities, part of the kraton was turned over to the new Gajah Mada University, which opened in 1946. Thus, as one of the sultan's advisers observed, in Yogya 'the Revolution could not

possibly smash the palace doors, because they were already wide open'.

When the Dutch occupied Yogya in 1948, the patriotic sultan locked himself in the kraton, which became the major link between the city and the guerillas who retreated to the countryside. The Dutch did not dare move against the sultan for fear of arousing the anger of millions of Javanese who looked upon him almost as a god. The sultan let rebels use the palace as their headquarters, and as a result of this support and the influence of the sultan, come independence Yogya was granted the status of a special territory. Yogya is now a self-governing district answerable directly to Jakarta and not to the governor of Central Java.

Under Soeharto's government, the immensely popular Sultan Hamengkubuwono IX was Indonesia's vice-president until he stepped down in March 1978. The sultan passed away in October 1988, and in March 1989 Prince Bangkubumi, the eldest of 16 sons, was installed as Sultan Hamengkubuwono X. The coronation involved great

CENTRAL JAVA

pomp and ceremony, and included a procession of dwarfs and albinos.

Leading up to the overthrow of Soeharto, Hamengkubuwono X was an outspoken supporter of reform, and when Jakarta attempted to appoint an outsider as governor in 1998, the people took to the streets demanding that the sultan become governor, forcing Jakarta to bow to popular pressure.

## Orientation

It is easy to find your way around Yogya. Jl Malioboro, named after the Duke of Marlborough, is the main road and runs straight down from the train station to the kraton at the far end, changing its name several times. The tourist office and many souvenir shops and stalls are along this street, and most of the cheap accommodation places are just off it in the enclave near the train line.

The old, walled kraton is the centre of the intriguing area of old Yogya, where you will also find Taman Sari, Pasar Ngasem (Bird Market) and numerous batik galleries. A second mid-range hotel enclave is south of the Kraton area around Jl Prawirotaman.

## Information

**Tourist Offices** The Tourist Information Office (☎ 566000), Jl Malioboro 16, is open from 8 am to 8 pm daily, except Sunday. It has useful maps of the city, produces a number of publications (including a calendar of events) and can answer most queries. Tourist office counters are also at the airport and on the eastern side of Tugu train station, facing Jl Pasar Kembang.

**Money** Yogya has plenty of banks and moneychangers for changing cash. Banks usually give better exchange rates, but moneychanger rates for US$ cash can be comparable.

The BNI bank, at Jl Trikora 1 opposite the main post office, is efficient and has reasonable rates for most currencies. The BCA bank, just north of the train station on Jl Mangkubumi, is also worth trying. Both have ATMs that accept Visa and MasterCard. Banks are open Monday to Friday only.

PT Baruman Abadi, at the front of the Natour Garuda Hotel, Jl Malioboro 60, is one moneychanger that gives excellent rates, often better than the banks. It is open from 7 am to 4 pm Monday to Friday, and to 3 pm Saturday. Plenty of other moneychangers can be found in the tourist areas and though the rates are lower than elsewhere, they are open long hours. Opposite the train station, PT Haji La Tunrung, at Jl Pasar Kembang 17, has so-so rates but is open until 9.30 pm daily.

The agent for American Express is Pacto (☎ 566328), in the Natour Garuda Hotel. It has another branch at the Raddisson Hotel, on Jl Gejayan.

**Post & Communications** The main post office, on Jl Senopati at the southern continuation of Jl Malioboro, is open from 8 am to 10 pm daily. For parcel post, go during business hours to the building next to the main office.

The Warposnet at the post office is open from 8 am to 9 pm Monday to Saturday and from 9 am to 8 pm Sunday for Internet services (1500 rp for 15 minutes).

You'll find Internet cafes all over town. In the Sosrowijayan area, Whizz Kids and CMC are on Gang I, and Warnet is on Gang II. The going rate is around 2000 rp for 10 minutes.

In the Prawiirotaman area, on Jl Prawirotaman, is Protech 8; the slightly more expensive Metro Internet is in the Metro Guesthouse on Jl Prawirotaman II. The Pujayo restaurant to the north of the city has the cheapest Internet cafe at 1500 rp for 15 minutes.

For international calls, convenient *wartels* are those behind the post office at Jl Trikora 2 and opposite the train station at Jl Pasar Kembang 29. The Telkom office, 1km east of Jl Malioboro on Jl Yos Sudarso, is open 24 hours and has Home Country Direct phones. Home Country Direct phones can also be found in the lobby of the Natour Garuda Hotel (also chip card phones) on Jl Malioboro and at the Putri Restaurant on Jl Prawirotaman.

**Language Courses** Realia (☎ 564969), Pandega Marta V/6, Pogung Utara, is highly regarded but expensive, and there are plenty of other language schools. Even one-day courses are arranged for travellers – try the Via Via Cafe on Jl Prawirotaman.

**Dangers & Annoyances** Yogyakarta has its fair share of thieves – of the break-into-your-room, snatch-your-bag, steal-your-bicycle-and-pick-your-pocket varieties. You should be particularly wary when catching buses to Borobudur and Prambanan. Bag snatchings by motorcycle riders have also been reported.

Yogya is crawling with batik salespeople who'll strike up a conversation on Jl Malioboro or follow you around Taman Sari, pretending to be guides or simply instant friends. Inevitably you'll end up at a gallery where you'll get the hard sell, and they'll rake in a big commission if you buy. A time-honoured ploy is the special batik exhibition that is being shipped to South-East Asia and this is your last chance to buy – at maybe 50 times the real price. Variations on a theme are the special student or *koperasi* (co-operative) exhibitions. Get rid of anyone who leads or follows you to shops, and be wary of anyone who strikes up a conversation on the street.

You soon get tired of the 'hello, excuse me, where are you from, where are you staying' of the batik peddlers, but the constant, hopeful cries of the *becak* (trishaw) drivers are even more wearisome. They're just trying to drum up business and make a living, but many are also batik peddlers. Their 'special rates' of 500 or 1000 rp for one hour are just another way of getting you into a batik gallery.

## Kraton

In the heart of the old city, the huge palace of the sultans of Yogya is effectively the centre of a small walled-city within a city. Over 25,000 people live within the greater kraton compound, which contains its own market, shops, batik and silver cottage industries, schools and mosques.

The buildings of the innermost group, where the current sultan still lives, were built between 1755 and 1756, although extensions were made over almost 40 years during the long reign of Hamengkubuwono I. European-style touches to the interior were added much later by the sultans of the 1920s, but structurally this is one of the finest examples of Javanese palace architecture, providing a series of luxurious halls and spacious courtyards and pavilions. The sense of tradition holds strong in Yogya, and the palace is attended by very dignified and elderly retainers who still wear traditional Javanese dress.

The centre of the kraton is the reception hall known as **Bangsal Kencana**, or Golden Pavilion, with its intricately decorated roof and great columns of carved teak. A large part of the kraton is used as a museum and holds an extensive collection, including gifts from European monarchs and gilt copies of the sacred *pusaka* (the heirlooms of the royal family), gamelan instruments, and a huge, bottle-shaped wooden alarm gong. One of the most interesting rooms contains the royal family tree, old photographs of grand mass weddings and portraits of the former sultans of Yogya. Another section houses the Royal Doulton, glassware and beer urns.

An entire **museum** within the kraton is dedicated to Sultan Hamengkubuwono IX, with photographs and personal effects of the great man. Other points of interest within the kraton palace include the small European bandstand at the entrance, with stained-glass images of musical instruments. In another part of the kraton are 'male' and 'female' entrances indicated by giant-sized 'he' and 'she' dragons, although they look pretty much alike. Outside the kraton, in the centre of the northern square, are two sacred *waringin* (banyan trees) where, in the days of feudal Java, white-robed petitioners would patiently sit, hoping to catch the eye of the king. In the *alun alun kidul* (southern square), two similar banyan trees are said to bring great fortune if you can walk between them blindfolded, without mishap.

The kraton is open from 8 am to 2 pm daily, except Friday, when it closes at 1 pm. It is closed on national holidays and for special kraton ceremonies, but don't trust the batik touts who will intercept you on the way to the kraton – they'll tell you it's closed just to lure you away to Taman Sari and a batik gallery.

The entrance is on the north-west side and easy to find if you are coming down Jl Malioboro, but more difficult if you are coming on foot from the south. Admission is 3000 rp (plus a 500 rp camera fee), which includes a guided tour. In the inner pavilion from 9 or 10 am to 11 am or noon, you can see *gamelan* on Monday and Tuesday, *wayang golek* on Wednesday, classical dance on Thursday and Sunday, wayang kulit on Saturday, and Javanese singing on Friday.

## Taman Sari (Water Castle)

Just west of the kraton is Taman Sari, or Fragrant Garden. Better known in Yogya as the Water Castle, this was once a splendid pleasure park of palaces, pools and waterways for the sultan and his entourage. The architect of this elaborate retreat, built between 1758 and 1765, was a Portuguese from Batavia, and the story goes that the sultan had him executed to keep his hidden pleasure rooms secret. They were damaged first by Diponegoro's Java War, and an earthquake in 1865 helped finish the job. Today, most of the Water Castle has tumbled down amid dusty alleys, small houses and batik galleries, but it's an interesting place of eerie ruins with underground passages and a large subterranean mosque.

The bathing pools have been restored, not terribly well perhaps, but it is possible to imagine life in the harem. Once surrounded by gardens, the sultan and ladies of the harem relaxed here, and from the tower overlooking the pools the sultan was able to dally with his wives and witness the goings-on below.

The entrance to the restored bathing pools are on Jl Taman, open daily from 9 am to 3 pm, and cost 1000 rp entry. Expect to be hassled by batik touts who will lure you away from the entrance before you even get there or pretend to be official guides and inspect your ticket. They will offer a free guided tour that will inevitably end at a batik gallery. Establish a price for a guided tour first or be prepared to put up with the hard sell at the end. Better still, shake them off. They can be informative, but even if you agree to pay them for a tour only, they'll still take you to a batik gallery.

After you have passed through the bathing pools, you come to another carved wall, the same as at the entrance. From here, head right past the batik gallery and take the alleys north through the kampung to the high broken walls at the edge of Pasar Ngasem. The underground mosque is a little off to the west at the base of the walls – ask for the *mesjid bawah tanah*. It is hard to find without a guide, but it doesn't matter – getting lost is half the fun in this interesting area dotted with ruins.

Alternatively, wander through from Pasar Ngasem to the old ruins and the underground mosque before proceeding to the bathing pools.

## Pasar Ngasem (Bird Market)

At the edge of Taman Sari, Pasar Ngasem is a colourful bird market crowded with hundreds of budgies, orioles, roosters and singing turtle-doves in ornamental cages. Pigeons are the big business here and Yogya residents are great pigeon fanciers – for training, not eating. Lizards and other small animals are also on sale, as are big trays of bird feed consisting of swarming maggots and ants. From the back of the bird market, an alleyway leads up to the broken walls of Taman Sari for fine views across Yogya.

## Pasar Beringharjo

Yogya's main market, on Jl A Yani (the continuation of Jl Malioboro), is lively and fascinating. The renovated front section has a wide range of batik, mostly cheap *cap*, but some good *tulis* work can be found if you know your stuff. The 2nd floor is dedicated to cheap clothes and shoes, and the top floor has a small Matahari department store and supermarket.

The most interesting area is the old section behind. Crammed with warungs and small stalls selling all manner of fruit and vegetables, this is still very much a traditional market. Check out the *rempah rempah* (spices) on the 1st floor. Essential cooking ingredients such as lemon grass, *laos* (a fragrant, ginger-like root) and smaller but related *puyang* are on sale. Other oddities include tentacle-like *protowali* used in cooking and *lerak*, black nuts used as a colour-fastener for washing batik. On the 3rd floor in the south-west corner, woven goods such as matting and baskets are on sale, and this is the place to pick up that conical Javanese farmer's hat you've always wanted to wear.

The market is open from 5 am to 4 pm daily. As the signs say – *awas copet* (beware of pickpockets).

## Other Palaces

The smaller **Pakualaman Kraton**, on Jl Sultan Agung, is also open to visitors and has a small museum, a *pendopo* (audience hall), which can hold a full gamelan orchestra, and a curious colonial house with fine cast-iron work. The kraton is open from 9.30 am to 1.30 pm Tuesday, Thursday and Sunday.

**Ambarrukmo Palace**, on the grounds of the Ambarrukmo Palace Hotel on Jl Solo, was built in the 1890s as a country house for Hamengkubuwono VII, and is another good example of Javanese palace architecture.

## Museums

On the north side of the main square in front of the kraton, **Sono-Budoyo Museum** is the pick of Yogya's museums. Though not particularly well maintained or labelled, it has a first-rate collection of Javanese arts, including wayang kulit puppets, *topeng* masks, *krises* (traditional daggers) and batik, and an outside courtyard which is packed with Hindu statuary. Artefacts from farther afield are also on display, including some superb Balinese carvings. It's open from 8 am to 1.30 pm Tuesday to Thursday, to 11.15 am Friday, and to noon Saturday and Sunday. Entry is 750 rp. Wayang kulit performances are held here every evening from 8 to 10 pm.

Between the kraton entrance and Sono-Budoyo Museum in the palace square, the **Museum Kareta Kraton** holds some opulent chariots of the sultans. It's open from 9 am to 1 pm daily, and admission is 500 rp.

Dating from 1765, **Benteng Vredeburg** is the old Dutch fort opposite the main post office at the southern continuation of Jl Malioboro. The restored fort now houses a museum with dioramas showing the history of the independence movement in Yogya. The fort architecture is worth a look, but the dioramas are mostly for Indonesian patriots. Opening hours are from 8.30 am to 1.30 pm Tuesday to Thursday, to 11 am Friday, and to noon Saturday and Sunday. Entry is 750 rp.

Until his death in 1990, Affandi, Indonesia's internationally best known artist, lived and worked in an unusual tree-house studio about 6km from the centre of town overlooking the river on Jl Solo. The **Affandi Museum** on the grounds exhibits his impressionist works, as well as paintings by his daughter Kartika and other artists. Affandi is buried in the backyard. The museum is open from 8 am to 3 pm daily.

**Sasmitaluka Jenderal Sudirman**, on Jl B Harun, is the memorial home of General Sudirman, commander of the revolutionary forces. Wasted by tuberculosis, Sudirman reputedly often led his forces from a litter. He died shortly after the siege of Yogya in 1948. The house is open every morning, except Monday.

The **Museum Sasana Wiratama**, also known as Monumen Diponegoro, honours the Indonesian hero, Prince Diponegoro, leader of the bloody but futile rebellion of 1825-30 against the Dutch. A motley collection of the prince's belongings and other exhibits are kept in this small museum built at the site of his former Yogya residence. There's still a hole in the wall which Diponegoro is supposed to have shattered with his bare fists so that he and his supporters could escape. The museum is open from 8 am to 1 pm daily.

The **Museum Biologi** at Jl Sultan Agung 22 has a collection of stuffed animals and plants from the whole archipelago. It is closed on Sunday. The **Museum Perjuangan**, in the southern part of the city on Jl Kol Sugiyono, has a small and rather poor collection of photographs documenting the Indonesian Revolution. The large **Army Museum** (Museum Dharma Wiratama), on the corner of Jl Jenderal Sudirman and Jl Cik Ditiro, displays more documents, home-made weapons, uniforms and medical equipment from the revolution years. Records also trace Soeharto's rise in the ranks of Yogya's Diponegoro Division. It is open from 8 am to 1 pm Monday to Thursday and until noon on weekends.

## Kota Gede

Kota Gede has been famous since the 1930s as the centre of Yogya's silver industry, but this quiet old town, now a suburb of Yogya, was the first capital of the Mataram kingdom founded by Panembahan Senopati in

**KOTA GEDE**

1582. Senopati is buried in the small, mossy graveyard of an old mosque near the town's central market. The sacred tomb is open from around 9 am to noon Sunday, Monday and Thursday, and from around 1 to 3 pm Friday. Visitors should wear conservative dress. On other days, there is little to see here but a murky mandi and a few goldfish.

The main street leading into town from the north (Jl Kemasan) is lined with busy silver workshops where you're free to wander around and watch the silversmiths at work. Most of the shops have similar stock, including hand-beaten bowls, boxes, fine filigree and modern jewellery. See under Shopping later in this section for information on Kota Gede's silversmiths.

Kota Gede is about 5km south-east of Jl Malioboro – take bus No 4 or 8. You can also take a becak, but andongs (about 2000 rp) are cheaper, more agreeable and more humane. Cycling is also pleasant on the back road and it is flat most of the way.

## Other Attractions

If you are bored in the evening, you can always head along to **Purawisata**, east of the kraton on Jl Brigjen Katamso. This amusement park is noted more for its dance performances, but there are also rides, fun-fair games and a Pasar Seni (Art Market) with a basic collection of souvenirs.

Yogya's **Gembira Loka Zoo** has its fair share of cramped cages but, on the whole, it is spacious and has some interesting exotica, such as Komodo dragons. It is open from 8 am to 6 pm daily, and entry is 2000 rp.

## Batik Courses

There are lots of batik courses and classes in Yogya. Plenty of places in Sosrowijayan (such as Lucy's, opposite New Superman's) and Prawirotaman (ask at the Via Via cafe) areas offer short courses (one or two days), and you get to make a batik T-shirt. High art it ain't, but the courses provide a good introduction for around 25,000 rp. Tiyos (Sutiyoso Wijanarko, ☎ 0274-512812), Sosrowijayan Wetan GT1/7A, has been recommended by readers.

Hadjir Digdodarmojo (☎ 377835) has been teaching batik for years and has three- and five-day courses, but they are expensive at US$25. His studio is on the left of the main entrance to Taman Sari at Taman Kp 3/177.

## Organised Tours
Yogya is the best place on Java to arrange tours. Tour agents can be found on Jl Prawirotaman, Jl Sosrowijayan, Jl Dagen and Jl Pasar Kembang – there are so many offering similar tours at competitive prices that it is difficult to recommend one in particular. The big national travel agents are also represented in Yogya – Pacto, Nitour, Natrabu etc – but prices are much higher.

Typical day tours and per person rates if you go through the budget operators are: Borobudur (25,000 rp), Dieng (35,000 rp), Prambanan (20,000 rp), Parangtritis and Kota Gede (30,000 rp), Gunung Merapi climb from Selo (50,000 rp), and Gedung Songo and Ambarawa (50,000 rp). Longer tours, such as to Gunung Bromo and on to Bali (100,000 rp, two days/one night) are also offered. Tours are often dependent on getting enough people to fill a minibus (usually a minimum of four), and prices will vary depending on whether air-con and snacks are provided. The prices usually don't include entrance fees, and many also stop at batik or silver galleries to earn extra commission for tour operators.

If you want to put together your own tour, operators also arrange cars with driver at some of the best rates on Java, if you bargain.

## Special Events
The three special Garebeg festivals held each year are Java's most colourful and grand processions. Palace guards and retainers in traditional court dress and large floats of flower-bedecked *gunungans* (mountains) of rice all make their way to the mosque, west of the kraton, to the sound of prayer and the inevitable gamelan music. These are ceremonies not to be missed if you're anywhere in the area at the time.

## Places to Stay – Budget
Yogya has hundreds of hotels and cheap guesthouses, which means that competition keeps the prices down. The Sosro area has the really cheap places and the most central location, while the Prawirotaman area, a couple of kilometres south of the kraton, has mostly mid-range places. Most of the big hotels are stretched out along Jl Solo.

Fierce competition among the many hotels means that discounts are often available, especially outside the peak July/August tourist season and public holidays.

**Sosrowijayan Area** Most of the cheap hotels are in the Sosrowijayan area, immediately south of the train line between Jl Pasar Kembang and Jl Sosrowijayan. Running between these two streets are the narrow alleyways of Gang Sosrowijayan I and II, with most of the cheap accommodation and popular eating places. More good places to stay are in other small *gangs* (alleys) in this area. Despite mass tourism, the gangs are quiet and still have a kampung feel to them. The area is central, and Jl Malioboro is a short stroll away.

Gang Sosrowijayan I has some very basic and very cheap places, but they are dingy and cater mostly to locals. *Losmen Beta* fits into this category, but they don't come much cheaper at 5000/8000 rp for singles/doubles. A bit farther along this gang is the *Losmen Superman*, behind the restaurant of the same name. Light, clean rooms with shared mandi are 8000 rp; the rooms with mandi for 10,000 rp are darker but have interesting rock-garden bathrooms. *New Superman's* has almost identical rooms a couple of doors from the restaurant.

Just off Gang I, *Losmen Lucy* has basic rooms with mandi for 15,000 rp. The *105 Homestay* (☎ 582896) is more appealing and has had a post-modern makeover. Bright rooms with bathroom and pastiche tiling are better than most and cost 15,000/20,000 rp.

On Gang Sosrowijayan II, the *Hotel Bagus* is a passable cheap place. Clean rooms with fan cost 7000/8500 rp. Farther south, the *Gandhi Losmen*, in its own garden, has very

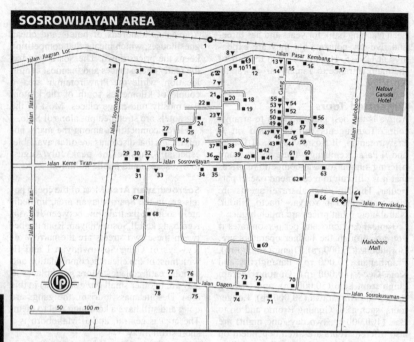

**SOSROWIJAYAN AREA**

basic rooms, but is friendly and cheap at 5000 rp per person. *Suprianto Inn*, down an alley by itself, has bright, well kept rooms with foam mattresses for 7500/10,000 rp.

There are a host of small losmen around Gang II and the small alleys off it, most of them in a similar rock-bottom price range. *Hotel Selekta* is popular and friendly. It's roomier and lighter than most. Rooms with mandi cost 15,000 rp, including breakfast. Nearby is the *Monica Hotel* (☎ 580598), a newer, more substantial hotel among the cheapies. Good rooms around a garden cost 25,000 rp. Of the other cheap losmen along this alley, the *Utar Pension* is more hotel-like, and rooms cost 12,500 rp. The *Lita Homestay* is a friendly place with light rooms for 9000 rp, or 12,500 rp with mandi.

Between Gang I and Gang II, the friendly *Dewi Homestay* (☎ 516014) has a pleasant garden and cafe, but the rooms with mandi

for 20,000 rp require bargaining. *Hotel Harum* (☎ 513043) has a better class of room for 22,000 rp, but is soulless.

*Hotel Indonesia* (☎ 587659, Jl Sosrowijayan 9) is popular and well run. This is more a regular hotel, with pleasant court-yard gardens, but the rooms and mattresses need an upgrade. Rooms with mandi cost 10,000 rp, 15,000 rp and 17,500 rp.

**Prawirotaman Area** This area has some cheaper places like the very friendly *Kelana Youth Hostel* (Vagabond, ☎ 371207, Jl Prawirotaman MG III/589). Dormitory beds cost 10,000 rp, and singles/doubles cost 12,500/20,000 rp with shared mandi. Student and HI card holders can get a small discount.

Jl Prawirotaman II has some cheaper options. The *Post Card Guest House*, run by the bigger Metro, has rooms from 15,000/

## SOSROWIJAYAN AREA

| PLACES TO STAY | | |
|---|---|---|
| 2 | Hotel Kota | |
| 3 | Berlian Palace | |
| 4 | Nusantara | |
| 5 | Hotel Mendut | |
| 9 | Batik Palace Hotel | |
| 10 | Hotel Asia-Afrika | |
| 12 | Hotel Ratna | |
| 15 | Kencana Hotel | |
| 16 | Trim Guest House | |
| 17 | Hotel Trim | |
| 18 | Supriyanto Inn | |
| 19 | Losmen Setia Kawan | |
| 20 | Hotel Bagus | |
| 22 | Losmen Setia | |
| 24 | Isty Losmen | |
| 25 | Utar Pension | |
| 26 | Dewi II | |
| 27 | Hotel Selekta | |
| 28 | Monica Hotel | |
| 29 | Yogya Inn | |
| 30 | Hotel Karunia | |
| 31 | Oryza Hotel | |
| 34 | Wisma Gambira | |
| 35 | Bakti Kasih | |
| 37 | Jaya Losmen & Heru Jaya | |
| 38 | Gandhi Losmen | |
| 39 | Losmen Atiep | |
| 40 | Dewi Homestay | |

| | | |
|---|---|---|
| 41 | Losmen Rama | |
| 42 | Losmen Happy Inn | |
| 43 | Hotel Jogja | |
| 47 | New Superman's Losmen | |
| 50 | Hotel Rejeki | |
| 51 | Losmen Sastrowihadi | |
| 52 | Sari Homestay | |
| 55 | Losmen Beta | |
| 56 | 105 Homestay | |
| 57 | Losmen Lucy | |
| 59 | Lima Losmen | |
| 60 | Hotel Aziatic | |
| 61 | Hotel Kartika | |
| 62 | Hotel Indonesia | |
| 63 | Marina Palace Hotel | |
| 66 | Hotel Cahaya Kasih | |
| 67 | Ella Homestay | |
| 68 | Hostel Yogya Backpackers | |
| 69 | Hotel Batik Yogyakarta II | |
| 70 | Wisma Perdada | |
| 71 | Sri Wibowo Hotel | |
| 72 | Lilik Guest House | |
| 73 | Blue Safir Hotel | |
| 74 | Peti Mas | |
| 75 | Kombokarno Hotel | |
| 76 | Wisma Nendra | |
| 77 | Puntodewo Guest House | |
| 78 | Hotel Kristina | |

| PLACES TO EAT | | |
|---|---|---|
| 7 | Cafe Sosro | |
| 8 | Mama's Warung | |
| 13 | Borobudur Bar & Restaurant | |
| 14 | Cheap Warungs | |
| 23 | Anna's Restaurant | |
| 32 | Bladok Restaurant & Losmen | |
| 33 | Caterina Restaurant | |
| 44 | Murni Restoran | |
| 45 | Bu Sis | |
| 46 | New Superman's Restaurant | |
| 53 | N & N | |
| 54 | Superman's Restaurant & Losmen | |
| 58 | Eko Restaurant | |
| 64 | Legian Restaurant | |

| OTHER | | |
|---|---|---|
| 1 | Tugu Train Station | |
| 6 | Wartel | |
| 11 | PT Haji La Tunrung Money-changer | |
| 21 | Warnet Internet | |
| 36 | Warpostal | |
| 48 | Whizz Kids Internet | |
| 49 | CMC Internet | |
| 65 | Ramayana Department Store | |

18,500 rp; or much better, quiet rooms with mandi for 22,000/27,500 rp.

Some of the mid-range accommodation on Jl Prawirotaman is only marginally more expensive. The *Guest House Makuta* or the *Muria Guest House* (☎ 387211) are cheaper options than these.

## Places to Stay – Mid-Range

**Sosrowijayan Area** Jl Pasar Kembang, opposite the train station, has a number of mid-range hotels.

The *Asia-Afrika* (☎ 566219, Jl Pasar Kembang 21) is a good place to start looking. It has a small pool, attractive garden cafe and good rooms with bathroom for 40,000 rp (fan), 60,000 rp (air-con) and 90,000 rp (TV and hot water).

The *Hotel Mendut* (☎ 563435) at No 49 is similar and also has a pool, but is expensive, with rooms from 90,000 rp to 200,000

rp, plus 21% tax and service. Expect discounts. The *Hotel Istana Batik* (☎ 589849, Jl Pasar Kembang 29) has a nice garden, a murky pool and rooms with hot water from 78,000/94,000 rp, before discount.

At the western end of Jl Pasar Kembang, the small, renovated *Hotel Kota* (☎ 515844, Jl Jlagran Lor 1) has oodles of colonial charm. Rooms have high ceilings, intricate and original tilework, air-con and hot water. A few tiny singles have cold water showers for 35,000 rp, but most have hot water for 63,000 rp. Substantial singles/doubles with all the trimmings are 87,500/122,500 rp, and 20% discounts were on offer when we were there. The rooms at the back are quieter and face courtyard sitting areas.

Jl Sosrowijayan also has some good mid-range hotels. *Oryza Hotel* (☎ 512495) at No 49 is an old villa with some style. Simple rooms with shared mandi cost 30,000 rp, and rooms with private bath (cold water) cost 43,000 rp or 53,000 rp with air-con.

At No 78, the very friendly *Hotel Karunia* (☎ 565057) is a cheaper alternative, straddling the budget and mid-range, with a rooftop restaurant. Fan rooms cost 16,500/20,000 rp, rooms with mandi cost 22,500/25,000 rp and air-con rooms are 40,000 rp, all plus 10% – a good deal.

*Bladok Losmen & Restaurant* (☎ 560 452, Jl Sosrowijayan 76) is one of the better mid-range buys in the Sosro area. It has a small pool, excellent restaurant and good rooms with nice touches that the others lack. Rooms with mandi are 35,000/38,000 rp; or rooms with European bathroom cost from 52,000/55,000 rp, up to 82,000/85,000 rp for the quite luxurious VIP rooms with air-con, TV and minibar.

Jl Dagen, one street farther south from Jl Sosrowijayan, is another mid-range enclave. The stylish *Peti Mas* (☎ 561938, Jl Dagen 37) has a pool, manicured gardens and an attractive restaurant. The air-con rooms around the garden for 107,500/122,500 and 130,000/145,000 rp are the ones to go for, while the cheaper rooms from 66,000/79,500 rp are dark and unappealing. Expect a discount.

*Hotel Batik Yogyakarta II* (☎ 561828) is an oasis in the quiet back alleys just north of Jl Dagen. Only a short stroll from Jl Malioboro, it has spacious grounds, a large pool and a restaurant. Plain rooms cost 104,000/124,000 rp, or attractive bungalows

are 128,000/152,000 rp to 168,000/196,000 rp. Bungalows have air-con, TV, hot water and a touch of kraton-style but are not luxurious, so expect a discount.

Nearby, the *Hotel Cahaya Kasih* (☎ 580 360, Sosromenduran GT I/280) is just 50m back from Malioboro down a quiet alley. This good, lower mid-range hotel has bright, tiled rooms for 44,000 rp with fan, or air-con rooms are 52,000 rp to 69,500 rp.

**Prawirotaman Area** This street, a couple of kilometres south of the city centre, is a more upmarket enclave than Sosrowijayan, but most hotels offer good value. Many of the hotels are converted old houses that are spacious, quiet and have central garden areas. Swimming pools are the norm. Prices can vary markedly between hotels of the same standard. After the rupiah crash, some hotels raised prices dramatically while others hardly changed. Negotiation is often possible.

The high-density *Airlangga Hotel* (☎ 378 044, Jl Prawirotaman 6-8) has a pool, restaurant and bands on Saturday night in the bar (avoid the rooms directly above). For a long time the best hotel on Prawirotaman, it is now looking a little frayed, but it is good value. Comfortable singles/doubles with air-con, TV and hot water are 50,000/60,000 rp; or lighter rooms upstairs are 60,000/70,000 rp, including breakfast.

At the lower end of this range, and without a pool, the small *Indraprastha Hotel*

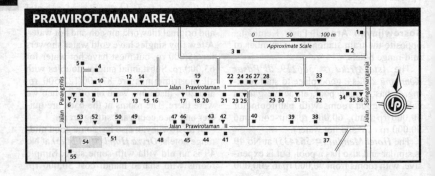

PRAWIROTAMAN AREA

(☎ 374087), down the alleyway opposite, has bright rooms with shower and toilet facing the garden for 30,000 rp.

Farther down the street, the very popular *Prambanan Guest House* (☎ 376167) at No 14 has a small pool, attractive garden, good service and the rooms have nice touches. It's a shame about the price. It's expensive at US$11/16 to US$16/21 for fan rooms and US$24/29 to US$32 for air-con rooms, even at 4000 rp to the dollar.

At No 26, the big *Hotel Duta* (☎ 372064) is one of the more luxurious places, and the garden and pool are very inviting. It is favoured by European tour groups, who can doubtless get bigger discounts than the 50% normally on offer. Before discount, rooms with outside mandi are a ridiculous 77,000/ 110,000 rp, rooms with bathroom start at 132,000/165,000 rp and the attractive rooms facing the garden are 242,000/ 275,000 rp to 385,000/440,000 rp.

The popular *Hotel Rose* (☎ 377991) at No 28 has a larger than normal pool and a restaurant next to it. It is good value, with prices lower than the others, but so are room standards. A few rooms cost 25,000/ 30,000 rp with shared mandi, but most have attached mandi starting at 30,000/ 40,000 rp (5000 rp extra with hot water) up to 60,000/70,000 rp for air-con and hot water.

A lot of the guesthouses in the old villas are pleasant enough, but the rooms can be dingy. *Sumaryo* (☎ 373507) at No 22 is one of the better ones. It has a pool and rooms from 25,000 rp up to 60,000 rp for a big air-con room. Others with pool in the same price range are the *Wisma Indah* (☎ 376021) at No 16 and the *Sriwijaya* (☎ 371870) at No 7.

Quiet *Hotel Kirana* (☎ 376600) at No 38 doesn't have a pool but is furnished with antiques and has colonial style. Rooms cost 40,000/55,000 rp with fan or 50,000/ 65,000 rp with air-con, less with discount. Rooms in the main building are a little faded but have the most character.

Around the corner from Jl Prawirotaman, the *Ayodya Hotel* (☎ 372475, Jl Sisingamangaraja 74) is a large, modern hotel with a big pool. Air-con rooms with hot water and TV cost 115,000/125,000 rp, or bigger rooms with mini-bar are 140,000/ 150,000 rp. If it were better maintained the rooms might be worth that; otherwise, expect a discount.

## PRAWIROTAMAN AREA

**PLACES TO STAY**

| | |
|---|---|
| 1 | Ayodya Hotel |
| 2 | Kelana Youth Hostel |
| 3 | Wisma Harto |
| 4 | Puri Pertiwi |
| 5 | Indraprastha Hotel |
| 8 | Wisma Gajah |
| 9 | Airlangga Hotel |
| 10 | Borobudur |
| 11 | Hotel Putra Jaya |
| 12 | Sriwijaya Hotel |
| 15 | Prambanan Guest House |
| 16 | Wisma Indah |
| 18 | Sumaryo |
| 21 | Hotel Duta |
| 23 | Hotel Rose |
| 24 | Mas Gun Guest House |
| 26 | Rumah Makan Asri |
| 28 | Perwita Sari Guest House |
| 29 | Wisma Parikesit |
| 30 | Prayogo Guest House |
| 32 | Galunggung Guest House |
| 34 | Hotel Kirana |
| 35 | Hotel Sartika |
| 37 | Post Card Guest House |
| 38 | Hotel Palupi |
| 39 | Wisma Kroto |
| 40 | Agung Guest House |
| 41 | Guest House Makuta |
| 43 | Metro Guest House |
| 44 | Metro Guest House |
| 46 | Sumaryo |
| 47 | Muria Guest House |
| 49 | Delta Homestay |
| 50 | Mercury Guest House |
| 55 | Sunarko Guest House |

**PLACES TO EAT**

| | |
|---|---|
| 6 | Tante Lies (Warung Java Timur) |
| 7 | Laba Laba Cafe |
| 13 | Palma Restaurant |
| 14 | Hanoman's Forest Restaurant |
| 17 | La Beng Beng Restaurant |
| 19 | Griya Bujana Restaurant |
| 22 | Putri Restaurant |
| 25 | Yuri |
| 27 | French Grill Restaurant |
| 31 | Via Via |
| 33 | Dalton Family Cafe |
| 36 | Going Bananas |
| 42 | Agni Restaurant |
| 45 | Lotus Breeze |
| 48 | Restaurant Java |
| 51 | Bamboo House Restaurant |
| 52 | Lotus Garden |
| 53 | Little Amsterdam |

**OTHER**

| | |
|---|---|
| 20 | Protech 8 Internet Cafe |
| 54 | Pasar Pagi (Morning Market) |

CENTRAL JAVA

The next street south is Jl Prawirotaman II (sometimes it's called Jl Gerilya and the numbering system is completely illogical), where Pasar Pagi (Morning Market) is located. This street is quieter than Jl Prawirotaman I, and the hotels are not as flash. The *Metro* (☎ 372364) at No 71 is the most popular, and has a garden area and an Internet cafe. The rooms range from 15,000/18,000 rp to 65,000/75,000 rp with air-con and hot water showers, but many are looking shabby. The best value are the mid-priced rooms in the annexe across the street, where you'll find the pool.

The *Agung Guest House* (☎ 375512) at No 68 has a tiny pool and is also popular for a cheaper room. It costs from 19,000/22,500 rp to 56,000/60,000 rp with air-con, less with negotiation. The attractive *Delta Homestay* (☎ 378092) at No 597A, another in the Duta chain, has a small pool and simple but good rooms for 27,500/44,000 rp up to 90,000/100,000 rp with air-con. Prices are after discount, but a further discount wouldn't go astray.

The *Mercury Guest House* (☎ 370846) at No 595 has kraton-style architecture and a wonderful dining area with antique furniture and floor cushions. The rooms are simple but very well kept, and cost 30,000/45,000 rp with hot water showers, before discount.

**Other Areas** The *Indraloka Home Stay* (☎ 564341, Jl Cik Ditiro 18) is north of the city centre near Gajah Mada University (Universitas Gajah Mada), so it is popular with overseas students and longer term visitors. Singles/doubles with air-con and hot water in this fine old colonial house are discounted as low as 50,000/60,000 rp, which is very good value. Tours are organised, and a travel agent and wartel are attached.

## Places to Stay – Top End

Yogya has a glut of luxury hotels, and heavy discounting has always been the norm. US dollar rates are quoted in brochures but a request for the rupiah rates will readily bring big reductions. If you are arriving by air, the Indotel (☎ 512144) hotel booking desk at the airport usually has very good deals. Ask to see its discount list. It is the second booking desk (avoid the first) as you come out of arrivals. All of the following places to stay have swimming pools, and most include breakfast, tax and service in the price.

The *Natour Garuda Hotel* (☎ 566353, Jl Malioboro 60), right in the action, was once a grand colonial edifice, Yogya's premier hotel in Dutch times. Numerous renovations over the years have seen it lose most of its colonial grace and the rooms are now run-down. Singles/doubles are 250,000/270,000 rp and suites start at 375,000/425,000 rp.

Right behind and connected to the Malioboro Mall, the new *Hotel Ibis* (☎ 516 977, Jl Malioboro 52-58) is very convenient. Small rooms with shower are discounted as low as 165,000 rp, plus 21%, though you might be told that these are full or only for Indonesian residents, in which case the bigger rooms with bath are 312,000 rp.

Just to the east of Jl Malioboro is the huge, Spanish-owned *Melia Purosani Hotel* (☎ 589521, Jl Suryotomo 31). The central location and superior facilities make this one of Yogya's most desirable hotels, but it is expensive at 423,500 rp (including breakfast).

Many of Yogya's big hotels are stretched out along the road to Solo. The road changes names many times but is usually referred to simply as 'Jalan Solo'. Close to Jl Mangkubumi and the centre of town, the *Hotel Phoenix* (☎ 566617, Jl Jenderal Sudirman 9-11) is a smaller hotel with some class. Rooms with private balconies cost around 200,000 rp – the price is negotiable.

Nearby and also central, the four star *Hotel Santika* (☎ 563036) is popular with business travellers and is noted for its good service. Rooms start at US$100 but discounts bring it down to 300,000 rp.

Farther east, the *Novotel Hotel* (☎ 580 929, Jl Jenderal Sudirman 89) is an excellent new hotel in a good position next to the Galeria shopping mall. Rooms are discounted to 240,000 rp and 301,000 rp.

Nearby, the *Radisson Plaza* (☎ *584222, Jl Gejayan*) is near the RRI Auditorium. Plush rooms start at US$110/120, discounted to 240,000 rp.

On Jl Solo about 5km from the centre of the city, the *Ambarrukmo Palace Hotel* (☎ *588488, Jl Adisucipto*) is a 1960s Soekarno-inspired construction and contains the old Ambarrukmo Palace on its grounds. For long the most prestigious hotel in Yogya, this government-run hotel is now looking tired, but discount rates of 160,000/180,000 rp make it a good buy.

Many other big hotels are on the way to the airport, including the five star *Hotel Aquila Prambanan* and the top of the range *Sheraton*. The new luxury *Hyatt Regency*, built in the style of Borobudur, is on Jl Palagan Pelajar on the northern outskirts of the city. All are a long way from the city centre.

## Places to Eat

**Sosrowijayan Area** This area is overrun with cheap eating houses featuring western breakfasts and meals, as well as Indonesian dishes. The food is distinguished by low prices.

A whole host of good warungs line Jl Pasar Kembang, beside the train line, but *Mama's* is No 1 in the evenings. At No 17, *Borobudur Bar & Restaurant* has average fare at high prices, but it has unlimited cold beer and bands after 9.30 pm.

Gang Sosrowijayan I is a favourite place for cheap eats. The famous *Superman's* is one of the original purveyors of banana pancakes and has been around for decades. The owner, Pak Suparman, re-spelt his name and adapted his food to conform with western sensibilities. Its offshoot, *New Superman's*, a bit farther down Gang I, is more popular, and has breakfasts for 5500 to 7000 rp, pizzas, steak, Indonesian and Chinese food. The 10% tax added to the bill gives the place pretensions it doesn't deserve. The no-frills *N & N* is popular for its low prices and, in a back lane off Gang I, *Eko Restaurant* has cheap steaks. The alcohol-free *Murni Restoran* serves tasty curries with flakey *parathas* and good iced juices. For the cheapest eats on Gang I, head to the little cluster of wall-hugging *warungs* at the train station end.

Gang II also has a few options. *Anna's* is popular for its low prices, while the *Cafe Sosro* has the best decor, and reasonable western and Indonesian food. The *Heru Jaya* at the Jaya Losmen has a big menu of cheap western, Indonesian and Chinese food. Its speciality 'French grills', such as steak and *frites*, are double the other items at around 10,000 rp, but pretty good. The beer is about the cheapest around.

Jl Sosrowijayan also has some good restaurants. *Chaterina* at No 41 has a varied menu, low prices and you can dine sitting on mats at the back. One of Sosro's best is *Bladok Restaurant*, opposite at No 76, a classy little place with predominantly European food.

**Jalan Malioboro** After 10 pm the souvenir vendors pack up and a *lesahan* area (where diners sit on straw mats) comes alive along the north end of Malioboro, staying open till early morning. Food stalls serve Yogya's specialities, such as *nasi gudeg* (rice with jackfruit in coconut milk) and *ayam goreng* (fried chicken). Young Indonesians sit around strumming guitars and playing chess into the wee hours. Dine cross-legged on mats and take in the nightlife.

Hidden away upstairs on the corner of Jl Malioboro and Jl Perwakilan, the *Legian Restaurant* has Indonesian, Chinese, French and Italian food served by Balinese waiters in a roof-garden setting. It's very classy and it does a great claypot *gudeg ayam* (chicken with jackfruit) and good Balinese specialities.

Malioboro Mall would not be complete without fast food, and *McDonald's* takes pride of place at the front of this monument to western-style consumerism. The mall has some reasonable cafes inside, including *Ciao* for pizzas, pasta, cappuccino and ice cream. It's also a popular gay pick-up spot. The top floor has a *food stall area*. Another good food-stall area is on the top floor of *Ramai shopping centre*, farther down Malioboro.

*Cherry Cafe*, upstairs at Jl A Yani 57, the southern extension of Jl Malioboro, is a good restaurant above the shopping mayhem on Jl Malioboro. It serves tasty western, Chinese and Indonesian dishes in the 7500 to 12,500 range (steaks 17,500 rp). The *opor ayam* (chicken in coconut milk) is particularly good.

*Griya Dahar Timur (Jl A Yani 57)* is a cheaper place which has Chinese, Indonesian and European dishes, more expensive steaks and some excellent iced juices. *Cirebon Restaurant (Jl A Yani 15)*, a few doors farther south, is an old-fashioned Chinese restaurant with good juices and vegetarian food.

**Prawirotaman Area** Prawirotaman I has the bulk of restaurants. Most have virtually identical menus, from *gado gado* to the snapper meurniere, and most are mediocre. 'Indonesian' dishes are usually a horrible travesty – tourist-oriented, without spices and such – but some restaurants offer half-decent attempts at western fare. Fortunately, there are some exceptions to the norm.

For Indonesian food, the long-running *Tante Lies* (Aunt Lies), at the Jl Parangtritis intersection, is the main budget recommendation. Sate, *nasi pecel*, *soto ayam* and other Central and East Javanese dishes are served at reasonable prices.

*Laba Laba Cafe (Jl Prawirotaman 2)* has a typically mixed menu of western, Indonesian and Chinese food, and though more expensive than most, the food is innovative. It stays open late and the bar attracts patrons until midnight. *Via Via (Jl Prawirotaman 24B)* is a very popular Belgian-run travellers cafe and meeting spot. As well as providing good food that includes a changing menu of Indonesian dishes, it organises a variety of activities from bicycle trips around Yogya to Indonesian cooking, language and batik courses.

*Hanoman's Forest Restaurant* has mediocre Indonesian and western cuisine, but classical Javanese dance, wayang golek or wayang kulit is performed most nights for a cover charge of 7500 rp.

Jl Tirtodipuran, the continuation of Jl Prawirotaman I, is home to the *Dutch Cafe* at 47A, which features good steaks, a few Dutch-inspired dishes and Indonesian fare. It has a bar with good music and draught beer, open until 1 pm. It's definitely the place for homesick Hollanders, with Drum, Heineken and Dutch books on sale.

Farther down the street, *Kedai Kebun* at No 3 is notable mostly for its beautiful garden setting, with an art gallery at the back.

**Other Areas** Good eats can be found to the north of the city out towards Gajah Mada University. *Pujayo (Jl Simanjuntak 73)* is Yogya's best food-stall restaurant. A dozen food vendors split over two floors serve an array of dishes and drinks at low prices in ultra-hygienic surroundings. Karaoke is upstairs, and downstairs is an Internet cafe.

The well known *Pesta Perak, (Jl Tentara Rakyat Mataram 8)*, about 1km west of Jalan Malioboro, has a delightful garden ambience and sometimes puts on gamelan music. Lunch and dinner buffets for 15,000 rp (plus 21%) feature a range of Javanese dishes, though the *krismon* (monetary crisis) seems to have been responsible for a proliferation of bland vegetable dishes. Still, it's good value. The *Pandan Perak* restaurant is a branch on the North Ring Rd, next to the Yogya Kembali monument, 3km north of the centre.

The famous Yogya fried chicken leaves the colonel's recipe for dead. Yogya chicken is boiled in the water of young coconuts and then deep fried – absolute heaven when done well. One of the most famous purveyors was Mbok Berek out on Jl Solo just before Prambanan, and in her wake a host of eateries have appeared nearby with similar names. *Nyonya Suharti (Jl Adisucipto 208)*, just past the Ambarrukmo Palace (to the east of Yogyakarta), has restaurants all over Java and is popular with tour groups.

Some of the big hotels put on good-value buffets. The *Novotel* has a Java Buffet on Sunday, with a wide selection for 43,000 rp, and the hotel has other changing buffets during the week.

## Entertainment

Yogya is by far the easiest place to see traditional Javanese performing arts, and performances of one sort or another are held every day of the week. Dance, wayang or gamelan are performed every morning at the kraton and are a good introduction to Javanese arts. Check with the tourist office for any special events.

Most famous of all performances is the spectacular *Ramayana* ballet held in the open air at Prambanan in the dry season. See under Prambanan later in this chapter for details.

Most performances follow a regular schedule, but with the downturn in tourism, some performance times have become less reliable. Check with the tourist office.

**Wayang Kulit** Leather-puppet performances can be seen at several places around Yogya on virtually every night of the week. Most of the centres offer shortened versions for tourists but at *Sasono Hinggil*, in the *alun alun selatan* (south square) of the kraton, marathon all-night performances are held every second Saturday from 9 pm to 5 am.

Abbreviated wayang kulit performances are held daily, except Saturday, at the *Agastya Art Institute*, Jl Gedong Kiwo MD III/237, where *dalangs* (storytellers) are trained. The two hour show (5000 rp) begins at 3 pm.

*Sono-Budoyo Museum*, near the kraton, also has popular two-hour performances every evening from 8 pm for 7500 rp. The first half hour or so involves the reading of the story in Javanese, so most tourists skip this and arrive later.

**Wayang Golek** Wooden-puppet plays are also performed frequently. *Nitour (Jl Dahlan 71)* has tourist-oriented shows at 11 am daily, except Sunday, for 12,500 rp. These are mostly for tour groups and can be easily skipped.

On Saturday there are wayang golek performances at the *Agastya Art Institute* from 3 to 5 pm.

**Dance** Most dance performances are based on the *Ramayana*, or are at least billed as 'Ramayana ballet' because of the famed performances at Prambanan. Tickets are readily on sale in Yogya and include transport to Prambanan (see under Prambanan for details). The Prambanan event is one of the must-see performances.

Dance performances at the *Purawisata theatre* (☎ 374089) in the amusement park on Jl Katamso are also excellent; they are performed nightly from 8 to 9.30 pm. The *Ramayana* story is performed in two parts on consecutive nights. Performances are outside at the *Gazebo Garden restaurant* and cost 30,000 rp; dinner will cost an extra 18,000 rp.

One of the finest troupes used to perform at Ndalem Pujokusuman at Jl Katamso 45, but their program has been suspended. Hopefully it will start up again.

**Schools** The *Indonesia Institute of Arts* (ISI) Dance Faculty, on Jl Colombo in north Yogya, is open Monday to Saturday, and you may see dance practice. Bagong Kussudiarja, one of Indonesia's leading dance choreographers, has a school at Padepokan, 5km south of Yogya, where he runs courses for foreign students.

**Other Performances** *Ketoprak* (folk theatre) performances are held at the *RRI Auditorium*, on the corner of Jl Colombo and Jl Gejayan, from 8 pm to midnight on the first Saturday of every month.

Some of the big hotels, such as the Ambarrukmo Palace and the Garuda, have gamelan music in their lobbies during the day. Other hotels and restaurants have gamelan or wayang performances. On Jl Prawirotaman, *Hanoman's Forest Restaurant* has different wayang performances most nights of the week.

## Shopping

Yogya is a noted batik centre, but other craft industries in and around Yogya include silver, leather, pottery and wayang puppets. Even if you don't intend to buy, galleries and workshops are open free of charge for visitors to observe traditional Javanese craftspeople in action.

For serious shoppers, Yogya has a great array of crafts and antiques, primarily from Java, but bits and pieces from all over the archipelago can be found.

Jl Malioboro is one great long colourful bazaar of souvenir shops and stalls, and is a good place to start shopping. The street stalls offer a wide selection of cheap cotton clothes, leatherwork, batik bags, topeng masks and wayang golek puppets. They are the cheapest place to buy souvenirs, depending on your bargaining skills. Look in some of the fixed-price shops on Jl Malioboro to get an idea of prices. Mirota Batik, Jl A Yani 9, is a good place to start. It specialises in batik but also has a wide selection of handcrafts at reasonable prices. Malioboro's labyrinthine and newly renovated market, Pasar Beringharjo, is always worth a browse, especially for cheap batik and textiles.

The other major area to shop is Jl Tirtodipuran, the continuation of Jl Prawirotaman. Here you'll find a string of expensive batik factories, galleries and art shops. This is an interesting, more upmarket shopping stretch, with furniture, antiques, and a variety of crafts and curios from Java and farther afield.

Other less interesting shopping options include the Yogyakarta Craft Centre on Jl Adisucipto, opposite Ambarrukmo Palace, which has overpriced souvenirs. The Purawisata amusement park also has souvenirs and crafts. Taman Sari is infamous for its batik painting galleries, and a few other craft shops can be found on Jl Ngasem at the entrance to the Pasar Nasem bird market.

**Batik** Batik in the markets is cheaper than in the shops, but you need to be careful about quality and be prepared to bargain. A good place to start looking is the Terang Bulan shop, Jl A Yani 108 (just before the market as you head south on Jl Malioboro), which will give you an idea of what you should be paying. Other shops in town include Ramayana

Batik, Jl Ahmad Dahlan 21, specialising in Yogya-style batik, and the more expensive Batik Keris, a branch of the big Solo batik house on Jl A Yani 71. Many other reasonably priced shops are on Jl Malioboro/A Yani.

Most of the batik workshops and several large showrooms are along Jl Tirtodipuran, south of the kraton. Many, such as Batik Indah (Rara Jonggrang) at No 6A and Batik Winotosastro at No 54, give free guided tours of the batik process. These places cater to tour groups, so prices are very high – view the process and shop elsewhere.

**Batik Painting** In the 1960s some of Yogya's innovative painters began experimenting with batik techniques to express traditional and modern themes. Their paintings were uniquely Indonesian and attracted attention nationally and overseas.

In the 1970s the style gave rise to a host of imitators who turned out all sorts of generic rubbish to cash in on the tourist trade. Batik painting galleries sprung up all over Yogya, and gallery touts had a field day. Now, sadly, much of the interest in batik painting has faded and the new generation of Indonesian artists has abandoned batik in favour of oil and other media. The copycat galleries and the increasingly hungry touts remain, and given that the batik painting industry is Yogya's biggest blight, perhaps the best advice is to avoid it altogether.

That said, batik paintings can be attractive souvenirs, and small paintings (around 300mm x 300mm) can be as cheap as 20,000 rp (if you are taken to a gallery by a prattling Malioboro tout, the asking price might be 200,000 rp). Most of the mass-production galleries are found around Taman Sari. It pays to shop around for something unique, and always bargain hard.

A few artists who pioneered and grew famous from batik painting still produce some batik works. Amri Yahya's gallery (open daily, except Monday) at Jl Gampingan 67 has a few early batik works on display, though he mostly produces abstract oil paintings these days.

Business as usual in a market in Yogyakarta.

Becak driver waiting outside Beringharjo Market, Yogyakarta.

The human face of Yogyakarta, the cultural heart of Java and proud of its tradition of independence.

**Antiques, Curios & Furniture** While a few antiques can be found, they are best left to collectors who know their stuff. Yogya art shops spend an inordinate amount of time defacing wayang golek puppets and topeng masks in the name of antiquity, and many other items get similar treatment.

Along Jl Tirtodipuran, you can buy artefacts from all over Java and Indonesia. Shops to try include Dieng at No 50, which has an interesting collection with bits and pieces from all over Indonesia. Kasumba, next door, has a very tasteful and expensive gallery, while Borneo Boutique at No 49 specialises in textiles, particularly *ikat* from Nusa Tenggara. Prices are generally very high here – bargain furiously, or get an idea of quality and look around for somewhere else to shop.

Furniture, mostly modern copies of antiques, can be found on Jl Tirtodipuran and in the back lanes nearby. Mirota Moesson, around the corner at Jl Parangtritis 107, has a large and interesting collection of furniture. A number of smaller shops are on Jl Sisingamangaraja at the end of Jl Prawirotaman II. The larger places can arrange shipping, but prices are high.

**Silver** Silverwork can be found all over town, but the best area to shop is in the silver village of Kota Gede. Fine filigree work is a Yogya speciality, but many styles and designs are available. Kota Gede has some very attractive jewellery, boxes, bowls, cutlery and miniatures.

You can arrange a guided tour to see the silverwork process, with no obligation to buy, at the large factories, such as Tom's Silver, at Jl Ngeski Gondo 60, HS, at Jl Mandarokan I, and MD, at Jl Pesegah KG 8/44, down a small alley off the street. Tom's has an extensive selection and some superb large pieces, but prices are very high. HS is marginally cheaper, as is MD, but always ask for a substantial discount off the marked prices. Kota Gede has dozens of smaller silver shops on Jl Kemesan and Jl Mondorakan, where you can get some good buys if you bargain.

**Other Crafts** Yogya's leatherwork can be excellent value for money, and the quality is usually high, but always check the stitching etc. Shops and street stalls on Jl Malioboro are the best places to shop for leatherwork.

Good quality wayang puppets are made at the Mulyo Suhardjo workshop at Jl Taman Sari 37 and also sold at the Sono-Budoyo museum shop. Swasthigita, Ngadinegaran MJ 7/50, just north of Jl Tirtodipuran, is another wayang kulit puppet manufacturer.

Kasongan, the potters' village a few kilometres south-west of Yogya, produces an astonishing array of pottery, mostly large figurines and pots.

Along Jl Malioboro, *stempel* vendors create personalised stamps hand-carved on leather. Expect to pay 10,000 rp or less for a reasonably sized stamp with name, address and a simple design.

## Getting There & Away

**Air** Garuda (☎ 565835) in the Ambarrukmo Palace Hotel has direct flights to Jakarta (503,000 rp), Denpasar (470,000 rp) and Mataram (580,000 rp), with onward domestic and international connections. Merpati (☎ 514272), Jl Diponegoro 31, has one flight daily to Surabaya (269,000 rp). Mandala (☎ 564559), Jl Suryotomo 31, also flies to Jakarta, while Bouraq (☎ 562664), Jl Mataram 60, had, at the time of writing, cancelled all Yogya flights.

The big travel agents can sell domestic tickets at a small discount. Try one of the many agents in the Ambarrukmo Palace Hotel, such as Satriavi, or Pacto in the Hotel Garuda.

**Bus** Yogya's Umbulharjo bus terminal is 4km south-east of the city centre. From Jl Malioboro, take city bus No 4. Plans are afoot to move the terminal outside the city to the South Ring Rd, but it will most likely be years before this happens.

From Umbulharjo bus terminal, buses run all over Java and to Bali. Ordinary/air-con buses include Solo (2000/3500 rp, two hours), Magelang (2000 rp, 1½ hours), Semarang (4000/7000 rp, 3½ hours), Wonogiri

(3000 rp, 2½ hours), Purwokerto (6000/ 10,000 rp, 4½ hours), Bandung (16,500/ 25,000 rp, 10 hours), Jakarta (17,000/35,000 rp, 12 hours) via Purwokerto and Bogor, Surabaya (10,000/20,000 rp, eight hours), Probolinggo (17,000/32,000 rp, nine hours), and Denpasar (24,000/40,000 rp, 16 hours).

For long hauls, you are better off taking the big luxury buses. It is cheaper to buy tickets at the bus terminal, but it's less hassle to simply check fares and departures with ticket agents along Jl Mangkubumi, Jl Sosrowijayan near the Hotel Aziatic, or on Jl Prawirotaman. These agents can also arrange pick-up from your hotel. Typical fares are Denpasar (55,000 rp to 60,000 rp), Surabaya and Malang (30,000 rp), Bandung (35,000 rp), Bogor (40,000 rp), and Jakarta (45,000 rp to 55,000 rp). Check more than one agent – some charge excessive commission.

From the main bus terminal, local buses also operate regularly to all the towns in the immediate area: Borobudur (2000 rp, 1½ hours), Parangtritis (2500 rp, one hour) and Kaliurang (1000 rp, one hour). For Prambanan (1000 rp), take the yellow Pemuda bus. For Imogiri (500 rp, 40 minutes), take a colt or the Abadi bus No 5 to Panggang and tell the conductor to let you off at the *makams* (graves). Buses to Imogiri and Parangtritis can also be caught on Jl Sisingamangaraja at the end of Jl Prawirotaman.

Apart from the main bus terminal, colts operate to the outlying towns from various sub-stations. The most useful is the Terban colt station to the north of the city centre on Jl Simanjuntak. From here, colts go to Kaliurang (1500 rp) and Solo (3000 rp), passing the airport en route.

Buses, and colts in particular, to the tourist attractions around Yogya are renowned for overcharging. Know the correct fare before boarding and tender the right money, but expect to pay extra if you have luggage taking up passenger space.

**Minibus** Door-to-door minibuses run to all major cities from Yogya. Many companies are found on Jl Diponegoro, and the Sosrowijayan and Prawirotaman agents also

sell tickets. Most will pick up from hotels in Yogya, but not for the short runs like Solo (they will drop you off at your Solo hotel, however). They provide a good service, but some of the minibuses are ageing and may not have air-con.

On Jl Diponegoro, SAA (☎ 584976) at 9A has minibuses to Solo (7000 rp air-con, two hours) every hour between 7 am and 7 pm, Jakarta (45,000 rp, 14 hours) at 4.30 pm, Cilacap (12,500 rp, five hours) at 2.30 pm, Semarang (8000 rp, three hours) every two hours from 2 am to 6 pm, and to Purwokerto (12,500 rp).

Rahayu (☎ 561322) is another big agent at No 15, with frequent non-air-con minibuses to Solo, Wonosobo (8000 rp), Kudus (9000 rp), Pekalongan (11,000 rp) and numerous other destinations.

Madya (☎ 566306) at No 27 has air-con minibuses to Bali (60,000 rp) and Surabaya (30,000 rp). Rosalih Indah (☎ 541604), around the corner at Jl Mangkabumi 43, also has frequent minibuses to Surabaya and Malang (23,000 rp).

Two popular tourist shuttles operate from Yogya. Direct bus-ferry-bus tickets to Pangandaran cost 30,000 rp, and the less than wonderful Yogya Rental door-to-door service to Gunung Bromo costs 50,000 rp (see under Gunung Bromo in the East Java chapter for more details).

**Train** Yogya's Tugu train station (☎ 589 685), in the Sosrowijayan area, is conveniently central, and handles all the bisnis and eksekutif trains. Economy trains depart from and arrive at Lempuyangan station, 1km to the east.

The *Fajar Utama Yogya* day trains and *Senja Utama Yogya* night services to Jakarta (36,000/76,000 rp, bisnis/eksekutif, 8½ hours) originate in Yogya, with departures at 7 and 9 am, and 6 and 8 pm. Other express services to Jakarta come through from Solo or Surabaya. See the Getting There & Away section in the Jakarta chapter for more details of Jakarta-Yogya trains.

For Solo, the best option is the *Prambanan Ekspres* leaving at 7.25 and 10.30 am,

1.20 and 4 pm. It costs 3000 rp in bisnis class and takes just over an hour – the quickest and most convenient way to get to Solo.

To Surabaya, the *Sancaka* (25,000/40,000 rp, 4½ hours) at 3.25 pm is the pick of the trains and quicker than the buses. Numerous other night trains from Jakarta, such as the *Bima* and *Mutiara Selatan*, stop in Yogya on the way to Surabaya.

Three daily trains operate on the Yogya-Banjar-Bandung route. Most trains come through from Surabaya. The night expresses, such as the *Mutiara Selatan* (33,000 rp bisnis) and *Turangga* (45,000 rp bisnis, 75,000 rp eksekutif), provide the best services and take about 7½ hours.

From Lempuyangan, most ekonomi services are through night trains between Surabaya and Jakarta (14,000 rp, 11 hours) and Bandung (9000 rp, 10 hours). The *Purbaya* provides a reasonable ekonomi service to Surabaya (6000 rp, seven hours) leaving at 10.13 am, if you can get a seat. In the other direction it goes to Cilacap. The *Sri Tanjung* at 7.30 am goes to Surabaya, Probolinggo and Banyuwangi. The *Matarmaja* to Malang (14,000 rp, seven hours) departs at 11.55 pm.

## Getting Around

**To/From the Airport** Taxis from Yogya's Adisucipto airport, 10km to the east, cost 10,000 rp to the city centre. It's slightly cheaper when you go to the airport on the meter.

If you stroll out to the main road, only 200m from the airport, colts run to Yogya's Terban colt station (about 1.5km from Jl Sosrowijayan), or buses go to Umbulharjo bus terminal (about 1km from Prawirotaman) for 500 rp.

**Bus** Yogya's city buses *(bis kota)* operate on dozens of set routes around the city for a flat 500 rp fare. They work mostly straight routes – going out and then coming back the same way – and all start and end at Umbulharjo bus terminal.

Bus No 2 is one of the more useful services. It runs from the bus terminal and turns down Jl Sisingamangaraja, past Jl Prawirotaman, then loops around, coming back up Jl Parangtritis and on to Jl Mataram a block from Jl Malioboro, before continuing to the university and returning.

Bus No 4 runs down Jl Malioboro to Umbulharjo bus terminal. From the terminal, it goes on to Jl Ngeksigondo at Kota Gede – get off at Tom's Silver and walk 1km south to the centre of the village. Bus No 8 from the bus terminal runs through the centre of Kota Gede.

**Becak & Andong** Yogya is over-endowed with becaks, and it is impossible to go anywhere in the main tourist areas without being greeted by choruses of 'becak'. They cost around 500 rp a kilometre, but the minimum fare for tourists is usually 1000 rp and the asking rate is a lot more. The trip from Jl Prawirotaman to Jl Malioboro costs at least 2000 rp. Fares do vary – depending on the weather, whether it is uphill or downhill etc. Avoid becak drivers who offer cheap hourly rates, unless you want to do the rounds of all the batik galleries that offer commission. There are also horse-drawn andongs around town, costing about the same, or cheaper, than the becaks.

**Car & Motorcycle** Travel agents on Jl Sosrowijayan and Jl Prawirotaman rent cars with driver for trips in and around town at around 10,000 rp per hour, including petrol. They have lists of prices for longer destinations such as Solo, Borobudur and Dieng, but you can usually get a car or small minibus with driver for 100,000 rp per day or less. Work out exactly what is included in the price before you hire a car, and expect to bargain.

Bali Car Rental (☎ 587548), in front of Adisucipto airport, is a registered car rental agency for self-drive hire, but rates are very high at US$26 for a Suzuki Jimney. Travel agents will rent you a small minibus from 75,000 rp a day, but insurance is not in the deal.

Motorcycles can be hired for around 15,000 rp a day. An international licence is required by law, but no-one seems to bother.

**Taxi** Taxis in Yogya are metered, efficient and cost 1500 rp for the first kilometre, then 750 rp for each subsequent kilometre. Waiting time is 10,000 rp per hour and some taxis have a 3000 rp minimum.

**Bicycle** Yogya traffic is becoming increasingly heavy, but bicycle is still a viable way to explore the city. Pushbikes can be rented from hotels and agents for as little as 3000 rp a day. On Gang I in Sosrowijayan, try the shops at the southern end. Bicycle theft is a problem. Make sure your bike is always locked and look for bicycle *parkirs* who will look after your bike for a couple of hundred rupiah – you'll find them at the train station, the market and the post office.

## AROUND YOGYAKARTA
### Imogiri

Perched on a hilltop 20km south of Yogya, Imogiri was built by Sultan Agung in 1645 to serve as his own mausoleum. Imogiri has since been the burial ground for almost all his successors and for prominent members of the royal family, and it is still a holy place. The cemetery contains three major courtyards – in the central courtyard are the tombs of Sultan Agung and succeeding Mataram kings, to the left are the tombs of the susuhunans of Solo and to the right those of the sultans of Yogya. The tomb of Hamengkubuwono IX, the father of the present sultan, is one of the most visited graves.

The point of major interest for pilgrims is the **tomb of Sultan Agung**. The tomb is only open from 10 am to 1 pm Monday, and from 1.30 to 4 pm Friday and Sunday, and there is no objection to visitors joining the pilgrims during these times.

It's an impressive complex, reached by an equally impressive flight of 345 steps. From the top of the stairway a walkway circles the whole complex and leads to the real summit of the hill. Here you have a superb view over Yogya to Gunung Merapi.

Colts and buses from Yogya (500 rp) stop at the parking lot, from where it is about 500m to the base of the hill and the start of the steps. As at most pilgrimage sites, there will be various, insistent demands for 'donations'. The only compulsory entry charge is payable when you sign the visitors' book, inside the main compound at the top of the stairs.

To enter the tombs you must don full Javanese court dress, which can be hired for a small fee.

### Kasongan

This is Yogya's pottery centre. Dozens of workshops produce pots and some superb figurines, including 2m-high dragons and pony-sized horses. Kasongan pottery is sold painted or unpainted – very little glazing work is done.

**Getting There & Away** Catch a Bantul-bound bus and get off on the main road at the entrance to the village, 6.5km south of Yogya. It is then about a 1km walk to the centre of the village and most of the pottery workshops.

### Parangtritis
☎ 0274

Twenty-seven kilometres south of Yogya, Parangtritis has rough surf and a long sweep of shifting, black sand dunes backed by high, jagged cliffs. It's a place of superstition and, like so many places along the south coast, a centre for the worship of Nyai Loro Kidul, the 'Queen of the South Seas'. Legend has it that Senopati, the 16th century Mataram ruler, took her as his wife and thus established the strong tie between the goddess and the royal house of Mataram. Their sacred rendezvous spot is at **Parangkusumo**, 1km west down the beach, where the sultans of Yogya still send offerings every year at Labuhan to appease this consort of kings. Just beyond Parangkusumo are hot springs at **Parang Wedang**.

The crashing surf and undertows at Parangtritis are dangerous, and a sign in Indonesian proclaims that swimming is forbidden, but those who are experienced in surf conditions may want to enter the water. Just don't wear green – it's Nyai Loro

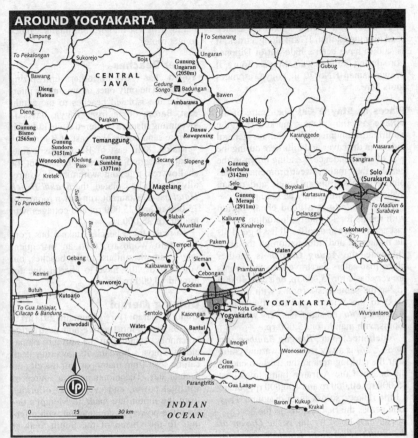

## AROUND YOGYAKARTA

Kidul's favourite colour. You can swim safely in freshwater pools *(pemandians)* at the base of the hill near the village, where spring water spills out through high bamboo pipes from the hilltop.

The beach promenade of straggling warungs and souvenir stalls is nothing to rave about, but you can go for long, lonely walks along the beach, or up into the sand dunes and the cliffs. This is a quiet, simple place for a break from Yogya during the week, when the hotels are empty. Avoid

weekends and holidays, when the beach is swamped by mobs from Yogya.

Trails along the hills above the sea to the east of Parangtritis lead to caves used for meditation. A couple of kilometres from town past the Queen of the South resort is **Gua Langse**, reached by narrow trails, rickety bamboo ladders and ropes down the cliff face to the cave opening. Branches of the cave extend deep into the hillside, where would-be mystics sit in contemplation, sometimes for days on end.

To the north-east of Parangtritis is another cave, **Gua Cerme** – 9km on a back road to Imogiri, then 1.7km along a track. It is said to have been a hide-out of Diponegoro during the Java wars. Moyasi Tours, Jl Prawirotaman I No 20 in Yogya, arranges tours here.

**Places to Stay & Eat** The centre of the village is the plaza, marked by the Sudirman monument. The famous general hid out in the caves and hills here during the war of independence. Leading down to the beach, the main street/promenade has plenty of basic cheap hotels and rumah makans. Bargaining may be required.

*Hotel Widodo* is a good cheap option with rooms for 15,000 rp, including breakfast and free tea and coffee. It has a good little restaurant and information on the area. Opposite, the *Agung Garden* is another place that caters for travellers, but rooms are very basic for 15,000 rp, or it asks 40,000 rp for the same basic rooms with air-con. Next to the Widodo towards the beach, *Wisma Lukita* (no sign), has very well kept rooms with mandi for 15,000 rp.

A definite step up, *Rangdo Bamboo Hut* (**☎** 367726) is away from the warung cram, near the parking area at the western end of the beach. Cute A-frame bungalows cost 45,000 rp, 60,000 rp and 100,000 rp, but are a little rickety, so ask for a discount. They look across the rice paddies to the beach.

The best hotel by far is the *Queen of the South* (*Puri Ratu Kidul*, **☎** 367196), perched on the clifftops high above town. It has excellent views, a fine pendopo-style restaurant and a swimming pool. Comfortable bungalows cost US$82 and US$90 plus 21%, but even with a 50% discount they are very expensive in rupiah terms.

**Getting There & Away** Buses for the one hour journey from Yogya's Umbulharjo bus terminal leave throughout the day. You can also catch a bus at the end of Jl Prawirotaman. The last bus back from Parangtritis leaves at around 5.30 pm. The cost is 2500 rp (including 1100 rp entry to Parangtritis), but the price is *very* variable. You can also reach Parangtritis via Imogiri, but this is a much longer route.

### Other Beaches

Yogya has several other uninspiring beaches. The only ones of any minor interest are the isolated beaches to the southeast. **Baron**, 60km from Yogya, has safe swimming inside a sheltered cove. **Kukup** is a white sand beach 1km east of Baron.

**Krakal**, 8km east of Baron, has a fine, usually deserted, white sand beach, but the shallow reef rules out swimming. If you really want to be isolated, the *Krakal Beach Hotel* has a restaurant, run-down rooms for 15,000 rp and 25,000 rp, and cottages with mandi for 35,000 rp.

To reach these beaches, take a bus from Yogya to Wonosari, then an infrequent *opelet* (small minibus) to the beaches, but you will usually have to charter one for around 10,000 rp.

### Gunung Merapi

Gunung Merapi (Fire Mountain, 2911m) is one of Java's most active and destructive volcanoes. Standing at the northern pinnacle of Yogya's borders, its towering peak can be seen from many parts of the city on a clear day. The mountain is a source of spiritual power, and every year offerings from the kraton are made to Merapi's destructive power, in conjunction with offerings to the Queen of the South Seas at Parangtritis.

Merapi has erupted numerous times, with at least four major eruptions and dozens of minor ones in the past century. Some have even theorised that a massive eruption of Merapi caused the sudden and mysterious evacuation of Borobudur and the collapse of the old Mataram kingdom in the 11th century.

Merapi's violent reputation was confirmed on 22 November 1994, when the volcano erupted, killing 69 people. Being so close to major population areas, the volcano is constantly monitored by posts all around the mountain, and advance warnings were issued. Nearby villages were evacuated, but a wedding party ignored the warning and its members were caught in the rain of ash. Many of the party were killed by deadly gases escaping through fissures on the flank of the mountain.

Merapi has been on the boil ever since. In June 1998, it spewed lava down its western flank, but though it damaged farm land, there were no casualties.

The hill resort town of Kaliurang, 25km north of Yogya, is the main access point for views of Merapi and makes a wonderful break from the city. Climbing to the top of Merapi is possible from the small village of Selo, on the other side of the mountain, but only if Merapi is quiet. Even in quieter times extreme caution is advised.

Merapi issues smoke and a regular stream of lava that flows away down the Sungai Boyong valley from the crater. Check the latest situation in Kaliurang, but with Merapi constantly threatening more eruptions, the climb to the peak from Kaliurang is off-limits. However, it is possible (and much easier) to walk partway up the mountain for unique views of Merapi's lava flows. See under Kaliurang for details.

Yogya travel agents also sell night trips for drive-in views of the lava flows from Pos Babatan, on the western side of the mountain. Take the road to Muntilan, then it is 5km up the mountain. Unless Merapi is in full force, it is unlikely you'll see the great streams of lava shown in tourist photos.

**Climbing Merapi** From Selo, it takes four hours to the top, so a 1.30 am start is necessary to reach the top for the dawn. After a 2km walk up through the village to Pos Merapi, the abandoned vulcanology post, the steady but steep climb begins. It is a tough, demanding walk, but manageable by anyone with a reasonable level of fitness.

The last stages are through loose volcanic scree, but guides may stop short of the top. Check with your guide if it is possible – or if he is willing – to go to the top before setting off. Climbs from Selo are not always well organised. Guides, at least the better

ones, will advise against the trip if it looks dangerous, but some will do anything for money. While they don't want to endanger lives, they may be prepared to take risks. Merapi is very unpredictable. There are two vents where lava can be seen, but it is not advisable to approach them, whatever your guide says. Even during quieter periods, Merapi can suddenly throw out a stream of lava.

## Kaliurang
☎ 0274

Kaliurang, 25km north of Yogya, is the nearest hill resort to the city, standing at 900m on the slopes of Gunung Merapi. Pick a clear, cloudless day during the week when it's quiet, and this is a great place to escape from the heat of the plains. There are good forest walks and superb views of the smoking, fire-spewing mountain.

Day-trippers can explore **Hutan Wisata Kaliurang**, the excellent forest park on the slopes of the mountain. Maps at the park entrance show where you are allowed go. Heed them and don't venture farther. In a sudden eruption, lava can flow down the mountain at 300km per hour. Currently you can walk 15 minutes to the Promojiwo viewpoint for great views of Merapi. Take the right-hand trail from the entrance. From the viewpoint, the trail leads on to the **Tlogo Muncar waterfall**, which is just a trickle in the dry season, then back to the entrance. The observatory at Pos Plawangan (1260m), the vulcanology post that monitors Merapi, is currently off-limits. The park is open from 8 am to 4 pm; entry is 450 rp.

Another good viewpoint of the mountain is at **Gardu Pandang**, just off the road on the western side of Kaliurang village. Kaliurang also has the **Museum Budaya Jawa** (Javanese Cultural Museum), attached to a compound owned by the Sultan, but entry is only for groups and must be arranged in advance (☎ 895161).

Kaliurang is a delightful place to spend a day or two, and Christian Awuy at Vogels Hostel arranges mountain walks to see the lava flows. Only registered rescue guides with radio contact can undertake the trek to the lava viewpoint. The five hour return trek starts at 3 am – to see the glowing lava at its best – and costs 15,000 rp per person. Overnight camping trips, village tours and birdwatching walks can also be arranged. A minimum of four is required for all trips.

**Places to Stay & Eat** *Vogels Hostel* (☎ 895208, Jl Astamulya 76), owned by Christian Awuy, has deservedly been the travellers' favourite for years. As well as being the local tourist information office, it also has a great travel library, with books on Indonesia and farther afield. There is a variety of rooms to suit most tastes and budgets, starting at 5000 rp in the dorm; doubles cost 10,000 rp, and good mid-range bungalows at the back with bath are only 20,000 rp. HI card holders get a small discount. The old part of the hostel, the former residence of a Yogya prince, has a good, very cheap restaurant. This is the place to arrange treks to Merapi and other good walks.

At the nearby, modern *Christian Hostel*, spotless rooms with mandi provide excellent accommodation for 25,000 rp (22,500 rp for HI members). The rooftop sitting area has views of Merapi and the lava flow.

Kaliurang has over 100 other places to stay. It is a downmarket resort with no star-classified hotels, but some of the guest-houses are pleasant, older-style places. The *Wisma Gadjah Mada* (☎ 895225, Jl Wreksa 447) is owned by the Universitas Gajah Mada. Built in 1919, the guesthouse has Indo-European architecture, with a Minang-kerbau roof atop a Dutch-style building. Two-bedroom villas with hot water cost 50,000 rp and 75,000 rp. The guesthouse is towards the top of the village, about 500m from the park entrance.

On Jl Astarengga, *Wisma Merapi Indah* (☎ 895224) is a three bedroom colonial villa costing 30,000 rp per room (with hot water), or you can rent the whole villa for about 80,000 rp (with negotiation). Other nearby options include the older-style *Wisma Wijaya Kusuma* and the newer *Satriafi*.

One kilometre south of Vogels, *Villa Taman Eden* (☎ 895442) is the most luxurious and has a swimming pool. Good rooms with TV and hot water are 75,000 rp, or a three bedroom villa with kitchen and huge, well appointed sitting room is 300,000 rp.

For meals, *Vogels Hostel* has a varied menu; the *Restaurant Joyo* is a bright, clean place with good Chinese and Indonesian food.

**Getting There & Away** From Yogya's Terban colt station, a colt to Kaliurang costs 1500 rp, or a bus from the main bus terminal costs 1000 rp. The last colt leaves Kaliurang at 4 pm, the last bus at 6 pm. Buses and colts pass through Pakem before Kaliurang. From Pakem, there are buses to Prambanan; for Borobudur take a bus from Pakem to Tempel, then another to Borobudur.

## Selo

On the northern slopes of volatile Gunung Merapi, 50km west of Solo, Selo is just a straggling village with limited amenities, but it has a few basic homestays where guides can be arranged for the climb up Merapi. The views of the mountain from the village are superb.

From Selo, it is a four hour trek to the volcano's summit. It is dangerous to attempt the hike around the side of the peak from Selo to see the crater. See the earlier Climbing Merapi section for more details.

**Places to Stay** Hospitable Pak Darto has been guiding trips to the top of the volcano for years, and runs a popular homestay known as *Pak Auto*. A misspelling in a French guidebook resulted in Pak Darto assuming the 'Auto' tag, which he did rather than confuse his customers. Accommodation is very basic but clean, and costs 9000 rp per person. Elderly Pak Darto rarely ventures far these days, but he can give good advice and arrange other guides. Prices are very variable, depending on the guide, your fitness, the number of people and the risk factor. Count on around 30,000 rp to 40,000 rp for two to three people.

The crumbling *Hotel Agung Merapi* is a little less basic and has a restaurant. Rooms cost 20,000 rp up to 39,000 rp with mandi. But standards are very poor for that price, so try bargaining. A dorm bed costs 6000 rp. Staff ask whatever they can get for guides and their advice is dubious.

**Getting There & Away** Selo is most easily reached from Solo. Take one of the Tri Karya buses from Solo to Magelang, stopping at Selo (1500 rp, two hours) on the way. The last bus leaves Solo at 5 pm. From Yogya, take a Magelang bus to Blabak, then a colt or bus to Selo. Travel agents in Solo and Yogya arrange climbing trips of Merapi via Selo.

## PRAMBANAN
☎ 0274

On the road to Solo, 17km east of Yogya, the temples at Prambanan village are the cream of what remains of Java's period of Hindu cultural development. Not only do these temples form the largest Hindu temple complex on Java, but the wealth of sculptural detail on the great Shiva Temple makes it easily the most outstanding example of Hindu art.

All the temples in the Prambanan area were built between the 8th and 10th centuries, when Java was ruled by the Buddhist Sailendras in the south and the Hindu Sanjayas of Old Mataram in the north. Possibly, by the second half of the 9th century, these two dynasties were united by the marriage of Rakai Pikatan of Hindu Mataram and the Buddhist Sailendra princess Pramodhavardhani. This may explain why a number of temples, including Prambanan Temple and the smaller Plaosan group, reveal Shivaite and Buddhist elements in their architecture and sculpture. On the other hand, you find this mixture to some degree in India and Nepal, too.

Following this two century burst of creativity, the Prambanan Plain was abandoned when the Hindu-Javanese kings moved to East Java. There is said to have been a great earthquake in the mid-16th century which toppled many of the temples and, in the centuries that followed, their destruction was ac-

celerated by greedy treasure hunters and local people searching for building material. Most of the restoration work of the last century has gone into the preservation of Prambanan, and the buildings have now been restored, at least to some extent. Most people only visit the temples of the main Prambanan complex, but if you have the time and energy, it can be pleasant getting out into the countryside to see the other, smaller temples.

## Orientation & Information

The Prambanan temples *(candis)* straddle the border between Yogyakarta and Central Java, and are usually visited from Yogya (17km away) but can also be visited from Solo (50km). The main temple complex lies on the Yogya-Solo highway, opposite Prambanan village. From the main entrance on the eastern side it is a short walk to Shiva Mahadeva Temple, the largest of the temples, locally called Candi Loro Jonggrang, or 'Slender Virgin'. Behind it, on the western side near the highway, is the outdoor theatre where the *Ramayana* ballet is performed on full-moon nights.

To the north of the Shiva Madeva, which is flanked by the smaller but still impressive Brahma and Vishnu temples, is the archaeological museum (entry is included in the ticket price), and farther north are smaller, partly renovated temples leading to Sewu Temple, 1km north. A shuttle trolley goes to Sewu Temple. All of these temples form the main, fenced-off Prambanan complex.

The temple enclosure is open daily from 6 am to 6 pm, with last admission at 5.15 pm. Entry costs 10,000 rp and, as at Borobudur, this includes camera fees and entry to the museum. Guides are no longer included in the ticket price, but they know their stuff and can be a good investment at 15,000 rp for one to 20 people. Tours last up to one hour. An audio-visual show on Prambanan plays every 30 minutes for another 2000 rp.

At the temple complex there is little in the way of free brochures or maps – you can buy a copy of the *Guide to Prambanan Temple*, which is detailed and covers most of the temple sites on Prambanan Plain.

CENTRAL JAVA

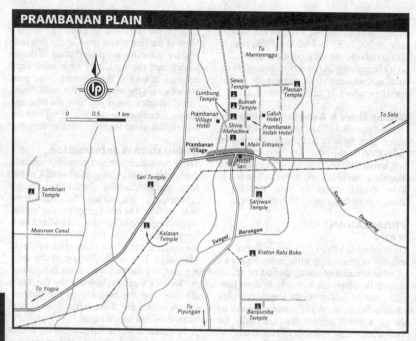

## PRAMBANAN PLAIN

Most of the outlying temples are spread within a 5km radius of Prambanan village. You'll need at least half a day to see them on foot, or they can be explored by bicycle if you ride to Prambanan. A standard entry fee of 500 rp applies to most of the outlying temples.

As with any of Java's major tourist attractions, the best time to visit Prambanan is early morning or late in the day when it's quiet, though you can never expect to get Prambanan all to yourself. Very few people visit the other sites, and the walk can be as much of a pleasure as the temples themselves.

### Prambanan Temple Complex

The huge Prambanan complex was constructed in about the middle of the 9th century – around 50 years later than Borobudur – but remarkably little is known about its early history. It's thought that it was built by

Rakai Pikatan to commemorate the return of a Hindu dynasty to sole power in Java. Some have even suggested it was intended as a counterpart to Borobudur, but more likely it was a counterpart to Candi Sewu, a Buddhist complex 3km away.

Prambanan was in ruins for years and, although efforts were made in 1885 to clear the site, it was not until 1937 that reconstruction was first attempted. Of the original group, the outer compound contains the remains of 244 temples. Eight minor and eight main temples stand in the highest central courtyard, and most have been restored.

**Shiva Mahadeva Temple** Dedicated to Shiva, this is not only the largest of the temples, it is also artistically and architecturally the most perfect. The main spire soars 47m high and the temple is lavishly carved. The 'medallions' which decorate its base have the characteristic 'Prambanan motif' – small lions in niches flanked by 'trees of heaven' (*kalpaturas*) and a menagerie of stylised half-human and half-bird heavenly beings (*kinnaras*). The vibrant scenes carved onto the inner wall of the gallery encircling the temple are from the *Ramayana* – they tell how Lord Rama's wife, Sita, is abducted and how Hanuman the monkey god and Sugriwa his white monkey general eventually find and release her. To follow the story, ascend the main eastern stairway and go around the temple clockwise. The reliefs break off at the point where the monkey army builds a bridge to the island of Lanka; the end of the tale is found on the smaller Brahma Temple.

In the main chamber at the top of the eastern stairway, the four-armed statue of Shiva the Destroyer is notable for the fact that this mightiest of Hindu gods stands on a huge lotus pedestal, a symbol of Buddhism. In the southern cell is the pot-bellied and bearded Agastya, an incarnation of Shiva as divine teacher; in the western cell is a superb image of the elephant-headed Ganesha, Shiva's son. In the northern cell,

Relief, Brahma temple

Durga, Shiva's consort, can be seen killing the demon buffalo. Some people believe that the Durga image is actually an image of Loro Jonggrang, the 'Slender Virgin' who, legend has it, was turned to stone by a giant she refused to marry. She is still the object of pilgrimage for many who believe in her, and the name of the cursed princess is often used for the temple group.

**Brahma & Vishnu Temples** These two smaller temples flank the large Shiva Mahadeva Temple. The Brahma Temple to the south, carved with the final scenes of the *Ramayana*, has a four-headed statue of Brahma, the god of creation. Reliefs on the Vishnu Temple to the north tell the story of Lord Krishna, a hero of the *Mahabharata* epic. Inside is a four-armed image of Vishnu the Preserver.

**Nandi Temple** This small shrine, facing Shiva Mahadeva Temple, houses one of Prambanan's finest sculptures – a huge, powerful figure of the bull, Nandi, the vehicle of Shiva.

The shrines to the north and south of Nandi may once have contained Brahma's vehicle, the swan, and Vishnu's sun-bird, the Garuda.

Shiva Mahadeva temple

PETER TURNER

CENTRAL JAVA

**Sewu Temple** The 'Thousand Temples', dating from around 850 AD, originally consisted of a large central Buddhist temple surrounded by four rings of 240 smaller 'guard' temples. Outside the compound stood four sanctuaries at the points of the compass, of which Bubrah Temple is the southern one.

The renovated main temple is interesting for the unusual, finely carved niches around the inner gallery, with shapes resembling those found in the Middle East. Once these would have held bronze statues, but plundering of the temple went on for many years – some of the statues were melted down and others disappeared into museums and private collections.

Sewu Temple lies about 1km north of the Shiva Mahadeva, past the small, partly renovated Lumbung Temple and Bubrah Temple. The crowds that hang around the main temple rarely get this far north, though there is a 'mini train' from the museum (1000 rp) that loops to Sewu, saving a hot walk.

## Plaosan Temples

This north-eastern group of temples is 3km from the Prambanan complex. The temples can be reached on foot by taking the road north from the main gate, past Sewu Temple at the end of the main complex, and then a right turn. Keep on this road for about 2km.

Believed to have been built at about the same time as the Prambanan temple group by Rakai Pikatan and his Buddhist queen, the Plaosan temples combine both Hindu and Buddhist religious symbols and carvings. The temples are comprised of the main Plaosan Lor (Plaosan North) compound and the smaller Plaosan Kidul (South), just a couple of hundred metres away.

Plaosan Lor comprises two restored, identical main temples, surrounded by some 126 small shrines and solid stupas, most of which are just a jumble of stone.

Two giant Dwarapalas (temple guardian statues) stand at the front of each main temple, which are notable for their unusual three part design. These are two-storey, three-room structures, with an imitation storey above and a tiered roof of stupas rising to a single larger one in the centre. Inside each room are impressive stone Bodhisattvas on either side of an empty lotus pedestal and intricately carved *kala* (dragon) heads above the many windows. The bronze Buddhas that once sat on the lotus pedestals have been removed.

Plaosan Kidul has more stupas and the remnants of a temple, but little renovation work has been done.

Guards produce a visitors' book (always a bad sign) and ask for a 2000 rp donation.

## Southern Group

**Sajiwan Temple** Not far from the village of Sajiwan, about 1.5km south-east of Prambanan, are the ruins of this Buddhist temple. Around the base are carvings from the *Jatakas* (episodes from the Buddha's various lives).

**Kraton Ratu Boko** Perched on a hill overlooking Prambanan, Kraton Ratu Boko (Palace of King Boko) is believed to have been a huge Hindu palace complex which dates from the 9th century and was part of the central court of the great Mataram Empire. Little remains from the original complex, though it is possible to get an idea of the scale of this palace complex. Renovations are only partly successful and a lot of new stonework has been included, but you can see the large gateway, walls, the platform of the main pendopo, Candi Pembakaran (Royal Crematorium) and a series of bathing places on different levels leading down to the nearby village. The view from this site to the Prambanan Plain is magnificent, especially at sunset, and worth the walk by itself.

To get to Ratu Boko, take the road just west of the river 1.5km south of Prambanan village; near the 'Yogya 18km' signpost, a steep rocky path leads up to the main site. It is about a one hour walk in total. The site can be reached by car or motorcycle via a much longer route that goes around the back of the mountain.

## Western Group

There are three temples in this group between Yogya and Prambanan, two of them close to Kalasan village on the main Yogya road. Kalasan and Prambanan villages are 3km apart, so it is probably easiest to take a colt or bus to cover this stretch.

**Kalasan Temple** Standing 50m off the main road near Kalasan village, this temple is one of the oldest Buddhist temples on the Prambanan Plain. A Sanskrit inscription of 778 AD refers to a temple dedicated to the female Bodhisattva, Tara, though the existing structure appears to have been built around the original some years later. It has been partially restored during the 20th century and has some fine detailed carvings on its southern side, where a huge, ornate kala head glowers over the doorway. At one time it was completely covered in coloured shining stucco, and traces of the hard, stone-like 'diamond plaster' that provided a base for paintwork can still be seen. The inner chamber of Kalasan once sheltered a huge bronze image of Buddha or Tara.

**Sari Temple** About 200m north of Kalasan Temple, in the middle of coconut and banana groves, Sari Temple has the three part design of the larger Plaosan temples, but is probably slightly older. Some students believe that its 2nd floor may have served as a dormitory for the Buddhist priests who took care of Kalasan Temple. The sculptured reliefs around the exterior are similar to those of Kalasan but in much better condition.

**Sambisari Temple** A country lane runs to this isolated temple, about 2.5km north of the main road. Sambisari is a Shiva temple and possibly the latest temple at Prambanan to be put up by the Mataram rulers. It was only discovered by a farmer in 1966. Excavated from under ancient layers of protective volcanic ash and dust, it lies almost 6m below the surface of the surrounding fields and is remarkable for its perfectly preserved state. The inner sanctum of the temple is dominated by a large

*linga* and *yoni* (stylised penis and vulva) typical of Shiva temples.

## Places to Stay

Very few visitors stay at Prambanan, given its proximity to Yogya, but there are plenty of hotels. This could be a pleasant option, but budget accommodation is not good. On the main highway opposite the main complex, *Hotel Sari* (☎ 496595) has rooms from 15,000 rp, but it is noisy and basic.

The quiet road on the east side of the main complex has a dozen budget hotels strung out over a kilometre or more, but they are seedy places that rent rooms by the hour. The big *Prambanan Indah* (☎ 497 353, Jl Candi Sewu 8) at least claims to be a real hotel, and has a few economy fan rooms for 20,000 rp. Air-con rooms are 60,000 rp to 120,000 rp.

Much better is the sparkling new *Galuh Hotel* (☎ 496854, Jl Manis Renggokm 1), one road east but more than 1km from the main complex. This big block hotel lacks sympathy with the surrounding rice paddies, but has good rooms, a pool and a large restaurant. Four-bed bunkrooms with shower cost 40,000 rp, double fan rooms are 60,500 rp, and deluxe rooms with minibar and TV are 84,700 rp and 133,100 rp.

The other main tourist hotel is the peaceful *Prambanan Village* (☎ 496435), down a quiet country lane at the north-west corner of the temple complex. Attractive bungalows next to the *sawah* (rice field) cost 200,000/240,000 rp for singles/doubles. The hotel has a pool, pleasant gardens and a restaurant, but is overpriced.

## Entertainment

The famous *Ramayana* ballet, held at the *outdoor theatre* in Prambanan is Java's most spectacular dance-drama. The story of Rama and Shinta unfolds over four successive nights, once or twice each month of the dry season (from May to October) leading up to the full moon. With the magnificent flood-lit Shiva Mahadeva Temple as a backdrop, nearly 200 dancers and gamelan musicians take part in a spectacle of monkey armies, giants on stilts, clashing battles and acrobatics.

Performances last from 7.30 to 9.30 pm. Tickets are sold through the Tourist Information Office and travel agents in Yogya at the same price as at the theatre box office, but they usually offer packages that include transport direct from your hotel for 5000 rp to 10,000 rp extra. Tickets range from 10,000 rp up to 35,000 rp for VIP. There are no bad seats in the amphitheatre – all have a good view and are not too far from the stage, but the cheapest seats are stone benches which are side on to the action. Cushions can be hired for an extra 1000 rp. VIP seats right at the front are padded chairs.

Alternatively, the *Ramayana Ballet Full Story* is a good two hour performance, condensing the epic into one night, and alternates with the four-part episodic performances. It features fewer performers but is still a fine spectacle, held at the same open air theatre from May to October. The rest of the year in the wet season, it moves indoors to Prambanan's *Trimurti covered theatre*. Performances start at 7.30 pm every Tuesday, Wednesday and Thursday.

Also worth seeing at Prambanan is the **Tawur Agung festival**, held one day before Nyepi, the Hindu new year. It usually falls around March, and thousands flock to see the procession or make offerings to the gods. Tawur Agung is held principally to ward off Ogoh Ogoh, a manifestation of Shiva's fearsome son Kala, who eats children. Kala particularly preys on only children. Families with two children of the same sex, or mixed twins, among other combinations, are also at risk. Kala is appeased by Ruwatan ceremonies, widely held throughout Java when they can be afforded. The children and families of potential victims are invited, and a special dalang will stage a wayang, usually based on stories of the first king of Java.

### Getting There & Away

**Bus** From Yogya, take the yellow Pemuda bus (1000 rp, 30 minutes) from the main bus terminal; or from the Sosro area, take bus No 4 along Jl Mataram and get out at the Jl Cik Ditiro/Jl Terbau corner, then take a bemo to Prambanan bus station. From Solo, buses take 1½ hours and cost 1500 rp.

**Bicycle** By bicycle, you can visit all the temples. The secret is to avoid as much of the Solo road as possible, though the main highway has a bicycle lane of sorts for much of the way, if you can endure the fumes and noise. The most pleasant route, though a longer ride, is to take Jl Senopati out past the zoo to the eastern ring road, where you turn left. Follow this right up to Jl Solo, turn right and then left at Jl Babarsari. Go past the Sahid Garden Hotel and follow the road anticlockwise around the school to the Selokan Mataram (Mataram Canal). This canal, built in Dutch times, runs parallel to the Solo road, about 1.5km to the north, and has a quiet, paved path running next to it – a little bumpy in parts but otherwise ideal for cycling. Follow the canal for around 6km to Kalasan, about 2km before Prambanan.

To view the western temples, you really need to come back via the Solo road. The turn-off north to Candi Sambasari from the Solo road crosses the canal before leading another 1km to the temple. You can visit the temple, backtrack to the canal path and continue back to Yogya.

### SOLO (SURAKARTA)
- pop 517,000    ☎ 0271

Only 65km north-east of Yogya, the old royal city of Surakarta competes with Yogya as a centre of Javanese culture. More popularly known as Solo, Surakarta has two palaces. One of these is even older than Yogya's, for Solo was the seat of the great Mataram Empire before Yogyakarta was split off from it.

Though it is larger than Yogya, Solo is more traditional and unhurried. It can also rightfully claim to be more Javanese than Yogyakarta, which as a university town has a large population of non-Javanese students.

Solo also attracts many students and scholars to its academies of music and dance. The city is an excellent place to see traditional performing arts. Traditional crafts are also well represented, especially batik, as Solo is a major centre for high quality batik and other textiles.

Wander around the back streets past white-washed palace walls and down alleyways through the kampungs, and you will discover Solo's graciousness. It can be visited on a day trip from Yogya, but Solo is worth far more than a day and there are a number of attractions outside the city. It has a good range of accommodation, and, though tourist services are not as developed as in Yogya, tourism is far less commercialised.

## History

Surakarta's founding in 1745 has a mystical past. Following the sacking of the Mataram court at Kartasura in 1742, the susuhunan, Pakubuwono II, decided to look for a more auspicious site. The transfer of the capital had something to do with voices from the cosmic world – according to legend, the king was told to go to the village of Solo because 'it is the place decreed by Allah and it will become a great and prosperous city'.

But Solo had already reached the peak of its political importance, and within 10 years the realm of Mataram had crumbled, split by internal conflict into three rival courts, of which Yogya was one. From then on the ruler of Surakarta and the subsidiary prince of Mangkunegara remained loyal to the Dutch, even at the time of Diponegoro's Java War.

Pakubuwono X (1893-1938) was a mystical ruler who revived the prestige of the court. He was looked upon as the rightful king of Java and his popularity challenged Dutch authority. After WWII, the royal court fumbled opportunities to play a positive role in the revolution and lost out badly to Yogya, which became the seat of the independence government. With the tide of democracy in the 1940s, the palaces of Solo became mere symbols of ancient Javanese feudalism and aristocracy.

Solo was a stronghold of the communists in the 1960s and the atrocities following Soekarno's overthrow saw many slaughtered. With the overthrow of Soeharto, the city erupted, one day after the Jakarta riots, in May 1998. For two days rioters went on a rampage, systematically looting and burning every shopping centre and department store in Solo. The shells of burnt-out buildings are dotted all around the city, and it will be years before Solo recovers.

## Orientation

The oldest part of the city is centred around Kraton Surakarta to the east, where Pasar Klewer, the main batik market, is also located. Kraton Mangkunegara is the centre of Solo. Away from these tranquil palaces Solo can be as busy as any other Javanese city, but it is less congested than its younger sister city, Yogya, and not overwhelmed by tourists. It is perhaps the least westernised of Java's cities, and there are corners with narrow walled streets and a strong village atmosphere.

Jl Brigiend Slamet Riyadi, the broad tree-lined avenue running east-west through the centre of Solo, is the main thoroughfare. Here, the city's double-decker buses run their course and a couple of trains a day ply Solo's main street. The tourist office is at the west end and most of the banks are at the east end, near Kraton Surakarta. Solo's Balapan train station is in the northern part of the city, about 2km from the city centre, and the main bus terminal is a few hundred metres north again. Most hotels and restaurants are on, or just off, Jl Slamet Riyadi.

## Information

**Tourist Offices** The Solo Tourist Office (☎ 711435), Jl Slamet Riyadi 275, has useful pamphlets, a map of Solo, and information on cultural events in town and places to visit in the area. The office is open from 8 am to 5 pm daily, except Sunday. A branch office is at the bus terminal.

**Post & Communications** The efficient main post office on Jl Jenderal Sudirman is open from 8 am to 8 pm daily for most postal services. The Warposnet for Internet

CENTRAL JAVA

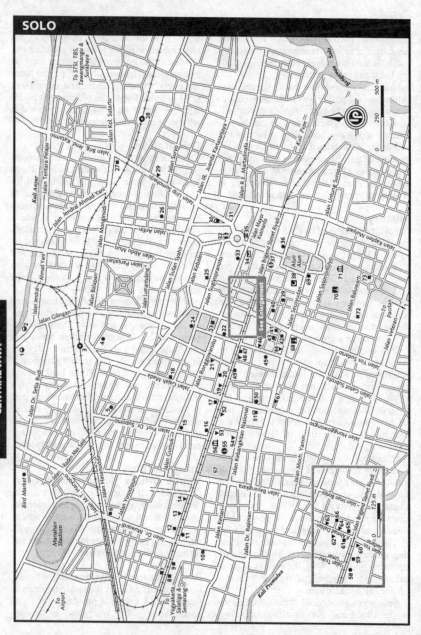

**SOLO**

| PLACES TO STAY | | PLACES TO EAT | | | |
|---|---|---|---|---|---|
| 6 | Hotel Agas International | 13 | Galael Supermarket & | 15 | Toko Bedoyo Srimpi |
| 7 | Hotel Bringin | | KFC | 22 | Pasar Triwindu |
| 8 | Riyadi Palace Hotel | 14 | Adem Ayam | 24 | Kraton Mangkunegara |
| 9 | Hotel Putri Ayu | 19 | Tio Ciu 99 | 26 | SMKI School |
| 10 | Ramayana Guesthouse | 21 | Kafe Atria; Atria | 28 | Jebres Train Station |
| 12 | Solo Inn | | Supermarket | 30 | Nirwana Disco |
| 16 | Hotel Dana | 29 | Timlo Solo | 31 | Pasar Gede |
| 17 | Novotel Solo | 44 | McDonald's | 32 | BNI Bank |
| 18 | Hotel Said Raya Solo | 46 | Bu Mari | 33 | Lojikom Internet |
| 20 | Pendhawa Homestay | 48 | Cafe Wina | 34 | Main Post Office |
| 23 | Lucie Pension | 52 | Cipta Rasa | 35 | Telkom Office |
| 25 | Kusuma Sahid Prince Hotel | 53 | Pujosari | 36 | Balai Agung |
| 27 | Hotel Asia | 54 | Restoran Boga | 37 | BCA Bank |
| 39 | Remaja Homestay | 60 | Kusama Sari | 38 | Mesjid Agung |
| 40 | Mama Homestay | 62 | Warung Baru | 45 | Batik Danarhadi |
| 41 | Paradiso Guest House | 63 | Cafe Gamelan | 50 | Batik Danarhadi |
| 42 | Westerners | 64 | Monggo Pinarak | 51 | Legenda Disco |
| 43 | Cendana Homestay; | 67 | Kafe Solo | 55 | Tourist Office |
| | Warung Biru | | | 56 | Radya Pustaka |
| 47 | Hotel Wisata Indah | **OTHER** | | | Museum |
| 49 | Hotel Cakra | 1 | Tirtonadi Bus Terminal | 57 | Sriwedari |
| 59 | Hotel Kota | 2 | Gilingan Minibus Terminal | | Amusement Park |
| 61 | Hotel Sekar Kedaton | 3 | Balapan Train Station | 58 | Wartel |
| 65 | Hotel Keprabon | 4 | Radio Republik | 68 | Vihara Rahayu |
| 66 | Istana Griyer | | Indonesia (RRI) | | Chinese Temple |
| 72 | Hondra Guesthouse | 5 | Batik Semar | 69 | Pasar Klewer |
| 73 | Dagdan's | 11 | Akuarius | 70 | Kraton Surakarta |
| | | | | 71 | Kraton Museum |

connections is closed. It may open again, but Solo has plenty of alternatives. Lojikom, Jl Ronggowarsito 2A, is open from 9 am to 9 pm. C-21, an Internet cafe buried among the warungs at the Pujosari warung centre on Jl Slamet Riyadi, is open from 9 am to 10 pm. Both charge 5000 rp per hour. For Internet cafes, Monggo Pinarak, on Jalan Dahlan, (7500 rp per hour) and the Kafe Atria (open from 11 am to 11 pm, 6000 rp per hour) are the best options.

A Telkom wartel is on Jl Mayor Kusmanto near the post office, and it has a Home Country Direct phone. Otherwise, wartels can be found everywhere, including in the Hotel Kota, Jl Slamet Riyadi 125, and at No 275 in the Sriwedari Amusement Park.

## Kraton Surakarta

In 1745, Pakubuwono II moved from Kartasura to Kraton Surakarta (also known as Kraton Kasunanan) in a day-long procession which transplanted everything belonging to the king, including the royal banyan trees and the sacred Nyai Setomo cannon (the twin of Si Jagur in old Jakarta), which now sits in the northern palace pavilion. Ornate European-style decorations were later added by Pakubuwono X, the wealthiest of Surakarta's rulers, from 1893 to 1939.

Entry to the kraton is through the north entrance, fronting the alun alun. Here the Pagelaran is the main audience hall where the susuhunan held court in front of his people. Across the street behind the Pagelaran is the kraton proper, though the main gateway is not open to the public and entry is from around the east side at the museum/art gallery.

Much of the kraton was destroyed by fire in 1985, and the Solonese blamed the susuhunan's lack of observance of tradition. Many of the inner buildings, including the pendopo, were destroyed and have been re-

CENTRAL JAVA

## House of Mataram – Java's Royalty

The sultanates of Yogyakarta and Surakarta are the successors of the Mataram kingdom, which was founded at Kota Gede by Senopati in 1575. Bearing the same name as the great Hindu-Buddhist empire of 600 years earlier, Mataram was an Islamic kingdom, though its mystical principles and court customs were Hindu Javanese.

Mataram's greatness is attributable to Sultan Agung, who created the most powerful kingdom on Java since Majapahit. A great warrior shrouded in mystical glory, he moved his court to Kerta in 1622, from where he ruled most of Java. Following Agung's death and internment at Imogiri, Mataram rapidly disintegrated.

Dutch military intervention in Javanese politics helped fragment the empire as Java was torn by internecine wars between rival states and contenders to the throne. The court of Mataram was to move three more times: to Plered in 1647, Kartosuro in 1680 and finally, under Pakubuwono II, to Surakarta (Solo) in 1745.

The Third Javanese War of Succession (1746-57) finished Mataram. Pakubuwono II's main rivals to the throne, his brother Prince Mangkubumi and nephew Mas Said, rebelled against Pakubuwono II's capitulation to Dutch demands. No side could dominate, so the Dutch brokered a settlement to end its expensive military involvement.

Prince Mangkubumi was granted the principality of Yogyakarta and assumed the title of Sultan Hamengkubuwono (Bearer of the Universe). The realm of Pakubuwono (Nail of the Universe) was divided further when Mas Said surrendered in 1757 and was given the smaller territory of Mangkunegaran. After the British attack of 1812, Yogyakarta was also further divided and the sultan's brother, who assisted the British, was rewarded with the small principality of Pakualaman.

Pakubuwono X was the most revered susuhunan of Surakarta and regarded by many in his time as the rightful king of Java.

The sultanates vied for the title of the rightful successor to Mataram, but despite

built. One that has survived is the distinctive tower known as Panggung Songgo Buwono, built in 1782 and looking like a cross between a Dutch clocktower and a lighthouse. Its upper storey is a meditation sanctum where the susuhunan is said to commune with Nyai Loro Kidul (Queen of the South Seas).

A heavy carved doorway leads through from the museum across the inner court-

yard of shady trees to the pendopo, but most of the kraton is off-limits and is in fact the *dalem*, or residence, of the susuhunan. The main sight for visitors is the Sasono Sewoko museum/art gallery; exhibits include fine silver and bronze Hindu-Javanese figures, Javanese weapons, antiques and other royal heirlooms.

Admission is 2500 rp, which includes entry to the kraton complex and museum

## House of Mataram – Java's Royalty

early threats of war, they remained independent. Though they ruled as heads of state in name, the courts increasingly turned their attention to the arts as the Dutch assumed political control. The rivalry between Yogyakarta and Solo became cultural, and both still compete as centres of Javanese culture.

The principalities' fortunes have waxed and waned with their rulers, and the royal houses have had their fare share of profligates and dilettantes. In the 20th century, able rulers helped restore prestige. The charismatic and mystical Pakubuwono X was enormously popular and goaded the Dutch by touring the countryside with his retinue, attracting admiring crowds that looked upon him as the real king of Java. Mangkunegoro VII and Pakualam VII were instrumental members of Budi Utomo, an early modernist organisation that helped pave the way for nationalist aspirations.

Hamengkubuwono IX, above all others, carved a place for the traditional rulers in post-independence Indonesia. His crucial role in support of the revolutionary government saw Yogyakarta gain special territory status after independence, while the kratons of Surakarta and Mangkunegara failed to play a positive role and were absorbed into Central Java.

Though many question their relevance in the modern world, the rulers still command a great deal of respect as the upholders of Javanese tradition. Each of the kratons has developed its own arts and traditions, but they are united by the inheritance of Mataram.

Like the ancient god-kings, the present rulers are expected to carry out the rituals necessary to ensure the harmony and prosperity of the realm. Nyai Loro Kidul, the Queen of the South Seas, is the spiritual wife of the sultans and the protector of the House of Mataram. She requires special favour and spiritual union through meditation.

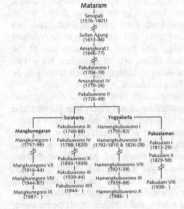

The successors of Mataram (with the exception of Mangkunegaran) are all buried at the royal tombs of Imogiri, alongside Sultan Agung.

---

and a guide. Entry is only from the north side opposite the alun alun, and the kraton is open daily, except Friday, from 8 am to 2 pm. Dance practice classes for children can be seen on Sunday from 10 am to noon, while adult practice is from 1 to 3 pm. The palace souvenir shop at the entrance sells a few craft items, crockery with the kraton emblem and even beer glasses with faces of the susuhunans on them.

## Kraton Mangkunegara

In the centre of the city, Kraton Mangkunegara, dating back to 1757, is the palace of the second ruling house of Solo. It was founded after a bitter struggle against the susuhunan, Pakubuwono II, launched by his nephew Raden Mas Said, an ancestor of Madam Tien Soeharto, the late wife of the former president. Though much smaller in scale and design, this kraton is better maintained and obviously wealthier than the more important Kraton Surakarta. Tours also tend to be better organised. Members of the royal family still live at the back of the palace.

The centre of the palace compound is the pendopo pavilion, bordered on its northern side by the dalem, which now forms the palace museum. The pavilion has been added to over the centuries and is one of the largest in the country. Its high rounded ceiling was painted in 1937 and is intricately decorated with a central flame surrounded by figures of the Javanese zodiac, each in its own mystical colour. In Javanese philosophy, yellow signifies a prevention against sleepiness, blue against disease, black against hunger, green against desire, white against lust, rose pink against fear, red against evil and purple against wicked thoughts. The pavilion contains one of the kraton's oldest sets of gamelan, known as 'Kyai Kanyut Mesem', which translates as 'drifting in smiles'.

The museum here is a real delight, and the guided tours are much less hurried and more informative than those in Solo's main kraton. Most of the exhibits are from the personal collection of Mangkunegara VII. Among the items are gold-plated dresses for the royal Srimpi and Bedoyo dances, jewellery and a few oddities (including huge Buddhist rings, a gold genital cover for a queen and a rather small penis cover for a king). There's also a collection of masks from various areas in Indonesia, a series of royal portraits and a library collection of classical literary works by the Mangkunegara princes.

The palace is open from 8.30 am to 2 pm daily, except Sunday, when it closes at 1 pm. Admission is 3500 rp. At the pavilion, you can see excellent dance practice sessions on Wednesday morning from 10 am until noon. The palace shop sells good wayang golek and other craft items.

### Radya Pustaka Museum

This small museum, next to the tourist office on Jl Slamet Riyadi, has good displays of gamelan instruments, jewelled krises,

wayang puppets from Thailand and Indonesia, a small collection of *wayang beber* (scrolls which depict wayang stories) and the Raja Mala, a hairy, muppet-like figurehead from a royal barge. Offerings must be made regularly to the Raja Mala – otherwise, it is said, it will exude a pungent odour. Official opening hours are from 8 am to 1 pm Tuesday, Thursday and Sunday, and to 11 am Friday and Saturday, but it often closes early. Entry costs 500 rp.

## Markets

**Pasar Klewer** is the ever-busy, crowded textile market near Kraton Surakarta. This is the place to look for batik, if you know your stuff and are prepared to bargain. It is open from 8 am to 4 pm.

Solo's antique market, **Pasar Triwindu**, is always worth a browse. It sells all sorts of bric-a-brac (not all of it old), though half the market is also devoted to car and motorcycle parts.

**Pasar Gede** is the city's largest everyday market, selling all manner of produce, while **Pasar Depok** is Solo's bird market, at the north-west end of Jl RM Said.

## Other Attractions

On the west side of the alun alun, **Mesjid Agung** (Grand Mosque) is the largest and most sacred mosque in Solo, featuring classical Javanese architecture.

The **Sriwedari Amusement Park** has fairrides, side-show stalls and other somewhat dated diversions in the THR (Taman Hiburan Rakyat, or People's Amusement Park) complex. Unlike similar amusement parks in other cities on Java, Sriwedari can still draw a crowd on a Saturday night. The main reason to come is for the nightly wayang orang and other regular cultural performances. Tuesday *dangdut* (pop music inspired by Indian movies) nights are very popular.

## Swimming

Most of the big hotels will allow nonguests to use the swimming pool for around 7500 rp. The Kusuma Sahid Prince Hotel has a good pool and the Hotel Agas has a warm water pool.

## Meditation

Solo is a noted centre for contemporary mystical groups of different philosophies and religions, which come under the broad umbrella of Kebatinan (Mysticism). A few schools in Solo have western followers, and most gatherings are generally held informally at private homes. Meditational practices and philosophy are Hindu/Buddhist, with a distinct Javanese world view. Islamic mystics also abound in Solo, but they don't attract westerners for some reason.

Pak Suprapto Suryodarmo (Prapto) at Plesungan Mojosonango (☎ 635210) follows Buddhist philosophy and practises meditation through movement, something like *Taijiquan* (t'ai chi). Pak Suwondo, Jl Sidikoro 10A, teaches the traditional theory and practice of Javanese meditation with a Hindu perspective, and has a reputation as a patient teacher. Ananda Suyono is a Javanese 'New Age' eclectic who lives at Jl Ronggowarsito 60.

On the eastern side of the kraton, opposite the museum, Pak Hardjanto's Pura Mandira Seta is about as Hindu and as ascetic as they come. Meditational practices include sun meditation (lying out in the midday sun in a black sack) and moon meditation (sitting in big pots of water up to the neck while meditating on the moon). Arrange your own medical insurance.

The guesthouses can help steer you towards a school.

## Batik Courses

Mama at Mama Homestay (see under Places to Stay in this section) offers a one day introductory batik course for 20,000 rp – you supply the T-shirt – or longer courses are available. Warung Baru, never to be outdone, also offers batik courses.

## Organised Tours

Various travel agents around town run tours, and many guesthouses, hotels and travellers cafes will book them. Most are expensive and require a minimum of two people. They include visits to Sukuh and Tawangmangu (50,000 rp), and trekking to the summit of Merapi (55,000 rp). Inta Tours (☎ 56128), Jl Slamet Riyadi 96, is one conveniently located tour operator, and there are many others nearby. Mandira Tours & Travel (☎ 718558), Jl Gajah Mada 77, opposite the Hotel Said Raya Solo, is another well established operator with a wide variety of tours and services.

Warung Baru and many of the homestays run bicycle tours of Solo and sites outside the city limits. These tours are reasonably priced and are perennial favourites. For 20,000 rp, one full-day tour takes you through beautiful countryside to see batik weaving, gamelan making, and tofu, arak and rice-cracker processing.

## Places to Stay – Budget

Solo has an excellent selection of friendly homestays. Almost all offer good travel information, tours, bus bookings, bicycles, breakfast, free tea and drinking water.

The *Westerners* (☎ 633106, *Kemlayan Kidul 11*), on the first alley north of Jl Secoyudan off Jl Yos Sudarso, is spotlessly clean, well run and secure. Solo's original homestay, it is still popular, if a little cramped, but prices are very reasonable. The dormitory costs 6000 rp, small singles cost 6500 rp and good-sized doubles with mandi are 17,500 rp.

On the same alley at No 1/3, the *Paradiso Guest House* (☎ 54111) is a classy little place with a pendopo-style lobby/sitting area. The all-white rooms are good, if expensive, at 9500 rp with shared mandi, and 27,500 rp to 44,000 rp with mandi. Look for the sign offering 'Westerner's' accommodation, an attempt to lure the competition's trade.

Off another alley to the north, the well run *Cendana Homestay* (☎ 46169, *Gang Empu Panuluh III No 4*) has well kept rooms from 9000 rp, and from 13,000/17,000 rp with bathroom. The good Warung Biru restaurant is attached.

*Mama Homestay* (☎ 52248, *Kauman Gang III*), also off Jl Yos Sudarso, has basic rooms for 10,000/15,000 rp, or better but dark rooms with mandi for 15,000/20,000 rp, including breakfast. Standards are below the others but many people enjoy the homey atmosphere. Mama gives a one day batik course for 20,000 rp (you provide the T-shirt) and bicycle tours are also offered.

They don't come any cheaper than the nearby *Remaja Homestay* (☎ *47758, Jl Cokro 1 No 1)*, where extremely basic but airy rooms cost 7500 rp, including breakfast. The old couple who run it don't speak much English but are natural hosts.

*Istana Griyer* (☎ *632667, Jl A Dahlan 22)* is a friendly new homestay in a good position down a lane off Solo's main cafe strip. Rooms are spotless and more hotel-like in standards, but also much more expensive. Singles/double are 22,500/27,500 rp with shared mandi, and from 30,000/35,000 rp with mandi up to 47,500/52,500 rp with air-con, hot water and TV.

*Lucie Pension* (☎ *53375, Jl Ambon 12)* is another new, switched-on homestay near Mangkunegaran kraton. Spotless rooms have tatami-style mats and mattresses on the floor for 9000 rp to 12,000 rp. The upstairs sitting room is very pleasant.

Another option is the *Pendhawa Homestay* (☎ *52219, Jl Jawa 31A),* but others have more appeal. Gloomy rooms cost 15,000 rp.

Other guesthouses popular for longer stays are on the south side of Surakarta kraton. *Dagdan's* (☎ *54538, Jl Sidikoro 42)* is one block south of Kraton Museum. It has just a few attractive rooms and rents by the week. Recommended by long-term visitors is *Hondra Guesthouse (Joyokusuman, ☎ 54842, Jl Gajahan 7),* which has large old bungalows and tranquil grounds in a former prince's mansion.

Solo has dozens of hotels, but they tend to be anonymous places. *Hotel Keprabon* (☎ *632811, Jl Ahmad Dahlan 8-12)* is right near Solo's travellers cafes and is a reasonably priced option, with old-style rooms from 12,500 rp. Rooms with hot water cost 25,000 rp, and air-con rooms are 30,000 rp and 40,000 rp.

*Hotel Kota* (☎ *632841, Jl Slamet Riyadi 125)* is very central. This double storey place, built around a large open courtyard, has rooms from 15,000 rp up to 45,000 rp with air-con.

## Places to Stay – Mid-Range

Many of the hotels in this bracket are strung out along or just off Jl Slamet Riyadi, west of the city centre. At the bottom of this range, *Hotel Putri Ayu* (☎ *711812, Jl Slamet Riyadi 331)* is a friendly place, with quiet rooms around a courtyard for 34,500 rp with mandi, fan and TV. Air-con rooms with bath are 54,000 rp.

*Ramayana Guesthouse* (☎ *712814, Jl Dr Wahidin 22)* is an attractive house with a garden. It has reasonable doubles with bath for 27,000 rp to 30,000 rp, or rooms with air-con and hot water for 40,000 rp to 50,000 rp. Add 20% tax and service to the rates, but breakfast is included.

*Hotel Sekar Kedaton* (☎ *661884, Jl Ahmad Dahlan 7)* is very central but shielded from traffic noise. Spotless but simple rooms with bathroom cost 60,000 rp; with air-con the price is 70,000 rp and 90,000 rp. This new place hasn't worked out what the competition is charging and is way overpriced. Expect a discount – 40% is about right.

Conveniently located across the street from the tourist office and museum is the *Hotel Dana* (☎ *711976, Jl Slamet Riyadi 286).* This fine colonial hotel has undergone extensive renovation, not all of it sympathetic, but it still has plenty of grace, extensive gardens and excellent rooms, most with private sitting areas. Rooms are 102,000 rp and 150,000 rp, and suites are 150,000 rp to 270,000 rp, including breakfast. Regularly offered discounts make it one of the best choices in this range, but watch your gear here.

Solo has plenty of older mid-range hotels on Jl Slamet Riyadi, such as the faded *Solo Inn* (☎ *716075, Jl Slamet Riyadi 366),* where rooms with fridge, hot water and TV cost 165,000 rp to 270,000 rp, before a big discount. *Hotel Wisata Indah* (☎ *46770, Jl Slamet Riyadi 173)* has dark older rooms with air-con and hot water from 65,000 rp, or very good new rooms for 110,000 rp and 120,000 rp. *Hotel Cakra* (☎ 45857, *Jl Slamet Riyadi 201*) is the best of this older bunch and has a swimming pool. Rooms cost 160,000 rp to 246,000 rp, but expect a 30% discount.

Farther west, the *Riyadi Palace Hotel* (☎ 717181, *Jl Slamet Riyadi 335*) is a reasonable choice. Well appointed rooms range from 129,500 rp to 275,000 rp, but discounts to as low as 87,500 rp make it good-value. Across the street, *Hotel Bringin* (☎ 726 232, *Jl Slamet Riyadi 392*) is a motel-style place; because it's new, the rooms are a touch better than most. Air-con rooms are 75,000 rp, or fancier rooms with carpet and hot water are 95,000 rp.

*Hotel Asia* (☎ 661166, *Jl Monginsidi 1*) is a new high-rise hotel and good value. Well appointed rooms with all the trimmings are 90,000 rp to 120,000 rp, but discounts have seen the price drop to as low as 54,000 rp. The drawbacks are that it is a long hike from the centre and is on the very busy road to Surabaya.

## Places to Stay – Top End

The following hotels all have swimming pools and restaurants. Considering the low numbers of tourists and business travellers who visit, Solo has a glut of luxury hotels, and big discounts make its luxury hotels some of the cheapest in Asia.

*Hotel Agas International* (☎ 720746, *Jl Dr Muwardi 44*) is a smaller hotel without the large facilities of the others, but it has everything you need, including a heated swimming pool. Good singles/doubles cost 245,000/277,000 rp, but ask for *paket* rates, which are as low as 130,000/145,000 rp.

The grand *Kusuma Sahid Prince Hotel* (☎ 46356, *Jl Sugiyopranoto 20*) has been designed around a former Solonese palace and is set in extensive grounds. Though it is an older hotel, most rooms have been renovated, and it has a large pool and more style than most. Published rates are around US$100, but it has been discounting as low as 175,000 rp for a room.

The *Hotel Said Raya Solo* (☎ 714144, *Jl Gajah Mada 82*) is a big high-rise hotel with all the trimmings. Rooms cost US$110 and US$142, but expect a huge discount.

Grandiose plans to turn Solo's airport into an international hub caused a rush to build luxury hotels in 1996-7, and these new hotels are the top of the heap in Solo. The *Novotel Solo* (☎ 724555, *Jl Slamet Riyadi 272*) is the most popular because of its excellent central position. Discount rates start at 240,000 rp, but the hotel can fill its rooms, so discounts may be hard to get.

Solo's newest hotel is the *Quality Hotel Solo* (☎ 731312, *Jl Ahmad Yani 40*), 3km west of the centre. This big hotel has impressive facilities but opening rates are only 145,000 rp, making it exceptional value.

The most luxurious of all hotels is the *Sheraton Solo* (☎ 724500, *Jl Adisucipto 47*), which has stylish buildings in luxuriant gardens, but it is 5km from town, out in the middle of nowhere on the airport road. The lack of guests makes it very quiet, and rooms from US$110 to US$170 are discounted to 285,000 rp.

## Places to Eat

For the cheapest food, listen for the weird and distinctive sounds which are the trademarks of the roaming *street hawkers*. The bread seller sings (or screeches) a high-pitched 'tee'; 'ding ding ding' is the sound of the *bakso* seller; 'tic toc' is *mie*; a wooden buffalo bell advertises sate; and a shrieking kettle-on-the-boil sound is the *kue putu*. Kue putu are coconut cakes, which are pushed into small bamboo tubes, cooked over a steam box and served hot, sprinkled with coconut and sugar.

Nasi gudeg is popular, but the speciality of Solo is *nasi liwet*, rice cooked in coconut milk and served with side dishes. Another local speciality to try at night is delicious *srabi*, the small rice puddings served up on a crispy pancake with banana, chocolate or jackfruit topping – best eaten piping hot.

Jl Ahmad Dahlan is the centre for budget travellers' eateries. The most popular travellers' meeting place is the long-running

*Warung Baru* at No 23. It has a huge menu featuring a bit of everything, and while it might not be *haute cuisine*, the prices are hard to beat. Various travel services, including bike tours of Solo and batik courses, are also offered.

Across the street, *Monggo Pinarak* (Javanese for 'please sit down') is the most stylish of the travellers cafes and has a library, Internet terminals and eclectic music (a nice change from Bob Marley). The well travelled Bangladeshi owner serves up excellent Indian food, western dishes and good breakfast fare. A couple of doors along, *Steak Warung* has steaks and is open late for a beer.

Farther down at No 28, the friendly *Cafe Gamelan* is another good travellers cafe, with a varied menu of Indonesian and western dishes and a range of travel services.

In the main homestay area, *Warung Biru* at the Cendana Homestay has good food and vegetarian meals. The small *Cafe Wina (Jl Slamet Riyadi 183)* has a limited menu, but is a friendly meeting spot, good for a drink. It offers a full range of travel services, including bicycle and motorbike rental.

Some of the cheapest and best food is to be found in Solo's numerous warungs. Everyone has a favourite. You can get a feed any time of the night at numerous dusk-to-dawn warungs dotted around the streets. On Jl Gatot Subroto, look for the *Bu Mari* warung, which has miniature chairs around a low table on the footpath. It has great nasi gudeg and chicken curry with rice and *sambal*, and it is open until the wee hours of the morning.

The small depots on Jl Teuku Umar are good for an inexpensive taste of local specialities like nasi liwet, as well as seafood, noodles, bakso – a bit of everything. Most of them offer lesahan dining (on mats). Lesahan dining is very much a part of eating in Solo. On fine evenings, straw mats are laid out on the pavements all around Solo, especially on Jl Slamet Riyadi, and all sorts of goodies, including sate, are offered.

*Pujosari* is a good selection of warungs next to the museum and tourist office in the Sriwedari Amusement Park area. It offers a wide range of Solonese and other Indonesian dishes. The biggest places are *Lezat*, a 24 hour lesahan place, and the more restaurant-like *Oriental*. The Lezat does a mean *ayam kampung* (village chicken), and the busy Oriental has a wide range of good Chinese dishes, including seafood. *Cafe Champion* is another, more salubrious, warung serving steak and other dishes.

Cheap Chinese restaurants along Jl Slamet Riyadi include the *Cipta Rasa* at 245 and the popular *Tio Ciu 99*. The unpretentious Cipta Rasa has cheap, filling fare, though for a little extra the Tio Ciu 99 is a better bet for good Chinese food.

The *Adem Ayam (Jl Slamet Riyadi 342)* is split into two restaurants, one serving Chinese food and the other Javanese. The gudeg is its best dish. *Timlo Solo (Jl Urip Sumohardjo 94)* is a Solo institution serving up Javanese specialities such as nasi liwet, gudeg and nasi timlo in its pack 'em in, move 'em out, laminex dining hall.

Apart from at the travellers cafes, a Pizza Hut and a McDonald's, few places in still-traditional Solo serve western food. One exception is the *Kusama Sari*, on the corner of Jl Slamet Riyadi and Jl Yos Sudarso, which has seductive air-con, good hot platter grills and ice creams. It is also one of those rarities in Indonesia – a nonsmoking restaurant. Another branch is next to the BCA bank.

In a similar vein, *Kafe Atria*, above the supermarket of the same name on the corner of Jl Ronggowosito and Jl Kartini, is a smart new restaurant serving mostly grills, some Asian dishes, iced juices etc. It also has an Internet cafe, views over the city and live music in the evening.

*Kafe Solo*, on Jl Secoyudan, is Solo's most stylish restaurant, housed in a restored colonial building. The menu is vaguely Chinese and Indonesian, with a few interesting variations and a smattering of western dishes. Meals cost from around 5000 rp up to 22,000 rp for imported steaks.

*Restoran Boga*, behind the Sriwidari Amusement Park, is another old-money restaurant popular with Solo's middle classes for good Chinese/Indonesian food. It has a peaceful aspect overlooking fish ponds.

## Entertainment

Solo is an excellent place to see traditional Javanese performing arts.

The *Sriwedari Theatre*, at the back of Sriwedari Amusement Park, behind the tourist office on Jl Slamet Riyadi, has a long-running wayang orang troupe. It's not what it used to be – you can see better wayang orang on Indonesian TV – but it only costs 1000 rp to sample this unique vaudeville style of telling the classics, complete with singing, comedy and action drama. Come and go as you please – the only time the theatre is even half full is on a Saturday night. Performances are staged from 8 to 10 pm nightly, except Sunday.

Various cultural performances are held at the broadcasting station of *Radio Republik Indonesia (RRI, Jl Abdul Rahman Saleh 51)*. The RRI performances are popular and often excellent. The station has all-night wayang kulit shows on the third Saturday of every month, from 9 pm to around 5 am; on the second Tuesday evening of the month there is wayang orang from 8 pm to midnight. Ketoprak performances are held on the fourth Tuesday of the month, from 8 pm to midnight.

At *Sekolah Tinggi Seni Indonesia* (STSI), the arts academy, you can see dance practice from around 7.30 am to noon, Monday to Saturday. STSI is at the Jl Kentingan campus in Jebres, 4km north-east of the city. *SMKI*, the high school for the performing arts on Jl Kepatihan Wetan, also has dance practice every morning, except Sunday, from around 9 am to noon.

Both kratons also have traditional Javanese dance practice: Wednesday from 10 am to noon at *Kraton Mangkunegara*, and Sunday morning and afternoon performances at *Kraton Surakarta*.

The tourist office has details of other cultural events around Solo. Wayang kulit shows are performed by the famous dalang,

Ki Anom Suroto, at Jl Gambir Anom 100, Notodiningran, in the area behind the Hotel Cakra. You can count on all-night performances there every Tuesday Kliwon of the Javanese calendar, which occurs every five weeks. All-night wayang kulit is also held at *Taman Budaya Surakarta (TBS, Jl Ir Sutami 57)*, the city's cultural centre, to the east of the city, on Friday Kliwon of the Javanese calendar. Anom also occasionally performs at the Sriwedari Amusement Park. Ki Mantep Sudarsono is one of Indonesia's most famous dalang, and performs all around Java and overseas. He sometimes has performances in his village, 27km from Solo, near Karangpandan.

Solo's title of the 'city that never sleeps' refers more to its all-night warungs than to raging nightlife, but the city has a few lively nightspots. *Legenda (Jl Honggowongso 81A)* is Solo's most popular pick-up spot, but it's small and incredibly dark – the strobe seems to operate on a 40W globe. Entry is 10,000 rp, as are the beers. Other discos include the *Nirwana (2nd floor of Pasar Besar, Jl Urip Sumoharjo)*, and the more modern *Freedom* on Jl Ahmad Yani, to the north-west behind the stadium at Balai Kambang. The bars at the *Novotel* and *Quality* hotels have pop cover bands and expensive beers. A few restaurants, such as *Akuarius (Jl Slamet Riyadi 317)*, have bands that kick on after dinner until around 1 am. If none of this interests you, on Saturday night you could check out the effete bikers, with their amazing collection of Vespa scooters, who hang out on Jl Slamet Riyadi.

## Shopping

Solo is one of Indonesia's main textile centres, producing not only its own unique, traditional batik but every kind of fabric for domestic use and export. Many people find it better for batik than Yogya, though Solo doesn't have Yogya's range for other handcrafts and curios.

For everyday shopping, try the markets or the shops on Jl Secoyudan. Solo has no big department stores. Its few shopping

CENTRAL JAVA

centres were destroyed in the 1998 riots, and the only modern supermarkets left are the rebuilt Gelael on Jl Slamet Riyadi and the new Atria on Jl Ronggowarsito.

**Batik** Pasar Klewer, a three storey market near Kraton Surakarta, has hundreds of stalls selling fabrics. This is a good place to buy batik, mainly *cap* (motifs are applied with a metal stamp), but you can also find *tulis batik* and *lurik* homespun (traditional striped cloth worn by kraton guards). Bargaining is obligatory and it pays to know your batik and prices

The big manufacturers have showrooms with a range of often very sophisticated work. You can see the batik process at the big Batik Keris factory, Kelurahan Cemari, in Lawiyan, west of the city, open from 8 am to 5 pm Monday to Saturday. A showroom is at the factory. Ask a becak to take you there. Another big Solonese manufacturer is Batik Danarhadi, with shops at Jl Slamet Riyadi 205, and on Jl Gatot Subroto and Jl Honggowongso. It has a good range of batik fabrics and ready-made clothes. Batik Semar, Jl R M Said 148, is good for modern cotton and beautiful silk batiks.

Smaller batik industries include Batik Srimpi, Jl Dr Supomo 25; and Batik Arjuna, Jl Dr Rajiman 247.

**Curios** Pasar Triwindu on Jl Diponegoro is Solo's flea market. All kinds of bric-a-brac plus a few genuine antiques are sold here – old buttons and buckles, china dogs and fine porcelain, puppets, batik tulis pens, lamps, bottles, bell jars and furniture – but if you're looking for bargains, you have to sift carefully through the rubbish and be prepared to bargain hard. Many of the 'antik' (antiques) are newly aged. Some of the dealers have larger collections at their homes, so it is worth asking if they have other pieces.

Toko Bedoyo Srimpi, Jl Ronggowarsito 116, is the place for wayang orang dancers' costumes and theatrical supplies such as gold gilt headdresses and painted arm bands. It also sells masks and wayang kulit puppets.

Jl Dr Rajiman (Secoyudan) is the goldsmiths' street. Buy gold in the Chinese shops and have it verified by the street-side gold testers along Jl Dr Rajiman and the side street of Jl Reksoniten. With their scale and little bottles of chemicals, they can confirm weight and purity.

Krises and other souvenirs can be purchased from street vendors at the east side of the alun alun to the north of Kraton Surakarta. Gem sellers there have a mind-boggling array of semi-precious stones. Vendors at Sriwedari Amusement Park also sell souvenirs. Pak Fauzan has a wide variety of krises for sale, and you can see the process of kris making at his small home workshop in Kampung Yosoroto Rt 09 No 21, just north off Jl Slamet Riyadi, about 200m from the Riyadi Palace Hotel.

At the Balai Agung, on the north side of the alun alun in front of Kraton Surakarta, you can see high-quality wayang kulit puppets being made. Gamelan sets, for around 40 million rp, are also on sale, but these are produced in the village of Bekonang, 5km from Solo.

## Getting There & Away

**Air** During the Soeharto era, Solo's airport was upgraded to an international airport in preference to the more logical Yogyakarta. Why? Some say it is because the ex-president's wife came from Solo and it is his adopted home (Soeharto has a mansion just off the western end of Jl Slamet Riyadi – any becak driver can show you). The only problem is the lack of demand for international flights. Only Silk Air flies to Singapore, on Tuesday and Saturday for around US$160 return. Even domestic services have been pared to the bone. Garuda (☎ 630 082), in the Hotel Cakra, flies daily to Jakarta. And that's it.

**Bus** The main Tirtonadi bus terminal is just north of the train station, 3km from the centre of the city.

Frequent buses go to Prambanan (1500 rp, 1½ hours), Yogya (2000/3500 rp normal/air-con, two hours), Semarang (3000/5000 rp to 8000 rp air-con, 2½ hours) and Salatiga (1600/2800 rp, 1½ hours).

To East Java, buses include those to Tawangmangu (1300 rp, one hour), Pacitan (3600 rp, four hours) and Madiun (3300/6000 rp), and there are numerous bus in all classes to Surabaya (six hours) and Malang. The Mila air-con bus goes direct to Probolinggo (eight hours) at 6pm. Luxury buses also do the longer runs, and agents can be found at the bus terminal and in the main tourist area around Jl Yos Sudarso/Slamet Riyadi. The homestays and travellers cafes also sell tickets. Luxury buses to Denpasar cost around 60,000 rp; to Jakarta, it's 45,000 rp.

Near the main bus terminal, the Gilingan minibus terminal has express minibuses to nearly as many destinations as the buses. Door-to-door minibuses include Yogya (7000 rp), Semarang (8500 rp), Blitar (21,000 rp), Surabaya or Malang (25,000 rp) and Bandung (50,000 rp). Homestays, cafes and travel agents also sell tickets. They also sell tickets to Bromo on the Yogya Rental bus for around 40,000 rp.

**Train** Solo is on the main Jakarta-Yogya-Surabaya train line, and most trains stop at Solobalapan, the main station, 2km north of the centre.

The quickest and most convenient way to get to Yogya is on the *Prambanan Ekspres* (3000 rp bisnis, one hour) departing at 6 and 9 am, noon, and 2.40 pm.

For Jakarta, the express trains are far preferable to the ekonomi trains. The *Argo Lawu* (115,000 rp eksekutif, 9½ hours) is the most luxurious day train, departing at 6 am. The *Senja Utama* (40,000/80,000 rp bisnis/eksekutif, 11 hours) departs at 6 pm. The eksekutif *Bima* and bisnis class *Jayabaya* both come through Solo from Surabaya on the way to Jakarta. For Bandung, the *Senja Mataram* (30,000/52,000 rp, nine hours) departs at 8.15 pm. The *Turangga* (45,000/75,000 rp) and the *Mutiara Selatan* (33,000 rp bisnis) are other night trains to Bandung.

Numerous trains run between Solo and Surabaya. The *Sancaka* is a good bisnis/eksekutif train to Surabaya (25,000/40,000 rp, 3½ hours) at 4.30 pm. The *Sri Tanjung* (7000 rp, five hours) is a bookable ekonomi service at 8.20 am that continues to Probolinggo and Banyuwangi (14,000 rp, 13 hours). Other ekonomi trains from Solobalapan run to Malang, Madiun and Kediri, as well as to all the big cities on the main line.

Solo Jebres station, in the north-east of Solo, has a few ekonomi services to Semarang and the north coast – the bus is a better option. From Purwosari station in the west, a slow ekonomi service runs to Wonogiri, right along the main street, Jl Slamet Riyadi.

### Getting Around

A taxi from Adi Sumarmo airport, 10km north-west of the city centre, costs 14,000 rp by taxi, or take a bus to Kartasura, then another to the airport. A becak from the train station or bus terminal into the city centre costs around 2000 rp, or a taxi from the taxi counter at the railway station costs 7500 rp. Solo's taxis have meters, but drivers won't use them from the bus or train station. The orange minibus No 06 costs 500 rp to Jl Slamet Riyadi.

The city double-decker bus runs between Kartasura in the west and Palur in the east, directly along Jl Slamet Riyadi, and costs a flat fare of 500 rp.

Many homestays and travellers cafes can arrange bike hire for around 5000 rp, or a motorbike will cost around 25,000 rp. Cars with driver can also be arranged, but prices are higher than in Yogya.

### AROUND SOLO
### Sangiran

Fifteen kilometres north of Solo, Sangiran is an important archaeological excavation site, where some of the best examples of fossil skulls of prehistoric 'Java Man' *(Pithecanthropus erectus)* were unearthed by a Dutch professor in 1936.

Sangiran has a small **museum** with a few skulls *(*one of *homo erectus)*, various pig and hippopotamus teeth and fossil exhibits, including huge mammoth bones and tusks.

## Java Man

Charles Darwin's *Evolution of the Species* inspired a new generation of naturalists in the 19th century, and his theories sparked acrimonious debate across the world. Ernst Haeckel's *The History of Natural Creation*, published in 1874, expounded further on Darwin's theory of evolution, tracing the evolution of primitive humans from a common ape-man ancestor, the famous 'missing link'.

One student of the new theories, a Dutch physician named Eugene Dubois, set sail in 1887 for Sumatra, where he worked as an army doctor. In 1889, he went to Java after hearing of the uncovering of a skull at Wajak, near Tulung Agung in East Java. Dubois worked at the dig, uncovering other human fossils closely related to modern man. In 1891, at Trinil in East Java's Ngawi district, Dubois unearthed an older skull and other remains that he later classified as *Pithecanthropus erectus* – a low-browed, prominent-jawed early human ancestor, dating from the Middle Pleistocene era. His published findings on 'Java Man' caused a storm in Europe and were among the earliest findings in support of Darwin's theories.

Since Dubois' findings, many older examples of *homo erectus* have been uncovered on Java. The most important and most numerous findings have been at Sangiran where, in the 1930s,

Ralph von Koenigswald found fossils dating back to around 1,000,000 BC. In 1936 at Perning near Mojokerto, the skull of a child was discovered and some (possibly sensationalist) estimates have dated it as 1.9 million years old. Most findings have been along the Bengawan Solo river in Central and East Java, though Pacitan, on East Java's south coast, is also an important archeological area.

Discoveries in Kenya now date the oldest hominid human ancestors, *Australopithecine*, to 2.5 million years old. Ancient man migrated from Africa to Asia and came to Java via the land bridges that once existed between the Asian mainland and the now insular Indonesian lands. It is thought that Java Man eventually became extinct and that the present inhabitants are descendents of a much later migration.

*Pithecanthropus* skull found at Sangiran, exhibiting the low brow and prominent jaw of early humans.

Souvenir stalls outside sell bones, 'mammoth tusks' carved from stone and other dubious fossil junk. Guides will also offer to take you to the area where fossils have been found – there are shells and other fossils in the crumbling slopes of the hill.

The museum is open from 9 am to 4 pm daily, except Sunday. Admission is 1000 rp. From the Tirtonadi bus terminal in Solo,

take a Purwodadi bus to Kalijambe (800 rp). Ask for Sangiran, and you will be dropped at the turn-off, 15km from Solo. It is then 4km to the museum (2000 rp by *ojek*).

### Gunung Lawu

Towering Gunung Lawu (3265m), on the border of Central and East Java, is one of the holiest mountains on Java. Mysterious

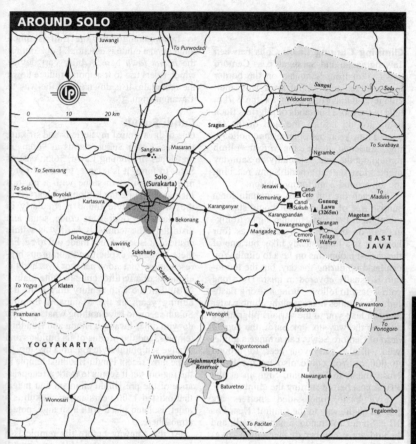

## AROUND SOLO

Juwangi
To Purwodadi
Sungai
Solo
Widodaren
0    10    20 km
Sragen
Sangiran    Masaran
To Surabaya
To Semarang
Ngrambe
Solo
(Surakarta)
Jenawi    Candi
Ceto
To Maduin
To Selo    Kemuning
Boyolali    Kartasura    Karanganyar    Candi    Gunung
Sukuh    Lawu
Karangpandan    (3265m)    Magetan
Bekonang    Mangadeg    Tawangmangu    Sarangan
Delanggu    Cemoro    Telaga    EAST
Juwiring    Sewu    Wahyu    JAVA
To Yogya    Sukoharjo
Klaten    Sungai    Solo
Prambanan    Purwantoro
Wonogiri    Jatisrono
To
YOGYAKARTA    Ponogoro
Wuryantoro    Gajahmungkur    Nguntoronadi
Reservoir    Tirtomaya    Nawangan
Wonosari    Baturetno
Tegalombo
To Pacitan

Hindu temples dot its slopes, and each year thousands of pilgrims seeking spiritual enlightenment climb its peak.

Although popular history has it that when the Majapahit kingdom fell to Islam, the Hindu elite all fled east to Bali, Javanese lore relates that Brawijaya V, the last king of Majapahit, went west. Brawijaya's son, Raden Patah, was the leader of Demak and led the conquering forces of Islam against Majapahit. But rather than fight his own son, Brawijaya retreated to Gunung Lawu

to seek spiritual enlightenment. There he achieved nirvana as Sunan Lawu, and today pilgrims come to seek his spiritual guidance or to acquire magic powers.

The unique temples on the mountain, the last Hindu temples built on Java before conversion to Islam, show the influence of the later 'wayang' style of East Java, though they incorporate elements of fertility worship. Most famous is the temple of Candi Sukuh, while Candi Ceto is another large temple complex that still attracts Hindu worshippers. Some villages in the area still resist conversion to Islam.

**Climbing Gunung Lawu** Colts between Tawangmangu and Sarangan pass Cemoro Sewu, 5km from Sarangan on the border between East and Central Java. This small village is the starting point for the 6.7km hike to the top. Thousands of pilgrims flock to the top on 1 Suro, the start of the Javanese new year, but pilgrims and holidaying students make the night climb throughout the year, especially on Saturday night. Most start at around 8 pm, reaching the top around 2 am for meditation.

To reach the top of the mountain for a sunrise free of clouds, you should start by midnight at the latest, though super-fit hikers can do the climb in as little as four hours. It is a long, steady hike, but one of the easiest mountains on Java to climb. You can head up during the day, but the mountain is usually covered in mist. The stone path is easy to follow – bring a strong flashlight – or guides make a night climb easier and can lead you to the various pilgrimage sites on the way up. Pak Sardi, the *kepala desa* of Cemoro Sewu, can arrange a guide, who will also carry your gear, for around 40,000 rp. You could also try the Hotel Nusa Indah in Sarangan. Sign in at the PHPA post before starting the climb.

Five basic, open-sided shelters are passed on the way to the summit. Near Pos III is Sumur Jolotundo, a natural well, and behind are a number of meditation caves with doors. Legend has it that one is the entrance to a tunnel that leads to Gunung Merapi and Parangtritis, with Gunung Lawu forming the third point of this mystic triangle. Farther up is Sendang Derajat, a holy spring, where pilgrims should bathe with the icy waters seven times to achieve wealth and influence. Pilgrims spend the night in meditation at **Argo Dalam**, some 500m before the top. It is said that Sunan Lawu appears at this bedecked shelter to the pure at heart, and only those who are spiritually fit can make the final climb to the summit.

An alternative trail begins at Cemoro Kandang, a few kilometres west on the way to Tawangmangu, but the trail is much longer and a guide is essential. Look out for the *becak lawu* here, a billy cart device which riders use to transport produce down the mountain. It is downhill all the way to Tawangmangu.

## Candi Sukuh

One of Java's most mysterious and striking temples, Candi Sukuh stands at 900m on the slopes of Gunung Lawu, 36km east of Solo. In form, it is a large, truncated pyramid of rough-hewn stone with a curious Inca look. While the sculpture is carved in the 'wayang' style found particularly in East Java, the figures are crude, squat and distorted. The temple is hardly as wildly erotic as it is sometimes made out to be, but there are fairly explicit and humorous representations of a stone penis or two, and the elements of a fertility cult are quite plain.

Built in the 15th century during the declining years of the Majapahit Empire, Sukuh seems to have nothing whatsoever to do with other Javanese Hindu and Buddhist temples, and the origins of its builders and strange sculptural style remain a mystery. It is the most recent Hindu-Buddhist temple in the region, yet it seems to mark a reappearance of the pre-Hindu animism and magic that existed 1500 years earlier. Sukuh is a quiet, isolated place with a strange, potent atmosphere.

At the gateway before the temple is a large stone linga and yoni. Flowers are still often scattered over them, and there's a story that the symbol was used mainly by villagers to determine whether a wife had been faithful or a wife-to-be was still a virgin. The woman had to wear a sarong and stride across the linga – if the sarong tore, her infidelity was proven. Other interesting cult objects stand farther in among the trees. These include a tall-standing monument depicting Bima, the *Mahabharata* warrior hero, with Narada (the messenger of the gods) in a stylised womb followed by another statue with Bima dropping through at his birth. In the top courtyard, three enormous flat-backed turtles stand like sacrificial altars.

There are superb views from the site to the west and north across terrace fields and mountains. A paved trail leads downhill most of the way to Tawangmangu.

**Getting There & Away** From Solo, take a Tawangmangu bus to Karangpandan (1000 rp), then a Kemuning minibus to the turn-off to Candi Sukuh (750 rp). On market days (Wage and Pahing in the Javanese calendar), a 9 am bus from Karangpandan stops right beside the temple; otherwise, it's a couple of kilometres uphill walk to the site. The trip takes about 1½ hours in total. You'll find that the ubiquitous visitors' book will appear here as well.

## Candi Ceto

Farther up the slopes of Gunung Lawu, Candi Ceto was constructed in the same era as Candi Sukuh. Combining elements of Shivaism and fertility worship, it is a larger temple than Sukuh, and spreads over terraces leading up the misty hillside. It is a spartan complex, with little carving, and the closely fitted stonework, some of it new, gives the temple a medieval atmosphere. Along with Sukuh, it is reputed to be the most recent Hindu temple on Java, built when the wave of Islamic conversion was already sweeping the island.

Because of the difficulty in reaching Ceto, few visitors make it here – one of the attractions. Ceto is 9km by road past the Sukuh turn-off. Take a bus as far as Kemuning, then an ojek, though it is more pleasant to walk the 6km through the hills covered in tea plantations, clove trees and vegetable plots.

## Tawangmangu
☎ 0271

Trekkers can make an interesting 2½ hour walk from Candi Sukuh, 6km along a paved path to Tawangmangu, a hill resort on the other side of Gunung Lawu. This path is steep in parts but also negotiable by motorbike. You can also reach Tawangmangu by

bus from Solo via Karangpandan, which is just as fine a trip along a switchback road through magnificent tightly terraced hills. Tawangmangu is packed on Sunday – go during the week.

On the back road in Tawangmangu, about 2km from the bus terminal, **Grojogan Sewu** (entry 1500 rp) is a 100m-high waterfall and a favourite playground for monkeys. This is perhaps the most famous waterfall on Java, though apart from its height, it is not all that spectacular. It's reached by a long flight of steps down a hillside, and you can swim in the very chilly and dirty swimming pool at the bottom. From the bottom of the waterfall a walking trail leads to the path to Candi Sukuh, and ojeks also hang out at the junction on weekends.

The cave of **Gua Maria** is a 3km walk from the road. Another 2km-long walking trail leads up through vegetable plots from in front of the Hotel Garuda and joins the main road at the top of the village. There's a wartel about 100m uphill from the Wisma Yanti.

**Places to Stay & Eat** In Tawangmangu, the *Pak Amat Losmen* is right by the bus terminal. Dirty rooms with enclosed verandahs cost 15,000 rp, more like 10,000 rp after bargaining. The mandis are disgusting and the food in the attached restaurant is almost as foul.

Prices and quality increase as you head up the hill, a long grunt from the bus station. The *Pondok Garuda* (☎ 97239), about half a kilometre uphill, is a good mid-range place but a little expensive. Rooms with hot water and TV cost 35,000 rp and 40,000 rp, or renovated suites with fine views cost 125,000 rp.

*Wisma Yanti* (☎ 97056, Jl Raya Lawu 65) is managed by the Hotel Sahid Raya in Solo, though it's hard to believe. It needs a thorough renovation, not to mention a good scrub, but this fine colonial villa is one of the cheapest around. Rooms with mandi at the back cost 20,000 rp and 25,000 rp. Better are the 30,000 rp rooms inside the main house, which has a wonderful sitting/dining room. On weekdays you'll most likely have the whole house to yourself.

Farther up the hill, the modern *Wisma Lumayan* (☎ 97481, Jl Raya Lawu 10) is another good choice. Clean rooms with mandi cost 20,000 rp, or a larger room with TV and sitting room is 35,000 rp. A three bedroom villa with hot water costs 90,000 rp. Next door, the more basic *Losmen Arto Moro* has rooms for 20,000 rp.

Nearby, the friendly, good-value *Pondok Indah* (☎ 97024, Jl Raya Lawu 22) has well kept rooms with sitting room, hot water and TV for 45,000 rp. Two- and three-bedroom villas cost 90,000 rp to 135,000 rp.

The best place in town is the *Komajaya Komaratih Hotel* (☎ 97125, Jl Raya Lawu 150-151), near the turn-off to the waterfall. It is favoured by tour groups, and rooms with hot-water showers and TV in the old wing cost 50,000 rp to 88,000 rp. Newer rooms and suites which accommodate up to four people cost from 118,000 rp. Add 21% to the prices. The hotel has a small restaurant and bar.

For good, cheap Indonesian dishes, eat at the *Sapto Argo* on Jl Raya Lawu opposite the Wisma Lumayan. It serves *sate kelinci* (rabbit sate), the local speciality, and also gives out rough maps of Tawangmangu. Also on Jl Raya Lawu, the tranquil *Lesahan Pondok Indah* has excellent food, and you can enjoy it while seated cross-legged on bamboo mats. At front of the Wisma Yanti, a little no-name warung serves a mean nasi goreng and *kopi susu* made from *susu segar* (fresh milk). The *Rumah Makan Bangun Trisno* on Jl Balaikambang, the road opposite the Komajaya Komaratih Hotel, is also worth trying and has elevated views.

**Getting There & Away** Buses go to Solo (1300 rp) and colts to Sarangan (2500 rp). Minibuses (500 rp) loop through town from the bus terminal up the main road, across to the waterfall and around the back to the bus terminal. They are frequent on Sunday, but they wait forever on other days and won't budge until they are jam-packed.

## Sarangan
☎ 0351

An interesting alternative to backtracking to Solo is to take a colt to Sarangan, 18km from Tawangmangu on the mountain road to Madiun. It is just over the provincial border in East Java, though most foreign visitors come via Solo. On weekends, local crowds pack the place, many from as far away as Surabaya.

This picturesque hill town lies on the slopes of Gunung Lawu, with hotels clustered at the edge of **Telaga Pasir**, a crater lake. At 1287m, it has a refreshing climate, and this is one of the most pleasant hill resorts on Java. It is cooler and more attractive than Tawangmangu, and the lake provides opportunities for boating and water-skiing. You can walk around the lake, and **Tirtosari Waterfall** is a pleasant, one hour return walk from the far side of Telaga Pasir through the countryside and small villages. Sarangan is also a good base for tackling the ascent of Gunung Lawu.

A few kilometres downhill on the road to Madiun is the smaller lake, **Telaga Wahyu**. This lake is less popular because, apart from its poorer aspect, legend has it that courting couples will separate if they visit the lake.

**Places to Stay** Many hotels are on the main road as you enter town, where a 1000 rp entry is payable at the town's entrance gate. Accommodation prices are higher than elsewhere, and guides will follow you into hotels to get a commission. Shake them off and negotiate for a room.

*Hotel Nusa Indah* (☎ 888021, Jl Raya Telaga 171) is the most popular. It is friendly, well kept and can arrange English-speaking guides (50,000 rp) to climb Gunung Sewu. Rooms with hot water cost 20,000 rp to 35,000 rp, and villas with sitting rooms are 75,000 rp to 90,000 rp.

Nearby, the *Sari Rasa Guest House* (☎ 888050) also has clean rooms from 25,000 rp. Across the road, the *Hotel Asia Jaya* (☎ 888027) has rooms from 28,000 rp to 70,000 rp, before discount.

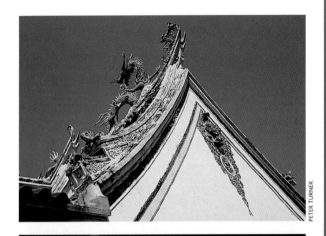

PETER TURNER

**Top:** Tay Kak Sie Temple, Semarang, Central Java.

**Bottom:** Figure in Sam Po Kong Temple, Semarang, Central Java – a fine example of traditional woodcarving.

PETER TURNER

**Top:** Fishing boats, Karimunjawa, Central Java.

**Bottom:** Ship mast, Karimunjawa, Central Java.

Turn left to find, right on the lake shore, the big but soulless *Hotel Telaga Mas* (☎ *888761, Jl Telaga Sarangan)*. It is hardly the 'international' hotel it claims to be, but rooms with hot water, bath, TV and sitting rooms are the best in Sarangan and cost 150,000 rp or 250,000/350,000 rp for two/three-bedroom villas.

Back from the lake beside the Telaga Mas, the *Wisma Moro Dadi* (☎ *888704, Jl Bantarangin 211)* is reasonably priced at 25,000 rp for rooms with TV and hot water mandi. Next door, the *Hotel Rejeki* (☎ *888 140)* has a good, cheap restaurant but rooms from 50,000 rp are overpriced, even with a 20% discount.

From the main street, turn right at the lake and you come to the *Hotel Indah* (☎ *888 012)*, a more upmarket motel-style place, with double rooms from 59,000 rp to 89,000 rp and family rooms from 116,000 rp, all including breakfast.

At the top of the village, with fantastic views of the lake, *Hotel Sarangan* (☎ *888 022)* has colonial charm and is very popular with Dutch tourists. Rooms, most sleeping four or more people, cost 95,000 rp to 145,000 rp and have their own sitting rooms with open fire places. Ask for a discount.

**Getting There & Away** Regular colts run to Tawangmangu (2500 rp), passing Cemoro Sewu for the climb to Gunung Lawu. Buses also run to Magetan and Madiun, from where there are buses all over Java.

## Mangadeg

Near Karangpandan, a road branches south from the main Solo-Tawangmangu highway. About 5km on this road to Mangadeg is the **burial hill** of Solo's royal Mangkunegoro family. Make a small donation and visit the graves, or simply take in the superb views across the countryside.

A couple of kilometres away in the same sacred hills, the lavish **Astana Giribangun** has been built by the former president as the final resting place for himself and the Soeharto family. Madam Tien Soeharto is buried here, and her grave is open to pil-

grims. They flocked here in their thousands after her death in 1996, but in the post-*reformasi* era, no one is interested in paying homage to the Soehartos any more.

On the way to Mangadeg is **Pablengan**, the former bathing pools of the Mangkunegoro. The ancient bathing pavilions are in disrepair. The springs emit seven different types of water with various curative powers. Water from one of the springs is also drunk to induce abortions.

## SALATIGA
● pop 103,000      ☎ 0298

This provincial city between Semarang and Solo lies at the foothills of Gunung Merbabu and is noted for its Satya Wacana Christian University, which takes foreign students who study Indonesian. It is a clean and attractive city and has a hill station feel, as well as some fine colonial architecture.

The tourist office (☎ 26244), Jl Diponegoro 10, produces a brochure but not much English is spoken. Most of the hotels are on the main street, Jl Jenderal Sudirman, near the sprawling central market and the big Salatiga Plaza, which are both worth a browse. One alley north of the Salatiga Plaza is Kafe Globy, an Internet cafe.

### Places to Stay & Eat
*Hotel Beringin* (☎ *26129, Jl Jenderal Sudirman 160)* is right in the action and is the pick of the hotels. Reasonable budget rooms cost 22,500 to 27,500 rp, or well appointed mid-range rooms with hot water are 55,000 rp to 100,000 rp. A wartel and a good Chinese restaurant are attached.

Jl Jenderal Sudirman has a few other restaurants, including the recommended *Tamansari*, but the widest dining selection is offered by the numerous *warungs* that set up in the evening down the southern end of the street.

*Hotel Maya* (☎ *23179, Jl Kartini 15A)* is about 1.5km from the centre and a little run-down, but it has spacious grounds, a restaurant and a swimming pool open to the public. Rooms cost 20,000 rp to 50,000 rp.

**CENTRAL JAVA**

## Getting There & Away

The bus terminal is 4km from the city centre on the Solo-Semarang highway. Frequent buses run to Semarang (2000 rp) and Solo (1600 rp), as well as to numerous other destinations. For Kopeng, take a No 2 angkot to the turn-off on the highway south of town, then hop on a Magelang bus or a Semarang-Kopeng bus.

## AROUND SALATIGA

Nearby **Lake Rawapening** is a popular local picnic spot, and **Kopeng** is a small, scruffy hill-resort 19km from Salatiga on the slopes of Gunung Merbabu. Kopeng has a waterfall and dirty hot spring pools, but the main point of interest here is the walk to towering **Gunung Merbabu**, a nine hour hike with a night spent on the mountain. In Kopeng, the faded, colonial *Hotel Kopeng (☎ 26344)* is exceptional value, and costs 11,000 rp up to 27,500 rp for a two room flat.

## AMBARAWA

At the junction where the Bandungan road branches from the Yogya-Semarang road, just off the Solo-Semarang road, this market town is the site of the **Ambarawa Train Station Museum** (Museum Kereta Api Ambarawa). Originally opened in 1873 as the Koening Willem I station, the museum has rail memorabilia and 21 steam locomotives built between 1891 and 1928. The oldest is a Hartmann Chemnitz SS300. Most (14) of the locos were made in Germany, but there are also Dutch (3), English (2) and Swedish (1) engines. The museum is open from 7 am to 5 pm daily. Pak Setio speaks Dutch and is an informative guide.

Though the railway line has closed, groups of up to 100 passengers can charter a train for the 18km round trip from Ambarawa to Bedono for 1,300,000 rp. Book through the Ambarawa station (☎ 0298-91035). It requires a few days notice to get the old cog steam engine and antique carriages ready. Alternatively, charter a little diesel *lori* on the spot for a fun trip to Ngampin (10,000 rp return, 5km away) or to Jambu (20,000 rp, 10km).

The museum is a couple of kilometres outside town, just off the road to Magelang. Ambarawa has hotels but Bandungan is a nicer place to stay.

## Getting There & Away

Ambarawa can be reached by public bus from Semarang (2000 rp, one hour, 40km) and Yogya (2½ hours, 90km) via Magelang. From Solo, you have to change buses at Salatiga.

## BANDUNGAN
☎ 0298

Bandungan, at 980m, is a pleasant enough hill resort and allows you to savour the mountain air, but the main attraction is nearby Gedung Songo. It is a busy little market town, noted for locally grown fruit, vegetables and cut flowers.

## Places to Stay

Bandungan has dozens of losmen and more expensive hotels. The cheapest places are in the town, while the better options are farther out on the road to Gedung Songo.

In the town, *Hotel Parahita (☎ 711017)*, just down the back road to Semarang from the market, is a typical basic place with rooms for 15,000 rp. The *Hotel Santosa* next door is similar. Owned by the railways, *Hotel Bandungan Indah (☎ 711078)* has huge grounds and an impressive main building, but hasn't seen maintenance since the Dutch left. The swimming pool is a cholera swamp. Rooms are 30,000 rp to 80,000 rp.

One kilometre west of town, the *Hotel Rawa Pening Eltricia (☎ 711134)* is the best value. Perched on a hill with great views and a terraced garden, it has a lovely old colonial-style restaurant, a small pool and tennis court. A big variety of well appointed rooms are scattered around the grounds – from 45,000 rp up to 162,000 rp for a four bedroom cottage. Farther along, the related *Rawa Pening Pratama (☎ 711 134)* has a similar aspect and facilities, but less style. Rooms start from 60,000 rp.

At the top end is the newer *Hotel Nugraha Wisata (☎ 711501)*, which has a swimming pool, a huge restaurant and rooms for 80,000 rp to 225,000 rp (50% more on weekends).

## Getting There & Away
Buses run directly from Semarang to Bandungan (2000 rp), or if you are coming from the south, get off at Ambarawa, then take a colt to Bandungan (500 rp).

## GEDUNG SONGO TEMPLES
These nine small Hindu temples (Gedung Songo means 'nine buildings' in Javanese) are scattered along the tops of the foothills around Gunung Ungaran. Like the temples in Dieng, the Gedung Songo are small and simple, among the oldest Hindu temples on Java. The architecture may not be overwhelming, but the setting is simply superb. This 1000m perch gives one of the most spectacular views in Java – south across the shimmering Danau Rawa Pening to Gunung Merbabu with, behind it, smouldering Gunung Merapi, and west to Gunung Sumbing and Gunung Sundoro.

Built in the 8th and 9th century, and devoted to Shiva and Vishnu, five of the temples are in good condition after major restorations in the 1980s, but most of the carvings have been lost. The temples were first discovered by the Dutch in 1740 and Raffles called them the Gedung Pitoe (Seven Buildings) after a visit in 1804. But it wasn't until 1930 that all the ruins were catalogued.

A well trodden path ventures up the hill past three groupings – the temples at the third grouping are the most impressive. Halfway, the trail leads down to a ravine and gushing hot sulphur springs, then up again to the final temple and its expansive views. The 3km loop can be walked in an hour, but allow longer to savour the atmosphere. Horses can also be hired.

The site is open from 7 am to 5 pm daily. Get there early in the morning for the best views.

## Places to Stay & Eat
It is possible to stay in the tiny settlement outside the gate for unsurpassed morning views, but facilities are very limited and the nights are freezing cold. Opposite the single, grotty warung is the *Hotel Melati I,* where simple but very clean rooms with mandi cost 10,000 rp. The *Hotel Rahayu,* back from the road, is similar.

## Getting There & Away
The temples are about 6km from Bandungan. From Bandungan, take a Sumawono bus (only 100 rp) 3km to the turn-off to the temples. Buses also run from Semarang and Ambarawa (1250 rp). From the turn-off, take an ojek for the final 3km uphill to Gedung Songo (2000 rp).

## BLEDUG KUWU
East of Puwodadi, which is 56km north of Solo and 38km west of Demak, Bledug Kuwu is one of Java's stranger natural phenomena. This 'mud volcano' erupts every few minutes. Hot water and steam under the grounds percolate up through mud, causing a bubble to swell to the size of a weather balloon, which then bursts with a great slap as the mud falls back to ground. It's not exactly Merapi, but it's worth a look if you are passing.

To reach Bledug Kuwu, head east about 15km from Purwodadi on the main Semarang to Surabaya highway and take the signposted turn-off at Wirosari. It is then about 5km on a paved road to the ramshackle tourist complex. Wooden walkways venture out on to the mudflats – don't stray off them.

## NORTH COAST
For many centuries Java's north coast was the centre for trade with merchants from Arabia, India and China. Through trade, the north coast came in contact with different cultures and ideas, and became the birthplace of Islam on Java. During the 15th and 16th centuries, Islam was adopted by the rulers of the trading principalities, in opposition to the Hindu kingdoms of inland Central Java.

Islam in Indonesia immortalised the *wali songo*, or nine saints, who are credited with

CENTRAL JAVA

the establishment of Islam in Java. With the exception of Sunan Gunungjati in Cirebon, the tombs of the saints all lie between Semarang and Surabaya, and are important pilgrimage points for devout Muslims. A number of these places lie on the road to Surabaya and can also be visited using Semarang as a base.

While the coast attracts many pilgrims, few tourists venture north. The flat, hot coastal plain bordered by low hills doesn't have fine beaches or the spectacular scenery of the central mountains. The massive monuments of ancient Java are missing, and apart from some impressive mosques, the reminders of the north coast's trading heyday are not obvious. Yet, while the north coast doesn't have any 'must-see' tourist attractions and is conspicuously absent from tour group itineraries, it has an interesting mix of cultural influences, a relaxed Middle Eastern atmosphere and makes an interesting diversion for the more adventurous with time to spare.

## PEKALONGAN
- pop 324,000    ☎ 0285

On the north coast between Semarang and Cirebon, Pekalongan is known as Kota Batik (Batik City), and its batiks are some of the most sought-after in Indonesia. Once positioned on the trading routes between China, India and Arabia, the city absorbed many influences, and these are reflected in its style of batik. Pekalongan batik is less formal, more colourful and innovative in design compared with the traditional styles of Yogyakarta and Solo.

Pekalongan is a must for batik freaks; otherwise, it is not a tourist destination. The town has a neglected, old-fashioned atmosphere and a mixed population. While the

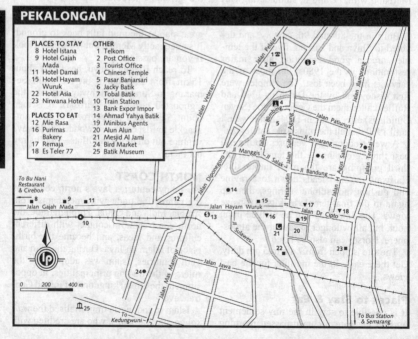

**PEKALONGAN**

PLACES TO STAY
8 Hotel Istana
9 Hotel Gajah Mada
11 Hotel Damai
15 Hotel Hayam Wuruk
22 Hotel Asia
23 Nirwana Hotel

PLACES TO EAT
12 Mie Rasa
16 Purimas Bakery
17 Remaja
18 Es Teler 77

OTHER
1 Telkom
2 Post Office
3 Tourist Office
4 Chinese Temple
5 Pasar Banjarsari
6 Jacky Batik
7 Tobal Batik
10 Train Station
13 Bank Expor Impor
14 Ahmad Yahya Batik
19 Minibus Agents
20 Alun Alun
21 Mesjid Al Jami
24 Bird Market
25 Batik Museum

To Bu Nani Restaurant & Cirebon

Jalan Gajah Mada
Jalan Pelajar
Jalan Veteran
Jalan Blimbing
Jalan Sultan Agung
Jalan Patiunus
Jalan Ilamprang
Jl Semarang
Jalan Terata
Jalan Diponegoro
Jl Manggis
Jl Salak
Jl Hasanudin
Jl Bandung
Jl H Agus Salim
Jalan Hayam Wuruk
Jalan Dr Cipto
Jl Sulawesi
Jalan Mas Mansyur
Jalan Jawa

0    200    400 m

To Kedungwuni

To Bus Station & Semarang

main street, Jl Gajah Mada/Hayam Wuruk, can bustle, Pekalongan is relatively quiet for its size, especially during the afternoon siesta.

## Information

The tourist office (☎ 41092), Jl Jatayu 3, in the town hall (Balai Kota) will try to answer most queries.

The main post office (Kantor Pos dan Giro) is opposite the Balai Kota. For international telephone calls, the Telkom office is next door at Jl Merak 2.

Change money at Bank Expor Impor on Jl Hayam Wuruk.

## Things to See

Pekalongan's small **Batik Museum**, 2km south of the train station on Jl Majapahit, exhibits examples of batik styles, with explanations in Indonesian. It's open from 9 am to 1 pm daily, except Sunday. Of more interest than this rather dull museum is the **bird market** nearby on Jl Kurinci.

The most interesting area of town is around **Pasar Banjarsari**, a lively market and a good place for batik shopping. Nearby on Jl Blimbing is the old **Chinese quarter**. Along this street is a Chinese temple and old terraced houses. To the east, on Jl Patiunus and the streets leading off it, is the **Arab quarter**, and this is also a good area for batik (see under Shopping in this section).

Facing the alun alun, **Mesjid Jami Yasmaja** has impressive Arabic architecture enclosing an older Javanese-style mosque.

## Places to Stay

Budget hotels are directly opposite the train station on Jl Gajah Mada. The friendly *Hotel Gajah Mada* (☎ 22185) at No 11 has singles/doubles from 10,000/12,500 rp, and is better than the *Hotel Damai*.

In the centre of town, a popular mid-range option is the *Hotel Hayam Wuruk* (☎ 22 823, Jl Hayam Wuruk 152-54). A variety of fading rooms with mandi cost 28,000/33,000 rp up to 57,000 rp for those with TV, air-con and hot water (maybe).

The *Hotel Istana* (☎ 23581, Jl Gajah Mada 23) is a better mid-range hotel, with fan rooms from 40,000 rp and air-con rooms from 60,000 rp. It has a disco – about the only nightlife in Pekalongan.

The *Nirwana Hotel* (☎ 22446, Jl Dr Wahidin 11) is by far the best hotel in town. It has a large pool, coffee shop and restaurant. Air-con rooms cost 62,000/70,000 rp to 108,000/119,000 rp, including breakfast.

## Places to Eat

On Jl Merdeka, just north of the main road near the market, the *Mie Rasa* is a spotless little place with noodle dishes and iced fruit juices. At the *Remaja* (Jl Dr Cipto 30), good and reasonably cheap Chinese food is available and seafood is served. For the best seafood, head 2km west of town along Jl Gaja Mada to *Bu Nani* (Jl Raya Tirta).

The *Purimas Bakery* (Jl Hayam Wuruk) has good cakes, pastries, cold drinks and a sit-down area in which to enjoy them. A smaller branch is on Jl Gajah Mada nearby.

## Shopping

Pekalongan batik is constantly evolving and new designs are more suited to western and modern Indonesian tastes. Traditional batik is still popular, however, and for formal occasions Indonesians are often required to don batik.

Street peddlers casually wave batik from the doorways of hotels and restaurants – mostly they offer cheap cloths and poor quality sarongs. Shops around town, many of them on Jl Hayam Wuruk, sell readymade clothes, lengths of cloth and sarongs in cotton and silk.

Pasar Banjarsari is a great place to browse for cheap, everyday batik, and some better pieces can be found. In the same area, Tobal, at Jl Teratai 24, is a large rag-trade business that produces clothes for the export market. You can view the process. Jacky, nearby at Jl Surabaya 5A, has a showroom down an alley, with a large range of clothes and lengths of good-quality cloth.

Most of the traditional batik is produced in the villages around Pekalongan. In the batik village of Kedungwuni, 17km south of town, Oey Soe Tjoen's workshop is famous for its intricate and colourful batik tulis. You can see it being made every day, except Friday.

### Getting There & Away

Pekalongan is on the main Jakarta-Semarang-Surabaya road and rail route. There is also a road linking Pekalongan and the Dieng Plateau.

**Bus** Pekalongan's bus terminal is about 4km south-east of the centre of town, 500 rp by colt or 2000 rp by becak. Buses from Cirebon can drop you off in town on their way through.

Frequent buses go to Semarang (3100/5000 rp air-con, three hours). Buses go to Cirebon (4000/7000 rp, four hours) supposedly every hour, but chances are you'll first have to take a bus to Tegal – they leave every half hour – and then another to Cirebon. There are a few buses to Wonosobo in the morning, or the most direct route to Dieng is to take a bus to Batur, then a pickup from there.

The agents for door-to-door minibuses are clustered together on Jl Alun Alun, just north of the square. Fares and journey times include Jakarta (50,000 rp air-con, 10 hours), Yogyakarta (11,000 rp air-con, five hours), Semarang (13,500 rp non-air-con, two hours) and Bandung (30,000 rp, eight hours). Hotels will ring for pick-up.

**Train** As Pekalongan is the midway point for most trains, it is hard to get a booking on the better express services, and ekonomi trains are crowded. The *Senja Utama* and *Fajar Utama* expresses run from Semarang to Jakarta and stop in Pekalongan and Cirebon. To Semarang and Solo, the ekonomi *Cepat* leaves at 3.05 pm.

### Getting Around

Pekalongan has plenty of becaks, costing around 500 rp per kilometre. Orange bemos run all over town for a standard 500 rp. For Keduwangi, take a bemo down Jl Mansyur.

## SEMARANG
• pop 1.35 million   ☎ 024

The north-coast port of Semarang, the capital city of Central Java Province, is a strong contrast to the royal cities of Solo and Yogyakarta. Under the Dutch it became a busy trading and administrative centre, and great numbers of Chinese traders joined the Muslim entrepreneurs of the north coast. Even in the depressed 1950s, great wealth flowed through the city, with sugar and other agricultural produce going out and industrial raw materials and finished goods coming in.

Today, Semarang is the main port in Central Java. Deep-water berthing facilities were built so that ocean-going vessels no longer had to anchor out in the mouth of Sungai Kali Baru.

Semarang is more a commercial centre than a city for tourists, and its main points of interest are the crumbling but fascinating old city and the Chinese Gedung Batu Temple. This little-visited city is a good starting point for trips along the north coast or south to the central mountains, and it makes a good stopover for a night or two.

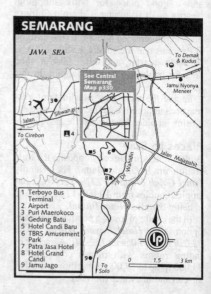

**SEMARANG**

JAVA SEA

To Demak & Kudus

See Central Semarang Map p330

Jamu Nyonya Meneer

To Cirebon

Jalan Majapahit

To Solo

1 Terboyo Bus Terminal
2 Airport
3 Puri Maerokoco
4 Gedung Batu
5 Hotel Candi Baru
6 TBRS Amusement Park
7 Patra Jasa Hotel
8 Hotel Grand Candi
9 Jamu Jago

0    1.5    3 km

## Orientation

Semarang is split into two parts. 'Old' Semarang is on the coastal plain, sandwiched between the two Banjir canals, while the new town has spread out to the wealthy residential areas in the southern hills of Candi. An important hub in the old town is Pasar Johar, on the roundabout at the top of Jl Pemuda.

Jl Pemuda, Semarang's premier boulevard in Dutch times, is still a major artery and shopping street, though nowadays the Simpang Lima (Five Ways) square, with its shopping malls and big hotels, is the real centre of Semarang.

## Information

**Tourist Offices** The city tourist office has a counter (☎ 414332) tucked away on the first floor of Plaza Simpang Lima in the north-east corner. It is open from 10 am to 2.30 pm and 3.30 to 7.30 pm daily, except Sunday. The head office (☎ 311220) is at Jl Siliwangi 29.

The Central Java tourist office (☎ 607 182) has lots of maps and brochures on the province, including a regional *Calendar of Events*. Unfortunately, it is well out of the city in the PRPP Complex, Jl Madukoro Blok BB, near Puri Maerakaca.

**Money** The BCA bank, Jl Pemuda 90-92, changes most currencies and its ATM accepts Visa. There are other big banks are nearby on Jl Pemuda, including the Lippo, which has a MasterCard ATM.

**Post & Communications** Semarang's main post office, on Jl Pemuda near the river, is open from 8 am to 10 pm for basic postal services, and normal office hours for parcel post. The W-Net Internet service next door is open from 8 am to 10 pm, and costs 2000 rp for 15 minutes. The Telkom office for international calls is at Jl Suprapto 7, and it has a Home Country Direct phone. Wartels are found all over town – one is directly behind the post office.

**Medical Services** The best hospital and first choice of the sizeable Semarang expat community is RS Saint Elizabeth (☎ 315 345), on Jl Kawi in the Candi Baru district.

## Old City

Semarang's old city is fascinating to wander around.

On Jl Let Jenderal Suprapto, the **Gereja Blenduk** is a Dutch church built in 1753 and still functioning. It has a huge dome, and inside is a baroque organ. This area was the main port area in Dutch times. Towards the river from the church are numerous **old Dutch warehouses**, many still housing shipping companies. Head south from here along the canal behind the post office for a glimpse of Amsterdam in the tropics. The imposing **PT Perkebunan building** in particular is a superb example of Dutch architecture. The **market street** here is the favourite haunt of traditional masseurs and other street-side medical *ahli* (experts) who claim to fix everything from kidney disease to sexual dysfunction.

Farther south, you plunge into the narrow streets of Semarang's old **Chinatown**. Though Chinese characters do not adorn the shops in a country where the Chinese language is still discriminated against by law, Semarang is Indonesia's most obviously Chinese city.

Chinatown's highlight is the brightly painted **Tay Kak Sie Temple**, one of the finest Chinese temples in Indonesia. This temple complex dates from 1772 and is on Gang Lombok, the small alley running along the river off Jl Pekojan. Also in Chinatown, **Pasar Cina**, also called Pasar Gang Baru, is a fascinating market to wander around. It's a morning market, at its best before 7 am. Wander along Gang Pinggir and the other bustling streets where Chinese businesses ply their trade and some old shop-houses can be seen.

Back towards the centre of the city, **Pasar Johar** is Semarang's most intriguing market. You can find a little bit of almost everything, from food to hardware to clothing, and it's worth an hour or so of wandering around. Semarang's **Grand Mosque** is facing the market.

# Gedung Batu (Sam Po Kong Temple)

This well known Chinese temple stands 5km south-west of the centre of the city. It was built in honour of Admiral Cheng Ho, the famous Muslim eunuch of the Ming dynasty, who led a Chinese fleet on seven expeditions to Java and other parts of South-East and West Asia in the early 15th century. Cheng Ho has since become a saint known as Sam Po Kong and is particularly revered in Melaka, Malaysia. He first arrived in Java in 1405 and is attributed with having helped spread Islam. This temple is also revered by Muslims.

The main hall of the temple complex is built around an inner chamber in the form of a huge cave flanked by two great dragons. Hence the temple's popular name, *gedung batu*, meaning 'stone building'. Inside the cave is an idol of Sam Po Kong.

To get to Gedung Batu, take Damri bus No 2 from Jl Pemuda to Karang Ayu, then a Daihatsu from there to the temple. It takes about half an hour from central Semarang.

# Puri Maerakoco

Often referred to as 'Taman Mini Jawa Tengah', this large theme park is Semarang's version of Jakarta's Taman Mini, with traditional houses representing all of Central Java's *kabupatens* (regencies). While mostly of interest to domestic tourists, it is well done and worth a look if you will be exploring Central Java in depth. Most of the houses have a small display of crafts and a map showing points of interest in their regency.

Puri Maerakoco is open from 8 am to 9 pm daily, and entry is 1500 rp. It is way out near the airport, and not accessible by public transport. Nearby is **Taman Rekreasi Marina**, a large swimming pool complex on the so-so beach, where jet skis can be hired. It is open from 5.30 am to 8 pm daily, and entry is 5000 rp.

# Jamu

Semarang is known for its two large *jamu* (herbal medicine) manufacturers – **Jamu**

**Nyonya Meneer**, Jl Raya Kaligawe Km 4, near the bus terminal, and **Jamu Jago**, Jl Setia Budi 273, about 6km from the city on the Ambarawa road. Jamu Jago is well known for its adverts that use a squad of dwarfs! Both have museums open from 8 am to 3 pm Monday to Friday, and tours of the factories are available upon request.

## Other Attractions

**Tugu Muda**, at the southern end of Jl Pemuda, is a candle-shaped monument commemorating Semarang's five day battle against the Japanese in October 1945. Nearby is an impressive European-style building, known to the Javanese as **Lawang Sewu** (1000 Doors). It was formerly Dutch offices, later headquarters of the Japanese forces, and is now Indonesian army offices.

**Simpang Lima** square is where you'll find Semarang's cinema complexes and big shopping malls. Crowds congregate in the evening and browse aimlessly through goods they can't afford to buy.

**Semarang harbour** is worth a look to see the *pinisi* (schooners) and other traditional ocean-going vessels, which dock at the Tambak Lorok wharfs.

The **Ronggowarsito Museum**, Jl Abdulrachman, is the provincial museum, with antiquities from all over the state. One of the most interesting exhibits is a recycled stone panel from Mantingan Mosque. One side shows later Islamic motifs, while the reverse shows the original Hindu-Buddhist scene. The museum is on Jl Abdulrachman, about 2km from the airport, and is open from 8 am to 2.30 pm daily, except Monday.

## Places to Stay – Budget

You don't get a lot for your money in Semarang. None of the budget hotels cater to travellers and some, like the Losmen Arjuna and Hotel Blambangan, are 'full' for foreigners. The main budget hotel area is close to the city centre on or just off Jl Imam Bonjol, 15 minutes' walk from Tawang train station (1500 rp by becak).

The friendly but noisy *Hotel Oewa Asia* (☎ 542547, Jl Kol Sugiono 12) gets a steady

## Jamu

Though the *apotik* (chemist) does more business than traditional medicine these days, *jamu* (herbal tonic) is widely consumed by those from all walks of life. Shops across the country sell jamu prepared by the big companies such as Sido Muncul, and Jamu Nyonya Meneer and Jamu Jago from Semarang. Roadside sellers are also common.

In Java, jamu vendors *(tukang jamu gendong)* sell from street carts, or more often women dressed in traditional kebayas and sarongs carry a cane basket on their backs filled with bottles. They can be found everywhere from street corners to petrol stations, ready to mix you up a murky-looking cure for just about anything.

Jamu has always been taken seriously. In 1775, a botanist named Rumphius published *Herbaria Amboinesis*, which explored the properties of traditional Indonesian herbs. The Dutch also conducted research at the Bogor Botanical Gardens.

A huge variety of ingredients are used but some of the more popular and commonly found are ginger, the related lempuyang and galingale, sepang (leaves of a tree also used for dyeing), brotowali (found in most Javanese markets), sambang, fennel, lemon and cinnamon.

Jamu comes in powders, pills and capsules but is most usually drunk as a liquid. It also comes as an ointment and is used in cosmetics. Traditional herbal baths and massages are a wonderful Indonesian beauty treatment.

Most often Jamu is taken as a pick-me-up to overcome tiredness, improve sexual energy and blood circulation or to ward off minor ailments like colds. There are also jamus for pregnant women, slimming, breath freshening or to cure more specific illnesses, from headaches to diabetes. Your local jamu supplier can mix up whatever you require, but mostly jamus are to improve general health and often come in specific mixtures for men or women.

A home-made, recreational jamu found in various parts of Indonesia involves mixing alcohol with herbs, including cinchona bark (from which quinine is extracted; it is therefore good for malaria). The crowning ingredient is the foetus of a deer, and the whole lot is left to ferment for years to improve the flavour, like a fine whisky or brandy. Yes, we have tried it and can confirm that it tastes much better than your average jamu.

trickle of travellers, so you won't be a total oddity here. Large but fairly basic rooms with fan and mandi cost 22,500 rp and have some colonial style; darker air-con rooms cost 30,000 rp and 35,000 rp.

Another colonial hotel is the pleasant *Hotel Raden Patah (☎ 511328, Jl Suprapto 48)*, in the colonial district. It is farther from the city centre but close to the train station. Spartan but good-value rooms cost 13,500 rp, or 17,000 rp with mandi and fan. Most rooms ring the inner courtyard and are sheltered from street noise.

If these two are full, and you can speak some Indonesian, Jl Imam Bonjol has a number of other options. The *Losmen Singapore* *(☎ 543757)* at No 12 has no-frills rooms with shared mandi for 12,500 rp and 14,500 rp. The *Hotel Rahayu (☎ 542532)* at No 35 has decent rooms with mandi for 25,000 rp, or 40,000 rp with air-con.

*Losmen Jaya (☎ 543604, Jl MT Haryono 85-87)* is a little far from the centre but has reasonable budget rooms from 16,000 rp, or 22,500 rp with mandi.

*Hotel Nendra Yakti (☎ 544202, Gang Pinggir 68)*, in the interesting Chinatown area, is more reminiscent of Chinese hotels in Malaysia or other parts of South-East Asia. Straddling the budget and mid-range categories, it has good service and spotless rooms with fan and mandi for 25,000 rp.

## CENTRAL SEMARANG

Better air-conditioned rooms with TV cost 55,000 rp, or 60,000 rp with hot water.

### Places to Stay – Mid-Range

In the city centre, the *Natour Dibya Puri* (☎ 547821, Jl Pemuda 11) is a rambling old hotel with loads of colonial atmosphere, but the place is sadly neglected. Large air-con singles/doubles with terraces overlooking the inner garden have hot water, TV and fridge for 55,000/65,000 rp to 100,000 rp, but nothing seems to work and rooms are

grubby for the price. The fan rooms without bathroom for 30,000/35,000 rp have towering ceilings and are the best value – you can savour the colonial ambience but don't have to pay for non-existent facilities.

Also central, Jl Gajah Mada has two older motel-style places, but they are overpriced like most mid-range hotels in Semarang. The partly renovated *Hotel Quirin* (☎ 547063) at No 44-52 is well run. Air-con rooms with bathroom for 74,000 rp are uninspiring, but the more expensive rooms

## CENTRAL SEMARANG

**PLACES TO STAY**

| | |
|---|---|
| 1 | Losmen Arjuna |
| 2 | Hotel Rahayu |
| 3 | Hotel Oewa Asia |
| 4 | Hotel Surya |
| 5 | Losmen Singapore |
| 6 | Hotel Blambangan |
| 7 | Natour Dibya Puri |
| 10 | Hotel Raden Patah |
| 15 | Metro Hotel |
| 22 | Losmen Jaya |
| 23 | Hotel Nendra Yakti |
| 25 | Quirin Hotel |
| 35 | Telomoyo |
| 36 | Hotel Graha Santika |
| 39 | Hotel Ciputra |
| 44 | Hotel Santika |

**PLACES TO EAT**

| | |
|---|---|
| 11 | Toko Wingko Babad |
| 16 | Sari Medan |
| 17 | Toko Oen |
| 20 | Loenpia Semarang |
| 24 | Rumah Makan Bintang Tiga |
| 29 | Rumah Makan Oriental |
| 33 | Bintang Laut |
| 34 | Rumah Makan Tio Cio |
| 43 | Mbok Berek |
| 45 | Timlo Solo |
| 46 | Istana Restaurant; |
| | Matsuri Restaurant |

**OTHER**

| | |
|---|---|
| 8 | Pelni Office |
| 9 | Gereja Blenduk |

| | |
|---|---|
| 12 | Telkom Office |
| 13 | Pasar Cina |
| 14 | Main Post Office |
| 18 | Pasar Johar |
| 19 | Tay Kak Sie Temple |
| 21 | Minibus Agents |
| 26 | Merpati |
| 27 | BCA Bank |
| 28 | Bouraq |
| 30 | Ngesti Pandowo Theatre |
| 31 | Lawang Sewu |
| 32 | Tugu Muda Monument |
| 37 | Mesjid Baiturrakhman |
| 38 | Ciputra Mall |
| 40 | Simpang Lima |
| 41 | Plaza Simpang Lima |
| 42 | RRI |

(up to 140,000) rp are better. The *Telomoyo* (☎ 545436) at No 138 is a better hotel, popular with local businesspeople. It has a few fan rooms for 30,000 rp, but most are comfortable air-con rooms for 79,500 rp to 138,000 rp.

The *Hotel Surya* (☎ 540355, Jl Imam Bonjol 28) is a newly renovated smaller hotel and slightly better value. Rooms with air-con and hot water cost 60,000 rp to 120,000 rp.

The *Hotel Santika* (☎ 412491, Jalan A Yani 189), a cousin of the big Graha Santika, is a better mid-range hotel, though the cheaper rooms are dark and not as flash as the lobby would lead you to believe. Rooms cost 125,000 rp to 190,000 rp, before discount.

The tranquil residential districts such as Candi Baru in the southern hills, 3km south-west of the Simpang Lima, have a number of hotels. The pick of these for colonial style is the *Hotel Candi Baru* (☎ 315272, Jl Rinjani 21) a magnificent, rambling old villa with panoramic views of the city. The hotel is fraying at the edges but good value. A few economy rooms cost 25,000 rp, or air-con rooms are 60,000 rp to 105,000 rp, all plus 21%. Check a few out – some are huge and have balconies overlooking the city. The On-On Pub at the hotel is the Hash House Harrier's hangout.

The three star *Metro Hotel* (☎ 547371, Jl H Agus Salim 3) is right in the city centre. Once Semarang's best hotel, it is now outclassed, but the rooms from 142,800 rp are well kept and fully equipped.

## Places to Stay – Top End

Most of these hotels cater to business travellers, but discounts are usually available.

The top class *Hotel Ciputra* (☎ 449888) has an unbeatable position right on Simpang Lima, Semarang's showpiece square. Rooms cost from US$105 plus 21%, but you'll have to try a travel agent for a discount.

The nearby *Hotel Graha Santika* (☎ 318850, Jl Pandanaran 116-120) is an older luxury hotel but is well maintained, with all amenities. Rooms cost 260,000 rp, after discount.

The other major hotels are near each other in Candi Baru. The *Patra Jasa Hotel* (☎ 314441, Jl Sisingamangaraja) is getting a little old but it has fine views of Semarang, good sporting facilities and has been offering discounts as low as 160,000 rp (its regular rates are 250,000/280,000 rp).

The new *Hotel Grand Candi* (☎ 416222, Jl Sisingamangaraja 16) competes with the Ciputra to be Semarang's best hotel, and has spacious grounds. Rates start at 500,000 rp, half that after discount.

CENTRAL JAVA

## Places to Eat

The *Toko Oen (Jl Pemuda 52)* is a large, old-fashioned tea room where white table-cloths and basket chairs hark back to gen-teel colonial times. Half of the original restaurant remains, but the other half has been remodelled and air-conditioned. The Chinese, Indonesian and European menu includes grills and ice cream – expensive but good food.

At night, there are dozens of warungs around *Pasar Johar* (or Pasar Ya'ik, as it is known in the evening), Semarang's best speciality market. Kaki limas around *Simpang Lima* are even more numerous in the evenings for lesahan dining. Simpang Lima's malls are the place for fast food. These include a *McDonald's* in Ciputra Mall, while the Plaza Simpang Lima has a *Pizza Hut* and a food court on the 4th floor. For something more upmarket, *Parkview Bar-BQ*, on the 5th level of Plaza Simpang Lima, has tasty grills, including Korean food, a bar, live music and good views.

Semarang is renowned for its *lumpia* (Chinese spring rolls). They can be found all over town, but one of the original pur-veyors is the small *Loenpia Semarang (Gang Lombok 11)*, near Tay Kak Sie Tem-ple. Other cheap, hole-in-the-wall places are on the same stretch – a good place to have a meal after touring Chinatown.

Another local speciality is *wingko babad*, delicious coconut cakes – buy them hot from the *Toko Wingko Badab bakery (Jl Cendrawasih 14)*.

Jl Gajah Mada has some excellent places for reasonably priced Chinese food with the emphasis on seafood. *Rumah Makan Tio Cio*, opposite the Telemoyo Hotel, is an open-sided restaurant, all steam and siz-zling woks in the evenings as it pumps out good food. The *Bintang Laut* nearby is similar. Farther north, the air-con *Rumah Makan Oriental* is more upmarket and has an ice-cream parlour outside at the front.

Another top spot for Chinese seafood is the hole-in-the-wall *Rumah Makan Bin-tang Tiga (Gang Pinggir 31A)* in China-town. Decor is bare but the fish is excellent.

The *Timlo Solo (Jl A Yani 182)* has good, inexpensive Javanese food. Try the *lontong timlo* or nasi timlo. A few doors away, *Mbok Berek* has Yogya-style fried chicken.

## Entertainment

The *TBRS amusement park* on Jl Sriwi-jaya, Tegalwareng, has wayang orang from 9 pm to midnight every night, wayang kulit every Thursday Wage and ketoprak every Monday Wage of the Javanese calendar. Wayang kulit is performed at the *RRI (Jl A Yani)* auditorium on the first Saturday of the month, and also in the courtyard of the *governor's office (Jl Pahlawan 10)* on the 16th of the month.

## Getting There & Away

**Air** Flight services have been slashed. Garuda (☎ 449331), in the Graha Santika Hotel, has direct flights to Jakarta (386,400 rp). Merpati (☎ 517137), Jl Gajah Mada 17, has direct flights to Surabaya (267,600 rp).

Merpati has suspended its flights to Kali-mantan but they may start up again. Deraya Air (☎ 604329) at the airport currently han-dles all flights to Kalimantan: Pangkalan-bun (298,600 rp), Pontianak (412,200 rp) and Ketapang (387,200 rp). It also offers charters to Karimunjawa (2,430,000 rp).

Departure tax is 9900 rp.

**Bus** Semarang's Terboyo bus terminal is 4km east of town, just off the road to Kudus. Destinations for non-air-con/air-con buses include Yogya (4000/7000 rp, three hours), Solo (3000/5000 rp, 2½ hours), Magelang (2500/6000 rp), Wonosobo (4000 rp, four hours), Pekalongan (3100/5000 rp, three hours), Cirebon (7500/13,000 rp, six hours), Kudus (2000/3000 rp, one hour) and Surabaya (10,000/15,000 rp, nine hours).

Ticket-agent offices for luxury buses and express minibuses are on Jl Haryono near the Losmen Jaya. Try the Rahayu agent (☎ 543935) at No 9 and the Nusantara Indah agent (☎ 548648) at No 9B, or Ar-mada Inter City (☎ 545144), around the corner at Kompleks Bubaan Baru 1-2. They have luxury buses for all major long-haul destinations, including Jakarta or Denpasar for around 50,000 rp. To Jakarta, it's a long 10 hour haul, and buses arrive at ungodly hours at Jakarta's remote Pulo Gadung bus terminal.

Non-air-con/air-con minibuses go to Solo (7500/11,000 rp) and Yogya (8000/11,500 rp) every hour from 7 am to 6 pm. Other non-air-con services include Kudus (11,000 rp), Wonosobo (11,000 rp) and Pekalongan (13,500 rp). Air-con buses include Surabaya (37,500 rp), Malang (35,000 rp), Bandung (35,000 rp) and Jakarta (50,000 rp).

**Train**  Semarang is on the main Jakarta-Cirebon-Surabaya train route, and there are frequent services operating to and from these cities. Tawang is the main train station in Semarang.

Good trains between Jakarta and Semarang are the *Senja Utama* and *Fajar Utama* (36,000/72,000 rp bisnis/eksekutif, 7½ hours). They stop in Pekalongan and Cirebon. The luxury *Argomuria* costs 115,000 rp does the run in six hours. The *Sembani* and a number of other trains also pass through Semarang between Surabaya and Jakarta, while the *Mahesa* goes to Bandung (40,000/70,000 rp, 12 hours).

Most of the ekonomi services depart from Poncol train station. To Jakarta, most are night trains, or the *Twangmas* (12,000 rp, nine hours) leaves at 7 am. All ekonomi trains to Surabaya are night through-trains, such as the *Kertajaya* (14,000 rp, eight hours). A few trains go to Solo but take four hours – buses are much quicker.

**Boat**  The Pelni office (☎ 555156), Jl Tantular 25, is near the Tawang train station. It's open from 8 am to 4 pm Monday to Friday, and to 1 pm on Saturday. Pelni's *Tilongkabila Lawit*, *Kelimutu*, *Binaiya* and *Sirimau* run between Semarang and the Kalimantan ports of Sampit (53,500 rp ekonomi to 174,000 rp 1st class), Kumai (46,000 rp to 152,000 rp), Banjarmasin (55,000 rp to 185,000 rp) and Pontianak (85,000 rp to 212,000 rp). Other Pelni boats are the *Pangrango* to Ketapang (Banyuwangi) and the

*Ciremai* to Ujung Pandang (98,500 to 333,500 rp). Occasional cargo boats go from Semarang to Kalimantan and take passengers – inquire in the harbour area.

## Getting Around

**To/From the Airport**  Ahmad Yani airport is 6km west of town. A taxi to town costs 8000 rp, less to the airport on the meter.

**Local Transport**  Semarang has becaks, taxis and a big Damri city bus service, supplemented by minibuses. City buses charge a fixed 300 rp fare and terminate at Terboyo bus terminal. Bus Nos 1, 2 and 3 run south along Jl Pemuda to Candi Baru. Minibuses cost 500 rp and operate all around town.

A becak from Tawang train station or the bus terminal to the Oewa Asia Hotel will cost about 2000 rp, as will most rides around town. Becaks aren't allowed along Jl Pemuda.

Semarang has metered taxis, which congregate around the big hotels, Simpang Lima and the post office. Private minibuses for hire can be found at the post office and bus terminal, but bargain furiously.

## Demak

Twenty-five kilometres east of Semarang on the road to Surabaya, Demak was once the capital of the first Islamic state – and the most important state – on Java during the early 16th century. Demak conquered the great Hindu Majapahit kingdom and helped spread Islam to the interior. At the time, this was a good seaport but silting of the coast has now left Demak several kilometres inland.

The **Mesjid Agung** (Grand Mosque) dominates the town of Demak and is one of Indonesia's most important places of pilgrimage for Muslims. It is the earliest mosque known in Java, founded by the wali songo in 1466. It's architecture combines Javanese-Hindu and Islamic elements, and legend has it that it was constructed entirely of wood by the wali songo in a single night. Four main pillars, called the *soko guru*, in the central hall were originally made by four of the saints but have been replaced and are now on display in front of the museum. One pillar, erected by Sunan Kalijaga, is said to be made from pieces of scrap wood magically fused together by the saints when no other wood could be found.

The Grand Mosque was extensively restored in 1987. The history and restoration of the mosque is outlined in a small **museum** (open from 8 am to 5 pm daily) to the side, and some of the original woodwork, including some magnificent carved doors, are on display.

The **tombs of Demak's rulers** are next to the mosque. These rulers include Raden Patah, Demak's first sultan, though it is the tomb of Raden Trenggono, who led Demak's greatest military campaigns, which attracts the most pilgrims. During Grebeg Besar, when various heirlooms are ritually cleansed, thousands of pilgrims flock to Demak.

The **mausoleum of Sunan Kalijaga** is at Kadilangu, 2km south of Demak.

The mosque is on the main road in the centre of town. Through buses can drop you on the doorstep. The bus fare is 750 rp to Semarang or Kudus.

## KUDUS
**☎ 0291**

Fifty-five kilometres north-east of Semarang, Kudus was founded by the Muslim saint Sunan Kudus. Like Demak, it is an Islamic holy city and an important place of pilgrimage. Its name comes from the Arabic *al-Quds*, which means 'holy', and it is the only place on Java that has permanently acquired an Arabic name.

Kudus is strongly Muslim yet, strangely, some old Hindu customs prevail, such as the tradition that cows may not be slaughtered within the town. Kudus is also a prosperous town and a major centre of Java's *kretek* (clove cigarette) industry.

The tourist office (☎ 35958), Jl Komplek Kriday Wisata, is in a children's recreation park to the east of town. The BII bank changes cash and has an ATM (Visa and MasterCard), or you could try the BCA.

## Old Town

West of the river on the road to Jepara, **Kauman**, the oldest part of town, can be an interesting place to wander around. Its streets are narrow and winding, stark white and almost Middle Eastern in atmosphere. Some of the buildings are colourful traditional houses with ornately carved wooden fronts.

In the centre of the old town, **Al-Manar** (or Al-Aqsa) **Mosque** was constructed in 1549 by Sunan Kudus. The mosque is named after the mosque of Jerusalem and, like so many of Java's early mosques, it displays elements of Islamic and Hindu-Javanese design, such as the old Javanese carved split doorways. In fact, it was probably built on the site of a Hindu-Javanese temple and is particularly famous for its tall red-brick minaret, or *menara*, which may have originally been the watchtower of that temple.

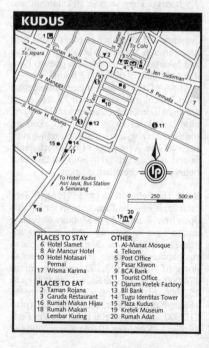

| PLACES TO STAY | OTHER |
|---|---|
| 6 Hotel Slamet | 1 Al-Manar Mosque |
| 8 Air Mancur Hotel | 4 Telkom |
| 10 Hotel Notasari | 5 Post Office |
| Permai | 7 Pasar Kliwon |
| 17 Wisma Karima | 9 BCA Bank |
| | 11 Tourist Office |
| PLACES TO EAT | 12 Djarum Kretek Factory |
| 2 Taman Rojana | 13 BII Bank |
| 3 Garuda Restaurant | 14 Tugu Identitas Tower |
| 16 Rumah Makan Hijau | 15 Plaza Kudus |
| 18 Rumah Makan | 19 Kretek Museum |
| Lembar Kuring | 20 Rumah Adat |

## Kretek Cigarettes

One of those distinctive 'aromas' of Indonesia is the sweet, spicy smell, almost like incense, of clove-flavoured cigarettes. The *kretek* cigarette has only been around since the start of the century, but today kretek addiction is nationwide and accounts for 90% of the cigarette market, while sales of *rokok putihs* (ordinary non-clove cigarettes) are languishing. So high is the consumption of cloves for smoking that Indonesia, traditionally a supplier of cloves in world markets, has become a substantial net importer from centres like Zanzibar and Madagascar.

The invention of the kretek has been attributed to a Kudus man, Nitisemito, who claimed the cigarettes relieved his asthma. He mixed tobacco with crushed cloves rolled in corn leaves, and these *rokok klobot* were the prototype for his Bal Tiga brand, which he began selling in 1906. Nitisemito became a tireless promoter of his product – on the radio, by air dropping advertising leaflets, and touring in a van, which took a musical troupe across Java in an attempt to sell the new cigarettes.

Kudus on Java became the centre for the kretek industry, and at one stage the town had over 200 factories, though today less than 50 cottage industries and a few large factories remain. Rationalisation in the industry has seen kretek production dominated by the big producers such as Bentoel in Malang, Gudang Garam in Kediri and Djarum in Kudus. Nitisemito became a victim of the industry he started and died bankrupt in 1953.

Although filtered kreteks are produced by modern machinery, non-filtered kreteks are still rolled by hand on simple wooden rolling machines. The manual process is protected by law. Women work in pairs, with one rolling the cigarettes and the other snipping ends. The best rollers can turn out about 7000 cigarettes in a day.

As to the claim that kreteks are good for smokers' cough, cloves are a natural anaesthetic and do have a numbing effect on the throat. Any other claims to aiding health stop there, because the tar and nicotine levels in the raw, slowly cured tobaccos used in kreteks are so high that some countries have banned or restricted their import. The Srintil tobacco from Muntilan is said to be the best.

Filtered kreteks now dominate the market, and popular brands include Bentoel, Gudang Garam and Sukun. The Bentoel company has even produced a 'light' range of kreteks, Sampoerna, though tar levels are still quite high. For the kretek purist, the conical, crackling, non-filtered kretek has no substitute – the Dji Sam Soe ('234') brand is regarded as the Rolls Royce of kreteks.

In the courtyards behind the mosque is the imposing **Tomb of Sunan Kudus**, which is now a shrine. His mausoleum of finely carved stone is hung with a curtain of lace. The narrow doorway, draped with heavy gold-embroidered curtains, leads through to an inner chamber and the grave. During Buka Luwur, held once a year on 10 Muharram of the Islamic calendar, the curtains around the tomb are changed and thousands of pilgrims flock to Kudus for the event.

### Kretek Production

The main kretek companies are Djambu Bol, Nojorono, Sukun and the Chinese-owned Djarum company, which started in 1952 and is now the biggest producer in Kudus. Djarum's modern factory on Jl A Yani is central, but it usually requires a week's notice to tour the factory. Sukun, outside the town, still produces some *rokok klobot*, the original kreteks rolled in corn leaves. For a tour, contact the tourist office for a recommendation of a factory to visit.

Also worth a visit is **Kretek Museum**, open from 9 am to 4 pm, closed Friday. Although explanations are in Indonesian, a number of interesting photographs and implements used in kretek production are on show.

## Other Attractions

Next to Kretek Museum, is **Rumah Adat**, a traditional wooden Kudus house which exhibits some of the fabulous carving work for which Kudus is famous. It is said that the Kudus style originated from Ling Sing, who was a 15th century Chinese immigrant and Islamic teacher. While nearby Jepara is now the more famous woodcarving centre, a few workshops in Kudus still make intricately carved panels and doorways. These are primarily works that have been commissioned by architects for public buildings, hotels or Jakarta mansions.

In front of Plaza Kudus, **Tugu Identitas**, styled after the menara, can be climbed for views over the town.

## Places to Stay

The central *Hotel Slamet (Jl Jenderal Sudirman 63)* is a colonial building with high ceilings, layers of dust and basic rooms for 11,500 rp. It's OK for a night, and cheap.

The small *Wisma Karima (☎ 31712, Jl Museum Kretek Jati Kulon 3)* has very clean rooms with mandi for 24,000 rp to 29,500 rp, and would be a good option if it were closer to the centre.

The motel-style *Air Mancur (☎ 32514, Jl Pemuda 70)* is a faded mid-range place. Passable doubles with mandi cost 25,000 rp to 50,000 rp. Expensive air-con rooms are 70,000 rp.

*Hotel Prima Graha (☎ 31800, Jl Agil Kusumadya 8)* has a variety of decent rooms with mandi from 25,000 rp, or from 60,000 rp to 85,000 rp with air-con and hot water. It is a reasonable hotel but dull.

*Hotel Notasari Permai (☎ 37245, Jl Kepodang 12)* is a good mid-range hotel, and the most popular place to stay. It has a swimming pool, restaurant and friendly staff. Dark rooms with mandi are 25,000 rp and 30,000 rp; much better air-con rooms start at 70,000 rp.

The *Hotel Kudus Asri Jaya (☎ 38449, Jl Agil Kusumadya)* is the best hotel in town, but it is a long way from the town centre, a few hundred metres north of the bus terminal. Rooms with mandi start at 25,000 rp, but most rooms are air-con and prices range from 95,000 rp to 145,000 rp for the suites. The hotel has a pool and a good restaurant.

## Places to Eat

Local specialities to try include *soto Kudus* (chicken soup) and *jenang Kudus*, which is a sweet made of glutinous rice, brown sugar and coconut. The best place for cheap eats and a wide variety of local specialties is **Taman Rojana**, a new food-stall centre with over a dozen stalls downstairs. You could also try the breezier **Rumah Makan Aneka Rasa** upstairs.

The **Rumah Makan Hijau Mas** *(Jl A Yani 1)*, near Plaza Kudus shopping centre, is cheap and good for Indonesian food and super-cool fruit juices.

The **Hotel Notasari Permai** restaurant is reasonably priced. The *Garuda (Jl Jenderal Sudirman 1)* is the town's best Chinese restaurant.

For ambience, the best restaurant is **Rumah Makan Lembar Kuring**, on Jl A Yani, with pleasant bamboo decor. Good Sundanese and Javanese dishes are served.

## Getting There & Away

Kudus is on the main Semarang to Surabaya road. The bus terminal is about 4km south of town. City minibuses run from behind the bus terminal to the town centre (500 rp), or you can take an ojek or becak.

From Kudus, buses go to Demak (750 rp, half hour), Semarang (1500/2000 rp, one hour, 54km), Purwodadi (1200 rp) and Surabaya (7000/14,000 rp to 20,000 rp, 286km). Brown and yellow minibuses go to Colo for 2500 rp. For Jepara (1000 rp, 45 minutes, 35km) and Mantingan, buses leave from the Jetak sub-station, 4km west of town (500 rp by purple minibus).

## AROUND KUDUS
### Colo
This small hill-resort lies 18km north of Kudus at an altitude of 700m on the slopes of Gunung Muria.

Colo is most famous for its **Tomb of Sunan Muria** (Raden Umar Said), one of the wali songo, who was buried here in 1469. The mosque surrounding the tomb is perched high on a ridge overlooking the plains to the south. It was built around the middle of the 19th century, though it has had many later additions. Pilgrims regularly come to pray at the tomb, and during Buka Luwur, held in Colo on 16 Muharram of the Islamic calendar, up to 10,000 pilgrims line the road to the top.

**Air Terjun Monthel** waterfall is 1.5km, or about a half-hour stroll from Colo village.

The government-run *Hotel Pesanggrahan Colo* (☎ 0291-35157) is good value, and has rooms with mandi for 10,000 rp and 18,000 rp, or comfortable villas are 22,000 rp to 44,000 rp.

### Mayong
Raden Ajeng Kartini (1879-1904) was born in this town, 12km north-west of Kudus on the road to Jepara. She was the daughter of the Regent of Jepara and was allowed, against Indonesian custom, to attend the Dutch school in Jepara along with her brothers. As a result of her education, Kartini questioned both the burden of Javanese etiquette and the polygamy permitted under Islamic law. In letters to Dutch friends, she also criticised colonial behaviour and vocalised an 'ever growing longing for freedom and independence, a longing to stand alone'.

Kartini married the Regent of Rembang, himself a supporter of progressive social policies, and they opened a school in Rembang for the daughters of regents. In 1904, Kartini died, shortly after the birth of her son. She was, perhaps, the first modern Indonesian writer, and Kartini's letters were published in 1911 in the original Dutch, as *Through Darkness to Light* (the English edition is available in paperback).

At Mayong is a **Kartini monument** which marks the spot where her placenta was buried, according to Javanese custom. Jepara and Rembang are other important places where ceremonies are held on 21 April to celebrate Kartini Day.

## JEPARA
☎ 0291
Jepara, only 35km north-west of Kudus, is famed as the centre for the best woodcarvers on Java. The road into Jepara passes workshops stacked high with furniture, so you get a fair idea of places to visit as you arrive.

Jepara is a small, peaceful country town, but it has a colourful history. An important port in the 16th century, it had both English and Dutch factories by the early 1600s and was involved in a violent dispute between the Dutch VOC (United East India Company) and Sultan Agung of Mataram. After some of the Dutch reputedly compared Agung to a dog and relieved themselves on Jepara's mosque, hostilities finally erupted in 1618 when the Gujarati (from Gujarat, in west India), who governed Jepara for Agung, attacked the VOC trading post. The Dutch retaliated by burning Javanese ships and much of the town. In 1619, Jan Pieterszoon Coen paused on his way to the conquest of Batavia to burn Jepara yet again and with it, the English East India Company's post. The VOC headquarters for the central north coast was then established at Jepara.

Jepara ('Jeporo' in Javanese pronunciation) is a conservative small town but the booming furniture business has brought signs of wealth, such as new hotels and a supermarket, a real focus for a town long-starved of modern amenities. Jepara was also going to be a centre for Indonesia's first nuclear power station, but the government finally quashed that idea after much criticism and doubts about safety.

### Things to See
Kartini's father was *bupati* (regent) of Jepara and she grew up in the bupati's

CENTRAL JAVA

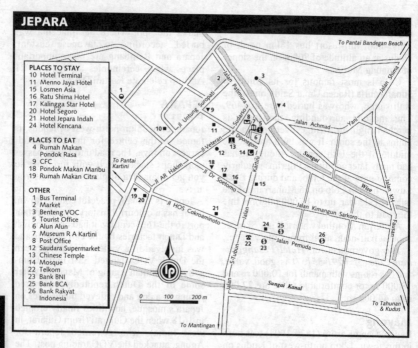

## JEPARA

**PLACES TO STAY**
10 Hotel Terminal
11 Menno Jaya Hotel
15 Losmen Asia
16 Ratu Shima Hotel
17 Kalingga Star Hotel
20 Hotel Segoro
21 Hotel Jepara Indah
24 Hotel Kencana

**PLACES TO EAT**
4 Rumah Makan Pondok Rasa
9 CFC
18 Pondok Makan Maribu
19 Rumah Makan Citra

**OTHER**
1 Bus Terminal
2 Market
3 Benteng VOC
5 Tourist Office
6 Alun Alun
7 Museum R A Kartini
8 Post Office
12 Saudara Supermarket
13 Chinese Temple
14 Mosque
22 Telkom
23 Bank BNI
25 Bank BCA
26 Bank Rakyat Indonesia

To Pantai Bandegan Beach
Jalan Shima
Jalan Patimura
Jalan Untung Suropati
Sudarso
Jl Untung Suropati
Jl Veteran
Diponegoro
To Pantai Kartini
Jl AR Hakim
Jl Dr Soetomo
Jl HOS Cokroaminoto
Jalan Kartini
Jalan Achmad Yani
Jalan Kimangun Sarkoro
Jalan KH
Jalan Fausan
Sungai
Wiso
Jalan S Tubun
Jalan Pemuda
Sungai Kanal
To Tahunan & Kudus
To Mantingan

0    100    200 m

---

house, Pendopo Kabupaten Jepara, on the east side of the alun alun. Though the building is still the bupati's residence, it is possible to visit Kartini's rooms inside if you contact the tourist office. Here, Kartini spent her confinement, known as *pingit* in Javanese. Traditionally, this was when pubescent girls were forbidden to venture outside the house, and from 12 to 16 girls were kept in virtual imprisonment.

The small **Museum RA Kartini**, next to the tourist office on the north side of the alun alun, has photos and furniture from the family home. It is open from 7 am to 5 pm daily.

Heading north from the museum, cross the river and veer left up the hill to the old Dutch fort, the **Benteng VOC**. Over the last 50 years, the stonework has been pillaged for building material and not much remains, but the site has good views across the town

and out to the Java Sea, and the nearby **cemetery** has some Dutch graves.

## Places to Stay

Budget options are rough and bargaining is required. Avoid the disgusting Hotel Terminal. The *Menno Jaya Hotel* (☎ *91143, Jl Diponegoro 40B*) used to be *the* budget place to stay, but since the erudite owner passed away his widow has had trouble maintaining the place. It's friendly but sadly neglected; rooms cost 20,000 rp.

The other budget option is the *Losmen Asia (Jl Kartini 32)*. It's passable, but the asking price for basic rooms is an inflated 25,000 rp.

The mid-range choices are much better. The friendly *Ratu Shima* (☎ *91406, Jl Dr Soetomo 13-15)* is a good choice. Fan rooms here start at 15,000 rp, and air-con rooms are 40,000 rp to 55,000 rp. A notch up in quality is the larger *Kalingga Star* *(☎ 91054, Jl Dr Soetomo 16)*. Rooms start at 16,500 rp, or from 37,000 rp with air-con. Both have decent restaurants.

*Hotel Segoro (☎ 91982, Jl Ringin Jaya 2)* is a motel with a range of immaculate rooms from 22,000 rp up to suites for 92,000 rp, and it has a good restaurant. *Hotel Jepara Indah (☎ 93548, Jl HOS Cokroaminoto 12)* is a cheaply built three star hotel, but far and away the biggest and best in Jepara. Rooms cost US$47/55 and US$68/73, plus 21%.

## Places to Eat

*Pondok Makan Maribu (Jl Dr Soetomo 16-19)*, next to the Kalingga Star, has a huge menu of Chinese food and western dishes – everything from spaghetti to lamb chops. The food is excellent and there's an air-con section or an open area with HBO cable movies on TV.

In the centre of town on Jl Diponegoro, *CFC* is a KFC clone. Just across the river from the alun alun, the *Pondok Rasa (Jl Pahlawan 2)* has a pleasant garden and a lesahan eating area to enjoy good Indonesian food. The *Rumah Makan Citra*, next to the Hotel Segoro, is Jepara's flashest restaurant and also specialises in seafood.

## Shopping

Intricately carved wooden cupboards, divans, chests, chairs, tables, relief panels and the like are carved from teak (*jati*) or sometimes mahogany. Jepara's consumption of teak is so high that demand is outstripping supply on Java. There are furniture shops and factories all around Jepara, but the main centre is in the village of **Tahunan**, 4km south of Jepara on the road to Kudus. The larger shops can arrange shipping, but you need to know your business – some buyers have had their fingers badly burned.

Brightly coloured ikat weavings using motifs from Sumba are sold on Bali, but they come from the village of **Torso**, 14km south of Jepara, 2km off the main road. Other designs are produced and the men do the weaving, allowing broader looms to be used. Srikandi Ratu and Lestari Indah are two workshops with fixed-price showrooms.

**Pecangaan**, 18km south of Jepara, produces rings, bracelets and other jewellery from *monel*, a stainless steel alloy.

## Getting There & Away

Frequent buses run from Jepara to Kudus (1000 rp, 45 minutes) and Semarang (2500 rp, 1½ hours). A few buses also go to Surabaya, but Kudus has more connections. Night buses to Jakarta cost 25,000 rp to 35,000 rp, Bumi Nusantara buses are the best.

Becaks are cheap and, from the terminal, about 1km west of the centre, 1000 rp will get you anywhere in town.

## AROUND JEPARA
## Mantingan

The **Ratu Kali Nyamat's mosque** and tomb are in this village, 4km south of Jepara. Kali Nyamat was the great warrior-queen of Jepara who twice laid siege to Portugal's Melaka stronghold in the latter part of the 16th century. The campaigns against Melaka were not successful, but Kali Nyamat scared the Portuguese witless.

The mosque, dating from 1549, was restored some years ago, and the tomb lies around the side. It is noted for its Hindustyle embellishments and medallions.

Mantingan is easily reached from Jepara. *Angkudes* (minibuses to villages) from the bus terminal can drop you outside the mosque for 500 rp.

## Beaches

Jepara has some surprisingly good white-sand beaches. **Pantai Bandengan**, also known as Tirta Samudra, 8km north-east of town, is the most popular and one of the best mainland beaches on Java. The main public section can be littered and is best avoided on Sunday, but just a short walk away, you'll find the sands are clean, the warm waters clear and swimming is safe. From Jepara, take a brown-and-yellow bemo (500 rp) from Jl Patimura, behind the tourist office. On weekdays, you will probably have to charter a whole bemo for around 5000 rp.

If it were closer to a main population centre or tourist area, Pantai Bandengan would be lined with hotels. As it is, the only option is the ***Pondok Bougenville*** (☎ *92693)*, which has rooms with mandi designed for groups, each with four beds or more for 30,000 rp a double, including breakfast, and 5000 rp per extra person (not including breakfast). Though fairly basic, it has a good beachside restaurant, an excellent stretch of sand out front and windsurfing equipment for rent. This is a great place to relax, looking out to sea and the offshore fishing platforms.

The most popular seaside recreation park is **Pantai Kartini**, 3km west of town. It is lined with warungs, but has no beach. However, you can rent a boat to **Pulau Panjang** (1km offshore) which has excellent white-sand beaches, for around 30,000 rp return.

## KARIMUNJAWA

These 27 islands, around 90km north-west of Jepara, have been declared a marine national park. Though they are being promoted as a tropical paradise, facilities are limited, the islands are difficult to reach and few visitors make it to this forgotten part of Java.

Like most north-coast destinations on Java, the islands are devoutly Muslim. Islam was brought here by Sunan Nyamplung, the wayward son of Sunan Muria, who banished his son to Karimunjawa. He made the journey in an outrigger canoe made from *dewadaru* wood, said to have sacred properties. Upon landing, he rammed one of the stays from his canoe into the ground and from it grew the first dewadaru tree on Karimunjawa. Traditionally, it was forbidden to take dewadaru wood off the islands, and legend has it that a ship carrying dewadaru will sink in the Java Sea.

Boats land at the main island of **Pulau Karimunjawa**, and homestay accommodation can be found in Karimunjawa village at the south-western tip of the island. The island's attractions are few. You can swim in the calm, clear waters but the island is mostly ringed by mangroves and has no decent beaches. The main attraction here is peace and quiet.

A road runs along the western side of the island, and about 6km from town, concrete steps lead up into the hills to the simple grave of Sunan Nyamplung. The road continues to a small bridge that crosses the mangroves separating Karimunjawa and the other large island of **Pulau Kemujan**. An airstrip has been built here in anticipation of a tourist boom that is still a long way off. Just offshore to the east of Kemujan is **Pulau Tengah**, a small island ringed by a reef and beautiful sandy beaches. It has the best accommodation in the islands.

Using Karimunjawa as a base, you can hire boats to visit other nearby islands, most of which live up to their billing as tropical paradises. **Pulau Menjangan Besar** is only a few hundred metres from Karimunjawa village and can be reached by canoe, but the beaches are not so good. Uninhabited **Pulau Burung** and **Pulau Geleang** have excellent white-sand beaches. Pulau Geleang has an extensive reef on the west side for snorkelling, but the scourge of South-East Asian coral – dynamite fishing – has done a lot of damage. Other more distant islands, with good beaches and snorkelling, are **Pulau Krakal Besar**, about 20km west of Karimunjawa, and **Pulau Sambangan**, 15km to the east. One of the westernmost islands, **Pulau Nyamuk**, is the other major island in the group, with a population of 2000 souls.

## Places to Stay

The main village of Karimunjawa has a handful of homestays charging around 15,000 rp, including meals. Pak Kholik and the Pak Abdul Mu'in have decent accommodation. Pak Ipong has rooms with mandi for 20,000 rp, with meals. The government-run ***Wisma Pemda*** has the best accommodation. Rooms with mandi cost 20,000 rp, and food costs an extra 6000 rp per meal. For something different, Pak Cuming rents rooms on a *karamba* fishing platform, 1km offshore, for 15,000 rp per night. Karimunjawa now even has a warung, *Bu Ester*. It serves standard fare and beer.

Pulau Tengah has quite luxurious two-bedroom cottages with separate sitting areas, but they are only available with expensive tours organised through Satura Tours (☎ 555 555), Jl Cendrawasih A-6, Semarang.

### Getting There & Away
Scheduled flights no longer operate but Deraya Air in Semarang offers charters for 1,300,000 rp. The airstrip is on Pulau Kemujan, which is linked to Pulau Karimunjawa by a bridge across the mangroves.

The ferry leaves from Pantai Kartini in Jepara (2000 rp by becak from the town centre) and costs 20,000 rp for the five hour journey. It leaves Jepara at 9 am Wednesday and Saturday, returning from Karimunjawa on Monday and Thursday, but schedules

change. The *Kota Ukir* (7500 rp, seven hours) carries cargo and passengers twice a month, but it doesn't carry life jackets or rafts and the Java Sea swells can whip up. Crossings in the wet season are rugged.

From Pulau Karimunjawa, it costs around 70,000 rp to 100,000 rp to charter a boat for a day trip to the nearby islands.

### BLORA
Blora's main claim to fame is the rise of **Saminism**, a unique religious/mystical sect that gained prominence in the early 20th century. Headed by a Javanese peasant, Surantika Samin, it followed the teachings of the prophet Adam, but owed little to Islam. Stressing the village structure, mysticism and sexuality, it was an early protest movement, and in 1914 the villages in the area refused to pay the new Dutch head tax. The sect was opposed to the local rulers as much as to the Dutch and survived until the 1960s.

# East Java

The province of East Java, or Jawa Timur, includes the island of Madura off the northwest coast and has a total population of 34 million and an area of 47,921 sq km. The majority of its population is Javanese, but many Madurese farmers and fishermen live in East Java. They are familiar faces, particularly around Surabaya, the bustling capital of the province and Indonesia's second city. In the Bromo area is a small population of Hindu Tenggerese.

Geographically, much of the province is flatter than the rest of Java. In the northwest there is lowland with deltas along the Brantas and Bengawan Solo rivers, vast rice-growing plains interspersed with countless villages and towns. But the rest of East Java is mountainous and contains the huge Bromo-Tengger Massif and Java's highest mountain, Gunung Semeru (3676m). This region is less populated and offers raw, natural beauty.

Major attractions include the impressive volcanic landscapes of Gunung Bromo (2392m), still one of Java's most active volcanoes. Most visitors only see Bromo and then scoot along the northern route through to Bali or Yogyakarta, but East Java has many other fine natural attractions far away from the crowds. Baluran National Park is the most accessible of Java's wildlife reserves, but the southern route through East Java is the most scenic. It is worth making the effort to get to the more remote areas such as the stunning crater lake of Kawah Ijen, and Meru Betiri and Alas Purwo national parks.

Then there's a host of other mountains, pleasant walks and fine hill towns, like Malang. The region is dotted with ancient Hindu-Buddhist temples, the most impressive of which is the Trowulan complex, once the capital of the great Majapahit Empire.

Finally, although East Java is closely related culturally to Central Java, the Madurese are best known for their rugged

## HIGHLIGHTS

- Gunung Bromo – a magnificent active volcano at the centre of the awe-inspiring volcanic landscape of the Tengger Massif
- Madura – a large and rugged island, especially famous for its bull races
- Trowulan – ancient site of the Majapahit kingdom
- Ijen Plateau – the hike to the serene crater lake of Kawah Ijen (Ijen Crater) is one of the finest in Java
- Malang – one of Java's most attractive hill towns
- Kalibaru – a small village with excellent accommodation and the chance to visit plantations
- Meru Betiri National Park – very difficult to reach but one of Java's finest parks, with coastal rainforest, beaches and considerable biodiversity

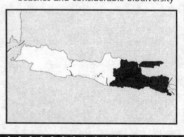

sport called *kerapan sapi*, the famous bull races which take place on the island during August and September.

## SURABAYA
- pop 2.4 million    ☎ 031

The capital of East Java, the industrial city of Surabaya is second only to Jakarta in size and economic importance. For centuries it

# EAST JAVA

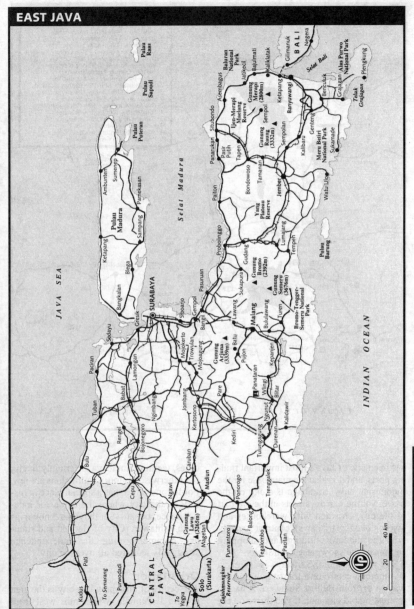

# ANTIQUITIES OF EAST JAVA

1 Trowulan – 14th-15th Century Hindu
2 Surawana – 14th Century Shivaite
3 Tigowani – 14th Century Shivaite
4 Selomangleng (Kediri) – 10th Century Buddhist
5 Gunung Penanggunan – 10th Century
   Vishnuite/Shivaite (Jalatunda & Belahan –
   14-15th Century Tantric/Shivaite)
6 Jawi – 14th Century Shivaite/Buddhist
7 Sumberawan – 14th-15th Century Buddhist
8 Singosari – 14th Century Shivaite/Buddhist
9 Panataran – 14th Century Shivaite
10 Goa Selomangleng – 10th Century Buddhist
11 Sumberjati – 14th Century Shivaite
12 Ganesha of Bara – 13th Century Shivaite
13 Kidal – 13th Century Shivaite
14 Jago – 13th Century Buddhist
15 Kedaton – 14th Century Shivaite

has been one of Java's most important trading ports, and it is also the main base for the Indonesian navy. Surabaya is a city on the move, yet the narrow streets in the old part of the city, crowded with warehouses and jostling *becaks* (trishaws), contrast strongly with the modern buildings and shopping centres of the showpiece central city.

For most visitors, Surabaya is merely a commercial centre or a transit point on the way to or from Bali or Sulawesi. It has an interesting old city and, if you thrive on big cities, teeming Surabaya is certainly lively; but otherwise, its tourist attractions are few. For Indonesians it has a special place in history as the city where the battle for independence began. Surabaya is known as Kota Pahlawan (City of Heroes) and statuary commemorating the independence struggle is scattered all over the city.

## Orientation

The centre of this sprawling city is the area around Jl Pemuda, which runs west from

## Antiquities of East Java

After the decline of Central Java, power shifted to East Java. Sendok's kingdom (929-47) produced the first temples of East Java and, though small, they showed great similarity to earlier temples from Central Java. The more important kingdoms of Airlangga (1019-47) and its successor, Kediri (1045-1222), blended Shivaism and Buddhism, and the arts flourished. Javanese literature and sculpture reached new heights. Many temples and meditational caves from this era dot the Kediri plain and surrounding mountains.

Singosari (1222-92) temples exhibit a strikingly distinct sculptural style in which figures are exuberantly carved in a two dimensional wayang form. Based around Malang, these temples are some of the more impressive and easily visited.

East Java peaked with the great kingdom of Majapahit (1294-1478). This left behind the greatest reminder of the Hindu-Buddhist period in East Java, including the remains of the city of Trowulan and the large Panataran complex near Blitar.

While East Java never produced awe-inspiring monuments like those of Central Java, the innovative East Javan temple style is an obvious prototype for later Balinese sculpture and architecture.

---

Gubeng train station past Plaza Surabaya, and a number of big hotels and banks. Jl Pemuda runs into Jl Tunjungan/Basuki Rahmat, another main commercial street where you'll find Tunjungan Plaza. Most of the hotels are in this area.

The old city is centred around the Jembatan Merah bridge and Kota train station to the north. Further north is Tanjung Perak harbour. Surabaya's zoo is 5km south of the city centre, and the main bus terminal, Purabaya, is just outside the city limits, 10km south of the city centre.

## Information

**Tourist Offices** Surabaya has plenty of tourist offices but little information. The Dinas Parawisata Daerah Surabaya (Surabaya Area Tourist Office, ☎ 5344710), Jl Basuki Rahmat 119, is at least central and if you wake up the staff they will try to answer your queries. It is open from 7 am to 2 pm, Monday to Saturday. Its *Surabaya Historical Tourism Guides* brochure outlines some of Surabaya's rich Dutch architecture from an independence perspective.

For information on Madura and the greater Surabaya area, the regional tourist office (☎ 5675448), Jl Darmokali 35, is 5km south of the city but hardly worth the effort. The East Java Regional Tourist Office (☎ 8531822) at Jl Wisata Menanggal, farther south of the city centre, has a few brochures on the province.

**Foreign Consulates** As Indonesia's second city, Surabaya has a number of foreign consular representatives, such as the USA, the Netherlands and France. The consulates have limited functions – you can try them in an emergency but, in general, visas and other functions are handled in Jakarta.

**Money** Surabaya has more than its fair share of extravagant bank real estate. Jl Pemuda has plenty – Bank Duta and BNI bank usually have good rates and their ATMs accept credit cards. Jl Tunjungan also has a string of banks.

**Post & Communications** Surabaya's main post office and poste restante, on Jl Kebon Rojo, is 4km north of the city centre. It is open from 8 am to 7.30 pm daily and has a Wasantara-net office next door for Internet connection, open from 7 am to 9 pm daily. Online time costs 1500 rp for the first 15 minutes then 150 rp/minute.

# SURABAYA

To Tanjung Perak Harbour
To Kalimas Harbour

Jalan Ampel Suci
Jalan Wamburungan
Jalan Patinus
Jalan Kertopaten

Jalan Rajawali
Jalan Katua RI
Jalan Pangung

Jalan Kembang Jepun
Jalan Kapasan
Jalan Smoverto

Jalan Merak Cendrawash
Jalan Jembatan Merah
Jalan Sikatan
Jalan Veteran
Jalan Waspada

Krem Barat
Jalan Indrapura

Jalan Kebon Rojo
Jalan Setasiun Kota
Jalan Pahlawan

To Terminal Oso Wilangun
Jalan Dupak

Jalan Tembaan
Jl Pasar Besar
Jalan Jagalan
Jalan Ngaglik

Jalan Cepu
Jalan Penghela

Kali Mas
Jalan Peneleh
Jalan Grogol
Jalan Undaan Kulon
Jalan Undaan Wetan
Jalan Kamboja
Jalan Kusuma
Bui Bui

Jalan Semarang
Jalan Bubutan

Jalan Ambengan

Jl Praban
Jalan Geteng Kali
Jalan Undaan

Jalan Raya Arjuno
Jalan Turjungan
Jalan Raya Jaksa

Jalan Embong Malang
Jalan Genteng Besar
Jalan Walikota Mustafab

Jalan Pasar Kembang
Jalan Kaliasin Pompa
Jalan Pemuda

Jalan Sos Sudirro

Basuki Rahmat
Jalan Embong Cerme

Jalan Panglima
Jalan Sumatra
Jalan Raya Guberg

Jalan Karimun Jawa

To Zoo, MPU Tantular Museum,
Bungurasih, Purabaya Bus Terminal,
Regional Tourist Office & Juanda Airport

0    250    500 m

EAST JAVA

## SURABAYA

| PLACES TO STAY | | PLACES TO EAT | | 13 | Pelni Office |
|---|---|---|---|---|---|
| 7 | Hotel Semut | 6 | Kiet Wan Kie | 14 | Tugu Pahlawan |
| 8 | Hotel Irian | 19 | Soto Ambengan | 15 | Pasar Turi Train Station |
| 9 | Hotel Ganefo | 20 | Cafe Venezia | 16 | Surabaya Mall |
| 23 | Hotel Paviljoen | 36 | Zangrandi Ice Cream Palace | 17 | Taman Hiburan Rakyat (THR) |
| 25 | Weta Hotel | 46 | Turin | 18 | Taman Remaja |
| 27 | Hotel Majapahit | 49 | Granada Modern Bakery | 21 | Tunjungan Centre |
| 28 | Westin Hotel | 53 | Galael Supermarket; KFC; | 22 | Sarinah Department Store |
| 29 | Sheraton Hotel | | Swensen's | 24 | Pasar Genteng |
| 30 | Hotel Tunjungan | 63 | Dunia Buah; Foodstalls | 26 | Andhika Plaza |
| 32 | Natour Simpang | 64 | Boncafé | 31 | Tunjungan Plaza; Wartel |
| 33 | Bamboe Denn | 65 | Ria Galeria | 34 | Governor's Residence |
| 37 | Garden Palace Hotel | 66 | Restoran Kuningan | 35 | Mitra Cinema |
| 38 | Garden Hotel | | International | 39 | World Trade Centre |
| 40 | Radisson Plaza Suite Hotel | | | 41 | Plaza Surabaya |
| 44 | Sahid Surabaya Hotel | OTHER | | 42 | Monumen Kapal Selam |
| 45 | Hotel Gubeng | 1 | Mesjid Ampel | 43 | Gubeng Train Station |
| 48 | Hotel Remaja | 2 | Pasar Pabean | 47 | BII Bank |
| 54 | Cendana Hotel | 3 | Kong Co Kong Tik Cun Ong | 50 | BNI Bank |
| 57 | Hotel Tanjung Indah | 4 | Jembatan Merah Bridge | 51 | Joko Dolog |
| 58 | Tanjung Hotel | 5 | Gedung PTP XXII | 52 | Bank Duta |
| 59 | Elmi Hotel | 10 | Kota Train Station | 55 | Minibus Agents |
| 60 | Hyatt Regency | 11 | Pasar Atum Market; Bandara | 56 | Goethe Institut |
| | Surabaya | | Terminal 1 | 61 | Bouraq Office |
| 67 | Puri Kencana Hotel | 12 | Main Post Office | 62 | Colors |

A convenient *wartel* (telephone office), open 24 hours a day, is in the basement level of Tunjungan Plaza.

**Useful Organisations** There is a French Cultural Centre (☎ 5620079) at the French Consulate, Jl Darmokali 10-12, and a Goethe Institut (☎ 5343735) at Jl Taman Ade Irma Suryani Nasution 15. The British Council (☎ 5689958) is at Jl Cokroaminoto 12A.

**Dangers & Annoyances** In most large Javanese cities it is hard to cross the street, but it is almost impossible on Surabaya's big, four-lane roads, which have constant traffic and few traffic lights or pedestrian bridges. The only way to cross the street is to wait for the traffic to subside (it never stops), head out onto the road and motion with one hand for the traffic to stop. Cross yourself in prayer with the other hand.

## Old City

This is the most interesting part of Surabaya, with fine Dutch architecture, a strong Chinese influence and an Arab quarter. If Indonesia were a rich country, this part of the city would have been renovated years ago to become fashionable real estate. As it is, much of this culturally mixed area is sadly run-down, but efforts have been made to clean it up.

It was at the **Jembatan Merah** (Red Bridge) that Brigadier Mallaby, chief of the British forces, was killed in the lead-up to the bloody battle of Surabaya for Indonesian independence. Some run-down but good examples of **Dutch architecture** can be seen here. Jl Jembatan Merah, running south of the bridge along the canal, is a grungy replica of Amsterdam. The area farther south around the post office and Pelni office also has some fine old buildings, though the most impressive is the Gedung PTP XXII, which is a government office building just west of Jl Jembatan Merah along Jl Merak Cendrawasih. This superb building is fashioned in the Indo-European style.

To the east of the Jembatan Merah is Surabaya's **Chinatown**, where hundreds of

EAST JAVA

small businesses and warehouses ply their trade. Becaks and hand-pulled carts are still the best way to transport goods in the crowded, narrow streets. **Pasar Pabean** on Jl Pabean is a sprawling, dark market where you can buy everything from Madurese chickens to Chinese crockery.

Farther north-east, on Jl Dukuh near the canal, **Kong Co Kong Tik Cun Ong** is primarily a Buddhist temple, but has a variety of Confucian and Taoist altars. On the full moon, *wayang* performances are held here at 10 am and in the evening.

The highlight of a visit to the old city is the **Mesjid Ampel** (Ampel Mosque) in the heart of the Arab quarter. From the Chinese temple, proceed north along Jl Nyamplungan and then take the second left down Jl Sasak. A crowd of becaks marks the way to the mosque. Through the arched stone entrance is Jl Ampel Suci, a narrow, covered bazaar lined with shops selling perfumes, sarongs, *pecis* (hats) and other religious paraphernalia. Follow the pilgrims past the beggars to the mosque. This is the most sacred mosque in Surabaya, for it is here that Sunan Ampel, one of the *wali songo* (saints) who brought Islam to Java, was buried in 1481. Pilgrims chant and offer rose petal offerings at the grave around the back.

From the old city you can then head north to the **Kalimas harbour**, where brightly painted *pinisi* schooners from Sulawesi and Kalimantan unload their wares. This is a far less touristed version of Jakarta's Sunda Kelapa.

## Surabaya Zoo

On Jl Diponegoro, 4km south of Jl Pemuda, the Surabaya Zoo (Kebun Binatang) specialises in nocturnal animals, exotic birds and fish. The animals look just as bored as they do in any other zoo, but the park is quite well laid out, with large open enclosures, a great collection of pelicans and lively otters. The rather dazed-looking Komodo dragons are the highlight for most visitors who haven't had a chance to see them elsewhere in Indonesia.

The zoo is open from 7 am to 4 pm. Entry costs 2000 rp. This park is popular with Surabayans and outside there are *warungs* (food stalls) and a permanent gaggle of vendors selling drinks and peanuts for the monkeys. Sunday is the big day and entertainment is often featured in the afternoon. Any bus heading down Jl Panglima Sudirman, such as P1 (1000 rp), will take you to the zoo, or take an M bemo (700 rp).

## MPU Tantular Museum

Across the road from the zoo, this small historical and archaeological museum has some interesting Majapahit artefacts, and is housed in a superb example of Dutch architecture. It is open from 8 am to 2 pm except Saturday (open from 7 am to 1 pm) and closed Monday.

Komodo dragon, found in the Surabaya Zoo.

## Taman Remaja & Taman Hiburan Rakyat (THR)

Taman Remaja, or 'Youth Park', is a neglected cultural park behind the big Surabaya Mall. The Aneka Ria theatre in the park is home to a *srimulat* (East Javanese folk comedy) company with performances on Thursday and Saturday from 8 pm. The cost is 3000 rp for this raucous, almost slapstick theatre. Other dance and theatre is held at the park, and on Thursday evenings the transvestites come out and *dangdut* music is performed.

Next door Taman Hiburan Rakyat (THR, or People's Amusement Park), Surabaya's amusement centre after dark, open from 5 to 10.30 pm, admission 1300 rp. It is quite lively from Thursday to Saturday with plenty of variations on the coconut shy, such as throw a ring around and win a bottle of Bintang, and other old-fashioned diversions.

## Monumen Kapal Selam

On Jl Pemuda, this attempt at riverside rejuvenation revolves around the *Pasopati*, a grounded Russian submarine commissioned into the Indonesian navy in 1962. This is yet another 'monument' glorifying the Indonesian armed forces, but the sub has some Boys' Own interest, and you can crawl through the person holes and play with the periscope. Entry is 1000 rp into the small landscaped park, which has a couple of cafes, and another 1000 rp into the sub. Don't bother with the navy video, it's all in Indonesian and costs another 1000 rp. The monument is open 8.30 am to 9 pm daily.

## Places to Stay – Budget

If you're staying in this busy port town – and many people do at least overnight between Yogyakarta and Bali – there's really only one very cheap place. The *Bamboe Denn (☎ 534 0333, Jl Ketabang Kali 6A)*, a 20 minute walk from Gubeng train station, is a Surabaya institution and has been the No 1 travellers centre in Surabaya for over 20 years. Beds in the large dorm are 9000 rp and a few tiny, very basic singles/doubles are

9500/17,000 rp. You may well get roped into a little English conversation with Indonesian students at the language school, which also runs from this youth hostel.

Across the river from the Bamboe Denn, the *Hotel Paviljoen (☎ 5343449, Jl Genteng Besar 94)* is the next best bet. This old colonial building has some style and the friendly owners speak Dutch as well as English. Rooms with *mandi* (Indonesian-style bath) cost 32,000 rp and 36,000 rp, or air-con rooms are approaching mid-range standard and cost 50,000 rp and 60,000 rp. Breakfast is included.

Most of Surabaya's other cheap accommodation is uninspiring and some of the mid-range hotels are only slightly more expensive and much better value.

The very basic *Hotel Gubeng (☎ 503 1603, Jl Sumatra 18)* is close to Gubeng train station if you can't be bothered going any farther. Rooms at the back with shared mandi cost 30,000 rp or noisy, high-ceiling rooms at the front with mandi cost 40,000 rp.

Plenty of cheap hotels can be found near Kota train station. The area is interesting but it is a long way from the centre and few travellers stay this far north. *Hotel Ganefo (☎ 364880, Jl Kapasan 169-71)* has a fantastic lobby with gigantic ceilings, stained glass, wood panelling and old furniture. Very simple rooms don't match the lobby and cost 30,000 rp with shared mandi, or big rooms with mandi are 40,000 rp. Rooms in the new section with mandi, air-con, TV and phone are 50,000 rp. The *Hotel Irian (☎ 20953, Jl Samudra 16)* has some colonial style. Basic rooms with shared mandi around the garden cost 30,000 rp. Rooms with mandi in the old colonial building cost 40,000 rp, or 42,000 rp to 50,000 rp with air-con.

## Places to Stay – Mid-Range

While cheap places are hard to find, Surabaya has a wide selection of mid-range accommodation and competition is fierce, particularly at the top of this range. All of these hotels have rooms with air-con, hot water and TV.

EAST JAVA

*Puri Kencana Hotel (☎ 5033161, Jl Kalimantan 9)* is a small, well-kept hotel near Gubeng train station. Standard rooms are small and some are dark but they are a very good deal at 45,000 rp. Larger and lighter rooms are 50,000 rp and 60,000 rp.

*Hotel Semut (☎ 3559850, Jl Samudra 9-15)*, in the old part of town, dates from the Art Deco era, and has good-sized rooms facing large verandahs around a central quadrangle. Air-con rooms are good value at 50,000 rp or 65,000 rp with minibar, plus 21%.

Surabaya has some mid-range hotels located centrally, just south of Jl Pemuda. Rooms are a little dark in these older hotels but they are well kept. *Hotel Remaja (☎ 534 1359, Jl Embong Kenongo 12)* is on a quiet street just behind Jl Pemuda and has tidy singles/doubles for 61,000/73,000 rp. Nearby, the *Tanjung Hotel (☎ 5344032, Jl Panglima Sudirman 43-5)* is a larger hotel with a variety of rooms from 81,000 rp to 127,000 rp, before discount. Just behind it is its newer, smaller offshoot, the *Hotel Tanjung Indah (☎ 535 3030, Jl Embong Cerme 1)* where rooms cost 72,600 rp, including breakfast.

Moving right up the scale, Surabaya has a number of three-star hotels that are exceptional value in dollar terms. The pick of them close to the city centre is the *Hotel Tunjungan (☎ 5466666, Jl Tunjungan 102-4)* right next to Tunjungan Plaza. Service may not be a strong point but the position is hard to beat. It has a pool, and large rooms have all the trimmings for 150,000 rp, including buffet breakfast. Nearby, the *Cendana Hotel (☎ 5455333, Jl Kombes Pol M Doeryat 6)* is another of the newer hotels and also a good buy, though it doesn't have a pool. Well appointed rooms with minibar cost 138,000 rp after discount, including buffet breakfast.

Of the older hotels, all charging around 150,000 rp, the sadly neglected *Natour Simpang (☎ 5342151, Jl Pemuda 1-3)* has a great position and a pool but not much else to recommend it. *Sahid Surabaya Hotel (☎ 5322711, Jl Sumatra 1)* has no pool but better rooms and is right next to Gubeng train station, which is handy if you're in transit. The *Elmi Hotel (☎ 532 2571, Jl Panglima Sudirman 42-44)* is more expensive at 200,000 rp but it has a fitness centre, large pool, renovated rooms and good service.

## Places to Stay – Top End

Surabaya has a glut of luxury hotels and competition is cut throat. All hotels in this category have a 21% service charge and government tax on top of the quoted rates, but big discounts are offered.

The *Garden Palace Hotel (☎ 5321001, Jl Yos Sudarso 11)* is an older four star hotel with rooms from US$90. It has been offering discounts as low as 137,500 rp, while better 'theme' rooms are 199,000 rp. The adjoining *Garden Hotel* is its cheaper sister with slightly run-down rooms from as low as 98,000 rp.

A better option nearby is the *Radisson Plaza Suite Hotel (☎ 516833, Jl Pemuda 31-7)*. This smaller hotel is in an excellent position. It has a pool (across the carpark from the hotel) and a variety of rooms and suites from US$180 to US$550, but discounts are as low as 300,000 rp.

The five star *Hyatt Regency Surabaya (☎ 5311234, Jl Basuki Rahmat 124-8)* has long been one of Surabaya's best hotels. Plush rooms start at US$180. Discounts are not so readily available unless you book through a travel agent.

The central *Hotel Majapahit (☎ 545 4333, Jl Tunjungan 65)* is a superb colonial hotel with a fine garden. Built in 1910, it was originally named the Oranje Hotel and bears a striking resemblance to Schomberg's hotel described in Joseph Conrad's *Victory*. In 1945, the returning colonial forces hoisted the Dutch flag, an incident that helped spark the Battle of Surabaya. Recent renovations have restored the hotel to one of Surabaya's finest. Brochure rates start at US$220, but discounts are as low as US$50.

Of all the new hotels, the *Sheraton (☎ 5468000, Jl Embong Malang 25)* has a great position adjoining Tunjungan Plaza. Superior rooms cost from US$140/150 for singles/doubles, but weekend packages start at 350,000 rp.

All the other big chain hotels are represented in Surabaya, including the Hilton, Shangri-La, Novotel and Westin.

## Places to Eat

For cheap eats, the **Genteng Market** on Jl Pasar Genteng, just across the river from the Bamboe Denn, has good night warungs. Most other eats in the city centre are mid-range restaurants found in the shopping centres.

The ground floor of Plaza Surabaya has the **Food Plaza**, with a range of restaurants serving Indonesian, Thai, Italian and American fast food. The best deal is the **Food Bazaar** on the 4th floor, with a large variety of moderately priced stalls.

Tunjungan Plaza has a much bigger selection of restaurants and fast-food outlets, starting on the lower level of Tunjungan Plaza II with **McDonald's** and **Kafe Excelso** for espresso and pastries. On the 4th floor, **Mon Cheri** is a classy ice-cream parlour with a view. Also on the 4th floor, the **New Singapore** has Chinese dishes and steamboats, or the cheaper **Es Teler 77** has Indonesian dishes. The 5th floor has a host of more expensive restaurants, including the **Winda Grill & Steak** and **Pizza Hut**. The 5th floor of the adjoining Tunjungan Plaza III has an excellent **food court**, **Suroboyo** for East Javanese dishes and **Jimbaran** for *ikan bakar* (barbecued fish).

**Zangrandi Ice Cream Palace** (Jl Yos Sudarso 15) is an old establishment parlour favoured by wealthy Surabayans. Relax in planters' chairs at low tables and somehow ignore the traffic noise. Another good place for ice cream and Chinese food is **Turin** on Jl Embong Kenongo.

**Kiet Wan Kie** (Jl Kembang Jepun 51) is an air-con retreat from the Surabaya heat, with dark but pleasant decor. This good Chinese restaurant has a varied menu.

At **Soto Ambengan** (Jl Ambengan 3A) enjoy Pak Sadi's lemon grass and coriander Madurese chicken soup, which is famed throughout the island. This simple restaurant

is a Surabaya institution or, if you prefer a more sanitised version, an offshoot is attached to the Suroboyo restaurant on the 5th floor of Tunjungan Plaza III.

**Cafe Venezia** (Jl Ambengan 16) is a very classy establishment in an old villa with a delightful garden. Considering the setting, the prices are very reasonable. The menu has steaks (around 16,000 rp), Korean BBQ, Japanese dishes and ice cream.

The best area for mid-range restaurants is south of Gubeng train station along Jl Raya Gubeng. Most are housed in impressive colonial buildings, like the **Restoran Kuningan International**, just off Jl Raya Gubeng at Jl Kalimantan 14. It has a large, mixed menu and seafood is a speciality. **Boncafé** (Jl Raya Gubeng 46) has a big menu of mostly western dishes and is noted for its steak, lamb chops and grills for around 20,000 rp. This pleasant restaurant also has an outside area for dining, and a large range of juices and ice cream.

Across the road, **Ria Galeria** (Jl Bangka 2) is housed in a beautiful old villa and is a great spot for Indonesian food. Numerous dishes from all over Java are served at very reasonable prices. Most mains are around 5000 rp to 7000 rp, while seafood costs more. Other restaurants on Gubeng Raya include **La Cafe** and **Fran's** for cakes and pastries. **Dunia Buah** is a big fruit supermarket and attached is a collection of *food stalls* for cheaper dining.

The big hotels are the places for fine dining at high prices, and some do good buffet deals. The **Primavera Restaurant** in the Hyatt Regency has innovative Italian food which is superb but *mahal* (expensive) – the daily set menu for 54,000 rp is a better deal. The **Garden Palace Hotel** has a different cuisine every day for lunch (28,000 rp) and dinner (37,000 rp) buffets.

## Entertainment

Bars at the big hotels are the happening places and they get some good bands. **Desperado's** at the Shangri-La Hotel, Jl May Jen Sungkono 120 (6km south-west of the city centre), has better bands than most and

**EAST JAVA**

always manages a lively crowd. The *Tavern* at the Hyatt Regency is another popular bar, open until 2 pm, but the bands can be ordinary. *Bongos* in the Sheraton is a fun pub in the city centre and though the bands may not scintillate, it has great decor in a Balinese/African 'primitif' style.

A beer in the big hotels will cost up to 15,000 rp, but *Colors (Jl Sumatra 81)* has cheaper beers (9000 rp) and a friendly atmosphere. This small venue is housed in an historic villa just east of the river and has bands every night until 2 pm. Meals and snacks are served.

Surabayans are also big on discos. Popular places include the *Top Ten* in Tunjungan Plaza and the *Bandara Terminal 1* in the Pasar Atum near Kota train station.

Surabaya's brothels are (in)famous, and the most well known of all is *Dolly*, a redlight district named after its madam founder. *Bangurejo* is another large red-light area, but less safe than Dolly.

Cinema complexes are found all around the city. *Mitra Cinema* at the back of the Balai Pemuda Building on Jl Pemuda, and *Tunjungan 21* in Tunjungan Plaza show recent Hollywood releases for around 8000 rp.

## Shopping

The huge Tunjungan Plaza is Surabaya's most upmarket and best shopping centre and is comprised of three adjoining centres – Tunjungan Plaza I to the north, II to the south and III behind it to the west. Construction of Tunjungan Plaza IV has stalled with the economic crisis. Two department stores and scores of shops sell almost everything, and it is particularly good for branded clothes. The lower ground level of Tunjungan Plaza III has an ice skating rink, open from 9.30 am to 10 pm. A skate will cost 11,000 rp including boots (14,000 rp on weekends).

Plaza Surabaya on Jl Pemuda is similar to Tunjungan Plaza but smaller. It has a Gunung Agung bookshop for books and maps.

The big Surabaya Mall on Jl Kusuma Bangsa is more downmarket and has the Mega and the Ramayana department stores for a big range of discounted goods. This is also Surabaya's computer centre for hardware, pirate software and games on the 1st and 2nd floors.

Electronics are reasonably priced in Surabaya with prices the same as Jakarta, but the range is not as big. Tunjungan Centre on Jl Tunjungan is Surabaya's main electronics centre.

Pasar Atum near Kota train station to the north of the city is a multi-storey market which is good for cheap clothes and shoes, video CDs and a bit of everything.

For handcrafts, Sarinah department store on Jl Tunjungan is a poor cousin of the Sarinah in Jakarta, but it has a decent selection of souvenirs from around Indonesia. Mirota Batik, Jl Sulawesi 24, about 200m south of Jl Karimun Jawa/Jl Raya Gubeng, has a big collection of batik and handcrafts from all over Java at very reasonable prices. A few hundred metres east of here in the back streets of Kampung Madura around Jl Raya Darmawangsa, many small antique shops sell a bit of everything, but mostly antique furniture. They are scattered around – ask for *barang barang antik*. Umar Putra, Guben Jaya II No 80, is one of the largest.

## Getting There & Away

**Air** Surabaya has a number of international connections, though services are rapidly diminishing. The most popular flights are the Singapore Airlines (☎ 5319218) and Garuda Indonesia flights to Singapore (US$180), and there are also flights to Kuala Lumpur, Bangkok and Hong Kong.

Surabaya is an important hub for domestic flights to Yogyakarta (269,000 rp), Denpasar (316,000 rp), Banjarmasin (526,000 rp), Bandung (531,000 rp), Jakarta (720,500 rp), Balikpapan (749,000 rp), Ujung Pandang (800,500 rp) and other connections.

Merpati Nusantara Airlines (☎ 5688111) is at Jl Raya Darmo 111, south of the city centre, and it has a convenient 24 hour office (☎ 5033991) at Gubeng train station. Garuda (☎ 5321525) is at the Hyatt Regency Hotel, Jl Basuki Rachmat 124. Bouraq (☎ 5452918) is at Jl Panglima Sudirman 70. Mandala (☎ 5678973) is at Jl Raya Diponegoro 73.

Looking into the caldera, Mt Bromo, East Java.

Crater lake, Kawah Ijen, East Java.

Collecting sulphur from the volcanic slopes of Kawah Ijen, East Java.

Batik cloth: each region has its own style.

'Antiques' are often new.

Topeng kartolo mask, East Java.

Decorative kris and scabbard.

Pottery from West Java.

Caneware stall, Pasar Cikini, Jakarta.

Travel agents can sell domestic tickets at a small discount and international tickets with a bigger cut. They are all over the city: Haryono Tours & Travel (☎ 5327300), Jl Panglima Sudirman 93, opposite the Bouraq office; and Vayatour (☎ 5319235) in Tunjungan Plaza are two big agents.

**Bus** Most buses operate from Surabaya's main Purabaya bus terminal, 10km south of the city centre at Bungurasih. Crowded Damri buses run between the bus terminal and the city centre – the P1 service (1000 rp) from the bus terminal is best and can drop you at the Jl Tunjungan/Jl Pemuda intersection. Buses along the north coast and to Semarang depart from Terminal Oso Wilangun, 10km west of the city.

Normal/*patas* (express) buses from Purabaya include Pandaan (1500 rp, one hour), Malang (2500/5500 rp, two hours), Blitar (3000/4500 rp, four hours), Probolinggo (3000/6000 rp, two hours), Banyuwangi (9500/17,500 rp, six hours), Bondowoso (7500 rp, 4½ hours), Solo (9000/15,000 rp, 6½ hours) and Yogyakarta (10,500/17,500 rp, eight hours). Buses also operate from Purabaya bus terminal to Madura and Semarang.

Luxury buses from Purabaya also do the long hauls to Solo, Yogyakarta, Bandung, Bogor, Denpasar and farther afield. Most are night buses leaving in the late afternoon and evening. Bookings can be made at Purabaya bus terminal, or travel agents in the city centre sell tickets with a mark-up. The most convenient bus agents are those on Jl Basuki Rahmat. Intercity buses are not allowed to enter the city, so you will have to go to Purabaya to catch your bus.

From Terminal Oso Wilangun, buses go to north-coast destinations, such as Gresik (1000 rp), Tuban (3000 rp), Kudus (8000 rp) and Semarang (10,500/17,500 rp air-con).

**Minibus** Door-to-door travel minibuses pick up at hotels, thus saving a long haul to the bus terminal, but they are not always quicker because it can take a long time to pick up a full load of passengers in sprawling Surabaya.

Minibuses run from Surabaya to all the major towns in East Java and to the rest of Java and Bali. Destinations and sample fares include Malang (12,000 rp), Denpasar (50,000 rp), Solo (27,000 rp), Yogyakarta (27,000 rp) and Semarang (37,500 rp). Hotels can make bookings and arrange pick-up, or a selection of agents can be found on Jl Basuki Rahmat, including Tirta Jaya (☎ 5468687, Jl Basuki Rahmat 64) and Tunggal (☎ 5323069, Jl Basuki Rahmat 70).

**Train** Trains from Jakarta, taking the fast northern route via Semarang, arrive at Pasar Turi train station. Trains taking the southern route via Yogyakarta, and trains from Banyuwangi and Malang, arrive at Gubeng and most carry on to Kota. Gubeng train station (☎ 5340080) is much more central and sells tickets for all trains regardless of where they depart.

Most Jakarta trains leave from Pasar Turi train station and range from the *ekonomi* services like the *Gaya Baru Malam Utara* (13,500 rp, 13 hours) to the luxury *Anggrek* (185,000 rp, nine hours) and the *Argo Bromo* (140,000 rp, nine hours). From Gubeng, night trains along the longer southern route via Yogyakarta range from the ekonomi *Gaya Baru Malam* (13,500 rp, 16 hours) to the *eksekutif* class *Bima* (115,000 rp, 12 hours).

The *Sancaka* is the best day train at 7.15 am to Solo (3½ hours) and Yogyakarta (4½ hours), costing 25,000/40,000 rp in *bisnis*/eksekutif to either destination. The trains are much faster than the buses. The 8.54 am *Purbaya* (6000 rp, seven hours) and the faster 1.14 pm *Sri Tanjung* (7000 rp, six hours) are reasonable ekonomi services to Yogya's Lempungan station via Solo.

Apart from services to the main cities, there are seven trains per day to Malang (two hours) and most continue to Blitar. The *Mutiara* goes to Banyuwangi (18,000/28,000 rp bisnis/eksekutif, six hours) at 8.15 am and 10.15 pm, or the ekonomi *Sri Tanjung* (7000 rp, 6½ hours) departs at 2.10 pm. They go via Probolinggo for Gunung Bromo.

**Boat** Surabaya is an important port and a major travel hub for ships to the other islands.

Popular Pelni connections are those to Sulawesi, with at least five Pelni ships running direct to Ujung Pandang (from 67,500 rp in ekonomi to 228,000 rp in 1st class) and to Kalimantan, with ships to Banjarmasin (48,500 rp to 162,500 rp) and Pontianak (83,000 rp to 282,000 rp). See the Getting Around chapter earlier in this book for Pelni route details.

The Pelni ticket office at Jl Pahlawan 112 is open Monday to Friday from 9 am to 3 pm, and on weekends (if there are ship departures) until noon. The front ticket counter can be chaotic but tourists often get preferential treatment. Boats depart from Tanjung Perak harbour – bus P1 or C will get you there.

Ferries to Kamal on Madura (550 rp, 30 minutes) leave every 40 minutes, also from Tanjung Perak at the end of Jl Kalimas Baru.

## Getting Around

**To/From the Airport** Taxis from the Juanda airport (15km) operate on a coupon system and cost 17,000 rp to the city centre. The Damri airport bus (3000 rp) runs infrequently between 8 am and 3 pm, and goes to Purabaya bus terminal, then on to the city centre.

**Bus** Surabaya has an extensive Damri city bus network, with normal buses (costing 300 rp anywhere around town) and patas buses (1000 rp per journey). They can be very crowded, especially the normal buses, and are a hassle if you have luggage.

One of the most useful services is the patas P1, which runs from Purabaya bus terminal past the zoo and into the city along Jl Basuki Rahmat. It then turns down Jl Embong Malang and continues to Pasar Turi train station, Pelni office and Tanjung Perak harbour. In the reverse direction, it runs to the zoo and Purabaya bus terminal, and can be caught on Jl Tunjungan or at the bus stop in front of the Natour Simpang hotel on Jl

Pemuda. The normal C buses also cover the same route.

Surabaya also has plenty of bemos labelled A, B, C etc, and all charge 500 rp to 700 rp, depending on the length of the journey. Bemo M runs to the zoo.

**Taxi** Surabaya has air-con metered taxis charging 1800 rp for the first kilometre and 900 rp for each subsequent kilometre. Typical fares from central Surabaya are Pelni office 5000 rp, Tanjung Perak harbour 9,000 rp, zoo 6000 rp, Bamboe Denn hotel to Gubeng train station 3500 rp and Purabaya bus terminal 12,000 rp. Surabaya also has yellow *angguna* pick-ups that are non-metered taxis; bargaining is required.

## AROUND SURABAYA
### Gresik

On the road to Semarang, 25km from Surabaya, this port was once a major centre for international trade and a major centre of Islam in the 15th century. Close by, at **Giri**, is the tomb of the first Sunan Giri, who is regarded as one of the greatest of the nine wali songo. He was the founder of a line of spiritual lords of Giri that lasted until it was overwhelmed by the Mataram kingdom in 1680. According to some traditions, Sunan Giri played a leading role in the conquest of Majapahit and ruled Java for 40 days after its fall – to rid the country of pre-Islamic influences. Gresik also has a colourful **pinisi harbour**.

### Pandaan

Pandaan is 40km south of Surabaya on the road to Tretes. At **Candra Wilwatika Amphitheatre** (☎ 31841) ballet performances takes place once a month from June to October, but performances have been irregular since the *krisis moneter* (monetary crisis). The varied program usually consists of dances based on indigenous tales and East Java's history. To reach the amphitheatre, take a bus from Surabaya, then a Tretes-bound colt. The theatre is 1km from Pandaan, right on the main road to Tretes.

Also on the main road to Tretes, a few kilometres from Pandaan before Pringen,

**Candi Jawi** is an early 14th century Hindu temple. Basically a Shivaite structure built to honour King Kertanegara, a Buddhist stupa was later added on top.

## Tretes
☎ 0343

This hill town, standing at 800m on the slopes of gunungs Arjuna and Welirang, is renowned for its cool climate and fine views. Tretes also has a reputation as a weekend red-light district. If you have to kill time in Surabaya, it can be a pleasant place to escape to. The **Kakek Bodo** (Stupid Grandfather), **Putuh Truno** and **Alap-alap** waterfalls are nearby, and there are a number of interesting walks around the town, including the trek to the Lalijiwo Plateau and Gunung Arjuna.

The **PPLH Environmental Education Centre** (☎/fax 0343-880884, email pplh@ sby.centrin.net.id) is near Trawas, a few kilometres north-west of Tretes. It has hiking/accommodation packages, mostly for groups, but interested volunteers are welcome and can stay in rustic bungalows or the dorm and do self-guided forest walks. Take a bus to Pandaan, then a Trawas bemo and then take an *ojek* (a motorcycle that takes passengers) – ask for Pay-Pay-eL-Ha.

**Places to Stay & Eat** Accommodation in Tretes is expensive but keep an eye out for special deals, especially at the big hotels.

The best places to stay are towards the top of the hill, and hotels lower down around Prigen are generally cheaper. Cottages can be rented for longer stays. Unattached males looking for a room to sleep in are considered an oddity, especially at the cheap hotels.

Starting near the top of the hill, the three star *Natour Bath Tretes Hotel* (☎ 81776) is in a commanding position. This 'old money' hotel has some style and a good range of facilities. Large, slightly run-down rooms cost US$60 and US$70. The smaller, renovated rooms cost US$80, but rooms have been discounted to as little as US$20.

Opposite the Natour, the *Kalimas Hotel* (*Jl Pesanggrahan 26*) has small but tidy rooms with bathroom and welcome hot water for 30,000 rp and 40,000 rp.

The *Lie Mas Hotel* (☎ 82091) on Jl Pesanggrahan, which leads uphill off the main road near the Natour, has fine views with rooms on different levels down the hillside. This good mid-range hotel has rooms from 80,000 rp (less during the week) with hot water.

On the main road near the Natour Bath Tretes Hotel, *Mess Garuda* is a 'bottom of the barrel' cheapie with rooms for 20,000 rp during the week. The *Wisma Semeru Indah* (☎ 81701, Jl Semeru 7) is below the main shopping area and has overpriced rooms from 40,000 rp.

The other luxury hotel competing with the Natour is the *Hotel Surya* (☎ 81991), a concrete-and-glass upstart with a huge heated pool, fitness centre and tennis courts, and good rooms from US$75.

For cheap eats, *Depot Abadi* (*Jl Raya 27*) opposite the Mess Garuda, has standard fare. A line of mid-range restaurants can be found along the road from the Natour Bath Tretes Hotel, including the *Mandarin* for Chinese food and the *Istana Ayam Goreng* for chicken.

**Getting There & Away** From Surabaya, take a bus to Pandaan (1500 rp) and then a minibus to Tretes.

## Gunung Arjuna-Lalijiwo Reserve

This reserve includes the dormant volcano **Gunung Arjuna** (3339m), the semi-active **Gunung Welirang** (3156m) and the **Lalijiwo Plateau** on the northern slopes of Arjuna.

Experienced and well equipped hikers can walk from Tretes to Selekta in two days, but you need a guide if you're going all the way. Alternatively, you can just climb Welirang from Tretes.

The easiest access is from Tretes. A well used hiking path, popular with students on weekends and holidays, begins in Tretes at the **Kakak Bodo recreation reserve**. Get information from the PHPA (Indonesia's national parks service) post at the entrance to the waterfall before heading off. It's a hard

EAST JAVA

five hour, 17km walk to the huts used by sulphur collectors, who collect slabs of sulphur from a crater on the side of Welirang.

It is usual to stay overnight at the huts in order to reach the summit before the clouds and mist roll in around mid-morning. Bring your own camping gear, food and drinking water, and be prepared for the freezing conditions.

From the huts it is a 4km climb to the summit. Allow at least six hours in total for the ascent, 4½ hours for the descent. You can also rent horses but hard bargaining is required.

The trail passes Lalijiwo Plateau, a superb alpine meadow, from where a trail leads to Gunung Arjuna, the more demanding peak. From Arjuna a trail leads down the southern side to Junggo, near Selekta and Batu. It is a five hour descent from Arjuna this way, and a guide is essential.

## Gunung Penanggungan

The remains of no less than 81 temples are scattered over the slopes of Gunung Penanggungan (1650m), a sacred Hindu mountain said to be the peak of holy Mt Mahameru, which broke off and landed at its present site when the holy mountain was being transported from India to Indonesia.

This was once an important pilgrimage site for Hindus. Pilgrims made their way to the top of the mountain and stopped to bathe in the holy springs adorned with Hindu statuary. The two main bathing places are **Jolotundo** and **Belahan**, the best examples of remaining Hindu art here. Both are difficult to reach.

Between Pandaan and Gembol, a rough road leads west and then a turn-off leads south to Genengan village, 4km away. From here an even rougher stone road leads 2km up through the fields and villages to **Candi Belahan**. The bathing pool is presided over by Vishnu's consorts Sri and Lakshmi, who once flanked the magnificent statue of Airlangga-as-Vishnu, which now lies in the Trowulan Museum. From Lakshmi's cupped breasts (and with the aid of plastic tubing), water spouts into the pool still used as a bathing spot by the villagers. From Belahan, the road continues farther up the hill, and the peak of Gunung Penanggungan lies 6km away.

**Candi Jolotundo** is the bathing place on the western side of the mountain. Dating from the 10th century, it is set into the hillside like Belahan but many of its carved reliefs have been removed. It lies about 6km south of Ngoro on the Gempol-Mojokerto road. Ojeks hang out around the turn-off and can take you to the temple along another bad road.

## TROWULAN

Trowulan was once the capital of the largest Hindu empire in Indonesian history. Founded in 1294 by Wijaya, a Singosari prince, it reached the height of its power under Hayam Wuruk (1350-89), who was guided by his powerful prime minister, Gajah Mada. During Wuruk's time, Majapahit claimed control over, or at least received tribute from, most of today's Indonesia and even parts of the Malay Peninsula. The capital was a grand affair – the *kraton* (walled city palace) formed a miniature city within the city, and was surrounded by great fortified walls and watchtowers.

Its wealth was based both on the fertile rice-growing plains of Java and on control of the spice trade. The religion was an open-ended version of Hinduism, with Shiva, Vishnu and Brahma being worshipped, although, as in the earlier Javanese kingdoms, Buddhism was also prominent. It seems Muslims were tolerated and Koranic burial inscriptions, found on the site, suggest that there were Javanese Muslims within the royal court, even in the 14th century when this Hindu-Buddhist state was at the height of its glory. The empire came to a sudden end in 1478 when the city fell to the north-coast power of Demak and the Majapahit elite fled to Bali, thus opening up Java for conquest by the Muslims.

The remains of Majapahit are scattered over a large area around the small village of Trowulan, 12km from Mojokerto. The Majapahit temples were mainly built from red clay bricks and did not stand the test of time. Many have been rebuilt and are relatively simple compared to the glories of Central Java such as Borobudur, but the numerous temples give a good idea of what was once a great city. It's possible to walk around the sites in one day if you start early, or you can hire a becak. Given the heat and the fact that the temples are spread over a large area, a car is the ideal way to see the temples.

## Trowulan Museum

One kilometre from the main Surabaya-Solo road, the museum houses superb examples of Majapahit sculpture and pottery from throughout East Java. Pride of place is given to the splendid statue of Kediri's King Airlangga-as-Vishnu astride a huge Garuda, taken from Belahan. The museum should be your first port of call for an understanding of Trowulan and Majapahit history, and it includes descriptions of the other ancient ruins in East Java. It is open from 7 am to 4 pm, and closed Monday and public holidays.

## Ruins

Some of the most interesting sites include **Kolam Segaran** (a vast Majapahit swimming pool); the gateway of **Bajang Ratu**, with its strikingly sculptured *kala* (guardian) heads; **Tikus Temple** (Queen's Bath); and **Siti Inggil Temple**, with the impressive tomb of Wijaya (people still come to meditate here and in the early evening it has quite a strange spiritual atmosphere). **Pendopo Agung** is an open-air pavilion built by the Indonesian army. Two kilometres south of the pavilion, **Troloyo cemetery** is the site of the oldest Muslim graves found in Java, the earliest dating from 1376.

## Getting There & Away

Trowulan can be visited from Surabaya, which is 60km to the east. Trowulan has a few restaurants on the highway but no accommodation. If you want to stay nearby, Mojokerto has plenty of hotels.

From Surabaya's Purabaya bus terminal it is a one hour trip to Trowulan. Take a

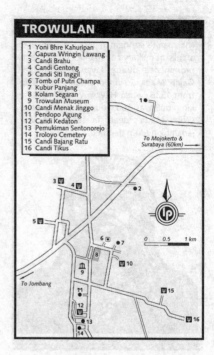

**TROWULAN**

1 Yoni Bhre Kahuripan
2 Gapura Wringin Lawang
3 Candi Brahu
4 Candi Gentong
5 Candi Siti Inggil
6 Tomb of Putri Champa
7 Kubur Panjang
8 Kolam Segaran
9 Trowulan Museum
10 Candi Menak Jinggo
11 Pendopo Agung
12 Candi Kedaton
13 Pemukiman Sentonorejo
14 Troloyo Cemetery
15 Candi Bajang Ratu
16 Candi Tikus

To Mojokerto & Surabaya (60km)

To Jombang

0    0.5    1 km

Jombang bus, which can drop you at the turn-off to the museum, or a Mojokerto bus that will stop at the bus terminal on the outskirts of town; then take a bemo (500 rp) to Trowulan. A becak tour of the sites will cost around 10,000 rp to 15,000 rp with bargaining.

When leaving Trowulan, flag a bus down on the road from Surabaya to Solo. Heading east to Probolinggo or south to Malang, take a bus or colt to Gempol and continue from there by public bus, which is cheaper. For Malang, an interesting alternative is to travel by bus via Jombang and the hill town of Batu.

## MOJOKERTO

Mojokerto can be used as a base to visit the Majapahit ruins at Trowulan. Mojokerto is in the centre of East Java's most populous region, the Brantas River Delta, but the city

**EAST JAVA**

## Gajah Mada

Majapahit's strongman prime minister was a brilliant military commander who rose to prominence during Jayanegara's reign. Gajah Mada assumed virtual leadership from 1336, when Hayam Wuruk became king but was too young to rule. After Gajah Mada's death in 1364, the Majapahit kingdom declined.

is not overwhelming. It has an old quarter of winding alleys, canals and old houses from the Dutch era.

The best bet for budget accommodation is the *Wisma Tenera*, Jl Cokroaminoto 1, where clean, quiet rooms with mandi cost 20,000 rp, including breakfast.

### Getting There & Away

Buses along the road from Surabaya to Madiun all pass outside Mojokerto. Some enter the city but others stop only at the bus terminal outside town on the main highway. If you stop off here for the night en route to Trowulan, you can pick up an *angkot* (small minibus, 500 rp), going that way from the road running parallel to Jl Majapahit (behind Pasar Kliwon) in the centre of town, rather than heading back out to the bus terminal.

## MADURA

• pop 3 million

Madura is a large and rugged island, about 160km long by 35km wide, and separated from Surabaya on the East Java coast by a narrow channel. It is famous for its bull races, the *kerapan sapi*, but also has a few historical sites, some passable beaches and an interesting, traditional culture. The sarong and peci are still the norm here, mall fever has not found its way to Madura and very few tourists go beyond a day trip to the bull races.

The people of Madura have settled widely in East Java, particularly in Surabaya, the north coast and around Banyuwangi. Up to 10 million Madurese live outside the island. Since independence, Madura has been governed as part of the province of East Java, but the island has had a long tradition of involvement with its larger neighbour, Java, and with the Dutch. The Dutch were not interested in the island itself, which was initially of little economic importance, but rather in the crucial role the Madurese played in Javanese dynastic politics.

Madurese men claim that the name Madura is derived from *madu* (honey) and *dara* (girl), and Madura's 'sweet' girls are famed throughout Java for their sexual prowess. Madura is, however, a very traditional and devoutly Islamic society. The Madurese are rugged *kasar* (unrefined) people (according to the Javanese), and are said to be adept at wielding knives when disputes arise. While the Madurese can be disconcertingly blunt at times, and in remote areas you may attract a crowd of curious onlookers, they can also be extremely hospitable.

The southern side of the island, facing Java, is shallow beach and cultivated lowland, while the northern coast alternates between rocky cliffs and beaches of great rolling sand dunes, the best of which is at Lombang. At the extreme east is tidal marsh and vast tracts of salt around Kalianget. The interior of this flat and arid island is riddled with limestone slopes and is either rocky or sandy, so agriculture is limited. There are goat farms, tobacco estates, some orchards

## Kerapan Sapi

As the Madurese tell it, the tradition of bull races began long ago when plough teams raced each other across the arid fields; this pastime was encouraged by an early king of Sumenep, Panembahan Sumolo. Today, when stud bull breeding is big business on Madura, the *kerapan sapi* (bull races) are as much an incentive for the Madurese to breed good stock as simply a popular form of entertainment and sport. Only bulls of a certain standard can be entered for important races, and the Madurese keep their young bulls in superb condition, dosing them with an assortment of medicinal herbs, honey, beer and raw eggs.

Traditional races are put on in bull-racing stadiums all over Madura. Practice trials are held throughout the year, but the main season starts in late August and September, when contests are held at district and regency level. The cream of the bulls fight it out for the big prize in October at the grand final in Pamekasan, the island's capital.

This is, of course, the biggest and most colourful festival. As many as 100 bulls, wearing fancy halters and yokes of gilt, ribbons and flowers, are paraded through town and around the open field of the stadium to a loud fanfare of drums, flutes and gongs. For each race two pairs of bulls, stripped of their finery, are matched against each other with their 'jockeys' perched behind on wooden sleds. Gamelan is played to excite the bulls and then, after being given a generous tot of *arak*, they're released and charge flat out down the track – just as often plunging right into the seething crowds of spectators! The race is over in a flash – the best time recorded so far is nine seconds over the 100m, which is faster than the human world track record. After the elimination heats, the victorious bulls are proudly trotted home to be used at stud.

Pamekasan is the main centre for bull races, but they can also be seen in the other regency centres, Bangkalan, Sampang and Sumenep, and in the surrounding villages. The *East Java Calendar of Events*, available from tourist offices in Surabaya, has a general schedule for the main races, but if you are in Madura in the main season on a Saturday or Sunday, you can be sure that races or practice will be held somewhere on the island. Surabaya travel agents also arrange day trips during the season.

and extensive stands of coconut palms, but the main industries of this dry, sunburnt land are cattle, salt and fishing.

### History

In 1624 the island was conquered by Sultan Agung of Mataram and its government united under one Madurese princely line, the Cakraningrats. Until the middle of the 18th century the Cakraningrat family fiercely opposed Central Javanese rule and harassed Mataram, often conquering large parts of the kingdom. Prince Raden Trunojoyo even managed to carry off the royal treasury of Mataram in 1677, which was restored only after the Dutch intervened and stormed Trunojoyo's stronghold at Kediri.

In 1705 the Dutch secured control of the eastern half of Madura following the First Javanese War of Succession between Amangkurat III and his uncle, Pangeran Puger. Dutch recognition of Puger was largely influenced by Cakraningrat II, the lord of West Madura. He probably supported Puger's claims simply because he hoped a new war in Central Java would give the Madurese a chance to interfere but, while Amangkurat was arrested and exiled to Ceylon, Puger took the title of Pakubuwono I and concluded a treaty with the Dutch which, along with large concessions in Java, granted them East Madura.

The Cakraningrats fared little better by agreeing to help the Dutch put down the

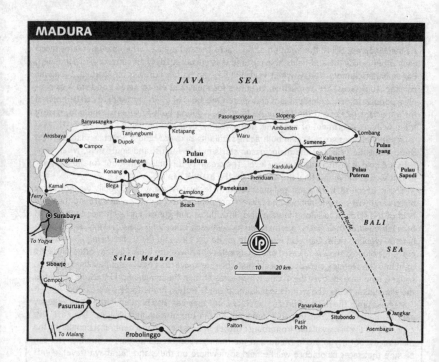

MADURA

*JAVA SEA*

Banyusangka

Pasongsongan · Slopeng

Tanjungbumi · Ketapang · Ambunten

Arosbaya

Campor · Waru · Sumenep · Lombang

Dupok

Pulau Iyang

Bangkalan · Tambalangan · Pulau Madura · Karduluk · Kalianget · Pulau Puteran · Pulau Sapudi

Konang · Prenduan

Kamal · Blega

Ferry · Sampang · Camplong · Pamekasan

Surabaya · Beach

To Yogya

BALI

*Selat Madura*

SEA

Siboarjo · 0  10  20 km

Gempol

Pasuruan · Panarukan · Jangkar

Paiton · Pasir Putih · Situbondo

To Malang · Probolinggo · Asembagus

Ferry Route

## Getting There & Away

rebellion in Central Java that broke out after the massacre of the Chinese in Batavia (Jakarta) in 1740. Although Cakraningrat IV attempted to contest the issue, a treaty was eventually signed in 1743 in which Pakubuwono II ceded full sovereignty of Madura to the Dutch. Cakraningrat fled to Banjarmasin and took refuge on an English ship but was robbed, betrayed by the sultan and finally captured by the Dutch and exiled to the Cape of Good Hope in South Africa.

Under the Dutch, Madura continued as four states, each with its own *bupati*, or regent. Madura was initially important as a major source of colonial troops, but in the second half of the 19th century it acquired greater economic value as the main supplier of salt to Dutch-governed areas of the archipelago, where salt was a profitable monopoly of the colonial government.

## Getting There & Away

From Surabaya, ferries sail to Kamal, the port town on the western tip of Madura, from where you can catch buses or colts to other towns on the island. It's a half hour trip by ferry (500 rp), which leave roughly every half hour around the clock. Buses go directly from Surabaya's Purabaya bus terminal via the ferry right through to Sumenep, but if you're already based in the centre of town, it's easier to take the P1 express city bus (1000 rp) or C bus to the ferry terminus at Tanjung Perak harbour, catch the ferry across to Kamal on Madura and then take local buses around the island.

Another possibility, if coming from the east, is to take the passenger and car ferry from Jangkar harbour (near Asembagus) to Kalianget (6500 rp, four hours) on the eastern tip of Madura. The ferry departs Thursday to Monday from Jangkar at 2 pm. To get to Jangkar, catch any bus heading along the main highway between Banyuwangi and Situbondo, and get off at Pasar Kambong in Asembagus. From the market, countless becaks make the 4.5km trip to Jangkar, or take an *andong* (horse-drawn cart) for 1000 rp. To Jangkar, the ferry departs from Kalianget at 8 am. To Kalianget, take an 'O' colt from Sumenep (500 rp, 11km).

## Getting Around
It's possible to pick up a through bus from Surabaya's Purabaya bus terminal. At least a dozen buses a day go to Madura across the island to Sumenep (6000 rp, 10,000 rp aircon) and most continue to Kalianget. There are also direct buses to and from Banyuwangi via Probolinggo, Denpasar, Malang, Semarang and Jakarta.

If you arrive on the ferry from Surabaya, you'll have to negotiate what can be a wild melee to find a colt to your destination. From Kamal, colts run along the main highway to Bangkalan (800 rp, half hour), Pamekasan (3500 rp, 2½ hours) and Sumenep (5000 rp, four hours). Colts travel along the northern route to Arosbaya, Tanjungbumi, Pasongsongan and Ambunten. Although the through buses are a better option, the colts are much more frequent and run all over the island. The drawback is that they can spend a lot of time picking up passengers.

To see something of the island, it's interesting to take a colt from Pamekasan inland through tobacco country to Waru, and another to Pasongsongan, from where you can head back to Sumenep via Ambunten and Slopeng.

Madura's roads are almost all paved and in excellent condition with relatively little traffic. As the island is mostly flat, Madura is a good cycling destination, though it does get very hot.

## Bangkalan
☎ 031
This is the next town north of Kamal along the coast, and because it is so close to Surabaya many visitors only make a day trip for the bull races. The **Museum Cakraningrat**

is a museum of Madurese history and culture, open from 8 am to 2 pm Monday to Saturday.

**Places to Stay & Eat** The *Hotel Ningrat* (☎ 3095388, *Jl Kahaji Muhammed Kholil 113*), on the main road south of town, is one of Madura's best hotels, though hardly luxurious. Small singles/doubles are 15,000/30,000 rp, and more comfortable rooms with mandi are 40,000 rp. The much more attractive air-con rooms are decorated in traditional Madurese style and cost 80,000 rp.

Closer to the centre of town, *Hotel Melati* (☎ 3096457, *Jl Majen Sungkono 48*) is a basic place with rooms for 15,000 rp. It is back from the street and down an alleyway.

For good Chinese food, try the *Agung Restaurant (Jl Jaksa Agung Suprapto 23)*.

## Sampang
Sampang, 61km from Bangkalan, is the centre of the regency of the same name and also stages bull races. It has a couple of hotels.

## Camplong
Camplong, 9km farther east, is a popular, if grungy, beach on the south coast. It's safe for swimming. The Pertamina storage tanks nearby do nothing for Camplong's visual appeal, but it is a breezy oasis from the hot interior of Madura. Impressive flotillas of twin-outrigger dugout canoes are used for fishing along the coast and the *prahus* (outrigger boats) carry huge, triangular striped sails.

**Places to Stay** At Camplong, the *Pondok Wisata Pantai Camplong (☎ 21569)* provides some of the best accommodation on Madura. Attractive cottages on the beach cost 37,500 rp to 60,000 rp.

## Pamekasan
☎ 0324
On the southern side of the island, 100km east of Kamal, the capital of Madura is a quiet and pleasant enough town, although during October each year it comes alive with the festivities of the Kerapan Sapi Grand Final. Bull races are held in and around

Pamekasan every Sunday from the end of July until the big day in early October.

To see *batik tulis* (hand-drawn batik) being made, visit Batik Kristal at Jl Jokotole 29, across the road from the BCA bank.

About 35km east of Pamekasan before Bluto, **Karduluk** is a wood-carving centre that produces mostly cupboards.

**Information** The BCA bank, just east of the *alun alun* (town square) on Jl Jokotole, changes money and travellers cheques at good rates and gives cash advances on credit cards.

**Places to Stay** In the centre of town opposite the alun alun, *Hotel Garuda (☎ 22589, Jl Mesigit 1)* has doubles with shared mandi at 6600 rp. Big, old rooms with mandi are 11,000 rp up to 28,600 rp with air-con. It's good value but lacks atmosphere.

Nearby on the road to Bangkalan, *Hotel Trunojoyo (☎ 22181, Jl Trunojoyo 48)* is clean, quiet and better. Rooms cost from 8000 rp up to 40,000 rp with air-con, including breakfast.

*Hotel Ramayana (☎ 22406, Jl Niaga 55)* is the best in town. A few small rooms with shared mandi cost 10,000 rp, but most are bright rooms with mandi from 20,000 rp. Air-con rooms start at 35,000 rp.

## Sumenep
☎ 0328

At the eastern end of the island, Sumenep is Madura's most interesting town. It is centred around the kraton, mosque and market, which is considered to be the most *halus* (refined) area of Madura. This small, quiet, easy-going town makes a fine base to explore the island.

Sumenep's decaying villas with white-washed walls, high ceilings and cool porches give the town a Mediterranean air, which is mixed with the Arabic influence typical of Java's north coast. Sumenep is also a champion bull breeding centre, and on most Saturday mornings practice bull races can be seen at Giling stadium.

The Festival of Sumenep celebrates the founding of the town on 31 October every year with various celebrations and cultural performances.

**Information** The post office is on the road to Kalianget and the Telkom office is farther out past the Chinese temple. Both the BCA bank, on Jl Trunojoyo, and the BNI bank change cash at poor rates.

**Things to See** The **kraton** and its **taman sari** (pleasure garden) are worth visiting. The kraton was built in 1750 by Panembahan Sumolo, son of Queen Raden Ayu Tirtonegoro and her spouse, Bendoro Saud, who was a commoner but a descendant of Muslim scholars. The architect is thought to have been the grandson of one of the first Chinese to settle in Sumenep after the Chinese massacre in Batavia. The kraton is occupied by the present *bupati* (the official in charge of a regency) of Sumenep, but part of the building is a small museum with an interesting collection of royal possessions, including Madurese furniture, stone sculptures and *binggels*, the heavy silver anklets worn by Madurese women. Opposite the kraton, the royal carriage house museum contains the throne of Queen Tirtonegoro and a Chinese-style bed reputedly 300 years old. Entry is 300 rp to the museum, and from here you will be taken on a guided tour of the kraton. On the first and third Sunday of the month, traditional dance or *gamelan* (orchestra) practice is held at the kraton.

Sumenep's 18th century **Mesjid Jamik** (mosque) is notable for its three tiered Meru-style roof, Chinese porcelain tiles and ceramics. Sumenep also has a **Chinese temple**.

The tombs of the royal family are at **Asta Tinggi cemetery**, which looks out over the town from a peaceful hilltop 2km away. The main royal tombs are interesting, and decorated with carved and painted panels, two depicting dragons said to represent the colonial invasion of Sumenep. The biggest mausoleum is that of Panembahan Notokusomo (1762-1811), but it is the grave of Tirtonegoro that attracts pilgrims from all over Madura and Java. One of the small pavilions in the outer courtyard still bears the

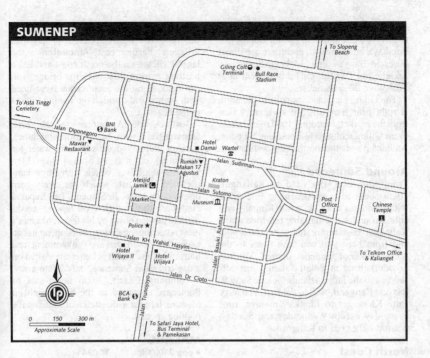

**SUMENEP**

mark of an assassin's sword from an unsuccessful attempt to murder Bendoro Saud.

**Places to Stay & Eat** The best place to head for is the *Hotel Wijaya I (☎ 21433, Jl Trunojoyo 45-7)*. Clean rooms cost 10,000 rp without mandi, from 17,000 rp with mandi, and air-con rooms cost from 35,000 rp. The sister *Hotel Wijaya II (☎ 21352, Jl KH Wahid Hasyim 3)* is also clean and well run. It is quieter, though many of the rooms are dark. Rooms cost 9000 rp up to 48,000 rp for the air-con rooms with mandi, fridge and TV.

The *Safari Jaya (☎ 21989, Jl Trunojoyo 90)*, on the southern outskirts of town, is a big hotel where rooms start at 8000 rp and go up to 20,000 rp with air-con. It is also good value, but dull and a long way from town. The other option is the very basic *Hotel Damai (☎ 21687, Jl Sudirman 39)*, where rooms cost 10,000 rp.

Decent restaurants to try around town include the *Mawar (Jl Diponegoro 105)* and *Rumah Makan 17 Agustus (Jl Sudirman 34)* serving both budget Chinese and Indonesian cuisine. There are good day and night *markets* in the area around the mosque. The *Hotel Wijaya I* has a good restaurant and ice cold beer.

**Shopping** Sumenep is a centre for batik on Madura, though Madurese batik isn't as fine as that in Java. Try the market, or you can visit home workshops around town.

The main business in town is antiques, but the best antiques are carted off by the truck-load to Bali and Jakarta. Every second house seems to have something for sale.

**Getting There & Away** The main bus terminal is on the southern outskirts of town, a 1500 rp becak ride from the town centre.

Buses leave roughly every 1½ hours between 6.30 am and 9.30 pm for Surabaya's Purabaya bus terminal, and there are direct buses to Banyuwangi, Malang, Semarang, Jakarta and Denpasar. The bus agent at Jl Trunojoyo 20 sells tickets.

The Giling bus stand for colts to the north is right near the bull-race stadium, 1.5km from the market, or around 1000 rp by becak. From Giling, colts go to Lombang, Slopeng, Ambunten and other north-coast destinations.

## Around Sumenep

From Sumenep, the road to **Kalianget**, 10km south-east, passes many fine villas with frontages of thick, white Roman-style columns under overhanging red-tiled roofs. Kalianget is a centre for salt production, and from here you can take boats to the other islands of Sumenep district. You can go snorkelling at **Pulau Talango** just offshore, and the larger islands include **Sapudi**, **Ras** and **Kangean**, well to the east. The ferry from Kalianget to Jangkar, in Java, runs every day except Wednesday and Sunday, when it only goes to Kangean.

## North Coast

Fishing villages and their brightly painted prahus dot the north coast. The coast is lined with sandy beaches, but Madura's beaches are not brilliant.

Near Arosbaya, 27km north of Kamal, the tombs of the Cakraningrat royalty are at **Air Mata** cemetery, which is superbly situated on the edge of a small ravine overlooking a river valley. The ornately carved *gunungan* (mountain range) headstone on the grave of Ratu Ibu, consort of Cakraningrat I, is the most impressive and is on the highest terrace. The turn-off to Air Mata is shortly before Arosbaya and from the coast road it's a 4km walk inland. *Air mata* means 'tears'.

The village of **Tanjungbumi** is on the north-west coast of Madura, about 60km from Kamal. Although primarily a fishing village, it's also a centre for the manufacture of traditional Madurese batik and Madurese prahus. On the outskirts is a beach, **Pantai Siring Kemuning**.

**Pasongsongan** is a fishing village on the beach where it may be possible to stay with villagers. Farther east, **Ambunten** is the largest village on the north coast and has a bustling market. Just over the bridge, you can walk along the picturesque river lined with prahus and through the fishing village to the beach.

Just outside Ambunten to the east, **Slopeng** has a wide beach with sand dunes, coconut palms and usually calm water for swimming, but it is not always clean. Men fish the shallower water with large cantilevered hand nets which are rarely seen elsewhere in Java . In Slopeng, Pak Supakra continues the tradition of *topeng* mask-making handed down by his father, Madura's most noted topeng craftsman. Slopeng has an expensive *pesanggrahan* (government rest house), but the beach is better off visited on a day trip from Sumenep, only 20km away.

**Lombang Beach**, 30km north-east of Sumenep, is touted as the best beach on Madura. It has a wide stretch of sand but it's nothing special.

## MALANG
● pop 710,000      ☎ 0341

Malang is one of the more attractive cities with a hill station feel in Java. Much smaller and quieter than Surabaya, it makes a good base for exploring East Java. Situated on the banks of Sungai Brantas, Malang was established by the Dutch around the end of the 18th century when coffee was first grown as a colonial cash crop in the area. In more recent years, local farmers have grown tobacco and apples; cigarette factories and the army have also set themselves up here. It's a cool, clean place with a well planned square, and the central area of town is studded with parks, tree-lined streets and old Dutch architecture.

The main attractions lie outside the city, but apart from being a good base for many points of interest in East Java, it is also worth a day or two visit for its own sake. Unlike many Javanese towns, which are planned on a grid pattern, this one sweeps and winds along the river bank, with surprising views and quiet backwaters to explore. The living is good and the atmosphere easy-going.

## Orientation

Life in Malang revolves around the alun alun and the busy streets of Agus Salim and Pasar Besar near the central market. Here are the main shopping plazas, restaurants, cinemas and many of Malang's hotels. The alun alun in particular is a very popular area in the evening, when families and students promenade and buskers perform. Northwest of the square along Jl Basuki Rachmat are banks, the Telkom office and restaurants.

## Information

**Tourist Offices** Malang has plenty of tourist offices but they are all a long way out and not really worth the effort. The East Java Government tourist bureau (DIPARDA, ☎ 368473), Jl Kawi 41, has brochures on East Java. The *kabupaten* (regency) tourist office (☎ 562680), Jl Gede 6, has information on the area around Malang, and the city tourist office is farther north-east in Taman Krida Budaya on Jl Soekarno Hatta.

**Money** Malang has plenty of banks, with ATMs, and moneychangers. Compare the BNI and BCA banks on Jl Basuki Rachmat for the best rates, or the Bank Lippo is opposite the alun alun.

**Post & Communications** The main post office is opposite the alun alun on Jl Kauman Merdeka. The Warposnet here, open from 8 am to midnight, has Internet terminals for 6000 rp per hour. Prima Warung Internet is an Internet cafe on Jl Basuki Rachmat.

The Telkom office on Jl Basuki Rachmat is open 24 hours. It has a Home Country Direct phone, as does the Toko Oen restaurant and the Kartika Graha Hotel. A Telkom wartel is on Jl Agus Salim, near the Hotel Santosa.

## Things to See & Do

The major attractions are outside town, but Malang has a few diversions to stave off boredom.

Malang is noted for its colonial architecture. The **Balai Kota** (Town Hall) on Jl Tugu Circle is a sprawling Dutch administrative building, and nearby are some old former mansions, such as the **Splendid Inn** and the **Wisma IKIP** next door on Jl Majapahit. For reliving colonial dreams, nothing beats the **Toko Oen restaurant**. Another good example of Art Deco colonial architecture is the **Hotel Pelangi** and its tiled restaurant with scenes of old Holland. Near the Toko Oen, the **Gereja Kathedral Kuno** is the old Dutch Reform Church. **Jl Besar Ijen** is Malang's millionaire's row. Most of the large houses date from the colonial era, but many have been substantially renovated, losing architectural detail in the process.

On the north-west outskirts of town, **Candi Badut** is a small Shivaite temple dating from the 8th century. West of town on Jl Besar Ijen, the modern **Army Museum** is devoted to Malang's Brawijaya Division.

Malang has some good markets. The huge central market, **Pasar Besar**, is always worth a browse. The flower market, **Pasar Bunga**, has a pleasant aspect down by the river, and it is the place to stroll in the morning. At the same time, you can also take in the nearby **Pasar Senggol**, Malang's bird market, which also sells butterflies. **Pasar Kebalen**, near the Eng An Kiong Chinese temple, is the most active market in the evening (until around 9 pm most nights).

## Organised Tours

A number of operators have tours to the Singosari temples (from 50,000 rp per person, minimum two), Batu (50,000 rp) and Bromo (via Tosari for around 85,000 rp). The private Tourist Information Service (☎ 364052) at the Toko Oen restaurant and the cheaper Hotel Helios are two well known operators, and staff speak Dutch as well as English. They can also arrange car hire with a driver from around 90,000 rp per day.

## Places to Stay – Budget

The best choice is the popular *Hotel Helios* (☎ 362741, Jl Pattimura 37). Doubles cost

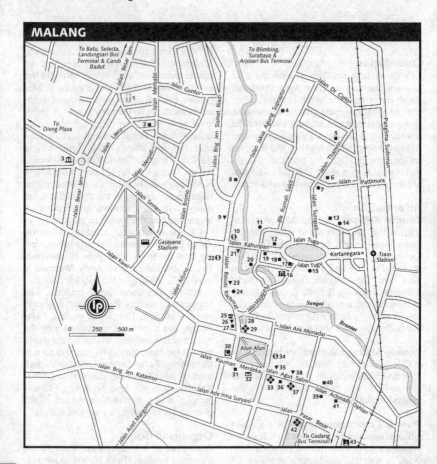

**MALANG**

To Batu, Selecta,
Landungsari Bus
Terminal & Candi
Badut

To Blimbing,
Surabaya &
Arjosari Bus Terminal

To Dieng Plaza

Gajayana Stadium

Jalan Besar Ijen
Jalan Merbabu
Jalan Guntur
Jalan Lawu
Jalan Merpati
Jalan Semeru
Jalan Bromo
Jalan Kawi
Jalan Arjuno
Jalan Basuki Rachmat
Jalan Brig Jen Slamet Riadi
Jalan Juksa Agung Suprapto
Jalan Dr Cipto
Jalan Thamrin
Jalan – Pattimura
Blk Rumah Sakit
Jalan Suropati
Jalan Kahuripan
Jalan Tugu
Kertanegara
Jalan Tugu
Jalan Majapahit
Jalan Aris Munadar
Sungai Brantas
Jalan Kauman
Alun Alun
Jalan Merdeka
Jalan Agus Salim
Jalan Achmad Dahlan
Jalan Brig Jen Katamso
Jalan Ade Irma Suryani
Jalan Ariel Margono
Jalan Pasar Besar
To Gadang Bus Terminal
Panglima Sudirman
Train Station

0   250   500 m

---

15,000 rp to 20,000 rp with shared mandi, and rooms with private bath for 27,500 rp and 37,500 rp. It's good value, clean, comfortable and all rooms have balconies overlooking the garden. Good travel information, bus bookings and tours are provided.

If the Helios is full, the *Hotel Palem II* (☎ 325129, Jl Thamrin 15) is a passable hotel only a short walk away. Rooms with mandi cost 22,500 rp to 32,500 rp.

In the lively central area, the friendly *Hotel Riche* (☎ 324560, Jl Basuki Rach-

mat 1) is well placed near the Toko Oen restaurant. Dark rooms at front cop the street noise but those at back around the courtyard are lighter, quieter and a good choice. Rooms, all with mandi, cost 25,000 rp to 40,000 rp.

Other central hotels include the *Hotel Tosari* (☎ 326945, Jl Achmad Dahlan 31) with bare but very clean rooms for 20,000 rp, or from 30,000 rp to 70,000 rp with mandi. The *Losmen Semarang* (Jl Achmad Dahlan 30) across the road has some old-fashioned

## MALANG

| PLACES TO STAY | | PLACES TO EAT | | 20 | Pasar Senggol; |
|---|---|---|---|---|---|
| 2 | Hotel Graha Cakra | 9 | Rumah Makan Minang Jaya | | Pasar Bunga |
| 4 | Hotel Taman Regent's | 21 | Jack's Cafe | 22 | BNI Bank |
| 5 | Hotel Palem II | 23 | Minang Agung | 24 | Prima Warung Internet |
| 6 | Hotel Helios | 26 | Toko Oen Restaurant | 25 | Telkom Office |
| 8 | Kartika Graha | 35 | Rumah Makan Agung | 28 | Gereja Kathedral Kuno |
| 12 | Hotel Kartika Kusuma | 38 | Gloria Restaurant | 29 | Sarinah Department Store |
| 13 | Hotel Menara | | | 30 | Mosque |
| 17 | Splendid Inn | OTHER | | 32 | Main Post Office |
| 18 | Tugu Park Hotel | 1 | Gereja Maria Bundel Karmel | 33 | Mitra Department Store; |
| 19 | Montana Hotel | 3 | Army Museum | | Gajah Mada Plaza |
| 27 | Hotel Riche | 7 | Wartel Suropati | 34 | Bank Lippo |
| 31 | Hotel Pelangi | 10 | BCA Bank | 37 | Malang Plaza |
| 36 | Hotel Santosa | 11 | Taman Rekreasi Senaputra | 42 | Pasar Besar; Matahari |
| 39 | Hotel Tosari | 14 | Wijaya Travel | | Department Store |
| 40 | Losmen Semarang | 15 | Balai Kota (Town Hall) | 43 | Eng An Kiong Chinese |
| 41 | Hotel Margosuko | 16 | Wisma IKIP | | Temple |

style and is cheap at 15,000 rp to 20,000 rp, but is run-down and unfriendly.

*Hotel Santosa (☎ 366889, Jl Agus Salim 24)* is right in the thick of things opposite the alun alun. Clean but uninspiring budget doubles cost 22,500 rp, or 35,000 rp with mandi. The mid-range rooms from 45,000 rp to 80,000 rp are a much better choice.

## Places to Stay – Mid-Range

In an excellent position right on the alun alun, the *Hotel Pelangi (☎ 365156, Jl Kauman Merdeka 3)* is a large, pleasant old Dutch hotel with spacious rooms. Simple 'driver's' rooms cost 25,000 rp to 35,000 rp, but you'll be directed to the more expensive but good value fan rooms with bath, hot water and TV costing 75,000 rp and 80,000 rp. Modern air-con rooms cost 115,000 rp and 130,000 rp. Add 10% tax to the rates, but a discount is usually possible and buffet breakfast in the delightful hotel restaurant is included.

Also in the centre, the *Hotel Margosuko (☎ 325270, Jl Achmad Dahlan 40-2)* has a flash new lobby, a small coffee shop and good service. Older, sometimes noisy, rooms with bathroom and TV cost 40,000 rp and 50,000 rp. The renovated rooms with air-con and hot water are much more luxurious, and cost 65,000 rp and 85,000 rp.

The most fashionable area to stay in is around Jl Tugu. This is the old Dutch administrative district, with impressive public buildings and old villas. The *Splendid Inn (☎ 366860, Jl Majapahit 2-4)*, just off the Jl Tugu Circle, is an excellent choice and good value. This fine old Dutch villa has time-worn but very comfortable rooms with hot water, TV and air-con from 60,000 rp to 70,000 rp, including breakfast. It has a small, murky swimming pool and a good restaurant and bar, which is the meeting place for the Hash House Harriers.

The newer *Hotel Kartika Kusuma (☎ 352266, Jl Kahuripan 12)* has well-kept rooms around a pleasant courtyard garden for 50,000 rp, or 65,000 rp with air-con and hot water. Some rooms are a little dark, but this is an attractive smaller hotel.

For something cheaper in Tugu, try the friendly, well run *Hotel Menara (☎ 362 871, Jl Pajajaran 5.)* All rooms have hot water and TV. Rooms start at 33,000 rp, or more luxurious rooms with air-con are 57,000 rp to 67,000 rp. The tariff includes breakfast, and there is a central restaurant for meals.

## Places to Stay – Top End

Malang has a couple of faded luxury hotels and two very classy boutique hotels.

EAST JAVA

The *Hotel Taman Regent's* (☎ *363388, Jl Jaksa Agung Suprapto 12*) has worn rooms from 175,000 rp after a 50% discount. The better maintained *Kartika Graha* (☎ *361 900, Jl Jaksa Agung Suprapto 17*) is a more modern hotel with a pool, restaurants, bar and rooms from 180,000 rp after discount.

*Hotel Graha Cakra* (☎ *324989, Jl Cerme 16*) is a superbly restored Art Deco building which has been converted into a hotel. It is tastefully furnished with antiques, and has a small swimming pool and restaurant. Rooms for US$60 and US$75 are a better class of mid-range room, while suites from US$95 to US$195 are luxurious. After discount, rates still start at a hefty 355,000 rp.

The *Tugu Park Hotel* (☎ *363891, Jl Tugu 3*) is one of the most delightful hotels in Java. Though neither large nor lavishly appointed, it has real style despite being a modern hotel. Rooms cost US$115, but it is worth the extra for the suites, all furnished in different Asian antique styles, costing US$140 to US$250. It has a pool, business centre, a good restaurant and a tea house facing the Tugu circle.

## Places to Eat

The *Toko Oen*, opposite the Sarinah department store, is an anachronism from colonial days, with tea tables and comfortable basket chairs. Relax, read a newspaper and be served by waiters in white sarongs and black pecis. It has Chinese and western dishes, plus good Indonesian food and delicious home-made ice cream. It's expensive but is a good place for breakfast and one of the most relaxing places for a meal. It's open daily from 8.30 am to 9 pm.

For a drink or snack, the *Melati Restaurant* in the Hotel Pelangi is even more architecturally impressive than the Toko Oen. This cavernous colonial relic has towering pressed metal ceilings, and painted tiles around the walls feature picture postcard scenes from old Holland. While guaranteed to make any Dutch person homesick, the Indonesian and western food is only average. The similarly named *Melati Pavilion Restaurant* in the Tugu Park Hotel serves

good Indonesian, Chinese and Continental cuisine at upscale prices. Dutch dishes are featured, and of course there is *rijsttafel*, which features a selection of East Javanese dishes.

For cheap and varied eats, head for Jl Agus Salim. Near the alun alun, *Rumah Makan Agung* at No 2F has good Indian dishes – savoury murtabak, biryani and chicken curry – as well as Indonesian dishes. The *Gloria Restaurant* at No 23 has good Chinese dishes. Try the *pangsit mie* – a bowl of delicious noodles, meat and vegetables served with a side bowl of soup for you to mix.

*Jack's Cafe* (*Jl Kahuripan 11A*) is a hip restaurant with a varied menu, popular with students and the alternative crowd. Bands play downstairs on Thursday, Friday and Saturday.

The *Rumah Makan Minang Jaya* (*Jl Basuki Rachmat 111*) has good Padang food at reasonable prices.

The big shopping centres have a variety of places to eat. The best is the *Food Centre*, sandwiched between Mitra department store and Gajah Mada Plaza. The busy food stalls here offer a great selection of dishes, including local specialities such as *nasi rawon* (beef soup served with rice). Street vendors on Jl Agus Salim also have tasty sweets and dumplings.

The shopping centres on Jl Agus Salim, as well as the Matahari on Jl Pasar Besar and Sarinah department store, have well stocked *supermarkets*. For western fast food, *KFC* and *Swensens* are in the Variety department store building next to Malang Plaza. *McDonald's* is next to Sarinah on Jl Basuki Rachmat. Sarinah also has the *Picnic Food Court* on the 3rd floor.

## Entertainment

*Taman Rekreasi Senaputra* is Malang's cultural and recreational park. Every Sunday morning at 10 am, *kuda lumping* 'horse trance' dances (*jaran kepang* in Javanese) are held here. The dancers ride plaited cane horses until they fall into a trance, allowing them to eat glass and perform other masochistic acts without harm.

On the last Wednesday of the month, *wayang kulit* (puppet plays) are performed at Senaputra from 10 pm. *RRI* (Radio Republik Indonesia), Jl Candi Panggung, 5km north-west of the city, has wayang kulit from 9 pm on the first Saturday of the month.

## Shopping

Malang's shopping is quite limited compared with Surabaya. For general shopping – clothes, shoes and a bit of everything – try the plazas on Jl Agus Salim and the nearby Matahari department store. Dieng Plaza, on Jl Raya Dieng on the western outskirts, is Malang's newest and brightest shopping centre, but it's small.

The best bookshops are Sari Agung, next to Sarinah department store, and Gramedia, on the other side of the street. Sarinah department store also has a small selection of crafts and souvenirs.

Malang is noted for its antiques, but most dealers operate out of their homes. Two to try are Dr Widodo (☎ 568402), Jl Terusan Taman Agung 7; and Mrs Herman (☎ 322 761), Jl Sulawesi 5.

## Getting There & Away

Malang can be approached from a number of directions. The back route between Yogyakarta and Banyuwangi takes you through some beautiful countryside. For an interesting trip, you could take a train from Solo to Jombang, then colts south to Blimbing, Kandangan, Batu and finally Malang.

**Bus** Malang has three bus terminals. Arjosari, 5km north of town, is the main bus terminal with regular buses mostly along the northern route to destinations such as Surabaya (2500/5500 rp, two hours), Probolinggo (3000/6000 rp, 2½ hours), Jember (6000 rp, 4½ hours), Banyuwangi (9500/17,500 rp, six hours) and Denpasar (12,000/20,000 rp, 10 hours). *Mikrolets* (small taxis) run from Arjosari to nearby villages such as Singosari (800 rp) and Tumpang (1000 rp).

Gadang bus terminal is 5km south of the town centre and has buses along the southern routes to destinations such as Blitar

(3000 rp, two hours), Kepanjan (800 rp), Lumajang (3200 rp), Dampit (1500 rp), and Trenggalek and Tulungagung.

Landungsari bus terminal, 5km northwest of the city, has buses to the west to destinations such as Kediri (2500 rp) and Jombang (3000 rp). Frequent mikrolets run to Batu (700 rp, half an hour).

Numerous bus companies offer deluxe services for the long hauls. Buses to Bandung (around 60,000 rp), Bogor and Jakarta (43,000 rp to 70,000 rp) leave around 2 pm. The numerous buses to Solo and Yogyakarta cost around 25,000 rp and leave around 7 pm. Night buses also do the run to Bali for around 28,000 rp to 35,000 rp, and some continue to Padangbai and Mataram (on Lombok). They leave from Arjosari bus terminal.

It is easiest to buy tickets from the agents found all over town. Jl Basuki Rachmat, south of the tourist office, has plenty of agents. Wartel Suropati (☎ 353089), Jl Suropati 42, near the hotel Helios books a wide range of buses, or try the travel agent at the Toko Oen restaurant.

**Minibus** Plenty of door-to-door minibus companies operate from Malang, and hotels and travel agents can book them. Wijaya Transport (☎ 327072), at Jl Pajajaran 7 next to the Hotel Menara, is a reliable agent. Destinations include Madiun (9500 rp) throughout the day, Jember (12,500 rp) via Probolinggo at 7 am and 2 pm, Solo (25,000 rp) and Yogyakarta (27,000 rp) at 9 am and 10 pm, Semarang (30,000 rp) at 9 am and 9 pm, and Denpasar (45,000 rp) at 7 pm. Minibuses to Surabaya (10,000 rp to 12,000 rp) will drop off at hotels in Surabaya, thus saving the long haul from Surabaya's bus terminal.

**Train** Some useful services, mostly ekonomi, operate out of Malang. The bisnis/eksekutif *Jatayu* is the best train to Surabaya's Gubeng train station (6000/9000 rp, 1½ hours) at 3 pm. It leaves Surabaya at 7.45 am. The *Pattas* is an express ekonomi service running between Surabaya and Blitar via Malang. The ekonomi/bisnis *Matarmaja* goes west from Malang to Solo, Yogyakarta (18,000/36,000 rp, seven hours), Cirebon and Jakarta at 4 pm. The *Regganis* goes to Banyuwangi (4500 rp ekonomi, eight hours) via Probolinggo. Most other services tend to go via Surabaya.

## Getting Around

Mikrolets run all over town from the main bus terminals and to other mikrolet stations. The most useful services are those running between the bus terminals and passing through the centre of town. These are marked A-G (Arjosari to Gadung and return), A-L (Arjosari-Landungsari), G-L (Gadang-Landungsari) etc. A trip anywhere around town costs 500 rp.

There are also becaks and metered taxis available.

## AROUND MALANG
## Singosari Temples

The Singosari Temples lie in a ring around Malang and are mostly funerary temples dedicated to the kings of the Singosari dynasty (1222-92), the precursors of the Majapahit kingdom.

**Candi Singosari** Right in Singosari village, 12km north of Malang, this temple stands 500m off the main Malang to Surabaya road. One of the last monuments erected to the Singosari dynasty, it was built in 1304 in honour of King Kertanegara, the fifth and last Singosari king, who died in 1292 in a palace uprising. The main structure of the temple was completed but, for some reason, the sculptors never finished their task. Only the top part has any ornamentation and the kala heads have been left strangely stark, with smooth bulging cheeks and pop eyes. Of the statues that once inhabited the temple's chambers, only Agastya, the Shivaite teacher who walked across the water to Java, remains. Statues of Durga and Ganesha were carted off to the Netherlands, but have since been returned and are now in the Jakarta Museum.

About 200m beyond the temple are two enormous figures of *dwarapala* (guardians against evil spirits) wearing clusters of skulls and twisted serpents. These may have been part of the original gates to the palace of the Singosari kingdom.

To reach Singosari, take a green mikrolet (800 rp) from Malang's Arjosari bus terminal and get off at Singosari market on the highway, then walk or take a becak.

**Candi Sumberawan** This small, plain Buddhist stupa lies in the foothills of Gunung Arjuna, about 5km north-west of Singosari. Originating from a later period than the Singosari temples, it was built to commemorate the visit of Hayam Wuruk, the great Majapahit king, who visited the area in 1359.

Take a colt from Singosari market on the highway to Desa Sumberawan, and from where the colts terminate, walk half a kilometre down the stony road to the canal, turn right and follow the canal through the picturesque rice paddies for a kilometre to the temple. This delightful walk is the highlight of the visit.

**Candi Jago** Along a small road near the market in Tumpang (18km from Malang), Candi Jago (or Jajaghu) was built in 1268 and is thought to be a memorial to the fourth Singosari king, Vishnuvardhana. The temple is in fairly poor condition but it still has some interesting decorative carvings – in the two-dimensional wayang kulit style typical of East Java – which tell tales from the *Jatakas* and the *Mahabharata*. The caretaker describes it as a Buddhist temple, but scattered around the garden are Javanese-Hindu statues, including a six armed death-dealing goddess and a *linga*, the symbol of Shiva's virility and male potency.

To reach Candi Jago, take a white mikrolet from Malang's Arjosari bus terminal to Tumpang (1000 rp). In Tumpang you can also visit the Mangun Dhama Art Centre (☎ 0341-787907), which is an East Javanese performing arts centre. It is noted for its dance classes, run by an American woman, and also has gamelan, wayang, batik and wood-carving courses.

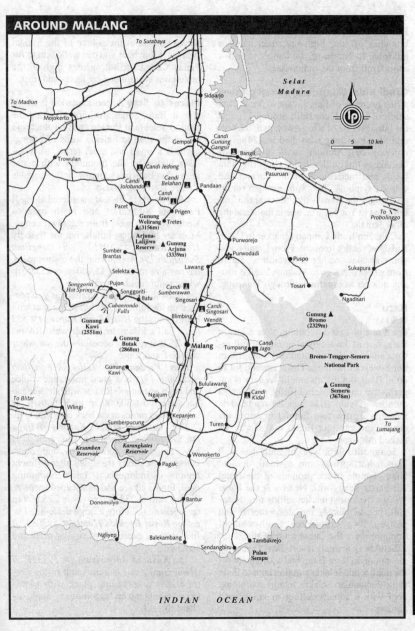

# AROUND MALANG

If you're coming from Singosari, go to Blimbing where the road to Tumpang branches off the highway, then catch a mikrolet. In Tumpang, the temple is only a short stroll from the main road.

**Candi Kidal** This temple, a small gem and a fine example of East Javanese art, is 7km south of Candi Jago. Built around 1260 as the burial shrine of King Anusapati, the second Singosari king who died in 1248, it is tapering and slender, with pictures of Garuda on three sides, bold, glowering kala heads and medallions of the *haruna* and Garuda symbols. Two *kala makara* (dragons) guard the steps – like those at the kraton steps in Yogyakarta, one is male and the other female.

Colts run from Tumpang market to Candi Kidal but are not frequent. From Candi Kidal you can take another colt south to Turen, from where buses go to Malang, but it is usually quicker to backtrack through Tumpang.

## Batu
☎ 0341
For a one or two day outing, take a bus to Batu, one of Java's most attractive hill resorts on the slopes of Gunung Arjuna, 15km north-west of Malang. There is not a lot to do in Batu, but the mountain scenery is superb, the climate delightfully cool and a number of side trips can be made. The Kusuma Agrowisata hotel has apple orchards you can tour (6500 rp), and an attached mini-zoo.

**Songgoriti**, 3km west of Batu, has well known hot springs and a small, ancient Hindu temple in the grounds of the Hotel Air Panas Songgoriti. Nearby is the Pasar Wisata, the tourist market selling mostly apples, bonsai plants, and stone mortar and pestles. Five kilometres south-west of Songgoriti are the **Cubanrondo Falls**.

**Selekta** is a small resort 5km farther up the mountain from Batu, and a kilometre off the main road. Selekta's main claim to fame is the Pemandian Selekta, a large swimming pool with a superb setting in landscaped gardens.

Farther up the mountain is the small mountain village of **Sumber Brantas**, high above Selekta at the source of the Sungai Brantas. From here you can walk 2km to **Air Panas Cangar**, a hot springs high in the mountains surrounded by forest and mist.

**Places to Stay** Accommodation is available in Batu, Songgoriti, and all along the road to Selekta at Punten and at Tulungrejo where the road to Selekta turns off. Songgoriti is a small and quiet resort, as is Selekta higher up the mountain with better views, but Batu has superior facilities and is a more convenient base.

Most hotels in Batu are scattered along Jl Panglima Sudirman, the main road to Kediri running west from the town centre. Most are mid-range hotels, but the friendly *Hotel Kawi* (☎ 591139, Jl Panglima Sudirman 19), 400m from the town square, has passable rooms for 15,000 rp, or 25,000 rp with mandi (cold water).

Prices and standards increase as you proceed up the hill. A better bet for a room with bathroom is the *Hotel Ragil Kuning* (☎ 593 051), half a kilometre farther west. Rooms cost 25,000 rp, and hopefully the hot water will be fixed soon.

*Hotel Perdana* (☎ 591104, Jl Panglima Sudirman 101) is a good mid-range choice and has a restaurant. Rooms with shower and hot water cost 30,000 rp to 50,000 rp, or large, newer rooms at the back cost 55,000 rp.

The upscale *Hotel Kartika Wijaya* (☎ 592 600, Jl Panglima Sudirman 127) has a delightful colonial lobby, and rooms in the new sections are styled after different regions in Indonesia. It has a swimming pool, fitness centre and landscaped gardens. Rooms start at 233,000 rp (from 275,000 rp on weekends), before a large discount. The newer *Royal Orchids Hotel* (☎ 593083, Jl Indragiri 4), nearby is of similar price and standard.

The *Kusuma Agrowisata* (☎ 593333, Jl Abdul Gani Atas) is 3km south of the centre and is a sprawling place with rooms from US$56 and an 'agrotourism' apple orchard to visit.

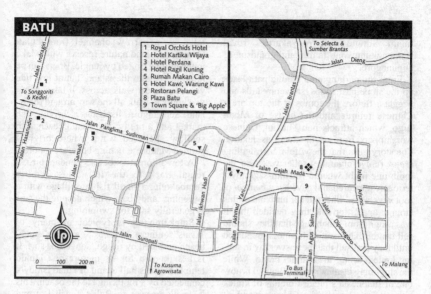

**BATU**

1 Royal Orchids Hotel
2 Hotel Kartika Wijaya
3 Hotel Perdana
4 Hotel Ragil Kuning
5 Rumah Makan Cairo
6 Hotel Kawi; Warung Kawi
7 Restoran Pelangi
8 Plaza Batu
9 Town Square & 'Big Apple'

Selekta has a couple of upper-notch hotels, such as the *Hotel Selekta* (☎ *91025*), near the swimming pool. On the main road in Tulungrejo are the *Hotel Santosa* and *Hotel New Victory*. *Aramdalu Hotel (Jl Aramdalu 2)*, in Songgoriti, has been recommended by readers. It has a swimming pool, and rooms with hot water cost 24,500 rp to 70,000 rp.

**Places to Eat** Jl Panglima Sudirman in Batu also has plenty of restaurants. Near the Hotel Kawi, *Restoran Pelangi (Jl Panglima Sudirman 7)* is an attractive restaurant serving East Javanese and Chinese meals at reasonable prices, with private bungalows around a garden at the back. Right next to the Hotel Kawi, *Warung Kawi* is a stylish little spot for buffet dishes and ice juices. Farther west, the *Rumah Makan Cairo* has martabak and Middle-Eastern-inspired fare for something a little different.

**Getting There & Away** From Malang's Landungsari bus terminal you can take a Kediri bus or one of the frequent purple mikrolets to Batu (700 rp, half hour). Batu's bus terminal is 2km from the centre of town – take another mikrolet (500 rp) from the bus terminal. For onward travel, buses can be caught along the main road to Pare, Kediri and Jombang. Batu Transport (☎ 592 218), Jl Agus Salim 2, has door-to-door minibuses to Surabaya and Kediri.

From the bus terminal, orange mikrolets run through town to Selekta (500 rp, half an hour) and Sumber Brantas (1000 rp, one hour), but they often hang out endlessly for a full complement of passengers. Mikrolets turn off to Sumber Brantas at Jurangkuwali village; for Air Panas Cangar continue 2km straight ahead. Cangar can be reached by car, but public transport won't tackle the twisting, dipping road.

**Gunung Kawi**

On Gunung Kawi (2551m), west of Malang and 18km north-west of Kepanjen, is the **tomb** of a Muslim sage, Kanjeng Penembahan Djoego, who died in 1871. Descended from Pakubuwono I, king of the Mataram kingdom, the sage is better known as Mbah

Jugo. Also buried in the tomb is Raden Imam Sujono, of Yogyakarta's royal Hamengkubuwono family and grandson of Diponegoro.

From the parking area, a long path leads up the slope past shops, souvenir stalls and beggars. Before the tombs at the top are a **Chinese temple** and the **house of Mbah Jugo**, which attracts non-Muslim, Chinese worshippers from as far away as Jakarta. The story goes that the wife of a struggling *kretek* (clove cigarette) seller was near the tomb one night when a Muslim sage mysteriously appeared and gave her a *bentoel* (a root vegetable). She told her husband of this strange apparition and they decided that it was a sign from Mbah Jugo that they should sell bentoel. The bentoel business foundered until they realised that the answer lay in selling kreteks using the bentoel brand. While the story may be apocryphal, Bentoel is now one of Indonesia's biggest brands of kretek cigarettes, and each year Chinese worshippers flock here in their thousands seeking prosperity and an answer to their prayers.

Malam Jumat Legi in the Javanese calendar is the most propitious time, but pilgrims visit Gunung Kawi throughout the year, especially at night – a regular procession visits the grave and perambulates the complex at midnight. Wayang performances are often staged at night because prayers are usually offered with the promise of a sacrifice if they come true. The most popular sacrifices include paying for a wayang performance or slaughtering a goat. Big pots of goat stew are often on the boil and dogs gnaw goat bones on the street.

This strange cross-religious mountain resort can be experienced on a day trip, or there are plenty of basic *penginapan* (simple lodging houses) and restaurants if you want to stay the night. Gunung Kawi can be reached by taking a bus to Kepanjan, 3km before the turn-off, and then a colt for the final 19km to Gunung Kawi.

## South Coast Beaches

The coast south of Malang has some good beaches, but facilities are limited. **Sendan-**gbiru is a picturesque fishing village separated by a narrow channel from **Pulau Sempu**, an island nature reserve with a lake in the middle ringed by jungle. Boats can be hired to cross to the island, but at low tide you can almost walk across. It takes about two hours to walk all the way around the island. Sendangbiru itself has a thriving fish market and a pretty white-sand beach with shallow sheltered water where brightly painted Madurese fishing boats are moored.

A few kilometres before Sendangbiru, a rough track to the left leads 3km to **Tambakrejo**, a small fishing village with a sweeping sandy bay, which despite the surf is generally safe for swimming.

**Balekambang** is typical of many of Java's southern beaches – a wide, sandy beach pounded by rough, dangerous surf. It is best known for its picturesque Hindu temple on the small island of Pulau Ismoyo, connected by a footbridge to the beach. This is Java's answer to Bali's Tanah Lot and was built by Balinese artisans in 1985 for the local Hindu community. Accommodation is limited to the very basic *Pesanggrahan Balekambang*. Balekambang is one of the most popular beaches and is crowded on weekends.

**Ngliyep** farther west is a rocky beach and is also very popular. It has a *pesanggrahan* for basic accommodation.

**Getting There & Away** Minibuses from Malang's Gadang bus terminal go to Sendangbiru (2500 rp, two hours, 69km), past the turn-off to Tambakrejo; otherwise, take a bus to Turen and then another to Sendangbiru.

For Balekambang buses run direct from Malang along the upgraded road for 2000 rp. The road to Ngliyep is also good, and occasional white minibuses run direct; otherwise, first take a bus to Bantur.

## Lawang
☎ 0341
Lawang, 18km north of Malang on the road to Surabaya, is a forgettable town, but the *Hotel Niagara* is a notable five storey Art

Nouveau mansion dating from the turn of the 20th century. This once grand hotel has seen better days but still has painted wall tiles, terrazzo floors and stained-glass lights. Tourists aren't encouraged to poke around, but you can stay in the run-down rooms from 40,000 rp.

Of more interest, the road just south of the Hotel Niagara leads a few kilometres west to the **Kebun Wonasari** (☎ 426032) tea estate. This agrotourism venture offers a variety of activities and tours – everything from tea plantation tours to tennis and a mini zoo. Best of all you can stay in this peaceful setting. The old plantation guesthouses now provide a variety of good accommodation from 30,000 rp to 250,000 rp. Bicycles can be hired and the estate will provide transport to and from Lawang (15,000 rp) and Malang (30,000 rp) with advance notice.

## Purwodadi

A few kilometres north of Lawang, the **Kebun Raya Purwodadi** are big dry-climate botanical gardens, open daily from 7 am to 4 pm. The entrance is right on the main highway, and if you want more information and maps of the gardens, visit the garden offices to the south of the entrance. The **Air Terjun Cobanbaung** is a high waterfall next to the gardens.

## BLITAR

• pop 125,000     ☎ 0342

Blitar is the usual base from which to visit Panataran, and is also of interest as the site of President Soekarno's grave. It's quite a pleasant country town to stay in overnight on the southern route between Malang and Solo.

Blitar is also the home of *ketok magik* (magic knocking), a mystical form of automotive panel beating that has spread all over Java and farther afield. Leave your dented car at the workshop and behind locked doors repairs are 'majikally' made by spiritual intervention, for a very reasonable price. It seems the residents are now more sceptical, and unlike almost every other town in Java, ketok workshops are hard to find in Blitar.

## Information

Change money at the BNI bank at Jl Kenanga 9 or the BCA bank on Jl Merdeka. The post office is next to the train station and has an Internet warung (6000 rp per hour) open until 3 pm daily expect Sunday. For international telephone calls, the Telkom office is at Jl A Yani 10 (the continuation of Jl Merdeka), about a kilometre east of the Hotel Sri Lestari.

## Makam Bung Karno

At Sentul, about 2km north of the town centre on the road to Panataran, an elaborate monument now covers the spot where former President Soekarno was buried in 1970. Soekarno is looked on by many as the 'father of his country', although he was only reinstated as a national hero in 1978 by the Soeharto regime. The leader of Indonesia from 1949 to 1965, he had been worshipped by the people (almost as a god) but by 1970 he was little more than a figurehead, suspected of having had ties with the attempted communist coup of 1965 and discarded by the army. His last two years were spent under house arrest, in isolation in Bogor and Jakarta.

Soekarno was given a state funeral but, despite family requests that he be buried at his home in Bogor, the hero of Indonesian independence was buried as far as possible from Jakarta in an unmarked grave next to his mother in Blitar. His father's grave was also moved from Jakarta to Blitar. It was only in 1978 that the lavish million-dollar monument was built over the grave and opened to visitors. Hundred of pilgrims come to all-but worship Soekarno, and the first president's rehabilitation meant that his grave has become more popular than ever.

A becak from the town centre will cost about 1500 rp, or take a Panataran *angkudes* (yellow minibus) and ask for the *makam* (tomb). Bemos turn off before the souvenir stalls, from where it is a walk of a few hundred metres.

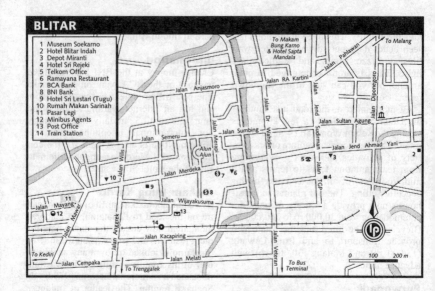

**BLITAR**

1  Museum Soekarno
2  Hotel Blitar Indah
3  Depot Miranti
4  Hotel Sri Rejeki
5  Telkom Office
6  Ramayana Restaurant
7  BCA Bank
8  BNI Bank
9  Hotel Sri Lestari (Tugu)
10 Rumah Makan Sarinah
11 Pasar Legi
12 Minibus Agents
13 Post Office
14 Train Station

On 21 June, which is the anniversary of Soekarno's death, thousands flock to Blitar to commemorate the event.

## Other Attractions

The house that Soekarno lived in as a boy functions as the **Museum Soekarno**. Photos and memorabilia line the front sitting room, and you can see the great man's bedroom and check out the old Mercedes in the garage, a former state car. The house, still owned by relatives of Soekarno, though they now live in Jakarta, is at Jl Sultan Agung 59, about 1.5km from the centre of town. The big new parking area is testament to Soekarno's revival in popularity.

Blitar's large **Pasar Legi**, next to the bus terminal, is also worth a look. In the northeast corner a few stalls sell *kris* (traditional daggers), woodcarvings and bronze walking sticks.

## Places to Stay & Eat

Blitar has plenty of hotels, many of them in the north of town, to cater to the Soekarno pilgrims. These hotels are quiet during the week but noisy when the big bus tours come on weekends. The pick of the them is the *Hotel Sapta Mandala* (☎ *802810, Jl Slamet Riyadi 31)*, 200m south of Soekarno's grave. It's clean, well run and good value, with rooms from 15,000 rp up to 40,000 rp with air-con, TV and hot water shower.

The best hotel in town, and most popular place to stay, is *Hotel Sri Lestari Tugu* (☎ *802766, Jl Merdeka 173)* right in the centre of town. It's undergoing renovations that will make it a fine boutique hotel, in the same style as the Hotel Tugu in Malang, which has the same owner. The krisis moneter may well slow the new work, but in the meantime a variety of cheaper rooms are still available from 15,000 rp for a few boxes out the back, while very comfortable mid-range rooms are 45,000 rp to 125,000 rp. The superb, renovated rooms in the old colonial building are decked out in antique style and cost 165,000 rp.

The *Hotel Sri Rejeki* (☎ *802770, Jl TGP 13)* is a cheaper mid-range hotel with good-value rooms to suit most budgets from 9000 rp, and from 30,000 rp to 60,000 rp with air-con. Farther east of town, **Hotel Blitar Indah** (☎ 802779, Jl Jend Ahmad Yani 60) is similar and has rooms from 15,000 rp to 40,000 rp.

Blitar has some good restaurants on Jl Merdeka, such as the large Chinese **Ramayana** (Jl Merdeka 65), east of the alun alun. **Rumah Makan Sarinah** has varied fare and does good sop buntut (oxtail soup) and ayam goreng (fried chicken). Farther east past the Telkom office, **Depot Miranti** has breezy bamboo decor and a varied menu. The Hotel Sri Lestari has an excellent, but slightly expensive, restaurant.

## Getting There & Away

Regular buses run from Blitar to Malang (3000 rp, two hours, 80km) and Surabaya (3000/4500 rp, four hours), as well as Kediri (1½ hours), Madiun (3½ hours) and Solo (six hours). The bus terminal is 4km south of town along Jl Veteran, 500m by angkot from the Pasar Legi market. Angkudes run from the bus terminal and the market to Panataran for 1000 rp and stop right outside the temple. They also pass near Makam Bung Karno, but the road in front of the grave is closed and they skirt around the side streets to the east.

Rosalia Indah (☎ 802149), Jl Mayang 45, opposite the market and bemo terminal, and Restu (☎ 802583), next door at No 47, have door-to-door air-con minibuses to Solo (23,000 rp), Yogyakarta (24,000 rp) and Semarang (30,000 rp).

The easiest way to reach Malang is by train. Of the several daily trains, the best service is the Pattas at 11.40 am, which goes to Malang (3000 rp, 40 minutes) and Surabaya (3800 rp, 3½ hours). It's an express ekonomi service, and seats can be booked for 1500 rp. The Dhoho runs east to Kediri (1300 rp, 1½ hours).

## PANATARAN

The Hindu temples at Panataran are the largest remaining Majapahit sanctuaries, and the finest examples of East Javanese architecture and sculpture. Construction began around 1200, during the Singosari dynasty, but the temple complex took some 250 years to complete. Most of the important surviving structures date from the great years of the Majapahit during the

---

### Ratu Adil

The Ratu Adil, or Just King, is a recurrent figure in a Javanese legend that came to light in the colonial period. According to this legend, when the age of destruction comes to Java a king arises and establishes a new, just kingdom from the ashes of the old. It is based on Muslim predictions of the Imam Mahdi, a messiah who leads the Muslim world against the infidels, and on the Hindu-Buddhist time cycles (yuga), represented in Indian lore by a cow. When the cow stands on four legs, peace, harmony and spiritual enlightenment rules in the world. Progressing through each of the four yugas, the world declines until the cow is standing on only one leg and chaos rule the world. With the final collapse, a new golden era is issued in and the cycle starts again.

The Ratu Adil prophecies peaked in the 18th and 19th centuries, when Dutch intervention broke down the existing social order. The peasantry was subjected to famine and great hardship and in the countryside a number of rebellions broke out. Based on the Prelambang Jayabaya, a Javanese religious text proclaiming the coming of the Just King, various mystics-turned-rebel-leaders, in the manner of Prince Diponegoro, claimed the title of Ratu Adil.

In more recent times, the tag was applied to Soekarno, who had an enormous following among the ordinary people of Java. At least part of the legend came true, in that Soekarno led the people of Indonesia against the Dutch to establish the new republic.

14th century and are similar to many temples on Bali.

Around the base of the first-level platform, which would once have been a meeting place, the comic-strip carvings tell the story of a test between the fat meat-eating Bubukshah and the thin vegetarian Gagang Aking.

Farther on is the small **Dated Temple**, so called because of the date 1291 (1369) carved over the entrance. On the next level are colossal serpents snaking endlessly around the **Naga Temple**, which once housed valuable sacred objects.

At the rear stands the **Mother Temple** – or at least part of it, for the top of the temple has been reconstructed alongside its three tiered base. If you walk around the temple anticlockwise, panels around the base depict stories from the *Ramayana*, with Hanuman's secret mission to Rawana's palace in Sri Lanka to find Sita, a drama of battles, flames and giants, Hanuman flying across the trees and monkeys building bridges across the seas. The more realistic people of the Krishna stories on the second tier of the base show an interesting transition from almost two dimensional representation to three dimensional figures. Behind is a small **royal mandi** with a frieze of lizards, bulls and dragons around its walls.

The temple complex is open from 7 am to 5 pm, and entry is by donation. As you enter the village if you continue straight ahead past the turn-off to the temples, the **Museum Panataran** is only 300m away. It contains an impressive collection of statuary taken from the complex, but labelling is poor and the museum is open irregular hours.

## Getting There & Away
Panataran is 16km from Blitar, and 3km north of the village of Nglegok. It is possible to see the Panataran temples comfortably in a day from Malang – and possibly from Surabaya.

## KEDIRI
- **pop 240,000**   ☎ **0354**
Kediri is a bustling city and a transit, not a tourist, destination. It is most famous as the home of Gudang Garam, the biggest kretek manufacturer in Indonesia. The factory's chimney towers above the city, belching smoke like a huge kretek.

Though Kediri is a noisy, busy city the main street, Jl Sudirman/Dhoho/Rachmat, is lined with rather dowdy Chinese shops and the town has few modern developments. Madiun is a more gracious city if travelling between Malang and Central Java.

## Places to Stay
The best reason to visit Kediri is to stay at the *Hotel Merdeka* (☎ *81262, Jl Jend Basuki Rachmat 4.*) After independence, almost every Dutch hotel in Indonesia was renamed the Hotel Merdeka and run by the government, which subsequently remodelled them and destroyed the architecture, but this one has retained its wonderful colonial ambience. Comfortable rooms with aircon, TV and hot water cost 60,000 rp to 131,000 rp. The hotel has a good restaurant and a disco.

The main street has plenty of other hotels, including the basic *Losmen Dhoho (Jl Sudirman 29)* with the cheapest rooms in town at 15,000 rp. Nearer the Hotel Merdeka, the *Hotel Panataran* (☎ *87799, Jl Dhoho 190)* is a good, but also an expensive, mid-range hotel with rooms from 40,000 rp to 150,000 rp. Better value is the *Hotel Safari Indah* (☎ *81588, Jl Urip Sumohardjo 66)* farther south of the city centre, with large grounds and a variety of rooms from 15,000 rp to 100,000 rp.

## Places to Eat
For the cheapest and most varied eats, numerous *kaki limas* (food carts) set up in the evening around the park at the corner of Jl Sudirman and Jl Katamso. Farther north on Jl Sudirman, the *Rumah Makan Pokang* is a good 'Mandarin' restaurant specialising in seafood and pigeon, but the prices are very high. On the other side of the street, *Pak Siboen* is famous in these parts for his excellent sate, and a couple of good sate places have borrowed his name. Farther north, on Jl Dhoho, the *Fiorenza* is a bright little fast

food restaurant for burgers, chicken and baked goods.

## Getting There & Away

The main Tamanan bus terminal, 3km south-west of the centre on Jl Semeru, has buses to all major cities in East Java and farther afield. Kediri is not on the main rail line but is serviced by a few trains. The bisnis/eksekutif class *Matamarja* departs at 7 pm for Kertosono, Madiun, Solo, Yogyakarta, Cirebon and Jakarta. In the other direction it runs to Malang via Blitar. Ekonomi trains also run to Blitar/Malang and on to Surabaya.

## PARE

☎ 0354

Pare, 20km north-east of Kediri on the road to Batu, is a small but busy town. It has grown substantially since the 1950s, when Clifford Geertz lived here researching his seminal work the *Religion of Java*, a fascinating social-anthropological study of Javanese society and beliefs. 'Modjokuto', the pseudonym Geertz gave the town, has changed substantially, as has much of Javanese society in general, but the layout and social structure of the town as described in the book and the related *The Social History of an Indonesian Town* are still relevant.

Pare's main interest is the two Hindu temples just outside the town. Though relatively small and not complete, they have unusual and very fine carvings.

Lying on the main Kediri-Batu road, at the intersection with the road to Jombang, Pare is well serviced by buses to those towns and Malang. The bus terminal is 4km east of town.

## Candi Surowono

About 5km north-east of Pare, this temple is the most lavishly carved. Only the base remains of this late 14th century temple and other carved stone blocks are scattered around it. Built as a shrine for Bhre Wengker of Majapahit, who died in 1388, the carvings around the base are wonderfully sensual though rarely erotic, as they have been described. The carvings depict everyday life and popular folktales, such as the exploits of the heroine Sri Tranjung, often in a jungle setting with great detail given to trees, plants and animals.

To reach the temple, head out about 3km on the Jombang road and follow the signs. It is then about a kilometre to a T-intersection – turn left and then right at the next road, another 1.5km in total through Surowono village with its numerous *lele* (a freshwater fish) ponds to the temple.

## Candi Tegowangi

Candi Tegowangi dates from the same period and is dedicated to Bhre Matahun, a brother-in-law of the Majapahit king, Hayam Wuruk. As with Surowono, only the base remains and one side is not carved, suggesting that the temple may not have been finished. Though not as impressive as Surowono, the carvings show the same cartoon-like style and fine detail, among the best in East Javanese temples. Reliefs show animals and comic tales from the *Sudamala* stories.

Walk up the steps to the top of this 5m high Shivaite temple, which has a large stone *yoni* (vulva), though the *linga* (penis) has been removed. A smaller temple lies off the side and there is a decapitated statue of Shiva astride the bull, Nandi.

To reach Tegowangi, take the road to Papar for 5.5km to the school (coming from the other direction it is 10.5km from Papar). Take the turn-off next to the school for 2km along a paved road and the temple is signposted off the road, 200m away.

## Places to Stay

Two hotels can be found in the centre of town near the Chinese shops on Jl Letjen Sutoyo. Set back off the main street, *Hotel Slamet* (☎ 391772, Jl Kandangan 1A) is an old colonial hotel with basic rooms from 15,000 rp, but the management is not welcoming. A few doors along, the friendly *Hotel Amanda* (☎ 391373, Jl Letjen Sutoyo 47) is Pare's best choice. Well kept rooms with mandi start at 25,000 rp while very good air-con rooms are 40,000 rp or 50,000 rp with hot water and sitting room.

Two other hotels are farther west of town, on Jl Sudirman, but are less convenient and no better than the Amanda.

## MADIUN
• pop 185,000          ☎ 0351

On the Solo to Surabaya highway, Madiun is a major travel hub in the western part of East Java and an important centre for the surrounding sugar and teak plantations. Lying on the plains below the Gunung Lawu massif, it was once regularly flooded by the Bengawan Madiun until the construction of a long retaining wall, locally dubbed the Berlin Wall.

This unhurried city has a turbulent past that earned it the moniker of 'Red City' after a communist takeover on 18 September 1948. After a battle with the republican

army in Solo, PKI supporters withdrew to Madiun, killed government officials and announced the formation of a National Front government. This premature attempt to start the revolution was short-lived. Soekarno galvanised opposition to the communists and government troops took the city a week later, chasing 10,000 or more communists into the countryside. In events reminiscent of 1965/66, blood-letting in the villages was rife, thousands died and up to 35,000 people were arrested.

Madiun has some interesting colonial architecture and is a pleasant place to spend the night on the way up the mountain to Sarangan, but its tourist attractions are mostly for train buffs.

## Information

The tourist office (Diparta, ☎ 463645), Jl Pahlawan 31, has an excellent free tourist map of the Madiun-Kediri area but not much else. Also on Jl Pahlawan, which is the main street, the post office is just north of the tourist office, and the main Telkom office is farther south opposite the Bank Lippo. Jl Pahlawan runs into Jl Sudirman, the main market street, where you'll find the BCA bank. Nearby, on Jl Dr Sutomo, is the BNI bank.

## Steam Locomotives

The city has a major train workshop, but of most interest are the old steam locomotives. One is on display near the train station and another near the bus terminal, but to see a still-working *loko*, visit the big PG Redjo Agoeng sugar mill in the north of the city. Narrow gauge steam locomotives still haul sugar cane between the mill and storage depots. Steam locomotives are also used at the PG Poewodadie mill, 15km from Madiun on the road to Ngawi.

## Places to Stay & Eat

Madiun has dozens of hotels. *Hotel Madiun (☎ 451680, Jl Pahlawan 75)* is a good, very central budget hotel. Clean rooms with mandi cost 11,500 rp to 16,500 rp, air-con rooms are 27,500 rp and 32,500 rp.

MADIUN

To
PG Redjo Agoeng,
Bus Terminal &
Sunabaya

Not to Scale

Sungai Madiun

Jalan A Yani

Jalan Pandan

Jalan Pahlawan

Jalan Sumatera

Jalan Jangka?

Jalan Bitton

Jalan Jawa

Jalan Dr Sutomo

Jalan Kemerdekaan

Jalan Merapi

Jalan Kalamantan

Jalan Sulawesi

Jalan
Semeru

Jalan Bali

Jalan Jendral Urip Sumoharjo

To
Surakarta

Jalan Kudang

Jalan Sudirman

Jalan Cokraaminoto

Jalan
Citandui

Jalan Merpati

| | |
|---|---|
| 1 Train Station | 8 Bank Lippo |
| 2 Steam Locomotive | 9 Hotel Kartika Abadi |
| 3 Post Office | 10 Hotel Madiun |
| 4 Tourist Office | 11 BNI Bank |
| 5 Hotel Merdeka | 12 BCA Bank |
| 6 Pasaraya Sri Ratu | 13 Hotel Bali |
| 7 Telkom Office | |

EAST JAVA

The relatively new *Hotel Bali* (☎ 493 086, Jl Citandui 11) is a mid-range hotel in a quiet side street south of the main market area. It has a good restaurant and spotless rooms from 15,000 rp to 90,000 rp. All but the very cheapest rooms have air-con, but some are dark.

*Hotel Kartika Abadi* (☎ 451847, Jl Pahlawan 54) is a much flasher business hotel with a big restaurant and a variety of tiled singles/doubles from 12,500/20,000 rp up to 75,000/85,000 rp. Suite rooms cost 130,000 rp and 250,000 rp.

The best in town is the *Hotel Merdeka* (☎ 462547, Jl Pahlawan 42.) Once the Grand Hotel, dating from 1904, it has lost most of its colonial charm, but it has an excellent airy cafe, a restaurant, and a public swimming pool. Rooms in the new wing are dark but good value at 35,000 rp, but you'll be directed to the rooms in the old wing which have all the trimmings and cost 75,000 rp to 150,000 rp. Add 21% to the rates but expect an even bigger discount.

Apart from hotel dining, you can find a few *rumah makan* (eating houses) along Jl Sudirman. The *Pasaraya Sri Ratu*, a big modern department store opposite the Hotel Merdeka, has a good food court on the ground floor.

## Getting There & Away

The train station (☎ 462014) is about 1.5km north of the city centre along Jl Pahlawan. Regular bisnis/eksekutif trains run to Solo and Yogyakarta (16,000/25,000 rp), Surabaya (16,000/25,000 rp), Semarang (36,000 rp bisnis), Cirebon (36,000/115,000 rp) and Jakarta (44,000 rp bisnis). Ekonomi trains also run along these routes and to Banyuwangi and Bandung.

The bus terminal is 2km farther north, on Jl Basuki Rahmat. Frequent buses run to Solo and Surabaya, and other destinations include Ponorogo (1000 rp), Ngawi (1200 rp), Kediri (3000 rp) and Malang (7000 rp). For Sarangan, first take a bus to Magetan (1000 rp) and change there. For Blitar, first take a bus to Nganjuk (1500 rp) or Kediri.

## AROUND MADIUN

Madiun is a jumping off point for the mountain resort of Sarangan (see the Central Java chapter) and you can continue through the mountains to Solo. To the east of Madiun is **Gunung Liman** (2563m), which has forest and a couple of waterfalls: **Air Terjun Malam**, past the village of Kare, and **Air Terjun Sedudo**, near Sawahan. **Gunung Liman** can be climbed from Ngiliman village, south of Sawahan.

**Ngawi**, 33km north-west of Madiun, is a sprawling provincial town. The bus terminal is on the southern outskirts on the road to Madiun, 2km from the centre. The *Hotel SAA Nuansa (Jl A Yani 38)* is a newer mid-range hotel with some cheaper rooms, but there is little reason to stay in Ngawi. The town's only attraction is **Benteng Pendem** on the north-eastern outskirts. This old Dutch fort (formerly Benteng Van Den Bosch) was built between 1839 and 1845 and parts of it are well preserved. Unfortunately, it is part of an army complex and written permission is required to visit.

In 1891 at Trinil, a Dutchman, Eugene Dubois, unearthed a skull of *Pithecanthropus erectus*, commonly known as Java Man. Dubois' discovery and his 'ape man' revelations in support of Darwin's theory of evolution caused a furore in Europe. A small museum displaying fossils found in the area has been built at the site, but the **skulls of Java Man** are only replicas. The remains of mammoths discovered in the area are more impressive. The museum is closed on Monday. Trinil is 11km west of Ngawi on the main highway to Solo, and it's a farther 3km to the musuem.

**Ponorogo**, 29km south of Madiun, is famed as the home of the Reyog dance, in which gaily costumed performers enact the battle between a court official of Ponorogo and the *singa barong*, the ruler of the forest. Combining elements of the horse trance dance, the Barong and possibly the Chinese lion dances, the Reyog is performed in Ponorogo's alun alun on 1 Suro (New Year) of the Javanese calendar, which falls around May.

## PACITAN
☎ 0357

On the south coast near the provincial border, the small town of Pacitan is on a horseshoe bay ringed by rocky cliffs. Pacitan's beach, **Pantai Ria Teleng**, is 4km from town and makes a good break from Solo. The sand is a dark yellow and the surf is rough, but it is very peaceful, and there are fine views of the coastline and the very scenic hills surrounding Pacitan Bay. Swimming is possible when the seas are calm – the safest area is towards the fishing boats at the south-western end of the bay, where there is also a swimming pool. Apart from picnickers on weekends, the beach is quiet, and you can wander farther along the beach to find a deserted spot.

### Information

The Bank Rakyat Indonesia on Jl A Yani will change US dollars and travellers cheques, as well as other currencies (cash only), but the rates are poor. Farther down towards the market, the BNI changes cash for a number of currencies, also at poor rates.

There is a wartel next to the Hotel Remaja, or the Telkom office is farther west on Jl A Yani.

### Places to Stay & Eat

The best place to stay is 4km out of town at Pantai Ria Teleng. **Happy Bay Beach Bungalows** (☎ 881474) has comfortable singles/doubles with bathroom for 25,000/ 30,000 rp, or private bungalows for 40,000 rp. Owned by an Australian and his Indonesian wife, Happy Bay is right opposite the beach, has a good restaurant, and you can rent bicycles and motorbikes.

The beach is the main reason to visit, so there a lot of reasons to stay in town. Budget hotels in Pacitan are along Jl A Yani, the main street. The **Hotel Pacitan** (☎ 881244, Jl A Yani 37) is close to the centre and good value. Rooms with mandi are 12,500 rp and 17,500 rp, or air-con rooms are 30,000 rp. Ask to see a selection of rooms, as some are internal facing and dark.

The best hotel in Pacitan is the **Srikandi** (☎ 881252, Jl A Yani 67) on the western edge of town. Spotless new rooms overlook the rice paddies and cost 50,000 rp with TV and fan, or air-con will cost another 20,000 rp. Attached is the town's best restaurant, a pleasant spot for cheap Indonesian dishes and fruit juices.

The next best dining option is **Depot Makan Bu Jabar** (Jl H Samanhudi 3) a block behind the police station on Jl A Yani. It has excellent *gado gado*, *nasi campur*, fish and fruit juices.

### Getting There & Away

Pacitan can be approached by bus from Solo (4000 rp, four hours), or hourly buses run along the scenic road to Ponorogo (2500 rp, 2½ hours), just south of Madiun. From Ponorogo, buses run to Surabaya via Madiun, and direct buses go to Blitar (four hours) throughout the day. From Blitar to Malang, take a colt or bus.

For Yogyakarta, head to Solo and take a bus from there.

Pacitan's bus terminal is half a kilometre from the centre of town on the road to Solo and the beach. Buses from Solo pass the turn-off to the beach and can drop you there. Happy Bay is a 500m walk away, or a becak from the terminal costs 3000 rp.

## AROUND PACITAN

Other isolated and undeveloped beaches accessible from Pacitan are **Watu Karung** (22km), the most well known to the west of Pacitan, and **Latiroco Lorok** (41km).

At Punung village, on the Solo road 30km north-west of Pacitan, is the turn-off to the limestone caves of **Goa Putri**, 2km away, and the much more impressive **Gua Gong**, 8km from the highway. Only open to the public since 1995, Gua Gong is the largest and most spectacular in this area famed for its caves. A stairway winds its way down into the cave for 400m and loops at the end, past many side caverns dripping with stalactites, some of them huge. The caves are lit, or you can hire torches to highlight the side caverns. Entry is 1500 rp and there are the usual warungs and souvenir sellers at the front. Any Solo-Pacitan bus can drop you at **Punung**, on the highway, from where you can either catch an infrequent minibus or hire an ojek for the journey along the winding road to Gua Gong.

The more famous **Gua Tabuhan** (Musical Cave) is 4km north on the highway beyond Punung, and then another 4km to the cave. This huge limestone cavern is said to have been a refuge for the 19th century guerilla leader Prince Diponegoro. Guides will give an excellent 'orchestral' performance, played by striking rocks against stalactites, each in perfect pitch and echoing pure gamelan melodies. You have to hire a guide and a lamp, and the concert lasts about 10 minutes. This is also agate country, and hawkers sell reasonably priced polished stones and rings.

## PROBOLINGGO
• pop 180,000    ☎ 0355

Probolinggo, on the Surabaya-Banyuwangi coastal road, is a transit centre for people visiting Gunung Bromo. It grows the finest mangoes in Java and its well stocked fruit stalls are a delight; but otherwise, Probolinggo is forgettable.

The main post office (which has Internet terminals), most of the banks (including the BCA and BNI) and most of the government buildings are on Jl Suroyo, which leads off the main street to the train station.

## Places to Stay & Eat

The *Hotel Bromo Permai (☎ 22256, Jl Panglima Sudirman 327)* is the most popular travellers hotel, and has comfortable, clean rooms from 12,500 rp, and from 35,000 rp to 45,000 rp with air-con. It is on the main road close to the centre of town at the eastern end.

The very well kept *Hotel Ratna (☎ 427 886, Jl Panglima Sudirman 16)* is 2km farther west. It is the best hotel in town and has good economy rooms for 12,500 rp, large rooms with TV and bathroom from 30,000 rp and air-con rooms from 55,000 rp to 70,000 rp.

The *Hotel Tampiarto Plaza (☎ 21280, Jl Suroyo 16)* is a fancier hotel, but has become run down and needs a good scrub. It has a pool but it is open to the public and usually full of screaming kids. Rooms start at 16,500 rp, or from 32,500 rp with air-con.

Most of the hotels have restaurants, and Probolinggo has some good Chinese restaurants. The *Restaurant Malang (Jl Panglima Sudirman 104)* has a wide range of items on the menu and the food is good. You'll find plenty of small restaurants and 'depots' at the night market around Pasar Gotong Royong.

## Getting There & Away

**Bus** Probolinggo's Bayuangga bus terminal is about 5km out of town on the road to Gunung Bromo. Yellow angkots run to and from the main street and the train station for 500 rp. The bus terminal is overrun with 'tourist office' bus agents offering dubious information and you'll be assailed by ticket sellers. Buses to destinations in East Java (eg Banyuwangi and Surabaya) are frequent, so avoid the agents and just pay on the bus. Advance bookings for long-distance executive buses will cost a little more – shop around.

Ekonomi/air-con buses include Surabaya (3000/6000 rp, two hours), Malang (3000/6000 rp, 2½ hours), Banyuwangi (6000/12,000 rp, five hours) via Situbondo, Bondowoso (3000/6000 rp), Yogyakarta (13,000/22,000 rp, eight hours) and Denpasar (16,000/25,000 rp).

Be careful on buses out of Probolinggo. Thieves are very common in East Java. They board the bus and sit behind you, waiting for you to put your day pack on the floor, when they'll slash it and get off the bus before you know it. Always wear a money belt for passport and travellers cheques when travelling on buses.

**Minibuses to Gunung Bromo** Green Colt minibuses from Probolinggo's Bayuangga bus terminal go to Cemoro Lawang (3000 rp, two hours) via Ngadisari (2500 rp, 1½ hours) until around 5 pm, sometimes later in peak tourist periods if there is demand. The late afternoon buses charge 3500 rp to

Cemoro Lawang, when fewer passengers travel beyond Ngadisari. Make sure the bus goes all the way to Cemoro Lawang when you board.

**Train** The train station is about 2km north of town, and 7km from the bus terminal. Probolinggo is on the Surabaya-Banyuwangi train line. Most services are ekonomi, or the *Mutiara Timur* costs 15,000/25,000 rp in bisnis/eksekutif to Surabaya (departing 1.40 pm) or Banyuwangi (departing 10 am). The pick of the economy services is the *Rengannis* to Banyuwangi (5500 rp) at 2.55 pm, via Jember and Kalibaru. The slow *Sri Tanjung* goes to Yogyakarta (10,000 rp) at 10.40 am via Solo.

## GUNUNG BROMO & BROMO-TENGGER-SEMERU NATIONAL PARK
☎ 0335

Gunung Bromo (2392m) is an active volcano lying at the centre of the **Tengger Massif**, a spectacular volcanic landscape and one of the most impressive sights in Indonesia. The massive **Tengger crater** stretches 10km across and its steep walls plunge down to a vast, flat sea of lava sand. From the crater floor emerges the smoking peak of Gunung Bromo, the spiritual centre of the highlands. This desolate landscape has a strange end-of-the-world feeling, particularly at sunrise, the favoured time to climb to the rim of Bromo's crater.

Bromo is the best known peak, and often the whole area is simply referred to as 'Mt Bromo', but it is only one of three mountains that have emerged within the caldera of the ancient Tengger volcano, and Bromo is flanked by the peaks of Batok (2440m) and Kursi (2581m). Farther south the whole supernatural moonscape is overseen by Gunung Semeru (3676m), the highest mountain in Java and the most active volcano in these highlands. The whole area has been incorporated as the Bromo-Tengger-Semeru National Park.

Legend has it that the great Tengger crater was dug out with just half a coconut shell by an ogre smitten with love for a princess. When the king saw that the ogre might fulfil the task he had set, which was to be completed in a single night, he ordered his servants to pound rice and the cocks started to crow, thinking dawn had broken. The coconut that the ogre flung away became Gunung Batok, and the trench became the Sand Sea – and the ogre died of exhaustion.

The Bromo area is also home to the Hindu Tengger people, who cultivate market vegetables on the steep mountain slopes and are found only on the high ranges of the Tengger-Semeru Massif. When the Majapahit Empire collapsed and its aristocracy fled to Bali to escape the tide of Islam in Java, the Tengger highlands provided a haven for Hindus left behind. Hinduism has in fact made a resurgence in the area, with growing cultural ties with Bali and the building of a Hindu temple near the base of Gunung Bromo.

Each year, Bromo is the site for the **Kasada festival**, with a colourful procession of Tenggerese who come to throw offerings into the crater at sunrise to pacify the god of the volcano.

Access is usually via Probolinggo, but Bromo can be approached from a number of routes. The ideal time to visit is during the dry season, April to October. At any time of the year it's cold on these mountains and night temperatures can drop to around 2°C to 5°C.

## Probolinggo Approach

This is the easiest and by far the most popular route. From Probolinggo, it's 28km to Sukapura, then another 14km to Ngadisari, and another 3km to Cemoro Lawang. Minibuses run all the way to Cemoro Lawang from Probolinggo. Just before Cemoro Lawang, you pay the 2100 rp entrance post.

As with mountain scaling anywhere in Asia, it is all important to be at the top of Gunung Bromo for the impressive sunrise.

From Cemoro Lawang, it's 3km down the crater wall and across the **Sand Sea** (Lautan Pasir) to Bromo, about a one hour walk. Get up at 4.30 am or earlier for an easy stroll

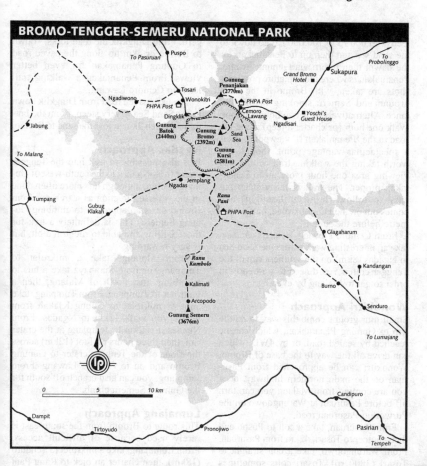

# BROMO-TENGGER-SEMERU NATIONAL PARK

To Pasuruan · Puspo

To Probolinggo

Grand Bromo Hotel ■ · Sukapura

Gunung Penanjakan (2770m) ▲

PHPA Post ·

Ngadiwong · Tosari · Wonokitri

PHPA Post · Dingklik

Cemoro Lawang ·

Yoschi's Guest House ■

Ngadisari ·

Jabung ·

Gunung Batok (2440m) ▲

Gunung Bromo (2392m) ▲

Sand Sea

Gunung Kursi (2581m) ▲

To Malang ·

Jemplang · Ngadas

Ranu Pani

· Tumpang

Gubug Klakah ·

PHPA Post

· Glagaharum

· Kandangan

Ranu Kumbolo

· Kalimati

· Burno

· Arcopodo

· Senduro

Gunung Semeru (3676m) ▲

To Lumajang

0    5    10 km

· Candipuro

· Dampit

· Tirtoyudo · Pronojiwo

· Pasirian

To Tempeh

across to Bromo. The white stone markers are easy to follow in the dark, not to mention all the other climbers. Horses can also be hired for 15,000 rp. By the time you've crossed the lava plain from Cemoro Lawang and started to climb Bromo (246 steps, one traveller reported), it should be fairly light. Bromo itself is not one of the great volcanoes of Indonesia – it is the whole landscape that is breathtaking – but from the top you'll get fantastic views down into the smoking crater and of the sun sailing up over the outer crater.

The colours are better at dawn, but don't despair if you miss it. Because of the rising hot air from the Tengger crater, visibility is good throughout the day in the dry season, even though the slopes below Cemoro Lawang may be covered in mist. Later in the day you'll also avoid the dawn melee, especially during school and other holiday periods. In the wet season the clouds and the dawn often arrive at the same time anyway.

From Cemoro Lawang, it is also possible to visit **Gunung Penanjakan** (2770m), the highest point on the outer crater. Hired jeeps (90,000 rp to 100,000 rp) go down to the sand sea and then up to Penanjakan for the dawn, then return via Gunung Bromo. Penanjakan is where those picture postcards shots are taken, with Bromo in the foreground and Semeru smoking in the distance. Alternatively, it is two hours on foot. Walk one hour (or charter a jeep) along the road to the 'Penanjakan II' viewpoint, itself a spectacular vantage point, though it's worth taking the walking trail behind this viewing area one hour more up to Penanjakan proper. The trail is fairly steep but easy to follow (bring a flashlight) and comes out on the Dingklik road, half a kilometre before the summit.

From Cemoro Lawang, trekkers can also take an interesting walk across the Sand Sea to Ngadas (8km) on the southern rim of the Tengger crater. You'd need to start early in order to get to Malang by evening.

## Wonokitri Approach

Small tour groups come this way to do the trip to Gunung Penanjakan, which can be reached by sealed road, or by 4WD, which can drive all the way to the base of Bromo. Wonokitri can be approached from Pasuruan on the main northern highway, or if you are coming from Malang you can turn off before Pasuruan at Warungdowo on the Purworejo-Pasuruan road.

From Pasuruan, take a colt to Puspo and then another to Tosari, 42km from Pasuruan. From Warungdowo, take a colt straight to Tosari (3000 rp). Tosari colts sometimes continue to Wonokitri; otherwise, take an ojek (2000 rp, 3km). Tosari and Wonokitri have accommodation (see Places to Stay later in this section).

At Wonokitri check in at the PHPA office on the southern outskirts of town and pay your 2100 rp park entry fee. In Wonokitri you can hire a jeep to Bromo for 125,000 rp return, or 150,000 rp including a side trip to Gunung Penanjakan. Cheaper ojeks can also be hired.

From Wonokitri, it is 2km along a good road to Dingklik. The views from Dingklik,

right on the edge of the outer crater, are superb. From Dingklik the road forks – down to Bromo or 4km up along the paved road to Gunung Penanjakan for even better views. From Penanjakan a walking trail leads to Cemoro Lawang.

The 6km paved road from Dingklik down to the Sand Sea is very steep. From the bottom it is then 3km across the sand to Bromo.

## Ngadas Approach

It is also possible to trek into the Tengger crater from Ngadas to the south-west of Gunung Bromo, although it is more often done in the reverse direction as a trek out from Bromo or as an approach to climbing Gunung Semeru. This is definitely a trek for those willing and able to rough it a bit, but is very rewarding.

From Malang, take a mikrolet to Tumpang, or from Surabaya take a bus to Blimbing, just north of Malang, then a mikrolet to Tumpang. From Tumpang, take another mikrolet to Gubug Klakah from where you walk 12km to Ngadas. From Ngadas it is 2km to Jemplang at the crater rim, then three hours on foot (12km) across the floor of the Tengger crater to Gunung Bromo and on to Cemoro Lawang. From Jemplang, you can also branch off south for the Gunung Semeru climb.

## Lumajang Approach

This route to Bromo from the south-east is rarely used because of difficult access. From Lumajang, take a mikrolet to Senduro (18km), then charter an ojek to Ranu Pani (25km) via Burno, from where you can walk to Bromo (14km) or Gunung Semeru.

## Climbing Gunung Semeru

Also known as Mahameru, the Great Mountain, Gunung Semeru has been looked on by Hindus since time immemorial as the most sacred mountain of all and father of Gunung Agung on Bali. It is a rugged three day trek to the summit, and you must be well equipped and prepared for camping overnight. Nights on the mountain are freezing, and inexperienced climbers have died of exposure. The best time to make the climb is May to October.

Hikers usually come through Tumpang, from where you can charter jeeps to Ranu Pani, the start of the trek; otherwise, take a mikrolet from Tampang to Gubuk Klakah and walk 12km to Ngadas, then on to Jemplang. It is also possible to cross the Tengger Sand Sea from Gunung Bromo (12km) to Jemplang, 2km from Ngadas at the Tengger crater rim. From Jemplang, the road skirts around the crater rim before heading south to Ranu Pani (6km, 1½ hours on foot).

Ranu Pani is a lake with a small village nearby. Pak Tasrep runs a *homestay*, and the *warung* serves basic meals. He can help organise a climb of Gunung Semeru, and you can rent a sleeping bag and other equipment. Ranu Pani is the usual overnight rest spot, and the *Ranu Pani PHPA post* is a few hundred metres past the lake. You can also stay here – accommodation is limited and Ranu Pani can be crowded with climbers. Register here and obtain advice on the climb. It can also help arrange guides.

The next day it is a couple of kilometres from the PHPA post to the shelter at the end of the road. Jeeps and motorcycles can make it this far. From here the trail climbs to the beautiful **Ranu Kumbolo** crater lake (2400m), 13km or about three hours away. Just past the lake is another shelter and the trail from here climbs to Kalimati (three hours) at the foot of the mountain. From Kalimati, it is a steep one hour climb to Arcopodo, where there is a campsite for the second night on the mountain.

The next day from Arcopodo, the fun begins. It is a short, steep climb to the start of the volcanic sands, the result of Semeru's eruption, and then a struggling three hour climb through loose scree to the peak. Semeru explodes every half hour and sends billowing smoke upwards. The gases and belching lava make Semeru dangerous – stay well away from the vent. From the top on a clear day, there are breathtaking views of Java's north and south coasts, as well as Bali. To see the sunrise, it is necessary to start at 2 am for the summit. It is possible to make it back to Ranu Pani on the same day.

## Places to Stay & Eat

**Cemoro Lawang** Right at the lip of the Tengger crater and the start of the walk to Bromo, Cemoro Lawang is the most popular place to stay. Prices for accommodation, and everything else, are inflated and bargaining brings few reductions. The national park information centre near the start of the walk is open sporadic hours.

*Cafe Lava Hostel (☎ 541020)* is the popular travellers place. Singles/doubles cost 15,000/20,000 rp, or 30,000/40,000 rp with cold water mandi. Rooms are very basic, but it's convivial and has a good restaurant.

The *Cemara Indah Hotel (☎ 541019)* is on the lip of the crater, with fantastic views and an excellent, airy restaurant. The very spartan rooms in the old block cost from 10,000/15,000 rp. Much better rooms with bathroom and hot water cost 65,000 rp. It also has a couple of overpriced rooms with TV for 165,000 rp.

One hundred metres past the Cafe Lava, the *Hotel Bromo Permai I (☎ 541021)* is the fanciest hotel and has a restaurant/bar, but don't expect luxury rooms. Those with shared mandi cost from 16,000 rp and 27,000 rp. Better rooms with attached bathroom and hot water are 60,000 rp to 106,000 rp.

The popular *Lava View Lodge (☎ 541 009)*, the fancier cousin of the Cafe Lava Hostel, is half a kilometre along a side road through the parking/souvenir stall area below the Hotel Bromo Permai I. It is right at the edge of the crater, with great views. Rooms with cold water cost 40,000 rp; or 60,000 rp and 100,000 rp with hot water, including a substantial breakfast. Service is excellent and it has a very good, but expensive, restaurant.

The PHPA's *Guest House Rumah Tamu (☎ 541038)*, opposite the Hotel Bromo Permai I, has two comfortable cottages, each with two bedrooms, sitting room, hot water and TV for 200,000 rp.

All the hotels have restaurants, or the *Adas Cafe*, next to the information centre,

**EAST JAVA**

has a limited but reasonably priced menu. The fancier **Venus Cafe** near the bus terminal has more varied fare.

**Ngadisari** Three kilometres down the mountain from Cemoro Lawang is Ngadisari village. *Yoschi's Guest House (☎ 541 018)*, just outside the village, is an excellent place to stay. This attractive, friendly inn has singles/doubles with shared mandi for 12,500/17,500 rp, or from 35,000/45,000 rp with shower. Comfortable family cottages with hot water are 65,000 rp to 125,000 rp. It has a great restaurant, and offers tours and transport to Bromo (4500 rp person).

A short walk away, the *Bromo Home Stay (☎ 541022)* has a restaurant and reasonable rooms with cold-water mandis for 15,000 rp, 25,000 rp and 40,000 rp. The Yogyakarta Rental minibuses stop here, and tickets to Yogyakarta or Bali cost 40,000 rp.

**Sukapura** The plush *Hotel Raya Bromo (☎ 581103)* is a few kilometres up the mountain from Sukapura village and a full 9km from the crater. If you want luxury accommodation and have a car, this may be your place. Otherwise, it is too far from the crater to be convenient. Rooms cost 242,000 rp to 726,000 rp, or cottages start at 726,000 rp, plus 21%, but it has been offering packages from 145,000 rp per room.

**Tosari & Wonokitri** The *Bromo Cottages (Surabaya ☎ 336888)* in Tosari are perched on the hillside, with fine mountain views and a restaurant. Posted rates are an expensive US$60, plus 21%, but discounts should be available.

It's also possible to stay with villagers in Wonokitri.

### Getting There & Away

Most visitors come through Probolinggo (see under Probolinggo earlier in this chapter for transport details). Hotels in Cemoro Lawang and Ngadisari can make bookings for onward bus tickets from Probolinggo for a large premium – 40,000 rp or more to Yogyakarta or Denpasar.

Travel agents in Solo and Yogyakarta book the Yogya Rental minibuses to Bromo for 40,000 rp to 50,000 rp. They are not luxury minibuses. Sometimes they run a bigger bus to Probolinggo and change there. Yogya Rental stops at the Bromo Homestay, Ngadisari. Specify if you want to go to Cemoro Lawang. There's a similar service to and from Bali. A two day tour – Yogyakarta/Solo to Bromo and Bali – costs around 100,000 rp from travel agents, but accommodation is at the less popular Bromo Homestay.

For Ngadas, frequent mikrolets go to Tumpang from Malang (600 rp). From Tumpang, irregular minibuses go to Ngadas, where jeeps go to Ranu Pani for 2500 rp per person. Jeeps can be chartered in Tumpang or Ngadas for high rates. From Tumpang, you can even charter a jeep to Bromo, but this is a long journey there and back.

Bromo tours are easily arranged in Malang, and you can also arrange jeep hire in hotels and travel agents there.

## PASIR PUTIH
☎ 0338

Roughly halfway between Probolinggo and Banyuwangi, on the north coast road, this is East Java's most popular seaside resort and is mobbed on weekends by sun'n'sand worshippers from Surabaya. It has picturesque outrigger boats and safe swimming, but its name (*pasir putih* means 'white sand') is a misnomer – the sand is more grey-black than white. This reasonable beach would make a pleasant enough stopover if the accommodation were better.

### Places to Stay

Pasir Putih's government-run hotels, sandwiched between the beach and the noisy main road, are dirty and overpriced. *Hotel Bhayangkara (☎ 91352)* is the cheapest. Dirty, stuffy rooms start at 15,500 rp; or dirty, larger rooms with mandi cost from 30,000 rp, more for air-con.

The *Pasir Putih Inn (☎ 91522)* is only slightly better and has singles/doubles with mandi from 20,000/30,000 rp. The *Mutiara Beach Hotel* is similar.

The *Hotel Sido Muncul (☎ 91352)* is the best of a bad bunch, but it too is not particularly clean and is badly in need of maintenance. Rooms facing the road with fan and mandi cost 25,000 rp, or air-con (don't bet on it working) rooms cost 38,000 rp to 65,000 rp for those facing the beach.

## BONDOWOSO
☎ 0332

Bondowoso, 34km south-west of Situbondo, is one of the cleanest towns in Java (in itself this is an attraction); otherwise, it is merely a transit point for nearby attractions such as Ijen. Bondowoso, like much of the north-eastern part of East Java, has a strong Madurese influence and Madurese, as much as Javanese or Bahasa Indonesia, is the lingua franca.

On weekends in **Tapen**, 15km from Bondowoso towards Situbondo, traditional Madurese horn-locking bullfights *(aduan sapi)* have been held, but these were recently cancelled for fear of exciting the Madurese population in a region that experienced a lot of krisis moneter problems and isolated looting.

### Places to Stay
*Hotel Anugerah (☎ 421870, Jl Sutoyo 12)* is very friendly and can arrange transport to Ijen for 150,000 rp return. Neat and tidy rooms cost 20,000 rp and 25,000 rp with mandi, or 30,000 rp with air-con. A good, cheap restaurant is attached.

The nearby *Palm Hotel (☎ 421505, Jl A Yani 32)* is the best in town, and has a swimming pool and good restaurant. This attractive hotel has a huge variety of rooms with mandi from 16,000 rp. Air-con rooms with TV and hot water start at 70,000 rp. It also arranges transport to Ijen.

### Getting There & Away
Buses from Bondowoso include Situbondo (1500 rp, one hour), Jember (1000 rp, 45 minutes), Probolinggo (3000 rp, two hours) and Surabaya (7500/12,000 rp air-con, five hours). For Tapen, take any Situbondo bound bus.

## IJEN PLATEAU
The Ijen Plateau, part of a reserve area that stretches north-east to Baluran National Park, was at one time a huge active crater complex, 134 sq km in area. Ijen is a quiet but active volcano, and the landscape is dominated by the volcanic cones of Ijen (2368m) and Merapi (2800m) on the north-eastern edge of the plateau, and Raung (3332m) on the south-west corner. Coffee plantations cover much of the western part of the plateau, where there are a few settlements. The plateau area has a number of difficult-to-reach natural attractions, but most visitors come for the hike to spectacular Kawah Ijen. There are few people in this unspoilt area.

### Kawah Ijen Hike
The magnificent turquoise sulphur lake of Kawah Ijen (Ijen Crater) lies 2148m above sea level and is surrounded by the sheer walls of the crater. Ijen's last major eruption was in 1936, though a minor ash eruption occurred in 1952. At the edge of the lake, smoke billows out from the volcano's vent and the lake bubbles when activity increases.

The vent is the source of sulphur and every day collectors make the trek up to the crater and down to the lake. With only a scarf around their faces to combat the caustic fumes, they prise off great chunks of sulphur rock and load up their baskets. With a full load of up to 100kg of sulphur rock jiggling on their shoulders, they weigh in at the monitoring post just below the crater and then head off down the mountain towards Banyuwangi. At Sodong, a long 10km away, trucks load up with the sulphur and take it to the factory in Banyuwangi, where it eventually ends in medicines, matches and other uses. For this backbreaking work the collectors are paid the princely sum of 150 rp per kg, but most do two trips a day, which is good money by village standards.

The best time to make the hike is in the dry season between April and October. Sulphur collectors hike up in the morning and return around 1 pm when the clouds roll in.

Trekkers are advised to do the same, but the clouds often disappear in the late afternoon. Make it for the dawn if you can.

The starting point for the trek to the crater is the PHPA post at Pos Paltuding, which is usually reached from Bondowoso but can also be accessed from Banyuwangi. Sign in and pay your 1000 rp entry fee here. The steep, well worn 3km path up to the monitoring post takes about one hour. Keep an eye out for gibbons and the prolific birdlife. Just past the post the road forks – to the left is the walk to the 'safety-valve' dam, which was built to regulate the flow of water into Banyu Pahit, the 'Bitter River'. The main interest lies along the right fork, a half-hour walk to the top of the crater and its stunning views, one of the most beautiful sights in Java.

From the crater, a steep, gravelly path leads down to the sulphur deposits and the steaming lake. The walk down takes about 20 minutes, and double this time for the walk back up. The path is slippery in parts and the sulphur fumes towards the bottom can be overwhelming. Take great care – a French tourist fell and died in 1997.

Back at the lip of the crater, turn left for the climb to the highest point on the crater (2368m) and magnificent views of the lake and the surrounding mountains. Or keep walking anticlockwise around the crater for even more expansive views of the lake. On the other side of the lake opposite the vent, the trail disappears into crumbling volcanic rock and deep ravines.

## Places to Stay & Eat

At Sempol, 13km before Pos Paltuding on the Bondowoso side, the Kebun Kalisat coffee plantation has a guesthouse, the *Arabika Homestay*, a kilometre from the main road. It is the best accommodation near Ijen, but expensive and run like an army camp. Rooms have attached bathrooms with hot water (maybe), but those for 50,000 rp are of *losmen* (basic, often family-run accommodation) standard. The main guesthouse building is better kept, and rooms cost 70,000 rp and 90,000 rp. A service charge of 10% is added to everything, including the

simple meals, which cost 3500 rp or 10,000 rp for buffet style. Otherwise, Sempol village has a couple of *warungs*. You can also visit the coffee groves and see the factory of this *agro wisata* (agricultual tourism) venture, but tourism is a neglected sideline to the fine arabica coffee produced here. Transport to Ijen can be arranged for 75,000 rp.

Pos Paltuding, the PHPA post at the start of the walk, has a small *shop* for provisions and a *cafe* serving noodles and not much else. There is an open-sided *shelter* for campers, or a bed in the cafe costs 10,000 rp per person. A new *guesthouse* lies off to the side, and while fairly bare, it is a relaxing spot and has comfortable beds. Rooms with mandi cost 35,000 rp. Blankets are not provided, so bring a sleeping bag – it gets extremely cold at this altitude. For something more substantial than noodles, guests can order meals.

The monitoring post just below the crater is not set up for guests, but there is a *wisma* (guesthouse) of sorts, and you can throw a sleeping bag on the floor for a small donation. The staff will gladly rent you their beds if you make it worth their while. Wake up to breathtaking views. This enterprising post also sells drinks and snacks, and will cook meals.

The coffee plantation also has another guesthouse, the more luxurious *Jampit Guesthouse*, 14km south of Sempol at Jampit. The accommodation is better than at the Arabika, but it is a long way from Ijen. Rooms cost 57,500 rp with outside mandi, and from 86,250 rp with hot water. The guesthouses have no phones, only radio contact, but they can be booked through PTP Nusantara XII in Surabaya (☎ 22360) and Jember (☎ 86861).

## Getting There & Away

It is possible to get most of the way to Kawah Ijen by public transport, but most visitors charter transport. The starting point for the hike to Kawah Ijen is the PHPA post of Pos Paltuding, which can be reached by road from Bondowoso or with more difficulty from Banyuwangi.

**Bondowoso** From Wonosari, 8km from Bondowoso towards Situbondo, an upgraded road runs via Sukosari and Sempol all the way to Pos Paltuding, 64km from Bondowoso. Apart from a few rough stretches, it's a good paved road and takes about two hours by car. Sign in at the coffee plantation checkpoints on the way. The Hotel Palm and the Hotel Anugerah in Bondowoso arrange day tours to Ijen for around 150,000 rp per vehicle.

Two minibuses per day run from Bondowoso to Sempol (3000 rp, 2½ hours) at around 7.30 am and 1 pm. You should be able to find someone in Sempol who will take you the 13km to Pos Paltuding on the back of their motorbike for around 15,000 rp one way, or the Arabika Homestay offers return transport, taking up to 10 people, for 75,000 rp. At the Pos Paltuding cafe there are usually a few motorbikes to take you back or on to Banyuwangi for 30,000 rp.

**Banyuwangi** Ijen is closer to Banyuwangi, but the road is very steep and has deteriorated badly. A 4WD is essential, but they are difficult to find in Banyuwangi and are outrageously expensive. Most people walk the last 8km along the road to Pos Paltuding.

From Banyuwangi's Blambangan bemo station, take a Lin 3 bemo to Sasak Perot (500 rp) on the eastern outskirts of town, then a Licin-bound colt that can drop you off in Jambu (1000 rp) at the turn-off to Kawah Ijen, which is a farther 17km away. Start at 5.30 am to reach the crater in time for good views. From Jambu, ojeks can take you 9km along the paved road to Sodong, through the plantations, for no more than 10,000 rp. Beyond Sodong, it is a hair-raisingly steep ride and ojeks are not keen to do it.

Sodong is nothing more than a small parking area at the edge of the forest where the sulphur collectors bring their loads to be taken by truck to Banyuwangi. Beyond Sodong, the washed out road is very steep and is just a slippery, rock strewn track for about 4km, though the last 4km is less steep

and is paved. The road was being upgraded and a new section built, but the krisis moneter put a stop to that.

The 8km walk from Sodong to Pos Paltuding is a tough three hours uphill, but is rewarded by brilliant, dense rainforest with towering ferns and palms. Halfway is the PHPA Pos Totogan, at the edge of the reserve, but it is not always staffed.

Only 4WD vehicles and motorcycles can make it all the way up, but cars and minibuses can go down from Pos Paltuding to Banyuwangi. It's a slow, bumpy ride in first gear with brakes on all the way.

## JEMBER
☎ 0331

Jember is the thriving service centre for the surrounding coffee, cacao, rubber, cotton and tobacco plantations. It has all the amenities of a large city, but is relatively uncongested and competes with Bondowoso for the tidy town award.

From Jember, groups can arrange a plantation tour, though Kalibaru is the usual centre for plantation visits. PT Perkubunan Nusantara XII (☎ 86861), Jl Gajah Mada 249, is the state-owned company that controls most of the plantations; it has day or overnight tours with accommodation on the plantations.

The *Hotel Widodo* (☎ *83650, Jl Letjen Suprapto 74)*, about a kilometre south of the town centre, is a good cheap hotel and on the ball with travel information. Good midrange hotels include the friendly *Hotel Seroja* (☎ *83905)*, Jl PB Sudirman 2, north of town on the highway to Bondowoso; and the more central *Hotel Safari* (☎ *81881)*, Jl Achmad Dahlan 7.

## Getting There & Away

The main bus terminal, Tawung Alun, 6km west of town, has buses to Probolinggo, Surabaya, Malang, Bondowoso, Banyuwangi and Kalibaru, but buses from Bondowoso usually terminate at the sub-terminal, 5km north of town, and there are also sub-terminals to the east (for Banyuwangi) and south (for Watu Ulo). Damri

JEMBER/BANYUWANGI REGION

city buses and yellow Lin bemos run from the terminals to the centre of town.

Jember is also on the train line that runs between Surabaya and Banyuwangi and the station is close to the centre of town.

## WATU ULO & PAPUMA
☎ 0331

Watu Ulo is popular on weekends, but like most of the beaches in Java's south coast, it has grey sands and crashing surf with dangerous swimming. The real surprise lies just west around the headland from Watu Ulo. Papuma is a small beach with white sand, turquoise waters and sheltered swimming. Farther around from Papuma, the rugged coastline with spectacular rocky outcrops is again pounded by the surf, but deserted patches of white sand can be found for sunbathing. Nearby caves and the **Wana**

---

### Ninja Killers

Quiet Banyuwangi hit the headlines in 1998 after mysterious serial killings claimed over 200 lives. The international press picked up on the killings, and Banyuwangi made headlines around the world as the centre for the strangest story to emerge from Indonesia's tumultuous times.

Local rumour has it that the killings began in a village south of Banyuwangi. When the identity of two *orang sakti* (black magicians) visiting the village became known, the villagers grabbed them, beat them up, then tortured them before dragging them around the village until they were dead. The police found it difficult to lay charges without arresting the whole village.

Black magicians are feared throughout Indonesia. Anyone with a grudge can employ the services of a black magician, who then casts a spell against the intended victim. The victim becomes sick and may die. Typically, it is said, the victim's stomach swells horrendously and they turn black.

Soon black magicians were turning up dead throughout Banyuwangi city and the surrounding district. Their throats had been cut or they had been hacked to death with knives. Then, conservative Muslim clerics were targeted. Many belonged to Nahdatul Ulama, the 40 million-strong Muslim organisation that belongs to the old school of syncretic Islam with a strong dose of mysticism. The killings had the hallmarks of an organised gang, dubbed the ninja killers because it is said they dressed in black and did their deeds at night.

Rumour was rife as the killings spread to Jember, then throughout East Java. Doors were locked at night and vigilantes set up roadblocks, searching vehicles for suspected ninjas.

In a country where the open transmission of information is relatively new, speculation is as much news as fact. Political leaders and newspapers, forever dreaming up conspiracy theories and blaming Indonesia's troubles on 'unknown forces', first claimed it was the work of the army. In response, the army pulled the red rabbit out of the hat and claimed it was communists. Opposition leader Amien Rais even claimed Soeharto was behind the killings in an attempt to deflect anger away from Rais himself and his cronies.

Abdurrahman Wahid, leader of Nahdatul Ulama, seemed nearer the mark when he hinted it was the work of rival Muslim groups, though many were random killings by hysterical mobs in this conservative, superstitious region. On Madura, three detectives were set upon and killed by a mob when a suspect they were chasing shouted out that the three were ninjas. In Malang, the severed head of a suspected ninja was paraded through the streets, but police had no idea of the victim's identity. In other incidents, those with mental disorders were killed.

Hundreds of suspects were arrested and a handful have been committed to trial. The violence is over, but it is unlikely that the killings were the work of a single organised gang. The real truth may never be known, though the killings mirror similar incidents in this region in the 1950s and 60s. Old grudges are resurfacing in Indonesia and are a constant threat to emergent democracy.

Wisata Londolapesan forest area can also be explored.

At Watu Ulo, the basic *Hotel Vishnu* (☎ *81028)* has rooms with mandi from 20,000 rp.

## Getting There & Away

In Jember, take a city bemo (500 rp) to the Ajung sub-terminal and then a *taksi* (the confusing name for a public minibus in these parts) to Ambulu (1000 rp, 25km). From Ambulu yellow bemos go to Watu Ulo (500 rp, 12km). Papuma is then a half hour walk along the paved road over the steep headland, though bemos can drop you at the beach.

## KALIBARU
☎ 0333

The picturesque road from Jember to Banyuwangi winds around the foothills of Gunung Raung (3322m) up to the small hill town of Kalibaru. On the way, kids position themselves on the hairpin bends and direct traffic, warning motorists of oncoming vehicles. Motorists throw coins to these enterprising village *parkirs* for their services.

Kalibaru has a refreshingly cool climate and makes a pleasant stop on the way between Jember and Banyuwangi. The village itself is unremarkable, but Kalibaru has excellent accommodation for such a small town and makes a good base for visiting the nearby plantations around **Glenmore**, 10km east. Java's finest coffee, both *arabica* and *robusta* varieties, is produced in the Ijen Plateau area, as well as cacao, cloves and rubber. In Kalibaru town, to the north of the train station, are smaller, easily visited plots of coffee and cloves.

## Tours

The area has many plantations, but the main plantation of interest is Kebun Kandeng Lembu, 5km south of Glenmore. Guides can be hired (35,000 rp) for groups to see rubber tapping and processing in the factory, and you can see cacao and coffee plantations, as well as the washing, drying and sorting processes. The easiest way to reach

the plantation is on a tour from Kalibaru. The Margo Utomo Homestay in Kalibaru has plantation tours for 101,000 rp for two people. It also organises transport and other fairly expensive tours to Kawah Ijen (250,000 rp per vehicle), Alas Purwo (195,000 rp) and Sukamade (400,000 rp), as well as river rafting (100,000 per person) in the dry season and *dokar* (horse cart) village tours (35,000 rp per person). The Hotel Kalibaru can also arrange coffee plantation tours for 15,000 per person, but caters mostly to larger groups.

The Kalibaru train station (☎ 897322) is also cashing in on the agrotourism boom and runs a Lorry Agricultural Tour. A small diesel lorry for eight people costs 170,000 rp (325,000 rp for two lorries taking 16 people) and goes 35km through impressive mountain countryside, across bridges and tunnels and past a coffee plantation.

## Places to Stay & Eat

Most visitors come to Kalibaru just to stay at the delightful *Margo Utomo Homestay (☎ 897123, Jl Lapangan 10)*, an old Dutch inn that has maintained its colonial feel. It has newer, colonial-style cottages with private balconies built around a pretty garden. Cottages cost US$19/25, including breakfast, and all-you-can-eat meals cost 15,000 rp for lunch or 20,000 rp for dinner. This hotel, and its offshoot, is the centre of tourism for many visitors to East Java.

The newer *Margo Utomo Cottages (☎ 897420, Jl Putri Gunung 3)* doesn't have the same colonial atmosphere, but it is in a superb, restful setting down by a river, 3km east of town and 200m south of the highway. Attractive bungalows cost US$22/27 – try to get one overlooking the river. It has a pool and a restaurant with similarly substantial meals.

*Wisma Susan (☎ 897289, Jl Lapangan 12)*, right next to the Margo Utomo Homestay, is a nice old colonial place with a garden. Simple rooms with verandah and mandi for 45,000 rp are overpriced.

The *Raung View Hotel (☎ 897214, Jl Jember 16)* has a swimming pool and restaurant, and is the best value in town. Rooms with hot water for 30,000 rp are a good deal, but it is worth paying 47,000 rp for the pleasant cottages at back overlooking the rice paddies.

*Hotel Kalibaru* (☎ 897333), 4km west of town on the Jember road, is a bigger, flasher hotel and also has a swimming pool. Rooms for 99,500 rp have pleasant, open-air bathrooms, and breakfast is included.

Glenmore also has two hotels, but Kalibaru has more appeal. The *Hotel Glenmore* (☎ 81306) has uninspiring rooms from 25,000 rp. The much better *Minak Jinggo* (☎ 81428) has a pool and rooms from 40,000 rp to 100,000 rp.

## Getting There & Away

Any bus between Jember (one hour) and Banyuwangi (two hours) can drop you near the hotels. The train station is right near the Margo Utomo Homestay, and Kalibaru is on the main train line: Banyuwangi-Jember-Probolinggo-Surabaya. It is a scenic run from Kalibaru to Banyuwangi (1100 rp ekonomi, 2½ hours) or the *Mutiara Timur* runs to Banyuwangi (12,000/20,000 bisnis/eksekutif) and Surabaya (14,000/24,000 rp). A 6.20 am train also goes to Malang via Bangil.

## MERU BETIRI NATIONAL PARK

Covering 580 sq km, Meru Betiri National Park is on the south coast, lying between the Jember and Banyuwangi districts. With magnificent coastal rainforest, abundant wildlife, beaches and superb coastal scenery, it is one of Java's finest parks, but it receives few visitors because of difficult access.

Named after Gunung Betiri (1223m) in the north of the park, the coastal mountains trap more rain than the surrounding area and the park is unusually wet for much of the year. The best time to visit is the dry season, April to October. Entry is impossible after heavy rains because the road into the park fords a river which easily floods. Even in the dry season, you may have to wade across the river and walk into the park.

The park's major attraction is the protected **turtle beach** at Sukamade, one of Indonesia's most important turtle spawning grounds, where five species of turtle come ashore to lay their eggs. Green turtles are the most common, but the giant leatherbacks come in the wet season from December to February. The huge female turtles, weighing up to 750kg, make their laborious climb up the beach at night and dig a deep hole where they lay up to 50 or more eggs. It's an amazing sight, but sightings are never certain. Olive-Ridley, hawksbill and the large loggerhead turtles also come to Sukamade. Park staff tag the turtles, and in an effort to stop poaching and natural predators, they collect the eggs and hatch them in tanks before returning the young to the sea. The beach is about 700m from Mess Pantai, the PHPA accommodation in the park, and staff can arrange a night trip.

Wildlife, mostly in the mountain forests, include leopards, wild pigs, deer, bantengs, black giant squirrels, civets and pangolins; the silvered-leaf monkey and long-tailed macaque are common. Birdlife is prolific and hornbills, including the rhinoceros hornbill, whoosh and honk overhead. Meru Betiri is most famous as the last home of the Javan tiger, but it is now believed to be extinct.

As well as the most extensive coastal rainforest in Java, there is mangrove, lowland swamp and bamboo forest. Endemic plants include the *Rafflesia zollingeriana*; the rafflesia is a parasitic plant that has the world's largest flower. *Balanphora fungosa* is another rare endemic parasitic plant.

Despite this rich biodiversity, the park is not all wilderness, and two plantations lie within its boundaries. The main plantation is **Sukamade** in the eastern part of the park, and the whole park and the turtle beach are often referred to as Sukamade. Sukamade plantation has a comfortable guesthouse, but it is about 5km from the turtle beach. The other plantation is in the west near Bandealit and it also has a small guesthouse, but the main interest is in the east. Visitors can tour the plantations, which include coffee, cacao, coconut and rubber.

EAST JAVA

## Tiger

The magnificent Javan tiger *(Pantera tigris sondaica)* once roamed right across Java, but by the 1960s, numbers were dangerously low. The last confirmed sightings were in 1972, despite full protection and the setting aside of habitats for the tiger. Though it once roamed Ujung Kulon National Park in West Java, the Javan Tiger's last home was Meru Betiri National Park. As late as the 1980s, four or five were still said to exist.

When he visited Java in 1861, the noted naturalist Alfred Russell Wallace reported that the tiger still roamed free. He told of a child mauled by a tiger in East Java, near Mojokerto, an area which is now a sea of towns and villages. The tiger's real decline was just beginning as the colonial government opened up more of Java to plantations and tiger hunting became a favoured sport of the well-to-do. In 1872 the Dutch government put a bounty of 3000 guilders on the head of a man-killer, resulting in indiscriminate slaughter. Tigers were still common at the beginning of the 20th century, but Java's massive population growth destroyed the tiger's habitat.

Tiger sightings – but not tigers – are still common in Java. In September 1997, the Indonesian press reported sightings at Gunung Merbabu in Central Java and more recently at Gunung Merapi, just outside Yogyakarta. As always, these sightings turned out to be leopards, which are also endangered and only number about 300 on Java.

Regular sightings are still claimed at Meru Betiri and examination of footprints and droppings give some credence to its existence, but the Javan tiger is believed to be extinct. The only known tiger to exist in the wild in Indonesia is the Sumatran tiger *(Panthera tigrissumatrae)* and its numbers are dangerously low. No more than 500 remain in Sumatra and only 5000 to 7500 tigers are left in the world.

Trails are limited in the park and a guide, arranged through the PHPA, is usually necessary. Apart from coastal walks, a trail leads about 7km north-west of the Sukamade estate to the **Sumbersari** grazing ground, part-way through rainforest and bamboo thicket. The cleared grazing ground is overgrown, but you may see deer and other animals. In the far west of the park, the **Nanggelan** grazing ground is home to bantengs.

The area is noted for its superb coastal scenery. **Rajegwesi**, at the entrance to the park, is on a large bay with a sweeping grey beach and a fishing village. Past the park entrance, the road climbs for expansive views over spectacular **Teluk Hijau** (Green Bay), with its cliffs and white sand beach framed by deep green sea. A trail leads a kilometre from the road down to Teluk Hijau, or it is about a one hour walk east from Mess Pantai. From Mess Pantai you can also walk west through forest to the beach at **Permisan**, an eight hour return walk. A couple of kilometres farther east is the beach at **Teluk Meru**, which is a four hour walk through forest from Bandealit in the west.

Other pretty beaches can be found on the coast on the way into the park. Most lie south off the main road, and include **Lampon**, just south of Pesanggaran, a passable beach that is popular on weekends. **Pancer**, on a sweeping bay, has a fine beach with good swimming and a small island, **Pulau Merah**, at one end. The Hindu community here has a temple and makes offerings at the island. The now-rebuilt Pancer was obliterated by a 1994 tsunami, with appalling loss of life.

### Places to Stay

The best place to stay for exploring the park is the PHPA *Mess Pantai*, in the forest a few hundred metres back from the beach. Simple, four-bedroom cottages with shared mandi cost 20,000 rp per room. Cooking facilities are provided and the staff may be able to help, but bring your own food. Stock up at the market in Sarongan on the way into the park. The Sukamade estate on the plantation also has a shop for basic supplies.

About 5km north of the beach, the plantation's *Wisma Sukamade* has much more comfortable accommodation with electricity and all creature comforts laid on. It has a variety of rooms from 60,000 rp, and meals are provided. Bookings can be made through PT Perkubunan Nusantara XII in Jember. Though the accommodation is good, it is not a convenient place to stay unless you have transport.

If you get stuck, the PHPA office at Rajegwesi at the park entrance can arrange something, but it is not always staffed. Outside the park, the nearest hotels are in Jajag. *Hotel Widodo* (☎ 0333-36147, Jl Sudirman 124) is basic but cheap. The *Hotel Surya* (☎ 0333-36126) has a swimming pool and is surprisingly luxurious for such a small town. It may also be possible to stay on the other plantations that you pass on the way into the park.

## Getting There & Away

This is one of the most isolated parts of Java, and it is a long bumpy trip, even by 4WD, which is how most visitors travel to the park.

From Banyuwangi, first take a bus to Pesanggaran (2300 rp, 2½ hours, 87km) or from Jember take a bus to Jajag (south of the highway), then a minibus to Pesanggaran (800 rp, 22km). From Pesanggaran take a taksi to Sarongan (2000 rp, one hour, 18km). The road is paved and goes through the plantations.

Sarongan is just a small town with a market, a few rumah makan and no hotels. Stock up on supplies, then take an ojek (around 15,000 rp) for the 18km trip to Sukamade. After 4km, you reach the Rajegwesi PHPA post at the entrance to the park, where you pay your 2000 rp entry fee. Check here on the condition of the river.

From Rajegwesi, the very rough road runs 10km to the river, crossing at Sumbosuko. This stretch climbs through brilliant dense forest before dropping down the mountain again. The views are stunning but the road is really only for 4WD vehicles – the few cars that do tackle it wish they hadn't.

If the river is low, ojeks can take you straight on to Sukamade or Mess Pantai; 4WDs can also cross. There are two river crossings – the deeper one farther south and the multiple, shallower crossing farther upstream. If the river is up but not flooded, you can wade across and get another ojek or walk the 4km to Mess Pantai.

Expensive 4WD tours with an overnight in Wisma Sukamade are organised by the Margo Utomo hotels in Kalibaru. Check on refund conditions if the river is not passable. Another way to reach the park is to charter a fishing boat from the beach at Rajegwesi, but this will require a lot of bargaining and depends on sea conditions – count on around 150,000 rp to drop off and pick you up on another designated day.

The western entrance into the park is rarely visited, as the main points of interest are in the east. From Jember, take a taksi to Ambulu (25km), then another along the rough road to Curahnongko (20km). Take an ojek for the last 19km to Bandealit.

## ALAS PURWO NATIONAL PARK

This 43,420 hectare park occupies the whole of the remote Blambangan Peninsula at the south-eastern tip of Java. The facilities are limited and it is not easy to reach, but Alas Purwo has fine beaches, good opportunities for wildlife spotting, and savanna, mangrove and lowland monsoon forests. Apart from day-trippers and local beach parties on weekends, the park gets few visitors.

Alas Purwo means 'first forest' in Javanese, for according to legend this is where the earth first emerged from the ocean. It is an important Hindu spiritual centre – Alas Purwo is regarded as the foot of Java, while Ujung Kulon is the head and Yogyakarta the heart. Many pilgrims, mostly Hindu but also Muslim mystics, come to pray and meditate at the **Pura Giri Selokah** temple, especially during Pagerwesi, the Hindu new year (which occurs every 210 days). A new temple has been built closer to the road, but the old temple is more sacred and said to be the gateway to a lost palace that lies buried in the jungle on the slopes of Gunung Tugu.

The waves at **Plengkung** on the isolated south-western tip of the peninsula have reached legendary proportions among surfers. The huge left-hand reef break, or rather a series of breaks stretching almost 2km, has made it world famous among surfers.

Surfers come by charter boat from Grajagan at the western end of the bay, but the usual entry to the park is by road via the village of Pasar Anyar, which has a large park office and an interpretive centre. Call in here to check on accommodation and the latest conditions in the park, or the head office is in Banyuwangi (☎ 424119), Jl Agus Salim 138. The actual gateway to the park is at Rowobendo, 10km south along a bad road – pay your 2000 rp entry fee at the guard post here. From Rowobendo, the road runs past the temple before hitting the beach at Trianggulasi, 2km away. Trianggulasi is the main camp and has hut accommodation, but not much else.

## Exploring the Park

This limestone peninsula is relatively flat – the rolling hills reach a peak of only 322m. Alas Purwo has plenty of lowland coastal forest, but few trails to explore it and vast expanses of the eastern park are untrammelled, even by park staff. Malaria has been reported in the park, mostly in the east, so take your pills and cover up against mosquitos at night.

Using Trianggulasi as a base, some interesting short walks can be made and the white-sand beach here is beautiful, though swimming is usually dangerous in the rough surf.

Herds of wild banteng cattle, kijang deer and peacocks are easy to see in the early morning and late afternoon at the **Sadengan** grazing ground, which has a viewing tower. This beautiful meadow, backed by forest, is a 2km walk from Trianggulasi along a road and then a swampy trail.

Alas Purwo also has a small population of *ajag* native dogs, one of the last packs in Java (ajags can also be found at Baluran National Park). Other wildlife includes jungle fowl, leaf monkeys, muncak (barking deer), rusa deer and leopards (mostly black panthers). The park guards can arrange night leopard-spotting expeditions for around 10,000 rp. A family of the big cats lives near the park entrance at Rowobendo and though sightings are not guaranteed, night walks are interesting.

Guards can also arrange a motorbike trip to the **turtle hatchery** at Ngagelan, or you can walk. It is 6km from Rowobendo along a rough road, or it is a 7km walk along the beach at low tide from Trianggulasi. This turtle-spawning beach attracts mostly Olive-Ridley *(Lepidochelys olivacea)* turtles, which lay their eggs in the dry season (June and July are the main months). Other turtles that visit the park are the Hawksbill, Green and the giant Leatherback turtles. Though Sukamade in Meru Beitiri is a more important turtle beach, Ngagelan makes an interesting trip, and the hatchery helps nature on its way by collecting the eggs and hatching them before returning the young to the sea.

It is also possible to walk along the beach all the way to Plengkung via other points of interest. From Trianggulasi, walk along the beach to **Pancur**, 3km south-east, or there is a trail through the forest. The trail is not always easy to follow, but it runs just inland from the beach, never more than 20m away, so you can't get lost. Pancur has a little mini-waterfall that comes out on the beach, and another PHPA post. There is a camping ground, but no one stays here unless Trianggulasi is full. The guards can also rent you a mattress on the office floor.

From Pancur, a trail heads 2km inland through some good forest to **Gua Istana**, which is a small cave that attracts meditating ascetics – one of many caves in this limestone landscape. Keep an eye out for monkeys and prolific birdlife on the way. Over 200 species of birds, mostly migrants, have been recorded in the park and hornbills are common. Two kilometres farther along this partly overgrown and sometimes wet trail is another cave, **Gua Padepokan**.

From Pancur, it is a further 11km walk (two hours) around Grajagan Bay to the fine beach at **Plengkung**, one of Asia's premier surfing spots, otherwise known as **G-Land** to the surfing fraternity. The Quicksilver Pro surfing championship is held here every year around June and is part of the ASP world championships. The surf camps at Plengkung are by no means five star, but provide unexpected luxury in the wilderness. Some surfers experienced the terrifying ride of their lives in 1994 when a tsunami hit the camps in the middle of the night, carrying huts and surfers 60m back into the jungle. How private accommodation is allowed to operate in the park is something of a mystery – KKN (an acronym for Soeharto-era Corruption, Collusion and Nepotism) seems a likely explanation. Bring plenty of money if you want a meal or drink at the expensive restaurants.

## Places to Stay & Eat

The PHPA's *Pesanggrahan* at Trianggulasi has elevated bungalows near the beach at 7500/12,000 rp for singles/doubles. Conditions are very basic. Rooms have a bed but nothing else, water is from a well and there is no electricity. The slightly more salubrious *Wisma Tamu* next door is a furnished bungalow costing 60,000 rp. It is wired for electricity but you have to bring your own generator! Though primitive, this is a lovely, relaxing spot and many who come for a day or two end up staying longer.

All food and drink *must* be brought with you. Trianggulasi has no warungs and is deserted if no guests stay, but the Pesanggrahan has a kitchen with a kerosene stove and hurricane lamps. The PHPA office at Pasar Anyar has a *shop* selling basic provisions such as Supermie packet noodles, but it is better to stock up in Dambuntung, where the bus drops you. Dambuntung's two *general stores* sell a wide range of packaged and fresh food. A guard stays at Trianggulasi if there are guests, and will cook for you if you share your food and, preferably, your beer (bring a few bottles with you).

There is also a *campground* at Pancur and a PHPA post.

The three surf camps back from the beach at Plengkung are for tours only. The biggest, *Bobby Camp*, is run by Wanawisata Alam Hayati (☎ 0333-421485) in Banyuwangi. *Plenkung Indah (☎ 031-53147)*, based in Surabaya, is the other main operator. The elevated bungalows are comfortable and have most of the facilities a surfer could want – cold beer, surf videos, pool tables and decent restaurants. The new *Bambang Camp* is a simpler place and not yet fully established, but it will allow walk-in guests (not that many make it on foot). Accommodation costs around US$30 a day at all the camps, but everyone comes on a surfing package that includes all transfers, usually from Bali. Most tours are sold on Bali – try the surf shops on Jl Legian in Kuta or Tubes Bar.

## Getting There & Away

From Banyuwangi's southern Brawijaya bus terminal, the Putra Jaya company has buses to Kalipahit (2200 rp, 1½ hours) via Benculuk and Tegaldelimo until 4 pm. 'Kalipahit' is the name of the region – the turn-off to the park is in the small village of Dambuntung. Stock up with food in Dambuntung, then take an ojek (motorbike taxi) from the turn-off. For around 10,000 rp they can take you first to the park office in Pasar Anyar, 3km from Dambuntung, to check on accommodation, then on to the park. The 12km road from Pasar Anyar to Trianggulasi is badly pot-holed, but flat and negotiable by car. It is a time-consuming trip, but Alas Purwo is much easier to reach than Meru Betiri National Park.

From Ketapang or Bali, a number of buses take the southern highway. Any bus that goes via Jember can drop you at Rogojampi on the highway, where you can pick up the bus to Kalipahit.

Surf tours to Plengkung come via boat from Grajagan.

## GRAJAGAN

At the western end of Grajagan Bay is the fishing village of Grajagan. The wide river estuary is dotted with brightly painted fishing boats, and farther around is a peaceful black-sand surf beach. The main point of interest is the forest park by the beach, 1.5km from the village, where *Wisma Perhutani Grajagan (Banyuwangi ☎ 0333-421649)* has very simple but attractive rooms with verandahs overlooking the beach for 27,500 rp. Meals can be ordered. It is very relaxing during the week, but the beach is not good for swimming. Most guests are locals on a weekend break or surfers who stay overnight before taking a boat to Plengkung in Alas Purwo National Park.

### Getting There & Away

From Banyuwangi, take a bus to Benculuk (see Getting There & Away under Alas Purwo National Park), from where buses run to Grajagan village for 1500 rp. For an extra 500 rp, buses will drop you at the wisma in the park. If coming from Jember, take a bus to Jajag and another to Benculuk.

A chartered speed boat for the half hour crossing to Plengkung will cost around 600,000 rp return, or about 400,000 rp for an outrigger fishing boat that takes two hours. Rates depend very much on negotiating skills, weather conditions and when you want to be picked up.

## BANYUWANGI
☎ 0333

Although there are no particular attractions to drag you here, schedules or just the urge to be somewhere different might take you to Banyuwangi, the ferry departure point for Bali. The ferry terminus, main bus terminal and train station are all at Ketapang, 8km north of town, so everyone goes straight though to Gunung Bromo, Yogyakarta or elsewhere. While Bali is teeming with tourists, Banyuwangi, just a stone's throw away, is a quiet, neglected backwater. The name Banyuwangi means 'perfumed water', from a legend that a Hindu king vanquished an evil usurper and threw him into the river, forever fragrant thereafter.

### Information

The Banyuwangi Tourist Office, Jl Diponegoro 2, is at the cultural centre/sports field. A branch in the passenger terminal in Ketapang is open sporadically. It is quite helpful, but also runs a sideline renting cars and drivers, so information may not always be unbiased.

The post office is opposite the tourist office and it has Internet terminals open from 8 am to 3 pm, Monday to Saturday.

Change money at the BCA bank on Jl Sudirman or the BNI south of the market, which also has an ATM that accepts Master-Card. Another BNI branch, at the Ketapang ferry terminal, has an ATM, and other banks at the ferry will change money at reasonable rates. There are no after-hours money-changers.

For information on Alas Purwo National Park and Kawah Ijen, the head office (☎ 424119) is at Jl A Yani 108, about 2km south of the town centre. The Baluran National Park head office (☎ 424119) is 2km farther south-west at Jl Agus Salim 138.

### Things to See

The main reason to stay here is to overnight on the way to Kawah Ijen or the national parks to the south. If you are desperate for something to do, the **Museum Daerah Blambangan**, opposite the alun alun on Jl Sritanjung, has a small collection of artefacts. Banyuwangi-style batik *(gajah oleng)* is produced in **Desa Temenggungan**, the *kampung* (neighbourhood) just behind the museum. Ask around to see it being made. The town's market, **Pasar Banyuwangi**, with its crowded, narrow alleyways, is also worth a look.

### Places to Stay

The *Hotel Baru (☎ 421369, Jl MT Haryono 82-4)* is the best of the cheap hotels. It's friendly and has a restaurant. Rooms, all with bathroom, cost 13,800 rp to 16,300 rp for fan rooms, 35,000 rp and 42,000 rp for air-con.

Nearby *Hotel Slamet (☎ 424675, Jl Wahid Hasyim 96)*, next to the old train station, is friendly enough but less inspiring. Rooms for 12,500 rp to 20,000 rp with mandi are depressing but the newer rooms with air-con and TV for 27,500 rp and 35,000 rp are good value.

For something better, the popular *Hotel Pinang Sari (☎ 423266, Jl Basuki Rachmat 116)* is on the main road north of the Blambangan bemo station. This excellent mid-range hotel has a very attractive garden and a restaurant. Rooms with bath cost 18,900 rp and 22,900 rp. A variety of stylish rooms and bungalows with air-con, TV and hot water cost 44,000 rp to 145,000 rp.

The *Hotel Ikhtiar Surya (☎ 421063, Jl Gajah Mada 9)* is the best in the town with large grounds and a huge variety of good-value rooms, all with bath, ranging from 17,000 rp up to the 129,000 rp 'sweet'. It is very quiet but a 1.5km hike west of the centre of town.

Banyuwangi's top hotels are at Ketapang. The big *Manyar Hotel (☎ 424741)*, a kilometre south of the ferry terminal on the road to Banyuwangi, has comfortable motel units, a restaurant, disco and pool. It's faded but good value, with discounted rates from 52,500 rp to 203,000 rp.

One kilometre farther south, the newer *Hotel Ketapang Indah (☎ 422280)*, facing the black sand beach and Bali, is marginally better and it has a pool. Bungalows back from the beach are 150,000 rp and 170,000 rp, or the well-appointed seaview rooms are 300,000 rp, before a substantial discount.

## Places to Eat
For snacks, Jl Pattimura has **night food-stalls**; here you'll find delicious *air jahe* (ginger tea) and *dadak jagung* (egg and sweetcorn patties), *ketan* (sticky rice topped with coconut) and fried banana.

Around the corner, the *Rumah Makan Surya (Jl W Hasyim 94)* has moderately priced Chinese food and serves a good ayam goreng. *Depot Asia (Jl Dr Sutomo 12)* also has good, if slightly expensive, Chinese food and boasts air-con. For the best Madurese-style sate in town, go to Pak Amat's warung on Jl Basuki Rachmat in the evenings.

## Getting There & Away
**Bus** Banyuwangi has two bus terminals. Terminal Seri Tanjung is 3km north of the Bali ferry terminal at Ketapang, and 11km north of town. Buses from here go to northern destinations, including Baluran (1000 rp, one hour), Probolinggo (6000/12,000 rp patas, four hours) for Gunung Bromo, Surabaya (9500/17,500 rp bisnis/eksekutif, six hours/five hours) and Malang (9500/17,500 rp). Buses also go right through to Yogyakarta, Jakarta and Denpasar (5000/10,000 to 15,000 rp, four hours including the ferry trip).

A few long-distance buses from Seri Tanjung take the southern route via Jember, but Terminal Brawijaya (also known as Karang Ente), 4km south of town, has most of the buses to the south, including Kalipahit (2200 rp, 1½ hours), Pesanggaran (2300 rp, two hours) and Jember (3200/6500 rp air-con, three hours).

**Train** The main train station is just a few hundred metres north of the ferry terminal at Ketapang. Most trains also stop at the Argopuro and Karang Asem train stations, on the northern and eastern outskirts of Banyuwangi respectively, but it is hard to get public transport to either.

The express *Mutiara Timur* leaves at 9.30 am and 10 pm for Probolinggo (15,000/25,000 rp in bisnis/eksekutif rp, four hours) and Surabaya (15,000/28,000 rp, six hours). Ekonomi trains include the *Blambangan* to Probolinggo at 1.05 pm, the *Regganis* to Malang (4500 rp, eight hours), the slow *Sri Tanjung* to Yogyakarta (14,000 rp, 13 hours) and the *Pandanwangi* to Jember (1700 rp, 3½ hours) via Kalibaru (1100 rp, two hours) at 5.30 pm. All trains take the southern route via Jember and on to Probolinggo. Trains can be very crowded at peak travel times, particularly Sunday.

**Boat** Ferries from Ketapang depart roughly every half hour around the clock for Gilimanuk on Bali. The ferry costs 1400 rp for passengers, 3600 rp for motorcycles and 18,000 rp for cars. Through buses between Bali and Java include the fare in the bus ticket and are the easiest option. Otherwise, check the buses on the ferry for a spare seat.

**EAST JAVA**

At Gilimanuk, it is 2km to the terminal by bemo or ojek (500 rp), and the ekonomi buses from Gilimanuk to Denpasar (5000 rp) can take a long time to fill up.

Pelni's *Tatamailau* stops in Banyuwangi on its route to Nusa Tenggara and Irian Jaya. It docks at Ketapang, along from the Bali ferry dock.

## Getting Around

Banyuwangi has a squadron of minibuses running between the bus terminals and ending at the Blambangan minibus terminal near the centre of town; they're marked Lin 1, 2, 3 etc, and charge a fixed 500 rp fare around town, or 800 rp from the ferry terminal. Lin 6 or 12 runs from Blambangan to the ferry terminal and on to the Terminal Seri Tanjung bus terminal. Lin 2 goes from Blambangan to the Hotel Baru area. Lin 3 goes from Blambangan to Sasak Perot, where you get colts to the Ijen Plateau. Private cars at the ferry terminal act as taxis but are expensive and not always easy to find.

## KALIKLATAK

Kaliklatak, 20km north of Banyuwangi, is another 'agrotourism' venture to tour large coffee, cocoa, rubber, coconut and clove plantations. *Wisata Irdjen Guesthouse (Kaliklatak ☎ 424061, Banyuwangi ☎ 424896)* offers excellent accommodation but is expensive and must be booked in advance.

## BALURAN NATIONAL PARK

On the north-east corner of Java, Baluran National Park covers an area of 250 sq km. Gunung Baluran (1247m), in the centre of the park, formerly overlooked extensive savanna grasslands. This explains the park's 'Indonesia's little bit of Africa' label. The park is still rich in wildlife, but the grasslands have gone, due to encroachment by Acacia thorn scrub. The park has undertaken major programs to eliminate the acacia, which was planted as a firebreak in the late 1970s, and a large area has been cleared to regenerate grass, but only scrubby growth has ensued.

Baluran supports internationally important populations of bantengs and ajags, plus rusa deer, muntjak (barking) deer, two species of monkey, wild pigs, leopards and other smaller carnivores. The bird population is depleted due to extensive illegal trapping for the caged-bird trade; however, green peafowl, red and green junglefowl, hornbills and bee-eaters are still easy to see.

On the hill above the guesthouses at Bekol is a viewing tower that has a panoramic view over a 300 hectare clearing. Banteng and rusa groups can be seen here and (if you are lucky) wild dogs can be seen hunting rusa, usually in the early morning. There are walking trails around Bekol.

From Bekol, you can walk or drive the 3km to Bama on the coast. Bama has accommodation and a half-decent beach where you can snorkel. The nearby coastal forest (follow the stony tracks) has numerous waterholes and is a good place to see water monitor lizards, monkeys and birds.

The main service town for Baluran is Wonorejo, on the main coast road between Surabaya and Banyuwangi, where food supplies can be bought – the PHPA office and visitor centre is on the highway. If you're not staying overnight, baggage can be left safely at the PHPA office. The park entry fee is 2000 rp.

Baluran can be visited at any time of the year, but the dry season (June to November) is usually the best time, as the animals congregate near the waterholes at Bekol and Bama. Recently, park projects, particularly those that allow villagers to harvest acacia seeds, have disrupted the wildlife. In view of this, the period between October and January (when the early rains cause new grass to sprout) may be the best time to see large mammals.

## Places to Stay

At Bekol, 12km into the park, the *Pesanggrahan* has seven rooms and costs 6000 rp per person; there's a mandi and kitchen, but you must bring your own provisions. *Wisma Tamu* next door has three very comfortable rooms with attached mandi for 10,000 rp per person, and the *Pondok Peneliti* costs 12,500 rp. The *canteen* at Bekol sells drinks and some provisions, but meals are cooked only for groups if advance notice is given. You might be able to arrange something with the PHPA staff, but bring your own food.

*Bama Guesthouse* is 3km east of Bekol on the beach and provides rooms for 6000 rp per person. It also has cooking facilities if you bring your own food. The newer *Rumah Panggung* is nearer the waterhole.

Bookings can be made in advance at the Baluran PHPA office in Banyuwangi or through the Baluran PHPA (☎ 0333-461 650). Most visitors tend to day trip, so accommodation is not usually full, but it pays to book, especially in the main June/July holiday period when school groups visit the park.

## Getting There & Away

Surabaya to Banyuwangi buses, taking the coast road via Probolinggo, can drop you right at the park entrance. Also, when leaving the park, these buses are easily flagged down. From Banyuwangi (or Ketapang ferry, if you're coming from Bali), it's only a half hour journey on the Wonorejo bus, which costs 1000 rp. Ask the driver to let you off at the park, and at the entrance ask a PHPA ranger to arrange an ojek (7,500 rp) to take you the 12km to Bekol along the badly rutted road. A private car (20,000 rp) can be arranged, but the park has no vehicles of its own. Coming from the west, Baluran is 3½ hours from Probolinggo/Gunung Bromo.

# Language

Java's three main languages are Javanese, which is spoken by nearly 60% of the people in central and eastern Java (or over one-third of the people of Indonesia), Sundanese, which is spoken in western Java, and Madurese, which is spoken on the island of Madura and in the eastern part of Java near Madura. Outside Jakarta and other main cities, these regional languages are often used in preference to Indonesian. Although these languages all belong to the Malayo-Polynesian branch of the Austronesian language family, they are mutually unintelligible.

Indonesian, or Bahasa Indonesia (*bahasa* means language), is the official national language of Indonesia and is spoken as a second language by most Javanese. It has become the language of government, commerce and education. In towns and cities people will often use Indonesian when speaking to others they don't know well, as it's considered a more appropriate language for formal communication and a preferable alternative to the complications and deferences of Javanese. In the villages and among older people, Indonesian is not always fluently spoken, but all educated people speak Indonesian proficiently. English is also widely spoken, particularly in the main tourist areas. It is taught in secondary schools, therefore young people will usually have at least a basic knowledge. Dutch is common among many of the older generation.

In addition to these main languages, various dialects are spoken in Java. Osing, a mixture of Javanese and Balinese, is spoken in the very east of Java, around Banyuwangi. It's closely related to Tenggerese, the language of the Hindu Tengger people of the Gunung Bromo area. In West Java, the isolated Badui tribe speaks a form of Old Sundanese. In Jakarta, the Orang Betawi (the original Indonesian inhabitants of the city during the Dutch colonial rule of the 19th century) used Malay as the common language of communication. The Betawi developed their own dialect, which uses some Jakartan slang. Many Betawi words have been incorporated into Bahasa Indonesia.

While it's fun to learn some words of the regional languages, travellers are much better off putting their efforts into learning Bahasa Indonesia, which is invaluable for travel off the beaten track.

## JAVANESE

Traditional Javanese society is hierarchical, and great importance is placed on politeness, humility and deference to superiors. This is not especially evident in the language, where different levels of speech are used between people according to their class, age, occupation, wealth etc. This hierarchical structure is comparable to Japanese but, linguistically, Javanese is related to Austronesian languages spoken throughout the Malay peninsula, Indonesia and the Philippines. It has a literature dating back to the 8th century and its own Indianised script, though Roman script is now more commonly used. The Old Javanese used in literature is called *kawi*.

The three main levels of modern Javanese are *krama*, *madya* and *ngoko* – high, middle and low. Pronouns, forms of address, and some verbs, nouns, prepositions etc change between these levels, depending on the relative status of the speakers. Someone of high status speaking to someone of low status will use *ngoko*, while the other will use the more formal *krama*. These levels are broken down into further levels and nuances of status. Another form of Javanese, *basongan*, is only used in the kratons of Yogya and Solo.

*Ngoko* and *krama* are the main forms used, though *ngoko* is most commonly used informally between friends and equals.

If two strangers of indeterminate status address each other there can be a quite complicated interchange of language as the speakers try to determine the correct level to use. Little wonder that most Javanese prefer to use Bahasa Indonesia for such exchanges rather than risk causing offence. There have also been attempts to reform the language by simply using *ngoko* to rid it of this feudal-like structure, which was inherited from the Hindu court tradition, and to make it more suitable for modern life.

## Javanese Dialects

Spoken Javanese varies from region to region. The *kejawen* dialect of Yogya and Solo is considered the most refined and correct. The more complex and varied levels of the language are used, and 'a' is pronounced halfway between 'a' and 'o', like 'aw'. Hence 'a' and 'o' are often interchangeable in the written language, so that *Solo* may also be written as *Sala*. Consonant formations include placing 'm' before 'b' (as in *mbak*, the polite word for addressing a woman). In the pasisir coastal district to the north, the dialect is similar but speech levels are simplified.

Javanese is also spoken farther along the coast in West Java, around Cirebon and Banten, where the Sundanese influence is noticeable. The Cirebon dialect is closer to Sundanese in pronunciation.

To the east, the arek dialect of the Surabaya region is considered very coarse, and krama is not used. Farther east along the coast, Madurese is the dominant language, while in the south-east corner of the Blambangan district, the Balinese influence is more pronounced.

## BAHASA INDONESIA

Bahasa Indonesia is almost identical to Malay. Pure Malay, as spoken by the Malaysians, is confined in Indonesia to Sumatra, but it has long been the common language of the Indonesian archipelago, having been the language of inter-island trade for centuries. Bahasa Indonesia is a relatively new language in Indonesia, but since independence its usage and complexity have expanded dramatically, through the media and its role as the linking language.

For the visitor who wants to pick up just enough to get by, Indonesian is very easy to

learn. Its pronunciation is uncomplicated, it uses the roman alphabet, there are no verb conjugations, genders or articles (the/an/a), and often one word can convey the meaning of a whole sentence.

You can learn enough Bahasa Indonesia to get by within a month. Once you get deep into the language it's as complicated as any other, but for everyday use it's easy to learn and pronounce.

Bahasa Indonesia is as its most developed in Java. Many people speak it fluently, with a wide vocabulary and developed grammar, but allowances are always made for those who take the time and trouble to learn Bahasa Indonesia, and Indonesians are delighted to hear foreigners speak their language.

A pronunciation guide to the language is shown here and we have also included some basic words and phrases. If you want a more comprehensive overview of Indonesian, see Lonely Planet's *Indonesian phrasebook*.

## Pronunciation

| | |
|---|---|
| a | as in 'father' |
| e | as in 'bet' when unstressed; when stressed, as the 'a' in 'may' |
| I | as the 'i' in 'marine' |
| o | as in 'bow' |
| u | as in 'flute' |
| ai | as in 'Thai' |
| au | a long 'ow', as in 'cow' |
| ua | at the start of a word, as 'w', eg *uang* (money), pronounced 'wang' |

The pronunciation of consonants is very straightforward. Most sound like their English counterparts, except:

| | |
|---|---|
| c | as the 'ch' in 'chair' |
| g | as in 'garden' |
| ng | as in 'singer' |
| ngg | as the 'ng' in 'anger' |
| j | as in 'join' |
| r | trilled, as in Spanish *pero* |
| h | like English 'h', but a bit stronger; almost silent at the end of a word |
| k | like English 'k', except at the end of the word, when it's more a closing of |

the throat with no sound, eg, *tidak* (no/not), pronounced 'tee-dah'

**ny** as the 'ny' in 'canyon'

## Stress

There is no strong stress in Indonesian, and nearly all syllables have equal emphasis. A general rule is to stress the second-last syllable. The main exception to this is the unstressed 'e' in words such as *besar* (big), pronounced 'be-SARRR'.

## Pronouns

| | |
|---|---|
| I | *Saya* |
| you | *anda* |
| he/she/it | *dia/ia* |
| we | *kita/kami* |
| they | *mereka* |

Pronouns are often dropped when the meaning is clear from context. As in the Javanese language, it is proper to show deference, especially to age, when using the second person. Speaking to an older man (especially anyone old enough to be your father) or to show respect, it's common to call him *bapak* (father) or simply *pak*. Similarly, for an older woman use *ibu* (mother) or simply *bu*.

*Mas* (older brother) is widely used in Java for a younger man, and *mbak* is the female equivalent. *Tuan* is a respectful term for a male, like 'sir', though it has colonial connotations of 'boss', while *Nona* (Miss) and *Nyonya* (Mrs) are also used. *Kamu* and *engkau* are used only among friends or to address children. *Anda* is used in written language, and this more egalitarian form is sometimes used for equals.

## Greetings & Civilities

| | |
|---|---|
| Good morning. | *Selamat pagi.* (until 11 am) |
| Good day. | *Selamat siang.* (11 am to 3 pm) |
| Good afternoon. | *Selamat sore.* (3 to 7 pm) |
| Good evening. | *Selamat malam.* |
| Goodbye. (said by the person leaving) | *Selamat tinggal.* |
| Goodbye. (said by the person staying) | *Selamat jalan.* |
| Please. (asking for help) | *Tolong.* |
| Please open the door. | *Tolong buka pinta.* |
| Please. (giving permission) | *Silakan.* |
| Please come in. | *Silakan masuk.* |
| Thank you (very much). | *Terima kasih (banyak).* |
| It's nothing. (You're welcome.) | *Kembali, sama sama.* |
| Yes. | *Ya.* |
| No/Not. | *Tidak.* |
| | *Bukan.* (used to negate nouns and pronouns) |
| I'm sorry. | *Ma'af.* |
| Excuse me. | *Permisi.* |
| Welcome. | *Selamat datang.* |
| How are you? | *Apa kabar?* |
| I'm fine. | *Kabar baik.* |
| What's your name? | *Siapa nama anda?* |
| My name is ... | *Nama saya ...* |
| Where are you from? | *Dari mana asal saudara?* |
| I'm from ... | *Saya dari ...* |
| Are you married? | *Sudah kawin?* |
| I'm not married yet. | *Saya belum kawin.* |
| I'm married. | *Saya sudah kawin.* |
| I (don't) like ... | *Saya (tidak) suka ...* |
| Good/Fine/OK. | *baik* |
| Great! | *bagus!* |

## Language Difficulties

| | |
|---|---|
| Do you speak English? | *Bisa berbicara bahasa Inggris?* |
| I understand. | *Saya mengerti.* |
| I don't understand. | *Saya tidak mengerti.* |
| What does this mean? | *Apa artinya ini?* |
| Please write that word down. | *Tolong tuliskan kata itu.* |

## Getting Around

| | |
|---|---|
| I want to go to ... | *Saya mau pergi ke ...* |
| Where is ...? | *Di mana ada ...?* |
| Which way? | *Ke mana?* |
| How many kilometres? | *Berapa kilometer?* |

## Bahasa Indonesia/Sunda/Jawa

Here are some common greetings and words, which travellers may find useful in basic communication and for deciphering place names. The words for greetings and civilities reflect the 'higher' or more polite levels of speech (*krama* in Javanese), while the words in Sundanese and Indonesian are from the more familiar or 'low' form (*ngoko* in Javanese). Where words of both levels are given, the higher form appears in brackets.

| English | Indonesian | Sundanese | Javanese |
|---|---|---|---|
| Thank you. | *Terima kasih.* | *Hatur nuhun.* | *Matur nuhun.* |
| You're welcome. | *Kembali.* | *Sami sami.* | *Sami sami.* |
| Please (giving permission) | *Silakan.* | *Mangga.* | *Monggo.* |
| Sorry. | *Ma'af.* | *Hapunten.* | *Ngapunten.* |
| Great! | *Bagus!* | *Sae!* | *Sae!* |
| Yes. | *Ya.* | *Sumuhun.* | *Inggih.* |
| No./not. | *Tidak/bukan.* | *Sanes.* | *Sanes.* |
| How are you? | *Apa kabar?* | *Kumaha damang?* | *Pripun kabaripun?* |
| I'm fine. | *Kabar baik.* | *Pangesto.* | *Pangestu.* |
| What's your name? | *Siapa nama anda?* | *Saha nami anjeun?* | *Sinten naminipuri panjenengan?* |
| My name is ... | *Nama saya ...* | *Nami simkuring ...* | *Nami kula ...* |
| north | *utara* | *kaler* | *lor* |
| south | *selatan* | *kidul* | *kidul* |
| east | *timur* | *wetan* | *wetan* |
| west | *barat* | *kulon* | *kulon* |
| beach | *pantai* | *sisi basisir* | *pesisir* |
| big | *besar* | *ageung* | *agung (gede)* |
| bridge | *jembatan* | *sasak* | *kreteg* |

What time does the ... leave/arrive? *Jam berapa ... berangkat/tiba?*
bus *bis*
train *kereta api*
ship *kapal*
aeroplane *pesawat terbang*

Stop here. *Berhenti disini.*
Straight on. *Terus.*
Turn right. *Belok kanan.*
Turn left. *Belok kiri.*
Please slow down. *Pelan-pelan.*
station *stasiun*
ticket *karcis/tiket*
first class *kelas satu*
economy class *kelas ekonomi*

Where can I hire a ...? *Dimana saya bisa sewa ...?*
car *mobil*
motorcycle *sepeda motor*
bicycle *sepeda*

## Accommodation

Where is a ...? *Dimana ada ...?*
hotel *hotel*
losmen *losmen*
cheap hotel *hotel yang murah*

Is there a room available? *Ada kamar kosong?*
What's the daily rate? *Berapa tarip hariannya?*

| | **Bahasa Indonesia/Sunda/Jawa** | | |
|---|---|---|---|
| **English** | **Indonesian** | **Sundanese** | **Javanese** |
| cave | *gua* | *guha* | *guwa* |
| (volcano) crater | *kawah* | *kawah* | *kawah* |
| forest | *hutan* | *leuweung* | *wono* |
| island | *pulau* | *pulo* | *pulo* |
| lake | *danau* | *situ, telaga* | *telaga* |
| mosque | *mesjid* | *mesjid/ mushola* | *mesjid* |
| mountain | *gunung* | *gunung* | *argo* |
| river | *sungai* | *walungan* | *kali* |
| road | *jalan* | *jalan* | *jalan (mergi)* |
| sand | *pasir* | *keusik* | *wedhi* |
| sea | *laut* | *basisir* | *segara* |
| waterfall | *air terjun* | *curug* | *grojogan* |
| 1 | *satu* | *hiji* | *siji (setunggal)* |
| 2 | *dua* | *dua* | *loro (kalih)* |
| 3 | *tiga* | *tilu* | *telu (tiga)* |
| 4 | *empat* | *opat* | *papat (sekawan)* |
| 5 | *lima* | *lima* | *lima (gangsal)* |
| 6 | *enam* | *genep* | *enem* |
| 7 | *tujuh* | *tujuh* | *pitu* |
| 8 | *delapan* | *dalapan* | *wolu* |
| 9 | *sembilan* | *salapan* | *songo* |
| 10 | *sepuluh* | *sapuluh* | *sepuluh (sedoso)* |
| 11 | *sebelas* | *sabelas* | *sewelas* |
| 100 | *seratus* | *saratus* | *satus (setunggalatus)* |
| 1000 | *seribu* | *sarebu* | *sewu (setunggalewu)* |
| 1,000,000 | *sejuta* | *sajuta* | *seyuta* |

| | |
|---|---|
| May I see the room? | *Boleh saya lihat kamar?* |
| Is there a better room? | *Ada kamar yang lebih bagus?* |
| I'd like to pay now. | *Saya mau bayar sekarang.* |
| for one day/week | *untuk satu hari/minggu* |
| for one/two people | *untuk satu/dua orang* |
| price list | *daftar harga* |
| bed | *ranjang/tempat tidur* |
| room | *kamar* |
| quiet room | *kamar tenang* |
| bathroom | *kamar mandi* |
| with private bath | *kamar mandi didalam* |
| with shared bath | *kamar mandi diluar* |

| | |
|---|---|
| air-con | *ac* (ah-say) |
| dirty | *kotor* |
| key/lock | *kunci* |
| noisy | *ribut* |
| sheet | *seprei* |
| towel | *handuk* |

**Around Town**

| | |
|---|---|
| Where's a/the ...? | *dimana ada ...?* |
| bank | *bank* |
| chemist/pharmacy | *apotek* |
| market | *pasar* |
| police station | *kantor polisi* |
| post office | *kantor pos* |
| postage stamp | *perangko* |
| public phone | *telepon umum* |

## Javanese Script

Javanese is now often written in roman script, through the traditional script is still used. Javanese script is based on the Devanegari script of South India and the Buddhist Pali script used in Sri Lanka and adapted by many South-East Asian languages. Javanese script has evolved through many incarnations into its modern form.

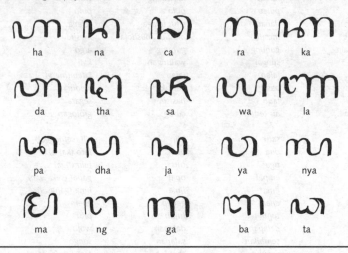

| | | | | |
|---|---|---|---|---|
| ha | na | ca | ra | ka |
| da | tha | sa | wa | la |
| pa | dha | ja | ya | nya |
| ma | ng | ga | ba | ta |

| | | | |
|---|---|---|---|
| restaurant | *rumah makan* | Can you lower the | *Boleh kurang?* |
| telephone number | *nomor telepon* | price? | |
| public toilet | *WC umum* (way say) | | |
| tourist office | *dinas pariwisata* | open/closed | *buka/tutup* |
| town square | *alun-alun* | too big | *terlalu besar* |
| | | too small | *terlalu kecil* |
| What time does it | *Jam berapa buka/* | more | *lebih* |
| open/close? | *tutup?* | less | *kurang* |
| What is the | *Berapa kursnya?* | cigarettes | *rokok* |
| exchange rate? | | clothing | *pakaian* |
| | | film (for camera) | *filem* |
| **Shopping** | | map | *peta* |
| Where is the/a ...? | *Dimana ada ...?* | matches | *korek api* |
| bookshop | *toko buku* | mosquito coil | *obat nyamuk* |
| grocery | *toko makanan* | mosquito net | *kelambu* |
| market | *pasar* | postage stamp | *perangko* |
| | | sanitary pads | *softex* |
| I want to buy ... | *Saya mau beli ...* | soap | *sabun* |
| What is this/that? | *Apa ini/itu?* | sunblock cream | *pabanox* |
| How much is it? | *Berapa harga?* | telephone card | *kartu telepon* |
| That's very | *Mahal sekali.* | toilet paper | *kertas wc* |
| expensive. | | toothpaste | *pasta gigi* |

## Time, Days & Months

| | |
|---|---|
| What is the time? | *Jam berapa?* |
| 7 o'clock | *jam tujuh* |
| 5 o'clock | *jam lima* |
| How many hours? | *Berapa jam?* |
| five hours | *lima jam* |
| When? | *Kapan?* |
| today | *hari ini* |
| tomorrow | *besok* |
| yesterday | *kemarin* |
| rubber time | *jam karet* |
| hour | *jam* |
| week | *minggu* |
| month | *bulan* |
| year | *tahun* |

| | |
|---|---|
| Monday | *Hari Senin* |
| Tuesday | *Hari Selasa* |
| Wednesday | *Hari Rabu* |
| Thursday | *Hari Kamis* |
| Friday | *Hari Jumat* |
| Saturday | *Hari Sabtu* |
| Sunday | *Hari Minggu* |

## Numbers

| | |
|---|---|
| 1 | *satu* |
| 2 | *dua* |
| 3 | *tiga* |
| 4 | *empat* |
| 5 | *lima* |
| 6 | *enam* |
| 7 | *tujuh* |
| 8 | *delapan* |
| 9 | *sembilan* |
| 10 | *sepuluh* |

After the numbers one to 10, the 'teens' are *belas*, the 'tens' are *puluh*, the 'hundreds' are *ratus* and the 'thousands' *ribu*. Thus:

| | |
|---|---|
| 11 | *sebelas* |
| 12 | *duabelas* |
| 13 | *tigabelas* |
| 20 | *duapuluh* |
| 21 | *duapuluh satu* |
| 25 | *duapuluh lima* |

### Emergencies

| | |
|---|---|
| Help! | *Tolong!* |
| Call a doctor! | *Panggil dokter!* |
| Call the police! | *Panggil polisi!* |
| It's an emergency! | *Keadaan darurat!* |
| I'm sick. | *Saya sakit.* |
| I'm lost. | *Saya kesasar.* |
| Thief! | *Pencuri!* |
| Fire! | *Kebakaran!* |
| Go away! | *Pergi!* |
| hospital | *rumah sakit* |

| | |
|---|---|
| 30 | *tigapuluh* |
| 90 | *sembilanpuluh* |
| 99 | *sembilanpuluh sembilan* |
| 100 | *seratus* |
| 200 | *duaratus* |
| 250 | *duaratus limapuluh* |
| 254 | *duaratus limapuluh empat* |
| 888 | *delapanratus delapanpuluh delapan* |
| 1000 | *seribu* |
| 1050 | *seribu limapuluh* |
| one million | *sejuta* |

A half is *setengah*, which is pronounced 'stengah', eg half a kilo is *stengah kilo*. 'Approximately' is *kira-kira*.

## Health

| | |
|---|---|
| My ... hurts. | *... saya sakit.* |
| I feel nauseous. | *Saya mau muntah.* |
| I feel dizzy. | *Saya merasa pusing.* |
| I'm pregnant. | *Saya hamil.* |

| | |
|---|---|
| I'm allergic to ... | *Saya alergi ...* |
| penicillin | *penisilin* |
| antibiotics | *antibiotika* |

| | |
|---|---|
| dentist | *dokter gigi* |
| doctor | *dokter* |
| hospital | *rumah sakit* |
| medicine | *obat* |

# Glossary

**ABRI** – Angkatan Bersenjata Republik Indonesia; the Indonesian armed forces
**adat** – traditional laws and regulations
**agama** – religion
**agung** – high, noble
**air** – water
**Airlangga** – 11th century king of considerable historical and legendary importance in East Java
**air panas** – hot springs
**air terjun** – waterfall
**ajag** – wild, native dog, an endangered species found primarily in the national parks of East Java
**alun alun** – main public square of a town or village. They are usually found in front of the residence of the *bupati* (governor) and were traditionally meeting areas and the place to hold public ceremonies. Nowadays they tend to be deserted, open grassed areas.
**anak** – child
**andong** – horse-drawn passenger cart
**angklung** – Sundanese musical instrument made of differing lengths and thicknesses of bamboo suspended in a frame
**angkot** or **angkota** – short for *angkutan kota* (city transport), these small minibuses ply city routes
**angkudes** – short for *angkutan pedesaan* (village transport), these minibuses run to nearby villages from the cities, or villages
**anjing** – dog
**Arjuna** – hero of the *Mahabharata* epic
**Ayodya** – Rama's kingdom in the *Ramayana*

**Bahasa Indonesia** – Indonesia's national language
**bajaj** – motorised rickshaw taxi found in Jakarta
**banyan** – see *waringin*
**bapak** – father; also a polite form of address to any older man
**barat** – west
**batik** – cloth made by coating part of it with wax, then dyeing it and melting the wax out. The waxed part is not coloured and repeated waxings and dyeings builds up a pattern.
**becak** – trishaw (bicycle-rickshaw)
**bemo** – minibus, a form of popular local transport. Originally a small, three wheeled pickup with a bench seat down each side in the back, these have all but disappeared in favour of small minibuses. The term bemo is now not commonly used but still widely understood.
**bensin** – petrol

**bis** – bus
**bouraq** – winged horse-like creature with the head of a woman; also the name of the domestic airline which mostly services the outer islands
**Brahma** – the creator; one of the trinity of Hindu gods, along with Shiva and Vishnu
**bukit** – hill
**bupati** – government official in charge of a regency (*kabupaten*)

**camat** – government official in charge of a district (*kecamatan*)
**candi** – shrine, or temple, usually an ancient Hindu or Buddhist temple of Javanese design
**candi bentar** – split gateway entrance to a Hindu temple
**cap** – metal stamp used to apply motifs to batik
**cipanas** – hot spring, from the Sundanese for 'hot water'

**dalang** – storyteller of varied skills and considerable endurance who operates the puppets, tells the story and beats time in a wayang kulit shadow puppet performance
**danau** – lake
**dangdut** – very popular modern music, influenced by the Indian pop music of Hindi films, with a strong beat and wavering vocals
**Dewi Sri** – rice goddess
**dinas pariwisata** – tourist office
**dokar** – horse cart, still a popular form of local transport in many towns and villages
**dukun** – practitioner of magic, usually a faith healer, herbal doctor or mystic
**dwipa mulia** – moneychanger

**Gajah Mada** – famous Majapahit prime minister
**gamelan** – traditional Javanese orchestra, usually almost solely percussion, with large xylophones and gongs
**Ganesh** – Shiva's elephant-headed son
**gang** – alley or footpath
**Garuda** – mythical man-bird, the vehicle of Vishnu and the modern symbol of Indonesia; this is also the name of Indonesia's international airline
**gereja** – church
**gua** – cave. The old spelling, *goa*, is also common.
**gunung** – mountain
**gunung api** – volcano (literally 'fire mountain')

**haji, haja** – Muslim who has made the pilgrimage *(haj)* to Mecca. Many Indonesians save all their lives to make the haj, and a *haji* (man) or *haja* (woman) commands great respect in the village.

**halus** – 'refined', high standards of behaviour and art; characters in wayang kulit performances are traditionally either *halus* or *kasar*

**harga biasa** – usual price

**harga touris** – tourist price

**helicak** – motorcycle taxi found in Jakarta

**homestay** – small family-run losmen

**hutan** – forest, jungle

**ibu** – mother; also polite form of address to any older woman; often shortened to *bu*

**ikat** – cloth in which the pattern is produced by dyeing the individual threads before weaving

**Jaipongan** – relatively modern, West Javanese dance based on Ketuktilu and danced by hostesses in nightclubs

**jalan** – street or road; Jl is abbreviation

**jalan jalan** – to go for a stroll

**jalan potong** – short cut

**jam karet** – 'rubber time'

**jamu** – herbal medicine; most tonics go under this name and are supposed to cure everything from menstrual problems to baldness

**kabupaten** – regency

**kain** – cloth

**kaki lima** – mobile food carts; literally 'five feet' – the three feet of the cart and the two of the vendor

**kamar kecil** – toilet, the traditional variety being a hole in the ground with footrests either side

**kampung** – village, neighbourhood

**kantor** – office, as in *kantor imigrasi* (immigration office) or *kantor pos* (post office)

**kasar** – rough, coarse, crude; opposite of *halus*

**Kawi** – classical Javanese, the old language of literature

**kebatinan** – Javanese mysticism or theosophical movement

**kebaya** – Chinese long-sleeved blouse with plunging front and embroidered edges. Traditional dress for a Javanese woman is kebaya and sarong.

**kebun** – garden

**kecapi** – Sundanese (West Javanese) lute

**kejawen** – 'Javanese knowledge', the term is more commonly used to designate the region around the courts of Yogyakarta and Solo, the centre of Javanese thought and culture

**kepala desa** – village head

**kepala stasiun** – station master

**kepiting** – crab

**ketoprak** – popular Javanese folk theatre

**ketuktilu** – traditional Sundanese dance in which professional female dancers (sometimes prostitutes) dance for male spectators

**kijang** – a type of deer; also a very popular brand of Toyota car, which is a cross between a family sedan and an off-road vehicle, often used for taxis

**KKN** – the acronym for Korupsi, Kolusi and Nepotisme (Corruption, Collusion and Nepotism). One of the buzz words of the post-Soeharto reform era, everyone claims to be trying to stamp out KKN.

**Konfrontasi** – catchphrase of the early 1960s when Soekarno embarked on a confrontational campaign against western imperialism, and expansionist policies in the region, aimed at Malaysia

**KORPRI** – Korp Pegawai Republik Indonesia; the Indonesian bureaucracy

**kraton** – walled city palace and traditionally the centre of Javanese culture. The most famous and influential kratons are those of Yogyakarta and Solo.

**kretek** – Indonesian clove cigarette

**kris** – wavy-bladed traditional dagger, often held to have spiritual or magical powers

**krisis moneter** – monetary krisis, often shortened to *krismon*

**KSDA** – Konservasi & Sumber Daya Alam; ie National Parks office

**ladang** – non-irrigated field, often using slash-and-burn agriculture, for dry-land crops

**langsam** – crowded, peak-hour commuter train to the big cities

**lapangan** – field, square

**laut** – sea, ocean

**lesahan** – traditional style of dining on straw mats

**losmen** – basic accommodation, usually cheaper than hotels and often family-run

***Mahabharata*** – great Hindu holy book, telling of the battle between the Pandavas and the Korawas

**Majapahit** – last great Hindu dynasty in Java, pushed out of Java into Bali by the rise of Islamic power

**mandi** – usual Indonesian form of bath, consisting of a large water tank from which you ladle water to pour over yourself like a shower

**Merpati** – Indonesia's major domestic airline

**meru** – multi-roofed shrines in Hindu temples and many old Javanese mosques; they take their name from the Hindu holy mountain, Mahameru.

**mesjid** – mosque

**mikrolet** – small taxi; a tiny *opelet*

**menara** – minaret, tower

**muezzin** – those who call the faithful to the mosque
**muncak** – 'barking deer' found on Java

**naga** – mythical snake-like creature

**ojek** – (or *ojeg* in West Java) motorcycle that takes passengers
**opelet** – small intra-city minibus, usually with side benches in the back

**Padang** – city and region of Sumatra that has exported its cuisine to all corners of Indonesia. See also *nasi Padang* in the food section of this glossary.
**pak** – shortened form of bapak
**parkir** – a parking attendant. Anywhere a car is parked, these often self-appointed attendants will be on hand to find drivers a parking spot, look after their cars and stop traffic while they back out, all for a mere 300 rp or so tip. They may also do the job of traffic cops, blowing their whistles and directing traffic for small gratuities thrown by passing motorists.
**pasanggrahan** – or pesanggrahan – lodge for government officials where travellers can usually stay
**pasar** – market
**pasar malam** – night market
**pasisir** – 'coast', specifically the north coast of Java, where pasisir culture is more traditionally Islamic and influenced by trade and external contact
**patas** – express bus
**peci** – black Muslim felt cap
**pelabuhan** – harbour, port, dock; also *bandar*
**pelan pelan** – slowly
**Pelni** – Pelayaran Nasional Indonesia, the national shipping line with passenger ships operating throughout the archipelago
**pemuda** – youth
**pencak silat** – form of martial arts originally from Sumatra, but now popular throughout Indonesia
**pendopo** – large, open-sided pavilion in front of a Javanese palace serving as an audience hall
**penginapan** – simple lodging house
**Pertamina** – huge state-owned oil company
**PHPA** – Perlindungan Hutan dan Pelestarian Alam; the Directorate General of Forest Protection and Nature Conservation, which manages Indonesia's national parks
**pesantren** – religious schools
**pinisi** – Makassar or Bugis schooner
**pompa bensin** – petrol station
**pondok** – guesthouse or lodge (also called *pondok wisata*); hut

**prahu** – traditional Indonesian outrigger boat
**priyayi** – aristocratic, old ruling class of Java
**pulau** – island
**pusaka** – sacred heirlooms of a royal family

**rafflesia** – gigantic flower found in Sumatra, with blooms spreading up to a metre
**raja** – king or lord
**Ramadan** – Muslim month of fasting, when devout Muslims refrain from eating, drinking and smoking during daylight hours
**Ramayana** – one of the great Hindu holy books; stories from the *Ramayana* form the keystone of many Balinese and Javanese dances and tales
**rattan** – see *rotan*
**Ratu Adil** – the Just Prince who, by Javanese prophecy, will return to liberate Indonesia from oppression
**rebab** – two stringed bowed lute
**rotan** – rattan; hardy, pliable vine used for handcrafts and furniture
**rumah adat** – traditional house
**rumah makan** – restaurant or warung (eating house)
**rumah sakit** – hospital, literally 'sick house'

**santri** – orthodox, devout Muslim
**saron** – xylophone-like gamelan instrument, with bronze bars struck with a wooden mallet
**sarong** – or sarung; all-purpose cloth, often sewed into a tube, and worn by women, men and children
**sawah** – an individual rice field, or the wet-rice method of cultivation
**selat** – strait
**selatan** – south
**Shiva** – one of the trinity of Hindu gods, along with Brahma and Vishnu
**sirih** – betel nut, chewed as a mild narcotic
**situ** – lake (Sundanese)
**slametan** – Javanese ritual feast in which neighbours and family are invited to celebrate and commune at a birth, name ceremony etc
**suling** – bamboo flute
**stasiun** – station
**Sunda** – West Java, home of the Sundanese people
**sungai** – river
**susuhunan** – king
**syahbandar** – harbour master

**taman** – ornamental garden, park, reserve
**taman nasional** – national park
**tari topeng** – type of masked dance peculiar to the Cirebon area
**tarling** – musical style of the Cirebon area, featuring guitar, suling and voice

**telaga** – lake
**teluk** – bay
**topeng** – wooden mask used in dances

**uang** – money
**udang** – prawn
**ular** – snake
**utara** – north

**Vishnu** – one of the trinity of Hindu gods
**VOC** – Vereenigde Oost-Indische Compagnie (United East India Company); the name of the Dutch trading monopoly established by the government to secure trade in the East Indies and represent Dutch interests. It was finally disbanded in 1799, when the Dutch government assumed direct control of its operations and territories in Indonesia.

**wali songo** – nine saints who brought Islam to Java
**waringin** – banyan tree; a large and shady tree with drooping branches which root and can produce new trees. It was under a banyan (bo) tree that Buddha achieved enlightenment. Waringin are found at ancient temples and many *alun alun.*
**Warposnet** – privately contracted Internet service found in post offices in main cities
**warpostel/warparpostel** – private post and telephone agency
**warung** – food stall; Indonesian equivalent to a combination of corner shop and snack bar
**wayang kulit** – shadow-puppet play
**wayang orang** – Javanese theatre or 'people wayang'
**wayang topeng** – masked dance drama
**wayang wong** – Javanese for wayang orang
**wisma** – guesthouse or lodge

# FOOD
## Menus

The following is a list of words which may be useful when ordering in a restaurant:

**asam manis** – sweet and sour
**bakar** – barbecued, roasted
**blimbing** – starfruit
**bon** – the bill
**bumbu** – combination of pounded ingredients used to flavour dishes
**daftar makanan** – the menu
**dingin** – cold
**durian** – fruit that 'smells like hell, tastes like heaven'
**Enak!** – Delicious!

**garpu** – fork
**goreng** – fried
**kelapa** – coconut
**makan** – to eat
**makanan** – food
**minuman** – drink
**minum** – to drink
**makan pagi** – breakfast
**makan siang** – lunch
**makan malam** – dinner
**nasi bungkos** – take-away food
**manis** – sweet
**nanas** – pineapple
**panas** – hot (temperature)
**pedas** – spicy hot
**pisau** – knife
**rebus** – boiled
**Saya mau makan** – I want to eat at ...
**sendok** – spoon

## Javanese dishes
These are some of the dishes you are likely to encounter in Java:

**abon** – spiced and shredded dried meat often sprinkled over *nasi rames* or *nasi rawon*
**acar** – pickle; cucumber or other vegetables in a mixture of vinegar, salt, sugar and water
**apam** – delicious pancake filled with nuts and sprinkled with sugar
**ayam** – chicken; *ayam goreng* is fried chicken

**babi** – pork. Since most Indonesians are Muslim, pork is generally only found in market stalls and restaurants run by Chinese, and in areas where there are non-Muslim populations, such as Bali, Irian Jaya and Tanatoraja in Sulawesi.
**bakmi** – rice-flour noodles, either fried *(bakmi goreng)* or in soup
**bakso** or **ba'so** – meatball soup
**bawang** – onion
**bubur ayam** – Indonesian porridge with chicken. The porridge is generally sweetened and made from rice, black sticky rice or mung beans.
**bubur kacang** – mung bean porridge cooked in coconut milk
**buncis** – beans

**cap cai** – pronounced 'chap chai', is a Chinese mix of fried vegetables, although it sometimes comes with meat as well.
**cassava** – known as tapioca to westerners, this is a long, thin, dark brown root which looks something like a shrivelled turnip
**cumi cumi** – squid

**daging babi** – pork
**daging kambing** – goat or mutton
**daging sapi** – beef

**emping** – is made of the seeds of the melinjo fruit *(gnetum-gnemon)*, pounded flat, dried and fried to make a crisp chip and served as a snack with a main course
**es krim** – ice cream. You can get western brands and also locally manufactured varieties.

**fu yung hai** – a sort of sweet and sour omelette

**gado gado** – another very popular Indonesian dish of steamed bean sprouts, various vegetables and a spicy peanut sauce
**garam** – salt
**gula** – sugar
**gula gula** – lollies (sweets, candy)
**gulai/gule** – thick curried-meat broth with coconut milk

**ikan** – fish. Understandably, there's a wide variety to choose from in Indonesia: *ikan laut* is saltwater fish and *ikan danau* is freshwater fish. *Ikan asam manis* is sweet and sour fish and *ikan bakar* is barbecued fish. If you're buying fresh fish (you can often buy it at a market and get your hotel to cook it up), the gills should be a deep red colour, not brown, and the flesh should be firm to touch.
**ikan belut** – eels. Another Balinese delicacy; kids catch them in the rice paddies at night.

**jahe** – ginger

**kacang** – beans, *kacang tanah* is peanuts
**kacang hijau** – mung bean sprouts. These can be made into a sweet filling for cakes and buns.
**kare** – curry; as in *kare udang* (prawn curry)
**kecap asin** – salty soy sauce
**kecap manis** – sweet soy sauce
**keju** – cheese
**kentang** – potatoes; usually the size found in the west. Used in various ways, including dishes of Dutch origin and as a salad ingredient.
**kepiting** – crab; features in quite a few dishes, mostly of Chinese origin
**kodok** – frog
**kroket** – mashed potato cake with minced meat filling
**krupuk** – made of shrimp and cassava flour, or of fish flakes and rice dough, cut in slices and fried to a crisp
**kueh** – cake

**lombok** – chilli. There are various types: *lombok merah* (large, red); *lombok hijau* (large,

green); and *lombok rawit* (rather small but deadliest of them all, often packaged with *tahu* etc).
**lontong** – rice steamed in a banana leaf
**lumpia** – spring rolls; small pancake filled with shrimp and bean sprouts and fried

**madu** – honey
**martabak** – found on food trolleys all over the archipelago. A martabak is basically a pancake but there are two varieties. The one that seems to be everywhere is the sickeningly sweet version guaranteed to set your dentist's bank account soaring when you get back home. But (at least in Java) you can also get a delicious savoury martabak stuffed with meat, egg and vegetables. Some people think the sweet version isn't all that bad.
**mentega** – butter
**mentimun** – cucumber
**merica** – pepper
**mie goreng** – fried wheat-flour noodles, which are sometimes served with vegetables, sometimes with meat
**mie kuah** – noodle soup

**nasi campur** – steamed rice topped with a little bit of everything – some vegetables, some meat, a bit of fish, a krupuk or two – a good, usually tasty and filling meal
**nasi goreng** – this is the most common of Indonesian dishes; almost like hamburgers are to Americans, meat pies to Australians, fish and chips to the British – popular at any time of day, including breakfast time. Nasi goreng simply means fried *(goreng)* rice *(nasi)* – a basic nasi goreng may be little more than fried rice with a few scraps of vegetable to give it some flavour, but sometimes it includes meat. *Nasi goreng istimewa* (special) usually means nasi goreng with a fried egg on top. The dish can range from dull and dreary to very good.
**nasi gudeg** – unripe jackfruit cooked in *santan* (squeezed grated coconut) and served up with rice, pieces of chicken and spices
**nasi Padang** – Padang food, from the Padang region of Sumatra, is popular all over Indonesia. It's usually served cold and consists of the inevitable rice, with a whole variety of side dishes, including beef, fish, fried chicken, curried chicken, boiled cabbage, sometimes fish and prawns. The dishes are laid out before you and your final bill is calculated by the number of empty dishes when you've finished eating. Nasi Padang is traditionally eaten with the fingers and it's also traditionally very hot (*pedas* not *panas*) – sometimes hot enough to burn your fingers, let alone your tongue! It can be wonderful, and it can

be very dull. It's also one of the more expensive ways to eat in Indonesia and you generally end up spending a couple of thousand rupiah on a meal, although it can be well worth it.

**nasi pecel** – similar to gado gado, with boiled papaya leaves, tapioca, bean sprouts, string beans, fried soybean cake, fresh cucumber, coconut shavings and peanut sauce

**nasi putih** – white *(putih)* rice – usually steamed; glutinous rice is mostly used in snacks and cakes

**nasi rames** – rice with a combination of egg, vegetables, fish or meat

**nasi rawon** – rice with spicy hot beef soup, fried onions and spicy sauce. A speciality of East Java.

**nasi uduk** – rice boiled in coconut milk or cream

**opor ayam** – chicken cooked in coconut milk

**pete** – a huge broad bean, quite spicy, which is often served in the pod

**pisang goreng** – fried banana fritters; a popular streetside snack

**rijsttafel** – Dutch for 'rice table'; Indonesian food with a Dutch interpretation, it consists of lots of individual dishes with rice. Rather like a glorified *nasi campur* or a hot *nasi Padang*. Bring a big appetite.

**roti** – bread. The stuff you get in Indonesia is nearly always snow white and sweet.

**sago** – a starchy, low protein food extracted from a variety of palm tree. Sago is the staple diet of the Maluku islands.

**sambal** – a hot, spicy chilli sauce served as an accompaniment with most meals

**sate** – one of the best known of Indonesian dishes, sate (satay) are small pieces of meat on a skewer served with a spicy peanut sauce. Street sate sellers carry their charcoal grills around with them and cook the meat on the spot.

**saus tomat** – tomato sauce; ketchup

**sayur** – vegetable; *sayur-sayuran* is mixed vegetables and *sayur asem* is a sour vegetable soup

**sembal pedis** – hot sauce

**sop** – clear soup with mixed vegetables and meat or chicken

**soto** – meat and vegetable broth, often a main meal eaten with rice and a side dish of sambal

**tahu** – tofu, or soybean curd; soft bean cake made from soybean milk. It varies from white and yellow to thin and orange-skinned. Found as a

snack in food stalls and sometimes sold with a couple of hot chillies or a filling of vegetables

**telur** – egg

**tempe** – made of whole soybeans fermented into cake, wrapped in plastic or a banana leaf; rich in vegetable protein, iron and vitamin B. Tempe goreng is pieces of tempe (tempeh) fried with palm sugar and chillies.

**udang** – prawns or shrimps

**udang karang** – lobster

## DRINKS

Popular drinks, alcoholic and non-alcoholic include:

**air** – water. You may get a glass of it with a restaurant meal. It should have been boiled (and may not have cooled down since), but often it won't be boiled at all. Ask for *air putih* (literally white water) or drink tea. Hygienic bottled water is available everywhere.

**air jeruk** – citrus fruit juice. *Jeruk manis* is orange juice and *jeruk nipis* is lemon juice.

**air minum** – drinking water

**Aqua** – the most common brand of bottled water, costing around 1000 rp for a 1.5L bottle.

**es juice** – Although you should be a little careful about ice and water, the delicious fruit drinks are irresistible. Just take one or two varieties of tropical fruit, add crushed ice and pass it through a blender. You can make mind-blowing combinations of orange, banana, pineapple, mango, jackfruit, soursop or whatever else is available.

**es buah** – more a dessert than a drink; a curious combination of crushed ice, condensed milk, shaved coconut, syrup, jelly and fruit. Sickening say some, wonderful say others.

**Green Sands** – a pleasant soft drink, made not from sand, but from malt, apple and lime juice.

**kopi** – coffee. Excellent coffee is grown in Java. It is made, Turkish style, by pouring boiling water on finely ground coffee beans spooned into a glass. Served sweet and black with the coffee granules floating on top, it gives a real kick-start in the mornings. *Kopi susu* is white coffee, usually made with sweetened, condensed milk.

**stroop** – cordial

**susu** – milk; fresh milk is found in supermarkets in large cities, although long-life milk in cartons is more common. Fresh milk (*susu segar*) is served in warungs in Yogya and Solo.

**the** – tea, usually served weak, sweet and without milk. *Teh tawar* or *teh pahit* is tea without sugar and *teh manis*.

# LONELY PLANET

## Phrasebooks

**L**onely Planet phrasebooks are packed with essential words and phrases to help travellers communicate with the locals. With colour tabs for quick reference, an extensive vocabulary and use of script, these handy pocket-sized language guides cover day-to-day travel situations.

- handy pocket-sized books
- easy to understand Pronunciation chapter
- clear & comprehensive Grammar chapter
- romanisation alongside script to allow ease of pronunciation
- script throughout so users can point to phrases for every situation
- full of cultural information and tips for the traveller

'...vital for a real DIY spirit and attitude in language learning'
— *Backpacker*

'the phrasebooks have good cultural backgrounders and offer solid advice for challenging situations in remote locations'
— *San Francisco Examiner*

Arabic (Egyptian) • Arabic (Moroccan) • Australian *(Australian English, Aboriginal and Torres Strait languages)* • Baltic States *(Estonian, Latvian, Lithuanian)* • Bengali • Brazilian • British • Burmese • Cantonese • Central Asia • Central Europe *(Czech, French, German, Hungarian, Italian, Slovak)* • Eastern Europe *(Bulgarian, Czech, Hungarian, Polish, Romanian, Slovak)* • Ethiopian (Amharic) • Fijian • French • German • Greek • Hill Tribes • Hindi/Urdu • Indonesian • Italian • Japanese • Korean • Lao • Latin American Spanish • Malay • Mandarin • Mediterranean Europe *(Albanian, Croatian, Greek, Italian, Macedonian, Maltese, Serbian, Slovene)* • Mongolian • Nepali • Papua New Guinea • Pilipino (Tagalog) • Quechua • Russian • Scandinavian Europe *(Danish, Finnish, Icelandic, Norwegian, Swedish)* • South-East Asia *(Burmese, Indonesian, Khmer, Lao, Malay, Tagalog Pilipino, Thai, Vietnamese)* • South Pacific Languages • Spanish (Castilian) *(also includes Catalan, Galician and Basque)* • Sri Lanka • Swahili • Thai • Tibetan • Turkish • Ukrainian • USA *(US English, Vernacular, Native American languages, Hawaiian)* • Vietnamese • Western Europe *(Basque, Catalan, Dutch, French, German, Greek, Irish)*

# Lonely Planet Journeys

**J** OURNEYS is a unique collection of travel writing – published by the company that understands travel better than anyone else. It is a series for anyone who has ever experienced – or dreamed of – the magical moment when they encountered a strange culture or saw a place for the first time. They are tales to read while you're planning a trip, while you're on the road or while you're in an armchair in front of a fire.

These outstanding titles explore our planet through the eyes of a diverse group of international writers. JOURNEYS books catch the spirit of a place, illuminate a culture, recount a crazy adventure or introduce a fascinating way of life. They always entertain, and always enrich the experience of travel.

## IN RAJASTHAN
### Royina Grewal

As she writes of her travels through Rajasthan, Indian writer Royina Grewal takes us behind the exotic facade of this fabled destination: here is an insider's perceptive account of India's most colourful state, conveying the excitement and challenges of a region in transition.

## SHOPPING FOR BUDDHAS
### Jeff Greenwald

In his obsessive search for the perfect Buddha statue in the backstreets of Kathmandu, Jeff Greenwald discovers more than he bargained for ... and his souvenir-hunting turns into an ironic metaphor for the clash between spiritual riches and material greed. Politics, religion and serious shopping collide in this witty account of an enlightening visit to Nepal.

## BRIEF ENCOUNTERS
### Stories of Love, Sex & Travel
### *edited by Michelle de Kretser*

Love affairs on the road, passionate holiday flings, disastrous pick-ups, erotic encounters ... In this seductive collection of stories, 22 authors from around the world write about travel romances. A tourist in Peru falls for her handsome guide; a writer explores the ambiguities of his relationship with a Japanese woman; a beautiful young man on a train proposes marriage ... Combining fiction and reportage, *Brief Encounters* is must-have reading – for everyone who has dreamt of escape with that perfect stranger.

**Includes stories by Pico Iyer, Mary Morris, Emily Perkins, Mona Simpson, Lisa St Aubin de Terán, Paul Theroux and Sara Wheeler.**

## Lonely Planet On-line

**W**hether you've just begun planning your next trip, or you're chasing down specific info on currency regulations or visa requirements, check out Lonely Planet On-line for up-to-the minute travel information.

As well as mini guides to more than 250 destinations, you'll find maps, photos, travel news, health and visa updates, travel advisories, and discussion of the ecological and political issues you need to be aware of as you travel. You'll also find timely upgrades to popular guidebooks which you can print out and stick in the back of your book.

There's also an on-line travellers' forum where you can share your experience of life on the road, meet travel companions and ask other travellers for their recommendations and advice.

And of course we have a complete and up-to-date list of all Lonely Planet travel products including travel guides, diving and snorkeling guides, phrasebooks, atlases, travel literature and videos, and a simple on-line ordering facility if you can't find the book you want elsewhere.

## Lonely Planet Diving & Snorkeling Guides

**B**eautifully illustrated with full-colour photos throughout, Lonely Planet's Pisces Books explore the world's best diving and snorkeling areas and prepare divers for what to expect when they get there, both topside and underwater.

Dive sites are described in detail with specifics on depths, visibility, level of difficulty, special conditions, underwater photography tips and common and unusual marine life present. You'll also find practical logistical information and coverage on topside activities and attractions, sections on diving health and safety, plus listings for diving services, live-aboards, dive resorts and tourist offices.

# LONELY PLANET

## Guides by Region

onely Planet is known worldwide for publishing practical, reliable and no-nonsense travel information in our guides and on our Web site. The Lonely Planet list covers just about every accessible part of the world. Currently there are nine series: travel guides, shoestring guides, walking guides, city guides, phrasebooks, audio packs, travel atlases, diving and snorkeling guides and travel literature.

**AFRICA** Africa – the South • Africa on a shoestring • Arabic (Egyptian) phrasebook • Arabic (Moroccan) phrasebook • Cairo • Cape Town • Central Africa • East Africa • Egypt • Egypt travel atlas • Ethiopian (Amharic) phrasebook • The Gambia & Senegal • Kenya • Kenya travel atlas • Malawi, Mozambique & Zambia • Morocco • North Africa • South Africa, Lesotho & Swaziland • South Africa, Lesotho & Swaziland travel atlas • Swahili phrasebook • Tanzania, Zanzibar & Pemba • Trekking in East Africa • Tunisia • West Africa • Zimbabwe, Botswana & Namibia • Zimbabwe, Botswana & Namibia travel atlas
**Travel Literature:** The Rainbird: A Central African Journey • Songs to an African Sunset: A Zimbabwean Story • Mali Blues: Traveling to an African Beat

**AUSTRALIA & THE PACIFIC** Australia • Australian phrasebook • Bushwalking in Australia • Bushwalking in Papua New Guinea • Fiji • Fijian phrasebook • Islands of Australia's Great Barrier Reef • Melbourne • Micronesia • New Caledonia • New South Wales & the ACT • New Zealand • Northern Territory • Outback Australia • Papua New Guinea • Papua New Guinea (Pidgin) phrasebook • Queensland • Rarotonga & the Cook Islands • Samoa • Solomon Islands • South Australia • South Pacific Languages phrasebook • Sydney • Tahiti & French Polynesia • Tasmania • Tonga • Tramping in New Zealand • Vanuatu • Victoria • Western Australia
**Travel Literature:** Islands in the Clouds • Sean & David's Long Drive

**CENTRAL AMERICA & THE CARIBBEAN** Bahamas and Turks & Caicos • Barcelona • Bermuda • Central America on a shoestring • Costa Rica • Cuba • Dominican Republic & Haiti • Eastern Caribbean • Guatemala, Belize & Yucatán: La Ruta Maya • Jamaica • Mexico • Mexico City • Panama
**Travel Literature:** Green Dreams: Travels in Central America

**EUROPE** Amsterdam • Andalucía • Austria • Baltic States phrasebook • Barcelona • Berlin • Britain • British phrasebook • Canary Islands • Central Europe • Central Europe phrasebook • Corsica • Croatia • Czech & Slovak Republics • Denmark • Dublin • Eastern Europe • Eastern Europe phrasebook • Edinburgh • Estonia, Latvia & Lithuania • Europe • Finland • France • French phrasebook • Germany • German phrasebook • Greece • Greek phrasebook • Hungary • Iceland, Greenland & the Faroe Islands • Ireland • Italian phrasebook • Italy • Lisbon • London • Mediterranean Europe • Mediterranean Europe phrasebook • Norway • Paris • Poland • Portugal • Portugal travel atlas • Prague • Provence & the Côte d'Azur • Romania & Moldova • Rome • Russia, Ukraine & Belarus • Russian phrasebook • Scandinavian & Baltic Europe • Scandinavian Europe phrasebook • Scotland • Slovenia • Spain • Spanish phrasebook • St Petersburg • Switzerland • Trekking in Spain • Ukrainian phrasebook • Vienna • Walking in Britain • Walking in Italy • Walking in Ireland • Walking in Switzerland • Western Europe • Western Europe phrasebook
**Travel Literature:** The Olive Grove: Travels in Greece

**INDIAN SUBCONTINENT** Bangladesh • Bengali phrasebook • Bhutan • Delhi • Goa • Hindi/Urdu phrasebook • India • India & Bangladesh travel atlas • Indian Himalaya • Karakoram Highway • Nepal • Nepali phrasebook • Pakistan • Rajasthan • South India • Sri Lanka • Sri Lanka phrasebook • Trekking in the Indian Himalaya • Trekking in the Karakoram & Hindukush • Trekking in the Nepal Himalaya
**Travel Literature:** In Rajasthan • Shopping for Buddhas

# Index

## Text

**Bold** indicates maps.

424

**Bold** indicates maps

**Bold** indicates maps

# Boxed Text

# MAP LEGEND

## BOUNDARIES

| | |
|---|---|
| ......................International |
| ......................State |
| ......................Disputed |

## HYDROGRAPHY

| | |
|---|---|
| ......................Coastline |
| ......................River, Creek |
| ......................Lake |
| ......................Intermittent Lake |
| ......................Salt Lake |
| ......................Canal |
| ......................Spring, Rapids |
| ......................Waterfalls |
| ......................Swamp |

## ROUTES & TRANSPORT

| | |
|---|---|
| ......................Freeway |
| ......................Highway |
| ......................Major Road |
| ......................Minor Road |
| ......................Unsealed Road |
| ......................City Freeway |
| ......................City Highway |
| ......................City Road |
| ......................City Street, Lane |
| ......................Pedestrian Mall |
| ......................Tunnel |
| ......................Train Route & Station |
| ......................Metro & Station |
| ......................Tramway |
| ......................Cable Car or Chairlift |
| ......................Walking Track |
| ......................Walking Tour |
| ......................Ferry Route |

## AREA FEATURES

| | |
|---|---|
| ......................Building |
| ......................Park, Gardens |
| ......................Cemetery |
| ......................Market |
| ......................Beach, Desert |
| ......................Urban Area |

## MAP SYMBOLS

| | | | |
|---|---|---|---|
| ✪ CAPITAL | National Capital | ✈ | ......Airport |
| ◉ CAPITAL | State Capital | ❾ | ......Bank |
| ● CITY | City | ⚐ | ......Beach |
| ● Town | Town | ⌒ | ......Cave |
| ● Village | Village | | ......Church |
| ○ | Point of Interest | | ......Cliff or Escarpment |
| | | ◔ | ......Embassy |
| ■ | Place to Stay | ✛ | ......Hospital |
| ▲ | Camping Ground | ☆ | ......Lighthouse |
| ⌑ | Caravan Park | ※ | ......Lookout |
| ☗ | Hut or Chalet | ▲ ⑪ | ......Monument, Museum |
| | | ☪ | ......Mosque |
| ▼ | Place to Eat | ▲ | ......Mountain or Hill |
| ⬮ | Pub or Bar | )( | ......Pass |

| | |
|---|---|
| ★ | ......Police Station |
| ✉ | ......Post Office |
| ❖ | ......Shopping Centre |
| 🏛 | ......Stately Home |
| △ | ......Stupa |
| ⌷ | ......Swimming Pool |
| ☎ | ......Telephone |
| 卍 | ......Temple (Buddhist) |
| ⛩ | ......Temple (Hindu) |
| ⚑ | ......Temple (Other) |
| ▣ | ......Tomb |
| ❶ | ......Tourist Information |
| ◓ | ......Transport |
| 🐾 | ......Zoo |

*Note: not all symbols displayed above appear in this book*

# LONELY PLANET OFFICES

**Australia**
PO Box 617, Hawthorn, Victoria 3122
☎ 03 9819 1877  fax 03 9819 6459
email: talk2us@lonelyplanet.com.au

**USA**
150 Linden St, Oakland, CA 94607
☎ 510 893 8555  TOLL FREE: 800 275 8555
fax 510 893 8572
email: info@lonelyplanet.com

**UK**
10a Spring Place, London NW5 3BH
☎ 020 7428 4800  fax 020 7428 4828
email: go@lonelyplanet.co.uk

**France**
1 rue du Dahomey, 75011 Paris
☎ 01 55 25 33 00  fax 01 55 25 33 01
email: bip@lonelyplanet.fr
minitel: 3615 lonelyplanet *(1,29 F TTC/min)*

**World Wide Web: www.lonelyplanet.com *or* AOL keyword: lp**
**Lonely Planet Images: lpi@lonelyplanet.com.au**